Systematic and Comparative Musicology: Concepts, Methods, Findings

Hamburger Jahrbuch für Musikwissenschaft

Herausgegeben vom
Musikwissenschaftlichen Institut
der Universität Hamburg

Redaktion:
Frederik Knop und Arne von Ruschkowski

Band 24

PETER LANG

Frankfurt am Main · Berlin · Bern · Bruxelles · New York · Oxford · Wien

Albrecht Schneider
(ed.)

Systematic and Comparative Musicology: Concepts, Methods, Findings

PETER LANG

Internationaler Verlag der Wissenschaften

Bibliographic Information published by the Deutsche Nationalbibliothek
The Deutsche Nationalbibliothek lists this publication in the Deutsche Nationalbibliografie; detailed bibliographic data is available in the internet at <http://www.d-nb.de>.

Gratefully acknowledging financial support by the University of Hamburg.

ISSN 0342-8303
ISBN 978-3-631-57953-4

© Peter Lang GmbH
Internationaler Verlag der Wissenschaften
Frankfurt am Main 2008
All rights reserved.

Printed in Germany 1 2 3 4   6 7

www.peterlang.de

Contents

Introduction

The volume at hand is titled *Systematic and Comparative Musicology: concepts, methods, findings*. Besides presenting fresh data and new insights, contributors were encouraged also to reflect upon disciplinary history and methodology. This seems apt since, reading some articles and books which appeared over the past years one could have the impression that Systematic Musicology was a discipline which had finally come to fruition because of recent developments in computation. Though such no doubt gave Systematic Musicology new momentum in regard of tools and experimental techniques as well as for theoretical considerations, the discipline of Systematic Musicology in fact was established, in its modern orientation, by scholars such as Hermann von Helmholtz and Carl Stumpf already before 1900. To comprehend what the goals, issues, and paradigms of our discipline were, and how it was transformed into current approaches, one should reconstruct the process of research done in central areas of systematic and Comparative Musicology including disciplinary and institutional history.

To illustrate in brief how complex developments are, I might point to the Institute of Musicology at Hamburg which offers Systematic Musicology as a subject that can be studied as a „major" (German: Hauptfach) in combination with a broad range of other subjects for a B.A., M.A., and PhD-degree, respectively. The process which, in 1975, finally led to independence of Systematic Musicology in terms of organization as well as building a special curriculum has been documented elsewhere (Karbusicky 1979). There were basically two reasons which played a central role in setting up Systematic Musicology as an academic subject of its own besides Historical Musicology. The first reflects a difference in subject matter both in regard of teaching and objects of research, the second a difference in theory and methodology.

As is well known, musicology as a modern academic discipline in Europe was established around 1860-1890. Notwithstanding the division into historic, systematic, and comparative approaches proposed by Adler (1885; see the articles of Elschek, Lothwesen, and Nettl, this volume), for a number of reasons musicology was centred in historic studies. The systematic branch flourished at Berlin and Vienna as well as at Leipzig and a few other places including, to some extent, also Hamburg (with the support of scholars from psychology who had an interest in psychology of music). In regard of Comparative Musicology, the picture was quite the same in that a mere handful of scholars were engaged in research as well as in teaching. Given this small number of scientists, the output in both the systematic and the comparative fields especially during the first decades of the 20th century was impressive. In effect, already by about 1920 it had become obvious that musicology comprised three specialized sub-disciplines, namely the historic, systematic, and comparative. Due to growing specialization, after 1950 or so very few musicologists were still capable to do research in at least two of the three sub-disciplines or fields of study, and the same holds true in regard of academic teaching (though some scholars felt that musicology had to offer a curriculum in all three areas).

At Hamburg, musicology had actually started with Comparative Musicology, by about 1930 when Wilhelm Heinitz (1883-1963) founded a small lab besides an archive of non-western music and European folk music within the Institute of Phonetics. During the

1930s, there were also lectures on topics of music psychology and aesthetics. Historic Musicology (and music pedagogy) emerged by the end of the 1930s. Lectures and seminars given in our institute even in the 1950s could be as diverse as covering medieval music, Javanese Gamelan, and „electron tubes as voltage amplifiers" (Reinecke 1999, 27). This was certainly unusual when, in most musicological institutes in Germany (and elsewhere) musicology meant, first of all, the historical study of European art music. One scholar who had adopted a different attitude towards musicology which was to become characteristic of Hamburg was Heinrich Husmann (1908-1983) who had studied, among others, with Erich Moritz von Hornbostel at Berlin. Husmann also had a background in mathematics, and a vivid interest in technological developments, in particular in electroacoustics. He wrote an introductory textbook for musicology (Husmann 1958) which included acoustics and psychoacoustics as well as other areas which were clearly outside the scope of conventional musicology. Moreover, Husmann had pursued a comparative perspective to allow for inclusion of phenomena from non-western music into the discussion of, for example, tone systems, scales, and perception of rhythm. The combination of systematic plus comparative aspects of course was what Stumpf and others had in mind when establishing Systematic and Comparative Musicology conceived as joint disciplines which both should study foundations of music perception and cognition plus the principles relevant for the organization of musical structures, in a transdisciplinary as well as a cross-cultural approach.

In the course of the 1950s and early 1960s, Husmann, his scientific co-worker Hans-Peter Reinecke (1926-2003), and Hans Hickmann (1908-1968), an ethnomusicologist with extensive field experience in Egypt and the Near East, offered a broad range of lectures and seminars devoted to Systematic and Comparative Musicology. Also, they had a reasonable number of students specializing in these areas, doing their own research for PhD-dissertations, etc. This naturally led to establishing a second ‚center of gravity' besides Historical Musicology (for details as well as for information regarding also the 1970s and later developments, see Schneider & Müllensiefen 1999). As a matter of fact, Systematic Musicology which was attracting more and more students, was acknowledged as a specialized field (not the least by colleagues from Historical Musicology), and became a subject of its own in the mid-seventies. Due to the untimely death of Hans Hickmann, Comparative Musicology and Ethnomusicology could not be covered as extensively as they should have, however, after Systematic Musicology was established, there always have been lectures and seminars on topics of „ethno" and „folk" music included in the curriculum, and we had (and have) a number of visiting professors and part-time teachers from Ethnomusicology to maintain the perspective of cross-cultural music studies.

The second reason which led to separating Historic and Systematic Musicology at Hamburg largely has to do with methodology. In Historic Musicology, methodology comprises, in the main, philological skills, description, music analysis, hermeneutic understanding and interpretation. In Systematic Musicology, methodology rests on measurement, experiment or other empirical investigation as well as on data analysis, statistics, and modelling. Though also researchers in Historic Musicology might employ statistics here and there, and researchers in Systematic Musicology will include music analysis in many of their studies, the two disciplines have different orientations which, in a broad sense, can be distinguished as „historic-philological-hermeneutic", on the one-hand, and „scientific-experimental-comparative", on the other. It goes without saying that there are still many relations between the two subjects as well as problems which call for close cooperation to be solved. Nonetheless, the difference in subject matter as well as in methodology was all too obvious. Beginning with the summer semester of 1976, Systematic Musicology was taught as a subject of its own, by Vladimir Karbusicky (1925-2002), Hans-Peter Reinecke, and also Horst-Peter Hesse (b. 1935) who later became professor at the Mozarteum of Salzburg. The range of teaching and research covered a broad spectrum from music acoustics and psychoacoustics to psychology of music, music sociology, semiotics and empirical aesthetics, plus „ethno" and „folk" classes (as well as seminars on jazz and pop) offered in between.

The *Hamburger Jahrbuch für Musikwissenschaft*, founded in 1974, from the very beginning was conceived to cover Historic and Systematic Musicology as well as, on occasions, also comparative and ethnomusicological research. In volume 1 (1974), topics are as diverse as Syrian sources of medieval liturgical music, Monteverdi, Händel, Haydn, aspects of modern music (Alban Berg, Lutoslawski), empirical rhythm research, changing attitudes in listening to music, an alternative approach to music psychology, experiments in pitch perception, finally, Islamic and African elements in the music of Northern Sudan. Except for Ingmar Bengtsson's report on the rhythm (and other) experiments performed at Uppsala, all other articles were contributed by colleagues from our institute.

After the first volume of 1974, there were some more which offered a combination of historic and systematic studies (e.g., Vol. 13: *Theorie der Musik. Analyse und Deutung.* 1995), or of systematic and comparative as well as ethnomusicologal studies as are contained in two volumes dedicated to Vladimir Karbusicky (Vol. 9: *Studien zur Systematischen Musikwissenschaft.* 1986), and György Ligeti (Vol. 11: *Für György Ligeti.* 1991), respectively. More recently, we added a volume devoted to popular music which contains several articles based on empirical and experimental methods (Vol. 19: *Musikwissenschaft und populäre Musik.* 2002).

In the present volume, articles are assembled some of which reflect on concepts and methods in Systematic and Comparative Musicology, whereas others report actual research and its findings. In some papers, both aspects are given about equal weight. A focus on concepts and methodology seems appropriate since Systematic Musicology, unlike its historic counterpart, publicly regarded as „music history" (by analogy to „art history"), often faces the problem to explain what is, or should be „systematic" in musicology. Of course, the term ‚systematic' refers to the notion of a ‚system' as well as to ‚systematization' as a specific task of scientific inquiry. Also, ‚systematic' has to do with research and the presentation of findings that is fundamental, thorough, and logical, based on explicit definitions (cf. Rudolph & Tschohl 1977). Further, a ‚systematic' approach was regarded as one directed to explaining the essence of a certain area or object of study as well as presenting the features and concepts characteristic for those areas in a well-ordered arrangement in which the areas or sub-disciplines make up a ‚system' (see, for example, Dilthey et al. 1908). Carl Stumpf used the term Systematic Musicology for an approach which should offer causal explanations of musical sound and of musical phenomena as related to perception, cognition, and appreciation. The systematic orientation had to be combined with a comparative perspective since findings obtained from the study of non-western music(s) could either confirm or refute views derived from European concepts of music (e.g., consonance, tonality, meter).

It is clear that our concepts of Systematic Musicology change with the phenomena we have to deal with according to cultural and social developments. Therefore, Systematic Musicology today is a much broader and much more diversified field of research (see, e.g., Leman 1997, 2006; Godøy & Jørgensen 2001) that – also as an implication of "systematic" – is transdisciplinary in approach because the problems we work on often require methodological tools and factual knowledge not confined to one area or discipline. To avoid the traps of cultural and scientific ethnocentrism as well as to enrich our understanding of music, a comparative view which includes regard for Ethnomusicology is needed (see Nettl, this vol.).

The volume at hand is the product of cooperation since most of the authors have been in contact with the Institute of Musicology of the University of Hamburg in one way or another, and several have also been involved in joint projects such as the International Summer School in Systematic Musicology. I am grateful that so many colleagues and friends contributed to this volume which is dedicated to the memory of Vladimir Karbusicky and Hans-Peter Reinecke, both academic teachers in Systematic Musicology at Hamburg and founding members of the International Cooperative in Systematic and Comparative Musicology. Finally, I'd like to thank Arne von Ruschkowski for providing most of the technical work necessary to publish this book.

Hamburg, February 2008 A.S.

References

Dilthey, Wilhelm et al. 1908. *Systematische Philosophie*. 2nd ed. Berlin, Leipzig: B.G. Teubner.

Godøy, Rolf Inge/H. Jørgensen (eds.), *Elements of Musical Imagery*, Lisse, Abingdon usw.: Swets & Zeitlinger 2001

Husmann, Heinrich 1958. *Einführung in die Musikwissenschaft*. Heidelberg: Quelle & Meyer (reprint Wilhelmshaven: Heinrichshofen 1975).

Karbusicky, Vladimir 1979. *Systematische Musikwissenschaft*. München: W. Fink.

Leman, Marc (ed.) 1997, *Music, Gestalt, and computing: studies in cognitive and systematic musicology*, Berlin, New York: Springer.

Leman, Marc 2006. *Embodied music cognition and mediation technology*. Cambridge, MA and London: MIT Pr.

Reinecke, Hans-Peter 1999. Vom Anfang der ‚Hamburger Schule' zur systemischen Musikwissenschaft. Konstruktion und Rekonstruktion musikhistorischer ‚Wirklichkeiten'. In In P. Petersen/H. Rösing (Hrsg.). *50 Jahre Musikwissenschaftliches Institut in Hamburg* (= *Hamburger Jahrbuch der Musikwissenschaft* Bd 16), Frankfurt/M.: P. Lang, 23-41.

Rudolph, Wolfgang/Peter Tschohl 1977. *Systematische Anthropologie*. München: W. Fink.

Schneider, Albrecht/Daniel Müllensiefen 1999. Vergleichende und Systematische Musikwissenschaft in Hamburg. In P. Petersen/H. Rösing (Hrsg.). *50 Jahre Musikwissenschaftliches Institut in Hamburg* (= *Hamburger Jahrbuch für Musikwissenschaft* Bd 16), Frankfurt/M.: P. Lang, 43-63.

Albrecht Schneider

Foundations of Systematic Musicology: a study in history and theory[1]

1. Introduction

After some twenty years of research often subsumed under „cognitive musicology", there are currently various proposals around to establish seemingly new or otherwise promising approaches to musicology labelled, for example, „empirical musicology", „experimental musicology", „interdisciplinary musicology", „systemic musicology". Apparently, there is a search for new directions and paradigms not only in musicology yet in other disciplines as well. Given the fast development of science in general, and a shift of paradigms within many disciplines, it seems appropriate to reflect on disciplinary history and methodology. This shall be done in this article in regard of foundations of systematic musicology which, as a modern scientific discipline, was formed in the course of the 19th century by scholars such as Hermann von Helmholtz, Carl Stumpf, Hugo Riemann, and others. Since much of its early development and disciplinary history took place in Germany and adjacent countries such as Austria, the focus of attention will be on German speaking countries where also the term *systematic musicology* (German: *Systematische Musikwissenschaft*, from here on SM) appears first. The present author is well aware, though, that research relevant for SM was undertaken quite early also in other countries (e.g., France, Italy, Great Britain).

As a matter of fact, SM from the very beginning centred in certain areas of research, in particular musical acoustics, organology, psychoacoustics, and psychology of music (including philosophical and aesthetic as well as some medical aspects), not to forget music theory which in itself comprises philosophical, aesthetic, psychological, and even acoustical facts and issues.

For a number of reasons which have to do, among other things, with research on the origins of music and a quest for principles fundamental to music perception and music making, SM from early on was close to, or even interrelated with, comparative musicology (hereafter CM; for a detailed account, see Schneider 1991, 1993a, 2006). To be sure, SM plus CM since the days of Helmholtz and Stumpf did stem from empiricism, experimental research, and certainly from a transdisciplinary perspective[2]. Also, systemic relations had been studied in acoustics and organology as well as in regard of music perception. Further, in particular SM did include a fair amount of cognitive aspects. As has been rightly stressed by Marc Leman (1995, 187), *the early systematic musicology is in many respects a cognitive musicology „avant la lettre"*.

---

[1] Parts of this article which condenses chapters from a book on the disciplinary history, theory and methodology of Systematic Musicology under preparation by the present author have been presented as an invited lecture at the Symposium *Future Directions in Musicology*, 13th Meeting of the FWO Research Society, University of Ghent, Belgium, 2nd of March, 2001.

[2] Recently, the term transdisciplinary has been used in general to denote an approach which is problem-orientated, and by tackling complex issues, surpasses boundaries of disciplines. It is distinguished from the interdisciplinary approach which is taken as a cooperation between scholars of several disciplines working together on certain problems.

Helmholtz and Stumpf (the latter with a number of co-workers; see below) took efforts to establish SM and CM as fields of scientific research and learning at the University of Berlin. Helmholtz, originally a physician and professor of physiology at the universities of Bonn and Heidelberg, respectively, became a most prolific scientist with major achievements in physics and mathematics, and with writings ranging from optics to epistemology, from non-Euclidean geometry to acoustics and systematic musicology. Acoustics did fit into his spectrum of interest as a scientist, auditory perception was part of his research when he was a professor in medicine. Stumpf, a philosopher with strong interests in music since childhood (for his autobiography, see Stumpf 1924), and an inclination towards empiric research in addition to theoretical work, was a professor of philosophy (at Würzburg, Prague, Halle, Munich, and, finally, Berlin[3]) who had specialized in areas of epistemology and logic, as well as in psychology. In those days, psychology meant one had to have professional training in philosophy as well as the motivation to contribute to philosophical reasoning besides doing theoretical or even experimental work in psychology (see Ash 1995, ch. 2). Further, a fair understanding of sensory physiology, psychophysics, and of experimental research in general was expected (see Boring 1950, Pongratz 1967). Stumpf was known to possess all these qualifications what, in 1893, did lead to a prestigous appointment as full professor at the university of Berlin. Though this professorship was assigned formally to philosophy, it was clear to all involved that Stumpf would divide his time and labour between both fields. Stumpf, considered by Dilthey and other colleagues at Berlin to be a „mild experimenter" (i.e., a philosophically minded psychologist not confined to experimental work), did set up his lab which, in the years to come, was the place where research into various problems of psychology was conducted (see Ash 1995, 2002; Sprung & Sprung 2002). It is known that Stumpf, his assistants, volunteer co-workers (e.g., Erich Moritz von Hornbostel, Otto Abraham), and his students (among them being Wolfgang Köhler, Kurt Koffka, Adhemar Gelb and – from 1902 to 1904 – Max Wertheimer) contributed significantly to what became *Gestaltpsychologie* (see below). Of the twenty-three doctoral dissertation Stumpf did supervise, six had a topic relating to psychoacoustics as well as to auditory (Gestalt) perception. Some of these dissertations, and important monographs written by Stumpf himself (see below), were published in a series he founded in 1898, titled *Beiträge zur Akustik und Musikwissenschaft*.

By 1900, Stumpf had also started a collection of sound recordings of (primarily) non-western music (see Simon 2000), and had published scholarly articles which were important to establish CM in Germany. By 1910 or so, one could see that SM and CM were flourishing at Berlin, and to some extent also at other places (most of all, Vienna; see below). However, due to World War I, and the aftermath it brought about (including political turmoil and severe economic problems), the situation became much more difficult. Stumpf retired as professor in 1921 (he continued his lectures, though, to the end of the twenties). His former co-worker, Erich M. von Hornbostel (1877-1935), who, in publications as well as in university teaching, did cover substantial areas of CM and SM, respectively, never was tenured at Berlin, and, as a so-called *außerplanmäßiger nichtbeamteter Universitätsprofessor*, was badly paid before finally being forced to

---

[3] Besides Stumpf's own account of his life and career (Stumpf 1924), there is detailed information now available from several articles (by E. and W. Baumgartner, J. Hoskovec, K. Schumann, H. and L. Sprung, M. Ash) in H. Baumgartner (ed.) 2002.

leave Germany, in 1934 (he died in Cambridge, England, in 1935). The Nazi regime of course was detrimental to further development of SM and CM. Given that these musicological sub-disciplines were small (considered by the number of researchers and academic teachers in relevant areas), a relatively large number of scholars from SM and CM plus many of their colleagues from psychology having also contributed to SM were to leave Germany (see Schneider 1993b).

In Austria or, rather, the Austrian lands before the collapse of the empire (in 1919), there had been also a strong movement into the direction of SM. In particular Ernst Mach (1838-1916), the scientist and philosopher, had addressed issues in acoustics, psychoacoustics as well as in sensation and perception of elementary musical stimuli (see Mach 1900/1922; Blaukopf 1995, ch. 13). Mach, a major proponent of empiricism, is respected to this day for his contributions to experimental physics as well as for his writings on epistemology and ‚philosophy of science‘ (see Haller 1993). For most of his scholarly life, Mach worked at the *Deutsche Karl-Ferdinands-Universität* of Prague[4]. Here he met Stumpf who did teach at Prague as a professor of philosophy from 1879-1884, and was completing the first volume of the *Tonpsychologie* (published in 1883) there. The two men were instrumental in securing a professorship in musicology for Guido Adler who spend the years from 1882 to 1898 at the Karls-Universität. Apparently, Adler was impressed by scientists like Ernst Mach and Ewald Hering (1834-1918), the latter known as an eminent figure in sensory physiology and psychophysics also teaching (from 1870 to 1895) at Prague (see Boring 1950, ch. 17). In 1885, Adler published his well-known essay on *Umfang, Methode und Ziel der Musikwissenschaft* in which he addresses briefly central concepts such as that of style and style history, the idea of development and ‚organic growth‘ of art as well as issues related to the tasks and methods of musicology[5]. An indication that Adler was aware of scientific concepts current at his time is his remark that art historians (including historic musicologists) will preferably make use of *inductive method*, the same as the natural scientist. That is, the researcher will find out what is common in a number of phenomena, separate things which are different, and also will use abstraction to determine such features which are essential (thereby neglecting others). Though Adler (1885, 15) does not explicitly refer to inductive generalization, this is what his approach, later exemplified in his writings on ‚style‘ in music, implies.

In his article, Adler introduces a system of musicology in which the discipline is divided basically into two parts, labelled historic and systematic. It is n o t that Adler did propose a self-contained discipline of SM, rather, he was looking for scholars doing research necessary to complement historical studies. For, according to his system, historical investigations will reveal the „highest laws" governing the organic evolution of (musical and other) art, whereas it is the task of (systematic) music theory then to

---

[4] Mach became professor of physics in Prague in 1867, and left for Vienna in 1895 where he had been appointed to professor of *philosophy, in particular history and theory of inductive sciences* (see Haller 1993, § 4). In 1896, Christian von Ehrenfels (1859-1932), author of the seminal article *Über Gestalt-qualitäten* (Ehrenfels 1890), came to the Karls-Universität as professor of philosophy.
[5] More on Adler's views related to music history, and to musicology in general will be found in Schneider 1984, Kalisch 1988; as to Adler's remarks on CM, see also Nettl, this volume.

order and explain such laws in a rational manner[6]. Further, aesthetics, as a part of the systematic division of musicology, in Adler's view should relate those „highest laws" to the idea of the beautiful in art, and also should establish criteria which define it. Finally, music pedagogy is allotted the task to incorporate the findings from historical studies into textbooks on harmony, counterpoint, etc.

More an appendix than an integral part of his system, Adler mentions *Musikologie* as the fourth part of the systematic division, meaning the then new sub-discipline of CM. We have to remember that Adler's article appeared five years before the Edison Phonograph (in a version usable for recording musical sound, not as the half-baked ‚talking machine' it was before ca. 1890) was ever brought to the field. By 1885, CM had just begun to take shape. The study of „primitive" music (by analogy to Edward Tyler's *Primitive culture*, 1873; see Schneider 2006), to be sure, among anthropologists, psychologists as well as a number of musicologists was believed essential to extend and enrich our knowledge of fundamentals of music, and it was also deemed useful to draw a more complete picture of the evolution of music from its most basic manifestations to complex textures.

Probably the first professorship ever assigned to a combination of SM plus CM was installed at the University of Vienna where, in 1896, Richard Wallaschek (1860-1917) took his Habilitation in *Musikästhetik und Psychologie der Tonkunst*. His academic background was in philosophy (and psychology), and his main interest was in psychophysiological foundations of aesthetic experience (see Allesch 1987, 388-90; Födermayr 2003, 387-89). Besides, he had monitored developments in anthropology and related fields. One has to be aware that, in the second half of the 19th century, various concepts of biological as well as social and cultural ‚evolution' based on writings of Darwin, Spencer, Haeckel, etc. had tremendous impact on almost all disciplines, including musicology. In 1908, Wallaschek became professor of CM at Vienna. Though he had published, in a predominantly classificatory approach based on a survey of anthropological and other literature, a book on *Primitive Music* (Wallaschek 1893/1903), his teaching was in areas of SM rather than in CM. In his book on the psychology of imagination (Wallaschek 1905, pp. 40), he treats, among other issues, melody perception whereby he explains the unity of a melody, being more than merely a sum of tones, as a „simultaneous picture". He held that it is achieved, in mental retrospect, from a sequence of successive notes which are condensed into one holistic structure.

Wallaschek was succeeded, in 1920, by Robert Lach (1874-1958), a former student of his and Adler's. Lach (1913, 1924) continued the genetical and historical approach to music as had been pursued, in different shadings and lines of argumentation, by his two teachers. He even went further and sketched a vision of CM, actually including quite many topics from SM, as a trans- and multidisciplinary science (Lach 1924, 1925). Lach, who had some experience as a field-worker, and was active also as a composer, saw CM based on a „synthetic" methodology of analysis, comparison, inference, and inductive generalization. Moreover, he (1924, 12) argued that, as much as the phenomena studied by CM, and the findings this discipline could offer would fall under natural

---

[6] Adler 1885, 11. As I have outlined earlier (Schneider 1984, 1993a), much of Adler's as well as of Robert Lach's concept of so-called *Entwicklungsgeschichte* is derived from Hegel's Philosophy of history, on the one hand, and from evolutionary speculations current in 19th century science (including disciplines such as anthropology and comparative linguistics), on the other.

laws, and would obey to processes observed in nature, a transition from CM into SM would take place. Apparently, Lach considered SM a science. This was well in line with the actual research that had been done, in particular by Helmholtz on sensations of tone (Helmholtz 1863, see below), and by him and others on musical acoustics (e.g., Jonquière 1898). Further, Stumpf had investigated foundations of music perception (Stumpf 1993, 1890, 1898) and similar issues.

The equation to be inferred from Lach's statement then would be that a *systematic* musicology is a *scientific* musicology, that is, a musicology which, in its methodology and practical research work, includes yet somehow goes beyond the usual empiricist approach of observation and experimentation, analysis of data, abstraction of features, statistical or other inference. In Lach's view, SM would be concerned with things, structures and processes which have a natural basis and which, in regard of music, govern and constrain cultural phenomena.

The idea that SM should investigate, in the first place, natural processes (up to the level of finding, or confirming, natural laws as they apply to music in some form) of course relates our discipline closely to certain philosophical and scientific concepts. Further, theoretical concepts are implied by the very term *systematic* which, in turn, refers to the notion of a *system*, and the scientific task of *systematization*. *System* and *systematization* play a major role in epistemology, and were treated as a special field of inquiry as well as scientific methodology, by philosophers and scientists of the 18th century. One can trace concepts of *system* and *systematization* from Lambert (1771, 1988) to Kant (1787), J.G. Fichte (1798), G.Fr.W. Hegel (1807, 1817, etc.), and other philosophers from the age of Enlightenment. During the 19th and 20th centuries, these considerations were continued by scientists and philosophers alike. More recently, the concept of *cognitive systematization* which is central to Kant's epistemology, has found a renewed and deepened interest (see Rescher 1979, 2000b) as has the problem of systematization in regard of natural science (cf. Rescher 2000a).

To understand what system and systematization mean, in a theoretical perspective, and to see the possible implications for SM, a discipline no doubt established by researchers with a strong philosophical background and inclination (as is most obvious in regard of Helmholtz, Wundt, Stumpf, Oettingen), the following chapter will discuss the notion of a system, the role of systematization as well as the term ‚systematic' which relates to both. Since the notion of a system and concepts of systematization are discussed in quite many scientific disciplines ranging from biology to philosophy, from cybernetics to economics and sociology (see, e.g., Dingler 1930, v. Uexküll 1928/1973, Bertalanffy 1968/1972, Löther 1972, Mayr 1975, Rescher 1979, 2000a/b, Stegmüller 1983, Keidel 1989, Luhmann 2004), the survey offered below considers such aspects which are relevant to SM in one way or another.

2. System, systematic, systematization

The notion of a system no doubt is basic to scientific thought. However, the term ‚system' can have various meanings depending on the view chosen. The notion of a system has been addressed from different angles to account for, most of all, (a) the ontological, (b) the epistemological, and the (c) methodological aspect. For the purpose of this article, these three aspects as well as certain levels of a ‚system' will be distinguished. (a) In regard of ontology, a system appears as a complex entity such as is nature as a whole, and as are biological organisms, in particular. A property of such complex entities is that they are highly structured internally whereby the parts which make up such structures have a specific architecture (e.g., anatomy and histology of the human brain). The architecture is 'functional' in that it may enable a sub-system to serve specific functions within the system. One of the most common functions is keeping the system as a whole stable.

Another aspect of a system is that of relations which are basically abstract so as in mathematical equations. On this level, the structure as such is of relevance though one of course can describe physical or biological systems which exist in the „real world" by means of mathematical relational systems. For example, transversal and axial vibrations {x[t], y[t]} of a xylophone bar can be adequately described by a system of coupled differential equations. Also, brain functions or the mechanics of the inner ear in regard of auditory perception can be modelled in a mathematical approach.

(b) The epistemological aspect of a system has been stressed by philosophers since antiquity. Human knowledge, regarding both each individual as well as mankind as a species, is not just accumulated yet is more or less ordered, and integrated into systems which should be as coherent and complete as possible. The most comprehensive and most extended system, in this respect, is science in total which, according to Husserl (1954), can be defined as a process of *continuous synthesis*. From a methodological point of view this implies that scientific findings must fit into a framework of concepts and facts, and that they should not contradict yet illuminate each other. Evidently, scientific disciplines such as physics or electrical engineering aim at organizing theories, methods, and findings of research into a coherent and well-ordered structure that can be called a system of that discipline.

Historically, the concept of a system as it goes back to Greek philosophy and musicology alike, means that one is dealing with an ordered set in which elements contribute to an overall configuration that is understood primarily by the relations between the elements. This was the case with, for example, tonal systems as they have been described in Greek music theory (see Vogel 1963; Barker 1989). The notion of σύστημα, however, did cover also entities such as nature or even the universe, and hence was used in an ontological sense. Both nature and universe were believed to be structured according to mechanisms that organize elements into coherent and stable wholes. Regarding in particular nature, Aristotle has argued that the high degree of order being characteristic of a system in its „final" state is achieved according to principles such as δύναμίς and εντελέχεια that bring about a process of continuous development (see Arist. Phys. lib. II). Once this process has reached its end (τέλος), the products of nature and the system they form remain almost stable.

The point which is of interest here is that Aristotle, especially in his book on metaphysics, draws parallels between an ordered entity as is nature, on the one hand, and science (επιστήμη), on the other. Though Aristotle distinguishes, in certain respects, between products of nature, and products of human creative labour (ποιησις), it is clear from his argument that sciences such as physics not only seek to understand principles of nature (φύσις), and of being (ουσια) in general, yet seek to be as coherent in their descriptions and explanations as is the object of their study (see in particular the chapter on science in Arist. Met. Δ11.1064a/b.). Since nature can be understood as forming a system that is governed by principles, science which adequately explores nature, again must yield a coherent system in its results. In short, one system (nature) which itself is ontological, is „mapped" onto another (science) which is epistemological. The science of nature by Aristotle *is seen as a systematic whole because it presents an account of the world that is similarly systematic* (Falcon 2005, 31).

The basic assumption in this model that has been adopted in disciplines such as physics and biology implies that the object of study indeed *is* a system which can be analyzed, described, and understood in objective terms. Physicists since the days of Newton, Huygens, etc. tended to analyse, describe and understand anorganic nature in terms of systems of differential equations (see, e.g., Mach 1898/1933, Truesdell 1950). Biologists since Linnaeus (Carl von Linné) tried to understand organic nature by methods of genetic classification. They established systematics of zoology and botany, respectively, which clearly is not just a descriptive approach yet one that involves exploration of principles as well (see Mayr 1975, Weberling & Stützel 1993). This becomes obvious in developments that have taken place in biology regarding such concepts as 'species', 'organism' and 'type' as well as in the role systematics play for the theory of evolution. Discussion of principles found to be relevant for biological „open" (versus closed) systems, in particular the capability of organisms to interact with an environment and to pick up information necessary to maintain certain processes and functions, in the 20th century has led to a broader perspective of general systems theory that considers funda-mentals of system behaviour not only for biological yet for various systems inside and outside nature (see Bertalanffy 1968).

The concept of a cognitive system perhaps was most clearly expressed by Immanuel Kant, who, in his *Kritik der reinen Vernunft* (KdRV; Critique of Pure Reason) and other writings on epistemology, argued that each individual builds up coherent knowledge during the span of one's life so that elements of this knowledge are integrated into a framework of categories rather than just being accumulated. Because we inherit certain fundamental categories such as space and time (which thus are innate), and conceive of the world and the manifold of objects therein, with the aid of more such basic categories (which Kant [1787,106] grouped into those of *quantity*, *quality*, *relation* and *modality*), knowledge is structured, ordered and hence, a system. The fundamental condition on which the integration of knowledge in each individual rests, by Kant is defined as the capability to perform an ongoing synthesis by means of apperception. This also constitutes our self-consciousness. Further, Kant argued that both perception and apperception (inner perception and awareness) operate according to certain cognitive rules. For example, he claims that human experience is synthetic because single percepts are integrated into more complex ones, and that all changes we register in a sequence of percepts are understood according to a scheme of causes and effects. This implies that intellectual activity even on the level of the individual is more or less „systematic" in that it aims at building up knowledge which is coherent, ordered, and as complete as is possible for a single person. The approach taken by Kant regarding the structure of human knowledge that is guided by categories and is based on cognitive rules, of course has been of influence to modern researchers (see, e.g., Rescher 1979, 2000a; Chomsky 1980).

(c) In the era of Enlightenment, an idea that gained prominence was that philosophical and other scientific knowledge has to be presented in an orderly fashion, according to certain principles. Science itself calls for a form of presentation where facts and rules make up a coherent, complete, and comprehensive system. Further, in order to gain such knowledge, research has to be conducted in a systematic manner. That is, research typically needs to be carefully planned and carried out according to methodological rules. In order to achieve valid results, there can be certain requirements defined by specifics of the object under study which must be met.

Though the systematic approach is somewhat different from the encyclopaedic one, the great *Encyclopédie ou dictionnaire raisonné des sciences, des arts et des métiers* of Diderot and d'Alembert (T. I-XXXV, Paris/Neuchatel/ Amsterdam 1751-1780) can be considered as one outcome also of the call for systematization of science. For philosophy, systematicity as a goal was proposed by, among others, Johann Heinrich Lambert (1771, 1988), a scholar whose writings on methodology and theory of science were known to Kant.

Kant himself (1787, 502, pp. 860) argued that knowledge cannot be offered adequately as an aggregate yet requires the *architecture of a system*. This he defined as the unity of a manifold of knowledge with respect to an idea (...*die Einheit der mannigfaltigen Erkenntnisse unter einer Idee*, KdRV B 860). Consequently, philosophy by Kant is understood as the system of all philosophical reasoning and knowledge. Systematic, in Kant´s opinion, is an approach suited to structure knowledge so that it becomes a system which is coherent, and is ordered with respect to certain principles and purposes. Thereby, the parts or elements of the system contribute to an overall meaningful configuration. It can be said that Kant's concept of a system incorporates aspects of cognitive systematization, of coherent inquiry and reasoning as well as of classification of scientific methods and findings. Further, the concept of system in Kant´s thought has some teleological aspects to it. He assumes, for example, that human rationality in itself bears a tendency towards integration of knowledge into a system. Kant, in his *Kritik der Urteilskraft* (Critique of judgement, Kant 1799) elaborates in great detail on the teleological status of nature, and of organisms, in particular. In this work, among other issues, he discusses the principle of purpose and expediency in nature. Nature in total by Kant (1799, pp. 279, pp. 388) is understood as a teleological system.

The concept of a ‚system‘, and the principle of ‚systematic‘ coherence of knowledge, in German philosophy were discussed by, among others, Johann Gottlieb Fichte (1798) and Jakob Friedrich Fries (1827, 1837). Both claim that coherent knowledge in philosophy and other disciplines can only be achieved if there are a number of logical and methodological principles to which all particular findings and statements can be related so that an ordered set of definitions, classifications, derivations, and conclusions is established. This ordered set makes up a configuration that, by its form, is called a system, and by its objective content is understood as a science (Fichte 1798, 47; Fries 1837, 206).

The concept of a ‚system‘ that, by Fichte and Fries, was viewed in a basically logical and formal approach, later has been addressed more and more from a teleological, evolutionary perspective as was the case in Hegel´s philosophy. Hegel (1807, 1827/1830), however, also re-established the ontological foundations of the notion of ‚system‘. His own *Encyclopädie der philosophischen Wissenschaften* (Encyclopedia of the philosophical sciences) deals not just with logic and epistemology, yet quite extensively with *Naturphilosophie*, and in particular with physics (including acoustics) and biology.

Friedrich Adolf Trendelenburg, a philosopher in the Hegelian tradition, maintained that different systems of science themselves are parts of an even larger system of all science. This, according to Trendelenburg (1870, p. 446) can be viewed as o n e organism that contains, and allows for, a complete image of the world. In this way, the „world" as an entity of things and beings is paralleled by science as an entity of principles and facts. Moreover, the metaphor of ,organism' of course points to order and coherence, and also to ideas of self-reference, of growth, and of teleonomy that are thus assigned to science.

Though this view of science as an „organic" system that covers the whole „world" may appear somewhat too optimistic today, it was this perspective that, in the 19th century, corresponded fairly well to rapid developments in almost all fields of science. To be sure, there are no serious doubts that scientific subjects, methods, and findings interrelate so as to make up systems which consist of sub-systems, of laws and facts (see Rescher 1984, ch. I). Rather, the question is whether such systems of knowledge can ever be completed. Also, the degree of logical as well as factual coherence apparently is different in several systems, and for various scientific disciplines. All in all, science is considered as an „open" system since there is a constant change in topics and methods to result in new findings, new hypotheses, new methodologies, etc.

Basically, the term ,systematic' has two meanings which, however, interrelate:

1. In case a certain field of learning is presented in a ,systematic' form, this indicates that the matter in question is treated according to certain principles, and in regard of definitions, concepts and other more theoretical and methodological aspects. Systematic treatment of a subject should be based on, as Wundt (1907, pp. 40) elaborated, (a) definitions, (b) classifications (which can be grouped into descriptive, genetic, and analytic classifications), and (c) various types of proofs. This scheme refers to the sciences, in the first place. It can be applied, however, also to disciplines such as anthropology where strict systematic approaches can be found (see Rudolph & Tschohl 1977). In regard of disciplines such as philosophy or psychology (both of which, to be sure, especially in the German scholarly tradition from Herbart to Külpe were often combined into ,philosophical psychology', see Boring 1950, Pongratz 1967), one further would expect a certain type of rational discourse for which Brentano's *Psychologie vom empirischen Standpunkt* (Brentano 1874) and Stumpf's *Tonpsychologie* (1883, 1890) are good examples. These works (as well as many other) incorporate definitions, elements of classification and typology, and make use of all kinds of empirical evidence. Yet the strength of both Brentano and Stumpf is the conclusiveness of arguments most of which are supported by logical thought *and* factual evidence. The systematic relevance of, for example, Stumpf's *Tonpsychologie* (which, to be sure, is as much a philosophical work as it is a psychological and psychomusicological treatise, see Schneider 1997b), rests on its conceptual organization, and especially on the consistency of ideas presented in a logical sequence of reasoning from one chapter to the next.

As regards the ,systematic' treatment of a subject, this is achieved more easily in case principles are found inherent in the matter under investigation. Typically, a field which is governed by objective principles can be given a systematic treatment. This holds true, for example, for acoustics as being a part of physics, or for tone systems as constructs ruled by mathematical laws as well as by physical factors. Consequently, works written on acoustics in general, on more specialized subfields such as vibrations or acoustics of musical instruments, or on foundations of tone systems, can be expected to reflect the order and consistency inherent in the subject matter itself (see, e.g., Morse & Ingard 1965, Meyer & Guicking 1975, Fletcher & Rossing 1991/1999, Lindley & Turner-Smith 1993).

2. The other meaning of ‚systematic‘ has to do with procedural and methodological aspects. In order to establish a system of knowledge concerning a field of study, one has to conduct research that needs to be broad enough to cover many if not most of the aspects relevant to the analysis, description, and understanding of phenomena belonging to that field. Research programmes therefore aim at being as complete and consistent in actual investigations as is possible. Explanations of phenomena should be based on theoretical considerations, on carefully formulated hypotheses, and on empirical evidence.

Ideally, systematic studies will be grounded in theory, and will stem from a methodological framework that leads to clear observations as well as to empirical data suited to allow for unambiguous explanations of the phenomena under review. ‚Systematic‘ research often is conducted in, for example, a comparative, typological or similar approach not restricted to individual cases. Systematic studies can, however, be undertaken to fill well-defined gaps in our current knowledge of a given subject. In many instances, systematic studies rather aim at finding certain (e.g., statistical) regularities, and sometimes they may lead to the formulation of ‚laws‘ or general rules derived from inductive generalization (see Hempel 1965).

Systematization of findings, of hypotheses and other scientific concepts is an ongoing process of empirical research and theoretical reasoning. There are various types of systematization including rational explanation and prediction (for which formal models such as developed by Carl G. Hempel and Paul Oppenheim exist; see Stegmüller 1983). The ultimate goal of systematization is to establish coherent systems of knowledge that should be free from any contradictions, and should be as complete in descriptions and explanations of the principles and phenomena of a certain field as is possible. The systematicitiy thus achieved is the result of cognitive systematization which, in principle, does not make any a priori assumptions about the systematicity of the objects which are studied (e.g., nature as a whole, or certain parts thereof; see Rescher 1979, 2000a, ch. 1). Rather, the systematicity of many natural phenomena (such as vibration, wave propagation, and sound) has been discovered in a long research process that is still continued.

It is plain to see that a truly ‚systematic‘ approach in this way will be of help in increasing, in particular the coherence and „explanatory power“ of our knowledge concerning a given field or discipline (see Rescher 1984, ch. I). In disciplines outside the exact sciences, however, such a systematic strategy perhaps is more difficult to pursue. Though it often is still possible to identify certain principles which are fundamental to a field of study as well as to understanding its subject matter, methodologies, etc. (see Rudolph & Tschohl 1977, Karbusicky 1979, Gigerenzer 1981, Schwarz 1985), establishing ‚laws‘ in the social sciences or even in the humanities is a goal difficult to achieve. One of the reasons is that, in the social sciences, such ‚laws‘ in many cases are based on statistics of data obtained from empirical measurements. Generalizations thereby rest on statistical inference, and can be considered as one form of ‚inductive‘

reasoning which, in most cases, „extrapolates" from some or even many observations. ,Incomplete induction' (see Mach 1905/1926) thereby has to estimate the validity of the generalization; for practical research, generalizations made on the basis of limited evidence often means that we offer the most plausible and most reasonable explanation that can be given at a certain time, and with a certain amount of factual evidence at hand (see Rescher 1980). This implies that inductive generalizations can be refuted, or corrected in the light of new findings.

To sum up this chapter, the concept of a ,system' has been briefly addressed here on several levels: (1) *nature* as being conceived of as an ordered, highly structured whole that becomes the object of scientific research directed at disclosing these structures, and the principles which govern the formation and persistence of such structures. As a special case of a ,living system' found in nature, the biological organism capable to maintain itself (as well as to undergo mutation) has been mentioned; (2) *science* in total as well as individual disciplines which, due to ,systematic' research, again make up ordered, highly structured wholes; (3) the individual *subject* that, as a 'cognitive system', investigates all kinds of things in order to acquire coherent knowledge of the „world" as well as of himself or herself. In a sense, individuals are capable to accumulate and synthesize knowledge in a way as ,systematic' as will be achieved by a scientific discipline comprising of many researchers. Undoubtedly, there have been scholars of universal as well as ,systematic' erudition such as Leonardo da Vinci or Hermann von Helmholtz. Further, regarding systematization, it has been suggested that ,inductive' reasoning became so powerful especially in empirical research because it strongly reflects our personal experience from processes such as repeated observation, abstraction from individual cases, and attempts at a generalization (Mach 1905/1926). In this respect, each individual trying to understand „the world" as completely as is possible needs to apply cognitive operations such as categorization and classification. Evidently, we systematize our knowledge in order to gain a coherent, structured and causal understanding of the phenomena we experience[7].

3. Foundations of Systematic Musicology

In certain respects, the beginnings of systematic musicology can be traced back to antiquity, and in particular to Greek scholars such as Archytas of Tarent who investigated mathematical models of tone systems (see Van der Waerden 1947/49, Vogel 1975), or to Aristoxenos who apparently did some experiments on perception and on tuning of melodic and harmonic intervals. The breakthrough of experimental work in acoustics and music, however, happened in the 17th and 18th centuries, respectively, and was accompanied by theories relevant to vibration in strings, air columns, and solids as well as attempts at calculating absolute frequencies from vibrations observed in strings (for details, see Dostrovsky & Cannon 1987). By about 1800, much of what is found in a modern textbook on fundamentals of musical acoustics had been investigated by great scientists like Marin Mersenne, Isaac Beeckman, Christiaan Huygens, John Wallis, Joseph Sauveur, Leonard Euler, Jakob and Daniel Bernoulli, Brook Taylor, and many

---

[7] The problems involved are discussed, from quite different angles, in Husserl 1939/1976, Estes 1994, Rescher 1979.

others. Another field that had become important to organology, music theory and practice alike, was tuning and temperaments. Especially during the 17th century, and well through the 18th, writings on tuning systems (including scordaturae) and keyboard temperaments make up a fairly large portion of the musicological literature (see Rasch 1983, Lindley 1987, Lindley & Turner-Smith 1993). Many of these publications, written by practitioners (organists, organ builders, etc.) with a background in music, music theory and organology, aim at relating temperaments calculated from irregular or regular divisions of the octave to actual tuning practice. Conversely, treatises on harmony (such as Rameau's and Tartini's works) not only reflect current issues in acoustics, tunings, etc. yet also discuss aspects of music perception and appreciation. Even compendia which treat musical composition and performance of music in a more technical perspective (e.g., Heinichen's *Der Generalbass in der Komposition* of 1728 or some of Mattheson's writings) deal with aspects of tunings and temperaments as well as with other material that one would attribute to „systematic" musicology rather than to the historical branch of the field. Perhaps the main reason is that many of these works were conceived so as to treat musical matters in a comprehensive and architectonic fashion. In particular Mattheson, who commanded an encyclopaedic knowledge (being by no means restricted to music), aimed at a truly systematic presentation, that is, the material he works on is systematized so as to form a coherent, rational treatise (see, e.g., Mattheson 1731, 1739). Up to about 1800, musicology in Germany maintained this rather systematic and rational approach. During the 19th century, historiography in general as well as historical orientations in musicology were much influenced by Hegelian metaphysics of history, on the one hand. On the other, historical particularism emerged. Both combined into streams of „Historismus" (philosophical as well as factual historicism, see Schneider 1984) which were accentuating philology as well as hermeneutics as methodology. At the same time, empiricism dominated in the sciences, and spread into new disciplines such as sociology and psychology which adopted scientific methodology based on calculation, measurement, statistics, experimental and other empirical investigations. It is at this junction that humanities and sciences parted, and so did historical and systematic musicology.

Looking at the beginnings of systematic musicology in the 19th century in Germany, we see significant contributions to the field in acoustics, psychoacoustics, music theory, aesthetics, and other areas of research. As regards acoustics, there had been seminal publications by Ernst Florens Friedrich Chladni (1756-1827), one of the founders of modern experimental acoustics (Chladni 1805, 1817; see also Ullmann 1996). Chladni is perhaps best known for his research on vibration of tuning forks, bells and other idiophones and the method to demonstrate modes of vibration by means of *Klangfiguren* (sound figures). Further, Chladni invented some musical instruments. His seminal book on acoustics (1805) indeed tries to systematize phenomena of vibration and sound in regard of musical instruments, on the one hand, and hearing, on the other. The physicists Georg Simon Ohm (1789-1854) and August Seebeck (1805-1849) contributed to both acoustics and psychoacoustics. They engaged each other in a famous debate on the nature of pitch perception (see Hesse 1972, pp. 58, Schneider 1997a, pp. 131). Pointing to Fourier's theorem, Ohm claimed that the ear performs a frequency analysis whereby complex sounds are dissolved into their constituents. According to Ohm's view, the fundamental frequency should account for the sensation of pitch whereas the number and strength of harmonics would determine the timbre of a sound. Using sounds from a siren, Seebeck demonstrated that a periodic time signal was enough to bring about a sensation of a definite pitch. His findings which stressed the principle of periodicity inherent in wave trains were of consequence to theories of pitch based in the „time domain" (e.g., Hesse 1972, Schneider 1997a, 2000). Surprisingly, perhaps, Helmholtz took Ohm's side. The reason was that for Helmholtz (see below) Ohm's frequency theory could be explained on grounds of anatomical structures found in the mammalian cochlea whereas Seebeck's periodicity theory was difficult to interpret in the light of anatomical and physiological facts known at the time.

Pitch theories involving periodicity did of course have an experimental basis. The pulse trains produced by a siren are a special case of regular sequences of pulses. Such had been taken into account since long, and in particular in regard of intervals tuned on organ pipes by means of beats. Sauveur (1700, p. 137) had argued that the sounds of two pipes tuned into unison (or almost so) *s'accordoient à fraper l'oreille d'un même coup.* From this it can be inferred that not just unisons yet also other simple ratio intervals of two tones produce conjoined pulse trains entering the ear.

Hypotheses of pitch perception based on internal patterns or „rhythms" of pulse trains in Germany were issued by Friedrich Wilhelm Opelt, in 1834, and in more detail in 1852 (Opelt 1852). As early as 1834, Opelt also suggested a geometrical model of pitch relationships that later became known as the ‚tone column', and which maps a spiral of pitches onto a cylinder so that tones being an octave apart fall on the same vertical line[8]. This model was adapted by Moritz Wilhelm Drobisch (1802-1896), an eminent scholar in the field of mathematical psychology (e.g., Drobisch 1850) and logic who also contributed to systematic musicology. Drobisch devoted his musical studies to tone systems, temperaments and the perception of pitch and intervals. He developed fundamentals of the two-dimensional model of pitch which later became popular with Géza Revész' textbook *Grundzüge der Tonpsychologie* (Révész 1913). It was Drobisch (1855, pp. 35), however, who combined the circle of chromata, the identity of octave-equivalent tones and the dimension of tone height into one coherent model for which he gave a geometrical construction. This model contains the sequence of musical pitches as a logarithmic spiral wound around a cylinder whereby the position of each tone is defined by two criteria, namely (1) the divergence (*Abweichung*) of a given tone from the base tone (*Grundton*) which is due to the chroma circle, and (2) the elevation or raise (*Erhebung*) which is a function of the frequency of vibration. The decisive feature of the construct, according to Drobisch (1852, 38) is that it not simply yields a helix yet a curved plane as is visible in figure 1(a). The structure of horizontal and vertical lines, Drobisch says, result in a spiral staircase, that of musical pitch. If the fact is taken into account that frequency doubles with octaves, and that the absolute frequency difference between notes an octave apart is smaller in the lower octaves than in the higher ones, figure 1 (a/b) results which shows the ‚pitch staircase' for three octaves.

---

[8] Opelt's small booklet of 1834, titled *Ueber die Natur der Musik* (Plauen and Leipzig: Hermann und Langbein), was known to Drobisch (1855, 38). As to its content, see Auhagen 2000.

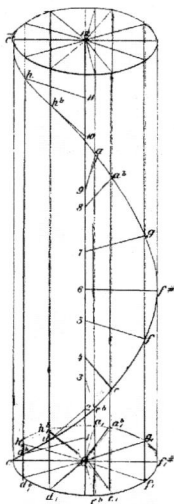

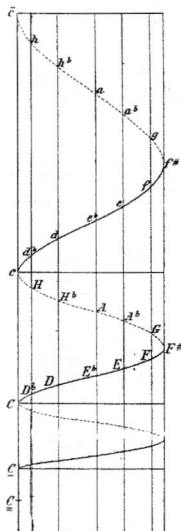

Figure 1 (a/b): Drobisch's construction of the 'pitch staircase' (1855)

The approach to ground models of perception on mathematical foundations had been advanced by Johann Friedrich Herbart (1776-1841), Kant's successor at Königsberg. Herbart (1812, p. 164; 1824/25, Vol. 1) had proposed a one-dimensional continuum of pitch which he had labelled *Tonlinie* (see Schneider 1997a, pp. 404). This model became influential for Stumpf (1883) who first held that, of three arbitrary tones a, b, c, only one can be in the middle position between the two other. This implies that the three notes must be located as „points" on a single dimension. Stumpf, a trained musician himself, of course knew that there are distinct tone qualities (or chromata) that repeat in each octave. Further, he had observed that there are several characteristics relevant to musical tones such as brightness, sharpness, volume, density etc. that can be distinguished by subjects. Stumpf (1883) proposed the one-dimensional model for the sake of, as he argued, simplicity as well as to avoid logical problems inherent in a multi-dimensional treatment of perceptual relations between stimuli. He later (1914) publicly corrected his view and accepted the two-dimensional model of pitch as had been advanced by Révész (1913).

For the early development of SM, it was essential that in Germany several scholars were active in the fields of acoustics, sensory physiology, psychophysics and experimental psychology (see also S. Vogel 1993, Boring 1950, chs. 2, 13-19). Among these scholars (whose individual contributions cannot be accounted for in this place) we find the physicist Wilhelm Weber (1804-1891) who, together with his brother Ernst Heinrich (1795-1878) conducted interesting experiments on pitch phenomena in organ reed pipes (see Jonquière 1898, p. 238). Ernst H. Weber is known for his contributions to psycho-physics, namely for experiments on jnd's which led to what is known (in the formulation of Fechner) as „Weber's law" $\Delta E = k \cdot \Delta S/S_0$ (E = sensation, S = stimulus). This work was continued by Theodor Gustav Fechner (1801-1887) whose textbook on psychophysics (Fechner 1860) not surprisingly points to sensation of musical pitch to exemplify the formula $E = K + k \cdot \log S$ (a.k.a. „Fechner's law"). Fechner's formula is derived from integration of a sequence of Weber fractions which, for the very nature of jnd's, form kind of a step function (see Schneider 1997a, 405-414). Fechner's formulation of the ‚psychophysical law' smoothes the steps (as well as extrapolates the regions where the logarithmic relation of stimulus magnitude and sensation applies). Fechner's ‚law' (the graph of the function is presented, in a schematic form, in figure 2), accounts well for octave equivalence of musical tones[9].

Pitch

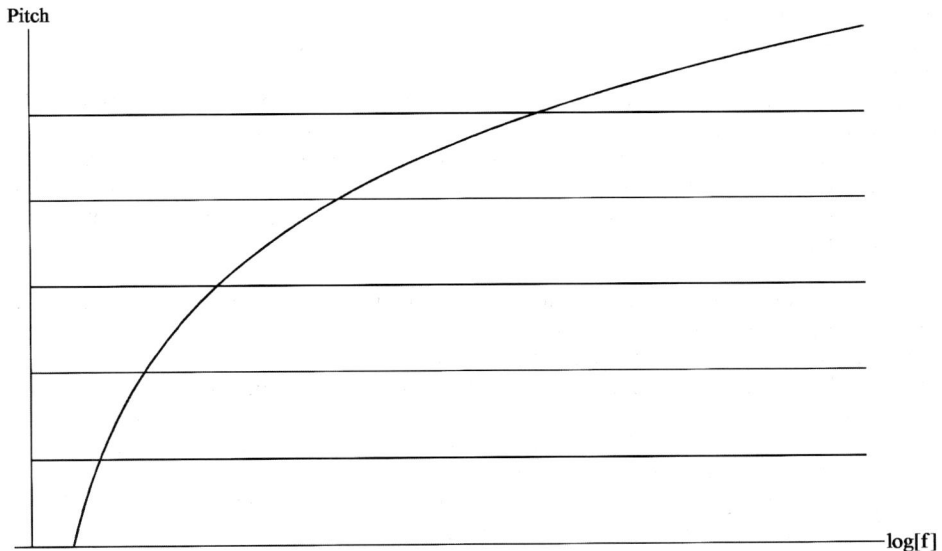

log[f]

Figure 2: Graph of Fechner's "law" plus octaves indicated as horizontal lines

This aspect, to be sure, had implications for the refutation of one-dimensional models of pitch. Fechner's ‚law' was further used by Stumpf (1901) in an attempt to explain the equidistant seven-note scale he had observed in „Siamese" (Thai) xylophones.

Among the experimental psychologists, Wilhelm Wundt (1832-1920) had included fundamentals of auditory perception, and even aspects of *Gehörvorstellungen* (auditory images), into one of his textbooks (Wundt 1873/74). Wundt was of importance to SM simply because much of the research carried out in his Leipzig laboratory had to do with sensation and perception, and in particular with psychoacoustics (see Boring 1950, 341). The dissertations of Carl Lorenz and Felix Krueger are but two of the experimental

---

[9] Fechner's law also applies fairly well to the scaling of the magnitude of loudness sensation. The difference between a Fechner scaling of loudness, and a Stevens scaling based on the ‚power law' $E = S^k$ is not very large (depending of course on the absolute values of the exponent k, and of the integration constant k, in Stevens' and Fechner's formula, respectively).

studies that came from Wundt's lab. The dissertation of Carl Lorenz (1890) on the perception of tonal distances became famous because it led to a public controversy between Stumpf (1890) and Wundt (1890). Felix Krueger's investigation of combination tones (1901) were part of his extensive research on consonance (Krueger 1905-1910). In particular in regard of hearing pairs of pure (sine) tones having harmonic frequency ratios (e.g., 3:2, 5:4), Krueger considered differential tones ($f_2 - f_1$; $2f_1 - f_2$) as significant for sensory consonance since these would add a fundamental to partials of a harmonic series. For example, the difference tone $f_2 - f_1$ of two pure tones of 500 and 400 Hz would be 100 Hz.

In addition to research done in Wundt's lab, there were more investigations in particular of sensation and perception of consonance and dissonance. Carl Stumpf did many experiments which led him to stress the principle of „Verschmelzung" as being relevant for consonance (see below). Theodor Lipps (1885,1905) advanced another theory of consonance based on „microrhythms". The essential idea is that periodicities inherent in a complex musical sound made up of several tones can have a common base periodicity, and that such periodicities found in signals might bring about corresponding periodicities in neural activity. This theory looks astonishingly modern as it contains elements of theories of hearing based on periodicity detection (see Schneider 1997a, 1997b, 2000). As far as the „microrhythms" are concerned, Lipps in part continued ideas issued by Opelt.

Besides acoustics and psychoacoustics, another field central to SM is music theory. In the European tradition, it is customary to distinguish between ‚speculative music theory', usually based on mathematical, physical and logical foundations, and ‚practical theory' relevant to actual composition and music analysis. This distinction in part relates to that of *musica theorica* and *musica practica* known from the Middle Ages and the Renaissance. Of course, both fields have been connected to some degree by various scholars. During the 18th century, acoustics had gained such a momentum that Rameau, perhaps most of all, incorporated findings of acoustics into his works on music theory (see Rameau 1737, 1750, Christensen 1987). There were other attempts at giving music theory ‚scientific' foundations (as is obvious, for example, in Tartini's treatise on harmony; see Tartini 1754/1966).

In the 19th century, it became customary to incorporate at least some basics of vibration, sound, and tone systems into textbooks on (‚speculative' as well as on more ‚practical') music theory. Typically, such books opened with a chapter which briefly outlines ‚fundamentals'. For example, the first volume of Gottfried Weber's *Versuch einer geordneten Theorie der Tonsetzkunst*, one of the most comprehensive works on music theory after 1800, starts with a chapter on hearing, on vibrations, and on sound in general[10].

It took decades, however, before a serious and systematic attempt was made to establish music theory, in particular harmony (often regarded as the most central part of music theory), on an acoustic, and thereby ‚scientific' basis. This work was carried out by Arthur von Oettingen (1836-1920), a physicist who proposed a new, elaborate system of tonal harmony (see below).

---

[10] Of this work, I had only the 3rd edition (4 vols, Mainz: Schott 1830-1832) at hand.

There were music theorists who did seek ways to ground music theory outside acoustics. One of the most educated was Moritz Hauptmann (1792-1868) who worked as a musician, composer and conductor. His argument, set forth in a book on foundations of harmony and meter (Hauptmann 1853/1873), basically is that music should be approached rather as a language that works according to grammatical principles. The framework of a theory suited to lay out principles of musical composition and musical apprehension, thereby would be guided by logic and grammar. Hauptmann's way of thinking and terminology were influenced by philosophical concepts elaborated by Hegel (see Rummenhöller 1963). Hauptmann in turn became influential for Hugo Riemann (1849-1919) though Riemann rejected Hauptmann's views of musical metrics, and proposed his own system instead (Riemann 1903). Before dealing with some of Hauptmann's ideas, with Riemann's struggle to build a systematic music theory as well as with basics of Oettingen's acoustic and psychoacoustic approach to music theory, two brief chapters on Helmholtz and Stumpf, respectively, will be inserted. The reason is that Helmholtz and Stumpf did provide comprehensive books and other publications relevant to SM that not only did built on the empirical research undertaken in the course of the 19th century yet did include important theoretical and methodological issues. It was Helmholtz who first presented a book that, because of its interdisciplinary and comprehensive approach to foundations of music perception and music theory viewed with respect to physics and physiological acoustics, can be regarded as paving the way for our discipline. Moreover, Helmholtz had done research on a variety of acoustical and musical problems that cover, among many other topics, sound production in a bowed string and the mechanism of bowing, theory of tone systems as treated in classical sources of Greece and the Near East, explanation of perceptual phenomena such as consonance and dissonance, etc. Stumpf complemented, in part corrected, and expanded the research work of Helmholtz, and also gave SM some explicitly ‚cognitive' directions. Further, he started CM in Germany as an important field of research.

3.1 Hermann von Helmholtz: empiricist open to cognitive issues

Hermann von Helmholtz (1821-1894), a scholar of world fame in physics, mathematics and other disciplines, can be regarded also to be one of the founders of systematic musicology in modern times. Though there had been a fair amount of experimental investigations especially in musical acoustics long before Helmholtz (see, e.g., Dostrovsky & Cannon 1987, Ullmann 1996, Beyer 1999), it was he who, throughout his work, most successfully did demonstrate interrelations of physical theory and experimentation, mathematical modelling, physiological investigations, and philosophical reasoning (see Cahan 1993). Helmholtz also underpinned the need to conduct experimental and other empirical research on music perception, organology and other fields that belong to systematic musicology .

Though Helmholtz, regarding theory of perception, accepted certain concepts of Kant´s transcendental idealism, he always stressed the role of experience as a prime force for cognitive development as well as for learning processes in general (see Helmholtz 1879). To Helmholtz, even perception in a single individual involves experimentation since one can explore the range of changes in perception which occur when we change the conditions under which certain stimuli are presented. Often, this can be achieved by simply moving our body. For example, when listening to sounds, one can explore the intensity and direction of the sound source by turning the head to the left and to the right. The approach is one which involves, on an elementary, subjective basis, ‚repeated measurement' which is effected by means of our sensory organs whose input is evaluated in perception. Experimentation, in this way, starts with ourselves acting as both ‚subject' and ‚experimenter'.

Regarding sensation and perception of musical and other stimuli, Helmholtz distinguishes at least three levels of processing:

1. the first level is based on sensation that is closely dependent on the anatomical structure and physiological functions of the peripheral sensory organ such ear and eye, respectively;
2. the second level is perception proper that is based on the sensory input. This is processed, however, with the help of so-called „unconscious inference" (*unbewusste Schlüsse*) that can be regarded as one type of mental associations. In contemporary cognitive approaches one could say that categorization of sensory input is achieved with the aid of knowledge gained from previous experiences that is stored in long-term memory. Repeated exposure to the same or to „similar" stimuli thus leads to stable perceptions as well as to knowledge that is expanding due to inductive generalization. It is from experience and learning that certain rules are established in each individual.
3. In case the „content" of perception is very distinct and clear to the subject perceiving, he or she reaches the level of apperception (*Anschauung*) that always involves cognitive acts such as comparison, classification, identification, etc.
4. Helmholtz also admits that subjects can have images (*Vorstellungen*) of phenomena which are actually not present regarding peripheral sensory input.

From this scheme it should be clear that Helmholtz indeed saw the basis of perception, and also of more complex knowledge, in experience that for each individual stems from observation and self-observation understood as experiments. An experiment, in a more narrow and technical sense, then can be defined as an observation achieved under such conditions which permit control of variables and parameters. Helmholtz, however, did not want to reduce perception, or even apperception, to processing of sensory input. It was his point of view (see Helmholtz 1879, 222) that perception results only in ‚symbolic' representations of the things in the world outside, and does not yield a true „picture" (*Abbild*) of objects perceived. According to Helmholtz, perception results in symbols, and not in icons. The claim he makes, however, is that the same object of perception will produce the same symbol in case the conditions under which perception is performed are the same.

Helmholtz (1870, 4) rightly says that, in music, sensations have a more immediate effect than they have in the other arts because, typically, sensations evoked by sound are not used to produce images of things and processes in the world outside. In the visual arts, according to Helmholtz, sensations have different functions: the appreciation we feel, for example, when viewing a marble statue, does not arise from the white light reflected from a marble statue yet from the image we form of a beautiful body which the statue depicts. Hence, sound structures that cause sensations are also the ‚perceptional object' in music whereas, in the visual arts, the ‚perceptional object' is embedded in

28

such sensations, on the one hand, yet different in quality from the sensory input, on the other.

Helmholtz' concept of ‚unconscious inferences' which, as it seems, did not meet full approval of psychologists at the time (cf. Stumpf 1895, 309), has been incorporated into more recent models in cognitive psychophysics where the perceptual response to a physical stimulus is regarded to make use of learning, memory, and estimation of meaning (see Marks 1992, 170, Fig. 3.13).

Perhaps the most significant aspect of Helmholtz' *Lehre von den Tonempfindungen* (1863, 1870, 1896) is that it presents a comprehensive, coherent and indeed systematic account. Helmholtz himself said that decisive parts of the book such as the chapters on sensory consonance and dissonance all rest on facts which can be o b s e r v e d. Helmholtz' treatise starts from basics of acoustics, hearing and psychoacoustics, to proceed to consonance and dissonance in regard of musical chords, and to tonality, scale types and other topics which fall into music theory (for which Helmholtz' book, as its title implies, intends to provide physiological [as well as psychoacoustic] foundations). Though Helmholtz includes aspects of psychology (e.g., memory for chordal structures, perceptual evaluation of different intonation of intervals and chords), and refers to (western and oriental) music history for the sake of description and elaboration of certain phenomena, his argumentation throughout the book is based on facts and principles which fall into the realm of science (i.e., anatomy of the inner ear, the sense of hearing, acoustics and psychoacoustics). In this respect, Helmholtz (1870, 369-374) restricts his competence to such aspects which can be explained in scientific terms, on the one hand, and seeks to avoid value judgements as well as the search for psychological motivations for certain developments in music, on the other. He argues that, notwithstanding the foundations music has in laws of (organic and anorganic) nature, the actual range of musical expression and musical forms found in various cultures in part has to be attributed to aesthetic principles and decisions. These have changed in the course of history, and are likely to change again. The task of science can only be to seek for the *technical* principles which are effective in different styles of musical production, whereas aesthetics might look for artistic motives from a psychological point of view.

3.2 Carl Stumpf: cognitive psychologist open to experimental research

Whereas Helmholtz stressed the role of sensation that is „shaped" by the specific structure of peripheral sensory organs, Stumpf held that perception is an active process centred in cognition rather than in processing of stimuli which evoke some physiological response (registered by the subject as a sensation). Of course, Stumpf – a doctoral student of the physician and philosopher Rudolf Hermann Lotze (1827-1881) – did not deny that sensations arise whenever certain stimuli are presented. Neither did he question the role of learning, and of experience in general. Stumpf had a broad philosophical background (from Platon to Kant, and from Aristotle to Hume), yet his own approach was shaped considerably by his teacher and friend, Franz von Brentano (1838-1917), who developed a specific way of empiricism coupled with minute theoretical considerations as is obvious in his *Psychologie vom empirischen Standpunkt* (Brentano 1874) as well as in writings ranging from problems in perception to mathematical and logical issues.

Stumpf's empiricism certainly had foundations in his reading of Aristoteles, as well as in Brentano's writings and personal instructions. Stumpf also was influenced by his academic teachers in physics, Wilhelm Weber (see above) and Friedrich Kohlrausch (1840-1910), the latter noted for his experimental skills. Stumpf himself conducted very many experiments regarding acoustical phenomena as well as perceptional issues such as consonance and dissonance, memory for intervals and melodies, discrimination and identification of timbres, etc. In regard of psychological experiments having to do with perception and apperception of music he, in general, followed the method of self-observation (*Selbstbeobachtung*; see Stumpf 1883, 1890, 1898a/b) which, to be sure, should not be confused with introspection[11]. The reason why Stumpf preferred self-observation (which he often calls *direkte Beobachtung*; see Stumpf 1898b), no matter if conducted by himself or by other skilled researchers (e.g., the philosophers and psychologists Alexius von Meinong and Stephan Witasek at Graz), was the degree of precision, validity and reliability of such observations he deemed necessary for scientific research (se Stumpf 1914, 307; 1919, 5). Stumpf (who played six instruments) and other scholars of that era (like Külpe, v. Hornbostel etc.) did have professional expertise which was lacking in persons without musical training and experience (*Unmusikalische*). Stumpf, therefore, always was reluctant to rely on judgements of musically untrained persons, notwithstanding there had been experiments with groups of non-musical subjects (in Stumpf's view, *Kollektivversuche an Unmusikalischen*).

The phenomenological approach to perception as was developed, in particular, by Stumpf (1883, 1890, 1898a/b; for theoretical considerations see Stumpf 1924, pp. 243, 1939, §§ 14-19), needed subjects which were capable intellectually to conduct precise observations of their perceptions and imaginations, and to report such observations in a way that was sound, and open to the control of other researchers, in their respective experiments[12]. In regard of Stumpf's theory of consonance based on *Verschmelzung*, there had been such experiments conducted at Graz by the philosophers and psychologists Alexius von Meinong and Stephan Witasek as well as by their student, Anton Faist (Meinong & Witasek 1897, Faist 1897), and at Berlin by Stumpf's own student, Max Meyer (1898). Also, another famous philosopher and psychologist, Oswald Külpe, had engaged in experiments on (auditory and visual) *Verschmelzung* as well as in a psychological explanation of *Verschmelzung* and of *Verknüpfung* (concatenation). Both can be regarded as cognitive processes directed at combining elements we perceive or imagine (see Külpe 1893, part II). One may call this approach „subjective" (what, in certain respects, it is, and deliberately so). The outcome of such experiments, however, was quite elucidating in regard not only of fundamentals of music perception, yet for psychology in general.

The point that distinguishes Stumpf from Helmholtz, in Stumpf's (1883:VI) own words, is this: regarding sensations of sounds, psychophysics as advanced by Helmholtz are concerned with the conditions and antecedents that lead to certain sensations, whereas psychologists are concerned with the effects such sensations have for music perception. To this day, Carl Stumpf's *Tonpsychologie* (1883, 1890) is regarded as a major work in cognitive psychology, with special emphasis on perception and

---

[11] As to introspection, see Boring 1953, Pongratz 1967.

[12] The same holds true, in principle, for the experiments Külpe and his co-workers conducted in the field known as *Denkpsychologie*; see Külpe 1922, pp. 297.

apperception of music. Stumpf (1883, 1890, 1906) found it essential to investigate, in particular, psychic functions (psychic acts if one applies the terminology of Stumpf's teacher and friend, Franz von Brentano [1874]) which include *perceiving* [or noticing] *of phenomena and the relations these may form, integration of phenomena into complexes, the formation of notions and concepts, comprehension and judgement, emotions, desire and will* (Stumpf 1907, 4/5). Psychic functions (acts, frames of mind, experience) are relevant to the perception of simple and more complex sound stimuli such as single notes, musical intervals, melodic and rhythmic patterns, chords, etc.

Though Stumpf underpins the active role our mind plays in perceiving, this point of view should not be mistaken in a modern „constructivist" way. The phenomena which we perceive *have* certain characteristics in an objective way, e.g., complex harmonic sounds have partials which can be detected in analytic hearing. The frequencies of such partials are in small integer ratios which results in perceiving a specific quality peculiar to configurations of partials in harmonic complex sounds, and of several such sounds played simultaneously in a chord. Stumpf labels the perceptual quality *Verschmelzung* (1890, 1898, 1906, 22/23; 1911, 1926, ch. 11; see Schneider 1997b). Though, cognitively, *Verschmelzung* is the result of apperception in that the relational structure of a tonal configuration is recognized as such, in regard of sensation and (simple) perception *Verschmelzung* is a property inherent in certain sound phenomena. Notwithstanding the awareness we derive of *Verschmelzung* when listening analytically, it is not a quality which would be generated only by the act of perceiving, and then attributed to the stimuli. According to Stumpf's own reports, he investigated phenomena of *Verschmelzung* while playing the keys of an organ where he had mixture stops activated. As is well-known, the groups of pipes which make up a mixture stop are tuned in just intonation. The effect of several such pipes sounding together is that a harmonic complex sound is generated which, by its constituents, appears as a highly consonant chord. According to Stumpf (1911a, 323), however, *Einheitlichkeit* (consistency, integrity) is not *Einheit* (unity, oneness)[13]. It is characteristic of the experience of *Verschmelzung* that we can switch, by focusing our attention, between (a) the percept of the chord as an highly integrated and homogeneous structure resulting from its constituents, and (b) single constituents being part of a sound structure which we can detect, „hear out", and identify by analytic listening. Further, we can (c) focus on the interval relations between two or more constituents, to find out which harmonic intervals are realized between constituents of the overall sound. As Stumpf (1939, pp. 229) elaborates, a musical chord is a specific configuration of relations between a number of tones. We yield the percept of a *Dreiklang* (triad) not because there are three notes (*drei Klänge*), yet because the relations between all tones integrate into one specific configuration (which Stumpf labelled *Verhältnisganzes*). Also, we can (d) judge various *degrees* of Verschmelzung (a quality which is scalable, see Schneider 1997a/b) as we are listening to different sound and chord structures.

Consequent to the distinction of phenomena and psychic functions, Stumpf (1906, 1924, 39; 1939) distinguishes between *external* (sensory-based) perception, and *internal* (psychic) perception (*innere Wahrnehmung*). Since the latter involves comprehension as well as conscious awareness of the psychic acts (and not just the content of the acts), the

---

[13] Attempts at understanding Stumpf's concept of *Verschmelzung* simply as *fusion* take but one of its characteristics into account, and, hence, fall short of the complexity of Stumpf's considerations.

notion of *apperception* as discussed by Brentano (1874), Wundt (1896/1928, pp. 244) and Külpe (1912, 167) may also be used.

Though Stumpf developed his theory of perception and apperception in great detail, in a number of psychological and philosophical writings (Stumpf 1873, 1883, 1890, 1898, 1907, 1919, 1924, 1939), some of the fundamentals of Stumpf's approach in regard of, in particular auditory perception, can be sketched thus:

Figure 3: Fundamentals of auditory perception (Carl Stumpf, 1883-1939)

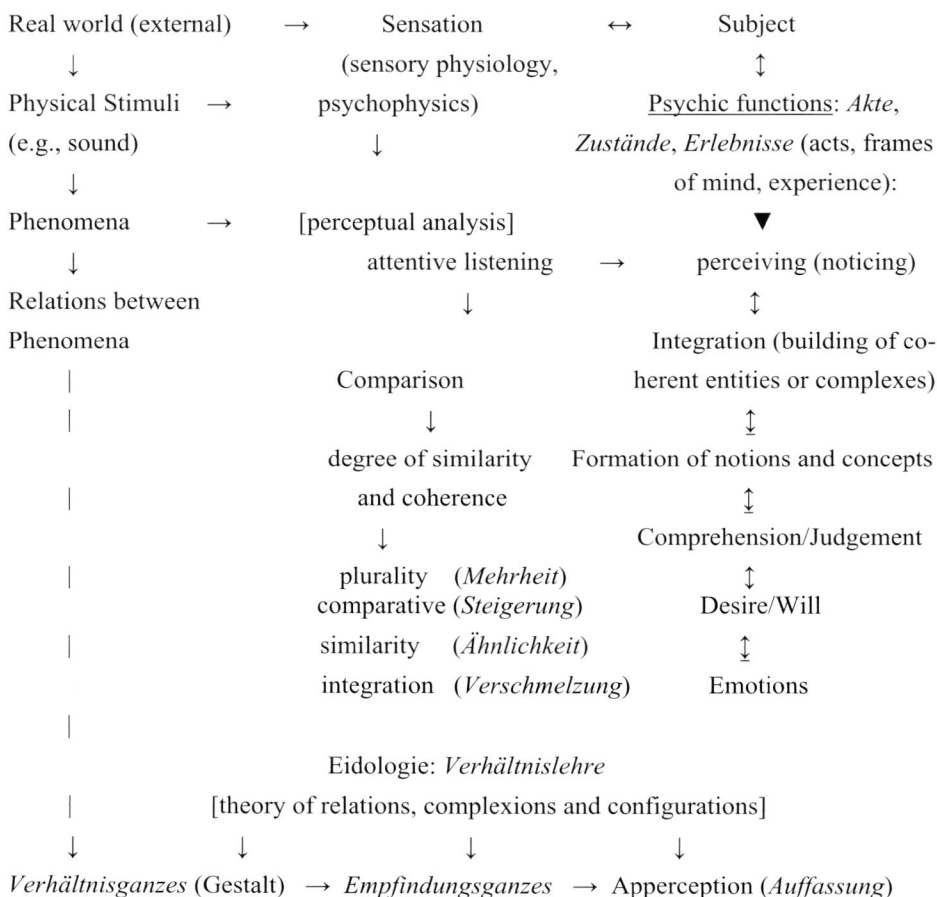

Real world (external)　→　　Sensation　　↔　　Subject
　↓　　　　　　　　　(sensory physiology,　　　　↕
Physical Stimuli　→　　psychophysics)　　　Psychic functions: *Akte*,
(e.g., sound)　　　　　　↓　　　　*Zustände, Erlebnisse* (acts, frames
　↓　　　　　　　　　　　　　　　of mind, experience):
Phenomena　　→　　[perceptual analysis]　　　▼
　↓　　　　　　attentive listening　→　　perceiving (noticing)
Relations between　　　　↓　　　　　↕
Phenomena　　　　　　　　　Integration (building of co-
　|　　　　　Comparison　　herent entities or complexes)
　|　　　　　　↓　　　　　　↕
　|　　　degree of similarity　Formation of notions and concepts
　|　　　　and coherence　　　↕
　|　　　　　↓　　　Comprehension/Judgement
　|　　plurality　(*Mehrheit*)　　↕
　　　comparative (*Steigerung*)　Desire/Will
　|　　similarity　(*Ähnlichkeit*)　↕
　　　integration　(*Verschmelzung*)　Emotions
　|
　　　　Eidologie: *Verhältnislehre*
　|　　[theory of relations, complexions and configurations]
　↓　　　　↓　　　　↓　　　　↓
Verhältnisganzes (Gestalt)　→　*Empfindungsganzes*　→　Apperception (*Auffassung*)

Stumpf assumes that the sensation of a stimulus undergoes some internal processing (*innerliche Bearbeitung der Empfindung*) which, first, leads to the perception of a stimulus. In a final state of cognitive processing, comprehension of the *specific* relational structure of, for example, musical formations (*Gebilde*) such as chords and chord progressions, leads to apperception as a mental act which gives us awareness (a) of the qualitative and quantitative features of the perceptual content as well as (b) of the act itself. Given a certain complexity of musical stimuli, to accomplish the task of apperception certainly needs attention, intensive training, and also categories on which judgements (*Urteile*) are based. The categories necessary as well as the conditions relevant for perception of musical formations are discussed in the first two volumes of Stumpf's *Tonpsychologie*. His *Konsonanz und Dissonanz* (Stumpf 1898) expands the topic of perception of musical intervals, the article *Konsonanz und Konkordanz* (Stumpf 1911a) treats perception and apperception of triadic and chordal structures. Taken together, these two publications contain much of vol. 3 of the *Tonpsychologie* (as announced by Stumpf 1890 in the preface to vol. 2 of this work; see also Stumpf 1924, 221). In addition, volume 4 should have dealt with affective and emotional aspects of tone sensation and perception.

Stumpf is often regarded as being one of the founders of Gestalt psychology (see Ash 1995). This view rests, at least in part, on the fact that major representatives of Gestalt psychology (e.g., W. Köhler, K. Koffka, M. Wertheimer) were Stumpf's students (Wertheimer, for unknown reasons, left Berlin in 1904 to take his Ph.D. at Würzburg, with Külpe as his supervisor; see Ash 1995, p. 105). Though Stumpf in several of his publications dealt with auditory phenomena in such a way that aspects of Gestalt perception were involved (e.g., 1898, 1911a), his main tool was the meticulous description and analysis of perceptions as well as of the psychic functions needed to accomplish such analysis. *Die Untersuchung der sinnlichen Erscheinungen als solcher* was what Stumpf (1924, 243) defines as phenomenology[14]. It starts at the empirical level yet involves most intricate epistemic problems (see Stumpf 1939, § 13). The concept of Gestalt is often implied in Stumpf's thought. He was certainly aware of the seminal article of Ehrenfels (1890), and of Meinong's contributions to Gestalt theory including reflections on so-called *Gegenstände höherer Ordnung* (Meinong 1891, 1899). Stumpf had debates with Meinong not only on the concept of *Verschmelzung* (see above) yet also in regard of Meinong's *Gegenstandstheorie* and other issues[15]. Gestalt theory and Gestalt psychology had to be developed to overcome limitations imposed on (empirical as well as ‚philosophical‘) psychology by earlier concepts which had favoured association as a means to explain the perception of complex objects (see Boring 1952, ch. 12). Associations still figured prominently in Wundt's psychology. Association, however, is a principle which refers to sequential and „additive" cognitive processing, and hardly accounts for the „holistic" perception of melodies, chords, rhythm patterns and other musical structures which, from about 1880 on, became the focus of Gestalt theory and Gestalt psychology, respectively.

---

[14] Stumpf's view basically is that of an empiricist addressing perceptual and cognitive issues. His understanding of phenomenology differs considerably from that of his one-time student, Edmund Husserl (as outlined in, for example, his *Cartesianische Meditationen*; Husserl 1969) though Husserl, in *Erfahrung und Urteil* (1939), includes many aspects of perception and cognition.

[15] Notably, Meinong's works on epistemics. One aspect which is not decisive in terms of theory and methodology yet interesting historically, is that most of the scholars who were involved in, first, Gestalt *theory* (the older generation, including Stumpf, Meinong, Ehrenfels, Marty), and then, empirical Gestalt *psychology* (including Köhler, Koffka, Wertheimer, Hornbostel, Gelb, Lewin) knew each other personally, and had exchanged letters and other personal communications. Also, Ehrenfels and Meinong had close contacts with Guido Adler, and with musicology in general. As to historical aspects, see Smith 1988, Ash 1995, Weber 1997.

When Gestalt psychology had gained momentum, around 1920, Stumpf gave a brief yet concise account of what *Komplex- und Gestalteigenschaften* were, and what their role is, in auditory perception (Stumpf 1926, ch. 11). At the end of his life, he offered a theoretical assessment of developments in philosophy and psychology where he is quite critical of, in particular, Husserl's approach to a „pure" phenomenology (which he said is a contradictio in se), and also reluctant to accept Gestalt psychology in some of its more radical versions (Stumpf 1939, §§ 13-15). Stumpf saw that certain assumptions of Gestalt psychology were hardly compatible with his or other experts' perception of musical structures, and moreover not well-founded in regard of theoretical considerations. Of his former students and co-workers, Hornbostel, in his *Psychologie der Gehörserscheinungen* (1926), incorporated elements of Stumpf's phenomenological approach as well as findings and ideas from Gestalt psychology which, in various lines of research, remained to be most influential for SM before and also after World War II[16].

For a number of reasons, Stumpf since about 1885 had engaged himself in research on non-western music. In major works on music aesthetics and music history alike, there had been views on the singular, outstanding achievements of western music and its theory (including notation) which thus were regarded as „the highest expression of musical art", and hence as the last stage in a long chain of cultural, in particular musical evolution (see Schneider 1984). Also, acoustic facts related to periodic vibration of strings and air columns, and to harmonic sound spectra comprising of partials, had been used again and again to derive the major mode in western music as being based on ,natural law'. Though Helmholtz (1863/1870) had warned that music, as an expressive art that appeals to aesthetic appreciation, cannot be reduced to acoustics and psychoacoustics (though these may constrain musical production and perception), the idea that western harmony is most perfect and „natural" because it conforms to acoustical laws was widespread.

Stumpf, who on occasions had met Indian musicians from America as well as from Siam (later to become Thailand) when touring Europe, and had done some experiments in regard of perception with them (Stumpf 1886, 1901), took an empiricist approach to the study of non-western music. He was familiar with speculations on the origins of music as had been discussed, most of all, in England by Spencer and other „armchair anthropologists" as well as by psychologists (see Stumpf 1885). Stumpf (1911b) gave a rather systematic account on the origins of music whereby ,origins' (*Anfänge*) were understood as „roots", with little concern for the factual (historic) beginnings. In fact, Stumpf presents examples for elementary musical formations which can be regarded as the basis of all music[17]. Stumpf gave a descriptive and analytical report of non-western

---

[16] The many contributions to SM by the psychologist (with a PhD in musicology from Robert Lach), Albert Wellek (1904-1972) deserve special notice. Much of Wellek's research up to 1960 is condensed in his *Musikpsychologie und Musikästhetik* (Wellek 1963). At our institute in Hamburg, Hans-Peter Reinecke (1926-2003) had based his Habilitationsschrift *Experimentelle Beiträge zur Psychologie des musikalischen Hörens* (Reinecke 1964) on Gestalt psychology.

[17] A similar approach was taken much later by Curt Sachs in his *Wellsprings of music* (Sachs 1962), published posthumously. Where Sachs (ch. 2, part V and VI) deals with *The oldest music*, he in fact treats structurally elementary forms, e.g., one-step melodies and similar examples found at the very „bottom" of an evolutionary scale ranging from „primitive" (meaning simple, rudimentary) to „developed" (complex, diversified).

(mostly „primitive") music which, in many instances, referred to sound recordings contained in the Phonogramm-Archiv at Berlin.

His interest in non-western music(s) did stem, at least in part, from personal and scientific curiosity to learn more about the broad range of musical phenomena outside Europe. More specifically, Stumpf took non-western music to test assumptions held in psychology and musicology at the time (see Schneider 1991, 1993, 2006). The objective study of non-western music provided the material to check foundations of western music as well as ideas related to the evolution of music which were current in musicology and other disciplines. CM, as Stumpf and his co-workers understood the field, was not only striving to collect and preserve music from abroad that had been neglected for too long (see Simon 2000). CM could be pursued, in a systematic manner, to deal with issues in perception and cognition as well. In this respect, CM was (and still is, see Graf 1980, Födermayr & Deutsch 1998, Schneider 1997a, 2001) complementary to SM.

Stumpf's research programme clearly combined SM with CM, as can be gathered from statements in his biographical and philosophical *Selbstdarstellung* (1924, pp. 257) as well as from a programmatic paper offered in cooperation with Erich M. von Hornbostel (Stumpf & v. Hornbostel 1911). However, essentials of his reasoning in regard of perception and cognition in general, and his views on music perception need to be reconstructed from various publications (Stumpf 1883, 1885, 1898, 1901, 1907, 1911b, 1926, 1939). According to Stumpf, SM means an empiric, interdisciplinary approach that aims at a full description, detailed analysis, and *causal understanding* of musical phenomena. These include sound, its production and sensation (see Stumpf 1926). Stumpf's approach certainly is interdisciplinary (or, given his personal work and that of his co-workers such as Otto Abraham and Erich M. von Hornbostel, transdisciplinary) in that he urges music research to integrate methods and findings from physics/acoustics, sensory physiology, psychology, anthropology/ethnology, aesthetics/philosophy, and music history. In Stumpf's view, SM has its center in psychology and music psychology (see Stumpf 1924, 258), with a focus on perception and cognition. In this respect, it differs from Helmholtz who had grounded SM in sensory physiology, acoustics and psychoacoustics.

SM as pursued by Stumpf would have to follow an intercultural, comparative approach aiming at thoroughly investigating phenomena. Besides objective description and analysis such an approach might be suited to finding regularities in a broad sample of musical expressions; by abstraction of essential features, one could then establish (basic as well as more complex) types of musical formations[18]. Further, this approach of SM combined with CM might finally yield the principles of music perception valid for many, if not all cultures. However, the approach had to be free from speculations, and instead had to be based on empiric methodology and the evidence gained from descriptive and analytic studies. Stumpf (1901, 1911b, Stumpf & Hornbostel 1911) and von Hornbostel (1910) argued that the results which CM had already achieved in a few decades were enough to question some assumptions concerning the universal validity of foundations of western music (see Schneider 1991, 1997a). With the help of sound recordings made all over world from 1890 on (when a version of the Edison phonograph usable in the field was available), CM had convincingly demonstrated the diversity of

---

[18] Typological methods, and studies directed to building typologies, were (and to some extent, still are) often pursued in CM as well as in folk song research; see Nettl 1983/2005, Schneider 1993, 2006.

musical phenomena as found in many cultures (see Nettl 1983/2005). The comparative approach was necessary to see whether this diversity could be systematized in regard of typologies as well as of concepts and principles (see Stumpf 1911b, Sachs 1962, Graf 1980, Schneider 2006, Nettl, this volume), and was also chosen to explore certain genetic and historic aspects.

3.3 Hugo Riemann: systematic music theorist

As much as Helmholtz had laid the foundations for SM in regard of acoustics and psychoacoustics, Stumpf had given it a thorough basis in regard of psychology. He also had integrated SM with CM, and had started a lab and an archive to further both. What was missing, to some extent, notwithstanding Helmholtz' attempt at providing the backbone also for the study of harmony, was a treatment of music theory that could claim the same level of scientific rigor and systematicity that had been achieved by Helmholtz (1863/1870), and later by Stumpf (1883, 1890).

As was briefly indicated above, there had been two major publications on systematic music theory contributed, around 1860, by Moritz Hauptmann (1853), and Arthur von Oettingen (1866), respectively. Their approach differed fundamentally in that Hauptmann, then a respected composer and conductor (he worked as Thomaskantor at Leipzig), treated music theory from a perspective of philosophical ideas applied to harmony and metrics, whereas Oettingen, the physicist with a musical background, aimed at giving music theory scientific foundations. Hugo Riemann drew from both when he (1872a, 1872b, 1873) set out to build his own, systematic music theory which, as Riemann claimed, would establish no less than a coherent, up-to-date *Musikalische Logik*.

Hauptmann, evidently influenced by Hegelian ideas, had offered a ‚deductive' approach to music theory (see Rummenhöller 1963). His construction of tonal relations in single triads as well as of cadences on the basis of numbers and ratios relates closely to the tripartite scheme of dialectics. For example, he considers the octave as *Einheit*, the fifth above a given note as *Zweiheit oder Trennung*, and the major third between the two as *Einheit der Zweiheit oder Verbindung. Die Terz ist die Verbindung der Octav und der Quint* (Hauptmann 1873, 20)[19]. The ideas Hauptmann elaborates for harmony and meter, respectively, give rise to a systematic treatment, however, they are quite normative (as might be expected within a deductive theory). In regard of perception of major triads, Hauptmann (1873, 19) states that there are (but) three immediately apprehensible (*direct verständliche*) intervals, namely (1) the octave, (2) the fifth, (3) the major third. His claim then is: *Sie sind unveränderlich*, meaning that they are the constituents of a system that, for its logical truth as well as its foundations in music and music perception, remains fixed. In this respect, Hauptmann differs clearly from Helmholtz (see above) and the empiricist point of view that calls for oberservations to allow ‚inductive' inferences based thereon.

The terminoloy employed by Hauptmann as well as his ‚deductive' reasoning pointing very much into the direction of *Musikalische Logik* was not greeted by everyone at the

---

[19] The terminology of *Einheit, Trennung, Ausser-sich-sein, Zu-sich-kommen* etc. reminds strongly of Hegel's *Phänomenologie des Geistes* (1807) which, to be sure, comes from a theological background (see Schneider 1984, pp. 84)

time. However, ideas such as viewing the basic cadence I – IV – I – V – I as if it constitutes a scheme of thesis, (first) antithesis, (preliminary) synthesis, antithesis, and (final) synthesis was appealing to philosophically trained musicologists like Riemann who, on the basis of *Quintengeneration*, saw a further opposition embedded in the cadence, that of *Unterquinte* and *Oberquinte* which results in a symmetric structure around a tonic, e.g.

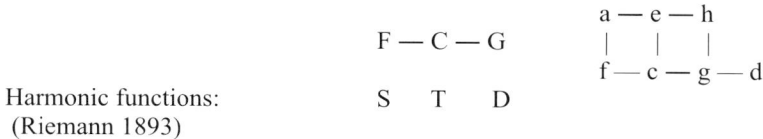

$$
\begin{array}{ccc}
 & a — e — h \\
F — C — G & \quad | \quad | \quad | \\
 & f — c — g — d \\
\end{array}
$$

Harmonic functions: S   T   D
(Riemann 1893)

Hauptmann's proposition of the octave (2:1), the pure fifth (3:2), and the just major third (5:4) as the (exclusively) *direkt verständliche Intervalle* implies that his system of tonal relations, and of harmony in general, is conceived on the basis of just intonation, on the one hand, and that it is ‚dualistic' in regard of major and minor tonalities, on the other.

Harmonic dualism is an approach to music theory that, as a full-fledged system, was outlined by Arthur von Oettingen (1866, 1903-1906, 1913, 1917; see Vogel 1966) yet which does have certain forerunners. Riemann (1877, 1905) shared the dualistic point of view, and defended it vigorously (see below.). Apparently, Riemann considered G. Zarlino (1517-1590) to have issued, in the *Istituzione harmoniche* (1558, 3rd ed. 1573) ideas which contained, at least in nuce, a differentiation of major and minor harmonies[20]. To be sure, harmony as based on textures of major and minor chords must not be equated with tonality in the modern sense of the major-minor-system. Zarlino (Parte terza, cap. 31, p. 210) indeed uses the term *Harmonia*, and distinguishes between two types of ‚harmony' which can be derived from the harmonic and the arithmetic division of a string. Riemann has been criticized for mistranslating Zarlino, allegedly on purpose to yield a ‚dualistic' interpretation of the text in question (Dahlhaus 1957). This criticism, as has been shown recently (Rehding 2003, 28), for the most part does not hold.

Harmonic dualism as proposed by Hauptmann and Oettingen, respectively, was not the result of, as Adorno has put in regard of Schönberg's twelve-tone theory, *losgelassene Spekulation*. It was a serious attempt at finding a solution for a problem that was discussed in works on music theory at least since 1700, namely the very ‚nature' of the major and the minor tonality. By nature, we have to understand natural (i.e., acoustical, physiological, etc.) foundations as well as logical explanations[21]. The former is what Oettingen had in mind when publishing his works on harmonic dualism, the latter is what is implied in Hauptmann's *Die Natur der Harmonik und Metrik*.

Many, if not most theorists since Rameau (1737) had derived the major tonality from the harmonic partials 4:5:6 as contained in a complex tone played, for instance, on a stringed instrument such as a harpsichord. Though it is possible, in principle, to derive a minor chord from the partials no. 10:12:15 acoustically, since these partials are present in the sound of a complex tone played on a harpsichord, and with relatively strong amplitudes in the spectrum (see Beurmann & Schneider 2003), it will be difficult (if

---

[20] Riemann (1898), Kap. 13; 2nd ed. 1920, p. 389; 1914b, 91.
[21] As in the German phrase *Die Natur der Sache* (the nature of a thing) which, as a type of logical explanation, is frequently used in legal arguments as well as in the sciences and engineering, respectively.

possible at all) to „hear out" these partials against the others. Rather, one hears o n e complex tone, and within this complex tone can identify (applying Stumpf's strategy of auditory probing for *Verschmelzung*; see above) a few of the lower harmonics (most likely, the partials no. 2, 3, 4, 5). Such experiments might be suited, in some way, to underpin the ‚natural' foundations of the major tonality. They do not really help in establishing the minor tonality which, as treatises from the 17th and first half of the 18th century show, was not always regarded as being „inferior" to major, or „sad" and „depressed" in character. As Mattheson (1739, Vorrede, p. 14) explained, the sequence of soft (minor [mollis]) and hard (major [durum]) thirds as found in the chords of the diatonic scale d – e – f – g – a – h – c is the consequence of (as he calls it) „physical" ratios whereby all chords of the diatonic scale are part of the same natural order. As can be checked empirically, composers especially before 1800 have made frequent use of the minor tonality, and theorists have treated major and minor as two different yet in principle equal modes of tonality. However, as already Helmholtz (1913, p. 477) had observed, in the course of the 19th century especially most of the modern popular dance music and songs were occupying the major tonality. Walter Wiora, in this respect, spoke of the *Verdurung* of folk song in Germany and adjacent areas during this period. In addition, Helmholtz saw that, in modern („serious") music of his time, the minor chord c – ēs – g (ēs indicating the just major third 4:5 below g) was used so as if c was its fundamental note (*Hauptton*); this, he said, gives the impression that the chord substitutes for a C-major chord which is slightly changed or blurred (*getrübt*). In fact, quite a few textbooks on harmony treat the minor tonality as if it were *tief alteriertes Dur*, thereby eliminating minor as a tonality in its own right.

The equal status a major and a minor chord have for many theorists was based on the simple fact that they are equal as to the intervals making up the ‚building blocks' for the respective major and minor chords, i.e., a major and a minor third. Though these are combined in two different ways (5/4 x 6/5 = 3/2; 6/5 x 5/4 = 3/2), the overall „content" of the two resulting chords does not differ. Also, if played on a harpsichord, the sound quality of, for example, an A-major compared to an a-minor chord changes very little in regard of brightness (spectral centroid) whereas there can be, in the sound of the a-minor chord, a slight increase in spectral inharmonicity which may account for a slightly higher sensation of roughness[22].

Since composers and music theorists accepted the minor tonality as a mode of meaningful musical expression, there had to be some explanation about the ‚nature' of the minor tonality. The harmonic series of string partials (see above) was not really suited to put minor on par with major since the partials needed to establish a minor chord are too far away from those of the major chord. A better choice was to make use of two distinct mathematical principles, the harmonic and the arithmetic division as applied to a string of given length. Harmonic and arithmetic divisions were known since antiquity in music theory (see Vogel 1975/1993). In fact there are several possible operations to derive a series of ‚undertones' that is perfectly symmetric to a series of ‚overtones' derived from harmonic division.

In result (leaving out a discussion of string sections, frequency ratios, etc. as detailed in Vogel 1975/1993), the overtones and undertones would form the following scheme:

---

[22] Beurmann & Schneider, unpublished measurements, 2002-2003.

tone	←b	c	d	f	as	c	f	c	c	c	g	c	e	g	b	c	d→
no.	←9	8	7	6	5	4	3	2	1	2	3	4	5	6	7	8	9→

When Riemann (a.k.a. Hugibert Ries[23]) began to publish on music theory (1872a), his draft of a *Musikalische Logik* did not yet relate to overtones, or undertones, or to acoustics at all. Instead, Riemann followed suit of Hauptmann's „dialectic" model of the cadence. Riemann's claim was: *Die Gestalt der Kadenz ist der Typus aller musikalischen Form.* In regard of the cadence, Riemann defines the tonic as thesis, the subdominant (plus the first return to the tonic) as anti-thesis, the dominant and the final return to the tonic as synthesis. However, this early paper was not confined to such rather formal constructs yet contained also remarks on intonation of certain notes in regard of establishing or changing the „meaning" (*Bedeutung*) of a chord which then, for instance, might no longer be the understood as the tonic of a certain cadence, yet might adopt a new function as is the case in modulation. The latter Riemann defines as *die Veränderung der logischen Bedeutung einer Tonstufe.*

Intonation has to be mentioned as a factor important for the study of tonal harmony that concerned Riemann for most part of his academic life, and is a central aspect still in his *Ideen zu einer ,Lehre von den Tonvorstellungen'* (1914-1916; see below). Just intonation, as a theory of tonal relations relevant for music practice, and for analysis of music alike (see Fokker 1944, Vogel 1975/1993, Blackwood 1985), was the basis for Helmholtz, Hauptmann, Oettingen, Stumpf, and Riemann

In his article *Ueber Tonalität* (1872b), Riemann continued the discourse on musical logics of cadences and tonality, however, he introduced, not without making some reservations, aspects of acoustics and psychoacoustics. According to Riemann, ‚speculative' music theory such as offered by Hauptmann, and experimental research as conducted by Helmholtz had to be brought together to allow for true understanding of music: *wir wollen begreifen, nicht nur was wir sehen, auch was wir hören.*

Riemann's point of view shifted again the following year. He (1873a, 29) criticizes Hauptmann for having missed to incorporate acoustical facts into his book in an appropriate way, and blames Helmholtz for being stuck in his lab, confined to experimental work. In short, Hauptmann is too „philosophical", lacking empirical backing to his theory, whereas Helmholtz is drowned in a multitude of observations yet fails to deliver *Definitionen.* Riemann's new hero then was Arthur von Oettingen who, as a physicist and music theorist, had combined the two areas in one approach that Riemann considered to be more on the ‚musical' side than Helmholtz' elaborations on harmony. In particular, Riemann was dissatisfied with what Helmholtz had to offer as explanations for dissonance. Though Riemann did not question sensations of roughness caused by detuned partials or inharmonic spectra, he apparently did not consider such phenomena sufficient to explain dissonance as a musical parameter. Hauptmann had even refused to review Helmholtz' (1863) book. Though he acknowledged Helmholtz' achievements in acoustics and psychoacoustics, he believed *Die Lehre von den Tonempfindungen* to fall short of genuine musical explanations: *das Psychologische im Sinne des Tonverständnisses, das, wodurch in der Musik ein musikalisch bestimmter*

---

[23] For personal and academic reasons, Riemann published his first articles which are of relevance for the present study under the pseudonym Hugibert Ries (= Riemann 1872a/b, 1873); see Arntz 2001.

Sinn auszudrücken ist, was Musik zur Sprache macht, wird im Buche nicht erklärt[24]. Helmholtz who, to be sure, did base his reasoning on the analysis of *sound*, and *sensations* evoked by sound, had not intended to address such issues in detail which he thought should be worked out by experts in music theory and music aesthetics. His book seeks to give music theory scientific foundations in regard of acoustics and psycho-acoustics which, as can be inferred from Helmholtz' treatment of scales, harmony, and tonality would pave the way for an e m p i r i c a l rather than a speculative approach.

In his article on *Tonverwandtschaft* (1873a, pp. 29), Riemann adopts simple integer ratios (such as 1:2, 3:2, 5:4) as a principle to classify the degree of relationship between harmonic partials, and also between the fundamental frequencies of tones in general. He argues that there is a series of tones which, in descending order, are apprehensible in regard of the ratios they form with a fundamental (*Grundton*). Apprehension is possible because the frequencies of such tones are commensurable to the frequency of the fundamental. From this principle, which he (1914b, 91) later attributed to Rameau (1737), Riemann refers to a series of *Obertöne* plus a series of *Untertöne* (derived from a symmetry operation), all in relation of one fundamental tone (*Grundton, Hauptton*). *Untertöne*, in this regard, simply means tones which are below the *Grundton*, and whose positions in relation to the fundamental is determined by the series of harmonic intervals taken downwards:

Figure 4: Series of overtones and undertones

Riemann (1873a) does n o t claim that *Untertöne* (undertones) do exist in the same objective way as do partials (*Obertöne*) in a harmonic complex tone. Quite to the contrary, he says that he, for a time, had believed that complex tones such as produced from playing a piano, could give rise to undertones (hitting the key of c' on the piano, Riemann thought he had heard c, F, C, As; see also 1873b). This impression, though probably attributable to faint resonances of strings in the piano when levering the damper, of course did not „prove" the existence of undertones in the sense that they were contained as partials in a complex tone. Riemann (1873a, 30), therefore, defined *Untertöne* simply as *verwandte Töne* (related tones) of a *Hauptton*. The reason of

---

[24] Hauptmann explains his resistance to Helmholtz in a letter to his friend, Otto Jahn (the well-known classical philologist, and biographer of Mozart). This letter was published in the *Allgemeine Musikalische Zeitung* N.F. 1, Nr. 40 (30. Sept. 1863) at Leipzig. A reprint of the article is found in Rummenhöller 1963 (Appendix, pp. V-XII).

relationship, as was stated above, in Riemann's opinion was that vibration frequencies of undertones are commensurable with the fundamental frequency of the *Hauptton*.

In the same article, Riemann, in agreement with Helmholtz, held that the partials of a complex tone which represent prime numbers {3,5,7,11}, even if sounded together, are apprehensible without any ambiguity, because of their specific relation to the fundamental.

From this principle of ,immediately apprehensible' tones (which he knew from Hauptmann's *direkt verständliche Intervalle*; see above), Riemann groups *Obertöne* and, in the same fashion, *Untertöne* (derived from a symmetry operation, see above) into three classes of consonance. He defines consonance as the sonority that results from tones which have the first degree of relationship, that is, which are derived from the same *Quintengeneration*, the latter being defined as the *Complex der auf den Grundton direkt bezogenen Töne*. To Riemann, only the pure major third (5/4) and the pure fifth (3/2) were of relevance (he did not want to deal with the natural seventh 7/4; see below).

It is in this article that Riemann adopts (a) the two-dimensional tone-net of pure fifths and pure major thirds that had been employed by v. Oettingen (1866). Not satisfied with Helmholtz' qualification of the minor tonality as *getrübtes Dur* (see above), Riemann (b) also follows Oettingen's approach to the minor tonality which implies harmonic dualism. According to Riemann (1873a, 55), the principal difference between a conso-nant major, and a consonant minor chord is simply that the first is derived from a given tone plus the *Obertöne* which belong to the first *Quintengeneration*, the second from a tone plus its *Untertöne*, also from the first *Quintengeneration*. Further, Riemann (c) adopts the terminology of *Tonicität* and *Phonizität*, and of *tonische* versus *phonische Dreiklänge*, from Oettingen who (1903, 64) defines *Tonicität* as the property of tones to be partials of the same fundamental, whereas *Phonicität* means that certain tones have partials in common. In this respect, the C-major chord in just intonation, given by Oetttingen as c – ē – g = c+ (with ē denoting that the tone is a syntonic comma, or 22 cent flat compared to the e which is the fourth fifth [c → g → d → a → e] above c), can be viewed to consist of the partials no. 4, 5, and 6 of a fundamental C, whereby the major chord is formed in upward direction. In a symmetrical operation, the a-minor chord which, in the dualistic perspective and terminology, becomes an e-*Unterklang* (= e° in Oettingen's, °e in Riemann's notation; see Oettingen 1903, 63; Riemann 1893) is formed so that the tone e does have a major third as well as a fifth below him.

Given that *Tonicität* is the property of an interval or chord to **be** part of a [harmonic series build upwards from a] fundamental, and *Phonicität* the property of an interval or chord to **have** partials in common (v. Oettingen 1904, p. 269), it follows that the major chord is *tonisch* consonant, and *phonisch* not consonant; the minor chord, adversely, is *phonisch* consonant but not *tonisch*. To be sure, Oettingen did consider the tones making up major and minor chords to be harmonic complex tones, that is, having a number of partials. Consequently, the tones of the minor chord, though conceived as forming intervals directed downwards from the fifth (which serves as the *Hauptton* of the chord), of course all have overtones to them. The effect described as *Phonicität* is that, in minor chords played in just intonation, a number of partials coincide. For example, in an a-minor-chord (e°) of three tones, each having ten partials, there will be five perfect coincidences plus five additional coincidences between partials an octave apart.

In the introductory chapter of his *Musikalische Syntaxis* (1877), dedicated to v. Oettingen, Riemann once more discusses the complementary structure of *Obertonreihe* and *Untertonreihe*, the latter being implied by the first in our images of tones (*Klangvorstellung*). In regard of a rational explanation of the minor tonality as well as the minor consonance, Riemann maintains that the difference between major and minor is *dass in der Mollkonsonanz die Töne durch eine polarisch entgegengesetzte Beziehungsweise zur Einheit verschmelzen als in der Durkonsonanz.* Riemann's line of argument in this chapter is much closer to psychology than to (psycho)acoustics though Riemann, in a discourse presented in lengthy footnotes (1877, 1-12), carries some remnants of his short-lived hypothesis of undertones as acoustic phenomena, inspired by reading Helmholtz' functional anatomy of the inner ear (1873b), side by side with philosophical and psychological considerations. The notion of *Tonvorstellung* as well as of *Klangvorstellung*, however, are of greater importance in this introduction which anticipates essentials of the *Ideen* Riemann elaborates in his essays 1914-1916.

As is well-known, Riemann was attacked by other theorists of the time, in particular Georg Capellen (1905) who questioned the dualistic approach to harmony and tonality, insisting on a ‚monistic‘ approach instead. Capellen (1905, 8) sums up the ‚monistic‘ Credo which goes: *In der Musik ist das monistische Grundprinzip die Erklärung aller Klänge von unten nach oben, mithin das Durprinzip, das der natürlichen Obertonreihe allein entspricht.* The sentence (spaced out in the original to underpin its importance) in fact contains three propositions, namely (1) all chords and sonorities have to be analyzed, and explained as tonal formations build upwards; (2) the standard hence is the major tonality, and (3) the template according to which chords and sonorities must be analyzed is the overtone series. In effect, the monistic position as claimed by Capellen meant a return to concepts found in Rameau's works (1737) which had emphasized the role of overtones as a means to demonstrate harmonic major (with rather weak constructions in regard of the minor tonality). Subscribing to the monistic credo as expressed by Capellen was equivalent to cancel attempts at dealing with the *Mollproblem* (as it was called before and after Riemann) in a way suited to find a solution which accounts for the independent status of the minor tonality, and for the consonance constituted by a minor chord.

Riemann, in a series of articles (1905), defended the dualistic position, claiming even that Rameau, with his treatise of 1737, had become a ‚dualist‘. He held against his adversaries that, in relying on the overtones 4, 5, 6 to „explain“ major, they had suppressed all higher overtones (such as 7, 9, 11, 13) which, in the actual sound of a complex tone as well as that of a harmonic chord, would be present, and, therefore, as „natural“ as the lower partials. Further, from a psychological point of view Riemann argued that a minor chord (such as °e or °g) appears as much as a perceptually congruent unit (*Einheit*) due to *Verschmelzung* of its parts as does the major chord. In pointing to *Verschmelzung*, Riemann of course relied on Stumpf (1890, 1898) to whom, as he said (1905, 25), we owe emancipation of music theory from the acoustic phenomena. Riemann, however, was dissatisfied with Stumpf because he, even in his treatise on consonance and dissonance (Stumpf 1898), had confined himself almost completely to a discussion of two-tone intervals, with little regard so far for chords. As long as Stumpf and his students were concerned only with intervals (*Zweiklängen*) instead of chords, Riemann (1905, 46) concludes, *befinden sie sich überhaupt noch nicht auf dem Gebiete des musikalischen Hörens.* Already a few years earlier, Riemann (1901), in a quite critical account of Stumpf's 1898 publication, recognized that Stumpf had got lost in discussing various details of interval perception, partly refuting, partly confirming findings and inferences of Helmholtz', and being unfavourable (though not totally opposed to) of Oettingen's attempts at giving harmonic dualism acoustic and psycho-acoustic foundations. By 1901, Riemann knew that there would be no real support from Stumpf's side, or from any other of the experimental psychologists (such as Wundt, Krüger, etc.) in regard of building new, scientific foundations for music theory, and in particular harmony. In his article on harmonic dualism, Riemann (1905, 24) also expressed doubts about some of Oettingen's concepts (which he, however, may not have properly understood; see v. Oettingen 1905, pp. 495).

Riemann (1905, pp. 43, pp. 57) took consequences and revoked most of what he had previously hypothesized about the acoustics or psychoacoustics of undertones. He also says that one has to refrain from explaining musical consonance by means of overtones or combination tones. He admitted, though, that such acoustical phenomena would have to be taken into account in regard of voice leading and other musical parameters. As to the foundations of harmonic dualism, Riemann (1905, 45) simply pointed to the reciprocal structure of the *Oberreihe* (not Ober*ton*reihe!) which is derived as a series of simple multiples of a given vibration frequency [i.e., n x f_i, n = 1,2,3,..., k], and the *Unterreihe* which is the series of multiples in regard of the length of a string (or several thereof).

With his retreat to the complementary structure of *Unterreihe* and *Oberreihe*, Riemann found a „neutral" explanantion which, however, is (a) time-honoured since it was a topic for music theory since antiquity, and (b) sufficient to allow for a rational explanation of the major and minor tonality, respectively (see Vogel 1975/1993). On the other hand, Oettingen, the physicist and systematic musicologist, continued his effort to integrate acoustics into music theory. According to one of his guiding principles (*Leitsatz*), elaborated in his last publication on harmonic dualism and on just intonation as well as on special instruments suited for this tone system and tuning, music and acoustics cannot be separated. To the contrary, they must be approached scientifically following the same principles: *In Musik und Akustik sind die gleichen Grundbestimmungen zu treffen* (v. Oettingen 1917, 158). This is what his dualistic system of harmony and his experimental work in acoustics and organology (1866, 1903-1905, 1913, 1917) tries to realize: integrating acoustics, psychoacoustics, music theory and performance of music again. For v. Oettingen (and later, Martin Vogel and others) there was no irrefutable evidence that the concept of musical consonance and dissonance is totally different, and more or less independent from the consonance or dissonance one perceives when listening to two-tone intervals, chords or whatever *Zusammenklänge*.

To illustrate the case, I may point to one simple example: if one tunes the oscillators of a digital synthesizer so that they produce a just major seventh chord, the resulting sound is stable, coherent, and gives rise to a maximum of *Verschmelzung* (as defined above), that is, sensory consonance[25]. Also, there can be no doubt about the musical structure of the chord. If the same chord is tuned in equal temperament, sensory consonance declines

---

[25] This sound and a number of musical cadences played with such sounds were generated by Martin Folger (1997) on Yamaha synthesizers. The tuning of the chords was as close as was possible techni-cally to just intonation pitch values.

considerably. The composition of such a musically elementary structure of course is recognizable, however, the seventh in the chord appears much weaker (less ‚decisive' if the chord would be used as a dominant seventh chord in a cadence). The difference between the two realizations becomes evident when the almost perfect intonation of the chord is compared to that in equal temperament in regard of spectral irregularity, whereby this is taken as a measure that expresses the relative degree of harmonicity[26].

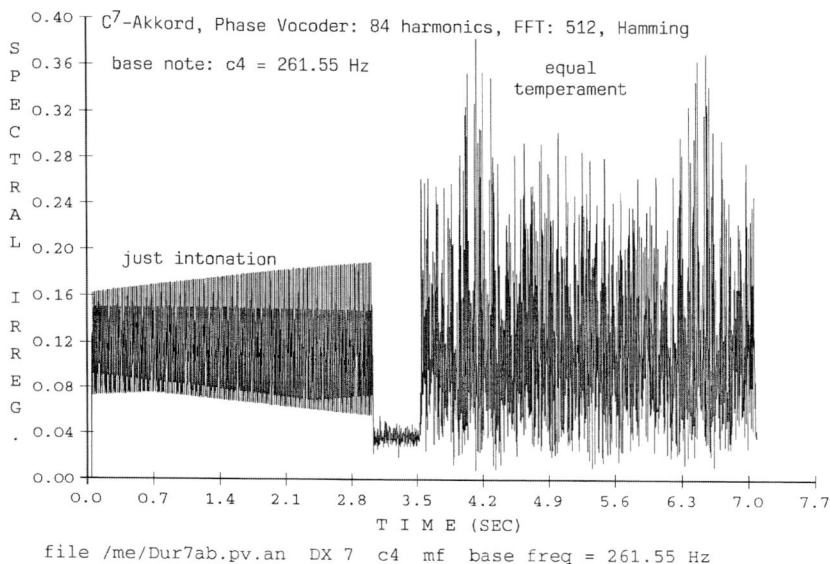

Figure 5: C^7 chord, just intonation ./. equal temperament

The same result is obtained if a full cadence $T - S - D^7 - T$ is played (a) in just intonation, and (b) in equal temperament. Again, the spectral irregularity is much higher in the equal temperament version due to spectral deviations between the notes of each chord, and the increasing amount of amplitude modulation in the dominant seventh chord.

---

[26] Spectral irregularity depends also on amplitude modulation of partials which increases with deviations of partials from small integer frequency ratios. The measurements were done with sndan (Beauchamp 1995) on a NeXT. The base frequency of the phase vocoder was set to the fundamental of the C7-chord, i.e. 261,55 Hz, and to 65,40 Hz for the measurement of the full cadence.

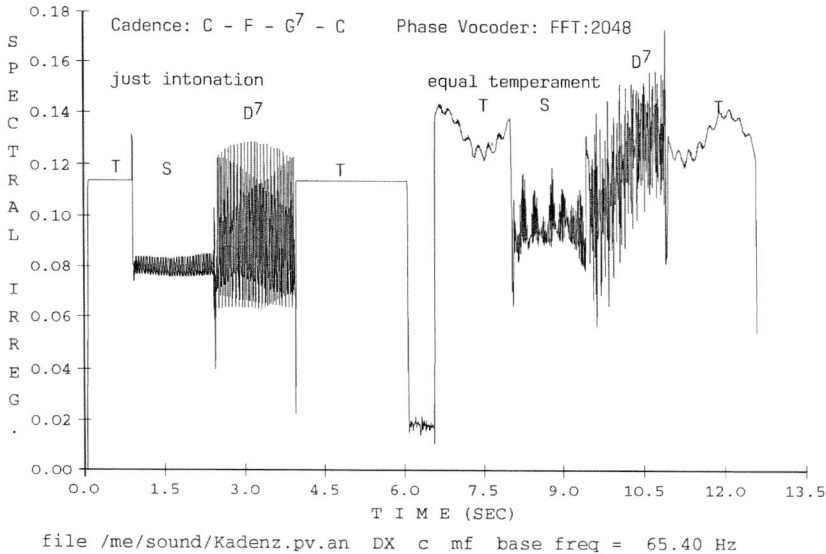

```
      0.18
  S        ┌─                                          
  P   0.16 ┤   Cadence: C - F - G⁷ - C    Phase Vocoder: FFT:2048
  E        │                                         D⁷
  C   0.14 ┤   just intonation          equal temperament
  T        │                    D⁷              T   S
  R   0.12 ┤   T   S                    
  A   0.10 ┤
  L   0.08 ┤
      0.06 ┤
  I   0.04 ┤
  R   0.02 ┤
  R   0.00 ┤
  E
  G
  .        └────┬────┬────┬────┬────┬────┬────┬────┬────┬────
             0.0  1.5  3.0  4.5  6.0  7.5  9.0 10.5 12.0 13.5
                            T I M E  (SEC)
```

file /me/sound/Kadenz.pv.an   DX   c   mf   base freq =   65.40 Hz

Figure 6: cadence of chords $C - F - G^7 - C$ (= $T - S - D^7 - T$), just intonation ./. equal temperament.

There can be no doubt that spectral irregularity, and, consequently, tonal ambiguity increases with the equal temperament version of the cadence since the tonal ‚meaning' of the dominant seventh chord is less clearly expressed in this realization compared to that in (almost) just intonation where modulation effects (caused, in this case, by tolerances within the digital synthesizers used in the production) are very slight.

One important goal of v. Oettingen's attempt at bringing acoustics and music theory together was to make sensation of musical sounds compatible with the apperception of musical structures. According to this view, musical consonance and dissonance must be realized in an acoustically appropriate way, that is, in just intonation in order to reduce perceptual ambiguity and, by means of correct intonation, strengthen the ‚meaning' (*Bedeutung*) of chords. This aspect becomes the more obvious the more complex harmonic structures in tonal music are (see Bister 1988, for examples from Verdi).

Riemann, Oettingen's one-time admirer, by 1905 had given up his ambitions of bringing music and acoustics as well as Stumpf's empirical investigations to congruence. Richard Münnich, assessing what had been achieved, and what went wrong, in Riemann's own *Festschrift*, left no doubt that the gap between experimental research in acoustics and psychoacoustics, on the one hand, and the type of ‚dogmatic' reasoning prevalent in treatises on music theory, had not been bridged yet[27]. Münnich (1909, 76) concluded that Riemann's theory of (musical) consonance would, essentially, fit to the facts relevant for musical listening (*musikalisches Hören*; spaced out in the original

---

[27] By ‚dogmatic', a certain type of reasoning coupled with claims in regard of ‚importance', ‚validity', and ‚truth' is meant. It is found frequently in philosophical, theological and similar contexts, however, also in treatises on music theory; see Rexroth 1971.

German text). He also said that there was no real alternative to the approach Riemann had taken to establish *Harmonielehre als tonale Logik*.

In fact, Riemann had begun his work with the aim to establish music theory as *Musikalische Logik* (see above). He had offered remarkable contributions (e.g., 1877, 1893, 1903) to this field which can be subsumed under the label of systematic music theory. When Riemann saw that his *Musikalische Logik* was not fully compatible with the findings of experimental research, yet could be based on musical considerations and phenomena, the choice was easy. However, as his 1905 essay testifies, he had neither given up harmonic dualism nor his inclination to regard the system of pitches established in just intonation as a reference or standard system. It was due to practical considerations in regard of equal temperament which, for the sheer annual production of pianos in countries such as Germany[28], had become predominant in music (including teaching) that Riemann, and similarly Stumpf, allowed for various compromises. Stumpf (1911a) introduced the concept of *Konkordanz* to deal, finally, with chord structures which he classifies into *konkordant* and *diskordant* according to certain structural features as well as criteria relevant also for consonance and dissonance (these two terms, Stumpf says, apply fully only to two-tone intervals). Stumpf's (1911a, 341) assertion was that *Konsonanz ist eine Sache der direkten sinnlichen Wahrnehmung, Konkordanz ist eine Sache der Auffassung und des beziehenden Denkens*. Therefore, he believes that (sensory) consonance and dissonance differ only gradually whereas *Konkordanz* and *Diskordanz* have a specific difference to them. Riemann (1914a, 49) interpreted Stumpf's concept of *Konkordanz* as supporting his own standpoint in regard of harmonic dualism as well as *Klangvertretung*[29].

Since an expert listener, by means of apperception (*Auffassung*) has to process various kinds of *Zusammenklänge* (concords), it follows that relational thinking (*beziehendes Denken*) is of prime importance, and, in regard of musical textures, rules out perception (which in turn is based on sensations brought about by sounds). Because apperception is the decisive stage of cognitive processing, it is suited to ensure correct understanding of musical structures notwithstanding poor, or even very poor intonation: *Man kann Dreiklänge noch musikalisch verstehen, d.h. als Dreiklänge auffassen, wenn die zulässige Schwelle der Unreinheit weit überschritten ist* (Stumpf 1911a, 342). To be sure, Stumpf did not vote for poor intonation, and he maintains that analysis of music and music theory in general have to be based on just intonation (which he [1926, ch. 11] presumes also to govern perception of musical sounds). His remarks on apperception account for the fact that music, as it is actually performed on a piano or other keyboard instrument tuned to equal temperament needs mental analysis so that the pitches which are ambiguous in regard of acoustics and psychoacoustics will be correctly interpreted musically. For example, whether a triad played on a piano has to be conceived as $c - e - gis$, or as $c - e - as$, is a matter of *Auffassung* which depends on the musical context.

Riemann had put forward elements of what became his *Ideen zu einer ‚Lehre von den Tonvorstellungen'* in, for example, the *Musikalische Syntaxis* (1877) where he speaks of

---

[28] From the figures available, piano production in Germany alone between 1870 and 1910 can be estimated to make up at least 200.000 instruments (the exact number might be considerably higher).

[29] It is not possible, in the present article, to discuss Riemann's concept of *Klangvertretung* though it played a central part in his theory of harmony (see Riemann 1983, 1905). See also Seidel 1966, pp. 62, Vogel 1975.

Tonvorstellung as well as *Klangvorstellung*. He (1877, 15) also points to a concept he calls *Oekonomie des Vorstellens* (economy of apperception) which became important not only for Riemann's own reasoning yet for others as well (Vogel 1975, p. 154). Riemann equated the *Oekonomie des Vorstellens* with a certain law of inertia (*ein gewisses Trägheitsgesetz*) which accounts for, among other issues, the cognitive strategy of listeners to regard the first chord, in a sequence of chords, as the *Hauptklang* (i.e., a reference or ‚anchor‘) as long as it makes ‚sense‘. As soon as we have reason to change our apperception, we will take another chord as *Hauptklang*. This is what listeners are likely to experience when following a complex modulation.

Another phenomenon for which Riemann and other music theorists claim economy of apperception is the broad range of mistuned intervals due to poor intonation, temperaments or other deviations from tone relations which, ideally, form simple integer ratios (such as 5/4 or 8/5). The actual diversity of intonations, according to Riemann (1914/15, 7), is not really a problem since we can always rely on our apperception which reduces complex tonal constellations to more simple ones. Riemann praised *die entschiedene Neigung unserer Auffassung, durch die Wirrnisse der endlosen Möglichkeiten der Ton-kombinationen (in Tonfolge und Zusammenklang) durch Bevorzugung einfacherer Ver-hältnisse vor komplizierteren bequem durchzufinden. Dies Prinzip möglichster Ökono-mie der Tonvorstellungen geht bis in die direkte Ablehnung komplizierterer Bildungen...*

Riemann combined the principle of economy of apperception still with just intonation theory. He (1914/15, 26) argued that we no doubt conceive tonal relations according to just intonation (*Daß wir durchaus im Sinne der reinen Stimmung die Tonverhältnisse vorstellen, steht außer Frage.*). This point of view was also expressed by v. Oettingen (1903, 380; 1913, 6). If our apperception works like prefering simple tonal ratios over more complex ones, this implies that melodies being sung somewhat out of tune, or chords being played on a poorly tuned instrument, will be corrected by means of *Auffassung* which, for Riemann and others, relates somehow to a template of just intonation pitches. These pitches can be abstracted into two- or three-dimensional tone nets which are constructed from series of pure fifths in horizontal lines, series of pure major thirds in vertical lines (see v. Oettingen 1866, 1903, pp. 385, 1917; Riemann 1873a) and, as a more advanced extension, pure natural sevenths (7/4) put in a third dimension (Vogel 1975/1993).

Remarkably, Riemann in his *Ideen* (1914/15, 26) announced a new part of theory which he labelled *enharmonische Identifikation*, and which should have expanded the principle of economy of apperception in a radical way. Riemann was of the persuasion that his concept of enharmonic identification (whatever it was) would overcome all contradictions which were still to be encountered between findings from psychological experiments, on the one hand, and the daily experience of practitioners in music, on the other. Riemann's death, in 1919, prevented that the theory of enharmonic identification was put to paper, and published to end all debates, and forever (*endgültig*, as Riemann puts it).

To assess the impact Riemann had on musicology in general, is beyond the scope of this article (see Arntz 1999, Rehding 2003). Even his achievements in regard of music theory are difficult to judge since Riemann, during the course of his academic life (1872-1919) changed his approach to harmony and other fields in many respects. For example, Seidel (1966) distinguishes three periods in regard of the development of Riemann's *Harmonielehre*. Even the notion *Musikalische Logik*, according to Nowak (2001), refers to quite different things which were important for Riemann at different times, namely first the logic of the musical cadence (as had been set out by Hauptmann, see above), then the logical structure found within individual works of music, and finally the *Tonvorstellungen* which are in the center of musical apperception. Riemann's consideration according to which expert listeners abstract correct tonal relations from diverse intonation patterns as are found in actual performance of music seems appropriate, at least in principle (see Schneider 1997c, 1999). Of course, one has to test such an assertion empirically in order to find the range within which it may apply.

All in all, Riemann's way of thinking in regard of *Tonvorstellungen* and intonation changed over the years as he, at the time of his doctorate (1873a/b), apparently influenced by Lotze and Helmholtz as well as Oettingen, tried to incorporate acoustics and psychoacoustics into a renewned theory of harmony. As was sketched in the preceding chapters, this ambitious project didn't come to fruition really, and by 1905 more or less was given up by Riemann who, seeing the logical and systematic aspect as the most important within his *Musikalische Logik*, concentrated on the cognitive analysis of musical structures and processes which are relevant for *Tonvorstellungen* (see Riemann 1914b, ch. 3: Tonvorstellungen (psychologisch)). Unfortunately, Riemann's move from an integrative approach including empirical science to one grounded more in music analysis and theoretical reasoning has been taken as evidence for a shift in paradigm whereby music theory in total is believed to have lost its normative and systematic character. Instead, it is suggested, we should focus on the analysis and interpretation of compositional techniques viewed in their proper historical context. The very idea behind such proposals is indeed to remove normative elements from music theory, and in particular dismiss whatever ,natural' foundations (western tonal as well as other) music might have. Thereby all the problems which systematic music theory before and after Riemann could not come to terms with would dissolve into „history"[30]. Riemann, though certainly interested in the history of music theory (1898/1920) as well as in the analysis of compositional techniques and individual works of music (as his analyses of Beethoven's piano sonatas amply demonstrate), never gave up his normative thinking. There can be no doubt that the *Lehre von den Tonvorstellungen* Riemann planned to develop in detail was not only conceived to replace Helmholtz' *Lehre von den Tonempfindungen* yet also regarded by Riemann (1914/15, 2) to offer, for the first time, the key to the innermost nature of music (*den Schlüssel zum innersten Wesen der Musik...*).

In a book on essentials of Riemann's music theory (which includes aesthetic and even moral aspects of a theory of music as an expressive art), the normative character of Riemann's way of reasoning in many of his works has been emphasized (Rehding 2003). In this book, Riemann is criticized more than once for his adherence to harmonic dualism, on the one hand, and for his belief in ,undertones', on the other. *Riemann's observation of audible undertones has been refuted; acoustical undertones simply do not exist in the soundwave. Along with this scientific certainty, Riemann's harmonic dualism is completely discredited in current thought* (Rehding 2003, 17). Though harmonic

---

[30] A critical discussion of historicism in musicology is found in Schneider 1984; as to Riemann's *Ideen* and questionable concepts of music theory in the realm of historicism, see also Schneider 1986.

dualism and the hypothesis of audible undertones for a limited period of time no doubt were combined in Riemann's thought, they did not have the same relevance for him (see above), and for their status and effects should be evaluated separately.

The concept of harmonic dualism was formed by Hauptmann, Oettingen, Riemann, and others, to deal with the minor tonality (the tonal *Mollgeschlecht*) in a serious way, treating minor as equal to major. The ‚undertones' Riemann introduced into this concept were not really supported by fact, and moreover unnecessary to justify the concept of harmonic dualism (see Vogel 1975/1993). They did fit, however, into discussions of combination tones and other psychoacoustic phenomena which were current at the time. Also, one has to take into account that Helmholtz' original model (1854, 1863) of the basilar membrane as a set of fibers under tension which are tuned to certain stimulus frequencies (not unlike the strings of a piano tuned to fundamental frequencies of musical tones), and react to stimuli by *resonance*, could give rise to interpretations such as the hypothesis of ‚undertones' put forward by Riemann. He was probably put on the track of finding audible undertones by Helmholtz who, experimenting with resonators he held close to his ear, refers to harmonic undertones of the resonator tone (1870, pp. 78, 1913, p. 75). Subharmonic relations, to be sure, are an element still contained in modern theories of pitch perception. Subharmonic matching processes, though, refer to virtual pitch (Terhardt 1974) whereas Riemann, one hundred years earlier, for a time believed there could be real undertones complementing the series of partials.

In fact, one can generate real sounding *Unterklänge*. Balthasar Van der Pol, one of the well-known scientists in the field of electronics before World War II, developed a method to generate series of subharmonics by means of frequency demultiplication which he used for musical demonstrations (see Van der Pol 1946, p. 18). Moreover, he did not find Riemann's ideas absurd yet said they could be realized with modern technology. One of the most interesting electronic instruments invented by Friedrich Trautwein, the *Trautonium*, operates on series of subharmonics which result in complex *Unterklänge* that have been used in the composition of new music, by Oskar Sala and others[31].

Admittedly, these developments took place after Riemann's death. However, subharmonics did play a part in music since long. As is well known (see Fokker 1944, pp. 56, Vogel 1975, pp. 50, pp. 79), difference tones were used in musical acoustics, organology as well as in musical performance practice[32]. They figured prominently in psychoacoustics, in particular in theories of consonance (see Krueger 1905-1910). It can be demonstrated that sounding a series of harmonic intervals yields a series of harmonic overtones as well as a series of difference tones which appear as *Untertöne* (Vogel 1975, p. 80).

Even if Riemann's impression of having heard undertones was wrong (he was fair enough to revoke his interpretations as early as in January 1873; see Riemann 1873a),

---

[31] Not too long before his death, Oskar Sala produced a CD with his (advanced) version of the Mixtur-Trautonium. Hear Oskar Sala. *My fascinating instrument*. Hamburg: Erdenklang 1990.

[32] In 1996, Pierre Dutilleux, formerly with the ZKM Karlsruhe, has produced instructive recordings where the difference tone f2-f1 was calculated from an actual performance (for example, of polyphonic music played on a cello), generated as sound by means of signal processing, and added (practically, in real-time) to the original cello sound as an additional voice. I'd like to thank P. Dutilleux for a copy of some of the recordings as well as for a paper of his on this computer music project.

this would not discredit harmonic dualism as a concept. Oettingen established harmonic dualism independent of Riemann, and with more regard for acoustics. Riemann (1905) tried to avoid being trapped in overtones and undertones, and based dualism on two complementary principles instead which gave it a more ‚neutral‘ explanation. The mathematical principles of harmonic and arithmetic division which are at hand to generate series of overtones and undertones, respectively, seems to have been the core of the dualistic approach (see Vogel 1975/1993).

Dualism of course can be critized for being too abstract, too far away from demands of „practical" music theory (in the tradition of *musikalische Handwerkslehre*; see Rexroth 1971, ch. 2), or rejected as contradicting everyday listening experience of chords which, as Capellen (1905) claimed, always have to be perceived and imagined bottom-up from a *Grundton*. A musical chord thereby is derived from a pile of thirds („Terzenturm") above a fundamental (*Grundton*) which itself is taken from a diatonic scale. Listening to Sala's music played on the so-called *Mixtur-Trautonium*, one gets an idea that a different apperception of chords, namely top-down, is at least feasible.

After Riemann and Oettingen, another attempt to ground harmonic dualism was undertaken by Sigfrid Karg-Elert (1877-1933). His *Polaristische Klang- und Tonalitätslehre* (1930), resulting from some thirty years of work (as its author states), took dualism to extremes, in a coherent, systematic treatment which, however, is difficult to follow for its complexity as well as the terminology Karg-Elert had to introduce to accommodate his system (for a brief introduction, see Schenk 1966). Karg-Elert, himself a renowned composer in his lifetime, certainly cannot be accused of mediocre musicianship (as was v. Oettingen). He also stayed clear of acoustical speculations. Karg-Elert's dualistic theory, in some more „practical" format (see Reuter 1950), found its way into the classroom of conservatories.

Martin Vogel (1923-2007) combined, in certain respects, essentials of v. Oettingens approach with some of Riemann's considerations as well as Karg-Elert's who, different from Oettingen, had accepted the natural seventh 7:4 as a fundamental musical interval (as was already suggested by Tartini 1754). Vogel's theory (1975/1993) which incorporates the prime numbers 3, 5 and 7, relates to a cyclic three-dimensional tone system of 171 pitches per octave (developed in cooperation with the mathematicians Rudolf Wille and Bernhard Ganter) suited to realize music in just intonation. The idea behind this systematic approach to dualism again is that an almost ‚objective‘ analysis as well as an acoustically unambiguous realization of the harmonic and melodic structure of musical works is possible (for examples, see Vogel 1975/1993, 1984, Bister 1988).

As is well known, Riemann's own concepts of harmony, due to his rather complicated system of tonal functions (including *Klangvertretungen*) as well as the notation of such functions, was not too popular outside central Europe. The generations of theorists after Riemann were determined to make his *Harmonielehre* more „practical" whereby his system was simplified again and again, to the point where not much of Riemann's concepts was visible anymore.

Recently, a certain movement of Neo-Riemannian theory established itself, predominantly in the U.S.A.[33]. If it will give systematic music theory new impetus remains to be seen.

---

[33] See the Special Issue: Neo-Riemannian Theory of the *Journal of Music Theory* Vol. 42, no. 2, 1998.

4. Conclusion

In this article, I have tried to sum up early developments of SM as well as CM in Germany and, at least in part, in the Austrian lands. Roughly, the focus was on the period 1850-1920 within which we find a large number of relevant publications which, besides presenting findings from empirical research, relate to many theoretical and methodological issues. This is what makes reading major works such as written by Hauptmann, Helmholtz, v. Oettingen, Stumpf, or Riemann still worthwhile.

In regard of these scholars and their work as well as SM in general, appropriate understanding is not possible without concern for the philosophical and methodological background. To gain an adequate approach to SM not only in a historic perspective yet also in regard of more recent, or even contemporary research, one needs to reflect what the notion of a system, the quest of systematicity of knowledge, and the continuing task of systematization imply. In addition to the discussion found in chapter 2 (see above), I may refer to some of my previous publications which had addressed issues in theory and methodology of SM and CM, respectively (Schneider 1991, 1993c, 1993d, 1997a, 1997b, 2001, 2003[34], 2006)[35].

Even earlier (1984), I had reason to deal with the idea as well as with concepts of ‚history‘ which, especially in the academic school of historicism (*Historismus*), play a central role far beyond the factual and descriptive level. The metaphysics of ‚history‘ as elaborated, perhaps most of all, in Hegel's philosophy, among his many epigones have been spun out, and have been adopted by scholars in many of the disciplines which, typically, are reckoned among the humanities. Historicism thereby was introduced also into musicology where it is cultivated, in certain quarters, to this day.

Different from the hermeneutics of historicism (which go along with aesthetic considerations and value judgements of various kinds; see Schneider 1984), the history of the sciences must seek to reconstruct theories, methodologies, and findings of our predecessors in a rational and objective way (as a good case in point, see Dostrovsky & Cannon 1987). Such an approach, moreover, seems necessary in regard of continuity of research as well as systematicity of its results. For example, theories of pitch perception from Ohm, Seebeck and Helmholtz to the present can be approached in a historic **and** systematic way whereby structural features of such theories as well as their strong and weak points will become evident. Similarly, it is well possible to trace the history of geometrical and other models of musical pitch from Herbart's one-dimensional *Tonlinie* to Drobisch's three-dimensional staircase of pitches, and further to modern concepts (see Schneider 1997a, Part III).

To obtain a more complete picture of the development of SM and CM, detailed studies of certain areas of research in a historic and systematic perspective will be needed. For example, a critical yet objective evaluation of various approaches to harmonic dualism could be a topic for rational reconstruction which, besides historical insight, could offer findings which might be useful for the theory of tonal music.

---

[34] This article was badly damaged in the editing of the respective volume which had to be reprinted, with corrected versions of my article as well as some other. Make sure that you have the corrected version of this volume at hand (the publishers have exchanged the defect versions for corrected ones)!
[35] See also Elschek 1986, 1992, Nettl 1983/2005, Leman 1995, Seifert 1993 for further information.

References

Adler, Guido 1885. Umfang, Methode und Ziel der Musikwissenschaft. *Vierteljahrsschrift für Musikwissenschaft* 1, 5-20.

Allesch, Christian 1987. *Geschichte der psychologischen Ästhetik*. Göttingen, Toronto: Hogrefe.

Arntz, Michael 1999. *Hugo Riemann (1849-1919): Leben, Werk und Wirkung*. Köln: Concerto-Verlag.

Ash, Mitchell 1995. *Gestalt Psychology in German culture, 1890-1967. Holism and the quest of objectivity*. Cambridge: Cambridge Univ. Pr.

Ash, Mitchell 2002. Carl Stumpf und seine Schüler: von empirischer Philosophie zur Gestaltpsychologie. In W. Baumgartner (ed.), *Carl Stumpf*, 117-148.

Auhagen, Wolfgang 2000. Die Musiktheorie Friedrich Wilhelm Opelts, In: *Musikwissenschaft – Musikpraxis. Festschrift für Horst-Peter Hesse zum 65. Geburtstag*, ed. by Kai Bachmann and Wolfgang Thies, Anif/Salzburg: Müller-Speiser, 13-25.

Barker, Andrew (ed.). *Greek musical writings*, Vol. 2, Cambridge: Cambridge U.Pr. 1989.

Baumgartner, Wilhelm (ed.). *Carl Stumpf*. (=Brentano-Studien, Bd 9). Dettelbach: Röll.

Bertalanffy, Ludwig von 1968. *General Systems Theory*, New York: Wiley, rev. ed. 1972.

Beurmann, Andreas/Albrecht Schneider 2003. Sonological Analysis of harpsichord sounds. *Proceedings of SMAC 03. Stockholm Music Acoustics Conference* 2003. Edited by R. Bresin, Stockholm: KTH, Vol. 1, 167-170.

Beyer, Robert 1999. *Sounds of our time. Two hundred years of acoustics*. New York: Springer.

Bister, Heribert 1988. Die Sept 7:4 in der Akkordfolge. Eine Untersuchung zu einigen harmonischen Zusammenhängen in Giuseppe Verdis *Ave Maria. Scala enigmatica armonizatta a 4 voci miste*. In H. Schröder (Hrsg.). *Colloquium. Festschrift Martin Vogel zum 65. Geburtstag überreicht von seinen Schülern*. Bad Honnef: G. Schröder, 11-34.

Blackwood, Easley 1985. *The Structure of recognizable diatonic tunings*. Princeton: Princeton U. Pr.

Blaukopf, Kurt 1995. *Pioniere empiristischer Musikforschung*. Wien: Hölder-Pichler.

Boring, Edwin 1950. *A History of experimental psychology*. 2nd ed. Englewood Cliffs, N.J.: Prentice-Hall.

Boring, Edwin 1953. A history of introspection. *Psychological Bulletin* 50, 169-189.

Brentano, Franz von 1874. *Psychologie vom empirischen Standpunkt*, Vol. 1, Leipzig.

Cahan, David (ed.) 1993. *Hermann von Helmholtz and the foundations of nineteenth-century science*, Berkeley/Los Angeles/London: Univ. of Cal. Pr.

Capellen, Georg 1905. *Die Zukunft der Musiktheorie (Dualismus oder „Monismus"?) und ihre Einwirkung auf die Praxis*. Leipzig: C. Kahnt Nachfolger.

Chladni, Ernst Fr. Fl. 1805. *Die Akustik*, Leipzig: Breitkopf & Haertel.

Chladni, Ernst Fr. Fl. 1817. *Neue Beyträge zur Akustik*, Leipzig: Breitkopf & Haertel

Chomsky, Noam 1980. *Rules and representations*, New York: Columbia Univ. Pr.

Christensen, Thomas 1987. Eighteenth-century science and the *corps sonore*: the scientific background to Rameau's principle of harmony. *Journal of Music Theory* 31, 23-50.

Dahlhaus, Carl 1957. War Zarlino Dualist? *Die Musikforschung* 10, 286-290.

Dingler, Hugo 1930. *Das System. Das philosophisch-rationale Grundproblem und die exakte Methode der Philosophie*, München: Oldenbourg.

Dostrovsky, Sigalia/Cannon, John 1987, Die Entwicklung der musikalischen Akustik 1600-1800. In: *Hören, Messen und Rechnen in der frühen Neuzeit* (=Geschichte der Musiktheorie, Bd 6), Darmstadt: Wissenschaftliche Buchgesellschaft, 7-79.

Drobisch, Moritz Wilhelm 1850. *Erste Grundlinien der mathematischen Psychologie*, Leipzig: Voss.

Drobisch, Moritz Wilhelm 1855. Über musikalische Tonbestimmung und Temperatur. In: *Abhandlungen der Math.-Phys. Kl. der Sächsischen Akad. der Wiss.* 2, 1-120.

Ehrenfels, Christian von 1890. Über Gestaltqualitäten. *Vierteljahrsschrift für wissenschaftliche Philosophie* 14, 249-292 (engl. translation in Smith 1986).

Elschek, Oskár 1986. Das Forschungskonzept der vergangenen und gegenwärtigen Musikwissenschaft. *Musicologica Slovaca* XI, 52-104.

Elschek, Oskar 1992. *Die Musikforschung der Gegenwart, ihre Systematik, Theorie und Entwicklung*. Bd 1 und 2. Wien-Föhrenau: Stiglmayr.

Estes, William K. 1994, *Classification and cognition*, Oxford, New York: Oxford Univ. Pr.

Faist, Anton 1897. Versuche über Tonverschmelzung. *Zeitschrift für Psychologie* 15, 102-131.

Falcon, Andrea 2005. *Aristotle and the science of nature. Unity without uniformity*. Cambridge: Cambridge Univ. Pr.

Fechner, Theodor Gustav 1860. *Elemente der Psychophysik*, Bd 1, 2. Leipzig: Breitkopf & Härtel (3rd ed. 1907).

Fichte, Johann Gottlieb 1798. *Wissenschaftslehre*, 2nd ed. Leipzig (many reprints).

Fletcher, Neville/Rossing, Thomas 1991. *The Physics of musical instruments*, New York, Berlin etc.: Springer (2nd ed. 1998).

Födermayr, Franz 2003. Vergleichend-systematische Musikwissenschaft. In K. Acham (ed.). *Geschichte der österreichischen Humanwissenschaften. Bd 5: Sprache, Literatur und Kunst*. Wien: Passagen-Verlag, 386-401.

Födermayr, Franz/Werner Deutsch 1998. Zur Forschungsstrategie der vergleichend-systematischen Musikwissenschaft. *Musicologica Austriaca* 17, 163-180.

Fokker, Adriaan D. 1944. *Rekenkundige Bespiegeling der Muziek*. Gorinchem: J. Noordduijn.

Folger, Martin 1997. *Neuere Forschungen zur Tonalitätswahrnehmung*. MA-Thesis, Univ. of Hamburg (Systematic Musicology).

Fries, Jakob Friedrich 1827. *Grundriß der Logik*, 3rd ed. Heidelberg: Winter.

Fries, Jakob Friedrich 1837. *System der Logik*, 3rd ed. Heidelberg: Winter.

Gigerenzer, Gerd 1981. *Messung und Modellbildung in der Psychologie*. München: Reinhardt.

Graf, Walter 1980. *Vergleichende Musikwissenschaft*. Wien: Stiglmayr.

Haller, Rudolf 1993. *Neopositivismus. Eine historische Einführung in die Philosophie des Wiener Kreises*. Darmstadt: Wissenschaftl. Buchges.

Hauptmann, Moritz 1853. *Die Natur der Harmonik und Metrik*, Leipzig: Breitkopf (2nd ed 1873).

Hegel, Georg Wilhelm Friedrich 1807. *Phänomenologie des Geistes*, Bamberg/Würzburg: J.A. Goebhardt.

Hegel, Georg Wilhelm Friedrich 1817, 1827, 1830, *Encyclopädie der philosophischen Wissenschaften im Grundrisse*, 1st, 2nd, 3rd ed. (the 2nd edition of 1827 and the 3rd ed. of 1830 are combined into a critical edition found in G.W.Fr. Hegel, *Sämtliche Werke. Kritische Ausgabe*, ed. by G. Lasson, Band V, Leipzig: F. Meiner 1905).

Helmholtz, Hermann von 1857. Über die physiologischen Ursachen der musikalischen Harmonien. (Vortrag, Bonn 1857). In H. v. Helmholtz. *Vorträge und Reden*. Bd 1, 4. Aufl. Braunschweig: Vieweg 1896, 119-153.

Helmholtz, Hermann von 1863. *Die Lehre von den Tonempfindungen als physiologische Grundlage für die Theorie der Musik*, Braunschweig: Vieweg (3rd ed. 1870, 5th ed. 1896, 6th ed 1913).

Helmholtz, Hermann von 1879. *Die Thatsachen in der Wahrnehmung* (=Speech, delivered at the Friedrich-Wilhelms-University of Berlin in August 1878), Berlin: A. Hirschwald; repr. in H. v. Helmholtz, *Vorträge und Reden*, Bd 2, Braunschweig: Vieweg 5th ed. 1903, 213-247.

Hempel, Carl Gustav 1965. *Aspects of scientific explanation and other essays in the philosophy of science*, New York, London: Wiley.

Herbart, Johann Friedrich 1812. Psychologische Bemerkungen zur Tonlehre. *Königsberger Archiv* 1, 158-192. (reprinted in J. Fr. Herbart. *Sämtliche Werke in chronologischer Reihenfolge*, hrsg. von K. Kehrbach und O. Flügel, Bd 3, Langensalza 1888, 99-118).

Herbart, Johann Friedrich 1824/1825. *Psychologie als Wissenschaft, neu gegründet auf Erfahrung, Metaphysik und Mathematik*, Bd 1 and 2. Königsberg: Hartknoch.

Hornbostel, Erich M. von 1910. Über vergleichende akustische und musikpsychologische Untersuchungen. *Zeitschrift für angewandte Psychologie* 3, 465-487.

Hornbostel, Erich M. von 1926. Psychologie der Gehörserscheinungen. In A. Bethe (Hrsg.). *Handbuch der normalen und pathologischen Physiologie*, Bd XI,1: Receptionsorgane. Berlin: J. Springer, 701-730.

Husserl, Edmund 1939. *Erfahrung und Urteil. Zur Genealogie der Logik*, Prag: Academia (5th ed. by L. Landgrebe Hamburg: F. Meiner 1976).

Husserl, Edmund 1954. *Die Krise der europäischen Wissenschaften und die transzendentale Philosophie*, ed. by W. Biemel, Den Haag: M. Nijhoff.

Husserl, Edmund 1969. *Cartesianische Meditationen. Eine Einleitung in die Phänomenologie*. Hrsg. von E. Ströker. Den Haag: M. Nijhoff (also Hamburg: F. Meiner 1977).

Jonquière, Alfred 1898. *Grundriss der musikalischen Akustik*, Leipzig: Th. Grieben.

Kalisch, Volker 1988. *Entwurf einer Wissenschaft von der Musik: Guido Adler*. Baden-Baden: Koerner.

Kant, Immanuel 1787. *Kritik der Reinen Vernunft*, 2nd ed. Riga/Königsberg: Hartknoch

Kant, Immanuel 1799. *Kritik der Urteilskraft*, 3rd ed. Berlin: Lagard

Karbusicky, Vladimir 1979. *Systematische Musikwissenschaft*, München: W. Fink

Karbusicky, Vladimir/Albrecht Schneider 1980. Zur Grundlegung der Systematischen Musikwissenschaft. *Acta Musicologica* 52, 87-101.

Karg-Elert, Sigfrid 1930. *Polaristische Klang- und Tonalitätslehre (Harmonologik)*. Leipzig: F. Leuckart (Reprint 2004).

Keidel, Wolf 1989. *Biokybernetik des Menschen*. Darmstadt: Wissenschaftl. Buchges.

Krueger, Felix 1901. Zur Theorie der Combinationstöne. *Philosophische Studien* XVII, 185-310.

Krueger, Felix 1903. *Das Bewußtsein der Konsonanz. Eine psychologische Analyse*. Leipzig

Krueger, Felix 1905-1910. Die Theorie der Konsonanz. *Psychologische Studien* 1 (1905/06), 305-387; 2 (1906/07), 205-255; 4 (1908/09), 201-282; 5 (1910), 294-411.

Külpe, Oswald 1893. *Grundriss der Psychologie*. Leipzig: Engelmann.

Külpe, Oswald 1912. *Die Realisierung. Ein Beitrag zur Grundlegung der Realwisssenschaften*. Bd 1. Leipzig: Hirzel.

Külpe, Oswald 1922. *Vorlesungen über Psychologie*. Hrsg. von Karl Bühler. 2nd ed. Leipzig: Hirzel.

Lach, Robert 1913. *Studien zur Entwicklungsgeschichte der ornamentalen Melopoie*. Leipzig: C. Kahnt.

Lach. Robert 1924. *Die Vergleichende Musikwissenschaft, ihre Methoden und Probleme*. Wien, Leipzig: Hölder-Pichler-Tempsky

Lach, Robert 1925. *Vergleichende Kunst- und Musikwissenschaft*. Wien, Leipzig: Hölder-Pichler-Tempsky

Lambert, Johann Heinrich 1771. *Anlage zur Architectonic oder Theorie des Einfachen und des Ersten in der philosophischen Erkenntnis*, Bd 1, 2, Riga: Hartknoch (repr. Hildesheim: Olms 1965).

Lambert, Johann Heinrich 1988. *Texte zur Systematologie und zur Theorie der wissenschaftlichen Erkenntnis*. Hrsg. von Geo Siegwart. Hamburg: Meiner.

Leman, Marc 1995. *Music and Schema theory. Cognitive Foundations of Systematic Musicology*. Berlin, New York: Springer.

Lindley, Mark 1987. Stimmung und Temperatur. In: *Hören, Messen und Rechnen in der frühen Neuzeit* (=Geschichte der Musiktheorie, Bd 6), Darmstadt: Wissenschaftliche Buchgesellschaft, 109-331.

Lindley, Mark/Ronald Turner-Smith 1993, *Mathematical Models of musical scales*, Bonn: Verlag für Systematische Musikwissenschaft

Lipps, Theodor 1905. Das Wesen der musikalischen Konsonanz und Dissonanz. In Theodor Lipps. *Psychologische Studien*, 2nd ed. Leipzig: Dürr, 115-230 [1st ed. Heidelberg 1885].

Löther, Rolf 1972. *Die Beherrschung der Mannigfaltigkeit. Philosophische Grundlagen der Taxonomie*, Jena: VEB G. Fischer

Lorenz, Carl 1890. Untersuchungen über die Auffassung von Tondistanzen. (Wundt's) *Philosophische Studien* VI, 26-103.

Luhmann, Niklas 2004. *Einführung in die Systemtheorie*. Hrsg. von D. Baecker. 2nd ed. Darmstadt: Wissenschaftl. Buchges.

Mach, Ernst 1898/1933. *Die Mechanik in ihrer Entwicklung historisch-kritisch dargestellt*. Leipzig: Brockhaus (Reprint of the 9th ed. 1933 Darmstadt: Wissenschaftl. Buchges. 1988).

Mach, Ernst 1900/1922. *Die Analyse der Empfindungen und das Verhältnis des Physischen zum Psychischen*. 2nd ed. Jena: G. Fischer (9th ed. 1922).

Mach, Ernst 1905/1926. *Erkenntnis und Irrtum. Skizzen zur Psychologie der Forschung*. Leipzig 1905, 5th ed. 1926 (Reprint Darmstadt: Wissenschaftl. Buchges. 1991).

Marks, Lawrence 1992. „What thin partitions sense from thought divide": Toward a new cognitive psychophysics. In D. Algom (ed.). *Psychophysical Approaches to Cognition*. Amsterdam: North Holland Publ., 115-186.

Mattheson, Johann 1731. *Große General-Bass-Schule*. 2nd ed. Hamburg: Kißner.

Mattheson, Johann 1739. *Der vollkommene Capellmeister*. Hamburg: Herold.

Mayr, Ernst 1975. *Grundlagen der zoologischen Systematik*, Hamburg: P. Parey.

Meinong, Alexius von 1899/1971. Über Gegenstände höherer Ordnung und deren Verhältnis zur inneren Wahrnehmung. In A. von Meinong. *Gesamtausgabe*, hrsg. von R. Haller et al., Bd 2, Graz: Akad. Druck- und Verlagsanstalt 1971, 377-471.

Meinong, Alexius von/Stephan Witasek 1897. Zur experimentellen Bestimmung der Tonverschmelzungsgrade. *Zeitschrift für Psychologie* 15, 189-205.

Meyer, Max 1898. Über Tonverschmelzung und die Theorie der Konsonanz. *Zeitschrift für Psychologie* 17, 404-421.

Meyer, Erwin/Guicking, Dieter 1974. *Schwingungslehre*, Braunschweig: Vieweg (2nd ed. 1981).

Morse, Philip/ Ingard, K. Uno 1968. *Theoretical acoustics*, New York: McGraw-Hill (repr. Princeton: Princeton Univ. Pr. 1986 [Paperback ed.]).

Münnich, Richard 1909. Von Entwicklung der Riemannschen Harmonielehre und ihrem Verhältnis zu Oettingen und Stumpf. In *Riemann-Festschrift. Gesammelte Studien. Hugo Riemann zum 60. Geburtstag überreicht von Freunden und Schülern*. Leipzig: Hesse, 60-76.

Nettl, Bruno 1983, 2005. *The Study of Ethnomusicology*. Urbana, Chicago: Univ. of Illinois Pr. (1st ed. 1983, 2nd enlarged ed. 2005).

Nowak, Adolf 2001. Wandlungen des Begriffs „musikalische Logik" bei Hugo Riemann. In T. Böhme-Mehner/K. Mehner (Hrsg.). *Hugo Riemann (1849-1919). Musikwissenschaftler mit Universalanspruch*. Köln, Weimar, Wien: Böhlau, 37-48.

Oettingen, Arthur J. von 1866. *Harmoniesystem in dualer Entwicklung. Studien zur Theorie der Musik*, Dorpat/Leipzig: W. Gläser (2nd ed. of this work = v. Oettingen 1913).

Oettingen, Arthur von 1903-1906. Das duale System der Harmonie. *Annalen der Naturphilosophie 2* (1903) 62-75, 375-403; 3 (1904) 241-269; 4 (1905) 116-338; 5 (1906) 449-503.

Oettingen, Arthur von 1913. *Das duale Harmoniesystem*, Leipzig: C.F. Siegel

Oettingen, Arthur von 1917. Die Grundlage der Musikwissenschaft und das duale Reininstrument. *Abhandlungen der Mathematisch-Physikalischen Klasse der Königlich-Sächsischen Akademie der Wissenschaften*. Bd 34, 2. Abhandlung, 155-307.

Opelt, Friedrich Wilhelm 1852. *Allgemeine Theorie der Musik auf den Rhythmus der Klangwellenpulse gegründet...*, Leipzig: J.A. Barth.

Pongratz, Ludwig 1967. *Problemgeschichte der Psychologie*. Bern, München: Francke.

Rameau, Jean-Philippe 1737. *Génération harmonique ou traité de musique théorique et pratique*. Paris: Prault fils.

Rameau, Jean Philippe 1750. *Démonstration du principe de l'harmonie servant de base à tout l'art musical théorique et pratique*. Paris 1750 (Translation into German by E. Lesser. Wolfbenbüttel, Berlin: Kallmeyer 1930).

Rasch, Rudolf 1983. Introduction to Andreas Werckmeister, *Musicalische Temperatur* (Qued-linburg 1691). Ed. by R. Rasch, Utrecht: The Diapason Press.

Rehding, Alexander 2003. *Hugo Riemann and the birth of modern musical thought*. Cambridge: U. Pr.

Reinecke, Hans-Peter 1964. *Experimentelle Beiträge zur Psychologie des musikalischen Hörens*. Hamburg: Sikorski.

Rescher, Nicholas 1979. *Cognitive Systematization. A systems-theory approach to a coherentist theory of knowledge*. Oxford: Blackwell.

Rescher, Nicholas 1980. *Induction. An Essay on the justification of inductive reasoning*, Oxford: Basil Blackwell

Rescher, Nicholas 1984. *The Limits of science*, Berkeley, Los Angeles: Univ. of Cal. Pr. (German edition Stuttgart: Reclam 1985).

Rescher, Nicholas 2000a. *Nature and understanding. The Metaphysics and method of science*. Oxford: Clarendon Pr.

Rescher, Nicholas 2000b. *Kant and the reach of reason. Studies in Kant's theory of rational systematization*. Cambridge: Cambridge Univ. Pr.

Reuter, Fritz 1950. *Praktische Harmonik des 20. Jahrhunderts. Konsonanz- und Dissonanzlehre nach dem System von Sigfrid Karg-Elert....* Halle: Mitteldeutscher Verlag.

Révész, Géza 1913. *Tonpsychologie*, Leipzig: Voss.

Rexroth, Dieter 1971. *Arnold Schönberg als Theoretiker der tonalen Harmonik*. PhD-dissertation, University of Bonn.

Riemann, Hugo 1872a. Musikalische Logik. Ein Beitrag zur Theorie der Musik. *Neue Zeitschrift für Musik* 68, 279-282, 287-288, 353-355, 363-364, 373-374. Reprinted in Riemann 1901, 1-22.

Riemann, Hugo 1872b. Ueber Tonalität. *Neue Zeitschrift für Musik* 68, 443-444, 453-454. Reprinted in Riemann 1901, 23-30.

Riemann, Hugo 1873a. Tonverwandtschaft. *Neue Zeitschrift für Musik* 69, 29-31, 42-43, 54-56.

Riemann, Hugo 1873b. *Ueber das musikalische Hören*. Phil. Diss. Göttingen 1873 (published under the title of *Musikalische Logik. Hauptzüge einer physiologischen und psychologischen Begründung unseres Musiksystems*. Leipzig: C. Kahnt 1874).

Riemann, Hugo 1877. *Musikalische Syntaxis*, Leipzig: Breitkopf & Härtel (repr. Wiesbaden: M. Sändig 1971).

Riemann, Hugo 1893. *Vereinfachte Harmonielehre*. London: Augener.

Riemann, Hugo 1898/1920. *Geschichte der Musiktheorie im IX. bis XIX. Jahrhundert*, Leipzig: Breitkopf & Härtel. (2nd ed. 1920).

Riemann, Hugo 1901. Zur Theorie der Konsonanz und Dissonanz. In H. Riemann. *Präludien und Studien*, Bd 3, Leipzig: H. Seemann Nachfolger, 31-46.

Riemann, Hugo 1903. *System der musikalischen Rhythmik und Metrik*, Leipzig: Breitkopf & Härtel.

Riemann, Hugo 1905. Das Problem des harmonischen Dualismus. *Neue Zeitschrift für Musik* 101, 3-5, 23-26, 43-46, 67-70.

Riemann, Hugo 1914a. *Grundriß der Musikwissenschaft*. 2nd ed. Leipzig: Quelle & Meyer.

Riemann, Hugo 1914b. *Handbuch der Akustik (Musikwissenschaft)*. 2nd ed. Leipzig: M. Hesse.

Riemann, Hugo 1914-1916. Ideen zu einer „Lehre von den Tonvorstellungen". *Jahrbuch Peters* 21/22 (1914/15), 1-26, 23 (1916), 1-26.

Rudolph, Wolfgang/ Tschohl, Peter 1977. *Systematische Anthropologie*, München: W. Fink

Rummenhöller, Peter 1963, *Moritz Hauptmann als Theoretiker. Eine Studie zum erkenntniskritischen Theoriebegriff in der Musik*, Wiesbaden: Breitkopf & Härtel.

Sachs, Curt 1962. *The Wellsprings of music*. Edited by Jaap Kunst. The Hague: M. Nijhoff.

Sauveur, Joseph 1700, Sur la détermination d'un son fixe [lecture given by Sauveur; the report was written by B. de Fontenelle, permanent secretary of the R. Academy]. *Histoire de L'Académie Royale des Sciences*, Année M.DCC, Paris 1703, 134-143. Reprinted in J. Sauveur, *Collected Writings on Acoustics*, ed. R. Rasch, Utrecht: The Diapason Press, 68-77.

Schenk, Paul 1966. Karg-Elerts polaristische Harmonielehre. In M. Vogel (Hrsg.). *Beiträge zur Musiktheorie des 19. Jahrhunderts*. Kassel: Bärenreiter, 133-162.

Schneider, Albrecht 1984. *Analogie und Rekonstruktion. Studien zur Methodologie der Musikgeschichtsschreibung und zur Frühgeschichte der Musik*, Bd 1, Bonn: Verlag für Syst. Musikwiss.

Schneider, Albrecht 1986. Tonsystem und Intonation. *Hamburger Jahrbuch für Musikwissenschaft* 9, 153-199.

Schneider, Albrecht 1991. Psychological Theory and Comparative Musicology. In B. Nettl and Ph. Bohlman (eds.). *Comparative Musicology and Anthropology of Music*. Chicago, London: Univ. of Chicago Pr., 293-317.

Schneider, Albrecht 1993a. Germany and Austria. In: H. Myers (ed.). *Ethnomusicology. Historical and regional studies*. New York, London: Macmillan Pr., 77-96.

Schneider, Albrecht 1993b. Musikwissenschaft in der Emigration: zur Vertreibung von Gelehrten und den Auswirkungen auf das Fach. In H.W. Heister/Cl. Maurer-Zenck/P. Petersen (eds.), *Musik und Musiker im Exil. Folgen des Nazismus für die internationale Musikkultur*, Frankfurt/M.: S. Fischer, 187 – 211.

Schneider, Albrecht 1993c. Zur Situation der Systematischen Musikwissenschaft: Aspekte und Annotationen, *Systematische Musikwissenschaft – Systematic Musicology – Musicologie systématique* 1, 73-93.

Schneider, Albrecht 1993d. Systematische Musikwissenschaft: Traditionen, Ansätze, Aufgaben. *Systematische Musikwissenschaft – Systematic Musicology – Musicologie systématique* 1, 145-180.

Schneider, Albrecht 1997a. *Tonhöhe – Skala – Klang. Akustische, tonometrische und psycho-akustische Untersuchungen auf vergleichender Grundlage*. Bonn: Orpheus-Verlag für Syst. Musikwiss.

Schneider, Albrecht 1997b. „Verschmelzung", tonal fusion, and consonance: Carl Stumpf revisited. In. M. Leman (ed.), *Music, Gestalt and Computing*, Berlin, New York, Tokyo: Springer, 117-143.

Schneider, Albrecht 1997c. Categorical perception of pitch and the recognition of intonation variants. In P. Pylkkänen et al. (eds.). *Brain, mind and physics*. Amsterdam, Tokyo: IOS Press, Ohmsha Publ., 250-261.

Schneider, Albrecht 1999. Über Stimmung und Intonation. *Systematische Musikwissenschaft – Systematic Musicology – Musicologie systématique* 6, 27-49.

Schneider, Albrecht 2000. Perception of inharmonic sounds: implications as to «pitch», «timbre», and «consonance». *Journal of New Music Research* 29, 2000, 275 – 301.

Schneider, Albrecht 2001. Sound, pitch, and scale: from „tone measurements" to sonological analysis in ethnomusicology. *Ethnomusicology* 45, 489-519.

Schneider, Albrecht 2003. Über systematische und systemische Musikwissenschaft. In K.W. Niemöller/B. Gätjen (Hrsg.). *Perspektiven und Methoden einer Systemischen Musikwissenschaft*. Frankfurt/M.: P. Lang, 31-40.

Schneider, Albrecht 2006. Comparative and Systematic Musicology in relation to Ethnomusicology: a historical and methodological survey. *Ethnomusicology* 50, 236-258.

Schwarz, Cécile 1985, *Systematische Logopädie*, Bern, Stuttgart, Toronto: Huber.

Seidel, Elmar 1966. Die Harmonielehre Hugo Riemanns. In M. Vogel (Hrsg.). *Beiträge zur Musik-theorie des 19. Jahrhunderts*, Regensburg: Bosse, 39-92.

Seifert, Uew 1993. *Systematische Musiktheorie und Kognitionswissenschaft*. Bonn: Verlag für Syst. Musikwiss.

Simon, Artur (Ed.). 2000. *Das Berliner Phonogramm-Archiv. Sammlungen der traditionellen Musik der Welt. The Berlin Phonogramm-Archiv 1900-2000. Collections of Traditional Music of the World*. Berlin: VWB – Verlag für Wissenschaft und Bildung.

Smith, Barry 1988. Gestalt theory: An Essay in Philosophy. In B. Smith (ed.). *Foundations of gestalt theory*. München, Wien: Philosophia Verlag, 11-81.

Sprung, Helga/Lothar Sprung 2002. Stumpf in Berlin (1894-1936). In W. Baumgartner (ed.), *Carl Stumpf*, 89-116.

Stegmüller, Wolfgang 1983. *Probleme und Resultate der Wissenschaftstheorie und Analytischen Philosophie, Bd I: Erklärung, Begründung, Kausalität*, 2nd ed. Berlin, New York: Springer.

Stumpf, Carl 1873. *Über den psychologischen Ursprung der Raumvorstellung*. Leipzig: Hirzel.

Stumpf, Carl 1883, 1890a. *Tonpsychologie*, Bd 1 und 2, Leipzig: Hirzel.

Stumpf, Carl 1885. Musikpsychologie in England. Beobachtungen über Herleitung der Musik aus der Sprache und aus dem thierischen Entwickelungsproceß, über Empirismus und Nativismus in der Musiktheorie. *Vierteljahrsschrift für Musikwissenschaft* 1, 261-349.

Stumpf, Carl 1886. Lieder der Bellakula-Indianer. *Vierteljahrsschrift für Musikwissenschaft* 2, 405-426.

Stumpf, Carl 1890b. Über Vergleichungen von Tondistanzen. *Zeitschrift für Psychologie* 1, 419-462.

Stumpf, Carl 1895. *Hermann von Helmholtz und die neuere Psychologie.* Archiv für Geschichte der Philosophie N.F. Bd 8, 303-314.

Stumpf, Carl 1897. Neueres über Tonverschmelzung. *Zeitschrift für Psychologie* 15, 280-303.

Stumpf, Carl 1898. *Konsonanz und Dissonanz*. Leipzig: J.A. Barth

Stumpf, Carl 1901. *Tonsystem und Musik der Siamesen*, Leipzig: J.A. Barth.

Stumpf, Carl 1907. *Erscheinungen und psychische Funktionen.* Berlin: Akad. der Wiss./D. Reimer (=Abhandl. der Kgl. Preuss. Akad. der Wiss., Jg. 1906, 4. Abhandl.).

Stumpf, Carl 1911a. Konsonanz und Konkordanz. Nebst Bemerkungen über Wohlklang und Wohlgefälligkeit musikalischer Zusammenklänge. *Zeitschrift für Psychologie* 58, 321-355.

Stumpf, Carl 1911b. *Anfänge der Musik*. Leipzig: J. Barth.

Stumpf, Carl 1914. Neue Untersuchungen zur Tonlehre. In: *Bericht über den 6. Kongress für experimentelle Psychologie in Göttingen*, April 1914, Leipzig: J.A. Barth, 305-344.

Stumpf, Carl 1919. *Empfindung und Vorstellung*. Berlin: Akad. der Wiss./D. Reimer (=Abhandl. der Preuss. Akad. der Wiss., Jg. 1918, Phil.-hist.Kl.).

Stumpf, Carl 1924. Carl Stumpf. In: Raymund Schmidt (ed.), *Die Philosophie der Gegenwart in Selbstdarstellungen*. Bd 5, Leipzig: F. Meiner, 205-265.

Stumpf, Carl 1926. *Die Sprachlaute*. Berlin: J. Springer.

Stumpf, Carl 1939. *Erkenntnislehre*, Bd 1, Leipzig: J.A. Barth.

Stumpf, Carl/Erich M. von Hornbostel 1911. Über die Bedeutung ethnologischer Untersuchungen für die Psychologie und Ästhetik der Tonkunst. *Bericht über den 4. Kongress für exp. Psychol. Innsbruck* 1910, Leipzig: Barth, 256-269.

Tartini, Guiseppe 1754/1966. *Trattato di musica secundo la vera scienza dell'armonia*, Padua (German translation and commentary by Alfred Rubeli, Düsseldorf: Gesellschaft zur Förderung der systematischen Musikwissenschaft e.V. 1966).

Terhardt, Ernst 1974. Pitch, consonance, and harmony. *Journal of the Acoustical Society of America* 55, 1061-1069.

Truesdell, Clifford 1960. The rational Mechanics of flexible or elastic bodies 1638-1788. In *Euleri Opera Omnia*, Series 2, Vol. II,2, Zürich: Orell-Füssli.

Uexküll, Jakob von 1928. *Theoretische Biologie*, Berlin: J. Springer (Frankfurt/M.: Suhrkamp 1973).

Ullmann, Dieter 1996. *Chladni und die Entwicklung der Akustik von 1750 – 1860*. Basel: Birkhäuser.

Van der Pol, Balthasar 1946. Music and elementary theory of numbers. *Music Review* 7, 1-25.

Van der Waerden. Bertil L. 1947/49, Die Arithmetik der Pythagoreer. *Mathematische Annalen* 120, 127-153; 676-700.

Vogel, Martin 1963. *Die Enharmonik der Griechen*, Bd 1, 2, Düsseldorf: Gesellschaft zur Förderung der systematischen Musikwissenschaft e.V.

Vogel, Martin 1966, Arthur von Oettingen und der harmonische Dualismus. In M. Vogel (ed.), *Beiträge zur Musiktheorie des 19. Jahrhunderts*, Regensburg: Bosse,

Vogel, Martin 1975/1993. *Die Lehre von den Tonbeziehungen*, Bonn: Verlag für Systematische Musikwiss. (Engl. translation: *On the relations of tone*, Bonn: Verlag für Syst. Musikwiss. 1993).

Vogel, Martin 1984. *Anleitung zur harmonischen Analyse und zu reiner Intonation*. Bonn: Verlag für systematische Musikwiss.

Vogel, Stephan 1993. Sensation of tone, perception of sound, and empiricism: Helmholtz's physiological acoustics. In: D. Cahan (ed.), *Hermann von Helmholtz and the foundations of nineteenth-century science*, Berkeley/Los Angeles/London: Univ. of Cal. Pr., 259-287.

Wallaschek, Richard 1893/1903. *Primitive Music*. London (enlarged German edition published as *Anfänge der Musik*. Leipzig: J. Barth 1903).

Wallaschek, Richard 1905. *Psychologie und Pathologie der Vorstellung. Beiträge zur Grundlegung der Aesthetik*. Leipzig: J. Barth.

Weber, Michael 1997. Empiricism, Gestalt qualities, and determination of style: some remarks concerning the relationship of Guido Adler to Richard Wallaschek, Alexius Meinong, Christian von Ehrenfels, and Robert Lach. In M. Leman (ed.), *Music, Gestalt, and Computing*. Berlin, New York: Springer, 42-56.

Weberling, Focko/Thomas Stützel, 1993. *Biologische Systematik. Grundlagen und Methoden*, Darmstadt: Wissenschaftl. Buchges.

Wellek, Albert 1963. *Musikpsychologie und Musikästhetik. Grundriss der Systematischen Musikwissenschaft*. Frankfurt/M.: Akad. Verlagsanstalt.

Witasek, Stephan 1897. Beiträge zur Psychologie der Komplexionen. *Zeitschrift für Psychologie* 16, 401-432.

Wundt, Wilhelm 1873/1874. *Grundzüge der physiologischen Psychologie*. 2 Teile. Leipzig: Engelmann. (3rd ed. [2 vols] 1874, 6th ed. 1908).

Wundt, Wilhelm 1890. Ueber Vergleichungen von Tondistanzen, (Wundt's) *Philosophische Studien* VI, 605-640.

Wundt, Wilhelm 1896, *Grundriss der Psychologie*, Leipzig: Engelmann (15th ed. 1928).

Wundt, Wilhelm 1907. *Logik*, Bd 2 (Logik der exakten Wissenschaften), 3rd ed. Stuttgart: F. Enke.

Oskár Elschek

Systematic Musicology – anachronism or challenge?
A perspective on disciplinary and scientific developments

1. Preliminary notes on systematic and comparative aspects

The term systematic in general designates a specific and effective scientific approach, i.e., a sophisticated, thought-out, and well-organized procedure of thinking and behaviour. As such, it stands in contradiction to nonsystematic or rather arbitrary, inconsistent access to observations and research. Throughout centuries, the systematic approach was understood as a profound methodical tool to organize knowledge as well as to differentiate fields of scientific learning. In the 19th century, systematic methodology was current in natural and social sciences as well as in the humanities. The systematic approach which is different from historical, regional, cultural and similarly specified studies is still in use in many disciplines. For example, in geography it is customary to differentiate between systematic and regional studies.

The comparative aspect and the methodical application of comparison made it possible to order a number of objects, structures, elements and items in relation to each other, of course, after having studied them systematically in regard of their distinctive features. Classification in comparative research in general was based on categories of similarity, identity, difference and variety. Such considerations were central in biology, anatomy, linguistics, anthropology, etc. Comparative methodology also was introduced into music research in regard of musical styles, tunes (e.g., the concept of ‚tune family' as found in folk song research), rhythmic and metrical formations, types of musical instruments etc.

Both frames of reference and methodical aspects – the systematic and the comparative – were developed from a certain intellectual and cultural background as can be seen when looking at the history of musicology, in particular at its beginnings as an academic discipline in the late 19th century. Some 120 years ago, both aspects were joined and implemented by Guido Adler in his system of musicology based on the dichotomy of historic and systematic aspects. Adler's system of was meant as a universal model which included fields of research that really did exist as well as some which were envisioned rather than established at the time.

However, Adler's sketch of a system of musicology was not haphazard or a game of chance. He simply followed ideas which were discussed in philosophy as well as in the natural sciences and humanities of the time.

Compared to music, modern musicology so far has had a relatively short life of about a century and a half, and has encountered many difficulties some of which were caused by exaggerating systematic as well as non-systematic activities. Music is a sophisticated system in which sounds are organized in time and space, and in which different elements blend into forms of artistic expression. Music is also a system of knowledge which enables the composer to "compose" what we receive as music, or what is presented by singers or players as a musical event. This system of knowledge and the creative use of it no doubt is also the key to understand music as well as for entering, in a scientific way, into the well-organized world of musical sounds and musical meaning.

The questions which I believe still call for an answer are: what are the reasons to deal with systematic musicology? What is its actual aim? Why should we, after a long history of use and misuse, return to the notion and concept of systematic musicology? Moreover: we have to notice that, in the past century, systematic musicology has lost, step by step, the endeavour to unite as well as to develop methods and procedures which could be understood as a challenging perspective for contemporary musicological research. Actually, musicologists have spent much more energy on building up highly specialized fields of knowledge, without an effective cooperation between musicological subdisciplines, or much regard for relations between different genres and traditions of music.

Neglecting Adler's central idea, musicology in recent decades has lost the goal which could have united the discipline, namely to hear, to see, to analyze, interpret, and understand music in its universal human and cultural perspective. Contradictions between separate fields grew up due to the vie for prestige and power, as well as because of a lack of tolerance. Not the least responsible for these malformations were, I regret to say, some leading representatives of musicology. We have to think of respectable musicologists being active in various areas of the field, each of them standing for certain institutions, universities, learned societies etc. Of course, each of them had or has a preferred and limited orientation in seeing and evaluating music. The view which took music as a historical and European phenomenon it seems prevailed.

Let us now return to the idea of a systematic approach and its disciplinary view. Adler's concept of musicology was to coordinate music studies, on the one hand, and to divide the labour to be done, on the other. This is clear from the role he assigns to the systematic subdisciplines (as „supporting" historical investigations), whereas comparative musicology (‚Musikologie' in Adler's terminology) is allotted the task of studying all kinds of music outside the European art music context.

The contradictions which came to light in the last years, perceived by many scholars, had very much to do with changes of music and music cultures and with the consequences such changes have for musicology. Changes which were reflected already decades ago, by Curt Sachs, evaluating the European art music tradition against the variety of non-western art and „primitive" music (including some European folk music, too). Concerning the idea of ‚progress', he stated: "But seeing and weighing the differences between the two worlds might help us in realizing that our gain is our loss, that our growth is our wane. It might help to understand that we have not progressed, but simply changed. And, when seen from a cultural viewpoint, we have not always changed to the better." (Sachs 1962, 222).

This conservative and may be rather pessimistic view reflected sociocultural change during the first half of the 20th century as well as a loss of faith in our idea of ‚progress'. Also, Sachs' in his last book (published posthumously), though still maintaining a comparative perspective, adopted some ideas from cultural relativism. In this respect, the concluding statement of his book quoted here has a real quintessence. Written more than a decade after World War II, by the time ethnomusicology was established as a discipline, and in a time of rapid political and sociocultural change all over the world, Sachs finally recognized that the approach of cultural evolution which had been prominent in anthropology as well as comparative musicology, and which did seek to classify cultural phenomena according to ‚stages of evolution', could not adequately account for the actual diversity of world music as well as the diversity of cultural standards. This did not prevent Sachs from seeking basic forms and structures of music found in many cultures, that is, the wellsprings from which so many musical cultures did draw. Also, different from many ethnomusicologists who did vote for particularism, and probably did overstate social and ritual contexts of music, Sachs never lost the universal perspective he had developed in a number of monographs written when still working in Berlin, and later as an emigrant refugee scholar teaching in New York.

In certain respects, Sachs took up Adler's universal programme for musicology according to which various subdisciplines should contribute to one common field of study, and from different angles, making use of different methodologies. Unfortunately, due to specialization and a lack of mutual understanding, the concept of a well balanced, integrative musicology was replaced by particularizing developments. This unpleasant situation has not changed in many respects over the past fifty years during which, moreover, systematic musicology hardly has gained the recognition it should have according to Adler's original concept.

Writing on systematic musicology, by taking into account the present situation, we have to recall some special aspects which refer to disciplinary history. In particular, we have to see how systematic musicology was conceived at various times, and in regard of the framework of musicology as a discipline, centered in a European tradition of scholarship and music (Elschek 2003), to understand certain developments. It is my understanding that systematic musicology can, in general, not be viewed as a field independent from the wider context of music research, and the disciplinary configuration of musicology as a whole. It is not my endeavour here to elaborate on the more than hundred years of disciplinary history of musicology. Rather, I want to shed light on some significant periods and changes.

2. Beginnings and some historic reflections

We can characterize systematic musicology from three points of view:

1. It is conceived as a part of the process of completing and building musicology as a closed and internally divided system of different subdisciplines.
2. It is meant in the sense as it appeared in Guido Adler (1885/1981) who proposed a dichotomous subdivision, separating musicology into two great disciplinary branches, the historical and systematic. The two-part structure became an essential element of musicological thought and remained inseparably connected with the beginnings of musicology. Adler's system is continually quoted and referred to as a ‚historical event' in the development of musicology. Unfortunately, Adler's concept up to now does not exert proper influence on musicological practice.
3. The term is joined with the long, varied and controversial process in which musicology was subjected to reduction and even disruption in that some traditionally accepted subdisciplines belonging to the systematic division were excluded or neglected. At the same time, some new fields were included into musicology. In musicology, the struggle to achieve a balance between specialized, complementary fields all active in music research is still going on.

Problems and difficulties in regard of systematic musicology were expressed, more than in other quarters, by scholars working in historical and philological music research. Musicology, they believe (see, e.g. Georg Feder 1987), centres in the study of music as a text which needs to be reconstructed and edited from sources, and which can be read and interpreted not unlike other types of texts. In this respect, musicology comprises source-criticism, biographic studies, music analysis based on scores, and aesthetic interpretation of individual works of music which belong, almost exclusively, to the western tradition of art music. This orientation of course has been followed in musicology since its beginnings in the 19th century. The reduction which this orientation implies (expressed, in similar ways, by J. Kerman in the United States; see Kerman 1985) was, and still is working against systematic musicology as well as comparative musicology and ethnomusicology (the latter two being closely related, though not identical in regard of subject matter and methodology; see Nettl, this volume). To this day, these musicological subdisciplines are barely recognized by members of the philological, historical and interpretative sections of musicology. The effect of this disregard, in short, is that musicology as a whole did not develop as fast and as intensely as it could have. As systematic and comparative musicology/ethnomusicology were denied proper status (including a sufficient number of professorships and other academic positions), these fields were kept marginal within the framework of musicology which in fact was reduced more and more to historical and philological approaches. One of the consequences was that, due to the lack of opportunities for systematic musicologists, a considerable portion of relevant research was, and still is done outside musicological institutes, by acousticians, psychologists, computer scientists, engineers and other professionals who took up a broad range of topics which clearly belong to the realm of systematic musicology (see Leman, this volume). Similarly, anthropologists and ethnologists as well as sociologists did relevant research on musical traditions and cultures outside western art music. For example, the anthropologist, Alan P. Merriam did write one of the most influential books on ‚music in culture' (Merrian 1966).

   The reduction of the disciplinary framework in musicology restricted, in a decisive way, the development of systematic subdisciplines, and of the systematic part of musicology in general. This, in return, affected the advancement of musicology and did harm to its academic reputation.

To clarify the points I made very briefly, let me return to some of the disciplines which were affected by the tendencies indicated above in an unpleasant way.

   a. Aesthetics, in the 19th century an important philosophical and cognitive analytical view on music, has lost in the 20th century much of its musicological substantiation. Music aesthetics, reflecting the apperception and appreciation of music by humans as well as the role of music in society, and in the life of man in general, is a subject which interests philosophers and aestheticians. Of their reflections and ideas, only few seem to have found the necessary resonance in general musicology. For that reason, I have (in a special study, see Elschek 2002) put up the topic of music philosophy and music aesthetics to show how they relate to each other, and that these fields can by no means be „deconstructed", or reduced so some marginal form of applied music criticism. To the contrary, philosophy and aesthetics of music remain an integral part of musicology (as Adler had correctly proposed).

b. A similar fate characterizes the position of psychology of music. We cannot understand music without its decisive physiological and psycho-physiological fundament. This was emphasized already by Hermann von Helmholtz who studied sensation and perception of music, and together with the philosopher, psychologist and musicologist Carl Stumpf, became one of the founders of systematic and comparative musicology (see Schneider, this volume). Stumpf, his co-workers (among them Erich Moritz von Hornbostel and Otto Abraham) as well as a small group of researchers from other universities established psychology of music in continental Europe where this discipline flourished in the first decades of the 20th century.

We may point to scholars such as the philosophically minded Ernst Kurth, to Geza Revesz who had contributed to psychoacoustics, or to Albert Wellek who investigated, among other issues, absolute pitch, musicality, and synaesthesia. In the United States, at the University of Iowa Carl Seashore and his group established a center for experimental music psychology which conducted research on intonation and synchronization in music as well as on many other aspects.

Music psychological examinations, many of them carried out in labs of psychological institutes, were not always recognized by musicologists notwithstanding musicological significance. Also, job opportunities for music psychologists within musicology were scarce.

Of the many efforts of the post war period, cooperation between acoustics and psychology should be mentioned. Also, there were attempts at renewing, in the 1980s and 90s, traditions of comparative, psycho-physiological, and psychoacoustic music studies (Schneider 1997a, Födermayr and Deutsch 1998). Besides conventional experimental investigations, psycho-biological (Cross 2003, 19), cognitive and theoretical research played a major role (Seifert 1993; Leman 1995) as did the field of music and artificial intelligence (Balaban et al. 1992). Further, music and the brain became an important issue as we look to studies in neuromusicology (Jourdain 1997/2001; Tervaniemi & Leman 1999, Deliége-Wiggins 2006, 273 seq.). We even find a revival of psychoanalytical methods (Oberhoff 2002).

c. Music theory is also a highly specialized field which was realized by Adler as a part of the systematic subsection. In his opinion, systematic musicology should be divided into three parts, namely (a) the music-theoretical section as such, which is speculative (in the medieval and Renaissance tradition of *musica speculative* and *musica theorica*), however scientific in its strive for general ‚laws' (Adler 1885, 11-13). The other two sections Adler had in mind are (b) music aesthetics, and (c) music pedagogy and didactics. In fact, music theory, in its systematic orientation as developed by, paradigmatically, Hugo Riemann (see Schneider, this volume) is quite different from ‚practical music theory' which is taught, at schools of music or conservatories, as a craft needed to analyze or write works of tonal music. The quest for a systematic music theory which includes philosophical aspects as well as findings from empirical science has gained new impetus in the past decades (see Seifert 1993).

d. Music pedagogy and didactics were understood by Adler as a field which puts the findings obtained in „speculative" (i.e., systematic) music theory to practical use. Music pedagogy did not yet gain full academic status in the decades after Adler as musicological research, on the one hand, and teaching of music, on the other, were largely kept separate. As Adler (1885, 14) had proposed, music pedagogy should apply the findings of systematic music theory, without doing research on its own. This view of course has changed, and quite drastically so. During the 1960s and 1970s, music pedagogy emancipated itself from (historical) musicology, and defined itself as an academic discipline (see Abel-Struth 1970) which began to conduct research also in areas relevant for music psychology (e.g., Kleinen and Motte-Haber 1982, 310). Thereby, relations between music pedagogy and other fields of systematic musicology were growing (see Lothwesen, this volume). In the United States, music pedagogy was continually changed as it pursued elaborate research projects (see Cowell 1992:Section B, pp. 73 seq.).

The programmatic concept developed by Adler for a long time certainly was of influence as a theoretical framework. It gave directions not all of which, however, were followed in the 20th century (when parts of Adler's system were probably outdated by both musical practice and scientific developments within specialized fields; see above). The question then is: if Adler's concept, at a certain time, was not adequate anymore, what could have been the appropriate way to substitute something new for Adler's system? Should we, for example, reduce the role of the systematic subdisciplines, or even omit them altogether? Or should we, on the contrary, reinforce and develop them?

In the course of the past fifty years, a number of proposals have been made which, as I see it, can be subsumed under four different considerations: (1) the first was to save Adler's system (for the lack of any real alternative) without substantial changes, and to modify it in part to adapt it to match the present situation (2) The second consideration was to make some corrections while accepting parts of the system, in particular those which refer to music history. At the same time, there were ideas to exclude most, if not all non-historical fields as well as those which do not focus on European (art) music in its different genres. (3) The third consideration reflects a relativistic tendency to get rid of various kinds of systematic thinking, and to give up all efforts of coordinating and integrating musicological research. Instead, one understands musicology as a bundle of more or less unrelated fields which are busy studying music in one way or another, however, without any hierarchy or systematic relation between them. (4) The fourth consideration was to propose new models for the disciplinary organization of musicology, however without following the dichotomic principle of Adler or similar bipartite concepts of ‚historic' and ‚systematic'. Instead of offering abstract systems, such models rather reflect actual research problems, methodological as well as interdisciplinary issues The aim of such models in general was to reform musicology by giving it some new direction.

As can be expected, the four considerations outlined here cannot always be completely separated. Also, in some cases additional motives can be detected which, for the most part, seem to reflect personal interest of individual scholars, or a specific focus as adopted by a certain subdiscipline.

In the following, I shall add some remarks on the four lines of argument:

In regard of (1), some authors identified themselves with the traditional system of Adler and accepted it with some corrections, thereby transferring the so-called auxiliary sciences (*Hilfswissenschaften*, in Adler's terminology) into the group of accepted systematic fields (Haydon 1941, 21). Other publications such as dictionaries and introductory texts for musicologists simply mentioned Adler, however as a historical reference, and without any actual meaning (Schwindt-Gross 1992, 22-23, Williams 2000, 2; Rösing and Petersen 2000, 94-95; Beard and Gloag 2005, 79). Adler's system was remembered in critical accounts of musicology, as by Joseph Kerman (1985, 11), but without going into details or even presenting alternative concepts in an appropriate way.

In regard of (2) and (3), it should be noted that the most thorough attempt to return to the ideas of Adler was undertaken in Austria, on the occasion of the centenary of his seminal publication. An international conference in 1985 offered some fifteen papers plus discussions, part of which were rather historic and apologetic whereas others were more stimulating because of offering new perspectives (see Lederer, Flotzinger and Födermayer 1986). Besides some insight into developments in systematic areas such as music psychology which barely could be denied, there were some old arguments and point of views reiterated, for example by Hans-Heinrich Eggebrecht who, as chairman of the closing session, had the following to say: *Ich beginne mit einer sehr provozierenden These: Die ganze auf die Musik gerichtete Wissenschaft ist (oder sollte sein) eine Wissenschaft, die es mit der Geschichte zu tun hat, also eine historische Musikwissenschaft, und alles, was sich nicht in diesem Sinne versteht, ist Hilfestellung dazu.* (H.H. Eggebrecht, in Lederer et al. 1986, 251). This sentence started a controversial debate which was characteristic of the situation of European musicology in the 1980s when, in certain quarters, a more or less general refusal of systematic musicology could be observed (Eggebrecht's plain statement being no singular case). It was an attitude which openly advocated exclusion of the systematic disciplines from ‚musicology' proper – that is, from a discipline which, in practice, believed musicology to be historic musicology. The „rest“ perhaps could do some „auxiliary“ work, if being accepted at all.

The same fate that was intended for systematic musicology, namely to vanish, was also intended for ethnomusicology. There were some rather weird arguments against ethnomusicology (Dahlhaus 1974) which called for some response (Elschek 1974). The attacks on, in particular ethnomusicology, continued (see below). These undesired trends indeed prove how far musicology had been drifted off the course once outlined by Adler. The idea that musicology as a discipline should allow for research activities in various fields was in fact repudiated.

On the occasion of Adler's anniversary, another set of scientific articles was published including an extended essay by the present writer on concepts of musicology in the past and the present (Elschek 1986). This article contains the following chapters: 1. The notion of a concept. 2. Musicological concepts of the past. 3. The current decomposition of the music historical research concept. 4. Between restitution und new orientation. 5. Research practice, criticism of methods, and new directions. 6. Disciplinary structure and the definition of musicology. 7. Ethnomusicology. 8. Systematic musicology. 9. Research in music history. 9. Principles of the present concept of research. 10. Consequences.

The article, intended as an attempt at clarifying disciplinary structures and developments, was written after some quite misleading and, as I see it, aggressive statements had been put forward, in the course of the 1970s, in which the reductionist view of musicology as philology cum history was advocated (see above). One leading proponent of those tendencies was Georg Feder (1980) who publicly questioned the quality of research on musical matters conducted outside historical musicology. Moreover, he questioned the validity and usefulness of musicological research based on empirical and experimental methodology. According to Feder's opinion, all results attained in regard of music by sciences other than musicology, should be qualified as of a second-hand character, that is, essentially non-musicological. To refuse, in effect, contributions to musicology from non-historians, and to classify scientific results into ‚musicological' and ‚non-musicological' certainly was one of the most curious ideas ever expressed by a professional musicologist.

Feder's initiative to „clean" musicology from unwanted areas of research did start from a certain background, namely two short yet influential papers known as the *Memorandum über die Lage der Musikwissenschaft in der Bundesrepublik Deutschland* (1976) and a supplement, published in 1977. The *Memorandum* was probably written by, or under the editorship of Carl Dahlhaus, the supplement apparently by Georg Feder. These two papers, if anything, documented unsurmountable contradictions in regard of disciplinary orientations of academic musicology as represented by the German Gesellschaft für Musikforschung in the 1970s. Basically, the memorandum and its supplement suggested a return to old concepts, cementing the dominance of historical musicology, and the focus on western music history.

As to (4), this position seemed natural, or even inevitable in regard of developments in various scientific disciplines related to systematic musicology (for example, acoustics, psychology, empirical aesthetics), on the one hand, and the unwillingness of conservative circles of musicologists to accept systematic and cross-cultural orientations, on the other.

Given the situation sketched above, it was inevitable to find ways for the autonomous development of disciplines understood as systematic, and to protect their status as musicological subdisciplines. Two ways to promote systematic musicology came into mind:

a. The first in fact was to detach key systematic disciplines, if necessary, from the traditional framework of musicology and to try to develop them in an independent institutional network, on the basis of a cooperation of systematic musicologists with other scientists. This seemed possible in regard of musical acoustics, psychoacoustics, music psychology, sociology of music, and some other fields which were attractive for disciplines outside conventional (i.e., historic) musicology;

b. The other was to reorganize and modernize the antiquated "building" of musicology by advocating a new, systematic model of the subdisciplines and relevant research areas. Thereby, also the status of systematic musicology as a major part of musicology could be improved (see Elschek 1973b, 1973c, and below).-

To strengthen as well as to adjust disciplines or subdisciplines, monographs are needed from time to time in which specialists try to give a synthesis of past and recent research, and where they will offer ideas for new endeavours as well. A collection of essays rather than a monograph was the small introductory book edited by Carl Dahlhaus (1971) in which specialists (Tibor Kneif, Helga de la Motte-Haber and Hans-Peter Reinecke) reflected the status, the achievements as well as the problems of some systematic subdisciplines (e.g., music psychology, music sociology). Dahlhaus, though not completely questioning the possibility of a discipline labelled systematic musicology, was critical of most of its tenets, concepts, and methods. It is certainly difficult to promote a field in whose fundaments one does not trust. The small book itself appeared quite heterogeneous and not well balanced (as if to confirm the scepticism of its editor).

About ten years later, the project basically was repeated, in a more voluminous issue, and with a couple of different authors, as part of the newly prepared *Neues Handbuch der Musikwissenschaft* (Dahlhaus and de la Motte-Haber 1982). The volume titled *Systematische Musikwissenschaft*, again presenting a collection of essays (of different scope, depth, and uneven quality), could not fully meet the expectations of providing a valid account of the field. Although the editors had, apparently, adopted essentials of Adler's concept, the contributions to this volume varied in many respects because of the actual preferences of the authors, and the choices they had made in regard of aesthetic, socio-political or other bias.

The volume received critical reviewing by the nestor of systematic musicology, Walter Wiora. In particular, he criticized the view reduced to European music, the lack of a more universal perspective, as well as the fact that some fundamental disciplines (acoustics, also organology etc.) are missing altogether. Also, Wiora saw the interrelations between systematic and historical branches of musicology not properly reflected. His review closed with the remark: *Es* [the volume in question] *bringt einerseits etliche psychologische, soziologische und andere Reflexionen, welche über die Grenze der Musik hinausgehen. Doch andererseits enthält es vieles nicht, was zum Überblick über den substantiellen Wissensschatz des Faches und zum Ausblick auf seine weiteren Aufgaben gehören dürfte* (Wiora 1984, 221). The volume is more of a recapitulation of the past than a vision of the future of musicology, especially systematic musicology.

The only true publication concerning systematic musicology as such was written by Vladimir Karbusicky (1979) who understood systematic musicology as an independent and special field of thinking about music as well as investigating music and musical behaviour. Moreover, Karbusicky was drawing attention to many interconnections inside and outside musicology.

His textbook was not so much directed to the disciplinary framework of musicology than it was to methodological and theoretical fundamentals common to a number of disciplines (with a focus on the humanities). Further, Karbusicky pointed to social, aesthetic, logical and structural commonalities relevant for studying and understanding music phenomena. His book is still worth reading because of the manifold of issues addressed therein.

A project intended to provide foundations for both systematic and comparative musicology was developed by Vladimir Karbusicky and Albrecht Schneider (1980), It was planned to be realized in cooperation with an international group of scholars.

Schneider had studied the history and methodology of comparative music research (Schneider 1976). Karbusicky, besides doing empirical research in music sociology, also had a background in ethnography. The combination of systematic and comparative issues seemed appropriate to overcome a Eurocentric, and to gain a cross-cultural as well as interdisciplinary perspective. For certain unfortunate circumstances, among them the untimely death of several co-workers, the ambitious project, outlined in some detail (Karbusicky and Schneider 1980), did not materialize.

At this point, I should explain my own considerations in regard of conceptualizing systematic musicology. By the end of the 1960s, it was obvious that the actual diversity of research activities in the realm of musicology as well as contributions from other disciplines had exceeded the original framework proposed by Adler (as well as some slightly expanded versions). Also, developments in the composition, production and distribution of music as well as in media technology in general and other changes had to be taken into account. All in all, a new approach to systematics seemed necessary. The problem, as I experienced it first in organology, forced me to consider solutions which would fit not only to research in organology yet which would be suited also for an appropriate musicological system. The first step was the analytical and comparative one, to summarize proposals and search for the most suitable solution. The first studies with this aim were published with reference to organology (Elschek 1969, 34). In order to clarify the state of musicology with its different approaches, a seminar *The systematics of contemporary musicology* was organized in 1970, in Moravany, Slovakia, where eleven papers were presented which were published later (Elschek 1973a).

My own proposals for a new systematics were published in 1973 (Elschek 1973a/b). They anticipated more or less the conservative resistance to change the status quo as was expressed clearly in the *Memorandum* of 1976/77 (and especially in its second part).

Therefore, it was inevitable to find and open potentials for future developments. The short communications I had published were supplemented by full versions, presenting the whole system designed to expand music research without any historical, ethnic, national, stylistic, structural, functional or methodical limitation. The focus was on music, and not on split-up musicological views. To the contrary, my aim was to reorganize and present a practicable system which indicates a network of possible cooperations in regard of the study of different musical forms, systems, and methods. In order to exemplify how the system works, a monograph was published, first in Slovak (Elschek 1984), and later in an enlarged German edition (Elschek 1992). In order to keep up with developments into the 1990s, a survey was added which concerns the actual structure systematic musicology had achieved (Elschek 1994). It was published in the journal *Systematische Musikwissenschaft/Systematic Musicology* which I had founded in 1993.

To find the best solution for a systematics, many alternatives had to be considered. One was the subdivision of musicology into theoretic and applied musicology. Such a division can be found in many fields of knowledge. Another possibility was to differentiate between theoretical (systematic) and regional (continental) research whereby systematic could be understood as fundamental research (Grundlagenforschung), as in the natural sciences. Within this frame twelve disciplinary fields have been proposed, ordered according to principles in a logical succession, and inspired by concepts known from information theory. In the two monographs more than twenty-seven models for the disciplinary differentiation of musicology, many of which had actually been proposed and used in the history of our discipline, have been discussed as examples for systematics (Elschek 1992, Vol. I, 31-89). As a result, it can be concluded that, in order to understand problems in regard of music research in an appropriate way, a flexible strategy which makes use of whatever tools and methods are available, seems more adequate than any static approach.

A similar scientific and educational project has to be mentioned, published 1988 by a group of editors and assisting authors, which appeared under the title Hudební *věda* (Musicology; Lébl, Poledňák and [Jiránek] 1988) and was intended as an encyclopedic overview on almost all fields of research, including also the systematic part of research in an international, but mainly Czech oriented perspective.

3. The actual practice of disciplinary division at present

Focusing on systematic or systematic-comparative musicology, we must relate them to other disciplines concerned with music. Without doubt we must consider three fundamental fields of musicology (or "musicologies"), each provided with a high degree independence: historical musicology (western [and non-western?] music history), ethnomusicology (ethnic and culture-specific aspects), and the field of systematic research which basically is not limited in regard of cultures, ethnic groups, or historical eras. Rather, its orientation is to look for fundamental principles in regard of sound and music as well as biological and anthropological or socio-cultural factors. The tripartite division in its modern form („hist/syst/ethno") was established in the 1950s. None of the three divisions, though seemingly autonomous in regard of methodology, research practice and organization, can in fact do without the others.

Further, each field does have limitations in itself. This is very obvious when looking at historical musicology which in fact mainly, if not exclusively is concerned with European art music and its offspring in a few other regions. Also, most of the music history which appears in textbooks as well as on the stage of the concert auditorium is from the 18th and 19th centuries, respectively. Moreover, there are shortcomings in regard of methodological reflection. It took decades, after Adler's essay on methods in music history (Adler 1919), before two books of similar scope appeared, written, however from quite different points of view (Dahlhaus 1977, Knepler 1977). As has been elaborated by Schneider (1984), the concept of history as it is derived in historic musicology (with a bias for written documents, neglect of oral history and, often, strong ideological inclinations) is questionable, to say the least.

Ethnomusicology emerged in the 1950s after the decline of the old comparative musicology. It was conceived as the, study of music in culture', based largely on fieldwork, with a focus on socio-cultural and other anthropological aspects (see Nettl, this volume). Ethnomusicology evolved quickly into one of the most extensive and comprehensive fields of music research, embracing field work, documentation (often with the aid of technical media), various types of analysis and, meanwhile, advanced techniques such as computer-based information retrieval. In the United States, a Society for Ethnomusiology was formed and a journal *Ethnomusicology* was founded (in 1955; the 50th anniversary volume appeared in 2005) to further the discipline. This story of success should not distract our view from the fact that comparative musicology and ethnomusicology had to struggle for recognition within „proper" musicology. Another field which complements ethnomusicology, and which also had to find its way outside mainstream musicology, is folk song research which had a main area in the musical folklore of Eastern Europe (see Elschek 1997).

As has been indicated above, one could observe, in the course of 1970s, attempts in Germany to reduce musicology to the historic section, at the cost of both systematic musicology and ethnomusicology. There were irrelevant proposals as well as arguments which were neither scientific nor fair. Though ethnomusicologists did defend their discipline (Laade 1976, Simon 1978), the troubles continued. The quest for a „different" musicology which would overcome old prejudices and limitations continued (see Weber 1990). In regard of scientific institutions and organizations relevant for ethnomusicology and folk song research, one has to remember that, after the ‚Cold War' was over, the Institute of Comparative Music Studies at Berlin (affiliated with the UNESCO) was closed down, and that the Academies of Science in many East European countries which had musicological institutes (in general with a focus on folk music research) did run into financial and other problems.

A new attack was started, with the provocative, unqualified article by Martin Greve (2002). He revitalized old differences between historic musicology and ethnomusicology, warming up old prejudices, enlarging them by ideological arguments as well as financial, cultural and other aspects, also offering some critical views on ethnology and anthropology. He summarized his "ideas" by pointing out: "Traditional areas of ethnomusicology are on the way to disappear and with them also its subject area. Even a new name can't stop its decline. On the contrary, for musicology with all its disciplines an intercultural opening is inevitable." (Greve 2002, 251). It is symptomatic that Greve's pamphlet was published in the central journal of German musicology, *Die Musikforschung*. On behalf of ethnomusicology, the response came from two German representatives of the field, Rudolf Brandl (2003) and Jürgen Elsner (2004), not to mention other reactions.

This short issue concerning ethnomusicology was included to show that systematic musicology is not the only discipline which had to defend itself against ignorance. The consequence of certain malformations was, and still is that each musicological discipline or field of research must build its own network of institutions and professionals to secure freedom and continuity of research. In this respect, it is imperative that systematic musicology and ethnomusicology (including the Austrian concept of comparative-systematic musicology) have their own periodicals and book series as well as their own conferences and other lines of communication to support exchange of information and opinions.

In order to demonstrate these paths of self-reliance in one single field, some periodicals should be mentioned which were important for the development of comparative musicology (since the days of C. Stumpf and E.M. v. Hornbostel) and ethnomusicology. We can start with journals which were established aside from the musicological mainstream, and then advance to some specialized journals, yearbooks and series. I would like to list the following:

1. Sammelbände für Vergleichende Musikwissenschaft (starting in Berlin, Germany 1922)

2. Zeitschrift für Vergleichende Musikwissenschaft (founded in Berlin, Germany 1933)
3. Journal of the International Folk Music Council (founded in London, GB in1948)
4. The World of Music (since 1952, for a number of years edited in Berlin, Germany)
5. Ethnomusicology (founded in the USA, in 1955)
6. Yearbook of the International Folk Music Council (founded in 1969 as a continuation of the Journal of the International Folk Music Council; since 1981as the Yearbook of Traditional Music, USA)
7. Jahrbuch für musikalische Volks- und Völkerkunde (since 1969, edited in Berlin)
8. Musikethnologische Sammelbände (since 1977, edited in Graz, Austria)
9. Culture Musicali. Quaderni di etnomusicologia (since 1982 edited and published in Rome, Italy)
10. British Journal of Ethnomusicology (London, GB, since 1991)
11. EthnoMusicologicum (starting 1992 in Bratislava, Slovacia)
12. East European Meetings in Ethnomusicology (Bucuresti, Roumania, from 1995 on).

The majority of these periodicals was or is prepared by international or national societies for ethnomusicology, centres and institutes for folk music research or similar organizations which have also their special informative bulletins (as, for example the Bulletin of the ICTM, ESEMpoint etc.). It is not my ambition to present a complete list, rather I would like to point out that such publications became instrumental for a process of self-reflection and emancipation of the field. They were led by personalities, research groups and societies with the aim to establish a forum for the exchange of information (including reviews, reports, discussions, etc.). The support for these periodicals from mainstream musicology and its institutional framework was negligible. Rather, attempts at establishing specialized journals and other periodicals which secured ethnomusicology independence were met with suspicion.

Of specialized book series in the field of comparative musicology and ethnomusicology, I should mention at least a few:

1. Beiträge zur Ethnomusikologie, founded bei Kurt Reinhard, since 1972
2. Veröffentlichungen des Museums für Völkerkunde Berlin, Abteilung Musikethnologie, ed. A. Simon
3. Intercultural Music Studies, ed. Max P. Baumann for International Institute of Comparative Music Studies and Documentation, Berlin (since 1990)
4. Vergleichende Musikwissenschaft, ed. By Franz Födermayr, August Schmid-hofer, Michael Weber, since 1994.
5. Chicago Studies in ethnomusicology, ed. By Philip V. Bohlman and Bruno Nettl

In the light of the information presented here concerning ethnomusicology, a similar development could be expected for systematic musicology. However, the process in this area was more complex because of the variety of subjects, research aims and disciplinary contexts which, taken together, make up systematic musicology. Traditio-nally, certain (sub)disciplines such as musical acoustics, organology, physiology, psychoacoustics and psychology of music, systematic music theory and music philosophy, music aesthetics as well as sociology of music are regarded as the ‚core' of systematic musicology. Within this group, some obviously are investigating musical sound and musical instruments in a specific way whereas others are relevant for understanding perception and cognition as well as for appreciation of music. A list of (sub)disciplines of course can only give some rough orientation. In practice, research in areas of systematic (and comparative-systematic) musicology from the very beginning (see Schneider, this volume) to this day meant a predominance of interdisciplinary and transdisciplinary investigations.

4. Notes on some recent developments in systematic musicology

Even though it might be difficult to characterize systematic musicology as a whole, we can describe certain (sub)disciplines, among them acoustics, organology, physiology, psychology, aesthetics, sociology and theory. It is a goal to find determining commonalities among them, and maybe a common history of their development. This might be possible in regard of their beginnings in the 19th century and also later, but in the second half of the 20th century each had made such a remarkable progress that the areas continued more or less independently. Of course, we must bear in mind that, for example the development of music psychology was in a decisive way determined by psychology at large; the same dependency is even more valid in acoustics. Looking at fields influenced by the natural sciences, these in particular profited much from the computer-based research methods and procedures which, in turn, was of influence as to the problems which could be investigated. Certainly we see an specialization leading to distinctive subdisciplinary fields, in disciplines such as music psychology (see Elschek 1992, 200). Further, achievements in biology and medicine played a significant role in clarifying fundamental cognitive processes in regard of underlying neurophysiological structures and brain activity, This was a decisive factor for improving our understanding of music perception, musical creativity, and musical performance. The many findings thus obtained certainly are of relevance for musicology no matter if certain investigations were carried out by systematic musicologists, or by professionally in neighbouring fields. If anything, the rapid growth of knowledge in particular in such fields as musical acoustics, cognitive musicology, and computer-based study of musical performance and analysis show how outdated and narrow ideas on „musicology proper" (such as expressed by Feder 1980, Kerman 1985, Eggebrecht 1986) were.

   In order to gain momentum, and proceed in an appropriate measure, the systematic (sub)disciplines had to establish their own specialized journals which have to cover a fairly wide area of research (probably even wider than that of ethnomusicology). In the following, I can give but a few examples of journals which played a major part in the development of the single disciplines as well as in the whole field of systematic and cognitive musicology. Previously, I had selected publications in monograph format (excluding articles in journals) to be assembled in four bibliographies covering the years 1980-1999/2000, each for one subdiscipline of systematic musicology. The bibliographies concern musical acoustics (Elschek 1998), organology (Elschek and Matúšková 1998), physiology of music (Elschek 1999), and psychology of music (Elschek 2000). In order to complete this overview some of the journal which are relevant for systematic musicology should be listed here; most of them were founded in the past two or three decades:

1. Journal of Music Theory (since 1956, Yale, USA)
2. Music Theory Spectrum (USA)
3. International Review of the Aesthetics and Sociology of music (Zagreb , Croatia, since1969)
4. Journal of New Music Research (since 1971, Ghent, Belgium; originally under the title of Interface)
5. Computer Music Journal (since 1976, USA)
6. Psychology of Music (GB)
7. Psychomusicology (USA)
8. Music Analysis (since 1982, GB)
9. Music Perception (Berkeley, USA, since 1982)
10. Jahrbuch Musik Psychologie (Germany, since 1984)
11. Computers in Music Research (USA, since 1989)
12. Systematische Musikwissenschaft - Systematic Musicology (Bratislava, Slovacia, since 1992)
13. Interdisciplinary Studies in Musicology (Poznań, Poland 1993
14. Musicae Scientiae (Liège, Belgium, since 1996)
15. Organised Sound (Cambridge, GB, since 1996)
16. Musik & Ästhetik (Stuttgart, Germany 1997)

The situation since about 1980 can characterized by the foundation of national and international journals, yearbooks, book series etc. which played an outstanding role in the advancement of the field(s) under review. Besides new book series such as Studies on New Music Research (ed. Marc Leman), older ones were continued (such as the ,Orpheus' book series edited by Martin Vogel, in which a number of relevant monographs have been published, since 1961). The rather positive aspect of the broad range of journals available to systematic and cognitive musicologists seems to be marred, unfortunately, by a trend towards separation, competition, and a strive for prestige whereby cooperation between such journals, and their respective editorial boards, publishers, etc. seems to be unsatisfactory in regard of the common goal we all should have to further scientific research in the relevant fields.

In regard of systematic and cognitive musicology it should be mentioned that, in the past decades, a number of learned societies have been founded with the aim to organize conferences, workshops, and similar conventions as well as to publish journals, book series, and to engage in whatever activity that one deems to be fruitful for a certain subdiscipline or field of research. Among such societies, we find, for example The Computer Music Society (USA), The Society for Music Perception and Cognition (USA), The European Society for the Cognitive Sciences of Music, The International Cooperative in Systematic and Comparative Musicology.

Besides fields such as acoustics and organology which have rather clear structures both in regard of content and organization, there are some which, for their psychological, sociological or aesthetic implications, fall into the realm of systematic musicology. One such field is popular music in its many genres and contexts, another is media (of course, these two are interrelated in many respects). As far as music nowadays has become an inseparable part of technical media as well as of medial policy, it is inevitable for systematic musicologists to deal with the relevant phenomena which also include psychological and psychophysical factors of medially transformed music (for references, see Elschek 2005, 53, 137 etc.).

Since there are many topics which are of concern for a number of disciplines, basically there should be opportunities for doing joint research. In regard of music research, David Greer (2000) speaks of *sister disciplines*. In practice, there are various strategies of conducting interdisciplinary or transdisciplinary research, the first meaning that colleagues from different subjects or departments work together as a group when solving certain problems, the second rather pointing to research which is done with little or no regard for whatever disciplinary boundaries might exist. Both approaches have been followed, and probably will be expanded over the years to come. At this moment, the amount of articles found in various musicological and anthropolical journals contributed by systematic musicologists, on the average is probably not more than 2-4% per year. One of the reasons for this situation is that most of the „proper" musicological journals hardly accept articles which fall outside the historical perspective. Another is that for certain subdisciplines such as music psychology, the number of specialized journals available to systematic musicologists is considerable.

5. Some challenges, tendencies, and views

It is certainly difficult, if not impossible to monitor all research activities which belong, for certain aspects (in regard of topic, method, result, implications, scientific organization etc.), to systematic musicology. Alternatively, one can focus on certain areas of research, or on developments in theory and methodology, etc. In the following, I would like to report on some problems which have been studied recently in order to indicate directions and approaches which have been taken.

1. First, let me point to one issue which has been debated, by musicologists, anthropologists, and scientists of various disciplines for a long time, that of the ‚origins of music' and the early phases of its development. As is well known, there have been various hypotheses issued by, among others, Lukrecius, Charles Darwin, Herbert Spencer, Karl Büchner, Karl Groos, Valentin Häcker, Fausto Torrefranca, Robert Lach. These (and many more authors) were seeking the origins of music in imitation of birdsong (as well as other animals), vocal expression cause by courting and arousal, excited speech, the need of signalling by voice over a large distance, human curiosity for games and subjectic expression, coordinated work in a group of people which leads to rhythm and meter, etc. Some of these hypotheses were mere speculation, some were based on observations. By about 1900, the question of ‚origins' was discussed in the light of „primitive music" (by, among others, Richard Wallaschek 1903; see also Nettl, this volume), and was shifted into the direction of musical roots and fundamentals, most of all by Carl Stumpf (1911). From recordings obtained in the field, especially in some remote areas of the world, it became clear that there were very elementary types of singing, or of musical instruments as well as of their use which could be regarded making up ‚The Wellsprings of [all] music' (see Sachs 1962). In addition to the anthropological and ethnological evidence, elaborate considerations in regard of the ‚origins of music' as a type of activity peculiar to humans, have been offered, from a

cognitivist point of view, by the famous Swiss conductor and mathematician, Ernest Ansermet (1965). Also, there were some serious attempts at discussing biological and neuobiological conditions prerequisite to the „birth" of, and relevant for, the development of music (e.g., Graf 1967, Wallin 1991) as well as investigations which made use of, among other methods, the analysis of bird song as well as of other bioacoustic and environmental sound sources (Szöke 1962, 1994; Tembrock 1978). The findings from such studies of course has to be related to archaeological and other sources whereby a more complete picture of the factual beginnings of music can be achieved (surveys of relevant material and a discussion of problems are found in Geist 1970, Schneider 1997b).

The problem of musical ‚origins' has been revisited recently (see essays in Wallin et al. 2000), and has been discussed, in part a in a controversial debate, in two issues of Music Perception (Vol. 23, 2005, no. 1 and 24, 2006, no. 1). Though one can adduce some factual evidence, and in addition can try to model certain processes of evolution, the very ‚origins' of music remain a topic for speculation (which, to be sure, is a genuine type of theory).

2. Another field in which substantial progress has been made is that of neurological research in regard of music, or ‚neuromusicology'. It has steadily grown since the 1970s (see Critchley & Henson 1977), and has incorporated more and more of cognitive aspects (see Tervaniemi & Leman 1999). Research was directed to central problems such as human auditory information processing, musical cognition and memory as well as to aspects of musicality and creativity (see articles in part vi of Deliège & Wiggins [eds.] 2006), synaesthesia, and other relevant phenomena. The aim of such research, most of all, is to understand the functional organization of what often is called the „musical brain" (for overviews, see Gruhn 1998, Spitzer 2002). In regard of musical performance, control of motor behaviour (e.g., handiness) and coordination in reading music and playing an instrument have been investigated. Also, the functional anatomy of brain regions has been studied in normal persons, and in patients have suffered brain lesions or similar defects. Clinical studies also did concern disorders such as musicogenic epilepsy, general amusia, autistic behaviour etc. The outcome of such studies in turn are useful formusic therapy based on the clinical research, on the one hand, and on psychological and musical methodology, on the other. Further, the study of the auditory system and its disorders (such as deafness caused by inner ear malfunctions) has made great progress over the past decades.

As to methodology in neuromusicology, a variety of techniques have been applied some of which are special event-elated EEG (Event-Related Desynchronization and Synchronization, ERD, ERS) as well as more traditional visualizing procedures which either give a snapshot of a state of a process at a certain time, or allow for continuous registration. Cognitive neuromusicology of course is an empirical, experimental science which requires modelling, statistical data analysis, and other tools (see Neuhaus, this volume). Research in cognitive neuroscience of music might, in the years to come, significantly improve our knowledge of how musical stimuli are processed along the auditory pathway and how they are ‚represented' in certain areas and specialized cell structures of the brain. Moreover, the goal is to look into such processes which are relevant for musical approciation or the experience of synasthesia.

Different from ‚cognitive neuromusicology' which is concerned with actual brain functions, approaches based on Artificial Intelligence rest on the analogy one can draw, between a brain and a computer, both taken as an ‚automat' (see Mainzer 2003). Artificial Intelligence concepts have been followed in studies in machine-learning of music and other areas. Relevant information will be found in Balaban, Ebcioglu and Laske 1992, the special issue on *Advances in AI for Music* of the Computer Music Journal (Vol. 16, 1992, no. 2), and the special issue *Music and Artificial Intelligence* of the Journal of New Music Research (Vol. 25, 1996, no. 3).

3. An important suddiscipline of systematic musicology no doubt is music theory which connects with other areas of systematic music research such as music philosophy and aesthetics, on the one hand, and acoustics, cognitive psychology of music and related fields on the other. As the history of music theory from antiquity into the 20th century (see Zaminer [ed.] 1984-2000) demonstrates, music theory, though at times with a strong orientation towards actual musical composition and execution, almost always had strong philosophical inclinations as well as scientific foundations. For example, one may point to music theory as outlined by Riemann and his contemporaries (see Schneider, this volume).

In the course of the 20th century, and in particular after ca. 1950, the (more or less coherent) theory of tonal music became a side phenomenon in many countries, and was replaced by a variety of theories composers had devised for their own work, or even for single works. Besides ‚theorizing' composers such as Boulez, Stockhausen, or Xenakis there were attempts at finding new concepts for musical composition and analysis by making use of mathematics (with a focus on set theory), or procedures derived from information theory etc. In many such studies, the aspect of formalization dominates whereas perception and cognition of music often are of little, if any interest. To be sure, theoretical inquiry since antiquity is a genuine part of music theory, however, it should be complemented with empirical considerations in regard of the actual listener as well as the performance of music.

The theory of tonal music took a new turn in the wake of the cognitive sciences when formalization indeed was paired with modelling of perception and cognition (see Seifert 1993). Also, there is a large number of studies from the 1980s on in which tenets of music theory have been tested empirically, by psychologists and musicologists alike. Mainly for practical reasons, many of the experiments are confined to smaller excerpts of existing works, and to works of the tonal tradition where the melodic, harmonic, metric, and rhythmic structures are not too complicated. There are some notable experiments, though, where music has been composed especially for the purpose of conducting experiments on cognition (e.g., Louven 1998).

A comprehensive account of music theory in the 20th is a task which needs, first of all, a critical examination of the various approaches which then would have to be subjected to an analysis of concepts and methodologies. To which extent the results could be systematized in order to determine general features, remains to be seen.

Without being able to go into details here, I may point to some relevant publications (outside journals devoted to music theory such as the Journal of Music Theory or similar periodicals) in which material is found relevant for a systematic investigation of music theory and its development in the recent decades in which interrelations between music theory, acoustics and electroacoustics, psychology etc. are of relevance. Such material will be found, for example, in several issues of the Journal of New Music Research (formerly Interface), namely vols. 16, 1987, no. 2; 24, 1995, no. 2; 27, 1998, nos. 1-2, 4 (Electroaoustic music); 28, 1999, nos. 1, 4; 30, 2001, no. 1 (Music and Mathematics); 29, 2000, nos. 1, 2; 35, 2006, nos. 2, 4.

Another aspect which needs at least to mentioned is music theory in regard of cultures outside western concepts of *Tonkunst* or diverse experimental directions new music took in the 20th century. Obviously, music cultures found in the Near East (e.g., Persia/Iran, the Arab speaking countries, Turkey and countries with populations speaking Turkish languages), in India, Indonesia, China, Japan and other regions each have explicit concepts about their music which can be studied and documented as such. The tripartite division of musicology mentioned above leaves these music cultures to be studied by ethnomusicology which in fact has devoted many of its publications to the music and music theory of the aforementioned regions and cultures. Also, concepts of African music cultures have been investigated in a growing number of studies. It should be clear, thereby, that music theory is by no means confined to „western" music, and that it calls for a comparative approach in order to determine such notions, concepts, rules, etc. which are common to a number of musical cultures, or which have equivalents among such.

In regard of the developments which took place in electroacoustic and computer music, on the one hand, and the experiences we have from ethnomusicology, on the other, it should be clear, finally, that music theory can neither restrict its view to written documents in which rules relevant for musical grammar and syntax are put to paper, nor can it exclude sound and sound structures. Since the 1980s, when computers and signal processing software became available to musicology, the latter aspect was the focus of many publications as found, for example, in the Computer Music Journal, Interface/Journal of New Music Research, in several issues of Systematische Musikwissenschaft/Systematic Musicology (e.g., Vol. 4, 1996: *Similarity and sound structure*), and in the journal Organised Sound.

4. In addition to the research areas and problems mentioned before, there is another field which relates to sound in several ways. It has to do, most of all, with the digitization of music which nowadays is common practice, and is extended backwards in time to transfer, for example, huge collections of traditional non-western and western folk and vernacular music from analogue to digital storage formats. (See the special issue *Digitizing world music*, Systematische Musikwissenschaft/Systematic Musicology 7, 2000, no. 2). Digitization of music which is stored, in large quantities, in data bases, however poses new problems in that, to allow for full access to the material, there has to be some form of ‚content management'.

Though there are various attempts at developing algorithms suited to extract salient features from audio sources (see, e.g., articles in Journal of New Music Research 28, 1999, no. 4), it has become clear over the past years that sufficient access to digital musical data cannot be adequately effected by relying on bottom-up signal processing alone. Rather, top-down aspects need to be included which account for subjective imaginations average users of such data bases might have of certain types or works of music (see Leman, this volume). In this regard, musical meaning and semantics is a factor which matters (see Karbusicky 1986, Sloboda et al., *Music and meaning: a syposium*, Musicae scientiae 2, 1998, 21-65).

5. Finally, the aspect of music in relation to other parts of (mainly western) culture has been emphasized once more, in a recent anthology of articles (Clayton et al. [eds.] 2003). The background of the views presented in this volume is manifold, ranging from ethnomusicology to British ‚Cultural Studies', gender, and beyond. One of the articles which deserves special notice is that of Martin Clayton (2003), titled *Comparing music, comparing musicology*. It is interesting to notice that the necessity to include a comparative perspective int ethnomusicology is acknowledged by someone writing, basically, from a culture-relativistic point of view (see also Nettl, this volume).

The cultural and social dimension of course is important in the study of popular music which, in the past thirty years, has grown into a specialized field with a number of scientific journals (e.g., Popular Music), and many monographs dealing with single artists, bands, genres, styles, etc. Because the sociocultural context of in many studies is the focus of attention, the music as composed and performed by certain musicians, and as sound produced live on stage, or in a studio, remains underexposed. There are, though, monographs which approach popular music as music, in the first place (see, e.g., Pfleiderer 2006).

6. Teaching, academic programmes, institutional cooperation

Under subsections 1-5 above, I have pointed to some areas of research which I believe are of importance in regard of systematic (as well as, in part, comparative) musicology. Looking at the field at large, there are very many relevant publications (journals, monographs, also electronic publications on the internet) which all address, in one way or another, music in its various manifestations and contexts. Due to a high degree of specialization, different subdisciplines have developed rather fast as is obvious in musical acoustics, psychology of music, neuromusicology, and areas which relate to computer science and electronics, respectively. Since there are so many publications where some problems are studied in detailed, the need to systematize and integrate the findings comes as a consequence. Also, as has been emphasized in this article, a comparative perspective should be encouraged in areas where such is appropriate (see, for example Schneider 1997a, Fördermayr & Deutsch 1998, Carterette & Kendall 1999, and Systematische Musikwissenschaft/Systematic Musicology vol. 3, 1995, no. 1: *Theory of music and psychoacoustics*). At present, in regard of research in many systematic subdisciplines it seems that there is a trend towards overspecialization going along with a lack of integrative and comparative approaches. Therefore, one would want to see more symposia bringing together professionals in order to find ways to systematize and integrate the huge amount of detailed studies which are the outcome of research done over the past decades. Besides, considerations in regard of academic teaching seem appropriate since a growing body of scientific results and research tools must be communicated to students in such a way that they are in position to do useful research on their own, on the one hand. On the other, they should have an adequate knowledge of research done in the past (for example, in Gestalt psychology in regard of music) and of fundamentals of methodology even if developed several generations ago (e.g., much of inferential statistics).

It was mainly for these reasons as well as a more general intent to improve communication between scholars from different countries, having a somewhat different background that a number of colleagues, most of which were teaching systematic musicology (or comparative musicology, or both), founded the International Cooperative in Systematic and Comparative Musicology, in 1993 (which was formally registrated as a non-profit scientific organization in 1995; see systematicmusicology.org), In 1993, we started a series of conferences the first of which took place in the castle of Moravany, Slovakia, the next in Hamburg (1994), and so on. Well before the fist conference, I had prepared a questionnaire in which I was asking for statements in regard of issues in systematic musicology which relate to its present status, disciplinary and institutional organization, educational aspects, etc. The answer from thirteen colleagues will be found in Systematische Musikwissenschaft/Systematic Musicology 1, 1993, no. 1, and most of the papers read at the first conference plus discussion from a round table are published in Vol. I, no. 2 (1993: *Theoretical and methodologoical aspects. State of research*) of that journal. It became obvious, besides other problems, that academic training, possibilities to study systematic musicology as a discipline, and actual curricula differed significantly from one country to the next, and even from one university to the next within one country. In addition to the first survey of 1993, we started a new one in 1997 (the responses are published in Systematische Musikwissenschaft/Systematic Musicology 5, 1997, no. 2: *Towards the 21st century*). One result of the surveys in both 1993 and 1997 was that, with a few exceptions, academic programmes for education in systematic (and comparative) musicology were much less developed than those in historic musicology, on the university level. (A few years later, thanks to an initiative of Jukka Louhivuori and Petri Toiviainen at Jyväskylä, Finland, a series of Intensive Programmes in Systematic and Cognitive Musicology was launched which was continued, in 2006 and 2007, at Ghent under the direction of Marc Leman). Further, with the implementation of the Bologna-style B.A. and M.A., there is a good chance that a Joint European Master in Systematic and Cognitive Musicology which is has been agreed upon, in principle, by several universities already in 2004, will be available to students soon. In fact, this would mean a significant step forward in regard of European integration as well as disciplinary independence of systematic musicology (including its subdiscplines and specialized directions such as cognitive musicology).

The change which is necessary to regenerate musicology becomes obvious if one looks at the imbalanced relation of historical and systematic musicology. As the following data demonstrate, there was, and still is, a dominance of historical musicology in regard of ist presence as an academic discipline. During the academic year 1978, for example in West Germany out of 432 courses (lectures, seminars, etc.) offered in musicology on the university level, 46 were of a general or technical nature, 41 were devoted to ethnomusicology, and 56 covered areas of systematic musicology. The vast majority of 286 courses by their content have to be regarded as historical musicology. The figures imply that about 13% of all courses were in systematic musicology, and less than 10% in ethnomusicology (see Elschek 1993, 16). The situation evaluated for the years 1999-2001, based on a record of 1655 courses offered at 21 German universities (and equivalent academic institutions) shows a similar structure, in that no more than 10% of the lectures and seminars can be attributed to systematic musicology (Adam, Heesch and Rode-Breyman 2002, 262). In fact, this means even a decline compared to the figures of 1978. Given these facts and figures, it is no wonder that many students in musicology are dissatisfied with the curriculum offered at most of the academic institutions. In this respect, it seems necessary to strengthen both systematic and comparative musicology as well as ethnomusicology since these can offer curricula which deal with phenomena of music in contemporary society, and in regard of modern media technology, on the one hand, and cultural diversity in a global perspective, on the other.

7. Conclusion

In the present article, I have tried to present an overview which, in paragraph 2, reconstructs some of the disciplinary developments of systematic (as well as parts of comparative) musicology from the time of Adler well into the 1970s and 1980s. For a number of reasons, the focus was on Central Europe, and in particular on Germany, Austria, and neighbouring countries. In paragraph 3, more recent concepts of disciplinary division were discussed. In paragraphs 4 and 5, I have addressed developments in some of the subdisciplines and areas of research which I believe were of importance in regard of finding new directions, or for the factual outcome as well as theoretical and methodological aspects of research. In paragraph 6, some problems in regard of teaching and studying systematic musicology are mentioned. As this article underpins once more, cooperation between professionals and institutions working in the wider field of systematic (including cognitive and comparative) musicology should be intensified .

References

Abel-Struth, Sigrid. 1970. Materialien zur Musikpädagogik als Wissenschaft. Mainz: Schott.

Adam, Nina, Florian Heesch and Susanna Rode-Breymann. 2002. Über das Gefühl der

Unzufriedenheit in der Disziplin. Die Musikforschung 55, 251-273.

Adler, Guido 1885/1981. Umfang, Methode und Ziel der Musikwissenschaft. Vierteljahrsschrift für Musikwissenschaft 1, 5-20. (engl. transl.: The Scope, method, and aim of musicology. Yearbook for Traditional Music XIII, 5-18)

Adler, Guido 1919/1971. Methode der Musikgeschichte. Leipzig (Repr. Hildesheim: Olms).

Ansermet, Ernest 1965. Die Grundlagen der Musik im menschlichen Bewußtsein. München: R. Piper Verlag.

Balaban, M., Ebcioglu, K. and Laske, O. eds. 1992. Understanding Music with AI:

Perspectives on Music Cognition. Menlo Park, Cambridge, MA: The AAAI Pr./MIT Pr.

Beard, David, Kenneth Gloag. 2005. Musicology. The Key Concepts. London and New York: Routledge.

Brandl Rudofl. 2003. Si tacuisses Greve – der notwendige Erhalt der Musikethologie. Die Musikforschung 56, 166-171.

Broeckx, Jan L. 1959. Methode van de Muziekgeschiedenis. Antwerpen: Uitgeverij Metropolis.

Carterette, Edward, Roger Kendall 1999. Comparative perception and cognition. In D. Deutsch (ed.). The Psychology of music. 2nd ed. Orlando: Academic Pr., 725-791.

Clayton, Martin, Trevor Herbert and Richard Middleton Eds. 2002. The Cultural Study of Music: A Critical Introduction. New York: Routledge.

Cowell, Richard, ed. 1992. Handbook of Research on Music Teaching and Learning. New York: Schirmer Books.

Cross, Ian 2006. Music and Biocultural Evolution. In Irène Dèliège and Geraint A. Wiggins (eds.). Musical Creativity. Multidisciplinary Research in Theory and Practice. Hove and New York: Psychology Press, 19-30.

Critchley, Macdonald and R.A. Henson (eds.) 1977. Music and the Brain. Studies in Neurology of Music. London: W. Heinemann.

Dahlhaus, Carl. 1971 (Ed.). Einleitung in die Systematische Musikwissenschaft. Köln: Gerig.

Dahlhaus, Carl 1974. Fragen an die Musikethnologie. Neue Zeitschrift für Musik 135, 150 and 493-494.

Dahlhaus, Carl 1977. Grundlagen der Musikgeschichte. Köln: Musikverlag Hans Gerig.

Dahlhaus, Carl and Helga de la Motte-Haber (eds.) 1984. Systematische Musikwissenschaft. Laaber: Laaber Verlag.

Delièxge Irène and Geraint A. Wiggins eds. Musical Creativity. Multidisciplinary Research in Theory and Practice. Hove, New York: Psychology Press.

Elschek, Oskár. 1969. Hudobnovedecká systematika a etnoorganológia (Musicological systematics and ethnoorganology). Musicologica slovaca I, 5-41.

Elschek, Oskar 1973a. ed. Muzikologický seminar "Systematika súčasnej hudobnej vedy" Musicologica slovaca IV, 145-268.

Elschek, Oskar 1973b. Gegenwartsprobleme der musikwissenschaftlichen Systematik. Acta Musicologica 45, 1-23.

Elschek, Oskar 1973c. Entwurf einer neuen musikwissenschaftlichen Systematik. Die Musikforschung 26, 421-434.

Elschek, Oskar 1974. Gegenfragen der Musikethnologie. Neue Zeitschrift für Musik, 135, 8: 491-493.

Elschek, Oskar 1984. Hudobná veda súčasnosti. Systematika, teória, vývin (Contemporary musicology. Systematics, Theory, Development). Bratislava: VEDA.

Elschek, Oskar 1986. Das Forschungskonzept der vergangenen und gegenwärtigen Musikwissenschaft. In O. Elschek (ed.). Entwicklungswege der Musikwissenschaft. Musicologica slovaca XI, 52-101. Bratislava:VEDA.

Elschek, Oskar 1992. Die Musikforschung der Gegenwart, ihre Systematik, Theorie und Entwicklung. Wien-Föhrenau: Verlag Stiglmayr. 2 volumes.

Elschek, Oskar 1993. Das Bildungsideal in der gegenwärtigen Musikwissenschaft und Musik-ethnologie. Musikethnologisches Kolloquium. Edited by Alois Mauerhofer. Musiketnologische Sammelbände 6: 9-23. Graz: Akademische Druck- u. Verlagsgesellschaft

Elschek, Oskar 1994. Aktuelle Fragen der Musikalischen Grundlagenforschung (I) Fachbereiche, Wechselwirkungen, Definitionen und Inhalte (I). Systematische Musikwisssenschaft II, 7-61.

Elschek, Oskar 1997. Entwicklungswege und Forschungsziele der europäischen Volkslied- und Volksmusikforschung. Festschrift Walter Wiora. Edited by Christoph-Hellmut Mahling and Ruth Seiberts, 44-60. Tutzing: Hans Schneider.

Elschek, Oskar 1998. Musikalische Akustik. Eine selektive Bibliographie (1980-1999). Systematische Musikwissenschaft - Systematic Musicology VI, 95-112.

Elschek, Oskar 1998. Organology – Instrumentenforschung. A selective bibliography - Eine selektive Bibliographie 1980-1999. Systematische Musikwissenschaft - Systematic Musicology VI, 255-284.

Elschek, Oskar (with A. Matúšková) 1999. Musikphysiologie – Physiology of Music. A selected bibliography (1980-1999). Systematische Musikwissenschaft - Systematic Musicology VI, 415-437.

Elschek, Oskar 1999. Musikpsychologie – Psychology of Music. A selective Bibliography 1980-1999. Systematische Musikwissenschaft - Systematic Musicology VII, 105-124.

Elchek, Oskar 2002. Die Beziehung zwischen Musikphilosophie und Musikästhetik. Musicologica Istropolitana I, Bratislava, 11-24.

Elschek, Oskar 2003. Gedankliche und methodische Konzepte der europäischen Musikwissenschaft. Musicologica Istropolitana II, Bratislava, 11-30.

Elschek, Oskar 2005. Medialna spolocnost' – jej kultúra, umenie a hudba [The medial society – its culture, art, and music]. In O. Elschek (ed.). Multimediálna Spolocnost na prahu 21. storocia, jej kultúra, umenie, hudba a neprekonané problemy. [Multimedial society at the door to the 21th century, its culture, art, music]. Bratislava: ASCO art & science, 13-138.

Elsner, Jürgen. 2004. Globalisierung, Verlockungen und Verirrungen. Deutsche Musikwissenschaft auf ausgetretenen Pfaden und die Heimkehr eines ´verlorenen Sohnes´ Ethnomusicologicum III, Bratislava, 199-217.

Feder, Georg. 1980. Empirisch-experimentelle Methoden in der Musikforschung. Kritische Bemerkungen zur Kompetenz und Eigenständigkeit der Systematischen Musikwissenschaft und zur Relevanz einiger ihrer Ergebnisse. Die Musikforschung 33, 409-431.

Feder, Georg 1987. Musikphilologie. Eine Einführung in die musikalische Textkritik, Hermeneutik und Editionstechnik. Darmstadt: Wissenschaftliche Buchgesellschaft.

Födermayr, Franz, and Werner, A. Deutsch 1998. Zur Forschungsstrategie der vergleichenden Musikwissenschaft. Musicologica Austriaca 17, 163-180.

Geist, Bohumil 1970. Puvod hudby [Origins of music]. Praha: Editio Supraphon.

Graf, Walter 1967. Biologische Wurzeln des Musikerlebens. Schriften des Vereins zur Verbreitung naturwiss. Kenntnisse in Wien 107; repr. in Graf 1980, 224-237.

Graf, Walter 1980. Vergleichende Musikwissenschaft. [Coll. Essays]. Wien: Stiglmayr.

Greer, David. 2000. Music and Sister Disciplines. Past, Present, Future. Oxford: Oxford University Press.

Greve, Martin. 2002. Writing against Europe. Vom notwenigen Verschwinden der „Musikethnologie". Die Musikforschung 55, 239-251.

Gruhn, Wilfried 1998. Der Musikverstand. Neurologische Grundlagen des musikalischen Denkens, Hörens und Lernens. Hildesheim: G. Olms.

Haydon, Glen. 1941/New.ed. 1959. Introduction to Musicology. Chapel Hill: University of North Carolina Press.

Jourdan, Robert. 1997/2001 (germ. transl.). Das wohltemperierte Gehirn. Wie Musik im Kopf entsteht. Heidelberg: Spektrum Akad. Verlag.

Karbusicky,Vladimir. 1979. Systematische Musikwissenschaft. Eine Einführung in Grundbegriffe, Methoden und Arbeitstechniken. München: UTB.

Karbusicky, Vladimir 1987. Grundriß der musikalischen Semantik. Darmstadt: wissenschaftl. Buchges-

Karbusicky, Vladimir and Albrecht, Schneider. 1980. Zur Grundlegung der Systematischen Musikwissenschaft. Acta Musicologica 52, 87-100.

Kerman, Joseph 1985. Contemplating music: challenges to musicology. Cambridge, MA: Harvard U.Pr.

Kleinen Günter and Helga de la Motte-Haber, 1982. Wissenschaft und Praxis. In C. Dahlhaus/H. de la Motte-Haber (eds.). Systematische Musikwissenschaft, 309-340.

Knepler, Georg. 1977. Geschichte als Weg zum Musikverständnis. Zur Theorie, Methode und Geschichte der Musikgeschichtsschreibung. Leipzig: Philipp Reclam jun.

Laade, Wolfgang. 1976. Musikwissenschaft zwischen gestern und morgen. Bemerkungen eines Musikethnologen zu einer Diskussion über Musikgeschichte und Musikethnologie. Berlin: Merseburger.

Lébl, Vladimír, Ivan Poledňá and [Jaroslav Jiránek]). 1988. Hudební věda. Histórie a teórie oboru, jeho světový a český vývoj. Vol. 1-3. Praha: SPN.

Lederer, Josef-Horst , Rudolf, Flotzinger, Franz, Födermayr, eds. 1986. Gedenkschrift Guido Adler. (=Musicologica Austriaca 6. Wien-Föhrenau: Stiglmayr).

Leman, Marc, 1995. Music and Schema Theory. Cognitive Foundations of Systematic Musicology. Berlin: Springer.

Louven, Christoph 1998. Die Konstrukttion von Musik. Theoretische und experimentelle Studien zu den Prinzipien der musikalischen Kognition. Frankfurt/M. P. Lang.

Mainzer, Klaus. 2003. KI – Künstliche Intelligenz. Grundlagen intelligenter Systeme. Darmstadt: Wissenschaftliche Buchgesellschaft.

Memorandum über die Lage der Musikwissenschaft in der Bundesrepublik Deutschland, ed. Carl Dahlhaus, Georg Feder. 1976, 1977. Die Musikforschung 29, 249-256; 30, 2-3.

Merriam, Alan P. 1966. The Anthropology of music. Evanston, Ill.; Northwestern U.Pr.

Oberhoff, Bernd. Ed. Psychoanalyse und Musik. Eine Bestandaufnahme. Gießen: Psychosozial-Verlag.

Pfleiderer, Martin 2006. Rhythmus. Psychologische, theoretische und stilanalytische Aspekte populärer Musik. Bielefeld: transcript Verlag.

Rösing, Helmut and Peter Petersen. 2000. Orientierung Musikwissenschaft. Was sie kann, was sie will. Reinbek bei Hamburg: Rowohlts Enzyklopädie.

Schneider, Albrecht. 1976. Musikwissenschaft und Kulturkreislehre. Zur Methodik und Geschichte der Vergleichenden Musikwissenschaft. Bonn-Bad Godesberg: Verlag für systematische Musikwissenschaft.

Schneider, Albrecht 1984. Analogie und Rekonstruktion. Studien zur Methodologie der Musikgeschichtsschreibung und zur Frühgeschichte der Musik. Bonn: Verlag für systematische Musikwissenschaft.

Schneider, Albrecht 1997a. Tonhöhe, Skala, Klang. Akustische, tonometrische und psychoakustische Studien auf vergleichender Grundlage. Bonn: Orpheus -Verlag für systematische Musikwissenschaft.

Schneider, Albrecht 1997b. Archaeology of music in Europe: an overview. In H.W. Heister (ed.). Musik – Revolution: Festschrift für Georg Knepler zum 90. Geburtstag. Hamburg: von Bockel, Vol. I, 39-66.

Seifert, Uwe. 1993. Systematische Musikwissenschaft und Kognitive Musiktheorie. Zur Grundlegung der kognitiven Musikwissenschaft. Bonn: Verlag für systematische Musikwissenschaft.

Sachs, Curt. 1962. The Wellspring of Music. The Hague: Martinus Nijhoff.

Simon, Artur. 1978. Probleme, Methoden und Ziele der Ethnomusikologie. Jahrbuch für musikalische Volks- und Völkerkunde 9, 8-52.

Spitzer, Manfred. 2002. Musik im Kopf. Hören, Musizieren, Verstehen und Erleben im neuronalen Netzwerk. Stuttgart New York: Schattauer.

Stumpf, Carl. 1911. Anfänge der Musik. Leipzig: J. A. Bartth.

Szöke, Peter 1962. Zur Entstehung und Entwicklungsgeschichte der Musik. Studia musicologica Acad. Scient. Hung. 2, 33-85.

Szöke, Peter 1994. Ist das hinter dem Horizont der Tonkunst verborgene säkulare Rätsel des Ursprungs der Musik unlösbar? Systematische Musikwissenschaft – Systematic Musicology 2, 71-108.

Tembrock, Günter 1978. Bioakustik, Musik und Sprache. Berlin (Sitzungsberichte der Akad. der Wiss. der DDR, Mathematik – Naturwissenschaften – Technik, Jg. 1978, Nr. 1/N).

Tervaniemi, Mari and Marc, Leman, eds. 1999. Cognitive Neuromusicology. Journal of New Music Research 28, no. 3.

Wallin, Nils, L. 1991. Biomusicology. Neurophysiological, Neuripsychological and Evolutionary Prespectives on the Origin and Purpose of Music. Stuyvesant, NY.: Pendragon Press.

Wallin, Nils, Björn Merker, Steven Brown (eds.). The origins of music. Cambridge, MA, London: MIT Pr.

Weber, Michael. 1990. Eine ´andere´ Musikwissenschaft. Vorstudien zur Theorie und Methodologie. Franfurt a.M.: Peter Lang.

Williams Alastair. 2000. Constructing Musicology. Aldershot-Burlington: Ashgate.

Wiora, Walter. 1984. Zum Systematischen Teil des "Neuen Handbuchs der Musikwissenschaft". Acta Musicologica 56, 211-221.

Zaminer, Frieder ed. 1984-1990. Geschichte der Musiktheorie. Vol. 1-11. Darmstadt: Wissenschaftliche Buchgesellschaft.

Marc Leman

Systematic musicology at the crossroads of modern music research

Abstract

The creative and cultural sector, of which music forms an important part, calls for a research basis that is grounded in a range of scientific disciplines with specialization in music-related technology and music-driven psychosocial interaction. In that music research space, there is a natural and emergent demand for an approach in which boundaries of object-centred and subject-centred research methodologies can be crossed. By putting music and embodied music experiences at the very centre of this research focus, systematic musicology can play an important role as moderator of a trans-disciplinary approach to music research. Evidence for the new position of systematic musicology in the modern European music research space is found in networks that foster systematic musicology, in a recent strategic roadmap for sound and music computing, commissioned by the European Commission, and in two recent National project initiatives, one in Finland and one in Belgium, that support long term research in the domain of systematic musicology.

Introduction

In a lecture entitled "Who stole systematic musicology?" (2003, Universität zu Köln), I once expressed my concern about "systematic musicology"[1]. The main reason for expressing this concern was that at the turn of the new millennium, the number of music

---

[1] The use of the term "systematic musicology" reflects the common distinction between "historical" and "systematic" musicology in academia. Apparently, the term "systematic musicology" is common in Continental Europe, but less common in the UK and the US. The term is often used in countries that were influenced by German music research. However, related approaches are sometimes called "cognitive musicology", "empirical musicology", "computational musicology", "systemic musicology", "interdisciplinary musicology" or simply: "musicology". It is assumed that systematic musicology is not restricted to any musical period, geographic area, musical genre or type of musical expression. Systematic musicology differs from the so-called historical musicology in that it is less involved with biographies of composers or the development of musical practices in a particular area or style period, but more with what these practices mean to people and more particularly how these practices can be understood, explained as a system (both from a psychoneuronal and social point of view), and possibly further explored and exploited (for example in connection with technology). The methodology of systematic musicology is particular in that it is often based on a mixture of methods from other sciences, including human sciences and natural sciences. The adjective "systematic" somehow points to the systemic character of the methodology and in fact, much of the discussion about the relevance of systematic musicology is related to the nature of this systemic aspect. The term "systemic musicology" was introduced by Fricke (1993), who defines it as "eine Sichtweise [...] die das komplexe Bedingungsgefüge [...] von naturgegebenen, genetischen, erlernten und kultur-abhängigen Faktoren in den Vordergrund stellt". The basic idea was that all sciences aim at being systematic in the sense of being planned, thorough and efficient, and that "systematic musicology" in fact means "systemic musicology", that is, affecting processes and connections between different levels of things that are constrained and linked together in a system (see also Schneider, 1993).

researchers had suddenly exploded and this formed a threat to the ongoing research practices of systematic musicology. After a decennium in which systematic musicology had positioned itself as an empirical and computational discipline[2], the amount of researchers working in music engineering and in neuroscience of music quickly outnumbered the small amount of researchers working in musicology departments. This was most noticeable at conferences on music information retrieval[3], where engineers convincingly showed that their tools outperformed almost everything that systematic musicology had explored so far in computational analysis and content-based representation. In a similar way, neuroscience[4] showed that the new brain scanning technologies could offer a fresh look at musical perception and performance, having an effect on our understanding of what music is about. I challenged my audience by saying that the sudden interest in music from engineering was probably driven by a rush for the chicken with the golden eggs, or more concretely, the rush for the over-all content-based search and retrieval system for music on the Internet (the "Music Google"). Equally threatening was the agenda of neuroscience, and the rush for brain localizations, the claim that all musical activities could be explained by just looking at the brain. The conclusion was clear: If music could be better studied by specialized disciplines, then systematic musicology had no longer a value. If everything could be accounted for by engineering and brain science, then systematic musicology would be no longer necessary. Systematic musicology could be classified "vertically", as we use to say for documents that are no longer needed, or it could be taken over by other disciplines, or it could just shrink its ambitions to music analysis, a smaller and less ambitious segment of music research.

In fact, my concern culminated in a discontentment about the fact that systematic musicology did not have a proper answer to this development. Other disciplines had discovered the music topic and they applied good empirical and computational methods. They got the money, they did the research, and they obtained the results. So what? What else could a systematic musicologist, living at the beginning of a new millennium, do than acknowledging the power of the new methods? What else could I do than becoming an engineer, psychologist, brain scientist, or perhaps, biologist ... and look to music from that perspective?[5]

---

[2] See e.g. "Journal of New Music Research", the journal "Systematische Musikwissenschaft/Systematic Musicology/Musicologie Systématique", as well as the journals "Music Perception", "Computer Music Journal", "Musicae Scientiae".

[3] Since 2000, a number of initiatives have shown the dynamism of the engineering approaches in music research. The conferences on Music Information Retrieval started in 2000 (see http://www.ismir.net/), the conferences on Computer Music Modeling and Retrieval started in 2003 (see http://www.lma.cnrs-mrs.fr/~cmmr2007/). Related conferences are the conferences on Digital Audio Effects, which started in 1998 (see http://www.dafx.de/), the international conferences on New Interfaces for Musical Expression, which started in 2001 (see http://www.nime.org/pastnimes.html), and the Sound and Music Computing conferences, which started in 2004 (see http://smc07.uoa.gr/SMC07%20Previous.htm).

[4] Reference can be made to the international conferences dedicated to the neurosciences and music in New York, 2000, Venice, 2002, and Leipzig, 2005 (with more than 400 people attending) (See Zatorre and Peretz, 2001; Avanzini et al., 2003; Avanzini et al., 2005).

[5] This feeling was quite different from the feelings that I experienced in 1993, when systematic musicologists from East and West Europe met, in an euphoric mix from old and young generations. Thanks to A. Schneider for inviting me to this particular setting at Moravany where I had the opportunity to meet the old generation of systematic musicologists from Central Europe. The

During the years before and after the lecture, I had the opportunity to get in close contact with many colleagues and many music research institutes in Europe. Invitations for short study periods at different institutes, among which the Music Technology Group of Pompeu Fabra University in Barcelona (June 2003), and later on that same year, the Kulturwissenschaftliches Forschungskolleg Media und Kulturelle Kommunikation (December 2003) of the University of Cologne, and the Max Planck Institute for Cognitive Neuroscience in Leipzig (May 2005) somehow stimulated my thinking about this problem. There, I saw groups of researchers at work that often had no background in musicology. Could they progress our knowledge about music? Around that period too, I was involved in a number of international meetings on music information retrieval (such as ISMIR, 2004 and CMMR, 2004), and I had my own projects both in a national and international context (e.g. MAMI, COST 287, S2S[2]) in which I collaborated with psychologists, engineers and brain scientists. In short, I travelled a lot all over Europe, and I could observe from very close how our colleagues actually dealt with "our stolen discipline" so to speak. And in fact, I must admit, those observations confirmed what I already had observed as editor-in-chief of Journal of New Music Research (from 1987 to 2004), namely, that non-musicologists could advance music research quite a lot. In fact, I had (and I still have) a great time with researchers from other disciplines. They enrich the field and they often contribute with excellent methods and approaches. But what about my own discipline? How could a systematic musicologist survive in such a context? Was there still a tiny little place for a researcher like me, or for the good old systematic musicology as a whole?

By the turn of the millennium, I had already realized that a proper answer to this question was needed. And in fact, raising the question "who stole systematic musicology?" was a strong incentive for reflecting on my own approach in relation to what I considered then to be the new upcoming music research space. Up to then, the entire paradigm of systematic musicology was still largely driven by the research paradigm of the cognitive sciences, to which I had contributed myself through empirical and computational modelling studies (e.g. Leman, 1995; Leman, 1997; Godøy and Jørgensen, 2001). Ultimately, thanks to some time for reflection in Köln (end of 2003), I decided to work on the research paradigm of systematic musicology in a more profound, say "systematic", way, and this finally resulted in my book on embodied music cognition, of which the first versions already circulated among collaborators and friends in 2005 (Leman, 2007).

In retrospect, my answer to the question about the need of systematic musicology in the modern music research space was much inspired by observations and discussions with colleagues from outside musicology. Somehow, I got strongly convinced that the modern music research space was much in the need of an approach, and a vision, that could go beyond the confines of the proper disciplines. Today, I am still convinced that the formulation of this vision, as well its implementation and validation is a major task

---

discussions at Moravany were about the future program of systematic musicology. Young researchers, like U. Seifert and myself at that time, pleaded for systematic musicology to play a role in cognitive science. For a state-of-the art of systematic musicology at the turn of the 1990ies, see the first volume of the journal Systematische Musikwissenschaft (1993), and the contributions from O. Elschek, H-P. Reinecke, J. Jiránek, F. Födermayr, W. Deutsch, L. Burlas, A. Schneider, J. Fricke, U. Seifert, M. Leman, H-W. Heister, B. Schabbing, M. Kartomi, V. Karbusicky and others. (See also Elschek, 1992).

of systematic musicology. Indeed, many researchers working in non-musicological disciplines of music-related research realise that music is more than just an application domain onto which their methodologies can be applied „out of the blue". Music is far too complex, far too multifaceted, and far too much integrated in our social and cultural environment to reduce it to a single approach or to conceive it merely as a domain of application. The study of how people move in accordance with music is a good example of this. A purely physical approach about how people move in response to music is likely to ignore the important role of cultural learning and goal-directed behaviour (intentionality) through posture and expressiveness. In a similar way, asking subjects to fill in a questionnaire about their social and cultural background and their intentions will hardly be sufficient for understanding their engagement in non-verbal forms of musical expression. It is even more likely that neither method may be sufficient, and that a proper method, involving the interaction of several disciplines and methodologies is needed. Similar observations can be made in the field of music information retrieval where user-oriented studies are needed that complement the engineering applications (Lesaffre et al., in press).

While it appeared to me that many researchers agreed that dealing with music necessitates a proper approach that is driven by the musical task, I observed at the same time that it was very rare that researchers went beyond the boundaries of their own disciplines. Apparently, academic careers depend more on the mastering of advanced measurement methods and analysis methodologies, than the ability to transcend the boundaries of the proper discipline, especially for a topic that is often considered to be fancy and pleasant. Hence the fact that music is more often seen as a domain for the application of proper methodologies than as a domain that can generate a proper methodological approach from inside. But I agree, one should be very careful in making such statements, because even when music is conceived as a domain for applying the "Eigen-methods" of the discipline, then the outcome may still be highly relevant for the cultural and creative music sector. There is a subtle balance between the goals, the means and the results of music research.

Anyhow, I got the feeling that all disciplines of modern music research were in the need for an approach and a vision that could link the different disciplines and their methodologies. Was this something of interest? Was this an opportunity for systematic musicology? I thought it was, although I realized that it would not be an easy bargain. Somehow, music researchers from outside musicology had to become convinced that the discipline of systematic musicology could offer something that is of value to them, a kind of glue that "cannot be stolen", so to speak. And therefore, the question was: What is this glue? What is of such a value in systematic musicology that it can appeal to a broad range of researchers working in other disciplines?

What follows is a state-of-the-art of this quest, showing how, in a world with a growing interest in music research, a new role for systematic musicology is gradually emerging. I will argue that the ability to transcend the proper discipline in response to the driving forces of the musical topic is one of the major characteristics of systematic musicology and that it is precisely this feature, combined with the attitude of putting music and people at the centre of the focus, regardless of whatever scientific method, approach, or discipline, is used, makes systematic musicology rather unique (and therefore quite necessary) in modern music research. However, the realization of this ambition is highly depending on a vision, a perspective, or a glue, that may appeal to all partners involved. In what follows, I will try to clarify what this vision and glue could be (or at least, how I see it at this moment) and how, by taking concrete actions to realize that vision, systematic musicology is gradually acquiring a new place in the modern music research space.

Transdisciplinary music research

Music research that goes beyond the boundaries of the involved disciplines can be called „transdisciplinary". The term "transdisciplinary", perhaps even more than the term "interdisciplinary"[6], suggests that music cannot be fully understood by a single discipline, or by different disciplines that are just put next to each other without much interaction.

Would transdisciplinarity be something of value and convincing for systematic musicology? For sure, transdisciplinarity has always been a core idea of systematic musicology. Since the late 19th Century, systematic musicology has been promoted as an integrated multidisciplinary approach involving disciplines such as psychology, sociology, acoustics, physiology, neurosciences, cognition sciences and computer and technology (Elschek, 1992, Schneider, 1993). Systematic musicologists aimed at understanding how people engage with music, how music perception and performance work, and how music appears as an aesthetic and social phenomenon. The approach was first related with Gestalt theory and, later on, with information psychology and cybernetics. In the 1970ies, with the advent of computers, this culminated in an approach that was closely related with the cognitive sciences. Up until today, the cognitive sciences still offer a main scientific research paradigm to systematic musicology. A key aspect of this paradigm is that it relies on scientific measurement for gathering empirical data, and on data-analysis and computer modelling for hypothesis testing (Leman and Schneider, 1997).

Since a few years, the terms "transdisciplinarity" and "multidisciplinary" have appeared in several contributions that aim at identifying the role of systematic musicology in relation to modern music research. Honing (2004) refers to a revitalization of systematic musicology that is based on empirical observation and rigorous method, the growing role of formalization and the notion of testability and falsification, and music cognition research. Parncutt (2007) claims that the diversity of systematic musicology is compensated by interdisciplinary interactions with the system of subdisciplines that makes up systematic musicology. He argues that the future development, and perhaps survival, of musicology will depend on the degree to which musicological institutions can achieve a balance between subdisciplines that are rooted in both natural sciences and humanities.

In short, transdisciplinarity has strong historical roots and it pops up as a key term in the actual discussion. The reason for using this term is that music is considered to be a

---

[6] Recent work on a roadmap for music research in the UK (http://music.york.ac.uk/dmrn/roadmap/) uses the term "transdisciplinary" extensively, whereas the (Continental) S2S^2-roadmap uses the term "multidisciplinary" (S2S^2, 2007). The difference between terms such as „multidisciplinary" and „transdisciplinary" and perhaps also „interdisciplinary" is subtle and I would propose to use the terms here as synonym, rather than considering "multidisciplinary" as the union of disciplines and "interdisciplinary" as the intersection of disciplines, whatever that may mean.

highly multifaceted phenomenon, involving all human faculties and very different social and cultural contexts. Single disciplines often focus on particular aspects of these faculties and therefore fail to address important aspects that go beyond the confines of the discipline. A transdisciplinary approach would thus address the subjective and context-dependent way in which humans deal with music, without neglecting the physical environment in which music is perceived either. However, the real question is: how does transdisciplinarity work in practice, and how could it work as an effective instrument leading to practical results that otherwise cannot be obtained?

Music's key role in society

The transdisciplinary nature of music research may be a strong asset to the development of activities that foster music's key role in personal development and social bonding. Let me first go a bit deeper into this aspect, because it provides a strong humanistic argument in favour of the necessity of a research discipline that supports this role. Afterwards, I come back to the way in which the umbrella term "trans-disciplinarity" can be deployed in music research and how systematic musicology is related to this.

It is known that the attractiveness of music is often rooted in the local cultures of people where it forms an important aspect of their active life. Music has appeal to active music makers, and it is used a lot for the accompaniment or support of social activities, such in religious activities, gaming or entertainment (dancing). Music is also known to strongly contribute to personal development, self-respect and pride, and it is considered to be a key factor of personal development. Music consoles, makes people happy, and it communicates cultural values and stimulates self reflection. Moreover, music is an excellent tool to promote respect for the diversity of social/cultural identity, the care of cultural heritage (preservation and archiving), openness to cultural change and new forms of expression, democratic access to culture and knowledge, and a culture of participation and participation in culture.

All this is of great value, and the intrinsic character of these values is a reason to put music in the centre of the picture. I claim that music is of such value that it requires our full attention as a topic, in such a way that other disciplines should support its study and contribute with methodological solutions that fully obey the requirements and the consequences of putting music at the centre. In other words, by putting music at the centre, we call upon musicology as a central research discipline. However, music is rooted in values that go beyond the study of its objective patterns. Music is experience, innovation, creation, expression, community, feeling of togetherness and knowledge, and much more. Therefore, these intrinsic values of music necessitate an approach that accounts for these values and that go beyond the confines of a single approach. Hence, driven by the values of the topic, the research approach should already be transdisciplinary. But there is more!

Music: a vibrant economical sector

According to a recent European study (KEA, 2006), music has a strong economic value as well. As an important part of a vibrant cultural and creative sector, the European music sector represents about 40% of the world-wide activity in this area, and employs about 650,000 workers in this sector. The study claims that the whole cultural/creative sector to which music belongs is in total twice as large as the auto-mobile sector, and as large as the ICT sector, with remarkable growth figures of about 20% over five years. The sector represents 2,6 % of the GNP (compared with chemistry and rubber/plastics industry: 2,3%). Total annual return is € 654 Billion.[7]

Interestingly, of all "content industries" (such as film, TV, art, heritage), music is the one which has been most affected by the digital revolution. Since the year 2000, the creation-production-distribution-consumption chain for music went almost entirely digital. Music is pushing broadband development (e.g. Napster and P2P) and mobile networks (GSM/GPRS, UMTS) and it has stimulated the uptake of broadband subscription and ICT by mass consumers (e.g. PCs, mobiles). Music stimulates e-business (e.g. iTunes), new management tools (e.g. Digital Rights Management, Audio-fingerprinting, Watermarking) and retrieval methods (Music information retrieval).

Moreover, music industry is currently transforming itself into a so-called experience-based economy. Musical audio is now distributed via large networks of ICT channels (broadband, mobile) and services start to provide an added economical and experiential value (Kusek and Leonhard, 2005). The impact of music on media consumption has been huge in recent years. Also in education, music has been a driver for young people to develop interest in science and ICT.

In short, music is a core economical factor whose innovative role in society (e.g. both with respect to technology development and new business models) requires its own line of research and support. It is justified to say that music is more than just a domain of application, and it is justified to say that music research requires a proper approach, given its wide scope and close relationship to a booming creative and cultural sector. Clearly, this is something that systematic musicology cannot handle on its own. Methods and approaches from different fields are needed, and in this perspective, the interest in music from other disciplines is a real opportunity, rather than a threat. Yet what is needed is a re-positioning of the discipline of systematic musicology in this new landscape for music research.

Music at the core of innovation

Apart from the social/cultural value and the economic value, I want to add a third value that is very specific for music, namely its value as incubator for innovation. This aspect too requires a very proper consideration because there are at least two reasons why music and art in general, may be expected to play an increasingly important role in modern society (Leman, 2005):

- First of all, music is so deeply connected with the technology of our society that it starts driving the development (of parts) of this technology. This is a quite natural thing to happen because if tools are used to be expressive, then one is always inclined to go beyond what is actually possible, and therefore, being expressive pushes innovation and drives new developments. Examples can be given from the development of electronic music in the 1950ies-1960ies, where analogue audio-equipment was used to create new musical sounds and where the first steps were taken to develop a content-based approach to musical information processing. The

---

[7] Compare with car industry = € 271 Billion in 2003, ICT factories = € 541 Billion in 2003.

recent quest for a „Music Google" can indeed be seen as an outcome of this development. In more recent times, there are signs that real-time interactive music systems push the frontiers of sensing, multi-modal multimedia processing and gesture-based control of technologies in a similar way as did the former research on synthesis and content-based processing. More researchers become aware of the fact that gesture technologies developed for interactive music and multimedia may also be useful in other areas.

– Secondly, music is so deeply connected with our social life that it starts driving new approaches to social communication, as art is always intended to be communicated and to involve social interaction. Recent developments in music research have pushed back the frontiers of networking into technologies that deal with semantics as well as new forms of human-human and human-machine interaction. Music is an excellent domain to develop technologies that focus on non-verbal communication patterns (related to gesture, corporeal articulation, kinetics and bioparametric sensing and related information processing) and therefore it is an excellent domain to develop patterns of communication that relate to corporeal social interaction.

In short, there is much to say in favour of the idea that music drives innovation in technology and in social interaction, because the context of music creation is constantly pushing for being more expressive, more human-friendly and more and different flavours. The interplay between music, technology and social interaction creates a huge market for innovation and creative development that links up with the ICT sector and the upcoming creative and cultural sector.

The intrinsic human value of music (e.g. for personal development and social bonding), the role of music in culture and economy (e.g., the development of new and massive internet-based business models), and its driving force for innovation and technology development (e.g. content-driven and socially embedded technologies), has forced systematic musicology to catch up with these activities. Could systematic musicology function as a moderator in this modern music research space? Could it become an agora for music research, a place where science meets art, a location where innovation and creation meets methodology and systematicity?

The modern music research space

Unfortunately, despite the enormous social-cultural, economical and innovative value of music, music research is still a rather small-scale enterprise in terms of number of people and institutes that work on innovation and supporting services for the cultural and creative sector. Even after the booming period of the millennium turn, the number of researchers working in music research is still rather limited. A survey [8] done within the context of the S2S²-project (S2S², 2007) reveals a trend that apart from a few exceptions (e.g. IRCAM in Paris), institutes working on music (in musicology, engineering, psychology, brain research) tend to be rather small (mean: about 2-3 professors, 10 PhD students), although the number of doctoral dissertations and internationally peer

---

[8] The website http://smcnetwork.org/ has recently been created to develop a better and more up to date statistics of music research.

reviewed papers has been growing over the past decennium. In general, the European music research space is characterized by a relative large number of small institutes and a small number of larger institutions which, together, form research networks through changing coalitions. The small-scale character of the institutes is compensated by the collaborative international networks that emerged during the past 10 to 15 years. This allows the centres to specialize in niche areas, such as sound synthesis (physical modelling), sound archiving, and interactive music systems and so on.

The ill-defined goals at long term and the bottom-up short-term emergent output structure (in contrast with a well-defined long term goal and a top-down long-term planned output structure) resembles the way research in microbiology is organized (although, admitted, institutes in biology tend to be much larger than those of music research). According to Nowotny et al. (2001), the uncertainty in large parts of modern science is an inherent feature of the research activity. Uncertainty does not mean that the field has no vision, or that a vision is impossible. Rather, it means that there is no concrete planned goal at long term, except some vague idea of what all these research activities are up to. Many things happen at the same time and it is rather unpredictable which output will survive, or what the effect of a small contribution will be on the whole field. In music research, the field is characterized by a multitude of objectives that focus on different music processing topics and a multitude of facets of how humans interact with music. The vision is not about a concrete scientific research goal, a concrete device or machine, but rather about what music may mean to people. In other words, the vision is about the relationship between music research and society. The vision is about goal-directed research in function of societal benefits. Clearly, in this context of discovery there is no single controlling instance, although the output is largely driven by society.

The control of the broad range of research activities is not something that systematic musicology should claim, or that any other discipline should claim. The music research field is simply too broad and the number of people working in systematic musicology is simply too small and not fully educated to cover all aspects involved. Therefore, collaboration with other disciplines is the only possibility, something that is highly needed in order to create a fruitful context of discovery that supports the creative and cultural sector. The role of systematic musicology in this universe or research can be that of a moderator, to help steering the development of a vision, to keep track of research outputs, to guarantee their relevance to music, that is, to make sure that psychosocial musical practices can profit from the developments, in other words, to keep focus on the music and what it does to people.

Surveys like KEA and S2S[2] show that Europe has a flourishing music research space that plays an important role in the development of a cultural and creative sector. This research space is based on multiple scientific disciplines, in which systematic musicology is one next to others. For example, in the S2S2 survey, with its focus on sound and music computing, a distinction is made between broad-focus content areas, in-focus content areas, and narrow-focus content areas. The broad focus areas include:

- Systematic musicology, covering music semiotics, score analysis, social-aesthetic aspects of music, computational models for music analysis and other aspects
- Auditory and music perception-action, covering psychoacoustics, music perception, computational approaches and models

- Auditory and music cognition, covering sound-based cognition, music cognition, artificial intelligence
- Music acoustics, covering acoustics of musical instruments, room acoustics
- Audio signal processing covering systems, sampling and quantization, spectral and time spectral representations, digital filters
- Hardware and software, covering sensors and actuators, real-time systems, output devices, software platforms, software engineering aspects.

In-focus content areas are:

- Sound modelling, covering models for sound synthesis, physically-based modelling, digital audio effects, artificial reverberation, binauralization, 3D sound and virtual acoustics
- Sound analysis and coding, covering auditory-based audio signal processing, perceptual coding, content-based audio processing and audio descriptors, content description and transmission languages, content-based transformations and synthesis
- Music information processing, covering feature extraction and classification, automatic transcription, music information retrieval, computer assisted composition
- Music performance, covering performance analysis, emotion and expression in music performance, computational models and control of music performance

Narrow-focus content areas are:

- Multimodal interfaces, covering multimodal perception, gesture and multimodal analysis, Representations of multimodal data, control mappings and interaction strategies, multimodal synthesis and rendering, assessment, evaluation, validation of models
- Sound design and auditory display, covering auditory warnings, sound in human computing interfaces, sonification, sound design
- Applications areas, covering digital and virtual musical instruments, interactive performing arts, museum interactive installations, edutainment, entertainment, multimedia and new media, therapy and rehabilitation

Obviously, in this list, systematic musicology has been assigned a specific role quite close to traditional approaches in musicology. This is certainly an area that is "difficult to steal" because it requires particular skills in music that are rather typical. However, the systemic basis of systematic musicology is in fact much broader, as it was influenced by the experimental research in psychology and computational modelling in engineering. The broad approach to systematic musicology covers other broad/in/narrow content areas that are situated in the psychosocial domain and it is likely to involve a number of other content areas as well that are not covered in this list, such as anthropology, ethnology, and perhaps even medialogy.

Anyhow, both the KEA study and the S2S[2] study show that Europe's potential power in music research, compared to US and Japan, is large. This can be attributed to

Europe's deep involvement with music over the past centuries, and its success in having produced strong musical paradigms rooted in very appealing music systems (such as modality, tonality and different historical styles from early medieval times up to the present), together with its long tradition in humanistic (read musicological) and scientific approaches to music. However, the US seems to be more versatile in terms of bringing a good idea into the market. The lack of continuity in research funding is often one of the major difficulties of the European small scale institutes, even more so when those institutes are operating in humanistic disciplines. The problem of discontinuous funding is more dramatic for small institutes than for large institutes. Core know-how in the hands of a small number of people makes these small institutes vulnerable to a sudden loss or a failure in getting a new project that could guarantee the position of a post-doc.

The European research space for music is organized as a network of small institutes, and temporary consortia are formed by changing coalitions among the members of the pool that defines music research. Transdisciplinarity in this context implies that small institutes have to cross the boarders of their own institute and establish collaborations with other institutes. This can be done at home (own university) or abroad, possibly at an international level. Often the dynamics of the research field also implies that young researchers have to be flexible and change institutes throughout Europe according to the available opportunities. Young systematic musicologists in Europe have to be active in this core music research business and they need to develop a healthy ambition to play a prominent role in this broader European music research space.

Identifying the challenge for music research

Given the above background, it is possible to go deeper into the major challenges for music research and to reconsider the claim that transdisciplinary will make systematic musicology attractive and necessary in the music research space. In other words, how can an umbrella term like "transdisciplinarity" or "interdisciplinarity" be deployed, and what can systematic musicology contribute to this?

When looking at the state-of-the-art of the disciplines that took music as their research topic it is of interest to ask to what extent these disciplines have encountered the boundaries of their own methodologies. It is my personal experience that young engineers, or brain scientists, sooner or later admit that research on music is a bit harder than expected. And the likely reason for this is often that the discipline handles music from a third-person viewpoint, that is, the viewpoint of music as an encoded physical energy, as a simple body movement, or as brain activation, whereas the human way of dealing with music is based on a first-person viewpoint, that is, based on actions, beliefs, intentions, interpretations, experiences, evaluations, and significations. Indeed, one could claim that in contexts where music is embedded in technology, music needs to be handled from the viewpoint of a physical signal and subsequent feature extraction and therefore, the engineering methods are appropriate. This reasoning is completely valid, but there is another side to it as well, namely that real users involve technologies in view of their intentions, values, beliefs and significations. Real users have a background. They are educated, belong to a particular culture, have a particular expectation, intention and so on. Hence, technology development needs much more than just signal processing and feature extraction. It also needs to take into account how people think, feel, experience, and interact with each other. At this point, it is clear that the engineering approach should be broadened with approaches from other disciplines. And it is also clear that this aspect is still insufficiently taken into account. Similar remarks hold for brain science in that brain activations may not reveal the semantic experience of the subject involved with music. Or can we reduce music to a disembodied brain? Can we deprive subjects from their environment, put them in a scanner and ask them not to move, while we know that 97% of the people do move when they listen to music? Clearly, more is needed to develop current music research practices in the direction of a more comprehensive approach.

The semantic gap that exists between music as third-person observation and as first-person experience is a serious problem and it forms a threat to music research as a whole. Indeed, access to music remains a problem when the retrieval technologies are insufficiently taking into account the user's search intentions, personal attitudes and social/cultural contexts. Interactive music making is problematic when the interaction is not sufficiently based on the subject's action-intended control of musical objects. Brain research is problematic when the technologies for brain measurement reduce musical experience to limited conditions where it can be measured.

More effort is needed to adapt these technologies to the study of realistic musical conditions. As my target is more related to the upcoming cultural and creative sector (and less to brain research at this moment) I will focus here mainly on engineering, arguing that the pure engineering approach to music is necessary but not sufficient for contributing to the cultural and creative sector. In similar terms it could be argued that brain research is necessary but not sufficient in that it needs more than just a series of photographs of how an individual human passively responds to music. In both approaches, it can be argued that there is a subjective, corporeal, and social component to be taken into account which is currently not taken into account at this moment, but which is necessary in view of the supporting services for the creative and cultural sector. I will argue that it is exactly at this point that systematic musicology can make the difference and regain its role as an attractive core discipline for music research.

Object-based approaches to the semantic gap problem

Consider the engineering approach in more detail. The classical approach to the semantic gap problem is object-based in the following sense: Starting from the sound, the approach uses feature extraction and classification methods to transform the sound (as object) into concepts which humans can mentally access. As such, it becomes possible to align musical audio with symbolic music scores, to use high-level semantic terms (such as "happy", "sad", "loud", "soft", "harmonious", "dissonant", "static", "dynamic") to search for music in a database, or to use musical gestures in an interactive system. However, many of the engineering solutions, not only those that make the connection with natural language, appear to be far from sufficiently robust for use in practical applications. In some cases, like in score transcription[9], it looks as if the use of

---

[9] In audio-to-score alignment, the target for audio analysis is known, namely as the musical score. Instead, in musical audio transcription the target is not known and each note must be recognized. In a polyphonic context, the latter poses a much more fundamental problem for feature extraction and classification.

more powerful stochastic and probabilistic bottom-up modelling techniques such as Hidden Markov Chains, Support Vector Machines, Neural Networks do not close this gap much further. In other words, it looks as if the bottom-up methods have reached their platform. Yet the semantic gap is not closed. To the contrary, there is evidence that the semantic gap problem cannot be solved with the current bottom-up engineering paradigm[10].

Among experts (see e.g. S2S², 2007), there is a growing understanding that the engineering techniques are excellent and necessary, but that the approach may be too narrow, and therefore insufficient. Briefly listed, the current approach can be characterized as follows:

- Unimodality: The focus has been on musical audio exclusively, whereas humans process music in a multi-modal way. Humans rely on multiple senses (modalities) such as visual information and movement.
- Structuralism: The focus has been on the extraction of structure from musical audio files (such as pitch, melody, harmony, tonality, rhythm) whereas humans tend to access music using subjective experiences (movement, imitation, expression, mood, affect, and emotion).
- Bottom-up: The focus has been on bottom-up (deterministic and learning) techniques whereas humans use a lot of top-down knowledge in signification practices.
- Perception oriented: The focus has been on the modelling of perception and cognition whereas human perception is based on action-relevant values.
- Object/Product-centred: Research has focused on the features of the musical object, whereas the subjective factors and the social/cultural functional context in musical activities (e.g. gender, age, education, preferences, professional, amateur) have been largely ignored.

In short, the approach starts from the object but does not take into account the proper context and the subjective factors that define how users would like to access music, such as knowledge of the domain or the context in which the technology is used.

Why human sciences are needed to solve the semantic gap problem

More input should come from a better analysis of the subjective human being and its social/cultural context. Such a subject-centred approach would involve:

---

[10] Paiva (2006) demonstrated that the classical bottom-up approach has reached its performance platform. In his study on melody extraction from polyphonic audio he showed that even the most advanced methods nowadays available show only a small increase in performance of the model. He used state-of-the-art techniques in auditory modelling, pitch detection and frame-concatenation into music notes and compared different methods. Yet, the results are still far from being sufficiently robust for use in practical applications. Similar observations have been made in rhythm recognition, timbre recognition, genre recognition and other applications that focus on the perception of musical structural features.

- Multi-modality: The power of integrating and combining several senses should be considered. Moreover, it is likely that the integration of auditory, visual, haptic, kinaesthetic sensing offers a reduction of the ambiguity of the perceived stimulus.
- Context-based approach: The study of the broader social, cultural and professional context and its effect on information processing is needed. Indeed, the context is of great value for the disambiguation of our perception. Similarly, the context largely determines the goals and intended musical actions.
- Top-down: Knowledge of the music idiom is needed in order to better extract higher-level descriptors from music so that users can have easier access to these descriptors. Traditionally, top-down knowledge has been conceived as a language model. However, language models may be extended with gesture models as a way to handle stimulus disambiguation.
- Action: Research may focus more on the action-oriented component of human behaviour. This implies a new approach to the perception of structural form (or Gestalt) as well because perception of structure is then conceived from the viewpoint of affordances. In other words, one could say that people do not move just in response to the music they perceive, rather they move to disambiguate their perception of music, and by doing this, they signify music. This aspect needs much more attention as it plays an important role in music mediation technologies.
- User-oriented: Research should involve the user in every phase of the research. It is very important to better understand the subjective factors that determine the behaviour of the user.

It is my understanding that the subject-centred approach which is prevalent in this viewpoint should be based on an empirical and evidence-based methodology, so that it connects with object-centred approach. Clearly, this subject-centred approach is not something that is readily available in engineering, nor is it readily available in experimental and/or cognitive psychology, and perhaps not even in systematic musicology as we know it today. Yet, I see it as a main task of systematic musicology to come up with a proper proposal of how to put music at the centre of human activities. In that sense, my proposal does not entail a rejection of the disembodied approaches in music research. Rather, what I propose is an extension of this approach with an embodied approach that puts the interaction between music and the subject in the centre. This can be done by a better linking of the currently prevailing object-centred account, which is characterized by a focus on audio, structural features, bottom-up data processing, perception oriented modelling and object/product-centred development, with a new type of subject-centred approach, which would be characterized by a focus on multi-modality, context-based processing, top-down data processing, action-based modelling, and user-oriented development.

Systematic musicology "transcends" natural and human sciences

In view of the above analysis it becomes clearer what the role of systematic musicology might be, namely, to foster the development of a transdisciplinary approach that uses object-centred and subject-centred methodologies for researching the relationship between music, mind, embodiment, social interaction and physical environment.

Systematic musicology has a certain tradition in dealing with transdisciplinarity and it offers an education that is much in the spirit of combining natural and human sciences. So yes, there is a value in having a transdisciplinary approach, and systematic musicology is well placed to contribute to problems in engineering and in brain science.

Closing the semantic gap with embodiment

The combination of object-centred and subject-centred approaches is an important point on the agenda of my conception of systematic musicology. Deep inside this approach is the viewpoint that music is related to the interaction between body, mind, and physical environment; in a way that does justice to how humans perceive and act in the world, how they use their senses, their feelings, their emotions, their cognitive apparatus and social interactions. I have tried to develop this core systemic topic in my book on embodied music cognition and mediation technology (Leman, 2007). In that book, I see the tight coupling between action and perception as a key to link all disciplines that deal with music research and I propose a solution for the semantic gap in terms of an embodied approach. In particular, I argue that music signification has a strong corporeal aspect and that this corporeal aspect is largely unexplored until today. The proposed (minimal) model is shown in Figure 1. The central idea of this model is that the human body supports action causation and perception from a musical goal to bio-mechanical, haptic, sonic, and visual energy. This proceeds back and forth via corporeal articulations and corporeal imitations, so that goal-directed action at the higher level of intentionality can be established. This intentional level is embedded within subjective experience, while the physical channels through which communication proceeds can be approached from an objective viewpoint.[11]

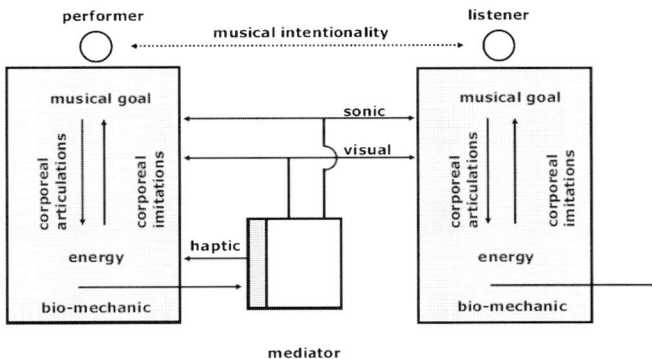

Figure1. Music communication: the body as link between mind and physical environment

Clearly, in this approach, mental musical activity is not reduced to physics, nor is gesture and meaning reduced to the biomechanics of the human body, or to a mere

---

[11] The approach is related with the perception theoretical notions of emulation and simulated perception (e.g. Berthoz, 1997). Historical roots can be found in the work of Piaget, Apostel, Maturana and Varela (e.g. Maturana and Varela, 1980). Reference can also be made to European projects (e.g. ENACTIVE, ConGAS, EMCAP).

disembodied approach of mental representation and cognition. Instead, the human body is considered to be a core component of a mediation system that relates the mental with the physical environment. In this context, transdisciplinarity means that disciplines which address the mental world, the physical environment and the human body are involved and used to focus on the musical aspect. Clearly, progress in this domain can only be made when the disciplines transcend their boundaries and take the relationship between music and humans as a goal to develop new methods and approaches. In my opinion, it is the task of systematic musicology to educate, promote and research into scientific methodologies that transcend the boundaries of limiting approaches. From that point of view, whatever can support music understanding should be used, including engineering, brain research, biology, cultural studies and so on, but in genuine music research, music and the tight connection between mind and body, and between the exchange of physical energy and the generation of interaction patterns at the level of intentionality (Figure 1), will always remain a central issue to which the methodologies have to be fine-tuned.

A role as moderator at the crossroads of modern music research means that systematic musicology is in charge of a discussion that makes sure that music research is conducted towards the realisation of a vision that fosters the development of our understanding and use of music as a cultural and societal value, as an economic value, and as a value for innovation and creation within an framework that subscribes the tight connection between musical mind, body, physical environment and social interaction. While this (I repeat) cannot be done by one single discipline, but instead by many disciplines that work together and transcend their boundaries, systematic musicology can clarify the vision and well as the transdisciplinary research paradigm that implements the realisation of this vision through empirical approaches and methodologies. Understanding the role of musical mind and body in relation to the physical and technological environment is a huge task but one that is absolutely necessary for all disciplines involved in music research.

Embodiment and social interaction

Thus, in the above model, a systemic approach to embodiment is proposed as the key feature that will help systematic musicology to develop solutions for core problems in music-related psychosocial interaction. By implementing this idea in research and in education[12], I believe that systematic musicology will be able to re-establish its position in the modern music research space.

Given the above model, there is a good reason for expanding embodiment with a component of social interaction. In fact, both embodiment and social interaction are strongly related with each other as they fit with the above-mentioned cultural and psychosocial value of music. Indeed, the articulations of the human body in music making and other musical activities such as listening and dancing are functioning in a natural context of social interaction. In this context, humans communicate expressive gestures along corporeal-based communication channels that are rooted in social cognition. It is likely that these expressive gestures form part of a social language that

---

[12] See the summer schools on systematic musicology (ISSSM), organized in Jyväskylä (1999, 2001) and Ghent (2006, 2007, 2008).

appeals to an essential component of human being. Therefore, concepts such as "behavioural resonance", "corporeal interaction", "expressive gesture", "synchronization" and "entrainment" are key concepts in our understanding what music is about. In my view, these concepts form the core concept of a new approach to systematic musicology (Leman and Camurri, 2006).

This new systematic musicology is different from the past in that it differs radically from the disembodied approaches of the cognitive sciences that were still dominant in musicology at the turn of the 21st Century[13]. However, it should be admitted that the focus on the perception of musical structures (such as pitch, rhythm, tempo, harmonic progression, articulation and so on) has been historically important and this will remain important in the future. Yet, a focus on musical structures is not sufficient to understand the complex phenomenon of music. What is needed is more attention for the values and goals of what music is all about, and what these values and goals mean to people[14]. In that sense, the role of systematic musicology is to push approaches towards elaborating the focus on structural aspects towards more comprehensive embodied approaches of music understanding. In retrospect one could say that what was „stolen" from systematic musicology was in fact the disembodied component, namely, the (wrong) idea that music is merely about structures, and that human involvement with music is merely about perception.

As the communication model of Figure 1 suggests, non-verbal communication patterns, for example, the responsive and expressive movements of body parts are key indicators of the musical communication. It can be assumed that they are also key indicators of the social embodied musical communication and the role of expressiveness in gesture. Up to now, the understanding of these corporeal types of non-verbal communication in their social interactive context is very poorly understood. I do believe, however, that certain states of social entrainment (based on the mutual adaptation of non-verbal expressive corporeal communication patterns) can be somehow perceived by the human mind as a state of optimal experience or "flow". This form of direct experience with music can be contemplated and the awareness of social entrainment that can be accessed in terms of semantic descriptions (i.e. descriptions of signification) as well. It is not excluded that these descriptions can be partly related to the (objective)

---

[13] The classical approach to systematic musicology is based on a theory that is rooted in the analysis of musical structures, their representation and inherent regularities. This approach has its roots in the Cartesian divide between moving bodies and the experienced self, and it is still dominating much of the music research today. In that respect, the modern and up to date music compendium by G. Loy (Loy, 2006) is still reminiscent to Descartes' Musicae Compendium of 1619. However, let it be clear that there is no reason to discard this good old mathematical "disembodied" approach to music at all. Instead, my plea is to extend this powerful approach with a new chapter that does justice to the embodied involvement with music. In that sense, I plea for an extension of tradition music cognition towards an embodied approach. Apparently, even Descartes, in his compendium, already suggested the need for doing this.

[14] As it will be clear by the previous paragraphs, I conceive the subject-centred approach in the sense of an empirical and computational approach, rather than in terms of a postmodern narration. However, the latter is a reality in (historical) musicology and therefore, this reality should be evaluated in terms of its possible contribution to a music research space that supports the cultural and creative sector. Unfortunately, and as far as I know, this has never been done, though I believe that embodiment may offer a possible point of connection.

measurements of the human body so that these descriptions can be used in connection with content-based technologies (e.g. the "Music Google"). We may assume that the process of signification, from corporeal signification to cerebral signification is a central factor that contributes to personal development and social well-being. This type of model, which connects mental, physical and social aspects, offers an attractive perspective which is much needed in music research. In my opinion, systematic musicology has the tradition and the competence to play a leading role in developing a transdisciplinary music research that focuses on these aspects.

Transdisciplinarity thus emerges from two sides, first, from a call for innovative services that support a broad range of activities in the creative and cultural sector, second, from a call for solving the semantic gap as the major obstacle for a breakthrough in content-based music technologies (the "Music Google"). In both cases, it is unlikely that solutions will come from one single discipline, say engineering or brain science. Instead, an approach that puts music at the centre and that further transcends the boundaries of objective and subjective descriptions, of mind and embodiment, of physics and intentionality, and of individual and social interactions is going to be transdisciplinary in that it combines methods and techniques from many different sciences, both natural sciences and human sciences. At the crossroads of music research, systematic musicology functions as a moderator of transdisciplinary viewpoints, approaches and methodologies. Without such a moderator, there would be more dispersion of the approaches as well as a risk that the research narrows down to risky commercial applications. An example of the latter is again related to our "Music Google". According to the current state of the art in content-based music retrieval, certain techniques work quite well for simple commercial music but not for classical music or other types of non-western music. Should these techniques be commercialized, then? Clearly, their usage would favour the retrieval of simple commercial music and disfavour the retrieval of more complicated, non-western, and non-commercial musical approaches. More people would get access to commercial music but the limitations of the technology would narrow down the broad spectrum of music that is actually available (even via internet). Therefore, there is clearly a task for systematic musicology to point to these dangers and to contribute to the development of technologies that can handle any type of music. Up to now, the state-of-the-art in music retrieval technology is too much focused on Western concepts and it is the task of systematic musicology to enlarge this viewpoint (see Moelants et al., 2007, Tzanetakis et al., 2007).

The S2S^2-project: a roadmap for transdisciplinary music research

Having revealed what makes systematic musicology in my view a necessary partner in music research, I now turn to the discussion of the research strategy that would guarantee impact on music research at long term. Having a good concept (although still open for discussion and refinement), the strategy is to implement that concept in the structures that support the creative and cultural sector. These structures involve the actual research, the educational system, and innovative industrial and social-cultural creative applications. Much of what follows is based on work of the S2S^2-consortium on a roadmap for sound and music computing research.

S2S^2 stands for Sound to Sense, Sense to Sound which, in fact, is exactly about this relationship between physical encoding of music and music as experience. The S2S^2-

project was based on an interdisciplinary consortium of music research laboratories in Europe, with the major task of writing a roadmap for sound and music computing. The consortium included the Media Innovation Unit, Firenze Tecnologia, Firenze, Italy (N. Bernardini), the Music Acoustics Group of the Kungliga Tekniska Högskolan in Stockholm, Sweden (R. Bresin), the Music Technology Group of the Universitat Pompeu Fabra in Barcelona, Spain (X. Serra), CSC - Dept. of Information Engineering, University of Padova, Italy (G. De Poli), the Austrian Research Institute for Artificial Intelligence of the Austrian Society for Cybernetic Studies in Vienna, Austria (G. Widmer), the Département d'Etudes Cognitives of the Ecole Normale Supérieure in Paris, France (A. de Cheveigné), the Laboratoire d'Etude de l'Apprentissage et du Développement of the Université de Bourgogne in Dijon, France (E. Bigand), the Institute for Psychoacoustics and Electronic Music of the Universiteit Gent in Ghent, Belgium (M. Leman), the Laboratory of Acoustics and Audio Signal processing of the Helsinki University of Technology in Espoo, Finland (V. Välimäki), the Vision, Image Processing and Sound Laboratory of the University of Verona, Italy (D. Rocchesso), and the Laboratorio di Informatica Musicale of the University of Genova, Italy (A. Camurri).

On the 16th of April 2007, this consortium launched a roadmap on Sound and Music Computing in the headquarters of the European Research Council in Brussels. The roadmap is in fact an ambitious document, of less than 100 pages, that aims at defining the major challenges for future music research. As a guide, it will have impact on the future strategic planning for sound and music research of the European Commission. In what follows, I will briefly introduce the rationale behind this roadmap and I show how transdisciplinary systematic musicology is inscribed as a core aspect of the European music research as it is envisioned for the future.

Content of the S2S²-project

The S2S²-project has produced three major outcomes, namely a book containing the state-of-the-art in sound and music computing[15] a series of summer schools that addressed the education of young music researchers[16] and of course, the roadmap itself, which is a text of about 100 pages. The first text was edited by X. Serra, M. Leman and G. Widmer and is available as pdf on the internet[17].

The S2S²-roadmap contains three parts, namely, (i) a description of the context and main trends in which music research operates, (ii) a state-of-the-art and identification of the research points and open issues, and (iii) a description of the research challenges.

---

[15] This book is currently edited by D. Rocchesso, to be published by LOGOS-Verlag in 2008.

[16] Reference can be made to the summer schools on sound and Music computing held in Barcelona 2004, Genova 2005, Barcelona 2006, Stockholm 2007.

[17] See http://smcnetwork.org/roadmap. Recently, this text has been reworked and polished to be published as a first frozen version in a special issue of the Journal of New Music Research, Vol. 36, Issue 3, 2008 (edited by N. Bernardini and G. De Poli). This issue contains the three main parts of the roadmap as separate articles, together with a roadmap from IRCAM (by H. Vinet) and a viewpoint from the US (by R. Dannenberg) and Japan (S. Hashimoto). See http://www.tandf.co.uk/journals/spissue/nnmr-si.asp

i.   Context: This consists of the research context, the educational context, the industrial context, and the social/cultural context. These contexts tell us about the societal framework in which music research is currently operative. It is mentioned that transdisciplinarity is necessary in research, for industrial development and cultural applications, but that it is rather difficult to implement the educational part.

ii.   The state-of-the-art then focuses on the main open issues. A distinction is made between research that focuses on sound and research that focuses on music. In between, there is the interaction between sound and music. For each research field (sound, interaction, music), there is an analytic and a synthetic component. The analytic component goes from encoded physical (sound) energy to meaning (sense), whereas the synthetic component goes in the opposite direction, from meaning (sense) to encoded physical (sound) energy. Accordingly, analytic approaches to sound and music pertain to analysis and understanding, whereas synthetic approaches pertain to generation and processing. In between sound and music, there are multi-faceted research fields that focus on interactive aspects. These are performance modelling and control, music interfaces, and sound interaction design. The nature of these distinctions reveals the inherent transdisciplinary character of the research field, as both the analytical (from sound to sense) and the synthetic (from sense to sound) approaches.

iii.   The challenges part looks ahead and identifies the key challenges for music research together with the strategies with which to face them. These challenges fit with the open problems that were identified in part (ii), and they are constrained by the contexts which were identified in part (i). It may be of interest to give a brief summary of the challenges that have been identified.

Challenge 1: to design better sound objects and environments

- Strategy 1: Seek directions in which to extend the notion of musical instrument
- Strategy 2: Improve technologies for pervasively producing, transforming and delivering sounds
- Strategy 3: Intensify research in sound modelling that goes beyond imitation towards capturing the communicative potential of sound
- Strategy 4: Promote research in fields involved in the shaping of natural, artificial and cultural acoustic ecosystems
- Strategy 5: Promote research on the effect of environmental constraints on artificially diffused sound and music
- Strategy 6: Promote studies aimed at reducing sound and music pollution in public and private ecosystems

Challenge 2: to understand, model, and improve human interaction with sound and music

- Strategy 1: Promote computational modelling approaches in human auditory perception and cognition research
- Strategy 2: Provide extensive augmented perception paradigms

108

- Strategy 3: Intensify research on expressivity and communication in sound and music
- Strategy 4: Develop an embodied, integrated approach to perception and action
- Strategy 5: Intensify multimodal and multidisciplinary research on computational methods for bridging the semantic gap in music
- Strategy 6: Intensify interaction with the arts

Challenge 3: to train multidisciplinary researchers in a multicultural society

- Strategy 1: Design appropriate multidisciplinary curricula for SMC
- Strategy 2: Promote broader integration of Arts and Sciences
- Strategy 3: Promote cross-cultural integration
- Strategy 4: Promote better coordination in Higher Education
- Strategy 5: Enhance education resources for Higher Education.
- Strategy 6: Promote the dissemination of available Higher Education in SMC.

Challenge 4: to improve knowledge transfer

- Strategy 1: Promote dissemination of SMC research and objectives among the general public
- Strategy 2: Promote projects containing artistic components
- Strategy 3: Promote the awareness of the various models of IP protection of research results
- Strategy 4: Promote venues for meeting industry experts
- Strategy 5: Promote direct industrial exploitation of research results
- Strategy 6: Promote academic quality standards.

Challenge 5: to address social concerns

- Strategy 1: Identify social needs relevant to SMC development; develop methods for the evaluation and assessment of SMC technologies in social contexts
- Strategy 2: Expand existing SMC methodologies (currently targeted at individuals) to understand music in its social dimension
- Strategy 3: Promote development of technologies and tools for broader collaboration, information and communication engagement; emphasise user-centred and group experience-centred research and development
- Strategy 4: Exploit cross-fertilisation between human sciences, natural sciences, technology, and the arts
- Strategy 5: Expand the horizon of SMC research through a multi-cultural approach.

Above, I have described how this roadmap relates systematic musicology to other disciplines. In this description of the main challenges, it is evident that the trans-disciplinary approach is a central feature. For example, in Challenge 2, Strategies 4-6 mention integration, multimodality, multidisciplinarity and interaction with arts. The notion of multidisciplinarity is taken up explicitly in Challenge 3, where the need for multidisciplinary curricula is addressed. In Challenge 4, the mentioning of cross-fertilisation between human sciences, natural sciences, technology, and the arts contains an explicit reference to multidisciplinarity. Reference to augmented perception, expressivity, embodiment and multimodality support the core challenges for music research. In Challenge 5, there is an explicit call to develop music technology in its social dimension. The latter aspect is not unimportant. After all, as mentioned, music is a very important aspect of all human cultures. Music gives meaning to life. It is a basic ingredient of cultural, group and personal identification and social bonding. Music affects the mental and bodily health of people.

Towards centres of excellence in Systematic Musicology

In the context of a flourishing European music research space, there have been a number of initiatives that contributed to the development of systematic musicology. Starting in 1993, the International Society for Comparative and Systematic Musicology (with seat in Hamburg) has organised a number of international conferences at Moravaný, 1993, Hamburg, 1994, Schloss Zeillern, 1995, Brugge, 1996, Berlin, 1997, Oslo, 1999, Jyväskylä, 2001, with several publications[18]. In recent years the Society has supported the educational activities of an international consortium of systematic musicology centres, consisting of the University of Hamburg, Köln, Jyväskylä, Oslo and Ghent. As a practical outcome, this consortium has organised several International Summers Schools on Systematic Musicology (ISSSM)[19].

The Conference on Interdisciplinary Musicology (CIM) is an initiative to create a forum for constructive interaction among all musically and musicologically relevant disciplines. CIM especially promotes "collaborations between sciences and humanities, between theory and practice, as well as interdisciplinary combinations that are new, unusual, creative, or otherwise especially promising". The first Conference on Interdisciplinary Musicology (CIM04) was held in Graz, 2004, then in Montreal, 2005, Tallin, 2007, and Thessaloniki, 2008.[20]

Recently, two centres for systematic musicology have received a substantial funding for long term (6 to 7 years) research in areas that affect the creative and cultural sector. Though these are national initiatives, they express a clear sign that countries are willing to invest more into systematic musicology research, provided that it supports the creative and cultural sector. The first centre is located in Jyväskylä and is supported by the Academy of Finland. The overall theme of the research in this so-called "Finnish Centre of Excellence in Interdisciplinary Music Research" is "the human as a listener, experiencer, and performer of music. Within this theme, research will investigate areas including perception and learning of music, musical emotions, and the connection between music and motion. The research is empirical and makes use of modern technology, such as brain imaging and motion capture devices as well as computer modelling". The centre combines the expertise of two research teams, namely, the Music Cognition Team (University of Jyväskylä, Department of Music, lead by Petri

---

[18] See http://www.uni-hamburg.de/Wiss/FB/09/Musik/systematicmusicology.html
[19] See e.g. www.ipem.ugent.be/ISSSM2007
[20] See http://www-gewi.uni-graz.at/staff/parncutt/cim.htm

Toiviainen) and the Brain and Music Team (Helsinki University, Department of Psychology, lead by Mari Tervaniemi).

The second centre is located at IPEM, Department of musicology, Ghent University, where a long-term ("Methusalem")-project has been started up on a topic related to embodied music cognition and mediation technologies for cultural/creative applications ("EmcoMetecca"). The project will focus on the development of empirical and computational approaches that foster embodiment and social interaction in music contexts. While the Finish project is build around collaboration between a music department and a department of brain science, the Belgian project is built around core research in systematic musicology with a substantial collaborative component in the area of electronic engineering. Both are example initiatives at the National and University level.

As both research groups start their activities in 2008 they will need some time to fully deploy themselves as a critical mass in the modern European music research space. As a matter of fact, these two projects are not the only projects in the field of systematic musicology but I mention these two projects because their amount of support is large and perhaps more endurable than the typical projects that could be obtained in the past by competition in university programs, national research programs and European research programs (lasting 2 to 4 years with typically 1 or 2 full time personnel). Hopefully, this is the start of a new trend in the building of a European space for music research. There are several larger institutes already operative in Paris (IRCAM, which is interdisciplinary and broad) and Barcelona (UPF-MTG, which is more focused on signal processing). The new groups in Finland and Belgium are not that large, and they are likely to focus more on niche areas within music research and systematic musicology. Yet the trend may be that Europe is re-shaping its music research space by building slightly larger research groups that have a more stable funding and that are more specialized in different niches of the music research space. The fact that systematic musicology is a player in this development should not come as a surprise. As I have tried to explain, its history and its empirical and computational orientation give this discipline a natural position in the centre of modern music research activities. However, it is necessary that more such centres become available so that a stable critical mass for research can be created and maintained. This is, I believe, the best guarantee for delivering outputs that can have an endurable value for society.

The above initiatives are by no means exhaustive. Rather, they are examples of activities that show the viability of systematic musicology in a rapidly changing European research space. It is very likely that systematic musicology has a bright future, provided that it can position itself at the crossroads of music research that supports the creative and cultural sector. In that sense, I believe that systematic musicology certainly has a value that appeals to a broad range of researchers with backgrounds in engineering, physics, psychology and neuroscience. Its necessity can be justified by pointing to its central role in transcending the boundaries of disciplines and its possible role in solving the semantic gap problem.

Towards centres for creation and public interaction

Supporting research for the creative and cultural sector implies research in areas that foster production, distribution and access to music. In the past, IRCAM[21] has been the main centre in Europe where this strategic alliance between artistic production and scientific research was actually implemented. From the very beginning, IRCAM's objective was to bring science and art together in order to widen the instrumentarium and to rejuvenate musical language. However, in Europe there is now a clear trend towards the creation of more such strategic alliances between art centres and research groups.

Casa Paganini[22] is an international centre in Genova for scientific and technological research in music and performing arts, artistic production of new music projects related to new technologies didactics, international schools and conferences. Casa Paganini is conceived as an incubator for new contemporary musical trends, for research in interactive multimedia systems and digital music technologies. The mission of Casa Paganini also includes research and developments with direct impact on therapy and rehabilitation, sport, edutainment and entertainment, in collaboration with industry (e.g., contributes to new multimedia interfaces and applications) and for cultural applications (museums, science centres). Casa Paganini is led by the University of Genova and in particular by the InfoMus Lab of DIST (A. Camurri) in collaboration with Regione Liguria, Provincia di Genova, and Comune di Genova.

The Sonic Arts Research Centre (SARC)[23] at Queen's University Belfast is a newly established (2004) centre dedicated to the research of music and sound. This interdisciplinary project has united internationally recognised experts in the areas of musical performance and composition, electrical engineering and signal processing, psychology, and computer science. The Centre is established in a purpose-built facility located alongside the engineering departments of Queen's University. The centrepiece of SARC, the Sonic Laboratory, provides a unique space for cutting-edge initiatives in the creation and delivery of music and audio. The Sonic Laboratory's uniqueness is vested in the degree of flexibility it can provide for experiments in sound diffusion, performance, and sound interaction, within a purpose-built, 3 story tall, variable acoustic space. The Sonic Laboratory contains a unique cluster of audience seats that are outfitted with sensors to measure audience and performer interaction.

A final example is the Bijloke Music Centre in Ghent. After many years of concert organisation, this centre opened its brand new infrastructure in 2007, including one large concert hall (located in a large and unique building dating from the 13th century), and a number of different smaller halls, of which two rooms are dedicated to multimedia performances (a former library and a former anatomy arena). The activities of Bijloke are no longer merely focused on concert organisation but they include many other activities related to music, like exhibits and multimedia workshops. Like Casa Paganini and SARC, Bijloke Music Centre wants to be operative as an incubator for new contemporary musical trends, for research in interactive multimedia systems and digital music technologies. Bijloke Music Centre has set up an agreement with Ghent

---

[21] http://www.ircam.fr
[22] http://www.casapaganini.org/
[23] www.sarc.qub.ac.uk

University to start up joint activities in multimedia performances and related experiments in the context of the "EmcoMetecca" project.

These are just three examples of recent initiatives that show how music research laboratories at universities (both in engineering, musicolog, and music performance) expand their activities in a domain that was up to recent rather separate from academic research. These examples are not meant to given an exhaustive overview of these developments. They just illustrate how music research is currently positioning itself inside one of the core activities of the creative and cultural sector, namely public performance and concerts. As new technologies allow new forms of artistic expression, and as artistic expressions constantly challenge the development of new technologies, it is likely that more institutes for music research will engage themselves in this type of alliances. It shows that the European music research in academia is ready to play a role in this creative and cultural sector and that systematic musicology can be a creative partner in this.

Conclusion

In this paper, I have argued that systematic musicology should take up its role as moderator at the crossroads of music research. The societal and economic value of the creative and cultural sector calls for a broad research basis grounded in different disciplines that specialize in technology, brain and social research. In that context, research on music is no longer the privilege of systematic musicology. On the one hand, it may appear that music research has been "stolen" from systematic musicology. On the other hand, these non-musicological disciplines bring in new and advanced methodologies that push music research into the frontiers of modern science.

I argued that music research in engineering and brain sciences often does not address signification practice and social interaction that makes music important for people. The main problem is the so-called semantic gap problem, that is, the difference between music as encoded musical energy and music as experienced meaning. The methodologies of non-musicological disciplines often do not allow a straightforward bridge from the physical/physiological domain to the relevant musical domain. This is perhaps due to the fact that these disciplines cannot afford investing too much in the musical domain which, by its nature, necessitates a transdisciplinary approach. A bridge between objective and subjective approaches in music is absolutely needed in a context of creative and cultural applications, such as in music information retrieval and interactive music systems. After all, music covers a broad range of phenomena. Music appeals to all human senses and it involves all faculties of human perception and action. It cannot simply be reduced to approaches that just consider either objective or subjective aspects.

Systematic musicology, by tradition, is naturally positioned to transcend the different non-musicological disciplines and motivate them to keep the focus on music. In the past, it is possible that systematic musicology has not been able to position itself in a sufficient way at the crossroads of music research. The reasons for this are manifold yet they may be have been related to the nature of the paradigm of the cognitive sciences which was, until recent, focused much on disembodied approaches (often influenced by linguistic paradigms) that distracted the focus from what music is really about. I consider the specific task of systematic musicology to develop the theory, the research paradigm and the methodology that is needed to transcend the contributions from different disciplines to music research. When music is put at the centre of music research, then there will always be the need for a discipline that somehow keeps the overview and the perspective. In contrast with previous approaches that were disembodied, I argue in favour of an embodied music research paradigm (Leman, 2007). In this paradigm, the human body is considered as the natural mediator between the mind and the physical environment. New mediation technologies can then be developed that extend the human body (the natural mediator) into domains where our mind has otherwise no access. These domains involve music and have a strong social component. In short, embodied music cognition and social interaction put music at the core of the research focus and they necessitate a new methodology that can only be developed by adopting a transdisciplinary perspective that integrates an object-centred account with a subject-centred account. While the former is characterized by the focus on audio, structural features, bottom-up data processing, perception oriented modelling and object/product-centred development, the latter is characterized by multi-modality, context-based processing, top-down data processing, action-based modelling, and user-oriented development. The present paper is a plea for making systematic musicology the discipline at the crossroad of the new music research space. The recent initiatives for long term research in small countries as Finland and Belgium show that after all, systematic musicology is a vital research area. The core of systematic musicology has not been stolen. How could it be stolen? What happened was just an expansion of the music research space, something that was needed to establish a broad interdisciplinary and transdisciplinary research basis for a sector that has both a high human, a high economic, and a high creative and innovative value.

References

Avanzini, G., Faienza, C., Minciacchi, C., Lopez, L., Majno, M. (2003). *The Neurosciences and Music*. New York, N.Y.: New York Academy of Sciences.

Avanzini, G. , Lopez, L., Koelsch, S., Majno, M. (2005). *The Neurosciences and Music II: From Perception to Performance*. New York, N.Y.: New York Academy of Sciences.

Berthoz, A. (1997). *Le Sens du Mouvement*. Paris: Editions O. Jacob.

Clayton, M., Sager, R., & Will, U. (2004). In time with the music: The concept of entrainment and its significance for ethnomusicology. *ESEM CounterPoint, Vol.1*, 82 pp.

Elschek, O. (1992). *Die Musikforschung der Gegenwart, ihre Systematik, Theorie und Entwicklung*. Wien-Föhrenau: Dr. E. Stiglmayr.

Fricke, J., (1993), Systematische oder Systemische Musikwissenschaft. *Systematische Musikwissenschaft* 1/2, 181-194.

Godøy, R. I., & Jørgensen, H. (Eds.)(2001). *Musical Imagery*. Exton, PA: Swets & Zeitlinger Publishers.

Honing, H. (2004). The comeback of systematic musicology: new empiricism and the cognitive revolution, *Tijdschrift voor Muziektheorie* 9/3, p. 242.

KEA. (2006). *The Economy of Culture in Europe*. http://ec.europa.eu/culture/eac/ sources_info/studies/ economy_en.html

Kusek, D., & Leonhard, G. (2005). *The Future of Music: Manifesto for the Digital Music Revolution.* Boston: Berklee Press.

Leman, M., & Camurri, A. (2006). Understanding musical expressiveness using interactive multimedia platforms. *Musicae Scientiae*, 209-233.

Leman, M., & Schneider, A. (1997). Origin and nature of cognitive and systematic musicology: An introduction. In M. Leman (Ed.), *Music, Gestalt, and Computing: Studies in Cognitive and Systematic Musicology* (pp. 13-29). Berlin, Heidelberg: Springer-Verlag.

Leman, M. (1995). *Music and Schema Theory: Cognitive Foundations of Systematic Musicology.* Berlin, New York: Springer.

Leman, M. (Ed.) (1997). *Music, Gestalt, and Computing: Studies in Cognitive and Systematic Musicology.* Berlin, New York: Springer.

Leman, M. (2005). Musical creativity research. In J. C. Kaufman & J. Baer (Eds.), *Creativity Across Domains: Faces of the Muse.* (pp. 103-122). Mahwah, NJ: Lawrence Erlbaum.

Leman, M. (2007). *Embodied Music Cognition and Mediation Technology.* Cambridge, MA: MIT Press.

Lesaffre, M., De Voogdt, L., Leman, M., Demeyer, H., Martens, J.-P., De Baets, B. (2008). How potential users of music search and retrieval systems describe the semantic quality of music, *Journal of the American Society for Information Science and Technology*, 59 (5), 1-13.

Loy, D. G. (2006). *Musimathics: The Mathematical Foundations of Music.* Cambridge, MA: MIT Press.

Maturana, H. R., & Varela, F. J. (1987). *The Tree of Knowledge: The Biological Roots of Human Understanding.* Boston: New Science Library.

Moelants, D., Cornelis, O., Leman, M., Gansemans, J., De Caluwe, R., De Tré, G., Matthé, T., Hallez, A. (2007) Problems and opportunities of content-based analysis and description of ethnic music. *International Journal of Intangible Heritage*, 2, 57-68.

Nowotny, H., Scott, P., & Gibbons, M. (2001). *Re-thinking Science: Knowledge and the Public in an Age of Uncertainty.* Cambridge: Polity Press.

Paiva, R. (2007). *Melody Detection in Polyphonic Audio.* PhD-thesis, University of Coimbra, Coimbra.

Parncutt, R. (2007). Systematic musicology and the history and future of Western musical scholarship. *Journal of Interdisciplinary Music Studies*, 1(1), pp. 1-32.

S2S[2] (2007). *A Roadmap for Sound and Music Computing (edited by X. Serra, M. Leman, and G. Widmer).* Brussels: The S2S[2] Consortium. (http://smcnetwork.org/). See also the special issue of Journal of New Music Research, Vol. 36, Issue 3, 2008

Schneider, A. (1993). Systematische Musikwissenschaft: Traditionen, Ansätze, Aufgaben. *Systematische Musikwissenschaft 1*, 145-180.

Tzanetakis, G., Kapur, A., Schloss, W.A., Wright, M. (2007). Computational ethnomusicology. *Journal of interdisciplinary music studies.* 1 (2). Online Journal http://www.musicstudies.org/fall2007.html.

Zatorre, R. J., & Peretz, I. (2001). *The Biological Foundations of Music.* New York: New York Academy of Sciences.

Rolf Inge Godøy

Reflections on Chunking in Music

1. Introduction

Although western musical discourse often assumes that large-scale forms such as symphonies and sonatas present meaningful experiences for listeners, as evident in innumerable writings on musical aesthetics, musical form, and music theory, and as epitomized in the Schenkerian notion of the grand-scale *Urlinie*, we actually know embarrassingly little about how listeners experience such large-scale forms. The few studies we have seen in this area (e.g. Karno and Konečni 1992, Eitan and Granot 2006) seem to suggest that we should be suspicious of claims about the importance of large-scale forms. My point here is not to reject the legitimacy or the efficacy of long stretches of musical sound (i.e. we do after all obviously enjoy listening to extended works of music), but rather to question at what level of resolution, meaning at what size of stretches of musical sound, we find the most salient elements of music. In other words: Are large-scale organizations of musical sound really so essential for our experience? And: Could small-scale fragments of music be edited together differently without destroying the overall experience of the music?

We should remind ourselves that the idea of concatenating small-scale musical fragments into various alternative larger-scale forms is not unknown in western music history, as for instance in the *Musikalische Würfelspiele* attributed to Mozart (but maybe falsely so, see Hedges 1978) that was supposed to make anyone without composition training capable of 'composing' music, or in various principles of collage and so-called 'open form' in the twentieth century, as for instance in Stockhausen's ideas of *Momentform* (Stockhausen 1963). However, what is missing in our musical discourse is the awareness, and more clear notions, of the status and role of fragments of musical sound, as well as the various aesthetic, perceptual, and cognitive constraints on both the formation and on the concatenation of such fragments. For these reasons, I shall in this paper present some *reflections on chunking in music*, meaning ideas on why fragments of musical sound are essential for our experience of music, and how such fragments emerge in our experience. The size of chunks I have in mind here is typically quite small, i.e. roughly in the 0,5 to 5 seconds range, as was suggested several decades ago by Schaeffer with his notion of the *sonic object* (Schaeffer 1966). The crucial role of chunks of this size in music is something that I shall argue is the result of several convergent constraints of our perceptual and motor apparatus, as well as something that is reflected in musical practice in the form of motives, ornaments, figures, grooves, etc., i.e. as various musically significant entities.

In music cognition and musical analysis, as well as in related domains such as linguistics and human movement science, we often come across terms such as 'segmentation', 'parsing', 'punctuation', and 'chunking', terms that sometimes are used synonymously, but also have different significations. I prefer to use the term *chunking* because in addition to signifying the cutting of something into smaller pieces, it also implies turning what is essentially ephemeral (as musical sound is) into something more solid in our minds. The *New Oxford American Dictionary* defines *chunk* as 'a thick, solid piece of something' or 'an amount or part of something', and the verb *chunking* as 'divide (something) into chunks' adding '(in psychology or linguistic analysis) group together (connected items or words) so that they can be stored or processed as single concepts' (McKean 2005, parentheses in the original). In cognitive psychology, the term chunking owes much of its significance to the seminal paper by G. A. Miller from 1957 (Miller 1957), where his main point was that there is a *re-coding* going on in perception in the sense that continuous and highly complex sensory experience is simplified by grouping into more tractable units in our minds, reducing memory load and enhancing our ability to think and act. This element of re-coding is essential in chunking, meaning that chunking has the twin elements of cutting a segment out of some larger context and of turning this segment into something that we can store in our minds as *Gestalts* or *shapes*, being subject to what I have previously termed 'flux to solid transformation' (Godøy 1997). The occurrence of visual terms in connection with chunking is not incidental, actually attesting to the close links between sound and action trajectories, making chunking here a multimodal phenomenon involving elements that can be seen (i.e. visual trajectories) and felt (i.e. sensations of effort) as well as heard (i.e. the acoustic signal).

There are good reasons for believing that chunking occurs spontaneously in listening (and also in musical imagery) as a result of various constraints of our perceptual-motor apparatus, and in this connection I see the following main reasons for studying chunking in music:

– We should find out more about what are the most significant units in musical experience, meaning how long stretches of musical sound we have to hear in order to have sensations of rhythmic, melodic, or textural patterns, of timbral features, of stylistic features, and of expressive intentions. Both informal observations and the few abovementioned more systematic studies of chunks in music seem to suggest that the chunk length for stylistic identification is typically quite short, probably roughly in the 5 second range.

– The chunk level allows for studies of significant features in all kinds of musical sound by a systematic multidimensional ordering of features, ranging from overall features such as the dynamic, timbral, textural, and pitch contour of the chunk, to the evolutions of various sub-features of the chunk, such as minute inflections of pitch, or various timbral or dynamic fluctuations, etc., in short, as presented in Schaffer's theories of the *typology* and *morphology* of the sonic object (Schaeffer 1966 and 1998, see Godøy 1997 and 2006 for overviews). Closely related to this is the strategy of *analysis by synthesis*, meaning making systematic and incrementally different variants of any musical sound in order to find out what are the perceptually salient features (Risset 1991), something that is best done at the chunk-level of resolution.

– We may understand more of music cognition in general if we find out more about what are the constraints of attention and memory that influence chunking in perception, as well as what are the constraints of biomechanics and motor control that condition chunking in sound-production. From an embodied cognition point of view, perception of musical sound is closely linked with our mental images of the production of sound, implying that musical sound also is a transducer of the kinematics and effort that go into the sound-production, a phenomenon I have earlier termed a *motormimetic* element in music (Godøy 2003). This means that music also is perceived as a script of concatenated action chunks, and that we may find out more about music by studying the nature of such action chunks.

This last point is what will be the focus of the present paper, but we shall first have a brief look at what may be significant chunking cues in musical sound, followed by an overview of some elements of our perceptual apparatus that may influence or even induce chunking. I shall then present a sketch of a model of chunking based on the idea of chunks as goal-directed action-units, a model I shall call *chunking by goal-points*, as well as some ideas on how to develop this model in future research.

2. Exogenous chunking

Although mainstream western musical discourse claims the efficacy of large-scale form, there is needless to say also a consensus that music may be divided into smaller sections. This is well known in various notions of *Formenlehre*, e.g. as in (Schönberg 1967) and in more recent music cognition theory, e.g. as in (Lerdahl and Jackendoff 1983), as well as in pattern recognition research, e.g. as in (Cambouropoulos 2006). Common to these otherwise rather different theoretical approaches is that they are notation-based, meaning that they look for segmentation cues in the musical scores. Also common to these approaches is that they are basically bottom-up in the sense that segmentation is deduced from the notes in the scores, albeit variably so by making recourse to various rules assumed to reflect our mental schemas for organizing notes into segments. The difficulties with such note-based, bottom-up, rule-directed approaches is that they are not well equipped for making transitions from discrete note symbols to more superordinate units of sound, i.e. are not well equipped to deal with emergent effects of chunking.

These and similar approaches that see the cues for segmentation as primarily coming from 'the music itself' is what I here shall classify as cases of *exogenous chunking* in the sense of seeing the source for chunking as outside our minds and bodies. Exogenous chunking can be contrasted with *endogenous chunking* in the sense that endogenous chunking sees chunking as emanating from our own active mental and/or corporeal rendering of what we hear. However, distinctions between these two approaches to chunking may not always be so clear-cut, and we have seen theories of segmentation that variably employ combinations of exogenous and endogenous elements in chunking. One important project that combines exogenous and endogenous elements has been that of Auditory Scene Analysis (Bregman 1990). Auditory scene analysis is based on continuous sound, i.e. on what is sometimes called the sub-symbolic level of music, and one of the main principles here is the combination of so-called *primitive* segmentations of sound, based on various low-level qualitative discontinuities and Gestalt principles for grouping, with what is called *schema-based* segmentations of sound, meaning our grouping of various sound elements into chunks based on massive previous experience of sound events. Classical auditory scene analysis is then a combination of bottom-up and a top-down approaches, but as has been the experience of machine-based auditory scene analysis (Rosenthal and Okuno 1998) and music information retrieval (http://www.ismir.net), advances in these fields seem to depend on enhancing the top-down schema-based elements, de facto developing better endogenous chunking capabilities in artificial systems.

Another combination of exogenous and endogenous chunking can be found in Schaeffer's notion of the sonic object. It should be mentioned that the initial idea of Schaeffer's sonic object came from the practical experience of working with sound fragments in the early days of *musique concrète*, i.e. before the advent of tape recorders, necessitating making loops called *sillon fermé* ('closed groove') on phonograph disks in order to allow for mixing and other manipulations of sounds. Because of this looping, Schaeffer and co-workers listened to innumerable repetitions of these sound fragments, and came to realize that such de-contextualized fragments of sound could acquire new and autonomous status if they listened to the fragment as a whole, as an object or shape having a beginning, a middle, and an end, regardless the initially arbitrary origin of the sound fragment. Later, Schaeffer used the metaphor of cutting a magnet into smaller pieces where each new piece of the magnet would have its polarities, hence, that any arbitrary sound fragment could be perceived as some kind of coherent chunk (Schaeffer 1998). But Schaeffer also took care to distinguish between such arbitrary originating sonic objects and sonic objects more based on naturally occurring qualitative discontinuities in any continuous stream of sound by the idea of *articulation-appui* ('stress-articulation' (Schaeffer 1998)[1], as well as a recourse to typological schemas for sound-production with the main categories *sustained*, *impulsive*, and *iterative* sounds. Each of these categories have distinct exogenous features that would trigger chunking in our listening experience, categories that we in our present research on music-related movement see correspond with quite distinct modes of sound-producing movement, i.e. sustained effort is quite distinct from impulsive, meaning continuous movement is biomechanically quite distinct from discontinuous movement, and iterative movement is a mid-category between sustained and impulsive in that it exploits rebounds that break continuous movement into a series of impulses as when stroking along the surface of a washboard (see Godøy 2006 for details on this).

Schaeffer emphasized that there is no simple one-to-one relationship between the signal and our mental images of the sonic object, but rather a relationship of what he called *anamorphosis*, meaning warping. In his discussions of the nature and status of the sonic object, Schaeffer concluded that the sonic object really is a mental image, what he called an *intentional unit*, hence that the sonic object ultimately is a matter of endogenous chunking, although the sonic object of course may be correlated with various features in the signal.

Actually, the associations of various sound-producing actions with sounds are an important element in music perception, as has been the topic of our own (Godøy, Haga, and Jensenius 2006) and other research (Leman 2007). In terms of exogenous and endogenous cues for chunking, sound-producing gestures may in many cases present quite clear discontinuities for chunking, such as in singular, non-overlapping impulsive events. However, in the case of more continuous action sequences where several action units occur in rapid succession or where we have long protracted and even overlapping actions, extracting cues for chunking from continuous motion may become difficult.

---

[1] 'Articulation' is defined as 'breaking up the sonorous continuum by successive distinct energetic events' (Schaeffer 1966, p. 396), and 'stress' as the prolongation of the sound, similar to vowels in speech (ibid, p. 366).

Thus, the challenges of chunking in musical sound are similar to chunking in sound-producing actions, as well as in dance or other music-related actions, or in human movement in general, for that matter.

As I shall try to demonstrate below, a possible solution to chunking of apparently continuous movement is to try to detect intentional focal point in human motion, meaning detecting certain goal postures in time, what I shall call *goal-points*. My understanding of chunking here will be based on an embodied perspective on music cognition, meaning on an active mental simulation of various actions we associate with musical sound. This also means that similar principles can be applied to both perception and action, because 'to perceive an action is equivalent to internally simulating it.' (Gallese and Metzinger 2003, 383) And: 'This enables the observer to use her/his own resources to penetrate the world of the other by means of an implicit, automatic, and unconscious process of motor simulation.' (ibid). This means that whatever sonic events or tones we may hear (or merely imagine), may be understood as included in action-trajectories, i.e. that perception is a matter of egocentric mental simulation of whatever we hear, including goal-points.

3. Endogenous chunking

The main idea of endogenous chunking is that although exogenous sensory cues may trigger chunking in perception, these exogenous cues may be insufficient for the simple reason that they are ambiguous (too many in rapid succession) or offer few or none qualitative discontinuities (as in long, protracted sounds, or as in continuously repeated events with no prominent discontinuities). One well-known case of this is the inclination to project meter onto a series of otherwise equal pulses, i.e. that listeners endogenously group events (Fraisse 1982). Ideas from different domains may be seen to converge in support of endogenous sources for chunking, and here are the most relevant in our context:

– We find remarkably lucid depictions of endogenous chunking in the writings of Edmund Husserl on temporal awareness. These writings, spanning several decades from 1897, but here referenced in (Husserl 1964), present an introspective analysis of our awareness in perception and thinking, stating that there has to be an element of discontinuity, meaning that awareness is only possible by intermittent flashes, or by what Husserl called 'now-points', of overviewing chunks of experience. If we were submerged in a continuous stream of sensory information, everything would only appear as an amorphous mass of indistinct and meaningless sensations. Interestingly in our context of chunking in music, Husserl uses the example of the melody to illustrate this idea of perception by discontinuous now-points, stating that if we are continuously submerged in the stream of tones, we will have no perception of the melody at all, and that it is only by somehow freezing the stream of tones and keeping all the tones we have heard (and expectations of what to hear as well) in consciousness for an instant, that we can have a perception of the melody. Later, Paul Ricoeur presented similar ideas on the need for discontinuity in our minds, concluding that *interruptions* of continuous sensations are necessary to make sense of the world (Ricoeur 1981). Actually, the question of continuity and discontinuity in awareness is general and encountered in various guises in music perception as well as in other cognitive sciences. As depicted in figure 1, it is a question of to what extent we perceive and think by discontinuous chunks, as well as to what extent sensations of continuity are preserved across various discontinuous chunks. In music (as well as in movement science) it seems quite clear that we have several temporal strata running in parallel so that we may have both awareness of chunks and awareness of the various continuous features within any chunk, e.g. we may be aware of the overall contour of a sonic event and at the same time be aware of its various features such as pitch and timbre and micro-fluctuations of pitch and timbre.

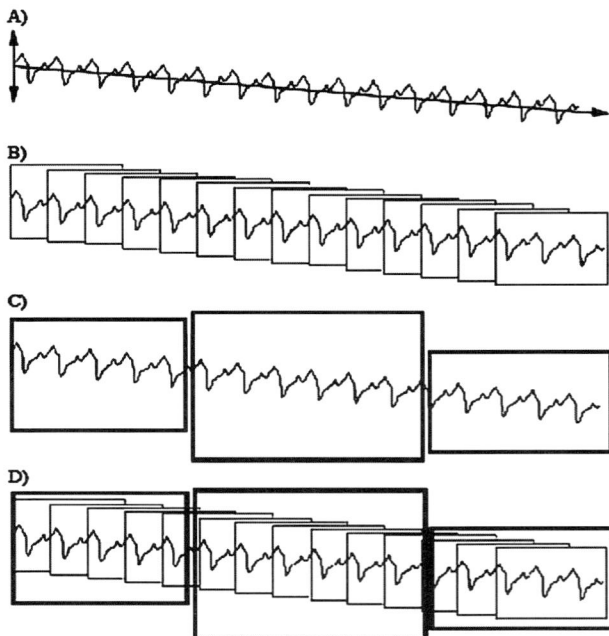

Fig. 1: Given A) a continuous stream of sensory impressions, be that sound, vision, or motion, is there B) a more or less continuous updating of our awareness by a 'sliding window', or is there C) a more discontinuous updating of our awareness by disjunct chunks, or is there D) a combination of continuity and discontinuity in our awareness?

– In many ways similar ideas of discontinuity in awareness seems to emerge in more recent neurophysiological research. Notions of discontinuity are here in part based on observable patterns of electrical activity in the brain, indicating certain moments of phase-coherence in different frequency regions, something that is understood as indicative of moments of experienced perceptual coherence and/or decision point for actions (Varela 1999, Engel et al. 2001). These notions of discontinuity are correlated with behavioral studies as in (Pöppel 1997), where it is suggested we may readily observe chunks of roughly 3 seconds durations both in perception and action, and that for phenomena lasting significantly longer than this time-frame of approximately 3 seconds, we will experience shifts of attention, similar to the figure-ground shifts of bi-stable images well known from Gestalt theory. Pöppel also refers to the large-scale study by Schleidt and Kien (Schleidt and Kien 1997) where it is documented that ordinary everyday human (as well as other primate) actions clearly tends to fall within this 3 second time-frame, concluding that perceiving and acting by chunks within such a time frame is deeply rooted in our cognitive apparatus. Finally, various studies of short-term memory also seem to suggest that there is a time frame of roughly 3 seconds at work in most situations of perception and action (Snyder 2000).

– As for the planning and execution of human actions, we find discontinuous elements with regards to biomechanical constraints of need for rests, for shifting between effectors, and for energy optimization. But in addition to such biomechanically induced chunking, there is also chunking with regards to motor control, in the sense that the actions may be pre-planned. To what extent such preplanning of movement determines entire action chunks, has been debated for more than a century since the presentation of the idea of an 'initial impulse' in human action in (Woodworth 1899). However, there seems now to emerge some kind of consensus that there is a combination of pre-planning with the possibilities of making adjustments in the course of the action chunk (Elliott, Helsen, and Chua 2001). Lashley raised a related question in (Lashley 1951) whether action could be regarded as a concatenation of several smaller action units, what was called 'response chaining', or whether the demands of everyday actions would make such chaining of smaller action units too slow and thus improbable, meaning that there had to be more superordinate action chunks at work. Recent research seems to support the view that there is indeed a considerable amount of pre-planning in human action, specifically by way of what is called *goal postures* and *motion between these goal postures*, alternatively referred to by the terms *keyframes* and *interframes* used in animation to denote respectively the most salient images and the intervening frames between these salient images (Rosenbaum et al. 2007). Undeniably, such a posture-by-posture or keyframe-by-keyframe model seems to resemble the phenomenological idea of perception and cognition by a series of 'now-points'.

– Lastly, some recent neurocognitive research seems to suggest that human action and perception in general is goal-directed, i.e. can be understood as organized primarily around a series of goal-states (Gallese and Metzinger 2003). Similar elements of goal-directed behavior is found in studies of imitative behavior, where it has been shown that the goals of actions are more robustly imitated than the intervening trajectories to these goals (Wohlschläger, Gattis and Bekkering 2003), something we have seen also in our own studies of air-instrument performance, where participating subjects, regardless level of expertise, seemed to focus on salient sound-producing events (Godøy, Haga, and Jensenius 2006). A similar capacity to determine points of salience on the basis of continuous sound is found in various studies of perceptual centers, also known as *p-centers* in auditory research. It has been shown that there the p-centers are often not in synchrony with acoustical peaks, e.g. amplitude peaks, implying that the subjective perception of peaks is based on a (as yet not well understood) holistic perception of more extended fragments of sound than just the acoustic peak points. Also, it has been shown that listeners have a capacity for determining peaks in sounds that are continuously changing, such as in sinusoidal motion (McAnally 2002).

What emerges from these different domains is the idea of *discontinuity* in the form of certain *goal-points* in action as well as in perception and cognition. Such a focus on goal-points does not mean that the motion between the goal-points is unimportant. On the contrary, the quality or mode of motion is just as essential as the goal-points for our experience; it is just that goal-points have a particular role in terms of chunking. For this reason, I shall in the next section present a sketch of a model of chunking centered around goal-points, and where the motion trajectories will be treated as shapes or envelopes in accordance with the typological and morphological principles of Schaeffer (Godøy 2006).

4. Chunking by goal-points

On the basis of these ideas of human action as motion between goal postures, we can thus understand chunking of musical sound, as well as music-related actions, as centered around what I shall here call *goal-points*. 'Goal-points' here means *goal postures at specific points in time*. Furthermore, the term 'goal posture' in our context designates both the *position of the effectors in space*, e.g. the hands at a certain place on a keyboard, the arms at a certain place in relation to the drums, etc., and the *shape of the effector*, e.g. the shape of the hand on the keyboard (meaning single tone, chord, etc.), the shape of the vocal apparatus (vowel shape), etc. Equally important is that these goal postures occur at *specific points in time*, e.g. that the hands hit the chord (goal posture) at the downbeat or some other salient point in time (goal time).

  Regarding perception and action as organized around successive goal-points will actually imply that we have to revise some traditional notions of chunking so that we regard the goal-points as the most important element in the formation of chunks, rather than focusing on the boundaries of where a chunk may start and end. This is admittedly a kind of 'Copernican revolution' in the sense that it is the center of the chunk, i.e. the goal-point, which constitutes the chunk, and not the start and the end points of the chunk.

  In music, these goal-points will be accent points in time, either in the form of downbeats or other kinds of accents, or in the form of other salient points in melodic or timbral trajectories. The movements to and from the goal-points are included in the chunk in the form of what I here shall call *prefix* and *suffix* respectively, meaning that the prefix will often be in the form of an upbeat trajectory, and that the suffix will be in the form of a rebound trajectory from the goal-point, see figure 2, illustration A). It will often be quite clear where a suffix ends and where a prefix for a new goal-point begins, but not always, and the prefix of a new goal-point may very well start when the suffix of the preceding goal-point is still resonating, see figure 2, illustration C). Chunking by goal-points also means that the various action components within a chunk are subsumed under the superordinate trajectory to and from the goal-point, i.e. under the prefix and suffix, effectively giving rise to *coarticulation* in the sense that otherwise individual events, or 'atom events', are fused into the prefix and suffix trajectories (Godøy in press), see figure 2, illustration B).

We could say that chunking by goal-points is related to the notion of the 'envelope' in musical acoustics, i.e. of there being a shape depicting the dynamical, pitch, timbral, etc. evolution of a sonic event, however with the essential addition here that there is always a prefix to the goal-point, i.e. that there always has to be an action trajectory to the goal-point, also in cases where the chunk starts directly on the audible downbeat and there is no audible upbeat, for the simple reason that the effector (hand, mallet, bow) has to make a trajectory to the goal-point. Generally speaking, the envelope of goal-point centered chunks would resemble any action trajectory that starts out from some kind of equilibrium or resting position, moves towards a goal, and then retracts back to the equilibrium or resting position, as for instance in what Kendon calls a *gesture unit* (Kendon 2004).

Furthermore, this goal-point model of chunking does resemble what is broadly known as *mass-spring* phenomena, both in a direct, physical sense and in a metaphorical or schematic sense: In a direct sense of how the effectors may rebound after the goal-point, e.g. the mallet bouncing back from the drum membrane, the arms bouncing upwards from the keyboard after an accented chord, etc., and thus also concerning how exploiting mass-spring phenomena in music performance may help optimize performance by energy conservation (exploiting the rebound energy, see Dahl 2006) and how this in turn shapes musical articulation. But the mass-spring model can also be applied in a more metaphorical or mental schematic sense of there being a building up of energy (the prefix trajectory to the goal-point), an impact or sudden release of energy at the goal-point, and a dissipation of the energy after the goal-point (the suffix trajectory).

Thinking of chunking by goal-points followed by rebounds or reverberations, or as a matter of *impulse-resonance*, could also serve as a metaphorical model of more long-term, contextual memory effects, similar to what has in fact previously been suggested in theories of memory by Lashley, by Hebb, and later by others such as Edelman (Snyder 2000), in that each goal-point will have a following resonance phase that overlaps into the subsequent chunk so that several chunks may linger in memory, i.e. beyond the confines of short-term memory. Modeling goal-point chunking as a mass-spring or an impulse-resonance phenomena is where we now are going in our research, and we shall be trying out various mathematical and physical models for simulating this, both as a direct biomechanical phenomenon in musical performance, and as a more metaphorical and conceptual model in music perception (see Ward 2002 for discussion of this and similar models). There is a schematic illustration of this in figure 2, showing first a prototype goal-point chunk with a prefix trajectory, a goal-point, and a suffix trajectory, as well as a similar goal-point chunk but with various coarticulated sub-movements included in the prefix and suffix trajectories, and lastly, a schematic illustration of how several goal-point chunks in succession with overlapping prefixes and suffixes could serve to create sensations of continuity in memory.

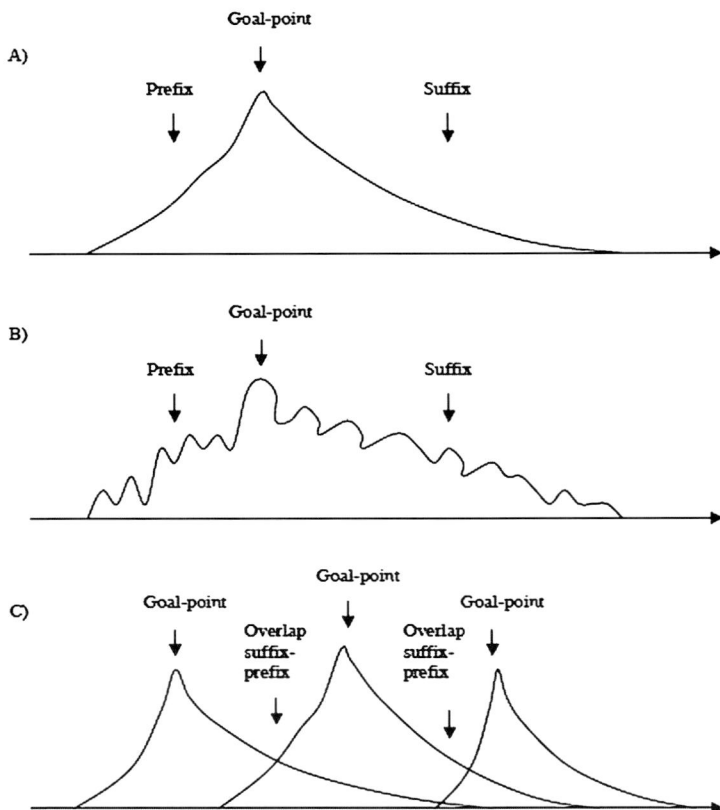

Fig. 2:. Schematic depiction of chunking by goal-points, A) with a singular chunk with just a prefix straight to the goal-point followed by a suffix from the goal-point, and B) with a prefix and a suffix containing several coarticulated sub-actions, and C), several goal-point chunks with overlapping prefixes and suffixes creating a sensation of continuity.

Besides this dynamical element of mass-spring action, chunking by goal-points also has some significant geometric features that we may suspect are important in the perception and cognition of musical sound. By having a prefix, a goal-point, and a suffix, any chunk may be thought of as an envelope shape, but in addition, there is also the position and shapes of the effectors at the goal-points: The *position* of the effectors signifies the position (as well as the *spread*, when there are more effectors involved as in two-hand keyboard performance) of the effectors on the instrument, and in a more metaphorical sense, in pitch space, typically with the left-to-right, low-to-high, organization based on the keyboards of western musical culture. But also the *shapes* of the effectors at these goal-points are important, e.g. the shape of the hand related to the features of the chord, the shape of the vocal tract or the mute, related to the formantic features of the sound, etc. In addition, there is also the geometry of the intervening movement between the

126

successive goal-points, meaning the shape of the trajectories in time-space, hopefully allowing us to correlate qualitative features of movement (e.g. calm, agitated, jerky, fluid, etc.) with motion measurement data (trajectory, speed, acceleration, deceleration, direction change, rest, etc.). Taken together, all these geometric elements enhance the notion of the chunk as a shape, as signifying the 'solidifying' aspect of chunking mentioned in the introduction.

Furthermore, the goal-point model of chunking could work both in anticipation and in retrospect: The element of anticipation is quite obvious as an action trajectory is planned in advance (cf. Rosenbaum et al. 2007), including advance preparation for the biomechanical elements of energy optimization, exploitation of momentum, rebound, fluency (or so-called 'minimum jerk'), etc. In perception, we have good reason to suspect that we project schemas of such action envelopes (based on massive previous experience) onto novel situations, so that we actively chunk what we hear (or imagine) by retrospectively mentally simulating the assumed sound-producing actions ourselves. Chunking by goal-points is then a schema that may be applied to various perceptual phenomena, such as understanding the thresholds for fusion vs. fission, similar to what is the case for stream segregation and principles of apparent motion (Körte's third law), where the variables are spatial distance in pitch space (analogous to actual spatial distance for flashing lights) and speed, i.e. temporal distance between tones (analogous to temporal distance between flashes), see (Bregman 1990) for a discussion and further references here. In our case of chunking by goal-points, the most important variable will in all probability be that of speed, grounded in biomechanical constraints on motion (amplitude and speed of effector motion) and on motor control principles of anticipatory planning, i.e. the extent to which action elements may be attended to individually. This means that with changes in speed and amplitude of movements, there may be shifts in the chunking of movements, and consequently, also shifts in the perceived chunking of the sounds. Such shifts are well known from dynamical theory as *phase shifts* (Haken, Kelso, and Bunz 1985), and have been studied in the case of bowing (Rasamimanana et al. 2007), however it remains to find out more what are the biomechanical and what are the motor control or more mental constraints at work in such phase shifts.

5. Applications

All in all, elements from several domains of the cognitive sciences and the human movement sciences converge in making this idea of chunking by goal-points reasonably well founded, although we have substantial challenges ahead in both getting a better understanding of how it works and of what are its biomechanical and neurocognitive bases. But we can already now see some interesting applications of chunking by goal-points in music:

- *In general*, regarding any sonic object as consisting of a trajectory towards a goal-point, a goal-point, and a trajectory away for the goal-point, however with highly variable degrees of salience, ranging from extremely clear to more indeterminate, e.g. as in cases of continuous, sinusoidal motion, or even stationary sounds. In the case of sinusoidal motion (or other continuous motion trajectories), we could assume principles of endogenous goal-point projection could apply as suggested by p-centre research (McAnally 2002), and in the case of stationary sounds, we

127

could speculate that similar principles of endogenously originating attention shifts beyond the roughly 3 seconds time frame as suggested by (Pöppel 1997) would apply, making these shift-points equivalent to the goal-points here.

– *Rhythmic patterns*, in particular cyclical (metrical) patterns where all sounds are perceived in relation to the goal-point, either as part of the upbeat or as part of the rebound, and this goes equally for non-periodic rhythms as well. A goal-point model of cyclical rhythmical patterns could well account for various offbeat accents, e.g. accented 2's in 2/4 meter, accents that acoustically may be stronger than the downbeat, i.e. the 1's, in that the cyclical motion has the 1's as the goal-points and accented 2's are just very energetic rebounds from the 1's goal-points. Similar principles could be applied to various textural patterns, with all occurring tones subsumed to the goal-points and the associated prefixes and suffixes.

– *Timbral contours* with evolutions of harmonic content, formantic peaks, and various micro textures, all perceived in relation to goal-points.

– *Melodic contours* as having one more or less prominent peak, and in cases of several competing peaks, or no peaks, there may be recourse more endogenously generated goal-points.

– *Tone semantic and modal features*, meaning that sequentially occurring tones have a contextual smearing so that all the tones in the action trajectories are perceived cumulatively and in relation to the goal-point.

– *Enhancing the geometric nature of musical sound* by making the position, spread, and posture of goal-points, as well as the intervening motion trajectories, all saliently present in consciousness, helping us understand the 'flux-to-solid' transformation of ephemeral musical sound in our mind (and could also be the basis for better computer visualizations of both musical sound and sound-related actions as keyframes and interframes).

– *Salience points*, meaning the goal-points as the basis for so-called *thumbnails* for large-scale works, i.e. in 'highlights' overviews of long stretches of musical sound and music-related actions, similar to what we see in movie trailers where the purpose of the trailer is to as rapidly as possible (typically in less than 30 seconds) present us with the gist of an entire two-hour movie.

6. Conclusion

The main objective of this paper has been to reflect upon how we chunk musical sound in listening and in imagery, motivated by the conviction that chunking is essential for our basic understanding of music, and that chunking is required for systematic explorations of musical sound by multidimensional models and by analysis by synthesis. It seems that exogenous elements in the form of various qualitative discontinuities are important, yet often insufficient for the formation of chunks in our minds. Fortunately, insights from various domains now seem to converge in suggesting that there may be endogenous origins of chunking, and that chunking may be based on perceiving goal-directed action, hence that chunking is focused on goal-points (goal postures at specific points in time). This implies a reversal in relation to other notions of chunking in that the borders of the chunk are seen as secondary to the goal-points of the chunk.

For the moment, this chunking by goal-points is at an hypothesis stage, and although I believe it has many attractive features, there are obviously very many challenges here:

We need more and better data on the movements that performers are actually making, hence we need better technologies and conceptual tools for motion capture, processing, and representation, and we need more and better simulations of the biomechanics and motor control issues involved in sound-production. But perhaps most of all, we need more insights from the cognitive sciences community on the enigmatic issues of continuity and discontinuity in human perception, cognition, and action, as well as mathematical and other conceptual tools for modeling this.

References

Bregman, A. (1990). *Auditory Scene Analysis*. Cambridge, Mass., and London: The MIT Press

Cambouropoulos E. (2006). Musical Parallelism and Melodic Segmentation: A Computational Approach. *Music Perception*, 23(3), 249-269.

Dahl, S. (2006). Movements and analysis of drumming. In Altenmüller, E., Wiesendanger, M., and Kesselring, J., (Eds.) *Music, Motor Control and the Brain*, pages 125-138. Oxford: Oxford University Press.

Eitan, Z., and Granot, R. Y. (2006). Growing oranges on Mozart's apple tree: "Inner form" and aesthetic judgment. In: M. Baroni, A. R. Addessi, R. Caterina, M. Costa (Eds.) *Proceedings of the 9th International Conference on Music Perception & Cognition (ICMPC9), Bologna/Italy, August 22-26 2006*, pp 1020-1027.

Elliott, D., Helsen, W., and Chua, R. (2001). A Century Later: Woodworth's (1899) Two-Component Model of Goal-Directed Aiming. *Psychological Bulletin*, Volume 127(3), May 2001, p 342–357

Engel AK, Fries P, Singer W. (2001). Dynamic predictions: oscillations and synchrony in top-down processing. *Nat. Rev. Neurosci*, Oct;2(10):704-16.

Fraisse, P. (1982). Rhythm and Tempo. In D. Deutsch (Ed.) *The Psychology of Music.* (1st ed.) New York: Academic Press, pp. 149-180,

Gallese, V. and Metzinger, T. (2003). Motor ontology: The Representational Reality Of Goals, Actions And Selves. *Philosophical Psychology*, Vol. 16, No. 3, pp. 338-365.

Godøy, R. I. (2003). Motor-mimetic Music Cognition. *Leonardo*, Vol. 36, No. 4, pp. 317-319.

Godøy, R. I. (2006). Gestural-Sonorous Objects: embodied extensions of Schaeffer's conceptual apparatus. *Organised Sound*, 11:2:149-157

Godøy, R. I. (in press). Coarticulated gestural-sonorous objects in music. In Gritten, A. and King, E. (Eds.) *Music and Gesture 2* (working title). Aldershot: Ashgate

Godøy, R. I., Haga, E., and Jensenius, A. (2006). Playing 'Air Instruments': mimicry of sound-producing gestures by novices and experts. In Gibet, S., Courty, N., Kamp, J.-F. (eds.): *GW2005, LNAI 3881*. Springer-Verlag, Berlin (2006) 256–67

Haken, H., Kelso, J.A.S., and Bunz, H. (1985). A theoretical model of phase transitions in human hand movements. *Biological cybernetics* 51(5) 347–356

Hedges, S. A. (1978). Dice Music in the Eighteenth Century. *Music & Letters*, Vol. 59, No. 2. (Apr., 1978), pp. 180-187.

Husserl, E. (1964). *The Phenomenology of Internal Time Consciousness*, ed. Martin Heidegger, trans. J. S. Churchill. Blomington, Indiana: Indiana University Press.

Karno, M. and Konečni, V.J. (1992). The effects of structural interventions in the first movement of Mozart's symphony in G minor, K.550, on aesthetic preference. *Music Perception*, 10, 63–72.

Kendon, A. (2004). *Gesture: Visible Action as Utterance*. Cambridge: Cambridge University Press.

Lashley, K. S. (1951). The problem of serial order in behavior. In L. A. Jeffress (Ed.), *Cerebral mechanisms in behavior* (pp. 112–131). New York: Wiley.

Leman, M. (2007). *Embodied Music Cognition and Mediation Technology*. Cambridge, Mass., and London: The MIT Press

Lerdahl, F., and Jackendoff, R., (1983). *A Generative Theory of Tonal Music*. Cambridge, Mass., and London: The MIT Press

McAnally, K. I. (2002). Timing of finger tapping to frequency modulated acoustic stimuli. *Acta Psychologica*, 109, 331–338

McKean, E. (Ed.) (2005). *The New Oxford American Dictionary, Second Edition*, Oxford University Press, electronic version in Macintosh OS X v. 10.4

Miller, G. A., (1956). The magic number seven, plus or minus two: Some limits on our capacity for processing information. *Psychological Review* 63: 81-97.

Miller, I. (1982). Husserl's Account of Our Temporal Awareness. In Dreyfus, H., ed., *Husserl, Intentionality, and Cognitive Science*. Cambridge, Mass., and London: The MIT Press, pp. 125-146.

Pöppel, E. (1997). A Hierarchical model of time perception. *Trends in Cognitive Science*, 1 (2): 56-61.

Rasamimanana, N., Bernardin, D., Wanderley, M. and Bevilacqua, F. (2007). String Bowing Gestures at Varying Bow Stroke Frequencies: A Case Study. In Miguel Sales Dias and Ricardo Jota (Eds.) *Proceedings of GW2007 - 7th International Workshop on Gesture in Human-Computer Interaction and Simulation 2007*, pp. 62-63

Ricoeur, P. (1981). *Hermeneutics and the Human Sciences*. Cambridge/ Paris: Cambridge University Press/Éditions de la Maison des Sciences de l'Homme.

Risset, J.-C. (1991). Timbre Analysis by Synthesis: Representations, Imitations and Variants for Musical Composition. In De Poli, G., Piccialli, A., and Roads, C. (Eds.) *Representations of Musical Signals*. Cambridge, Mass., and London: The MIT Press, pp. 7-43.

Rosenbaum, D., Cohen, R. G., Jax, S. A., Weiss, D. J., and van der Wel, R. (2007). The problem of serial order in behavior: Lashley's legacy. *Human Movement Science*, vol. 26, 4, August 2007, pages 525-554.

Rosenthal, D. F. and Okuno, H. G. (Eds.) (1998). *Computational auditory scene analysis*. Mahwah, NJ: Lawrence Erlbaum

Schaeffer, P. (1966). *Traité des objets musicaux*. Paris: Éditions du Seuil.

Schaeffer, P. (with sound examples by Reibel, G., and Ferreyra, B.) (1998, first published in 1967). *Solfège de l'objet sonore*. Paris: INA/GRM.

Schleidt, M., and Kien, J. (1997). Segmentation in behavior and what it can tell us about brain function. *Human Nature*, Vol. 8, No. 1, pp 77-111.

Schönberg, A. (1967). *Fundamentals of Musical Composition*. London & Boston: Faber and Faber.

Snyder, B. (2000). *Music and Memory: An Introduction. Cambridge*. Mass., and London: The MIT Press

Stockhausen, K. (1963)**.** Texte zur elektronischen und instrumentalen Musik, Band 1: Aufatze 1952-1962 zur Theorie des Komponierens. Cologne: M. DuMont Schauberg.

Varela, F. (1999). The specious present: The neurophenomenology of time consciousness in: J. Petitot, F. J. Varela, B. Pachoud and J. M. Roy (Eds.), *Naturalizing Phenomenology*, Stanford University Press, pp. 266-314.

Ward, L. M. (2002). *Dynamical Cognitive Science*. Cambridge, Mass., and London: The MIT Press

Wohlschläger, A., Gattis, M., Bekkering, H. (2003). Action generation and action perception in imitation: an instance of the ideomotor principle. *Phil. Trans. R. Soc. Lond. B,* 358 (2003) 501–515

Woodworth, R. S. (1899). The accuracy of voluntary movement. *Psychological Review*, *3*, (3, Suppl. 13), 1–119

Daniel Müllensiefen, Geraint Wiggins, David Lewis

High-level feature descriptors and corpus-based musicology: Techniques for modelling music cognition

1 Introduction

In recent years large electronic collections of music in a symbolically-encoded form have been made available. They have enabled music researchers to develop and test precise empirical theories of music on large data sets. Both the availability of music data and the development of new empirical theories creates a new perspective for Systematic Musicology, which, as a discipline, often sets out to explain or describe music through the induction of empirical laws, regularities or statistical correlations in relation to music objects or music related behaviour (see e.g. Karbusicky, 1979; Karbusicky & Schneider, 1980; Schneider, 1993; Huron, 1999; Parncutt, 2007). We present two methodological frameworks, feature-extraction and corpus-based musicology, which are the core approaches of a particular research project, M^4S, whose aim is to discover mechanisms of music cognition. These two frameworks are also very useful for many other empirical tasks in Systematic Musicology.

Before we go on to sketch a current project and to describe feature-extraction and corpus-based musicology, we need to clarify the term *symbolically-encoded music,* better to position our approach in the larger picture of contemporary music research. By "symbolically-encoded music", we mean music in a computer-readable format where the fundamental unit of representation is the note. Thus, symbols in these formats designate notes as might be performed by musicians, or played back by music software, or rendered to score notation by music engraving/publishing software. Well-known and widely-used symbolic computer formats include the Plaine and Easie Code (Brook, 1970), MIDI (International MIDI Association, 1988), kern** (Huron, 1995), MusicXML (Recordare, 2004/2007), and MuseData (Hewlett, 1997), Selfridge-Field (1997) gives a summary up to 1997. Symbolic formats can be contrasted with audio formats which, instead of capturing notes explicitly, encode the sonic aspect of a musical performance by representing sound as a complex waveform. The best known formats are audio CD, the WAV and AIFF formats used primarily in computers and iPods, and MPEG-1 Audio-Layer 3 (mp3) as a compression format used for web-based and portable applications.

The decision to use symbolic formats for our study lies in the fact that we are interested in objects of music cognition like melodies, rhythms, and harmonies, which seem to be mentally represented in a form comparable with symbolic encoding formats. Accordingly, our project will make use of experimental procedures that require the comparison, recognition or reproduction of pitch or rhythm sequences which also can be described most easily at a note level. To extract faithful representations of (monophonic) pitch or rhythm sequences from a polyphonic piece of music encoded in an audio format remains an unsolved problem. The procedures of instrument recognition, voice separation, and note segmentation necessary for our purposes currently suffer from unacceptably high error rates, especially when these procedures are combined to produce transcription from complex audio signals. But when we turn to symbolic formats the extraction of melodies, harmonies and rhythms as well as the extraction of features of these musical entities from polyphonic music becomes much easier, as we shall see below.

Context and goals of the M⁴S project

The project Modelling Music Memory and the Perception of Melodic Similarity (M⁴S) is a three-year project hosted in the Computing Department of Goldsmiths, University of London and aims to construct cognitive models of memory and of similarity perception for melodies, questions which fall in the areas of music psychology and music cognition. The way to arrive at these answers involves music analysis based on algorithms and the computation of distributions of analytic features. Therefore, scientific outcomes of the project can be found in the precise definition and evaluation of analytic features as well as in the identification patterns of musical features that are interesting for music analytic purposes (see section "Feature extraction").

The project is organised in four steps.

The first step involves the construction of a database for a large collection of symbolically-encoded music. This includes not only the incorporation of the raw musical data, but also the computation and integration of higher level musical structure (based on the concept of constituents, Smaill et al. 1993). Constituents denote musically meaningful groups, and are linked to sets of note events, allowing the annotation of a musical surface with structures and relationships.

The second step is an empirical evaluation of the defined features based on psychological experiments. As the number of potential implementations for any given feature is large, the goal of this step is to select the implementation of a feature that matches human perception most closely. Feature computation and evaluation will be explained in detail in the next section.

As a third step, the joined distributions of the selected features is computed. This includes the detection of associations or correlations between categories of different features which might be related to musical patterns. The distributions of feature categories and feature category combinations as they appear in the music corpus are recorded.

In a fourth and final step, these distributions are employed to model the data from a second series of psychological experiments. This time these experiments are focused on memory for music objects like melodies and rhythms.

The music corpus used for M⁴S is a collection of 14,067 transcriptions of pop songs from the 1950s to 2006 in the MIDI file format. These files were commercially acquired and were produced, to a high standard, by musicians for a distributing company (Geerdes MIDI Music; http://www.midimusic.de) which normally sells its MIDI files to studio musicians, entertainers or karaoke enterprises where they are used as backing tracks. The MIDI files may be considered accurate transcriptions of the original recordings and contain all the vocal and instrumental voices that are present in the original. In addition, the encoding conventions of the distributor allow us automatically to identify the lyrics, main tune (vocal), bass line, drums, and harmony instruments. Apart from these conventions, the files are not otherwise annotated: there is no indication of song sections, harmonic labels, or abstracted representations of rhythmic and harmonic patterns. In short, the raw data that the M^4S project has to deal with are effectively[1] faithful full-score transcriptions of pop songs.

Whilst MIDI is not a standard designed for representing scores (it was originally intended for real-time synthesizer control), and lacks even such basic information as enharmonic pitch spelling, it is a remarkably rich format. A MIDI file consists of a sequence of events indicating, in the case of notes, pitch, start and finish times, mix volume, timbral strength ('key velocity'), instrumental timbre, voice, stereo placement, pitch bend, etc. Lyrics, key and time signatures, and transposing instruments are also supported.

In M^4S, all this information is recorded in an indexed SQL database, allowing not only fast querying, but also the construction of compound (or higher-level) musical queries.

Musical objects provide information about sets of other musical objects. For example, a melody is a set of notes which may be considered as musically meaningful and distinct, to some extent, from their surroundings. A melodic contour, however, might refer to that phrase and indicate that it has, say, an arch structure, or a sentence object might group several musical phrases rather as the melody groups several notes (for an example of the power of reasoning with such constructs, see Smaill et al, 1993).

Whereas the lowest level of data in our database is specific to the particular encoding format and conventions of the collection, these higher-level constructs are progressively more abstract, allowing musical objects to be directly compared even if their source material originates from different corpora, represented with different encodings and even different notations—potentially, even audio representations may be treated similarly. Musical objects are defined in terms of how they behave and what information they contain, rather than by the details of their implementation, in a practice known as Abstract Data Typing, allowing the commonalities between representations to be emphasized and exploited, without undermining the integrity of genuinely different sources and types of information. This allows us to run our algorithms on diverse corpora without modification, whilst at the same time permitting the details (parameters) of how those algorithms are carried out to vary between corpora. This, in turn, permits us to draw inference about how music from different repertoires might be similar or different with respect to analytic features, even if the repertoires stem from completely different technological sources. Apart from the pop music collection which was imported from MIDI files, the database system also hosts other repertoires, including the Essen folksong collection (Schaffrath, 1995), a collection of Chorale melodies from J.S. Bach's cantatas and a set of Canadian folksongs which were all imported from kern** source files.

When we refer to features and feature extraction, we refer to these musical objects. To be more specific, any musical object that we view as being meaningful or useful in itself (as opposed to being an intermediate step towards a useful end) can be described as a

---

[1] "Effectively" because some musical constructions which would be denoted symbolically in a score, such as crescendi and tempo changes, are encoded as parameter changes in the MIDI file.

feature. Examples of features are the sequence of notes in a melodic phrase, a summary of the melodic arch, the prevailing harmony over a period of time, or a formal label.

Our 14,067 songs were selected from the full catalogue of the distributor in such a way as to be as representative as possible of the history of commercial western pop music. Most of the songs were chart-listed or recorded by commercially successful artists. While songs from Anglo-American artists represent about 70% of the corpus, the remaining 30% are distributed primarily across other European countries. Stylistically, the corpus comprises everything from Rock'n'Roll to Soul and Funk classics to modern day HipHop and Ragga. The reason for choosing a corpus of highly commercial pop songs lies in the fact that this musical repertoire can be assumed to be very familiar to the musically untrained Western listeners from which the primary group of participants in the project's experiments will be drawn.

The choice of this specific music corpus corresponds with the hypothesis at the heart of the modelling idea behind M^{4}S. The hypothesis is that cognitive processes like memory encoding and retrieval as well as similarity perception are influenced by the familiarity of the musical material that is to be processed. As it is impossible to determine directly and objectively the familiarity of a particular subject with a musical object/stimulus, a viable approach is to approximate the individual familiarity with the frequency that a musical object has been listened to or, in a further approximation, with its frequency of occurrence in a corpus of music that the subject is highly familiar with. This hypothesis makes M^{4}S also a project about implicit statistical learning of non-verbal material.

Thus, the project has an explicit cognitive focus which distinguishes it from previous research projects that dealt with large music corpora. Perhaps the most ambitious corpus-based musicology project was one based in Princeton University concerned with Josquin scholarship. From 1963 to the beginning of the eighties, researchers, led by Arthur Mendel and Lewis Lockwood, generated electronic scholarly editions of the complete works of Josquin (as defined by the research of the time), many including concordances, and relevant related works. From this, statistics for cadential progressions and modal indicators were compiled and subjected to statistical analysis primarily in order to study issues of authorship and stemmatic filiation (see, for example, Lockwood, 1970 and various papers in *Computers in the Humanities* between 1969 and 1978). The ambitions of this project, though great, never extended to revealing cognitive processes, being limited, essentially, to style analysis.

In folk music research, feature extraction and the use of computers have been employed as a means for the (automatic) classification of songs (mainly melodies) according to their musical characteristics. In a comprehensive study Steinbeck (1982) classified European folk melodies into six homogeneous groups by employing Ward's classification algorithm with 35 relatively simple features derived from the monophonic melodies. He was able to show that this classification was in close correspondence with the melodies' regional origin and functional uses. Although theoretically proposed in his concepts of "Determination" and "Gängigkeit" (prevalence or commonness), Steinbeck did not make any use of the frequencies of occurrence of his features for computing similarities or grouping pieces. Starting from a similar background and music repertoire, Damien Sagrillo (1999) carried out an exploration of frequently employed melodic formulae in folk songs from Luxembourg and Lorraine. Among the outcomes of

Sagrillo's work is the ordering and classification of a catalogue of more than 3,000 melodic phrases and the description and discussion of frequent melodic patterns in this particular folksong repertoire.

In contrast, David Huron in his work from the last two decades (e.g. 1988, 2006) has paid special attention to the frequencies of features over a range of different music corpora. The features Huron has been using can be characterised as mainly simple features derived from monophonic melodies, like interval direction and interval size or melodic phrase contour. As summarised in his latest book (Huron, 2006), he and his collaborators have also tested the relationship between the frequencies of features and cognitive behaviour experimentally. In many instances, Huron was able to show a strong relation between feature frequencies and cognitive expectation and, thus, considers statistical learning as the major mechanism for the creation of knowledge about music. Going one step beyond Huron, M^{4}S tries to better approximate the implicit knowledge that people have about a specific musical style by using a music corpus that should be representative of the experimental participants' musical experience. Secondly, M^{4}S tries to work with richer music representations than the pre-segmented monodies that Huron uses in many of his studies and to employ more complex features which might more accurately reflect the music percepts of untrained listeners. We call these features "higher-level features" and examples are given in the feature section below.

2 Corpus-based musicology

The ideas behind the concept of *corpus-based musicology* are not entirely new, and have been explored by some of the projects briefly discussed above (Lockwood, 1970; Steinbeck, 1982; Sagrillo, 1999; Huron, 2006). Corpus-based musicology might be regarded as one concrete instantiation of empirical musicology as envisioned by the contributors of the popular volume by the same name (Clarke & Cook, 2004). Nonetheless, by introducing the novel term *corpus-based musicology*, we would like to emphasize the motivations that drive the musicological aspects of the M^{4}S project. They can be summarized as follows:

1. Analytical observations about a musical object as they are made by automatic feature extraction or human analysis are only really meaningful in context of a music corpus. When experienced music analysts observe peculiarities about a musical object a reference corpus serves always as the basis for comparison—though it might not be explicitly named. Indeed, the reason why analytic works by experts in their respective fields are generally preferred is that they have a wealth of knowledge about a particular musical style at their disposal; one may think of Charles Rosen's Classical Style (1976) or Allan Moore's (1997) monograph on Sgt. Pepper's Lonely Hearts Club Band, for example. When we trust the computer to analyse music and to extract and compare feature value then we have to make a conscious effort to introduce the context of a music corpus in which feature comparison is meaningful.

2. Using a computer for music-analytic purposes forces a researcher to define very precisely what are the analytic markers, features and structures that she or he wants to observe. For example, it might seem perfectly clear to every knowledgeable analyst what a melodic phrase is, but if we attempt to design an

algorithm that is supposed to indicate phrase boundaries for every unsegmented stream of notes in a corpus of songs, the definition of a melodic phrase becomes a surprisingly hard problem. One has to know in advance what melodic phenomena might occur in the corpus and how they are expressed in the music data representation. Decisions must then be made about how to treat certain classes of phenomena in terms of the desired outcome (i.e. to assign a number of boundaries in reasonable locations for each monophonic melody). In designing these algorithms, the researcher creates his/her own tools for observation and it is necessary that the tools are designed with respect to the peculiarities of the music corpus. To give a simple example: one could think of a phrase segmentation algorithm that uses a completely different set of criteria and procedures according to whether it is employed for the segmentation of vocal tunes from popular music or repetitive bass lines from 1970s funk pieces. To summarise: knowledge of a reference corpus necessarily informs the choice and design of the analytical tools that are used to explore it. This circular relationship between theory, tools, and data is only rarely fully acknowledged when feature extraction and analysis algorithms are made available (e.g. the MIDI tool box, Eerola & Toiviainen, 2004, or Cory McKay's jSymbolic feature extractor, McKay, 2006).

3. One of the main motivations and potentially most useful outcomes that can arise from corpus-based analysis is the *quantification* of musical structures in a music corpus. Knowledge about the frequency of occurrence of musical objects or their combinations can not only serve as a backbone in models of music cognition but might also be very valuable for the design of music information retrieval systems for that corpus. In addition, information about the frequency of musical structures in combination with meta-data e.g. about the time and geographical origin of the musical works, their genre categories or their popularity in specific eras creates a new perspective on music analysis: quantitative information about musical structures can then be associated with categories of styles and popularity. The analysis of the usage of melodic and harmonic formulae over different times and styles that Allan Moore did paradigmatically for the "doo-wop progression" (Moore, 2006) could be extended with the help of the computer for all significant harmonic formulae as well as for melodic and rhythmic patterns that are frequently used in a similar fashion. This could make an important contribution to the study of evolution of musical style, at least in many areas of popular music.

Such an approach can offer two advantages. Firstly, it can facilitate the discussion of common factors and trends within a corpus. Secondly, it can reveal aspects of a work or group of works that appear unusual with respect to the reference corpus. Such investigations can be carried out in a manner that is quantifiable and whose confidence of prediction can, to some extent at least, be evaluated both in terms of the accuracy of its summary, but also in terms of the quality of coverage of the music under discussion the encoded corpus offers. Not only can we quote the accuracy with which our algorithms model observed human behaviour, but we can also observe the amount of data we have for a given area of the corpus, noting, for example, that our observation of trends in Latin-American music may be less reliable than those for classic rock music on the grounds, say, that the proportion of released recordings of the former that are

138

represented in our collection is smaller than that of the latter. The metrics used are less important than the fact that we can begin to make real, meaningful estimates of our uncertainties.

It is important to bear in mind, however, that the evaluation of musical relationships is not a task amenable to automation. The quantification discussed above is a statistical one and, whilst its usefulness will be greater as more information is provided to the system, it is cognitive experiment and musicological reasoning that must prove the final arbiter of the system's performance. Furthermore, such an approach can only offer limited assistance to those wishing to perform detailed analyses of single works—which is the standard paradigm in traditional music analysis. If we follow de la Motte's (1990, p. 8) tri-partition of the tasks of musical analysis for a single musical piece into a) identification of details (which we call features here), b) explanation of how details function as part of a whole and c) choosing a good perspective for presenting a convincing analysis, then corpus-based and computer-assisted musicology can only provide support for the first two tasks. Even identification of features is only possible automatically if each feature, or its components, are known to the system. Although Artificial Intelligence methods can lead to the identification of novel features, many musical features only make sense after the combination of a large number of smaller elements, with intermediate combinations having no meaning, and this makes algorithmic discovery difficult. Appropriate analysis algorithms can basically identify and count features and, by reference to frequency counts in a reference corpus, it is furthermore possible to determine whether the particular combination of features in a given piece is common, relatively infrequent or something in between. But the evaluation of what an infrequent combination of features means in cultural and aesthetic terms is still entirely up to the researcher that makes use of a corpus-based analysis system. In the context of the M^4S pop music database, an infrequent combination of features in a given piece can arise from, for example, compositional incompetence where the composer was unable to stay within the boundaries of a particular style, or it can arise from a masterpiece where a composer extended the boundaries of that style to achieve a special aesthetic effect. And of course, an infrequent combination of features can also indicate gross errors in transcription or MIDI encoding. It is important to remember that the interpretation of the (corpus-based) analysis remains the duty and the responsibility of the researcher and cannot be loaded onto the methodology.

The introduction of the term corpus-based musicology is also a deliberate link to the research paradigm of corpus-based linguistics which has seen a tremendous boom in recent times with fast-growing number of electronic text libraries and, of course, the internet as a virtually infinite source of digitally encoded texts. While there are many clear commonalities and differences between the methodologies of statistical natural language processing and statistical music analysis, we would like to mention here only a few of the obvious parallels between the two corpus-based approaches (see, e.g., the introductory chapter of Manning & Schütze, 1999, for the main ideas of the statistical approach in natural language processing). While grammaticality has been a central and binary category for analysing and describing linguistic units such as sentences for a long time it has become apparent in the last decades that the grammaticality of sentences is rather an attribute on a continuous scale which ranges from indisputably wrong to indubitably correct. The continuous nature of the attribute arises from the impact that usage frequencies of linguistic structures have upon human language processing. Language grammars try to fix a set of rules from which grammatical sentences can be derived. But it is easy to come up with examples of both grammatically correct but meaningless sentences or grammatically correct sentences where the correctness is very hard too judge and that are potentially ambiguous and hard to understand. In music, strict obedience to rules of music theory is also not a property through which a piece of music would be described as "wrong" or "right" in modern musicology. The notion that a music style or genre is better characterised by frequent structures, formulae, and note transitions is generally recognised as being more viable than compliance to music theoretic rules.

As musical styles and genres, especially in popular music, change much more quickly than the usage of linguistic structures in natural language, it is generally acknowledged that musical rules-of-thumb and frequent formulae change over time and that this change normally happens gradually. Analogously, the process of change in the usage of linguistic structures, although it generally happens much more slowly, is an established fact. Therefore, it is advisable to choose a corpus with elements (text documents or music pieces respectively) that were created within a limited time-span in which the change in frequency of linguistic or musical structures is negligible or where it can be controlled, e.g. by filtering according to meta-data.

Several of the major goals of linguistic and musical corpus-based analysis overlap to a large degree. This includes the detection of regularities or probabilistic grammars in a corpus, the retrieval of items from a corpus according to a query or search parameters, the grouping and ordering of items within a corpus according to similarity, and last but not least the inference about human cognition in the particular domain.

Finally it is worth mentioning that the statistic tools from corpus-based linguistics have been adopted quite successfully for music analysis in recent years (e.g. Downie, 1999; Conklin & Witten, 1995; Pearce & Wiggins, 2006; Potter, Pearce & Wiggins, 2007). While the basic elements and features (or tokens) over which statistics are computed naturally differ between linguistics and musicology, the statistical concepts that allow us to infer regularities within the specific domain are quite similar or nearly identical. Among the chief statistical concepts that can be derived from frequency counts of tokens/features, and that are employed in both fields, are Markov models, entropy and mutual information, association measures, unsupervised clustering techniques, and supervised classifiers such as decision trees.

3 High level feature descriptors

3.1 Introduction

As those researchers dealing with music information retrieval from audio recordings are made very aware, the music we hear, remember and describe is very hard to discover in the sound itself. Even fundamental concepts such as 'pitch' and 'note' clearly simplify and summarise a complex reality, whether that summary takes place in the ear or in the brain or some combination of the two. These apparently quite basic concepts can then be progressively combined and summarised into other more elaborate constructions, such as interval, melody, sequence, harmony, metre or form. We call all such musically-relevant constructions *musical objects* that can be described by and possibly computed from a set of features.

For our purposes, notes, and their attributes of pitch and rhythm are taken as basic or *atomic*, not because we believe them always to be so, but because in symbolic music, they are not explicitly dependant on any simpler elements, being provided by the representation itself. As we have indicated above, were we using recordings, or, for that matter, graphical scores, this might not be the case. In traditional computer-science style, we describe musical objects that are basic in the above sense as 'low level'. 'High-level' musical objects, then are those that are derived from combination of or deduction from other musical objects.

For conceptual clarity as well as for practical implementation reasons, it is helpful to distinguish between features that summarise emergent features of musical objects, such as a harmonic label, and those that model transformations of a sequence of basic musical events/concepts (i.e. notes) or musical objects. In the former case, the input to a feature computation procedure is a set of musical objects at a given structural level, and the feature, computed as output, is a more abstract set of information. By contrast, in the latter case, the feature is a one-to-one mapping between its input elements and its output elements, in sequence. Examples for these transformational features include accent strength values or entropy values for all notes in a melody notes. The distinction between these two types of features, i.e. summary and transformational features, is useful when correlations or associations between different features are computed and probability distributions of feature combinations are of interest (see description of music corpora as joint probability distributions, above). The toolbox for melodic feature computation, MELFEATURE, designed by Klaus Frieler and Daniel Müllensiefen is implemented to run in two modes, one of which transforms note events of a melody whereas the other one summarises them (Frieler, 2007).

Within the context of M^4S, we focus on some features that we expect to be relevant in connection with the cognitive processing of melodies. The following list contains the summarising features that will play a role in the project along with references to work from the M^4S environment:

- Melodic contour: see below for an in-depth discussion of this feature (Frieler et al., in press)
- Phrase segmentation: Segment a stream of melodic notes into meaningful 'chunks' or phrases (Müllensiefen et al., 2007)
- Harmonic labeling: Summarise the harmonic movement of a time window from a polyphonic piece of music by one or several chord labels in sequence (Rhodes et al., 2007).
- Rhythm classification: Describe the rhythm of a melodic sequence by classifying it into one of a few rhythm classes or by positioning it in a multi-dimensional perceptual rhythm space (Allan et al., 2007)
- Instrumentation/arrangement: Characterise the density and the type of instrumental ensemble playing over a region of a polyphonic music segment (Allan et al., 2007)

Among the transformational features to play a crucial role are:

141

- Accent structure: Determine the perceptual (accentual) strength of notes of a melody (Pfleiderer & Müllensiefen, 2006).
- Expectedness/Entropy/Information content: Determine the information content/ expectedness of each note in a melody (Pearce & Wiggins, 2006).

The literature contains several different versions of each of these features, which differ considerably with respect to how a feature is computed from symbolic music data and what feature value is assigned for a given musical object; the discussion of melodic contour as a feature, below, serves as just one example here. Our approach to the selection and/or construction of features is to implement various alternative and possibly competing versions of the same feature and test, in reliable music-psychological experiments, which versions of a feature best approximate those used by listeners when they cognitively process melodic content. A similar approach has been used successfully by Müllensiefen and Frieler (2004, 2007) for the comparative evaluation of melodic similarity measures.

In addition to the difficulty of choosing from a variety of versions of a particular feature, there are several dangers involved in building a feature model of music pieces in a corpus using high-level features. Since each high-level feature depends on those lower in the feature chain, the reliability of each is compromised by errors in other algorithms. Errors may be compounded to result in increasing inaccuracies, and natural ambiguities, which characterise many musical features, can be lost in the complexity. As an example one can think of melodic phrase contour as a high-level feature which depends on the extraction of a melodic line (i.e. the tune) from a polyphonic piece and subsequently on the segmentation of the notes of the melodic line into melodic phrases. By the time we use these incorrectly-segmented, inaccurately-extracted melodies to find melodic contours, the results may bear no relationship at all to the answers that a listener might produce – in fact they may well appear random. Errors on lower levels can easily propagate onto higher feature levels and may introduce noise in a resulting feature data set.

By comparing multiple algorithms (and parameter choices for each of them) with experimental data, we aim to minimise this sort of error accumulation. Furthermore, the data from the perceptual experiments can help to inform an assessment of the ambiguities in a given task (or even different schools of response to it) and enable an appropriate response.

3.2 Example: Melodic Contour

Melodic contour has a long history as being regarded as one of the most important features in the context of modelling music perception and melodic memory. The contour of a melody is believed to be abstracted early in the listening process and to remain a stable and reliable representation especially for novel melodies. On a very general level contour is conceptualised by most researchers as the pattern of up and down movements of a melody in pitch space over time (see below for several different realisations of this basic concept). Numerous psychological studies in the past have found contour to be a decisive mental representation of melodies or short melodic phrases which memory is based primarily upon, particularly after short retention intervals and for novel or non-standard melodies (for a full discussion of the importance of melodic contour for memory see Müllensiefen, 2004. The long list of melody contour studies includes Dowling & Fujitani (1971), Dowling (1978), Edworthy (1985), and Cutietta & Booth (1996).

Dowling (1978) proposes that the mechanism through which contour works as an effective memory representation can be summarised very briefly and superficially as follows. During listening the up and down movement of the melodic line (=contour) is recorded in memory. Encoding and retaining up and down movements requires the processing of much less information than, say, the retention of the exact size and direction of the melodic intervals and is, therefore, more efficient. At the same time the scale of the melody is abstracted as well. Then, to reconstruct the melody from memory, experimental participants seem to align the retained contour movements to scale degrees from the retained scale and thereby reconstruct melodic intervals. Dowling's scale and contour theory of melodic memory is widely cited throughout the literature and has been vastly influential. But regardless of whether melodic contour is used in exactly the way described here, experimental evidence suggests that contour is a very efficient memory representation.

In the greater part of the psychological literature, melodic contour is defined in a way that allows for a construction of experimental stimuli. Contour is often contrasted with the concept of melodic interval. The former is generally believed to encode only the direction of a melodic interval, or the direction and a gross indication of interval size (e.g. unison, step, skip). While this realisation might be sufficient to separate artificial experimental items in terms of factors in an ANOVA design, it is unsatisfactory from a music-analytical standpoint, and, indeed, musicologists have proposed a number different realisations of contour for analysing existing melodies. Without going into too much detail, we briefly outline five different realisations of contour from the literature that can be regarded as competing with regard to which representation listeners actually use when cognitively processing novel melodies.[2]

Huron Contour

David Huron (1996) proposed a representation of contour based on the pitch height of the first and last notes of a melodic phrase as well as the average pitch of all notes in between. Huron describes phrase contour by the relation the average[3] and the last note, respectively, has with its predecessor. The value of this relation is ordinal which means e.g. that the average note can be higher, lower or equal to the first note but no information about the amount that it is higher than its predecessor is encoded. From the combination of these two free parameters describing relative pitch height on an ordinal level, Huron defines creates distinct contour classes to which any melodic phrase can be assigned. Figure 1 depicts Huron's nine resulting contour classes.

---

[2] The names of the different contour realisations are used not as such in the literature but are assigned here by the authors to facilitate discussion.
[3] The average note is, of course, only an abstract note

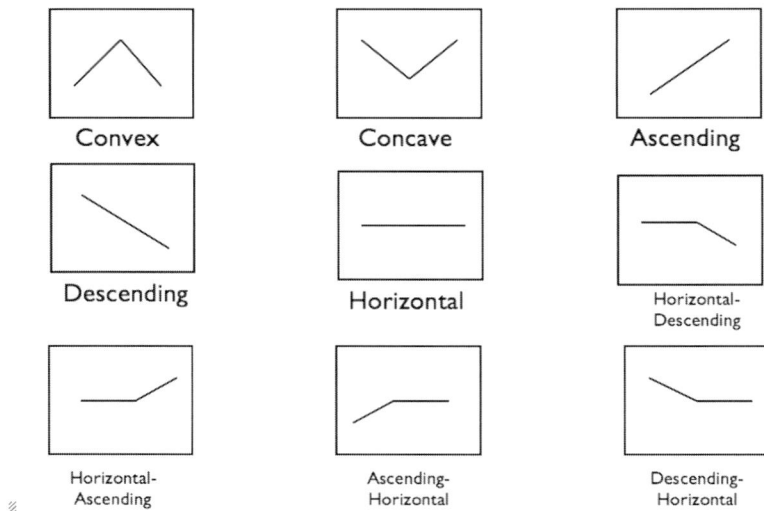

Figure 1: The nine classes of melodic phrase contour according to Huron (1996, p. 8).

The conceptual advantages of Huron's contour model are its computational simplicity and the restriction of the outcome to just nine classes or two free relation parameters. On the other hand, assigning all possible melodic phrases to one of nine contours may be too simple for a describing the cognitive representation of listeners especially if they have a stronger musical background. Another conceptual disadvantage arises from the inclusion of the contour classes which contain a horizontal relationship as one of the free parameters. These classes might have been included in the scheme primarily for the sake of combinatorial completeness but for a lot of melodic phrases found in existing music they might not reflect what was conceptually intended. Imagine the melodic phrase in Figure 2. The starting pitch is C_5 (=72 in MIDI pitch encoding), the last pitch is G_4 (=67) and the average of the intervening notes is $(76+74+66)/3 = 72$.

Figure 2: Example phrase leading to an assignment of a 'horizontal-descending' Huron contour.

This phrase would be classified as horizontal-descending according to Huron's scheme but it is not impossible to imagine that perceptions might tend rather towards a descending contour shape. It is easy to find similar examples where the inclusion of Huron's hyphenated contour shapes lead to counter-intuitive contour assignments. In fact, it may be more appropriate to define the few musical instances where these hyphenated classes actually do make sense. These instances would for example include a repetition of notes or a trill with a low ending note for the horizontal-descending class.

But for the remainder of this paper we will refer to the original formulation of the Huron contour classes, leaving any modifications or amendments to a future paper.

Extended Huron contour

Huron (1996) also suggests an extension of his nine classes to include 'M' and 'W' shapes. These shapes would be constructed analogously to the contour classes explained above but would comprise 4 free parameters describing ordinal relations instead of 2. Depending on how boundaries of melodic phrases are set in a music corpus—for his explorations of contour frequencies Huron relies mainly on the expert-marked phrase indications in the Essen folk song database—and how many notes a phrase comprises on average, either the extended Huron contour can be constructed as concatenation of two phrase contours or a decision has to be made where to position a middle note which represents the end of the first half and the beginning of the second. This could be either a note near the temporal middle of the phrase, a relatively long note in a middle region, or a contour turning point in a middle region, e.g. selected in such a way that the length of the melodic movement on both sides of the turning point is maximized.

Exploiting all possible combinations of the four 3-valued parameters would result in $3^4=81$ possible contour shapes. Even if part of these shapes can be thought of being equivalent (e.g. rising-rising = rising), there still seem to be far too many to be used cognitively efficiently, but one could propose solutions where several similar shapes are mapped onto the same category/class.

Interpolation contour

The idea behind interpolation contour is that melodic turning points are important and salient points in a melody and that notes in-between these turning points can be summarised by a line. The concept of summarising a general melodic movement by a line has been around in music analysis for a long time and was popularised e.g. by Heinrich Schenker's (for examples see Schenker, 1932), *Urlinie*. Wolfram Steinbeck (1982) was one of the first to adapt to the concept for the computer analysis of melodies. An example from his book of how an interpolated line is drawn is given in Figure 3. The beginning of the first note and the end of every contour turning point, as well as the end of the last note, are connected by straight lines in a two-dimensional time-pitch space. A melodic phrase is then characterised by a list of two vectors reflecting the length and the gradient of the interpolation lines. The number of free parameters for this interpolation line contour model is then *2(t+1)* with *t* being the number of melodic turning points and the values of the vector elements represent melodic contour on an interval level. This contour representation depends crucially on the method for identifying the melodic turning points in a phrase and differences have been found in a study of melodic similarity where two different realisations of interpolation line contour control for trivial change notes in a different way (see Müllensiefen & Frieler, 2004). Another conceptual difficulty is the variable length of the two vectors which is a function of the number of turning points found in the melodic phrase. This variable length makes comparisons between melodic phrases, that rely on the computation on correlation or difference coefficients of the two vectors, difficult. Zhou and Kankahalli (2003) use a very similar contour representation for a modern query-by-humming system by drawing straight lines ("slopes") between "peaks and valleys" of melodies and then working with the "pitch ranges" and "duration values" of the slopes. This is essentially and equivalent to using the gradient and length of the interpolation lines proposed by Steinbeck (1982) but Zhou and Kankanhalli employ a different terminology and apply this contour concept to a popular task from music information retrieval.

Instead of summarising melody notes by interpolation with a straight line, a curve can also be fitted to the melody notes to be summarised. Fitting a polynomial curve to the notes of a melody was originally proposed by Steinbeck (1982) as well, but due to the lack of computational resources not realised at that time. Frieler et al. (in press) took up that approach and fitted 2nd and 4th order polynomials to 989 melodic phrases taken from commercial pop songs from 1990-2005. Once the order of the polynomial is chosen, the polynomial coefficients can be regarded as a representation of the melodic contour. A comparison of contours of different phrases like in the clustering of polynomials coefficients that Frieler et al. carried out is possible. Using unsupervised model-based clustering via the expectation-maximisation algorithm (see Frayley & Raftery, 1998, for model-based clustering) Frieler et al. found four clusters derived from 2nd order polynomials that were comparably close to a subset of the contour classes proposed by Huron (1996) as Figure 3 shows.

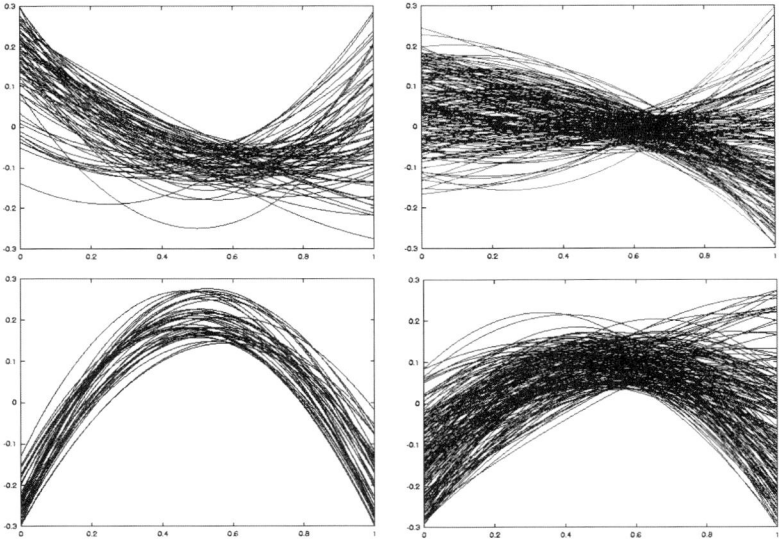

Figure 3: Clusters of interpolation curve contours as found by Frieler et al. (in press). Clockwise from top left: Cluster 1 (concave-descending); Cluster 2 (Mixture); Cluster 3 (Small arch); Cluster 4 (Big arch)

Just as for interpolation line contour, for polynomial curve interpolation contour, the free parameters represent contour on an interval level. But unlike the vectors of length and gradient resulting from the interpolation lines, the set of coefficients of the interpolation polynomial curves is limited to $o+1$ where o designates the order or the polynomials. So the researcher is free (or rather obliged) to choose the level of observational details for a given research question which might depend on the question to be answered and the musical repertoire at hand. While selecting, too high an order might overfit the melodic phrases and introduce noise into the data, the choice of too low an order might obscure important differences between phrases. In any case, post-processing procedures like principal component analysis might be helpful in reduce reducing noise in the data. Generally, the curve fitting approach to obtaining representations of melodic contour offers a vast set of possibilities which is currently completely unexplored and which includes potentially fitting b-splines, wavelets or procedures using other basis functions to the numerical values of the notes of a melody.

Step curve contour

Representing a melodic contour by a step curve contour can as well be depicted by a graph in time-pitch space where the height of the steps corresponds to pitch height, the beginning corresponds to onset times and length corresponds to the inter-onset interval between two successive notes. The information in this graph can be expressed as a list of two vectors containing length and relative pitch height of all notes in the phrase. This is the richest (= least abstract) contour representation and the only one that allows full reconstruction of the melodic phrase. 2n free parameters are necessary for this representation, where n is the number of notes. Instead of using this compact representation, it is more practical in certain application to sample from pitch values from a step curve at regular intervals (Juhász, 2000; Eerola and Toiviainen. 2004). When melodies are normalised in time, vector correlation and difference measures work straightforwardly for any pair of melodies, as vectors built from sampling necessarily have the same length. Figure 4 shows sample points taken at a sample rate of 4/beat from a step curve contour as presented by Eerola and Toiviainen (2004).

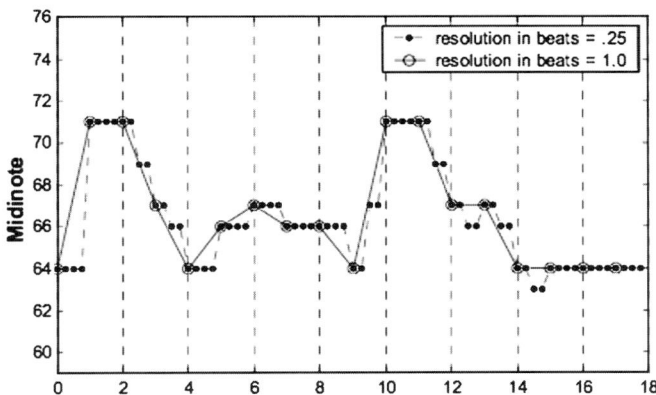

Figure 4: Sampling of melodic contour according to the step curve contour representation. Taken from Eerola & Toiviainen (2004).

The point of our rather detailed discussion of different versions of melodic contour was to show how diverse the formulations and computations of contour in the literature are. With a number of different contour definitions the question for the 'best' contour model or, in our context, rather the model that is cognitively most adequate (i.e. comes closest to the mental contour representation that listeners employ for cognising melodies) becomes very apparent. The way to deal with various competing versions or realisations of a feature within the framework of M^4S is to test it in a rigorous experimental paradigm and with participants from a population which should be as close as possible to the phenomenon to be modelled in the end, i.e. memory for melodies of people with no special music training. As we are unaware of any existing comparative study of different contour definitions, an experiment is current within M^4S which should give indications about which versions of contour are appropriate in the research context of the project. The basic paradigm is a cross-model recognition paradigm where a melody item is presented aurally and should subsequently be identified on a list of visually presented contour shapes. This paradigm exploits the fact that, even for untrained participants, the analogy between auditory movement in pitch space and visual movement on a vertical axis is easily understood and that the fact that all these versions of contour lend themselves naturally to interpretation as visual shapes. The experiment is due to be carried out in early 2008 and its results will be reported in due course.

4 Results

We present in this section some preliminary findings that show several different ways in which the corpus-based approach can generate interesting results. The four types of results presented fall into the categories a) comparison of feature distributions between music corpora, b) identification of generic patterns within a corpus, and c) the identification of specific, non-generic patterns in a corpus. As the M^4S project is an ongoing research enterprise, we will have to spare the application of corpus-based musical information for modelling human music cognition for a later publication.

Comparison of feature distributions between music corpora

If a feature is considered to correspond to a cognitive important entity in the process of music production or perception than comparing the distributions between two corpora can reveal something about why two music styles/corpora are perceived to be different and how large the difference is in quantitative terms.

We chose here melody contour as a feature which is believed to be of certain importance for music production and perception (see discussion above), and we choose Huron contour as an realisation of contour. This is not to mean that we believe Huron contour to be superior to the other contour realisations presented above. As said before the results of the comparative study on the cognitive validity of contour representations are still pending. But Huron contour has the advantage that the computation of the contour classes is relatively easy to understand and that empirical investigations have used this contour feature before (e.g. Huron, 1996).

We counted the frequencies of the nine contour classes for the melodic phrases in the European tunes from Essen folk song database and in the M^4S pop song database. The 5,739 folk songs contained a total of 33,504 melodic phrases. Phrase boundaries are marked up in the Essen collection and were originally generated by the individual transcriber or encoder of the song in question. Phrase boundaries might have been inserted according to the music-analytical understanding of the transcriber/encoder in most instances, but phrase segmentation might have also been carried out according to indications of the song's lyrics in other instances. As no phrase segmentation is provided in the original data of the M^4S boundaries, we used the SimpleSegmenter (Müllensiefen & Frieler, 2004) procedure to identify melodic boundaries which in turn provided us with 444,107 melodic phrases from the 14,067 pop songs. The results of the frequency counts are summarised in table 2 and contrasted with frequency counts over 33,504 melody phrases from the Essen folk song collection.

Contour class	Essen folk songs (%, n=33,504)	M4S pop songs (%, n=442,107)
Convex	33.66	23.99
Concave	7.37	11.55
Descending	24.87	16.29
Ascending	16.54	22.85
Horizontal	2.2	5.65
Horizontal-Descending	6.01	5.18
Horizontal-Ascending	1.95	3.53
Descending-Horizontal	2.64	3.7
Ascending-Horizontal	4.76	7.27

The main claim originally made by Huron (1996) on the basis of melodic phrase data from the Essen collection, can obviously be maintained when we look at the M^4S pop songs[4]: the melodic arch (i.e. a convex phrase contour) is the dominant model for the melodic movement on phrase level, although the difference in frequency between convex and other contour classes is much less pronounced in pop melodies than for the folk song phrases. This is also corroborated by the high frequency of the two ascending-horizontal and horizontal-descending contours which would form together an arch shape. An interesting difference between the two frequency distributions concerns the prevalence of descending vs. ascending phrases. While we count clearly more descending than ascending phrases in the folk song collection the reverse is true for the pop songs corpus. Also, the horizontal phrases and the partially horizontal contours account for a much larger percentage in the pop song corpus. However, we must be cautious at this stage about basing musicological interpretations on these numbers as we will have to investigate the role of the phrase segmenting algorithm onto subsequent

---

[4] There are minor differences between our count of the contour classes in the Essen corpus and the number that Huron published (1996) which are due to the fact that we only included European folk songs in our corpus, and that we rounded the average pitch to the nearest semitone. Huron did not round his averages but reasons in a recent personal email communication that "of course, rounding [the average pitch] "makes perfect sense".

contour determinations. Preliminary results from a comparative study on different phrase segmentation models show large differences between different approaches and a suboptimal performance of SimpleSegmenter (Müllensiefen et al., 2007).

Identification of generic patterns

The identification of generic or overly frequent patterns in a corpus can serve two purposes: Firstly, to find the basic building blocks from which longer and more complex musical objects are made from, or phrasing it more poetically, to establish the alphabet that the music of a particular style is written in. Secondly, only once it is know what the generic patterns of a particular corpus are, one is able to judge what a significant or original pattern within the context of a corpus is. We will exemplify this briefly by giving examples from the harmonic and melodic sequences of the M^{4}S pop database.

   Using the chord labelling algorithm based on Bayesian model selection proposed by Rhodes et al. (2007) we assigned chord labels to all bars of all the 14,067 pieces that had pitched instruments playing. For the current purpose we ignored information about functional bass notes and chord extensions and counted sequences of differing of chord modes (major/minor) and intervals between subsequent chord roots. A preliminary evaluation of the frequency table of harmonic sequences gave the following results:

   – 52% of all chord sequences of a maximal length of five subsequent chords are combinations of major chords that are 5, 7 and 2 semitones away from each other, or expressed in terms of a Roman Numeral analysis, we found mostly chord sequences chords in the pop music database that are combinations of I, IV, and V chords.
   – A very frequent group of chord sequences can be summarised as combinations I, vi, IV, and V chords. The sequences from this group cover 5% of all sequences in the database and appear at least once in 16% of all 14,067 songs. For the particular sequence of this group where the chords appear in the order given above, several researchers have proposed names like the "doo-wop progression" (Moore, 2006) or the turn-around formula (Kramarz, 2006).
   – Very frequently we also find alternations between I and vi or I and ii chords in our pop song database, each which makes for approximately 3.5% of all chord sequences.

It is difficult to draw a definite line between what can be regarded as generic harmonic patterns and what makes an original harmonic progression but the huge difference in frequency is certainly useful for distinguishing between the two.

   For melodic generic patterns we have a very similar picture with the most frequent patterns covering a large percentage of all melodic sequences in the database. For a preliminary evaluation we used only the melodic lines encoded on MIDI channel 4 of the original files which, by a convention used by our MIDI-file provider, contains the main vocal line. We ensured that the main melodic line of each song be a pure monody by an algorithm which adjusts note onset and note end times to avoid small overlaps and, where there are segments of true polyphony, favours louder, higher notes as the main voice. For all monodic lines in the corpus interval sequences of different lengths are counted. Among the most frequent sequences with a length of four intervals (five notes), while ignoring all temporal information, are:

Note repetitions (frequency rank #1)

Combinations of note repetitions and seconds, e.g. rising major second on third and falling major second down on the fourth interval (frequency rank #5)

The first interval sequence with a range of more than a major third appears at frequency rank number 35 and is the descending major scale.

Again it is difficult to define what a generic melodic pattern is but the three very frequent interval patterns we just presented can surely be regarded as the basic building blocks from which pop melodies are made.

Identification of relevant patterns in a corpus

In contrast to the generic patterns just discussed finding special or relevant patterns in a corpus appears to be a much more interesting retrieval task and can be potentially important for various goals, including the detection of cover songs and copyright infringements or for tracing citations and explicit musical references. Again, we have to limit ourselves here to a few examples.

The song *Brown girl in the ring* was at the core of a law suit that spanned almost 25 years in German courts (Pendzich, 2004, p.226). If we represent the six beginning notes of the melody as a sequence of tuples of pitch intervals and duration ratios ((0,1) (0,.75) (-2,.3) (-2,4) (+4,.75)) and query the M^{4}S database with this sequence we find 26 different songs where this melodic sequence is used. We would like to highlight the comparatively low number of occurrences of this melodic sequence, even though it is a very short and very simple sequence in musical terms. Among the songs that incorporate this melodic sequence are, apart from Boney M's famous version, Rick Astley's *Together forever*, The Beatles' *Maxwell's silver hammer*, and Bon Jovi's *In these arms*. It would be an interesting musicological task to evaluate the significance of this melodic sequence in the respective songs and to investigate whether and where there are any connections between the usage of this formula in Boney M's version or the original Jamaican children's rhyme and occurrence in the other 25 songs.

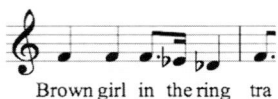
Brown girl in the ring tra

We carried out an analogous search for the opening harmonic sequence from *Yesterday* by The Beatles which was represented as sequence of chord modes and intervals between subsequent chord roots. In Roman Numerals this sequence can be written as I vii III vi IV. We found only 14 out of 14,067 songs that contained this harmonic sequence. The result set from the database query included apart from the Beatles song and one cover version *Make me smile* by Chicago and *Sara* by Jefferson Starship. Again, note that the number of occurrences of this harmonic sequence is by magnitudes lower compared to the doo-wop progression which we found in more than 2200 songs. Interestingly enough, Mauch et al. (2007) report a much stronger prevalence of this sequence in a corpus of Jazz pieces from the Real Book. Again, with the support of these quantitative findings an interesting socio-cultural explanation might connect the success of that chord sequence to the Beatles' interest in Jazz harmony at a certain time.

5 Summary and conclusion

The aim of this contribution has been to present a modern approach towards modelling human music cognition. This methodology is employed in the current M^4S project on melody cognition and memory processing for melodies. The main frameworks that support this approach are the automatic extraction of cognitively relevant features from symbolically encoded music and the statistical analysis of a large music corpus which is annotated in terms of the relevant features. The idea is to model the implicit knowledge of western pop music listeners by the proxy of a statistical description of the music corpus that the listeners build their listening experience on. The assumption is that using information about the prevalence of musical features in real music within the modelling framework is substantially better than merely applying musical features to relate music data to behavioural data as if a long enculturation in a musical culture had never happened or was irrelevant.

As the M^4S project is a still ongoing research work, we have not presented any results from the memory experiments that are due towards the end of the project to support our claims about the usefulness in cognitive modelling. Instead, we have focused on exemplifying the methodology by discussing in depth the feature of melodic contour and by outlining the concept of corpus-based musicology. Although grounded here in music cognition research, corpus-based musicology has potential as a very fruitful approach for a range of areas in music research. We provide a few examples of the type of results a corpus-based approach can generate, although, the true potential of this approach will only become apparent over time as researchers increasingly inform their methods with empirical and quantified knowledge about the corpus of music they are studying.

References

Allan, H., Müllensiefen, D., & Wiggins, G. (2007). Methodological considerations in studies of musical similarity. In *Proceedings of the 8th International Conference on Music Information Retrieval* (pp. 473–478).

Brook, B. (1970). The plaine and easie code. In B. Brook (Ed.), *Musicology and the computer: Three Symposia.* New York.

Clarke, E. & Cook, N. (Eds.). (2004). *Empirical Musicology: Aims, Methods, Prospects.* Oxford: Oxford University Press.

Conklin, D. & Witten, I. (1995). Multiple viewpoint systems for music prediction. *Journal of New Music Research, 24*(1), 51–73.

Cutietta, R. A. & Booth, G. D. (1996). The influence of metre, mode, interval type und contour in repeated melodic free-recall. *Psychology of Music, 18*, 45–59.

de la Motte, D. (1990). *Musikalische Analyse* (6. ed.). Bärenreiter.

Dowling, W. J. (1978). Scale and contour: Two components of a theory of memory for melodies. *Psychological Review, 85*(4), 341–354.

Dowling, W. J. & Fujitani, D. S. (1971). Contour, interval, and pitch recognition in memory for melodies. *The Journal of the Acoustical Society of America, 49*(2, Part 2), 524–531.

Downie, J. S. (2003). *Evaluating a simple approach to music information retrieval. Evaluating a simple approach to music information retrieval. Conceiving melodic n-grams as text.* Doctoral dissertation, Faculty of Information and Media Studies, University of Western Ontario, London (Ontario), Canada. Available from http://people.lis.uiuc.edu/~jdownie/mir_papers/thesis_missing_some_music_figs.pdf

Edworthy, J. (1985). Interval and contour in melody processing. *Music Perception, 2*(3), 375–388.

Eerola, T. & Toiviainen, P. (2004). Mir in matlab: The midi toolbox. In *Proceedings of the 5th International Conference on Music Information Retrieval.* Available from http://ismir2004.ismir.net/ proceedings/p004-page-22-paper193.pdf

Fraley, C. & Raftery, A. (1998). How many clusters? which clustering method? - answers via model-based cluster analysis. *Computer Journal, 41*, 578–588.

Frieler, K. (2007). Melodic feature machines: Melfeature & melex. Presentation held at Symposium on MIR, University of Utrecht. Available from http://www.cs.uu.nl/research/projects/witchcraft/mir2007/frieler.pdf

Frieler, K., Müllensiefen, D., & Riedemann, F. (in press). *Statistical search for melodic prototypes.* Staatliches Institut für Musikforschung.

Hewlett, W. B. (1997). Musedata: Multipurpose representation. In E. Selfridge-Field (Ed.), *Beyond MIDI: The handbook of musical codes* chapter 27, (pp. 402–447). Cambridge, MA: MIT Press.

Huron, D. The new empiricism: Systematic musicology in a postmodern age. lecture 3 from the 1999 Ernest Bloch lectures. Available from http://musiccog.ohio-state.edu/Music220/Bloch.lectures/3.Methodology.html

Huron, D. (1988). Error categories, detection, and reduction in a musical database. *Computers and the Humanities, 22*, 253–264.

Huron, D. (1995). *The Humdrum Toolkit: Reference Manual*. Menlo Park, California: Center for Computer Assisted Research in the Humanities.

Huron, D. (2006). *Sweet Anticipation: Music and the Psychology of Expectation*. Cambridge, MA: MIT Press.

International MIDI Association (1988). *Standard MIDI Files 1.0*. Los Angeles: International MIDI Association.

Juhász, Z. (2000). A model of variation in the music of a hungarian ethnic group. *Journal of New Music Research, 29*(2), 159–172.

Karbusicky, V. (1979). *Systematische Musikwissenschaft*. Fink.

Karbusicky, V. & Schneider, A. (1980). Zur Grundlegung der Systematischen Musikwissenschaft. *Acta Musicologica, 52*(2), 87–101.

Kramarz, V. (2006). *Die Popformeln*. Voggenreiter.

Lockwood, L. (1970). A stylistic investigation of the masses of josquin desprez with the aid of the computer: a progress report. In B. Brook (Ed.), *Musicology and the computer: Musicology 1966-2000: a Practical Program*. City University New York.

Manning, C. D. & Schütze, H. (1999). *Foundations of Statistical Natural Language Processing*. Cambridge, MA: MIT Press.

Mauch, M., Dixon, S., Harte, C., Casey, M., & Fields, B. (2007). Discovering chord idioms through beatles and real book songs. In *Proceedings of the 8th International Conference on Music Information Retrieval* (pp. 255–258).

McKay, C. (2006). jsymbolic: A feature extractor for midi files. In *Proceedings of the International Computer Music Conference* (pp. 302–305).

Moore, A. (1997). *The Beatles, Sgt. Pepper's Lonely Hearts Club Band*. Cambridge: Cambridge University Press.

Moore, A. (2006). What story should a history of popular music tell? *Popular Music History, 1*(3), 329–338.

Müllensiefen, D. & Frieler, K. (2004). Cognitive adequacy in the measurement of melodic similarity: Algorithmic vs. human judgments. *Computing in Musicology, 13*, 147–176.

Müllensiefen, D. & Frieler, K. (2007). Modelling experts' notions of melodic similarity. *Musicae Scientiae, Discussion Forum 4A*.

Müllensiefen, D., Pearce, M., Wiggins, G., & Frieler, K. (2007). Segmenting pop melodies: a model comparison approach. Presentation held at SMPC07, Montreal, Canada.

Parncutt, R. (2007). Systematic musicology and the history and future of western musical scholarship. *Journal of Interdisciplinary Music Studies, 1*, 1–32.

Pearce, M. T. & Wiggins, G. A. (2006). Expectation in melody: The influence of context and learning. *Music Perception, 23*(5), 377–405.

Pendzich, M. (2004). *Von der Coverversion zum Hit-Recycling*. LIT.

Pfleiderer, M. & Müllensiefen, D. (2006). The perception of accents in pop music melodies. In M. Baroni, A. R. Addessi, R. Caterina, & M. Costa (Eds.), *Proceedings of the 9th International Conference of Music Perception and Cognition (ICMPC9)* (pp. 1272–1280).

Potter, K., Wiggins, G., & Pearce, M. (2007). Towards greater objectivity in music theory: Information-dynamic analysis of minimalist music. *Musicae Scientiae*, *11*(2), 295–322.

Recordare (2004). Music xml definition 2.0. Website. Available from http://www.musicxml.org/xml.html.

Rhodes, C., Lewis, D., & Müllensiefen, D. (2007). Bayesian model selection for harmonic labelling. In *Program and Summaries of the First Internatinal Confernece of the Society for Mathematics and Computation in Music, Berlin, May, 18-20, 2007*.

Rosen, C. (1976). *The classical style: Haydn, Mozart, Beethoven*. London: Faber.

Sagrillo, D. (1999). *Melodiegestalten im luxemburgischen Volkslied: Zur Anwendung computergestützter Verfahren bei der Klassifikation von Volksliedabschnitten*. Bonn: Holos.

Schaffrath, H. (1995). *The Essen Folksong Collection in the Kern Format*. Center for Computer Assisted research in the Humanities.

Schenker, H. (1932). *Fünf Urlinie-Tafeln*. Wien: Universal Edition.

Schneider, A. (1993). Systematische musikwissenschaft: Traditionen, Ansätze, Aufgaben. *Systematische Musikwissenschaft*, *1/2*, 145–180.

Selfridge-Field, E. (1997). Describing musical information. In E. Selfridge-Field (Ed.), *Beyond MIDI: The handbook of musical codes*. Cambridge, MA: MIT Press.

Smaill, A., Wiggins, G., & Harris, M. (1993). Hierarchical music representation for analysis and composition. *Computers and the humanities*, *27*, 7–17.

Steinbeck, W. (1982). *Struktur und Ähnlichkeit: Methoden automatisierter Melodieanalyse*. Kassel: Bärenreiter.

Zhou, Y. & Kankanhalli, M. S. (2003). Melody alignment and similarity metric for content-based music retrieval. In *Proceddings of SPIE-IS&T Electronic Imaging*, volume 5021 (pp. 112–121).

Klaus Frieler

Metrical Circle Map and Metrical Markov Chains

Abstract

We propose a novel method, called Metrical Circle Map, for exploring the cyclic aspects of musical time. To this end, we give a concise formalization and introduce the notion of Metrical Markov Chains as n-th order transition probabilities of segments on the metrical circle, which leads naturally to the definition of zeroth- and first-order metrical entropy as a measure of metrical patterness and variability, and for "occupation accentuation". As a demonstration, we present an exemplary metrical analysis of five folk and pop melody collections.

1. Introduction

An important and distinctive feature of metrically bound music is the double nature of its musical time, linear on one hand, cyclic on the other. However, in most of musicological and other music-related research the focus was laid on linear aspects, while the cyclic nature of musical time was mainly investigated in the context of genuine meter and rhythm research, where rhythm and meters are occasionally illustrated using a circle representation (London, 2004; Toussaint 2004, Taslakian, 2006). But these representations were mostly limited to rhythmic patterns, e.g. clave patterns from African and Latin-American Music, or to the structural analysis of particular meters. In this paper, we like to extend and formalize this approach by introducing the Metrical Circle Map along with Metrical Markov Chains opening up several interesting possibilities of visualizing and analysing metrically bound music in a statistical way.

2. Metrical Circle Map

Events of metrically bound music are organized around underlying pulses (beats), which are grouped into higher-level units, notably the bar. Pulse is a function[1] of the sounding music, but in a certain way external to it, because it is created by listeners and performers, so it might be called "semi-autonomous". Our concept of meter will be solely based on the grouping of the pulse, in contrast to definitions incorporating accents already on a fundamental level (e.g. Temperley, 2004). Metrical accents are conceived here as a function of the grouping of the pulse (and of other musical features), playing only a secondary role. Meter can be described as a set of discrete time-points (the pulse) along with a grouping prescription. Consider a sequence of strictly monotonously increasing time-points b(i), regarded as a map from the integers into the reals. A partition of the integers is given by a mapping

$$S(k) = [i_k : i_{k+1}-1],$$

---

[1] Function in the mathematical sense here.

with $i_{k+1} - i_k > 0$, i.e. a collection of disjunctive intervals covering the integers.

A bar is then defined as grouping of pulses with respect to a certain partition, i.e. as the sets

$$B_k = b(S(k)) = \{ b(i_k), b(i_k + 1), \ldots, b(i_{k+1} - 1) \}$$

This is the basic procedure, for a full theory of meter a hierarchical procedure is needed, i.e. grouping of groupings and division of pulse, which cannot be done here due to space limitations. For the following we will only use the durations of the bars B_k given by $T_k = b(i_{k+1}) - b(i_k)$, and restrict ourselves to isochronous pulses and constant group lengths, so that the bar times T_k are all equal to a certain time T.

Consider now a rhythm conceived as an increasing sequence of time-points t_i, and an associated meter, possibly inferred from the original sequence by some beat and meter induction algorithm (e.g. Frieler, 2004), or given by manual annotation. The *Metrical Circle Map* M is then defined as a mapping from the reals into the complex unit circle S^1:

$$M_{T,\phi}(t_i) = \exp(2\pi i \frac{t_i - \phi}{T})$$

We have chosen the mathematical direction of counter-clockwise rotation, the complex-conjugated mapping would do the other way round.

The phase ϕ is a free parameter that can be used to gauge the map by aligning the downbeats (the beginnings of pulse groups) to a certain point on the circle. We fix for the following a gauge prescription, where the downbeats will be always aligned to the point (1,0) on the complex plane, i.e. zero phase or 3 o 'clock.

2.1 Metrical Markov Chains

The Metrical Circle Map (MCM) lends itself quite naturally to the definition of transition probabilities between segments on the metrical circle. To this end, we define N intervals on S^1 according to

$$I_k = \{ z \in S^1 \mid arg(z) \in [\frac{k-1/2}{N}, \frac{k+1/2}{N}] \}$$

with $0 <= k < N$. The intervals cover the unit circle with the N-th roots of unity as midpoints. We can transform now a sequence of time-points into a sequence of intervals on the metrical circle, in virtue of

$$\{t_i\} \rightarrow \{I^{-1}(M_T(t_i))\}$$

where I^{-1} denotes the interval index function yielding the interval index of a point z on the circle. For these sequences of interval indices we can define Markov transition probabilities. We will restrict ourselves to zeroth- and first-order transitions

$$p(k) = p(z_i \in I_k), \ p(k \mid j) = p(z_i \in I_k \mid z_{i-1} \in I_j)$$

For transition probabilities the choice of N is of course crucial. For example, for N=2 the first-order probabilities would refer to transitions between the two halves of a bar. For a more complete comparison, particularly of whole corpora with a full range of meters, a choice of N=48 seems appropriate in the most cases, which means a resolution of sextuplets in 4/4 meter or 32th notes in 3/4 meter.

Metrical Markov Chains can be visualized on a circle using the following procedure:

1. Zeroth-order probabilities are displayed by smaller circles at corresponding circle positions with radius and blackness proportional to probability
2. First-order probabilities are displayed by arrows with thickness and blackness proportional to probability.

In Figure 1 an example for a single melody metrical, the vocal line of *Mandy* by Barry Manilow. The signature is 4/4. We see a preference for events at beginnings and ends of bars with beat 2 being the most frequent position. Generally, the melody avoids the classical strongest metrical positions. The main rhythmic movement is in eighth notes with occasional 16th notes and some triplets at beat 2. There are some prominent syncopations, particularly the transitions from 4+ to 1+ and from 2+ to 3+.

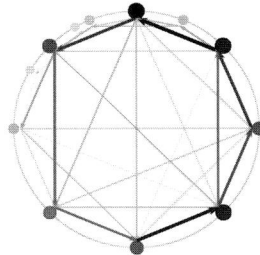

Figure 1: Vocal line of *Mandy* by Barry Manilow

Another example is shown in Figure 2. The composition "Cross-Fade" by Steve Coleman employs a considerably complex 4-bar drum groove in 9/4 time, played throughout the entire piece. Inferring the meter just by listening is even for trained musicians a highly demanding, if not impossible task. The groove is played with bass drum, snare drum, hi-hat and cowbell. The cowbell is rendering a highly asymmetrical clave pattern yielding actually a 36-beats period. The hi-hat serves as the main timekeeper playing nearly constantly on every quarter pulse. The snare drum shows a relatively simple pattern of 5 beats spread over two bars, whereby the even bars equal the odd bars plus an additional stroke on the downbeat. Finally, the bass drum repeats also only after the full 4-bar cycle, and avoids the downbeat. However, the bass drum pattern is the same in the first half of each bar with two or three varying kicks in the second half. The metrical characteristics of the groove, particularly the complexity of the cowbell pattern, are nicely reflected in the representation on the metric circle.

2.2 Metrical Entropy

Information entropy is often been used to describe stochastic distributions, which can be done for Metrical Markov Chains as well. Recall, that for a discrete probability distribution of N states with probabilities p_i, Shannon's information entropy is given by the formula

$$H = -\Sigma \ p_i \log_2 p_i$$

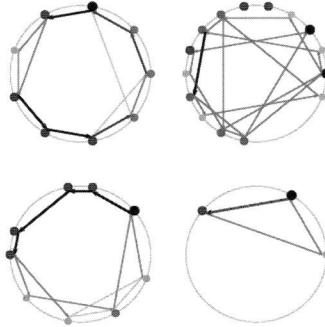

Figure 2: Single drum parts of the "Cross-Fade" groove. Top row from left to right: Hi-hat and cow bell. Bottom row from left to right: Kick and snare drum.

Information entropy measures the uncertainty of a probability distribution, which can be interpreted in terms of information (Shannon, 1948), The more confident an observer can be about the next event, the less information is provided, as nothing new (i.e. information) can be inferred from such events. The more concentrated (or "accented") the probabilities are, the lower the entropy will be. The maximum of the entropy is reached for uniform probability distributions, where each event is equally probable.

For the matter of comparison, we normalize the entropy by dividing by the maximum entropy $H_{max} = \log_2 N$, where N is the number of possible events. Hence,

$$h = -\Sigma \ p_i \log_2 p_i \, / \log_2 N$$

The parameter N determines the event space and thus influences critically the entropy. Fixing an N for the Metrical Circle Map means fixing the smallest possible subdivision of a bar, but perceptually this of course depends on absolute bar length, type of the meter, and tempo. Here we encounter a general problem of statistical measures in the field of humanities, because the true event space is often not determinable, and needs a definition *a forteriori*. This means, that any interpretation of metrical entropy in terms of absolute information content is not well justified, but for the purpose of comparison it is still useful, when careful interpreted. As Feldman & Crutchfield put it: "How is the [complexity] measure to be used? What questions might it help answer?" (Feldman & Crutchfield, 1998).

For Metrical Markov Chains we define normalized zeroth- and first-order metrical entropies h_0 and h_1, where the first-order Markov Chains are regarded as probability distributions with N^2 states. What is the interpretation of these entropies then?

The zeroth-order metrical entropy h_0 becomes maximal for a uniform distribution of metrical positions. The more different metrical positions occur in a rhythm and the more similar the probabilities of these positions are, the higher the entropy will be. Conversely, the fewer positions appear in a rhythm and the more imbalanced the probabilities are, the lower the entropy. This could be interpreted as an indicator of "patterness" on one hand, because any constantly repeated rhythmic pattern would receive higher entropy than a rhythm with an identical set of metrical positions, but with variations in such a way, that some metrical positions are preferred over other. Note, that form and phase of a repeated pattern does not matter. A sequence of quarter notes will always receive the same entropy, regardless how it is aligned to the beat, and any more rhythmically complex pattern, but with the same number of events, e.g. African timeline, would also gain the same zeroth-order metrical entropy. Moreover, this is also true for a rhythm jumping randomly from one metrical position to another with the number of events per bar being the same. Hence, zeroth-order metrical entropy is not fully sufficient as a measure of patterness. However, to distinguish the totally random case from the totally patterned case, the first-order entropy can to be taken into account. A totally random rhythm would have a more widespread and uniform distribution of first-order transitions, and thus higher first-order metrical entropy than a patterned rhythm, where the transitions are already completely fixed by the pattern. With the combined view of zeroth- and first order metrical entropies it is thus possible to make statements about the metrical patterness and variability of rhythms.

3. Metrical analysis of melody collections

For a demonstration of the just described methods, we analysed five different song collections: 61 Irish folksongs, 586 Luxembourgian folksongs, 149 East-polish chants from Warmia, and 207 German children songs (all taken from the Essen Folksong Collection, Schaffrath, 1995), and 53 contemporary Pop songs (data kindly provided by Frank Riedemann). Every song was transformed with the MCM using an N=48 segmentation of the circle. Subsequently, zeroth- and first-order transition probabilities were calculated for every song and also accumulated over all songs.

3.1 Distribution of Signatures

The distribution of signatures in Table 1 already shows remarkably differences. The German children songs, the Warmian chants, and the Pop songs are clearly dominated by duple meters (79,2%, 72,29% and 96,2% resp.), where Children songs clearly prefer 2/4 (70,5%), and the Pop songs almost all are in 4/4 meter (only two are written in 6/4 meter). Odd meters are only found in the Warmian chants, though to a fairly small amount (2,02%). The Luxembourgian collections contains also a high share of duple meters (60,8%), with a slight preference for 2/4 over 4/4 time (33,6% vs. 27%). The Irish songs are insofar distinguished from each other collection, as the share of triple and compound duple meters is higher (56%) than the share of duple meters (44%).

Signature	Children	Warmia	Luxembourg	Irish	Pop
2/4	70,5%	4,05%	33,6%	11%	
4/8			0,2%		
4/4	8,7%	72,29%	27%	33%	96,2%
8/4		2,02%			
3/8	3,9%	1,35%	2,0%		
3/4	12,1%	7,43%	21,5%	33%	
6/4		1,35%		3%	3,8%
6/8	4,8%	1,35%	15,7%	16%	
9/8				3%	
9/4		8,1%			
5/4		1,35%			
7/4		0,67%			
Total duple	79,2%	78,36%	60,8%	44%	96,2%
Total triple	20,8%	19,58%	39,2%	56%	3,8%
Total odd		2,02%			

Table 1: Distribution of signatures in the melody collections

3.2 Analysis of Metrical Markov Chains

The joint visualisations for zeroth- and first-order Metrical Markov Chains of the five melody collections can be found in Figures 3-7. As described above, the size and blackness of the small circles are proportional to the occupation probabilities, and the thickness and blackness of the arrows connecting two metric positions is proportional to the first-order transition probability. The downbeat lies at 3 o'clock, and time is running counter-clockwise.

By looking on the graphs, the squares and octagons from duple, and the triangles and hexagons from compound duple and triple meters appear as the most prominent shapes. The distributions of signatures in the collection is clearly reflected too, particularly the mixture of duple and triple meters in the Irish collection, and the smaller share of triple meters in the Children, Warmian and Pop songs. In all collections, the most frequent transitions are constituted by quarter- and eighth notes movement, which is of course not surprising. For the Pop songs a certain lack of quarter note movement along the main beats can be stated, however, we can find a rotated square here, stemming from syncopations. A further comparison with the other diagrams reveals that syncopations are almost exclusively present in the Pop song collection.

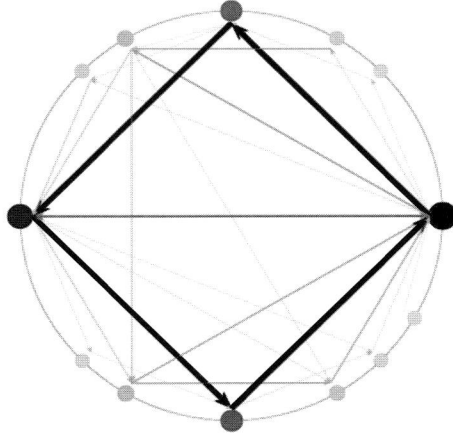

Fig. 3: Metrical Markov probabilities of German Children songs (N=207)

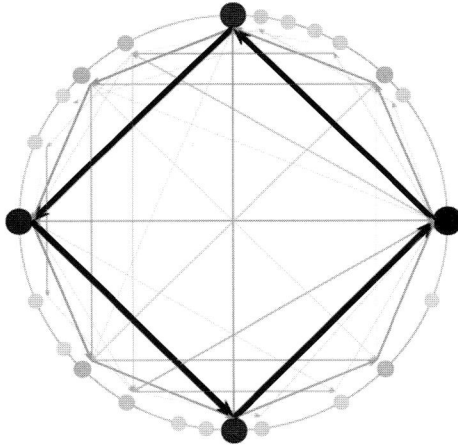

Fig. 4: Metrical Markov probabilities of Warmian chants (N=190)

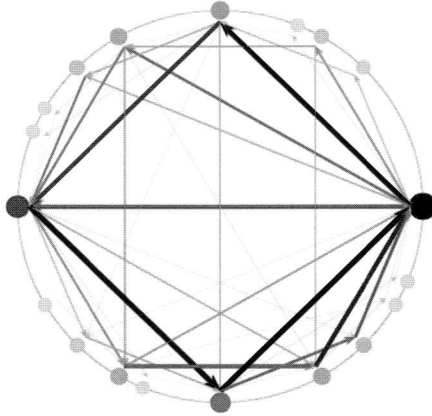

Fig. 5: Metrical Markov probabilities of Luxembourgian folk songs (N=586)

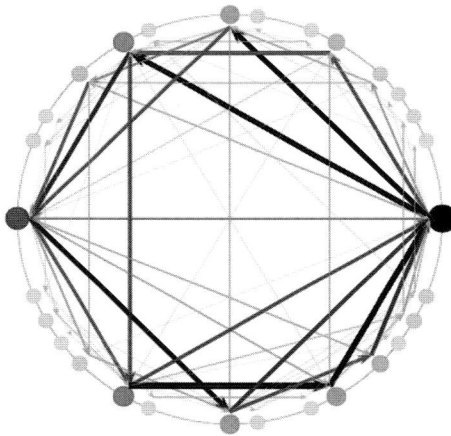

Fig. 6: Metrical Markov probabilities of Irish folk tunes (N=61)

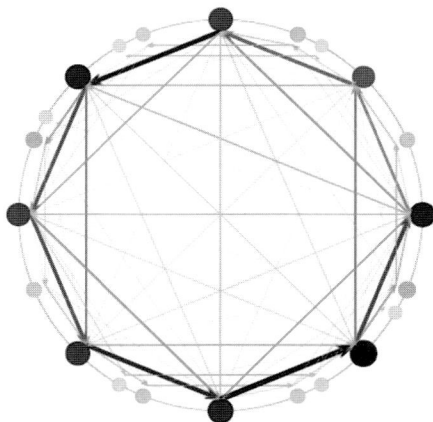

Fig. 7: Metrical Markov probabilities of the Pop songs (N=53)

An alternative display of the distribution of metrical positions is shown in Figure 9. Here the relative frequencies of metrical positions of all collections are plotted against the indices on the Metrical Circle. The downbeat is the most frequent position in every collection except one: the Pop songs. Here the anticipated one (4+) appears slightly more often than the downbeat. Similarly, the anticipated 3 (2+) occurs more frequent than the third beat itself. Generally, in the Pop songs every eighth-note position is quite equally probable indicating a high rhythmic and metric variability of the vocal lines, or, connected to this, a high amount of syncopation. The Children songs and the Warmian chants show distributions, which could be expected in the light of western metrical theory, and what might be termed "occupation accentuation". The classical hierarchy of metrical positions is nicely reflected in the occupation probabilities. The rank order of beats in 4/4 meter is then 1, 3, 4, 2, (or 1+, 2, 2+, 1+ in 2/4 time).[2] Similar statements for the Luxembourg and Irish collections hold as well as will be corroborated by the analysis of metrical entropies below.

---

[2] Looking at the German children songs this would suggest, that its most common 2/4 signature should be in fact written as 4/8.

165

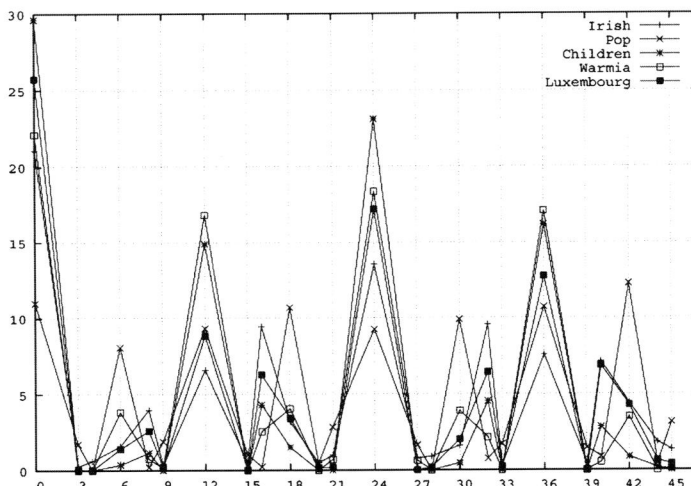

Fig. 9: Frequencies of metric positions with N=48 for the five melody collections.

An alternative display of first-order Metrical Markov Chains can be found in Fig. 10. The transition probabilities form an asymmetric 48x48 Matrix. The size of the bubbles at each grid point in the graph is proportional to the value of the corresponding matrix entry. The quarter- and eighth-note movement is reflected in the concentration of bubbles on the upper secondary diagonals. The lower right triangle contains much less bubbles, which means a lack of metrical transitions across bar borders. An exception is the concentration of bubbles on the x-axis, where the transitions to the downbeat can be found, which generally belong to the class of most frequent transitions. Another exception is the column of bubbles above index 42 (4+ in 4/4 time) on the outer right, belonging to the Pop songs. A similar column can be found above metrical position 6 (1+) in the upper left corner, also from the Pop songs. These transitions are due to phrase endings at the anticipated 1 with subsequent phrases beginning somewhere in the next bar, or due to transitions across the bar, touching not the downbeat but the delayed downbeat on 1+, as for example can be seen in *Mandy*. This is another indication for the high amount of syncopation in Pop songs.

166

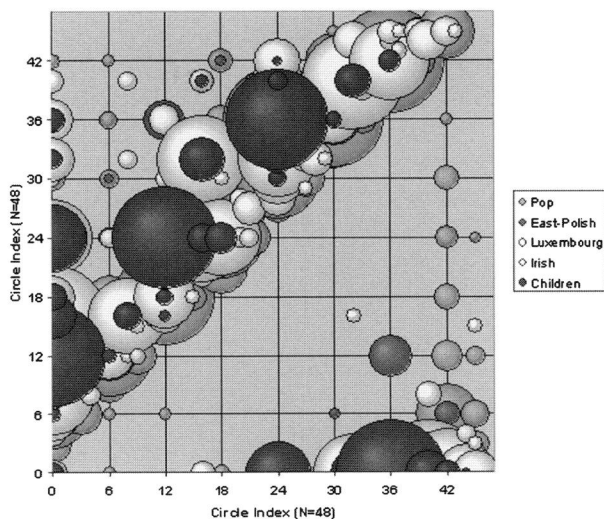

Fig. 10: Metrical Markov first-order transition probabilities.

	Children	Warmia	Luxembourg	Irish	Pop
h_0	0.38	0.44	0.43	0.48	0.59
h_1	0.24	0.28	0.27	0.31	0.40
σ_{avg}	0.031	0.059	0.047	0.065	0.05

Table 2: Means and averaged standard deviation of metrical entropies of the five song collections

As explained above, metrical variability can be measured using the zeroth- and first-order metrical entropies. Mean values and mean standard deviation are shown in Table 2. Boxplots of the entropy distributions are depicted in Figure 11. The metrical most homogenous collection of the most "accented" songs are the German Children songs. The Warmian and Luxembourgian tunes show quite similar distributions to each other with quite low average values indicating that these songs are also quite "occupation accented". The Pop songs have the highest metrical entropies, which confirms the observations from above, that the Pop songs have a close to uniform distribution of eighth-notes positions and the highest spread of metrical transitions. The Irish songs are somewhere in between, but more close to the folk songs with regard to average values, thus also showing metrical "occupation accentuation". However, they possess the highest variance of all distributions, stemming partly from the mixture of signatures here. On the opposite side, the most homogenous collections are the Children and the Luxembourgian songs, closely followed by the Pop songs and the Warmian songs.

To check, whether the distributions of metrical entropies are statistically different, we employed Welch's t-test and found all differences between all distributions of metrical entropies to be highly significant ($p<0.00$), except for the entropies of the Warmian and the Luxembourgian songs. A conclusion that can be drawn is, that metrical entropies can serve as distinction criterion between different genres and folksong styles, at least on the level of collections. And we believe, that in conjunction with other melodic and rhythmic features, classification of single songs should be possible as well.

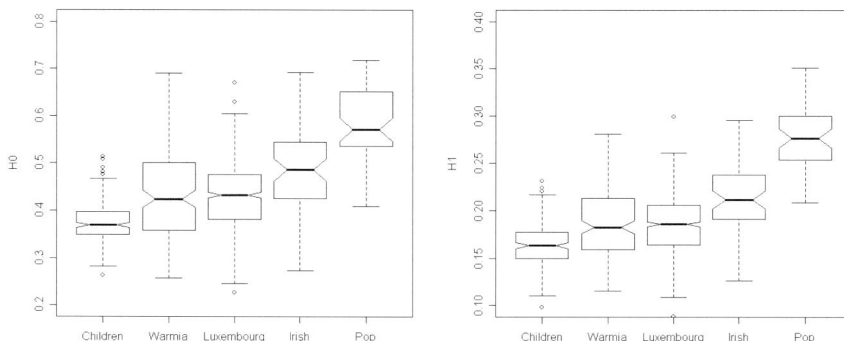

Fig. 11: Boxplots of metrical entropies. Left: Zeroth-order. Right: First-order entropies.

4. Conclusion & Outlook

We presented the methods of Metrical Circle Map and Metrical Markov Chains. Using metrical occupation and transition probabilities, melodies and entire corpora, as well as polyphonic music, can be analyzed and instructively visualized, thus giving deeper insights into the cyclic organization of music and in the metrical peculiarities of different music and styles.

Several extensions to the Metrical Circle Map, incorporating other dimensions of music, can be imagined. The pitch dimension of melodies could be reflected, for instance, in the radial dimension of the circle. By using a circle of fifth representation of pitch, we would arrive at toroidal representations of melodies. Linear time could be used as an additional coordinate as well, resulting in spirals on metrical cylinders. All these geometrical representations might possibly be used for similarity algorithms as well. Furthermore, drawing on distance measures for probability distribution, e.g. the Jensen-Shannon divergence, similarity measures for Metrical Markov Chains could be constructed as well.

We hope to explore some of these possibly fruitful extensions in the future.

References

Anku, Willie. "Circles and Time: A Theory of Structural Organization of Rhythm in African Music", *Music Theory Online*, 6(1), http://www.societymusictheory.org/mto, 2004.

Feldman, D. P. and Crutchfield, J. P. "Measures of Statistical Complexity: Why?", *Physics Letters* A 238 (1998) 244-252, 1998.

Frieler, Klaus. "Beat and meter extraction using gaussified onsets.", In *Proc. 5th International Conference on Music Information Retrieval*, Universitat Pompeu Fabra, Barcelona, Spain, 2004.

London, Justin. *Hearing in Time*. Oxford University Press, Oxford, England, 2004.

Temperley, D. *Cognition of Basic Musical Structures*, MIT Press, 2004

Schaffrath, H. The Essen Folksong Collection in the Humdrum Kern Format. D. Huron (ed.). Menlo Park, CA: Center for Computer Assisted Research in the Humanities, 1995

Shannon, C.E. "A Mathematical Theory of Communication", *Bell System Technical Journal*, vol. 27, pp. 379-423, 623-656, July, October, 1948

Toussaint, Godfried T. "A comparison of rhythmic similarity measures.", In *Proc. 5th International Conference on Music Information Retrieval*, Universitat Pompeu Fabra, Barcelona, Spain, 2004.

Taslakian, P. and Toussaint, Godfried T. "Geometric properties of musical rhythm", *Proceedings of the 16th Fall Workshop on Computational and Combinatorial Geometry*, Smith College, Northampton, Massachussetts, November 10-11, 2006.

Christiane Neuhaus

Auditory Gestalt perception and the dissociation between pitch and time: ERP studies on processing musical sequence structure

Introduction

Whenever psychology has to explain the processing of musical structure, proximity, closure, and other perceptual grouping principles once established by Wertheimer and other Gestaltists in the early 20th century, appear useful. Empirical proof of Gestalt theory, however, even though experiments are quite large in number, is mostly restricted to *particular* principles of perceptual organization (for an overview see e.g. Deutsch, 1994), while basic considerations of the forerunner von Ehrenfels (1890) are mainly brought in on the theoretical side.

As a starting point for the following experimental study, let us bring Ehrenfels' classic essay "Ueber Gestaltqualitäten" (1890) to mind. In his opinion, a "Tongestalt" is a consciousness-complex or mental picture, which consists of accumulated impressions of successively presented tones ("Erinnerungsbild", "Bewußtseinseinheit", 1890, p.252). The build-up or formation of a "Tongestalt" might therefore be described as a process of abstraction and transformation of the actual sound pattern.[1] This means, first, that for Gestalt formation, relationships between tones instead of absolute pitches are considered relevant. Second, that a piece of music is transposed from a tone-wise presented sound stream to a mental sound picture of *simultaneous* impressions. Third, that mental images map the sequential contents in a compressed form, and, fourth, that mental pictures include a new holistic property, the so-called "Gestaltqualität", which is not inherent in the sum of component parts of the actual melody (cf. the Ehrenfels criterion "Übersummativität" or "the whole is more than the sum of its parts").

Ehrenfels further points out that handling mental "Tongestalts" requires active listening strategies and selective attention ("eine eigens hierauf gerichtete Geistesthätigkeit", 1890, p. 254), which seems to include both, the segmentation and analysis of a given, ready-made melody as well as the conjunction of tone elements during Gestalt formation. Thus, Gestalt-building as such is a process of *perceptual synthesis* and, in this form, related to several cognitive concepts, including encoding and integration of tones as well as their expectancy and predictability. Each of these concepts seems to consist in a cognitive matching or comparison between the new acoustic input and the already existing context, taking place in working memory, and including long-term memory as a cognitive resource. In line with that, Patel (2003) remarks that melodies provide a valuable tool to study basic issues in cognitive neuroscience, such as the interaction of bottom-up and top-down processing during sequence perception.

---

[1] Original wording of von Ehrenfels (1890, 262, 265): "Unter Gestaltqualitäten verstehen wir solche positive[n] Vorstellungsinhalte, welche an das Vorhandensein von Vorstellungscomplexen im Bewusstsein gebunden sind, die ihrerseits aus von einander trennbaren (d. h. ohne einander vorstellbaren) Elementen bestehen. ... an Gestaltqualitäten [kann] der Abstractionsprocess vollzogen werden".

The *process* of melodic Gestalt formation also bears several similarities to the so-called "feature-integration theory of attention", proposed by Treisman and Gelade (1980). This theory assumes that features come first in perception, and that focal attention provides the "glue" to integrate initially separable items into unitary perceptual objects. Thus, zooming in on the detail, the process of building a melodic Gestalt, which is influenced by several cognitive concepts such as encoding, integration, and predictability, first seems to take place between touching items on the local level. According to this, spatio-temporal coherence between adjacent tones in terms of tone relationships and duration distances should be examined first.

In line with the "feature-integration theory of attention", Peretz and Morais (1989) as well as Deutsch (1994) propose that *pitch* and *time properties* of a melody are first processed as separate dimensions before being integrated to a perceptual unit.[2] In a broader sense, this suggestion leads to the still ongoing debate, if pitch and time are perceived independently from each other, or if, on the contrary, both dimensions perceptually do interact. Behavioural experimental psychology, however, does not seem to take sides. On the one hand, functional and neuroanatomical results of brain lesion studies provide evidence for the independence theory, as lesions in the right auditory cortex affect the processing of pitch distance while damage of the left auditory cortex causes impairments in rhythm discrimination (see Peretz & Zatorre, 2005, for a review). Similar conclusions can be drawn from judgments of phrase completeness (Palmer & Krumhansl, 1987), and from testing long-term memory, i.e. from retrieval ability (Hébert & Peretz, 1997; White, 1960). In these studies, familiar melodic patterns (folk songs and instrumental themes) were reduced to one of the two dimensions - either pitch or time - while the respective second parameter was set to an equitonal or equitemporal 'baseline'. In terms of musical phrase completeness, Palmer and Krumhansl (1987) demonstrated that judgments could well be made by pitch or temporal information alone, thus, proving the independence of both variables when building a percept. Moreover, scores of musical experienced listeners as participants were slightly better for isolated pitch in comparison to pure rhythm. Regarding information retrieval, Hébert and Peretz (1997) showed the primacy of pitch over time by evaluating the correct naming responses given by musicians and non-musicians for flattened uni-dimensional melodic sequences (49% vs. 6% of correct answers, while musical experience had no influence on the retrieval results).

Boltz (1999), by contrast, investigated the *interdependency* of pitch and time from the outset, by varying the type of instruction on learning various unfamiliar folk tunes. While focussing either on pitch, on duration, or on both during initial learning, non-musicians as participants had lowest reproduction scores after having focussed on pitch

---

[2] Deutsch writes the following: "Eine von den britischen Empiristen des 17. und 18. Jahrhunderts stammende Doktrin lautet, daß Objekte als ein Bündel von Merkmalsausprägungen wahrgenommen werden. Es wird z.B. angenommen, daß wir beim Sehen eines Objekts seine Form, Farbe, räumliche Position usw. getrennt erfassen, ferner, dass die unterschiedlichen Ausprägungen dieser Merkmale später vom Wahrnehmungssystem so kombiniert werden, dass daraus ein integriertes Perzept resultiert. In ähnlicher Weise wird angenommen, dass wir beim Hören eines Tons seine Tonhöhe, räumliche Position, Lautstärke usw. getrennt erfassen und wir diese Merkmalsausprägungen später so kombinieren, dass ein einheitliches Perzept entsteht." (1994, p. 349 et seq.).

while disregarding rhythm, and highest performance scores after attending to duration while pitch was considered as irrelevant.

The basic idea of the present study was to compare by experiment the processing of a well-structured melody to a fully randomised tone sequence for which contour, interval, and rhythm structure had been demolished. Our first objective was to investigate the build-up of a mental "Tongestalt", as stated by Ehrenfels, in contrast to the build-up of a tone sequence consisting of random elements in the sense of Wundt and his "Elementenpsychologie" (elementarism, structuralism; 1874). Our second objective was to examine, to what extent pitch and time as separate structural properties contribute to melodic Gestalt formation as a perceptual process. For these goals, we used the measures of modern neuroscience as well as four types of tone sequences differing in structure (see Figure 1), a) unfamiliar melodies with spatio-temporal cohesion between adjacent tones (condition $P^O D^O$)[3], b) sequences with pitch structure preserved, but time values at random (condition $P^O D^R$), c) sequences with time values preserved, but pitch structure at random (condition $P^R D^O$), and d) completely (pseudo)-randomised versions with pitch and time permuted over the entire set of tones (condition $P^R D^R$).

In a recent study with functional neuroimaging (fMRI), Levitin and Menon (2005) used a similar paradigm to investigate the development of musical expectancies and the processing of temporal structure. As stimuli, they contrasted familiar and unfamiliar 23-s musical excerpts to their scrambled versions, in which the original musical structure was demolished by cutting the sequence into arbitrary 250-350 ms particles regardless of rhythm, tonal function, and phrase structure, while spectral energy in each example was kept constant. The main result with non-musicians as participants was, that structured, but not scrambled versions activated the pars orbitalis region in the left prefrontal cortex (Brodmann Areal 47) and its right hemisphere homologue.

In the present study, brain-electrical activity was recorded by measuring event-related potentials (ERPs) which are the product of an averaging procedure. At each particular electrode, ERP traces show the electrical potential relative to the reference electrode after spontaneous brain oscillations have been evened out. Each ERP curve is time-related to the onset of a stimulus and consists of several components in sequence, which, according to general knowledge, reflect different phases of cognitive processing from the automatic bottom-up processing of stimulus properties to task-related processing, demanding focussed attention. The first high-amplitude ERP voltage deflections that originate in the cortex are called P1, N1, and P2 components. They are of opposite polarity (P stands for positive, N for negative) and occur roughly between 50 – 100 ms, 100 – 200 ms, and 170 – 250 ms, as measured from the onset of the respective tone.

In this study, we use two methods of display and analysis. First, the *grand average ERP* (see Figures 3, 7, and 8). It shows brain activity in compressed form over all tones per condition and might therefore correspond to the "Tongestalt" as a mental picture with 'simultaneous' impressions of all presented tones as the constituent parts. Second,

---

[3] P stands for pitch, D for tone duration, while O and R classify ordered versus random structure. Thus, to specify a sequence type, we used four types of abbreviation: PODO (melody), PRDO (random pitch and regular time order), PODR (regular pitch and random time order), and PRDR (double permutation of pitch and time).

the so-called *single-tone ERP* (see diagrams 4 to 6), in which amplitude values are plotted separately against each of the 15 initial tones per condition.[4] This way, for each 50-ms time range around the peak of components, the *time-course* of Gestalt formation was roughly displayed along the tone axis (see Data Analysis and Results sections).[5]

Taken together, our hypotheses are the following:

1. Early components (P1, N1, and P2) are more affected than late components (P3) during the successive processing of tones. - In line with this assumption is the result of Hillyard et al. (1998) that *spatial* attention to noise bursts, which are concurrently delivered from an array of seven loudspeakers, has a mere effect on early ERP components up to 200 ms, which indicate an initial stage of feature encoding.

2. Early components reflect the build-up of a unitary percept when tone progression is highly predictable. - The perceptual integration of tones to form a mental picture of simultaneous sound impressions, might be facilitated when a sequence has a rule-based structure and follows the Gestalt principles of perceptual organisation.

3. Late components indicate the processing of random in contrast to regular tone order. - Random tone sequences do not match with a melodic template or a set of structure-generating rules, for which mental representations in long-term memory might exist. According to this, the brain might identify random sequences as deviating from musical syntax, for which late components (P300, P600) are commonly regarded as the neural correlates (e.g. Patel, 1998).

4. The build-up of a melodic Gestalt basically relies on the processing of pitch. - Results supporting this claim have already been obtained with behavioural methods (see White,1960; Hébert & Peretz, 1997). Tone sequences with random pitch in contrast to random time order might therefore be processed with higher mental effort.

5. Sequence processing is influenced by formal musical training. The processing of orderless pitch or time structure yields larger amplitude differences in musicians than in non-musicians, and processing speed is also higher in musically experienced subjects. - Results of that kind might be likely as a major concern of musical education is the development of analytical listening strategies (see e. g. Sims, 1986).

6. Processing velocity depends on the structure of a sequence. It is lowest for double permutation of pitch and time (P^RD^R), higher for random tone duration (P^OD^R)

---

[4] Single-tone ERPs in this study show brain activity split up according to tone, which, however, is averaged over all subjects per group. Thus, although the display is different, single-tone ERPs are grand averages which, by definition, reflect brainvoltage activity merged *over subjects*.
[5] In order to find out at what time point Gestalt recognition and the identification of tone structure exactly take place, reaction time measurements might also have been a suitable method to learn more about sequence processing in music. However, behavioural data of that kind cannot be correlated with subjects' neural responses in an appropriate way, as the phases of stimulus evaluation measured with both methods are different. While reaction time measurements indicate the time point when structure identification is just completed, ERP recordings measure brain activity online, i.e. *during* the whole time period of listening and evaluation.

than for random pitch (P^RD^O), and highest for well-balanced melodies (P^OD^O). - Encoding and integration processes might be delayed when tone progression is difficult to predict.

7. Pitch and time properties of a tone sequence are processed in an interwoven manner. - The fact that both parameters depend on each other has already been demonstrated by Boltz (1999) using a learning paradigm. However, functio-anatomical results with brain damaged persons also gave evidence for the separate processing of pitch and time (see Peretz & Zatorre, 2005).

Methods

Subjects

Fourteen musically trained and 15 musically untrained students participated in the experiment. Musically trained persons (7 males, 7 females, mean age 23.5, range 18 to 30 years) had started playing an instrument at the average age of 8.93 years, and daily practicing at the point of measurement was between 0.5 and 3.5 hours. Their main musical instrument was the piano, the guitar, the saxophone, oboe, or French horn. Musically untrained persons (7 males, 8 females, mean age 25.17, range 22 to 30 years) were neither singing in a choir nor taking any music lessons at the time of the experiment, and, if at all, had played an instrument for altogether less than 1.6 years. In addition to that, only three of them were able to read and write musical note symbols.

Testing out handedness with the Edinburgh Handedness Inventory (Oldfield, 1971) revealed right-handedness of all participants (lateralization quotient for musicians and non-musicians 93.57% and 98.2%, respectively). All subjects reported to have normal hearing. They gave written informed consent before running the experiment. Due to muscle, eye, and electrode artefacts, data from one musician and two non-musicians were excluded from further analysis, so that the final number of data sets was 13 in each group.

Stimuli

We used four types of tone sequences to investigate the processing of ordered versus orderless structure. Sequences are exemplified in Figures 1a to d. Figure 1a shows the original form (condition P^OD^O), consisting of a tonal melody with symmetric phrase structure in four four (4/4), three four (3/4), or six eight (6/8) time, in accordance with the Gestalt principles of closure, temporal, and spatial proximity. Figure 1b shows the same sequence where rhythmical structure is left unchanged, but pitch values are randomised over the entire set of examples (condition P^RD^O). Vice versa, condition P^OD^R (Figure 1c) represents the overall randomisation of time values (i.e. tone duration plus proximate offset-onset distance) while pitch structure is preserved. Finally, condition P^RD^R (Figure 1d) describes double, but independent, permutation along the pitch and time axes. In all conditions, tone number is the same.

For each condition, 80 full-length examples were generated.[6] Original melodies (condition P^OD^O) were played on a programmable keyboard (Yamaha PSR 1000) that was connected with a PC. Each sequence was recorded in the sound color 'piano' and stored in MIDI format (using Steinberg ^{TM} Cubasis VST 4.0) for subsequent permutation of pitch and/or time values. Original sequences and modified MIDI versions were transformed to Soundblaster ^{TM} audio format, using the software package TiMidity (http://timidity.sourceforge.net) which enabled us to gain access to an open set of instrument samples for sound generation (Sound Font no. 0, 'acoustic piano'; see http//freepats.opensrc.org).

The original melody was played the natural way by connecting adjacent notes with movements of hand and fingers (legato effect). These duration overlaps had to be corrected when time values were permuted over the entire set of tones (see conditions P^OD^R and P^RD^R). In this way, the resulting minimum distance (inter-stimulus interval, ISI) between adjacent tones was at least zero or positive. Due to this adjustment, time values differed slightly among conditions. In the time-preserving conditions P^OD^O and P^RD^O, tones had an average length of 0.287 s ($SD = 0.254$), the ISI was 0.062 s ($SD = 0.115$), and the onset-onset interval (IOI) - due to legato effects - was 0.320 s ($SD = 0.206$). In the time-permuting conditions P^OD^R and P^RD^R, tones had an average length of 0.277 s ($SD = 0.250$), an ISI of 0.07 s ($SD = 0.107$), and an IOI of 0.348 ($SD = 0.257$).

According to the experimental paradigm (see Fig. 2 and task description below), an additional set of 80 tone excerpts per condition also had to be generated, for which we used either the initial or the final 2-second-section of each sequence. Thus, every condition (P^OD^O, P^RD^O, P^OD^R, P^RD^R) comprised 80 full-length examples as well as 40 initial and 40 final tone excerpts of 2-s length.

Paradigm, Task, and Procedure

Figure 2 shows a flowchart with the experiment set-up. In section 1, a full-length audio sequence was presented together with a fixation cross that had already been shown for attention purposes in the 2-s-time period before. In section 2, a 2-second-tone-excerpt was repeated that was or was not part of the previous full-length example. In section 3, the result of stimulus comparison was recorded via button press. The entire presentation flow was automated with ERTS (Experimental Run Time System, Version 3.11, BeriSoft 1995).

In section 1 of each trial, participants had to listen carefully and memorize the sequence. In section 2, they had to identify the tone excerpt as either congruous or incongruous compared to the prior full-length example. In part 3, subjects had to indicate their rating result by pressing the left or the right key of a response-device placed in front of the monitor.

---

[6] Tone sequences with preserved pitch structure (conditions P^OD^O and P^OD^R) had a mean interval size of 2.42 half tone steps ($\approx$ a major second; $SD = 2.13$), and the most frequent interval types were the minor second (471 times), the major second (756 times), the minor third (252 times), and the fourth (215 times). Sequences with randomised pitch structure (conditions P^RD^O and P^RD^R) had a mean interval size of 6.42 half tone steps ($\approx$ augmented fourth; $SD = 5.01$), and consisted mostly of major seconds (293 times), fourths (254 times), fifths (206 times), minor sixths, and larger intervals (763 times).

According to the general guidelines of ERP measurement (Picton et al., 2000), subjects were also requested to reduce eye blinks during recording and keep arms, hands, fingers, and facial muscles as relaxed as possible.

Each participant was comfortably seated in a soundproof, dimmed, and electrically shielded EEG cabin. Every experimental session comprised seven blocks with tone examples which were binaurally presented via loudspeaker at a device-to-subject-distance of approximately 1 m. Each block consisted of 36 full-length sequences randomised over conditions, and each sequence was followed by a congruous or incongruous initial or final tone excerpt. Block order was permuted between consecutive sessions.

A test trial was run before the EEG recording to become acquainted with the paradigm. In addition, stimulus intensity was balanced according to individual hearing abilities and preferences. After measurement, participants were requested to fill out a questionnaire about their musical education and their current state of health.

Data Recording

The EEG was recorded with a 32-channel-set-up, using an electrode cap (Electro Cap International Inc., Eaton, Ohio) with small inserted Ag/AgCl scalp electrodes placed according to the 10-10 system onto the head's surface (e.g., Oostenveld & Praamstra, 2001). The electrically inactive reference electrode was set at the left preauricular point (A1), and for the ground electrode, the sternum was chosen. EEG signals were recorded with an infinite time constant and were digitised with a sampling rate of 500 Hz. Ocular activity was recorded with a vertical and a horizontal electrooculogram (EOGV, EOGH) from above and below the right eye, and from the outer canthus of both eyes. At each electrode channel, impedance was kept below 5 kΩ.

Data Analysis

Preprocessing of Data

EEG raw data were subjected to a 0.50 Hz high-pass filter to bring slow potential drifts into line. EEG traces were then carefully examined for eye, muscle, and technical artefacts. Artefact-contaminated signal epochs, especially with blink amplitudes larger than 30 µV or 40 µV (EOGH and EOGV), were excluded from further processing. Experimental trials were defined as time windows from –200 to 800 ms, taking the onset of each of the 2389 tones per condition as a reference point. Averages were computed over all tones and conditions (Figure 3), as well as over all tones within the respective condition (Figures 7 and 8), and also separately for tone 1 to 15 of each condition ('ERP-single-tone diagrams', Figures 4 to 6). Signal preprocessing further consisted in the baseline-correction of ERP traces, using the 100 ms pre-onset interval for curve adjustment. ERPs were finally averaged over subjects, resulting in grand average curves separate for musicians and non-musicians.

For analysis and display, representative electrode channels were selected (frontal F3, Fz, F4, central C3, Cz, C4, and parietal P3, Pz, P4; Figs. 3, 7 and 8). Diagrams with ERP single tone responses (Figs. 4 to 6) were limited to brain activity at anterior (fronto) electrode placements within three selected time ranges (50 – 100 ms, 100 – 150 ms, and 170 – 220 ms; see next paragraph).

Statistical Analysis

We first computed a repeated-measures analysis of variance (ANOVA) over the entire time range of analysis (50 to 220 ms) without any further specification of time window, conditions, and channel (Fig. 3 and Table 1). This enabled us to ascertain if component activity per se differed significantly from the technical baseline to do further analyses separately by time window. In a second analysis, scattergrams were generated with Matlab by plotting the respective ERP amplitude value against each of the 15 initial tones per condition. Scatterplots were drawn separately for each time interval of analysis[7] (i.e. 50 – 100 ms for the P1 component, 100 – 150 ms for the N1 component, and 170 – 220 ms for the P2 component). The trend lines in Figures 4 to 6 show the predicted curve progression. They were modelled with an exponential function that approximated an asymptotic value along the time axis. It is assumed that the time point at which the regression line reaches 90% of the asymptotic value, roughly informs about the time needed to identify the structure of a sequence and indicates a kind of steady state of brain activation (see Table 2).

In a third analysis, we tested to what extent the average amplitude of *all* tones (see Figs. 7 and 8) could be explained by an independent or interwoven processing of pitch and time.[8] For this purpose, and provided that the four-factor ANOVA over the entire range of analysis - including 'window', 'pitch', 'time', and 'channel' as the repeated factors - had yielded significant results (see previous footnote), we computed a three-factor repeated-measures ANOVA separate for musicians, non-musicians, and time window. Within-subjects factors were PITCH (2 levels: ordered vs. orderless), TIME (2 levels: ordered vs. orderless), and brain topography CHAN (9 levels: F3, Fz, F4, C3, Cz, C4, P3, Pz, P4). An additional three-way-*between*-subjects ANOVA informed about possible significant results of PITCH and TIME depending on the between-subjects factor GROUP, i.e. on the level of 'musical expertise'. Whenever necessary, significance levels were adjusted with Huynh and Feldt's epsilon. Results were considered significant at p<.05, but marginally significant results (p <.08) are also discussed.

Results

Behaviour (button press)

Button press responses indicated how accurate subjects identified the 2-second tone-excerpts as congruent or incongruent in relation to the preceding full-length example. Response data of each participant were analysed according to the signal detection paradigm[9], and the precise number of correct recognitions ('hits' and 'correct rejections') as well as of omitted and erroneous detections ('misses' and 'false alarms') were statistically evaluated.

---

[7] Time ranges for statistical analysis were roughly determined after visual inspection of ERP traces. Each time window is a 50-ms interval with equal spacing around the component peak.

[8] Prior to our third analysis, a four-factor overall ANOVA was computed over the entire 50-to-220-ms time range, in which 'window', 'pitch', 'time', and 'channel' were the repeated variables. A significant third-order interaction WINDOW x PITCH x TIME x CHANNEL would show that curve progression per time window was different, so that further analysis of ERP components separate for each time window was justified.

[9] first applied by Tanner and Swets, 1954.

Altogether, performance scores for the detection of tone excerpts were quite similar between groups. Musicians had an error rate of 21.73%, non-musicians of 30.35% in total. Musicians identified 81.93% of the initial and 97.71% of the final excerpts correctly. Non-musicians recognized 82.72% of the initial and 95.39% of the final excerpts without mistake. In each subject group, differences between error rates for initial and final excerpts were highly significant (musicians: $t(12) = -4.31$, p < .001, non-musicians: $t(12) = -2.99$, p < .02, paired-samples t-test, two-tailed).

Overview of brain activity

Figure 3 shows compressed brain activity averaged over all notes and conditions, but separate for musicians and non-musicians. Visual inspection reveals peak activity in three 50 ms-time windows: 50 – 100 ms (P1), 100 – 150 ms (N1), and 170 – 220 ms (P2), and peak occurrence as such, showing different polarity, amplitude value, and topography per time range, was confirmed by the significant interaction WINDOW x CHANNEL (Table 1), which justified further separate analyses per time window.

ERP scattergrams for single tones

The scattergrams in Figures 4 to 6 show 15 peak amplitude values plotted against the respective first 15 tones per condition. Figures 4a and 4b map P1 amplitudes for musicians and non-musicians, and Figures 5a/b and 6a/b are similar illustrations for the N1 and P2 components. As distributions are most clear in the anterior part of the brain, scattergrams only refer to frontal activity merged over channels F3, Fz, and F4. Whenever the trend line, which is the product of an exponential function, approximates 90% of the asymptotic value of this function, we assume that brain activation according to sequence type has reached a kind of steady state, and that identification of sequence structure has happened in the time period before. Thus, we took each time point (tone number) in which the slope of the curve turns into a straight line as an indicator for the rough detection of pitch and/or time order as being either regular or random.

On looking through the scattergrams, we observe that the time point at which brain activity reaches the steady state is different for each condition and each time window (P1, N1, and P2), as well as between musicians and non-musicians (see Table 2). In the P1 range and with regard to the melody condition (P^OD^O), *musicians* approached the steady phase already at tone 3. For irregular pitch order (P^RD^O), approximation was at tone 4, while for randomisation of time order (P^OD^R and P^RD^R) the steady state was reached at tone 6. In the N1 range, tendencies for regular and for completely irregular structure (P^OD^O and P^RD^R) were the same as for the P1 (i.e. the steady state was approximated at tone 3 and 6). For randomised pitch (P^RD^O), the steady state was reached around tone 5, whereas for randomised time structure (P^OD^R), it was already approached at tone 4. With regard to the P2, the change-over point was fairly constant for the melody condition (approximately tone 3), but was quite early for the remaining conditions P^OD^R, P^RD^O, and P^RD^R. In these cases the steady state was already approached at tone 3.

Non-musicians, by contrast, surprisingly did not make any clear difference between conditions in terms of reaching the steady state of neural activation. They approached the steady state between tones 3 and 4, apparently regardless of sequence structure and time window.

179

ERP grand average

Figures 7 and 8 show the ERP grand average traces of musicians and non-musicians. They are the averaging result for the assumed steady state of brain activity, i.e. over all tones per condition except the six initial notes of each sequence example. For these initial tones, trend lines in the ERP scattergrams have revealed different slopes per sequence type which might indicate different processing velocity for identifying sequence structure until the steady state is reached (see diagrams 4 to 6 and previous section).

The ERP grand average traces show three distinct amplitude peaks in the early time range up to 250 ms as distinctive features of the P1, N1, and P2 components. No effects beyond 250 ms could be observed. Over all channels, musicians had slightly higher amplitude values than non-musicians.

For each component of the grand average ERP, we observed a different rank order of amplitudes depending on sequence structure (condition), which, for the most part, was congruent with the rank order of trend lines in the scattergrams. It was $P^R D^R / P^O D^R > P^R D^O > P^O D^O$ for the P1 and for the P2 in musicians, and $P^R D^R > P^O D^R / P^R D^O > P^O D^O$ ($P^R D^R > P^O D^R > P^R D^O > P^O D^O$) for the P1 (P2) in non-musicians. For the N1, amplitude-order at frontal channels[10] was $P^R D^R / P^O D^R > P^R D^O / P^O D^O$ and $P^R D^R / P^O D^R > P^R D^O > P^O D^O$ for musicians and non-musicians, respectively, i.e. between $P^R D^R$ and $P^O D^R$ on the one hand as well as $P^R D^O$ and $P^O D^O$ on the other, we found only marginal differences in amplitude, if at all. Thus, in all three components, amplitude peaks for well-ordered versus double permuted structure ($P^O D^O$ vs. $P^R D^R$) were the corner points, and deflections for simple time randomisation independent of pitch ($P^O D^R$) were larger than those for pitch randomisation independent of time ($P^R D^O$; see Figures 7 and 8).[11] Musicians, in particular, showed highest amplitude values for randomized time order independent of the ordering of pitches ($P^O D^R$ and $P^R D^R$), while both subject groups had lowest amplitude values for structured melodies.

We tested the effects with an ANOVA per time window, and separately for musicians and non-musicians. In both groups, statistical tests yielded a main effect of PITCH and of TIME for the P1 and P2, but not for the N1, indicating that P1 and P2 amplitude differences *may partly* result from an *independent* processing of pitch and time order. Furthermore, *musicians* in contrast to non-musicians showed a highly significant interaction PITCH x TIME in the P1 range, which was only marginally significant for the P2. Significant interaction results were specified by several one-way posthoc ANOVAs. In terms of the P1, musicians distinguished between order and disorder of either pitch or time, when the respective second factor was of regular structure. For the P2, the result was extended, in that musicians differentiated between time order and disorder when pitch structure was either regular or scrambled (see Table 3 for details). Musicians as compared to non-musicians also showed stronger and more frequent first and second order interactions with Channel in the N1 and P2 range, indicating that amplitude differences between factor levels (pitch order versus disorder and time order versus disorder) became smaller in anterior-posterior direction (fronto-central to

---

[10] slightly different at central and parietal electrode sites.

[11] The only exception is the P1 of non-musicians, revealing equal-sized amplitudes for conditions $P^O D^R$ and $P^R D^O$ at all electrode sites.

parietal), whereas no such differences could be observed in left-right direction, i.e. between hemispheres in both subject groups.

Non-musicians showed a significant interaction PITCH x TIME for the N1 component. Posthoc ANOVAs revealed that they distinguished between time order and disorder given that pitch structure was regular, which is similar to the P1 results in musicians (see Tables 3 and 4).

An additional between-subjects-ANOVA revealed a significant interaction PITCH x TIME x GROUP in terms of the P1, emphasizing that musicians distinguished quite early between time order and disorder when pitch was of regular structure. A similar significant interaction PITCH x TIME x GROUP could also be found for the N1. This time, effects were caused by non-musicians, who distinguished between time order and disorder whenever pitch was identified as regular.

Discussion

ERP single tone analysis

From the trend lines of the scattergrams it became apparent that the time for the brain to reach the steady state depends on the regularity of pitch and time dimensions. This may reflect the time needed to identify the structure of a sequence. Nonetheless, we have to specify these results according to musical expertise, i.e. according to different levels of skill in analytical hearing. Musicians seem to identify the type of sequence between tones 3 and 6, and structure recognition takes shortest for melodies, i.e. when pitch and time properties are balanced (condition P^OD^O). Recognition, on the other hand, takes longest when *time order* is at random, suggesting that this type of information might be more important than pitch. For non-musicians, however, recognition time over sequence type and ERP time window is almost the same. Obviously, they do not focus strongly on different structural aspects. Thus, formal musical training may indeed influence the strategy of processing sequence structure.

ERP grand average and the dissociation between pitch and time

We conclude from the ANOVA results that for identifying sequence structure, time and pitch should be considered equally important. The relevance of time was corroborated by highly significant main effects (F-values) in the P1 and P2 window, and was also underlined by the posthoc analyses of P1 and P2 interactions for musicians, revealing that pitch order could be distinguished from disorder when time as the second factor was of regular structure. Additional evidence was given by the visual display of ERP components, demonstrating that - against our fourth hypothesis - it is randomised time, regardless of preserved or permuted pitch/interval structure, that caused the largest peak values in all three components. This indicates a higher mental processing effort to integrate an incoming tone of unpredictable time value into the existing context, and selective attention might be more intense to build a perceptual object, if at all.

In this regard, our results differ from those obtained by Hébert and Peretz (1997), who found the converse relationship, i.e. superiority of pitch over time independent of musical expertise. In their study, recognizability of familiar excerpts was tested in such a way that either isochronous pitch or pure rhythm patterns contained the music information. Nonetheless, both authors tested the retrieval ability of subjects in this study, i.e. the recall of tunes when long-term memory had been activated. Thus, because of the task which points to another phase in cognitive processing, priority differences in comparison to our study are likely, in which subjects simply had to memorize a sequence.

With regard to the independence-interdependence debate in terms of processing pitch and time (for a review see Peretz & Zatorre, 2005), our chosen paradigm was well-suited to show that, apparently, both processes are interwoven and take place simultaneously, which supports the seventh of our hypotheses. In this regard, however, ANOVA results should be differentiated according to the level of analytical listening skills. On the one hand, significant main effects of PITCH and TIME without any first-order interactions are the basic result for non-musicians. It shows that during an early (P1) and a later (P2) processing stage time information may be encoded and identified *independently* from pitch structure and vice versa.

On the other hand, and for musicians in particular, posthoc analyses of the interactions between pitch and time shed light on two more aspects of musical sequence processing. First, structure identification of one dimension on the basis of a regular second dimension points towards a hierarchical manner of encoding. Second, pitch and time interactions occur earlier (P1) in musicians than in non-musicians (N1) so that, in accordance with our fifth hypothesis, formal musical training seems to be a decisive factor. When encoding a new type of sequence structure already in the preattentive processing phase, musicians, much more than non-musicians, might seek for a grid of metrical regularity in order to perceptually organise the actual tone input along the time axis. This explanation is in line with a computational model of Large and Palmer (2002) which assumes, that listeners perceive temporal fluctuations in a piece of music against an internal system of small and regular oscillations.

With regard to the specific role of ERP components, we tentatively share the view of Meeren et al. (2005), expressing that, from a top-down perspective, ERP components within the time range up to 200 ms, reflect the *same* stage of structural encoding, even though the mode of conscious awareness might be different. This means, in other words, that from the rank order of amplitudes in our study, which is quite similar between components and subject groups, it might be too vague to conclude, that each component represents a *different* processing stage in such a way, that the P1 might reflect the processing of ordered versus orderless time, and the N1 that of pitch structure, while the P2 might reveal the influence of tone predictability, possibly with recourse to mentally stored rules and representations. However, there is evidence in literature that, as regards *time processing* in the primary and secondary auditory cortex, a large number of duration-specific neurons of the little brown bat (*Myotis lucifugus*) do indeed respond differently to long in contrast to short stimulus duration (Galazyuk et al., 1997). Nonetheless, this result does not explain how the brain encodes temporal *cohesion*, i.e. the processing of tone durations in regular or irregular relationship to each other. In spite of this, Johnsrude et al. (2000) demonstrated in a brain lesion study that the right primary auditory cortex could process not only absolute but also relative tone information, i.e. when the direction of pitch change in tone pairs had to be evaluated. The result suggests a kind of higher order perceptual mechanism already for early processing stages and is in accordance with our results for identifying temporal order on the basis of pitch regularity, for which ANOVA yielded significant interaction results for the P1 in musicians and for the N1 in non-musicians.

Taken together, the objective of our study was to investigate, how pitch and time factors are processed either in spatio-temporal coherence (condition $P^O D^O$), in complete incoherence ($P^R D^R$), or when randomised independently ($P^O D^R$ and $P^R D^O$) while leaving the respective second factor unchanged. Our findings specify and extend the results of the former Gestalt study of Neuhaus and Knösche (2006), in which the authors arrive at similar conclusions, although restricted to both dimensions in coincidence (i.e. for regular versus completely randomised sequences $P^O D^O$ vs. $P^R D^R$).

Nonetheless, our ERP results are in an apparent contrast to the neuroimaging findings by Levitin and Menon (2005). This might partly result from the respective measuring method at hand. While our ERP study shows enhanced components for irregular time order, the fMRI study proves activation, when musical structure was *preserved,* but not when temporal cohesion between adjacent items was disrupted. Levitin and Menon explain their results by introducing a kind of "structure tracker", for which Brodmann Area 47 of the left inferior frontal cortex and its right hemisphere homologue are activated whenever musical syntax is detected. This "structure tracker" might therefore serve as a framework for identifying regularity similar to the metrical grid suggested by Large and Palmer (2002).

ERP and fMRI methods, however, investigate different aspects of functional brain activation, as the resolution in time and space varies between these methods. ERP can detect short processes within the time course of brain activity, but requires concurrent activation of a large mass of parallel pyramidal cells. FMRI, by contrast, can detect much smaller active brain areas, but tends to miss short activations that do not consume much energy. It is therefore quite plausible, that both methods measure partially different processes related to musical structure.

Conclusions

In this study on processing musical sequence structure, the grand average ERP depicted brain data in compressed form and separate per sequence type. Thus, we tried to produce a neurophysiological equivalent for the "Tongestalt" as a mental sound picture. However, the grand average for well-balanced sequences in contrast to orderless pitch and/or time structure did not reveal any *specific* component for the build-up of a perceptual unit or melodic Gestalt. This means that, in terms of the new holistic property named "Gestaltqualität", which is obviously inherent in the "Tongestalt", we could not find a neural correlate using the paradigm at hand.

Instead, our measurements show that sequence processing in music is a matter of encoding, and thus, early, but not late ERP components were affected in our study. In detail, amplitude size of the P1, N1, and P2 revealed that the amount of processing effort for tone encoding and integration depends on sequence structure, and that especially for trained musicians, time information is at least as relevant as pitch.

Furthermore, event-related potentials seem to be a suitable method to map the time-course of sequence processing in detail, as can be seen in the ERP scattergrams. According to this, basic identification of pitch and time order is between tones 3 and 6, and in this respect, musicians differ from non-musicians, in that lacking time information particularly hampers structure identification.

As regards the precedence of pitch over time, our grand average results showed, that priority order was equal or might be opposite. Thus, it was the encoding of irregular time values, either with or without regular pitch, that evoked the highest level of amplitude, especially in musicians. Furthermore, ANOVA statistics suggested two mechanisms of processing pitch and time, depending on the level of analytical listening skills. That is, while for non-musicians significant main effects point towards some degree of *independent* processing of pitch and time order, posthoc analyses of interactions showed the *interwoven* processing of both parameters for the P1, N1, and P2, in that structure identification of one dimension depended on the regularity of the second dimension. In addition to that, interactions between pitch and time occurred earlier (P1) in musicians than in non-musicians (N1), so that, in accordance with our fifth hypothesis, formal musical training seems to be a decisive factor.

In any case, the task in our experiment (listen carefully and memorize the sequence) shows the active role of mind during musical sequence processing, and top-down strategies such as attention, context matching, expectancy, and predictability of tone progression already seem to be effective in the early phase of sequence encoding. However, to study the influence of long-term memory on this process was beyond our scope and might be an issue for further studies.

In sum, pitch and time properties of a musical sequence may be processed in an independent as well as interwoven manner, depending on the level of musical expertise. Besides that, formal musical training seems to point out the role of temporal information in the recognition of sequence structure.

Acknowledgements

I owe thanks to Angela D. Friederici and Thomas R. Knösche for valuable discussions and statistical advice.
I thank Ina Koch for careful EEG measurements.
The current contribution is an extended and modified version of C. Neuhaus, & T. R. Knösche (2007). Sequential processing of pitch and time relations in music. 1 – 16 (submitted).

References

Boltz, M. G. (1999). The processing of melodic and temporal information: independent or unified dimensions? *Journal of New Music Research 28(1)*, 67 - 79.

Deutsch, D. (1994). Die Wahrnehmung auditiver Muster. In N. Birbaumer, D. Frey, & J. Kuhl (Series Eds.) & W. Prinz, & B. Bridgeman (Vol. Eds.), *Enzyklopädie der Psychologie: Vol. 1. Wahrnehmung* (pp. 339 – 389). Göttingen: Hogrefe.

Galazyuk, A. V., & Feng, A. S. (1997). Encoding of sound duration by neurons in the auditory cortex of the little brown bat, *Myotis lucifugus*. *Journal of Comparative Physiology A 180*, 301 – 311.

Hébert, S., & Peretz, I. (1997). Recognition of music in long-term memory: Are melodic and temporal patterns equal partners? *Memory & Cognition 25(4)*, 518 – 533.

Hillyard, S. A., Teder-Sälejärvi, W. A., & Münte, T. F. (1998). Temporal dynamics of early perceptual processing. *Current Opinion in Neurobiology 8(2)*, 202 – 210.

Johnsrude, I. S., Penhune, V. B., & Zatorre, R. J. (2000). Functional specificity in the right human auditory cortex for perceiving pitch direction. *Brain 123*, 155 – 163.

Large, E. W., & Palmer, C. (2002). Perceiving temporal regularity in music. *Cognitive Science 26*, 1 – 37.

Levitin, D. J., & Menon, V. (2005). The neural locus of temporal structure and expectancies in music: evidence from functional neuroimaging at 3 Tesla. *Music Perception 22(3)*, 563 – 575.

Meeren, H. K. M., van Heijnsbergen, C. C: R. J., & de Gelder, B. (2005). Rapid perceptual integration of facial expression an emotional body language. *Proceedings of the National Academy of Sciences 102(45)*, 16518 – 16523.

Neuhaus, C., & Knösche, T. R. (2006). Processing of rhythmic and melodic Gestalts - an ERP study. *Music Perception 24(2)*, 209 – 222.

Oldfield, R. C. (1971). The assessment and analysis of handedness: The Edinburgh inventory. *Neuropsychologia 9*, 97 – 113.

Oostenveld, R., & Praamstra, P. (2001). The five percent electrode system for high-resolution EEG and ERP measurements. *Clinical Neurophysiology 112*, 713 – 719.

Palmer, C., & Krumhansl, C. L. (1987). Independent temporal and pitch structures in determination of musical phrases. *Journal of Experimental Psychology: Human Perception and Performance 13(1)*, 116 – 126.

Patel, A. D., Gibson, E., Ratner, J., Besson, M., & Holcomb, P. J., (1998). Processing syntactic relations in language and music: An event-related potential study. *Journal of Cognitive Neuroscience 10*, 717 – 733.

Patel, A. D. (2003). A new approach to the cognitive neuroscience of melody. In I. Peretz & R. J. Zatorre (eds.), *The cognitive neuroscience of music* (pp. 325 – 345). Oxford: Oxford University Press.

Peretz, I., & Morais, J. (1989). Music and modularity. *Contemporary Music Review 4*, 279 - 293.

Peretz, I., & Zatorre, R. J. (2005). Brain organization for music processing. *Annual Review of Psychology 56,* 89 – 114.

Picton, T. W., Bentin, S., Berg, P., Donchin, E., Hillyard, S. A., Johnson, R., Miller, G. A., Ritter, W., Ruchkin, D. S., Rugg, M. D., & Taylor, M. J. (2000). Guidelines for using human event-related potentials to study cognition: Recording standards and publication criteria. *Psychophysiology 37,* 127 – 152.

Sims, W. L. (1986). The effect of high versus low teacher affect and passive versus active student activity during music listening on preschool children's attention, piece preference, time spent listening, and piece recognition, *Journal of Research in Music Education 34(3)*, 173 – 191.

Tanner, W. P., & Swets, J. A. (1954). A decision-making theory of visual perception. *Psychological Review 61*, 401 – 409.

Treisman, A. M., & Gelade, G. (1980). A feature-integration theory of attention. *Cognitive Psychology 12*, 97 – 136.

von Ehrenfels, C. (1890). Ueber 'Gestaltqualitäten'. *Vierteljahrsschrift für wissenschaftliche Philosophie 14*, 249 – 292.

White, B. W. (1960). Recognition of distorted melodies. *The American Journal of Psychology 73(1)*, 100 – 107.

Wundt, W. (1874). *Grundzüge der physiologischen Psychologie*. Leipzig: Engelmann Verlag.

Tables

Table 1. Repeated-Measures ANOVAs. Overview of brain activity merged over conditions and tones (the initial tone is excluded).

a. Two-factor, Overall; musicians

Source	df	F
Window x Channel	16,192	28.21***

b. Two-factor, Overall; non-musicians

Source	df	F
Window x Channel	16,192	27.53***

$^{(*)}p < .08$ $*p < .05$ $**p < .01$ $***p < .001$

Table 2. *ERP single tone activity separate for condition and subject group: Tone numbers and amplitude values when 90% of the asymptotic value is reached.*

ERP-Component	Condition	Musicians		Non-Musicians	
		Tone Number	Amplitude value [µV]	Tone Number	Amplitude value [µV]
P1	$P^O D^R$	6.4	1.64	3.4	0.96
	$P^R D^O$	3.8	1.34	2.7	1.07
	$P^O D^O$	2.8	0.95	2.8	0.76
	$P^R D^R$	6.2	1.57	3.1	1.16
N1	$P^O D^R$	4.0	-1.3	3.9	-1.10
	$P^R D^O$	5.7	-1.24	4.0	-0.91
	$P^O D^O$	3.5	-1.42	3.9	-0.85
	$P^R D^R$	6.8	-1.27	2.8	-1.12
P2	$P^O D^R$	3.3	2.43	3.6	2.33
	$P^R D^O$	2.8	2.33	2.5	2.31
	$P^O D^O$	2.5	1.98	2.5	1.75
	$P^R R^O$	2.9	2.30	2.5	2.49

Table 3. *Repeated-Measures ANOVAs; Musicians' group.*[12]

a. **Four-factor, Overall**

Source	df	F
Window x Pitch x Time x Channel	16,192	3.41*

b. **Three-factor, per Time Window:**
   50 - 100 ms (P1)

Source	df	F
Pitch	1,12	$4.10^{(*)}$

---

[12] For clarity, Tables 3 to 5 include only those effects for which ANOVA statistics yielded significant F values ($p < .08$).

Time	1,12	9.77**
Pitch x Time	1,12	22.42***
(post hoc: pitch $_{regular}$: Time	1,12	50.43***
time $_{regular}$: Pitch	1,12	20.46***)

100 - 150 ms (N1)

Source	df	F
Pitch x Time	1,12	4.18$^{(*)}$
(post hoc: time $_{random}$: Pitch	1,12	4.11$^{(*)}$)
Pitch x Time x Channel	8,96	5.38**

170 - 220 ms (P2)

Source	df	F
Pitch	1,12	7.31*
Time	1,12	28.51***
Pitch x Time	1,12	3.92(*)
(post hoc: pitch $_{regular}$: Time	1,12	31.01***
pitch $_{random}$: Time	1,12	11.59**
time $_{regular}$: Pitch	1,12	16.61**)
Pitch x Channel	8,96	3.37$^{(*)}$
Time x Channel	8,96	11.57***

$^{(*)}$p < .08   *p < .05   **p < .01   ***p < .001

Table 4. *Repeated-Measures ANOVAs; Non-musicians' group.*

a. Three-factor, Overall

Source	df	F
Window x Pitch x Time	2,24	3.82*

b. Three-factor, per Time Window:
50 - 100 ms (P1)

Source	df	F
Pitch	1,12	7.57*
Time	1,12	5.90*
Pitch x Channel	8,96	$3.20^{(*)}$
Time x Channel	8,96	4.17*

100 - 150 ms (N1)

Source	df	F
Pitch x Time	1,12	5.33*
(post hoc: pitch $_{regular}$: Time	1,12	5.67*)
Time x Channel	8,96	$3.23^{(*)}$

170 - 220 ms (P2)

Source	df	F
Pitch	1,12	21.06***
Time	1,12	73.35***
Pitch x Channel	8,96	5.82**

Time x Channel	8,96	13.38***
Pitch x Time x Channel	8,96	4.66**

(*)p < .08   *p < .05   **p < .01   ***p < .001

Table 5. *Repeated-Measures ANOVAs; between-subjects-comparison (Musicians vs. Non-musicians).*

Four-factor, per Time Window:
  50 - 100 ms (P1)

Source	df	F
Pitch x Time x Group	1,23	6.19*
(posthoc: pitch $_{regular}$: Time x Group	1,24	9.65**)

  100 - 150 ms (N1)

Source	df	F
Pitch x Time x Group	1,23	9.08**
(posthoc: pitch $_{regular}$: Time x Group	1,24	4.34*)
Pitch x Time x Channel x Group	8,184	4.20**

(*)p < .08   *p < .05   **p < .01   ***p < .001

Figures

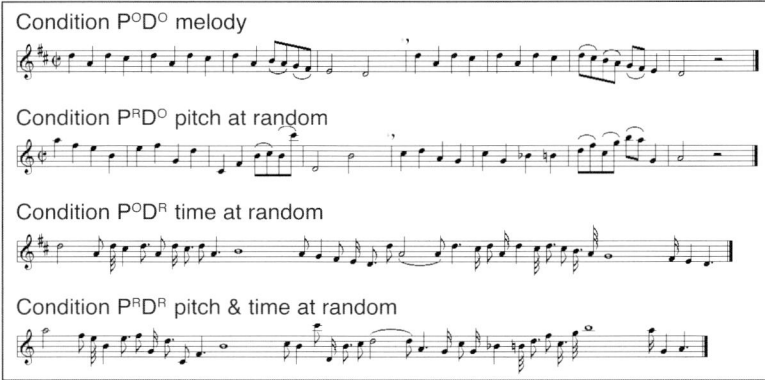

Figure 1: Note examples, illustrating tone sequence structure.
a. Condition P^OD^O (structured melody), pitch and time in balance (from a Sonata for two recorders and basso continuo by Robert Valentine, 1720).
b. Condition P^RD^O. Same instrumental piece with preserved time structure, but randomised pitch.
c. Condition P^OD^R. Pitch structure as defined in the original version. Time values scrambled over all note examples.
d. Condition P^RD^R. Pitch and time in randomised order.

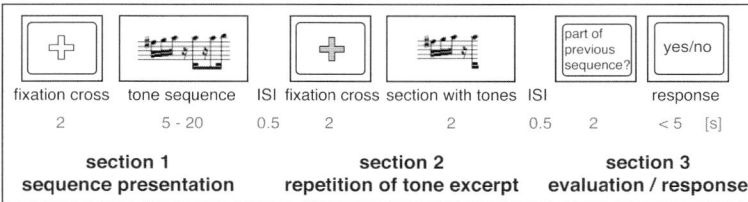

Figure 2.[13]: Flowchart of the experiment set-up.

---

[13] ISI = interstimulus interval; blank screen

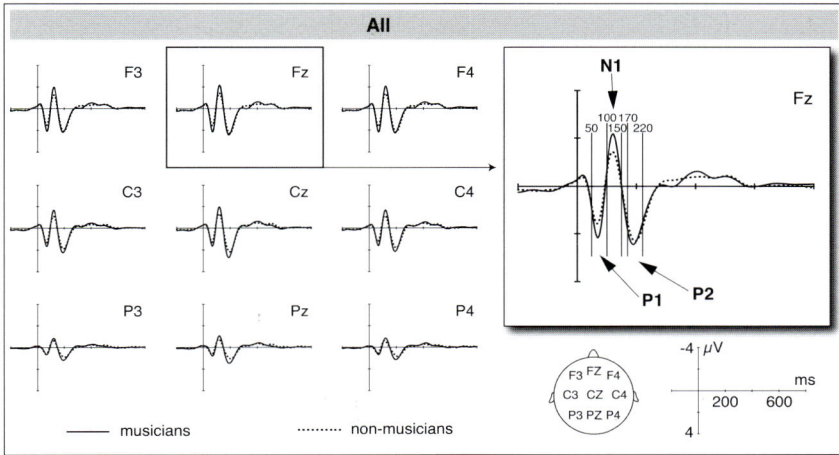

Figure 3: Overall grand average ERP over conditions and tones; responses of musicians and non-musicians. The shape-distorting initial tone (onset response) is omitted.

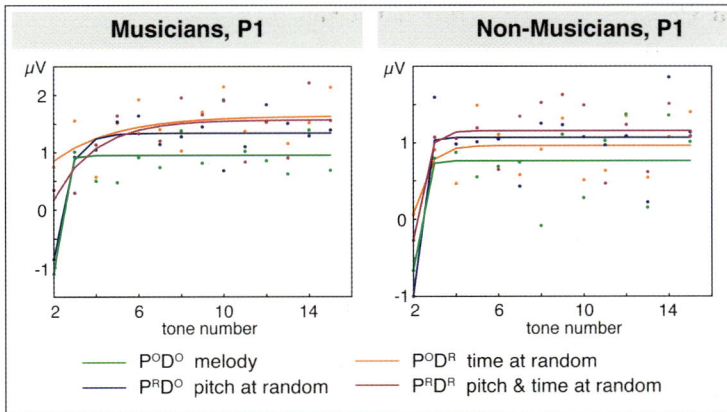

Figure 4: Scattergrams with trend lines. P1 amplitude is plotted against tone number (tones 2 to 15; conditions P^OD^O, P^RD^O, P^OD^R, and P^RD^R). Musicians' responses are in Figure 4a, non-musicians' responses are in Figure 4b, anterior part of the brain.

193

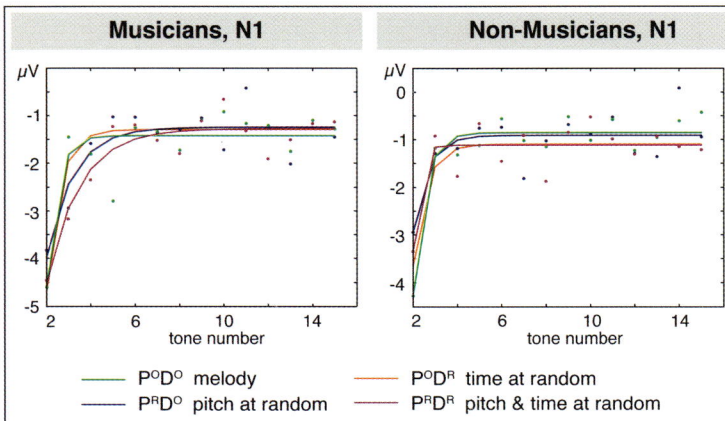

Figure 5: Scattergrams with trend lines, relating N1 amplitude and tone number. Musicians' activity in Figure 5a, non-musicians' activity in Figure 5b.

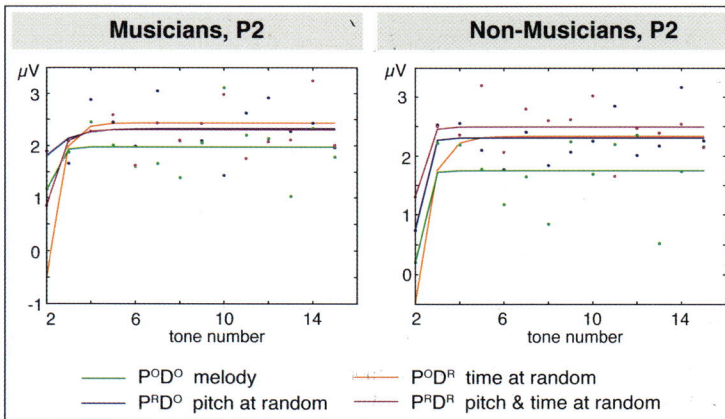

Figure 6: Scattergrams with trend lines, relating P2 amplitude and tone number. Musicians' activity in Figure 6a, non-musicians' activity in Figure 6b.

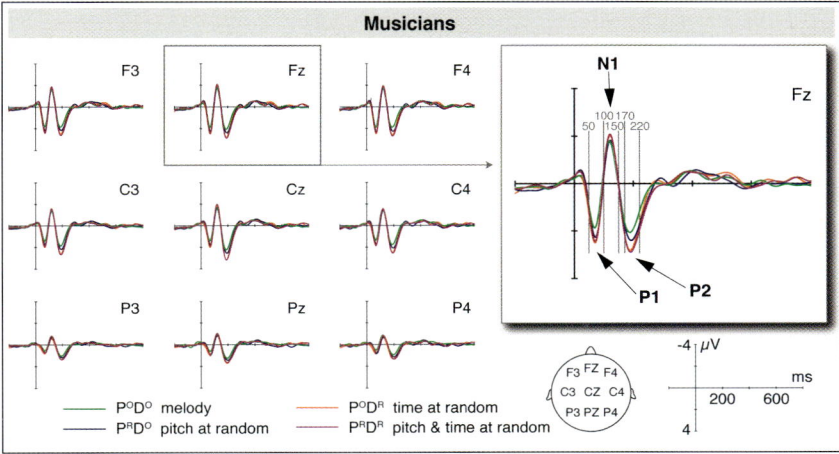

Figure 7: Grand average ERP of musicians at selected EEG channels. Compressed form of brain activity over all tones per condition (from tone 6 onward).

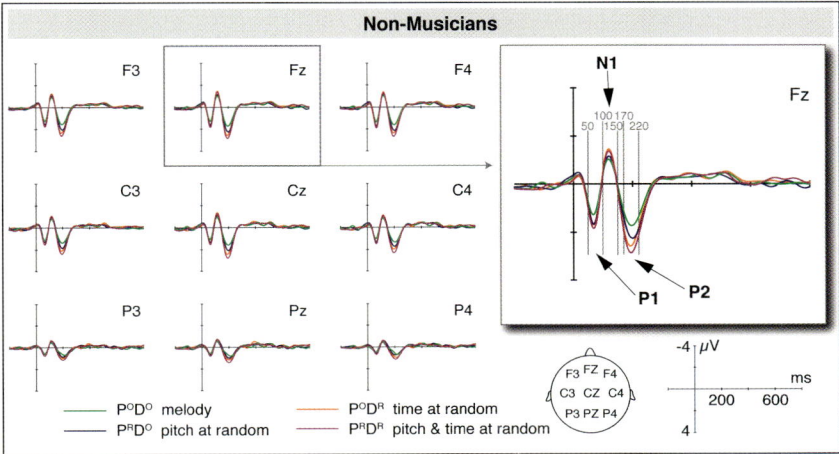

Figure 8: Grand average ERP of non-musicians; same form of compressed brain activity (from tone 6 onward).

195

Rolf Bader

Efficient Auditory Coding of a Xylophone Bar

Introduction

Efficient coding of auditory or visual signals is based on the idea of the sensory system efficiently processing the data which come into the sensory channels. Although the efficiency must be a relative term as the goals of sensing the world may vary. If one needs to perceive only a visual trigger the coding may take much less effort than if one wants to look at a painting for pleasure, or listen to a sound because of its beauty based on complexity. Nevertheless, in many cases a clear definition of efficiency can be given and redundant information may be excluded by data reduction.

So for vision, efficient models for detecting and perceiving pictures have been proposed, where redundant information is reduced by using edge detection [Schwartz & Simoncelli 2001] or other statistical and probabilistic models [Rao et al. 2002] in accordance with experimental findings. It shows up, that with visual objects the variance of filters analysing a visual field is not independent of the frequency analysed, a fact also true for auditory data. Another method widely used is the principle component analysis of visual data [Simoncelli & Olshausen 2001], where from an arbitrary pixel field the basic features are extracted by rotation and translation of the picture. This method is used in everyday life without a special notice, still for the neuronal system it is quite an effort to perform this task. So if one sees a cross which is distorted by looking at it from a side view, the main property of it being a cross is detected by subjects instantaneously without the need to analyse or think about it. But only by rotation and distortion, two orthogonal lines can be extracted which then are linear independent one from another. This linear independence – the features being orthogonal – is what makes them components.

This basic property of features being orthogonal is also needed when analysing sounds, which is automatically true if we perform a Fourier analysis of sounds. The spectrum is nothing but a set of orthogonal base vectors, independent one from another. Starting from these principle component bases, efficient models of auditory perception have been proposed [Dau et al. 1996a] [Dau et al. 1996b] [Lewicki 2002a] [Lewicki 2002b] [Olshausen 2002] [Smith & Lewicki 2005]. The basic idea is to reduce redundancy and still perceive the sound without loss. As the auditory nerve fibre output is then further processed, its output is used in the model which is mathematically similar to a gammatone, and so the cochlear is taken as a gammatone filter bank [de Boer & de Jongh 1978] [Patterson et al. 1991] [Patterson et al. 2003] [Van Immerseel & Peeters 2003] [Lopez-Poveda & Meddis 2001]. Here traditional filter bank models use the sound input and filter it according to 24 critical bands. These filter responses may then be processed further, for example, for pitch detection. Still this method uses redundant information as the temporal resolution may overestimate the information in the cochlear channels. Also neighbouring filters may represent signals twice to a certain extent, and thereby process more information to the brain than actually is present in the sound.

As confirmed by experimental results of cat nerve fibres, an efficient coding with gammatones is suited to predict the auditory output as gammatones with certain bandwidth, depending on different sound types like environment and cat sounds [Lewicki 2006]. The model trained with cat sounds alone overestimated, while the model trained with environment sounds alone underestimated the bandwidth of the experimental data. Only when training the model with both sound types they did fit to the experimental data. Here again the variance is not independent from the used frequency as was found with the visual data (see above). This means that the efficient model seems to be the way the auditory cochlear system is going to encode the sound coming to the ear.

Now, using the efficient model for musical instrument sounds could answer an important question concerning the complexity of sounds and also of musical instrument building and geometry. Are the instruments built to fit into the efficient coding behaviour of the cochlear? This would mean, that musical instruments are built in a way to have a certain complexity to be interesting for listeners while still being not too complex to overstrain the ear, and so they may not be encoded in that complexity. To turn the question around, one could also argue that musical instruments come close to natural sounds quite often, especially with percussion instruments or with flutes. Nevertheless all the natural instruments made out of wood or steel do have a natural damping behaviour and so reduce the energy of the higher spectral regions much faster than the lower ones.

To make a first step in this field, an efficient model was applied to a Xylophone sound. This sound was used because it comes close to natural sounds which are caused by a strike. This paper discusses the method used in detail and shows results for different gammatone codings to estimate the gammatone shapes of most efficient coding and compare them to measured data found in [Lewicki 2006].

Xylophone sound used in the model

An Orff Xylophone bar was used being struck not by a soft mallet but by a wooden hammer to enhance the higher overtones. The bar is 31.5 cm long, 3.6 cm wide and 2.7 cm in height, where the height differs from the edges of the width to the centre between 3.5 cm to 3.6 cm with the bar being a little bit round. It has a large cutoff in height over its length starting from 8.2 cm at both sides getting smoothly thinner up to its middle, where it is only .55 cm in height. It is supported by a resonance box enhancing the fundamental frequency of 260.1 Hz. The first overtone is at 1055.0 Hz which is nearly perfectly tuned with only 14.6 Hz apart from the second octave which would be at 1040.4 Hz. This is caused by the cutoff which tries to tune the second harmonic at the position of the second octave [Borg 1983] [Bader 2002]. Figure 1 shows the deformation shape of the first eigenfrequency of the bar calculated by a Finite-Element Method.

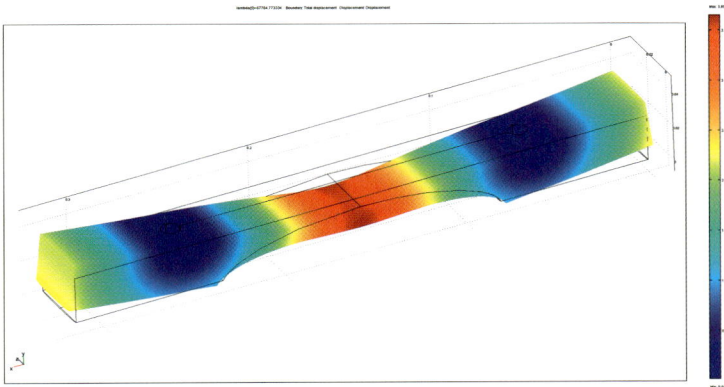

Fig. 1: Finite-Element eigenfrequency solution of the used xylophone bar for the first harmonic, measured frequency $f_m = 260.1$, calculated frequency $f_c = 260.4$. The bar is fixed at the two holes at the sides.

The sound itself is percussive in nature with a broad range of high frequencies. Figure 2 shows the time dependent Wavelet Transformation of the sound with the horizontal axis ranging in frequency from 100 Hz on the right to 10 kHz on the left in a linear way. The up axis is time from 0 ms on the top to 100 ms on the bottom. The amplitude scale is logarithmic. One can clearly see that from around 100 ms on the fundamental mode is the only one left. That is because of support by the resonance box. This continues while decaying for nearly 1 s. The sound used in the efficient coding calculation was chosen to be 200 ms long to keep more of the nearly pure sinusoidal part. This will also show a restriction of the calculation as a representation of a sinusoidal with gammatones which are decaying is problematic. But this will also show the behaviour of an overestimation of the cochlear when using wrong gammatone shapes.

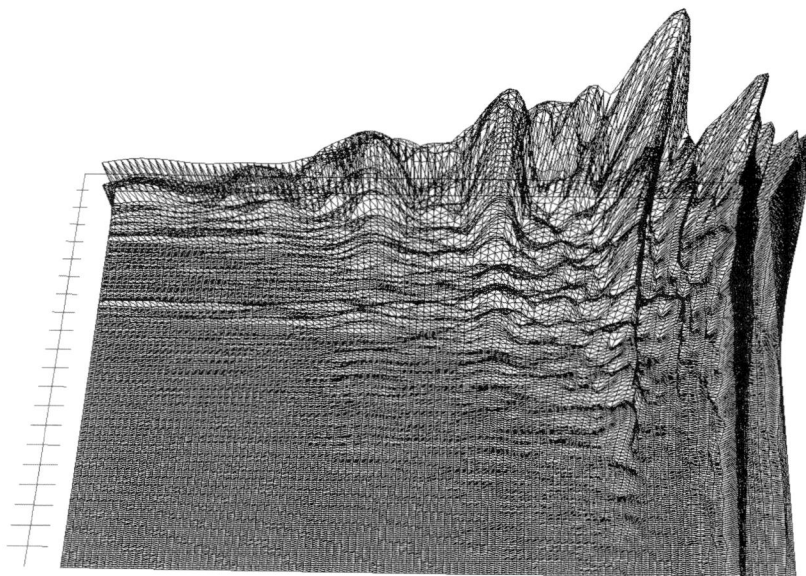

Fig. 2: Wavelet-Spectrum of the Xylophone bar. Horizontal axis shows the frequency range from 100 Hz (left) to 10kHz (right). Up axis is time ranging from 0 ms (up) to 100 ms (bottom).

Efficient coding algorithm using gammatones

The algorithm used here to predict the optimum shape of gammatones to represent the Xylophone sound changes the parameter b of the gammatone definition:

$$x(t) = b^{\eta}\left(\frac{t}{samfreq}\right)^{\eta-1} e^{-2\pi b t} Cos\left[\frac{2\pi fg\, t}{samfreq}\right].$$

Here, x(t) is the time series, $\eta = 2$, samfreq is the sampling frequency, and fg is the frequency of the spike. Different values of b change the length of the gammatone and therefore its bandwidth. Figure 3 shows three examples of one gammatone compared to a sound of a hammer knocking on a violin top plate. The knocking sound shows a rise and decay time of the amplitude shape and a fundamental frequency. The fit of one gammatone here would try to best match the knocking sound by adjusting the frequency and the amplitude shape of the sound, where Fig. 3 c) fits best. Here, the gammatone does not explain the whole knocking sound, so additional gammatones with different frequencies and adjusted rise and decay behaviour concerning the amplitude shape are needed.

In the method used by Lewicki [Lewicki 2006], the gammatones are also compared to the nerve fibre output of the hearing system of the cat. As these nerve fibres are only matched to one best frequency, only one gammatone is needed for each fibre output to fit the measured time series with very high precision.

200

a)

b)

c)

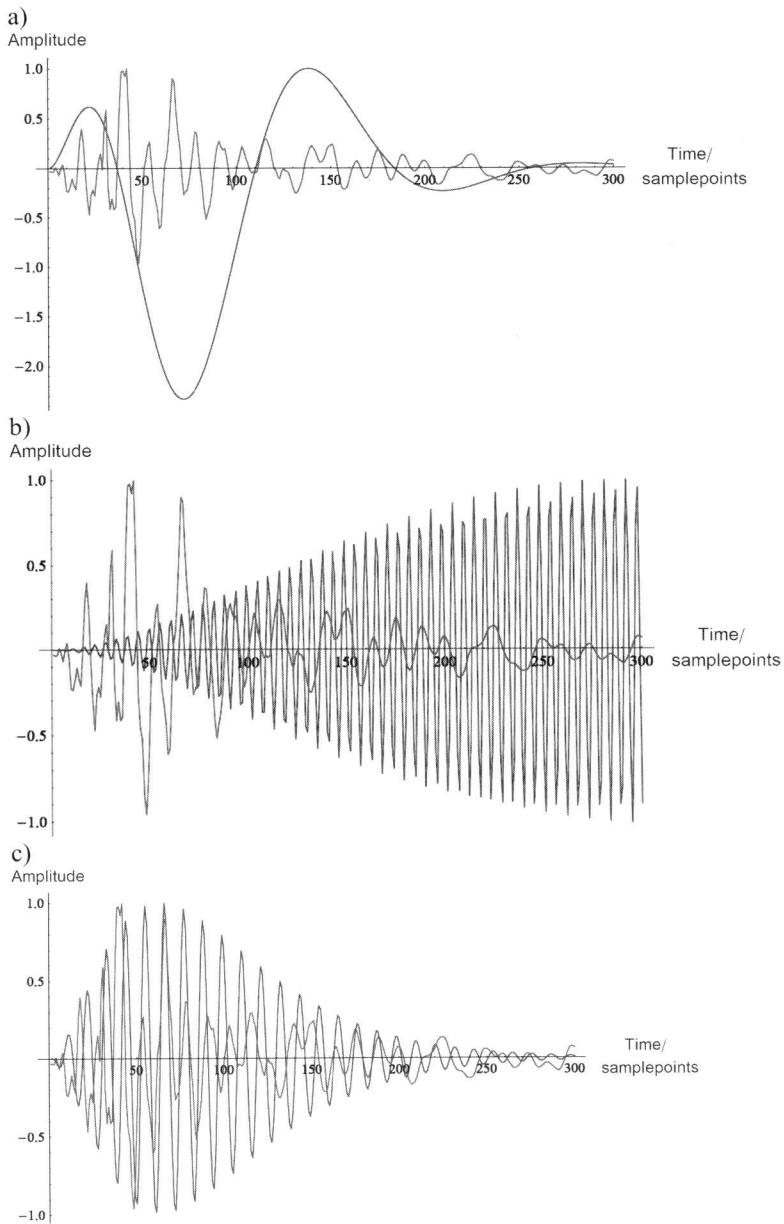

Fig. 3: Comparison between the sound of knocking on a violin top plate with different gammatones: a) frequency is too low, b) value of b is too low, c) good fit in terms of frequency and amplitude shape.

201

So the reasoning of efficient coding is, each sound can be decomposed in gammatones with different frequency and amplitude shape functions which are the nerve fibre outputs. These gammatones would on the one hand represent the sound perfectly and on the other hand do not show any redundancy, as no more than the gammatones used are needed by the system. When performing e.g. a Fourier transform as a waterfall plot where the time window is shifted, the amount of information gathered by the algorithm is much more than needed to reproduce the original time series perfectly again. This is not true for the efficient coding algorithm as the sound is decomposed only into as many gammatones as at least needed to reproduce the original sound again.

Still there are many kinds of gammatones in terms of different frequencies and amplitude shapes we could use for estimating the sound. So the aim of the efficient coding algorithm used here is to find the value of the amplitude shape (by varying the value of b of the gammatone function), which would represent the sound with as few gammatones as possible. The gammatones produced by this value of b are the most efficient way to represent a sound and if the audio system is working in terms of efficient coding, the nerve fibre outputs are about the same shape as the calculated most efficient gammatone amplitude shapes.

Method

So the algorithm was performed in several steps. The value of b in the gammatone function was varied in the range of $0.0004 <= b <= 0.00313$, using a range of gammatone shape functions, which lasted from very short gammatones to very large ones. Figure 4 shows three different gammatone shapes. Plot a) with a value of $b = 0.00313$ and with a frequency of fg = 200 Hz is showing a very short pulse. On the other hand the gammatone in plot c) with b = .0004 and fg = 1000 Hz shows an output of unreasonable long shape. Plot b) with b = .00313 and fg = 200 Hz is most suitable for the output of nerve fibres being of a medium length. So the calculations were performed within this region in 21 steps.

The sound was cut off after 200 ms and cut into 10 parts. The gammatone filter bank consisted of 64 channels ranging from 200 Hz < f < 4350 Hz, as the fundamental frequency of the bar was f_0 = 260.1 Hz .The frequencies above 5 kHz were skipped in this calculation to make it less time consuming. One calculation for one value of b took about a day of calculation time on the Linux parallel cluster of the RRZ (Regionales Rechenzentrum) at the University of Hamburg.

Now for each of the ten slices of the sound, all 64 gammatones were convolved with the normalized sound at all possible time shifts. Then the best fitting gammatone was chosen and substracted from the original sound. For this sound, all 64 gammatones over all possible time shifts were used again. This procedure was repeated until the best fitting gammatone had a threshold of c < 0.5. So the representation of the sound is not perfect in a way that all of the sound is explained. Still the results are comparable as the same threshold was used for every value of b and as shown below, the error as the relation between the original and the remaining sound was about the same for all 21 steps.

What should differ in the results is the amount of gammatones needed to represent the sound. If this amount changes from step to step in a systematic way, the auditory system would be able to adapt to the most efficient value.

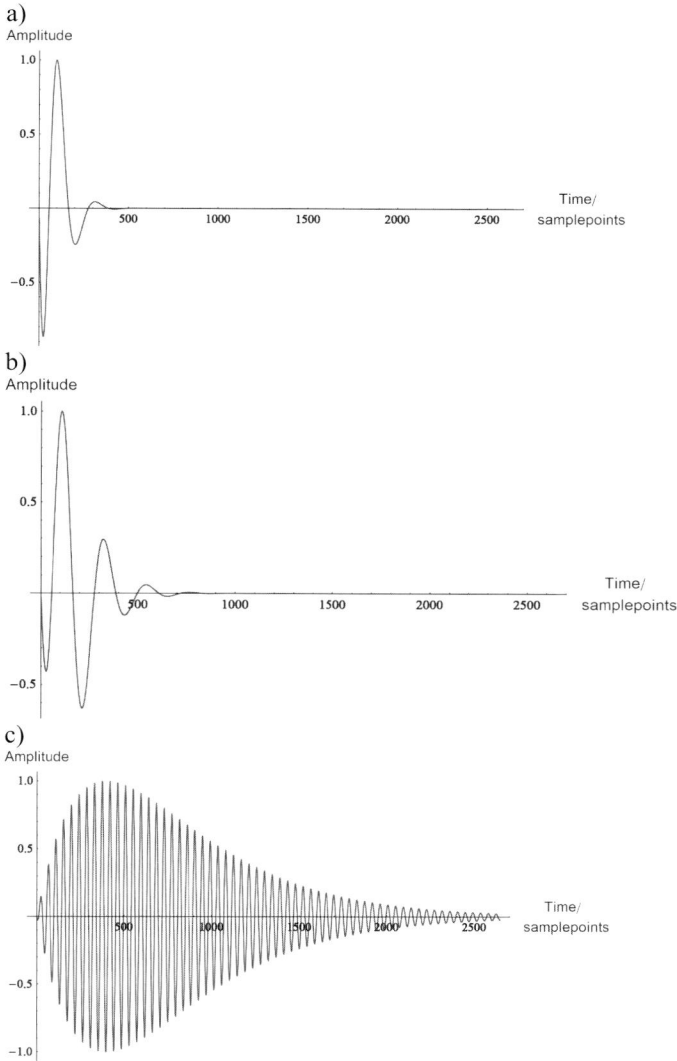

a)

b)

c)

Fig. 4: Different gammatones with varying values of b: a) b = 0.00313, fg = 200 Hz, b) b = 0.0017, fg = 200 Hz, c) b = 0.0004, fg = 1000 Hz. The gammatone of the b) plot is of reasonable shape.

Results

Figure 5 shows the time series of a) the original Xylophone sound, b) the restored sound, reconstructed by the gammatones and c) the error signal ε as the difference between original and reconstructed sound.

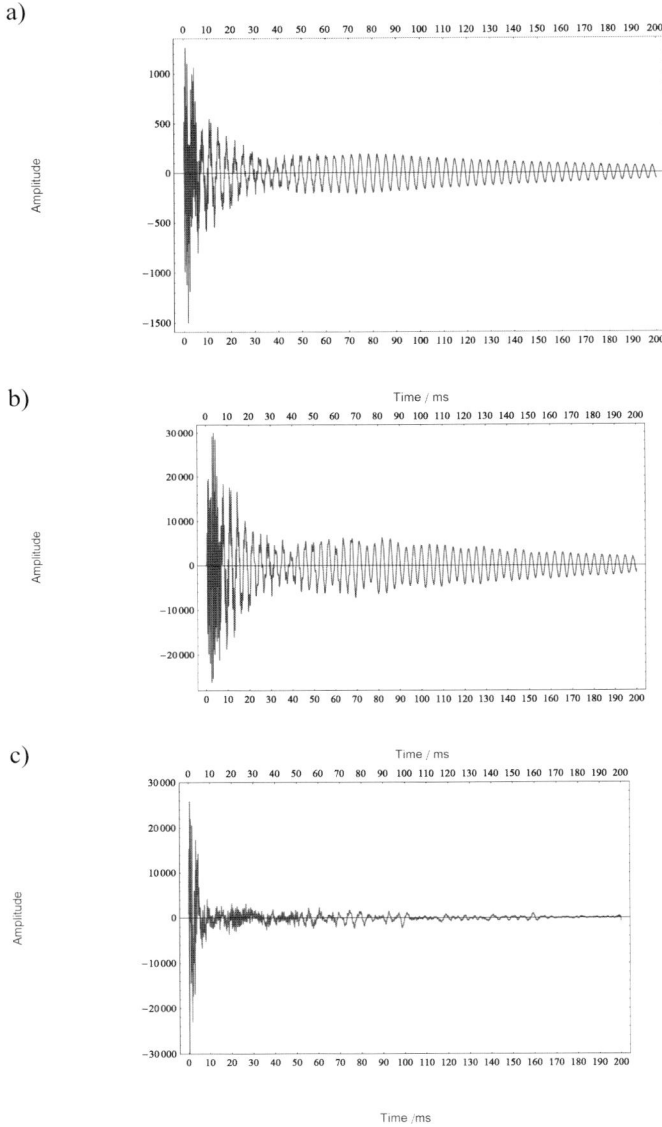

a)

b)

c)

Fig. 5: The Xylophone sound a) original, b) reconstructed and c) error as difference between a) and b).

The reconstructed signal shows some deviations in the initial transient. This is due to the fact that frequencies above 4.5 kHz were not used in the calculation, and so these frequencies remain. Much more interesting is the slight amplitude fluctuation that can be seen in the reconstructed signal. This is caused by the fact, that the gammatones do have a raise and a decay amplitude shape which is not the case for signals in their quasi-steady state. So a reconstruction of these signals with gammatones results in small amplitude fluctuations. This is an interesting finding, as most signals in nature are transient and therefore can easily be modelled with gammatones. Only sounds like musical instruments and other signals with a steady nature are represented much harder by gammatones. So the auditory system uses a periodicity detection here because otherwise it would need unreasonably many gammatones, which is not the case.

Coming back to our problem, the 'spikeograms' of the sounds for different values of b are shown in Fig. 6. The tendency is clear. The larger the value of b, the shorter the gammatones, and so less gammatones are needed to represent the sound. This is astonishing at first sight, as one might expect that larger gammatones would cover wider ranges of the sound. But as the initial transient gammatones need to be very short, large gammatones would overestimate the sound and so lead to unrealistic perception. This can clearly be seen in Fig. 5 a). In this case additional gammatones are needed after the initial transient phase to compensate the estimated gammatones from the beginning. Here, the algorithm still tries to fit the sound as good as possible and so needs to assume new gammatones which are in anti-phase to the wrongly estimated ones. This tendency clears out after about 140 ms, showing that the algorithm does not need additional frequency components anymore. Clearly such a perception would not be preferred, and indeed nerve fibres normally do not show such large gammatone outputs as presented in Fig. 4 c) above.

Additionally, in Fig. 6 a) and b) there are new components added to the sound between 40 ms and 140 ms in the frequency range between the fundamental pitch and the second partial. It is not quite clear yet, why these up-beams occur. One explanation is that the sound resulting after substraction of gammatones being too long could also be explained by frequency components in between.

The picture is getting much more realistic for values from b = .0017 on. In this case, the sound is represented reasonably and the artefacts are gone. This tendency continues for even shorter gammatones which can be seen in Fig. 6 d) for b = .00313. No further calculations were performed here as these gammatones are mostly shorter than one period of the sound – depending on the frequency of the gammatone. This seems not to be a likely representation because the auditory system would need to cut the sound within its very first period. This process would need additional functioning in the cochlea or the ear channel.

So indeed it seems to be, that the auditory system tries to fit its gammatone shapes in a way to efficiently encode the sounds. If they were shorter – less than one period – this representation would mean additional effort for the ear, if they would be longer, the representation would not be able to represent the sound correctly.

a)

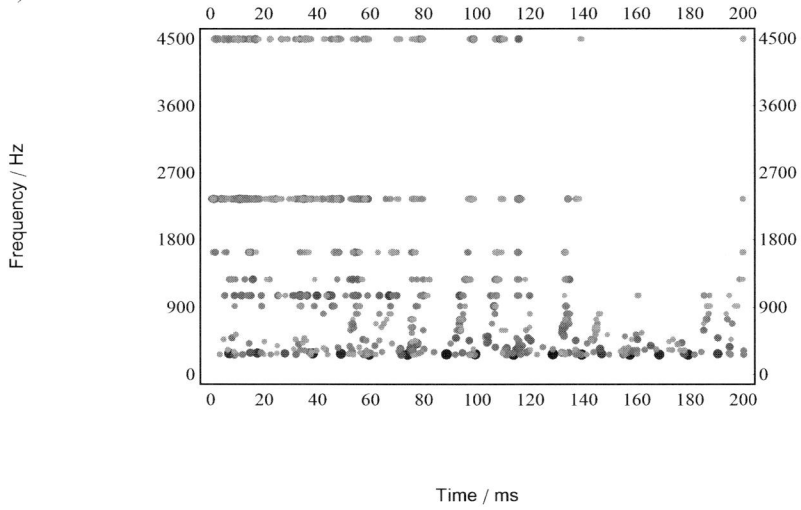

b)

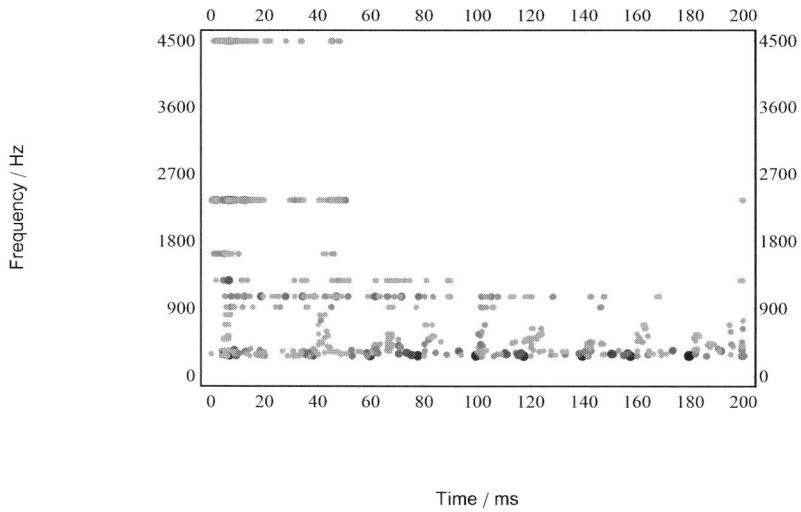

c)

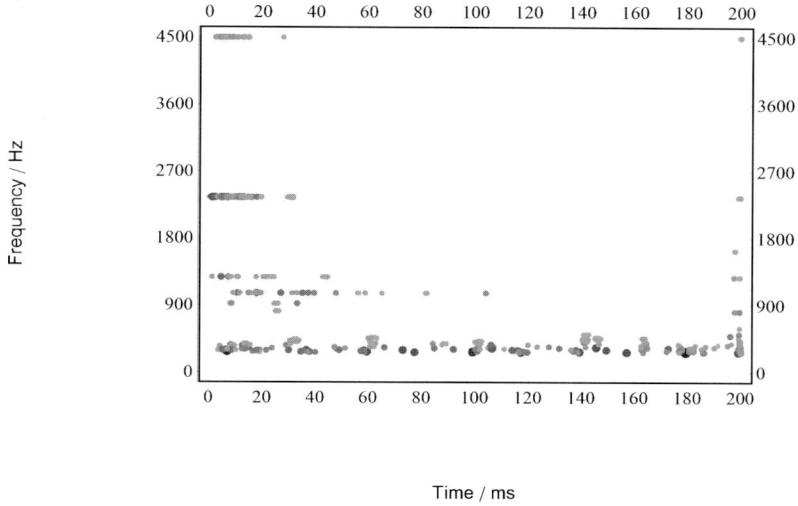

d)

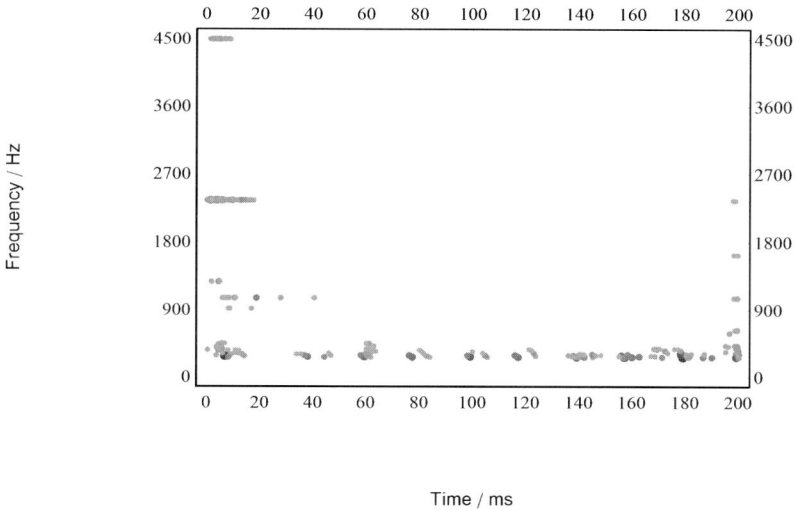

Fig. 6: Gammatone or spike representations of the Xylophone sound for different values of b. a) b = 0.00313, b) b = 0.00105 c) b = 0.0017 and d) b = 0.00313. The gray scale represents the amplitudes of the gammatones. The shorter the gammatones the less are needed to represent the sound.

a)

Amount spikes

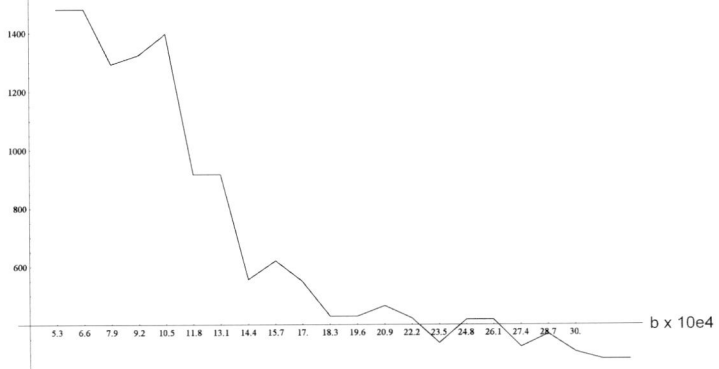

b)

ϵ^2

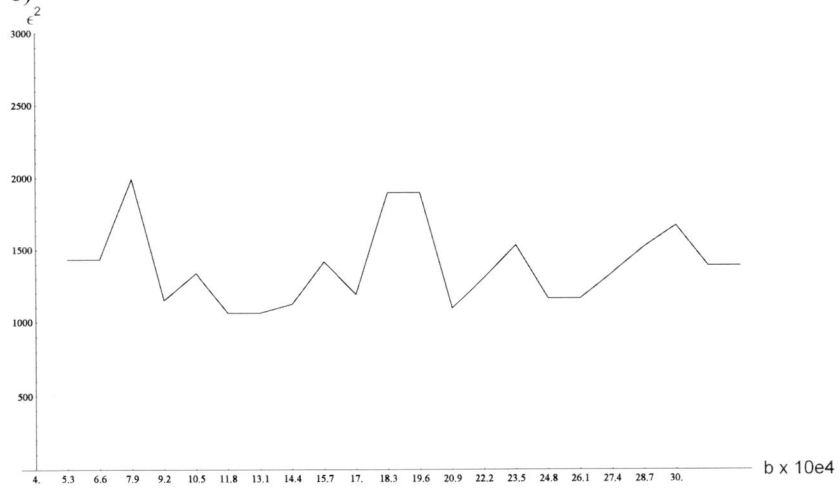

208

c)

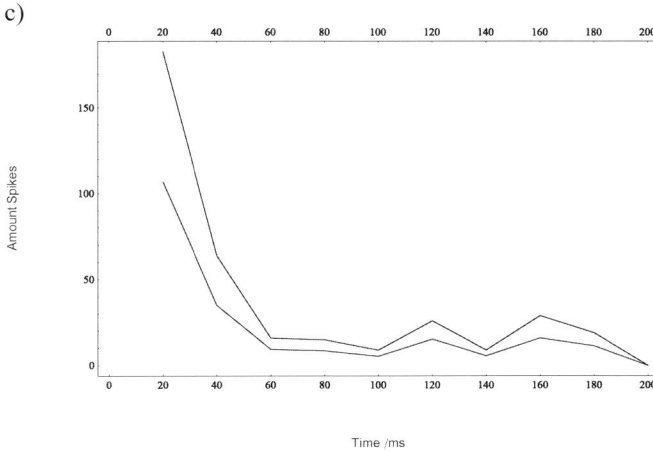

Time /ms

Fig. 7: a) Amount of spikes needed to fit the sound in a way, that convolution with gammatones are below a threshold of c = .5 for values of b of $0.0004 \leq b \leq 0.00313$; b) error ε^2 for these values of b; c) development of the amount of spikes over time for the value of b = 0.0017, absolute amount and weighted with amplitudes, where maximum amplitude was set to a max = 1.

Fig. 7 shows this tendency again. In a) the overall amount of gammatones needed to represent the sound in the used frequency region for a convolution threshold of c = .5 is shown. It decreases exponentially and starts converging from a value of about b = 0.0017 on. For this value in Fig. 7 c) the development of the amount of gammatones needed to represent the sound is shown as a function of time (also compare Fig. 6. c)). Values are shown for the absolute amount and for the amount weighted with the amplitudes of the gammatones. As this amplitude was normalized to a max = 1, the weighted curve must be below the one for absolute amounts.

Fig. 8 shows the gammatones for such a value of b = 0.0017, the value from which on the amount of gammatones needed to represent the sound is converging. They are all in reasonable shape compared to the measured data at auditory nerve fibres in terms of their length. So one could reason that this shape is chosen because it is most efficient in terms of representation of sounds by the auditory system.

209

Amplitude

b)
Amplitude

c)
Amplitude

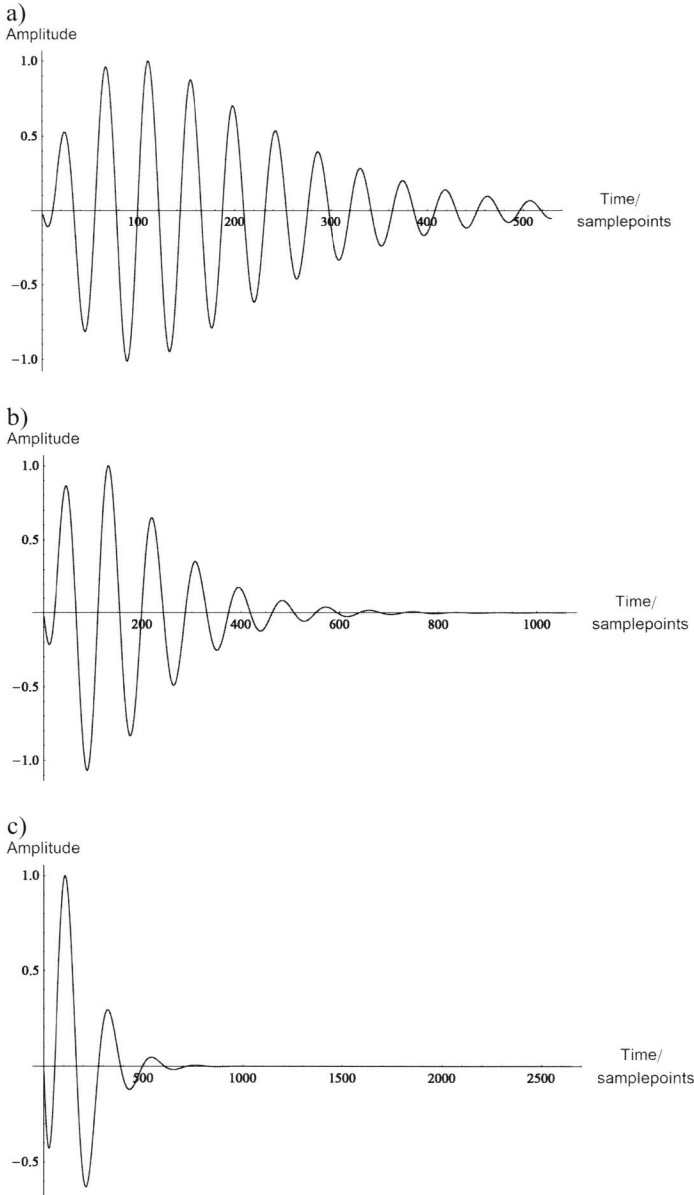

Fig. 8: Gammatones for the value of b = 0.0017 for a) 1000 Hz, b) 500 Hz and c) 200 Hz. They are all in reasonable shape compared to auditory nerve fibre output.

Conclusions

After the initial transient, the gammatone amount decays to a value of about 20 spikes per 20 ms. So for a steady-state sound of mostly one harmonic of frequency f = 260 Hz, roughly estimated, the efficient auditory coding is about 1000 spikes per second. This corresponds to the value found by Lewicki [Lewicki 2006] for transient sounds. The transient sounds he used also showed times of silence, so the values may be compared. For transient sounds, where the changes are constantly going on, we can again roughly estimate, that the auditory system would need about 10 000 gammatones for adequate representation. As a value of 1000 spikes per second seems to be usual with natural sounds and also with sounds of a steady-state with an initial transient, this value may be seen as a middle-of-the-road amount expected by the auditory system.

So it seems to be, that the Xylophone bar sound fits very good into the expected range of auditory nerve fibre output in terms of gammatone shape and the amount of gammatones per second. The reason for that may be, that the Xylophone is a percussion instrument and therefore it is close to natural sounds. But with a look at the results from quasi-steady state solutions of gammatone density (gammatones per time interval) this finding may hold also true for other musical instruments with a steady state like bowed, blown or plucked instruments. Still this needs to be investigated further, as more overtones are expected there and amplitude or frequency fluctuations may occur (vibrato, beating etc.). If these investigations would really point into that direction, we could argue, that 'analog' musical instruments – not electrical or electronical synthesized sounds - are built in a way to fit the gammatone density listeners are used to from everyday sounds or human speech.

References

[Bader 2002] Bader, Rolf: Fraktale Dimensionen, Informationsstrukturen und Mikrorhythmik der Einschwingvorgänge von Musikinstrumenten. PhD Hamburg 2002. http://www.sub.uni-hamburg.de/opus/volltexte/2002/598

[Borg 1983] Borg, Ingolf: Entwicklung von akustischen Optimierungsverfahren für Stabspiele und Membraninstrumente. PTB Report, Projekt 5267, Braunschweig 1983.

[Dau et al. 1996a] Dau, Torsten & Püschel, Dirk, Kohlrausch, Armin: A quantitative model of the "effective" signal processing in the auditory system. I. Model structure. In: J. Acoust. Soc. Am. 99 (6), 3615-3622, 1996.

[Dau et al. 1996b] Dau, Torsten, Püschel, Dirk & Kohlrausch, Armin: A quantitative model of the "effective" signal processing in the auditory system. II. Simulations and measurements. In: J. Acoust. Soc. Am. 99 (6), 3623-31, 1996.

[deBoer & de Jongh 1978] de Boer, E. & de Jongh, H.R.: On cochlear encoding: Potentialities and limitations of the reverse-correlation technique. In: J. Acoust. Soc. Am 63(1), 115-135, 1978.

[Lewicki 2006] Lewicki, Michael S.: Efficient auditory coding. In: nature Vol. 439 (23), 978-82, 2006.

[Lewicki 2002a] Lewicki, Michael S.: Efficient Coding of Time-Varying Signals Using a Spiking Population Code. In: Rao, Rajesh, P.N., Olshausen, Bruno A. & Lewicki, Michael S. (ed.): Probabilistic Models of the Brain. MIT Press, p. 243-56, 2002.

[Lewicki 2002b] Lewicki, Michael S.: Efficient coding of natural sounds. In: nature neuroscience, Vol. 5 (4), 356-63, 2002.

[Lopez-Poveda & Meddis 2001] Lopez-Poveda, Enrique A. & Meddis, Ray: A human nonlinear cochlear filterbank. In: J. Acoust. Soc. Am. 110 (6), 3107-3118, 2001.

[Olshausen 2002] Olshausen, Bruno A.: Sparse Codes and Spikes. In: Rao, Rajesh, P.N., Olshausen, Bruno A. & Lewicki, Michael S. (ed.): Probabilistic Models of the Brain. MIT Press, p. 257-72, 2002.

[Patterson et al. 2003] Patterson, Roy D., Unoki, Masashi & Irino, Toshio: Extending the domain of center frequencies for the compressive gammachirp auditory filter. In: J. Acoust. Soc. Am. 114 (3), 1529-42, 2003.

[Patterson et al. 1991] Patterson, R.D. Holdsworth, J. Nimmo-Smith, I. & Rice, P.: The auditory filter bank. MRC-APU Report 2341, Cambridge, 1991.

[Rao et al. 2002] Rao, Rajesh, P.N., Olshausen, Bruno A. & Lewicki, Michael S. (ed.): Probabilistic Models of the Brain. MIT Press, 2002.

[Schwartz & Simoncelli 2001] Schwartz, Odelia & Simoncelli, Eero P.: Natural signal statistics and sensory gain control. In: nature neuroscience Vol 4(8), 819-25, 2001.

[Simoncelli & Olshausen 2001] Simoncelli, Eero P. & Olshausen, Bruno A.: Natural Image Statictics and Neural Representation. In: Annu. Rev. Neuroscience 24, 1193-216, 2001.

[Smith & Lewicki 2005] Smith, Evan & Lewicki, Michael S.: Efficient Coding of Time-Relative Structure Using Spikes. In: Neural Computation 17, 19-45, 2005.

[Van Immerseel & Peeters 2003] Van Immerseel, Luc & Peeters, Stefaan: Digital implementation of linear gammatone filters: Comparison of design methods. In: Acoustics Research Letters Online 4(3), 59-64, 2003.

Arne von Ruschkowski

Loudness War

Introduction

The terms "Loudness War", "Level War" and "Loudness Race" describe the phenomenon of a constantly growing loudness of CDs containing popular music in the last two decades.[1] The expression "war" indicates that these terms not only describe the phenomenon itself, but also the negative side effects of increasing loudness. The terms have their origin in web forums, professional journals and books concerning mastering[2] and audio technology, where the topic is heavily discussed since approximately 1999.[3] Those threads and articles show that there is awareness for the issue both in the professional audio industry and among "ordinary music listeners". The ongoing discussions can be summarized in the following hypotheses:

- CDs with popular music are constantly getting louder since approximately 1990.
- Responsible for that are the artists as well as the producers and the A&R (Artists and Repertoire) Managers of the record labels. They want their CDs to be louder than the ones by competing artists.
- CDs are made louder mainly during the mastering process. The tools used for this are digital limiters and compressors.[4]
- The mastering engineers see the "Loudness War" as a negative trend, but they are forced to make CDs louder because otherwise they would lose jobs.
- The louder the CDs get the more distorted they are.
- There is no dynamics left on current CDs because of "overcompression".
- Music without dynamics is boring and hard to listen to.

---

[1] In the following, the term "Loudness War" is used because it is the most common term.

[2] Mastering (or "Premastering") is the last stage in the production process of a CD that follows up the recording and mixing of songs at a recording studio. The mastering is done at a specific mastering studio. During the mastering process, changes in level, tonality or dynamic range are implemented in order to get the various songs of a CD to sit comfortably alongside each other. Additionally unwanted material gets removed from the songs, they are placed in the correct order and the length of the gaps between the songs is decided (White (2000), p. 10). And, last but not least, the CDs are made louder. Bobby Owsinski (Owsinski (2000), p. 1) describes the mastering process as follows: *"Mastering is the process of turning a collection of songs into a record by making them sound like they belong together in tone, volume, and timing (spacing between songs)."*

[3] see: http://recforums.prosoundweb.com; http://webbd.nls.net:8080/~mastering; www.hifi-forum.de; http://www.hydrogenaudio.org/forums; Grundman (2002), p. 2; Jones (2005), pp. 1; Fey (2005), pp. 30; Owsinski (2000), pp. 8; Katz (2002), pp. 109 and pp. 187; Tischmeyer (2006), pp. 73.

[4] You cannot make a CD louder by just boosting the level because the recording level of a CD is limited to 0dB$_{FS}$. A higher level leads to severe distortions. Thus, compressors and limiters (also called: dynamics processors) are the ultimate tools to make CDs loud because they reduce the dynamic range of the signal first through which the level can be boosted to a certain extent without distortion. For further information on dynamics processors and for detailed information on how they are working see e.g.: Katz (2002), pp. 117.

— The "Loudness War" is one of the reasons for the crisis in the record industry.

Altogether the "Loudness War" is regarded negative in all those discussions. Particularly, plenty of criticism comes from mastering engineers. Bob Ludwig, one of the best-established people in this business says: *"The levels getting louder and louder is an awful thing. It makes it hard to broadcast and hard to listen to!"*[5] Bob Katz (Digital Domain) adds: *„...the broadcast and music recording disciplines have entered a runaway loudness race leading to the chaos at the end of the 20th century."*[6] And Brian „Big Bass" Gardners' comment veers towards the same direction: *„And with our levels today - with having to deal with always operating on the threshold of distortion - well, that's always fun."*[7]

Basically, three questions arise from the derived hypotheses:

1. Do CDs really get louder? If yes, to what extent?
2. Why are CDs getting louder and who is making them louder?
3. What are the consequences of the "Loudness War"?

To answer these questions, a number of quantitative and qualitative studies have been carried out in recent years. In this context, the following sections describe methodology and results of a study carried out to determine the loudness of CDs.

Loudness measurements of CDs with popular music

Methods

The study included a selection of 32 individual songs and 36 complete CDs.[8] The first step was to determine measurement tools that are able to predict the loudness of music.[9] Helpful in the decision making was the research carried out by the SRG 3 ("Special Rapporteur Group") within the ITU-R (International Telecommunication Union Radiocommunication Sector). The SRG 3 aims to define a standard for broadcast loudness measurement. They have completed studies where the loudness of typical broadcast material (speech, music etc.) first had been measured with test persons in listening tests. Afterwards those subjective loudness measurement results were correlated with "objective" measured loudness values from loudness measurement tools. To summarize the results, an L_{eq} ("equivalent continuous sound level") measure with a slight (L_{eq}(RLB)) or no frequency weighting (L_{eq}(LIN)) is presently the best tool to measure the loudness of music and speech. The correlation between "subjectively" and "objectively" measured loudness values exceeds 95% for both methods. Surprisingly

---

[5] Bob Ludwig (2003) via email.
[6] Katz (2000): p. 2.
[7] Droney (2002a): p. 3
[8] For the complete study see von Ruschkowski (2006).
[9] The measurement of loudness is a quite complex issue (as it is for other sensations). For further information on this topic see e.g. Zicker, Fastl (2007) or Moore (2003).

complex loudness models like the one by Zwicker were not working properly when measuring "natural" sounds like music or speech.[10]

Thus L_{eq}(RLB) and L_{eq}(LIN) were chosen for the loudness measurements in this study. The L_{eq} corresponds to an (energy domain) average over a time interval T during which the sound level is measured. The unit of the L_{eq} is dB and it is mathematically defined as follows:

$$L_{eq}(W) = 10\log_{10}\left(\frac{1}{T}\int_0^T \frac{x_W(t)^2}{x_{\text{Ref}}(t)^2}\,dt\right) dB$$

$$= 20\log_{10}\sqrt{\frac{1}{T}\int_0^T\left(\frac{x}{x_{\text{Ref}}(t)}\right)^2 dt}\ dB$$

W stands for the chosen frequency-weighting filter and $x_W(t)$ for the frequency-weighted sound pressure of the measured signal at time t. $x_{Ref}(t)$ is the sound pressure of the reference signal. The second formula shows the L_{eq} as a root-mean-square (RMS) type of measurement which is transformed into dB.[11] The term RMS is frequently used instead of L_{eq}.[12] Fig. 1 shows the RLB-weighting-filter curve:

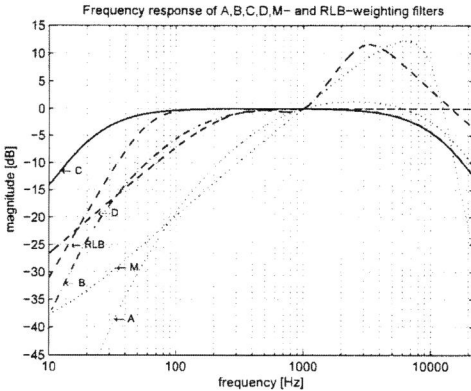

Fig.1: Frequency response of A, B, C, D, M- and RLB-weighting filters. The levels of the curves are chosen in a way that 0 dB is always reached for 1 kHz (Skovenborg, Nielsen (2004), p. 7).

---

[10] Soulodre (2004), pp. 8. For Zwicker's model of loudness see Zwicker, Fastl (2007), pp. 220. Why those complex loudness models are not working properly on "natural "sounds is not quite clear yet.
[11] Skovenborg, Nielsen (2004), p. 7.
[12] Soulodre (2004), p. 5; Spikofski (2004), pp. 6. The software Wavelab 6 by Steinberg which was used for the measurements presented in this paper also uses the term RMS.

For this study, two measurement devices on software basis were used. LMCU 1.3 by ABC Technology Research & Development, which measures L_{eq}(RLB) and Wavelab 6 by Steinberg, which measures RMS(LIN). Both programs were running under Windows XP on a laptop computer (Fujitsu Siemens Amilo M1425) with a 1,6 GHz processor and 512 MB RAM. The songs can be read into the programs for the measurement. There is just one loudness value for each song or CD, which was considered a problem at first glance. But further research showed that at least for popular music, one loudness value is quite representative for the loudness of a whole song and even for entire CDs.[13]

Both programs measure loudness (a sensation) in dB_{FS}, which is a physical unit. Hence there are some things to consider when interpreting the results. The values are at most on ordinal scale level (because it is a sensation) and thus absolute evidence regarding the changes of the loudness of CDs is not possible. As mentioned above, loudness models like the one by Zwicker that measure loudness in sone and thereby attempt to bring a sensation on a ratio scale level are not working properly. From this it can be concluded that with the measured loudness values from LMCU 1.3 and Wavelab 6 one just can make a statement such as: "*The loudness of CDs has increased heavily in the last 10 years.*" Conclusions like: "*The loudness of CDs has doubled in the last 10 years*" are not possible.

Media

For the study, only CDs that contain music released after 1982 (the year the CD was introduced to the public market) were used. For earlier recorded music, it is often uncertain if, how and particularly when the music has been mastered before being pressed on CD. Seven artists, altogether representing a big variety of musical styles, were chosen: Sting, David Bowie (rock and pop music), Beastie Boys (hip hop), Depeche Mode (electronic music), Danzig (hard rock/heavy metal), Prince (rhythm and blues) and Die Ärzte (punk). For four artists, the loudness of entire CDs was measured (number of CDs in parentheses): The Beastie Boys (6), Depeche Mode (10), Prince (12), Sting (8). For the other three artists, the loudness of individual songs was measured (number of songs in brackets): Die Ärzte (10), David Bowie (13), Danzig (9). The individual songs from the artists were chosen in a way that they had a similar character (ballad, up-tempo-song, rock song etc.) to ensure comparability.

Results

Fig. 2- Fig. 8 show the results of the study. The horizontal axis is the release year and the up axis the measured loudness value in dB_{FS}:

---

[13] von Ruschkowski (2006), pp. 78.

Beastie Boys

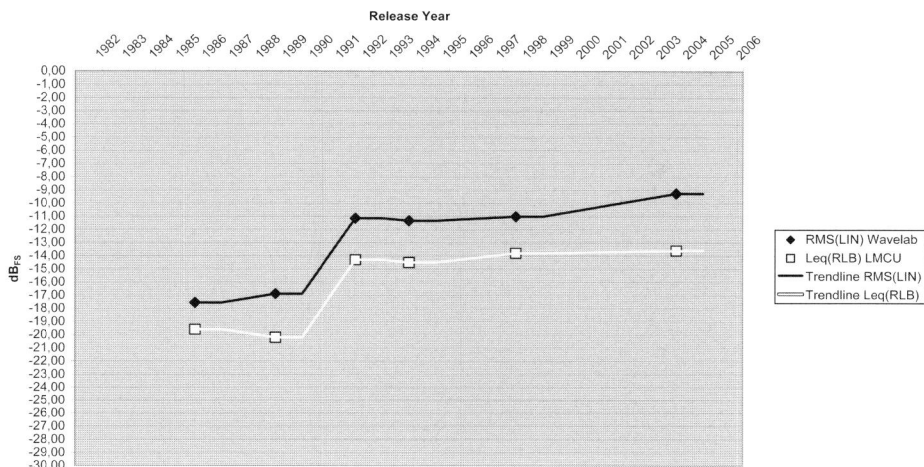

Fig. 2: Loudness values for six CDs of the Beastie Boys. Measured with LMCU 1.3 and Wavelab 6.

Depeche Mode

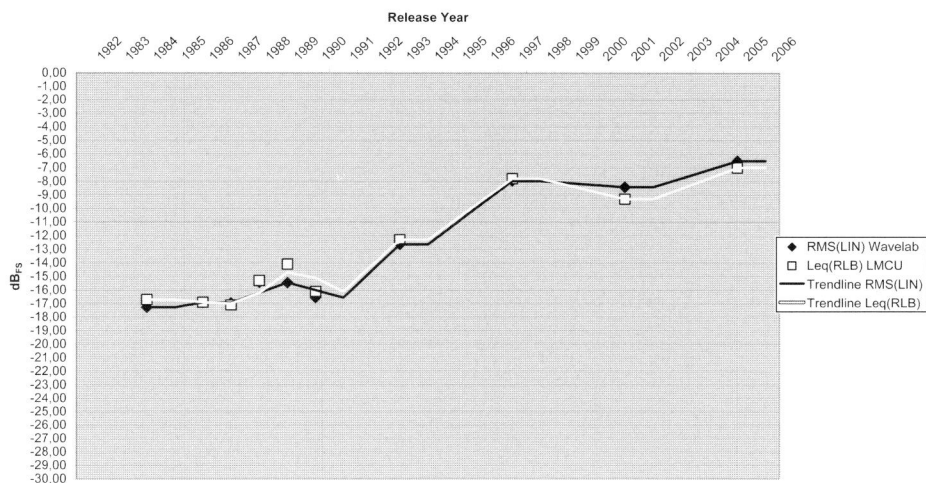

Fig. 3: Loudness values for ten CDs of Depeche Mode. Measured with LMCU 1.3 and Wavelab 6.

217

Prince

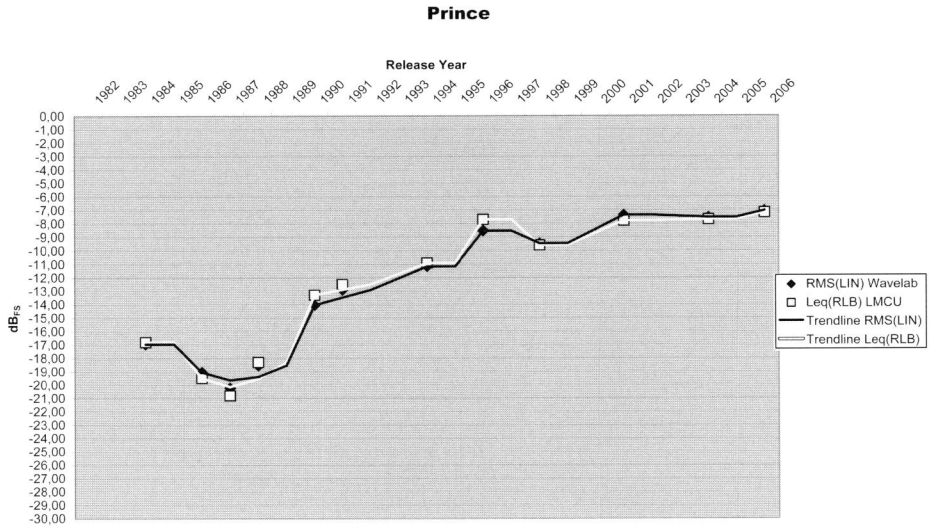

Fig. 4: Loudness values for twelve CDs of Prince. Measured with LMCU 1.3 and Wavelab 6.

Sting

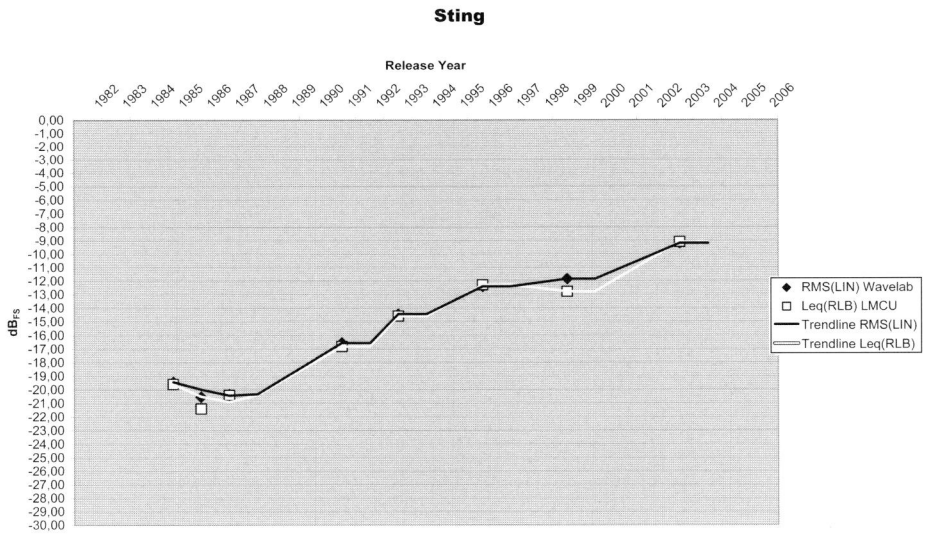

Fig. 5: Loudness values for eight CDs of Sting. Measured with LMCU 1.3 and Wavelab 6.

Die Ärzte

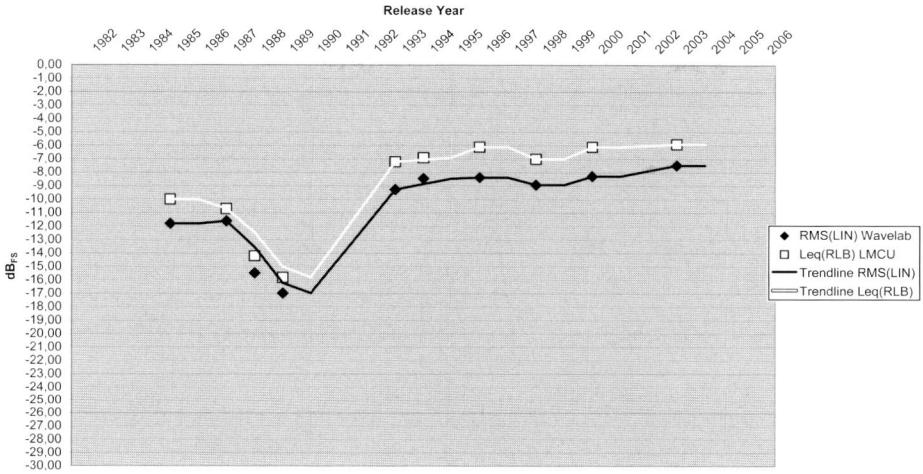

Fig. 6: Loudness values for ten songs of Die Ärzte. Measured with LMCU 1.3 and Wavelab 6.

David Bowie

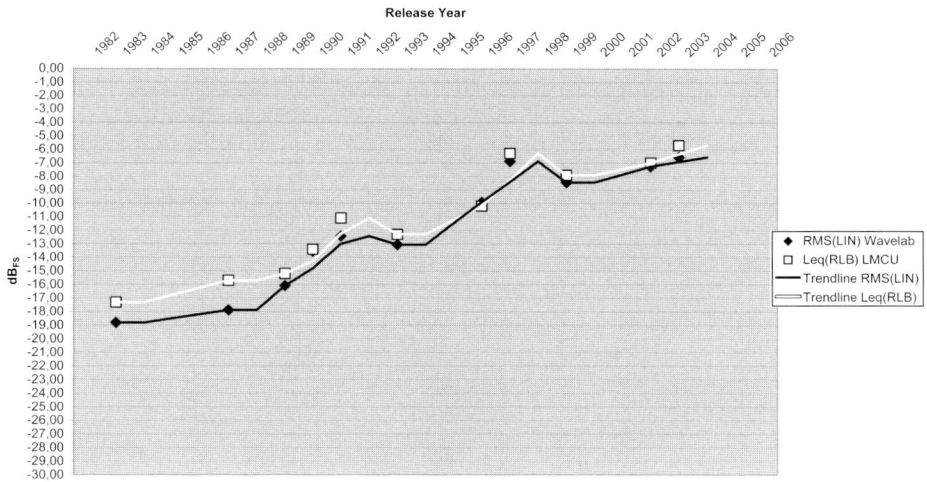

Fig. 7: Loudness values for thirteen songs of David Bowie. Measured with LMCU 1.3 and Wavelab 6.

219

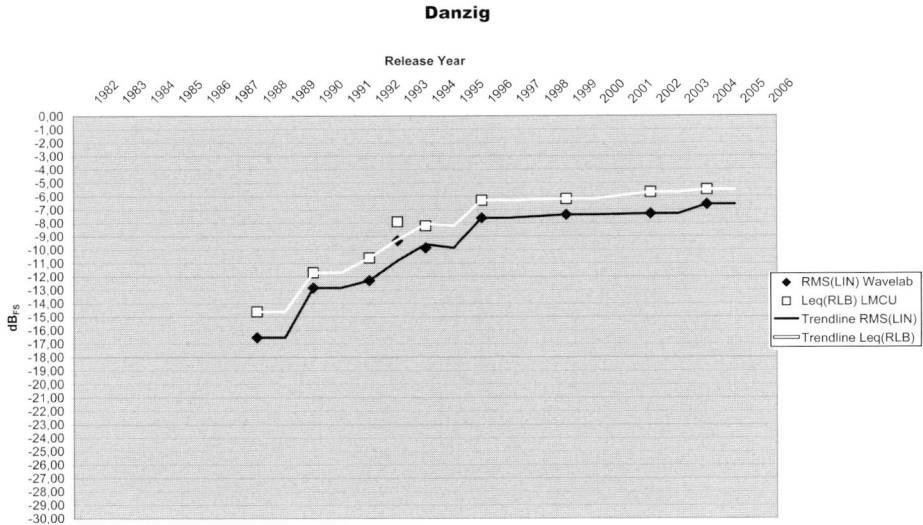

Fig. 8: Loudness values for nine songs of Danzig. Measured with LMCU 1.3 and Wavelab 6.

Overall it is visible that the loudness of the CDs has grown for all the artists. In all seven cases, the current CD was the loudest. Furthermore the following observations were made:

– For the 1980ies, the trend of the development of loudness shows to a lesser extent an increase of loudness, but rather a stagnation or a slight decrease. Only in one case the loudness increased. In two cases, the loudness stagnated and in three cases it decreased. In one case (Danzig) a trend could not be identified because of missing releases in the 1980ies.
– Towards the end of the 1980ies and at beginning of the 1990ies, the loudness increased nearly uninterrupted for all seven artists to this day. In six cases, the growth was more intense in the period from 1987 to 1994 than from 1995 to 2006. In one case, the maximum growth fell between 1995 and 2006.
– From the mid-1990ies on, the increase of loudness slowed down.
– For twelve of the fourteen cases, the overall increase of the RMS(LIN)- and L_{eq}(RLB)-values lay between 9-12 dB$_{FS}$ (Fig. 9).

220

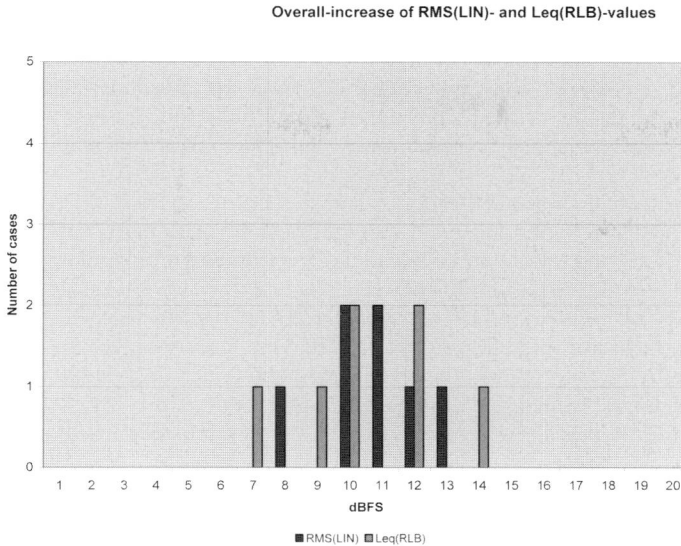

Fig. 9: Overall increase of RMS(LIN)- and L_{eq}(RLB)-values.

In one case the value is lower (6,6 dB_{FS}) and in one case higher (13,6 dB_{FS}). The arithmetic mean is 10,7 dB_{FS} for the RMS(LIN)-values and 10,5 dB_{FS} for the L_{eq}(RLB)-values. The standard deviation is 2 dB (RMS(LIN)) and 2,3 dB (L_{eq}(RLB)) respectively.

It has to be stated again, however, that the RMS(LIN)- and L_{eq}(RLB)- values in dB_{FS} are (when measuring a sensation like loudness) not on ratio scale level and thus absolute evidence about the changes of the loudness of CDs is not possible (see above). However those values show at least a clear trend: the loudness of CDs with popular music has increased heavily over the last two decades. Also noticeable is the trend of a disproportionately intense growth of loudness in the period from 1987 to 1994.

The following chapter tries to find an explanation for this phenomenon.

Premises and reasons for the „Loudness War"

Premises

The literature basically mentions two premises for the "Loudness War": The invention of the CD and the invention of digital limiters and compressors.

In vinyl-disc times, the possibilities to influence the sound of the recordings during the mastering were limited because of the technical limitation of the medium. Vinyl mastering was (and still is today) a compromise between sound, level and duration of the music. Technically, approximately 30 minutes of music are possible per side of a long-playing record, if losses in level and bass-frequencies are accepted. Music with a heavy bass can reduce playing time to approximately 10 minutes per side. A high level also reduces the playing time of a record, because more level leads to broader grooves.[14] In times when vinyl discs were the preferred sound storage medium compressors and limiters were also used to make the records as loud as possible. However the mastering engineer had to take care not to overuse the dynamics processors because otherwise with too much loudness the needle of the record player would jump out of the groove while playing the record. Music mastered too loud always bore the risk of financial losses due to not "playable" records.[15]

The situation changed in the mid-1980ies when the Compact Disc (CD) started to replace vinyl discs as the preferred sound storage medium. The mastering engineers were not constrained by the limitation of the sound storage medium anymore, like Bob Ludwig points out: "*It* [the invention of the CD] *gave us freedom to concentrate even more on the creative without having to worry about the mechanical worries of vinyl.*"[16] There is hardly any technical limitation for the CD. Playing time is neither depending on the amount of bass frequencies nor on the level. And, important in conjunction with the "Loudness War", heavily limited and compressed music causes no problems on a CD. Thus the invention of the CD is one premise for the fact that music is mastered as loud as it is nowadays.

The improvement of dynamics processors is another premise for the "Loudness War". Digital dynamics processors, which have been available since approximately 1990, caused a revolution in mastering like Bob Katz confirms: "*I can cut a CD that's 16 dB louder than the ones we made in the early 90's, before digital limiters became popular,....*"[17]

Hence digital dynamics processors are broadly seen as the main premise for the "Loudness War". This can be proved by statements from mastering engineers. Being asked about the main premises for the "Loudness War" Bob Ludwig points out: "*The invention of digital domain "look-ahead" compressors. Thank God they weren't invented when the Beatles made their music.*"[18] The measurement results also show evidence for a strong correlation between the "Loudness War" and the invention of digital dynamics processors. The first digital dynamics processors were available around 1990[19] and the results of the measurements show a trend of a disproportionately intense growth of loudness for just this period.

Altogether it seems like the phenomenon "Loudness War" is based on two premises that are linked with each other. On the one hand, music can be mastered as loud as it is today because digital dynamics processors give mastering engineers the chance to do so. On the other hand with the CD a music storage medium has been invented that is capable of storing music mastered that loud.

---

[14] Katz (2002), p. 257.
[15] Owsinski (2000), pp. 176, 212, 224; Jones (2005), pp. 1; Droney (2002b), p. 2.
[16] Bob Ludwig (2003) via email.
[17] Katz (2004). Q.v.: Owsinski (2000), p. 164.
[18] Owsinski (2000), pp. 10, 198. Similar: Sax; Pesche (2005) via email.
[19] Jackson (1999), p. 1; Owsinski (2000), p. 3; Daniel Weiss (Weiss Digital Audio) via email; Peter Poers (Jünger Audio) via email.

Reasons for the „Loudness War"

The most frequently named reason for the battle for the loudest CD is of an economical nature: The "Loudness War" stems from the desire of the people in charge (artists, producers, A&R Managers) to produce a CD that's louder than those by competing artists. There is a current opinion that louder CDs sell better on the market, in other words there is belief in that maximum loudness is appealing to the listeners.[20] A parallelism can be seen between this trend and a trend in broadcast where every radio station tries to have the loudest signal as Robert Orban and Frank Foti describe: *"Just as radio stations wish to offer the loudest signal on the dial, it is evident that recording artists, producers, and even some record labels want to have a loud product that stands out against its competition in a CD changer or a music store's listening station."*[21] In both cases a signal as loud as possible is produced to stand out from the crowd. During the mastering CDs from competing artists serve as a standard to outbid. This results in a vicious circle with a permanently increasing loudness because the pressure of being louder than the competitors always remains. Bob Katz describes the situation as follows: *"Producers don't seem to like making a CD that's even a little softer than the competition, so each succeeding CD is often a little bit hotter."* [22] Brian Gardner adds: *"They always wonder, "Can't you make this a little louder?" It keeps moving up...."*[23] An exploratory study showed the relevance of this issue for the music industry. Nine out of thirteen interviewed artists, A&R Managers and producers (69 %) confirmed that loudness plays an important role during the mastering of their CDs.[24]

The tendency to produce records with progressively increasing levels is not a new issue. The "Loudness War" has been existing since the 1960ies.[25] But the technical limitations of vinyl disc defined an upper limit for loudness. This upper limit ceased to exist with the invention of the CD and thus the pressure on the mastering engineers to produce louder records was growing.

The mastering engineers are forced to take part in the "Loudness War" against their will because otherwise they would lose business. Dave Collins describes his situation as follows: *"I have to play the game because if you want to stay in the business, you've got to compete on absolute level, but it's really a horrible trend."*[26] Bob Ludwig's comment points in a similar direction: *"And for me, I'm under pressure from A&R people and clients to have things loud,...."*[27]

Interestingly there is no scientific study until today that has proved a direct connection between loudness and commercial success. Nevertheless "louder" is often equated with "better".[28] This phenomenon is explainable in a certain way: With an unchanged volume

---

[20] for comparison.: http://recforums.prosoundweb.com; http://webbd.nls.net:8080/~mastering; www.hifi-forum.de; http://www.hydrogenaudio.org/forums; Grundman (2002), pp. 1; Jones (2005), pp. 1; Fey (2005), pp. 30; Owsinski (2000), pp. 8; Katz (2002), pp. 187; Tischmeyer (2006), p. 92.

[21] Orban, Robert; Foti, Frank in Katz (2002): p. 273. Similar: Droney (2002a), p. 3; Katz (2004), p. 7, Owsinski (2000), p. 177; Fey (2005), p. 30.

[22] Katz (2004): p. 8 Similar: Owsinski (2000), p. 213; von Ruschkowski (2006), p. 101.

[23] Droney (2002a): p. 3.

[24] von Ruschkowski (2006).

[25] Owsinski (2000), pp. 8, 176; Jones (2005), pp. 1; Katz (2002), p. 187.

[26] Owsinski (2000), p. 165. Similar: Fey (2005); p. 31; Jackson (1999), p. 2.

[27] Owsinski (2000), p. 198.

[28] Katz (2004), p. 6, Owsinski (2000), p. 177; Fey (2005), p. 30.

control the more compressed the music the louder it is. To a certain degree louder music contains more high and bass frequencies, a circumstance explainable with the "equal loudness contours". Those "extra" frequencies make the music sound more brilliant and warm, something that most listeners prefer. But after readjusting the volume of less compressed or uncompressed music the same effect can be observed. Therefore loud CDs only exhibit advantages in situations where the volume isn't usually readjusted, which is very rare (e.g. CD changers for background sound reinforcement in pubs). In most listening situations the volume is adjusted by the listener or the DJ. In those cases loud CDs do not have an advantage. In radio airplay, even disadvantages occur as radio stations compress and limit the signal before it is broadcasted and music that already has a reduced dynamic range causes undesired side effects like distortion.

The "Loudness War" might also be caused by the ongoing changes in the production process of music, i.e. that the music is inherently louder before it is mastered. But to what extent new technology (like digital audio workstations) has influenced the loudness of unmastered music is a controversial question. Some mastering engineers like Bob Olhsson report on a growing loudness of unmastered music: "...*that people are commonly going too far with compression during mixing so much that an awful lot of mixes can't be helped.*"[29] In contrast other mastering engineers like Brian Gardner don't observe any differences with the material that they master. He answers the question if the source material delivered for mastering is louder than in the past: "*No, not necessarily how it comes in; it's just they want the end product to jump.*"[30] It is likely that the changes in the production process of music did have an influence on the "Loudness War", but to what extent remains questionable.

Another reason for the "Loudness War" could lie in the fact that the way of listening to music has changed. Instead of listening at home, music is more and more consumed en-route via MP3 player or a car CD player. Hence with this way of listening to music other aspects than the sound become important. A reduced dynamic range (and thus a greater loudness) can help to prevent music that's listened to en-route from vanishing in the background noise.[31] The mastering engineers have to respond to this changing situation. Paul Stubblebine describes the new challenge as follows: "*Parallel to that trend over the last ten years we have seen an increase in the end-user listening environments that we have to consider. Back then, we concerned ourselves primarily with how the record would sound in the "average" living room and how it would sound on the radio. Now a large part of the audience listens on Walkman-style headphones. A substantial part of our audience is listening in a car.*"[32] Nowadays during the mastering session the mastering engineer has to find a compromise that satisfies all music listeners and all listening situations respectively. According to this, it is likely that this changed situation has an influence on the "Loudness War". However, the dynamic range is reduced to a

---

[29] Owsinski (2000), pp. 230. Similar: Tischmeyer (2006), p. 77.
[30] Droney (2002a): p. 3. Similar: Grundman (2002), p. 1.
[31] Owsinski (2000), p. 239; Katz (2002), pp. 127, 188; Jones (2005), pp. 1; Jackson (2006), pp. 1.
[32] Stubblebine (2007). Similar: Jones (2005), pp. 1.

larger degree actually necessary to allow the consumption of music en-route in a comfortable way.[33]

The consequences of the "Loudness War"

As consequences of the "Loudness War" the increase of audible distortion and the loss of the dynamics in popular music are frequently mentioned.[34] Distortion and reduced dynamic range are indeed detectable on a physical level. But how they affect the listener's sensation remains unknown. Scientific studies on those topics haven't been done yet. The following remarks base therefore on individual comments.

Distortion

The excessive use of dynamics processors results in measurable and audible distortion. Mastering engineer Bernie Grundman describes his sensations while listening to current CDs as follows: *"It's all smashed and smeared and distorted and pumping. You can hear some pretty bad CDs out there."*[35] Bob Katz states: *"To say nothing about distortion. Are we really in the business of making square waves? Why has the average sound quality of popular music CDs gone downhill since the introduction of the digital medium, ..."*[36] Those distortions arise from the exaggerated use of dynamics processors during the mastering process and are for the most part caused by the so called "clipping". Clipping occurs on the one hand if the signal overloads in the digital domain. This can be the case in every part of the (digital) recording chain. On the other hand "clipping" is used as mode of operation in digital limiters. The algorithms are programmed in a way that short peaks are cut out of the signal electronically to raise the level afterwards. Those "clipped" waveforms have a flat top (see Fig. 10) like a square wave:

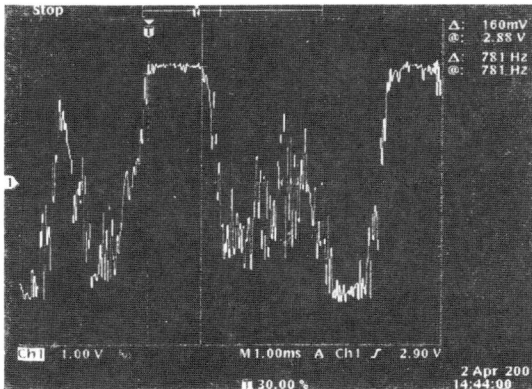

Fig. 10: „Clipped" Waveform (Katz (2002), p. 273).

---

[33] Jones (2005), p. 2.

[34] Katz (2002): p. 188; Owsinski (2002), pp. 9; Fey (2005), p. 31; Grundman (2002), p. 1.

[35] Owsinski (2002), pp. 9.

[36] Katz (2002): p. 188.

"Clipping" is not audible if only a few short peaks are "clipped". But nowadays with the excessive use of digital limiters in mastering a large part of the music signal is "clipped". Nielsen and Lund showed in a study that the number of "clipped" waveforms on CDs has grown in recent years. In consequence of that the total harmonic distortion (THD) increases, which results in audible distortion.[37] Moreover with those distorted signals further problems occur in broadcast, while using lossy data compression algorithms and in electronic devices from listening units like CD players.

In radio stations the dynamics of the broadcast signal is heavily processed with devices like the Orban Optimod. For music that already contains THD, the treatment makes everything worse like Robert Orban and Frank Foti conclude: *"Hypercompressed material does not sound louder on air. It sounds more distorted, making the radio sound broken in extreme cases."*[38] The European Broadcasting Union (EBU) is aware of this problem and warns their members of the excessive dynamics treatment of the broadcast signal.[39]

When music is listened to via a CD player, another problem may occur. Many of the built-in electronic devices (e.g. analog-to-digital converters) are not designed for operation with signal levels that hot like from current CDs. In consequence, the already existing distortion gets aggravated because of overloading electronic devices. Nielsen and Lund showed in a study that CD players of all price ranges have difficulties in handling those signals.[40] And not only CD players, but all kinds of digital music equipment. Thomas Lund recapitulates: *"We have documented that current consumer, music, film and broadcast equipment has not been designed for levels this hot."*[41]

If music is processed with lossy data compression algorithms like the popular MPEG-1 Audio Layer 3 (in short: mp3) similar problems occur. Those algorithms have difficulties with the processing of hot levels and are exceedingly susceptible for already existing distortion. The amount of THD rises proportionally with the diminishment of the bitrate. For a data reduction free of artefacts, for music it is necessary to reduce the level at least by 3 dB before processing.[42]

How an average music listener perceives the distortion caused by "clipping" in current music, and whether it is sensed at all remains unknown. Nielsen and Lund suppose that today's music is tiring because of the distortion but studies on this topic are lacking.[43] In this context again attention should be paid to the fact that the majority of the listeners nowadays consumes music en-route and/or in data reduced formats like mp3. This can be taken as an indication that the relevance of sound quality for the listeners is declining.[44] Eventually it remains questionable if someone who is used to listen to mp3 files downloaded from the internet in often miserable sound quality is bothered by an increase of THD.

---

[37] Nielsen, Lund (2003), pp. 1.
[38] Katz (2002), p. 273. Similar: Tischmeyer (2006), p. 77.
[39] EBU (2006).
[40] Nielsen, Lund (2007), p. 11.
[41] Lund (2004), p. 4.
[42] Nielsen, Lund (2003), pp. 6. Similar: Tischmeyer (2006), p. 90, Lund (2004), p. 5.
[43] Lund (2004), p. 6; Nielsen, Lund (2003), p. 2.
[44] Jones (2005), p. 2.

Loss of musical dynamics

A further consequence of the "Loudness War" is the ongoing loss of musical dynamics in today's popular music. In some cases the dynamic range has been reduced to 2-6 dB.[45] But how the missing dynamics affect the listener's sensation remains unknown. Scientific studies on this topic are not available yet and so the only useable sources of knowledge are comments on this topic from individuals, mostly from audio experts with trained ears.

It is said that the absence of dynamics makes music lifeless and boring and that listening to "overcompressed" music is exhausting and stressful because of the missing transients. Bob Ludwig describes that as follows: "*To me, it's a fact that highly compressed music is tiring to the ear and doesn't make you want to listen to something over and over again.*"[46] He assumes that this situation is one of the causes for the decreasing record sales over the past years: "*Could this be one of the reasons for the record industry's demise?*"[47]

However it remains questionable if average listeners sense "overcompressed" music in the same way. Their way of listening to music differs from the analytic listening of mastering engineers and other professionals of the audio sector. Music is listened to more and more en-route and in that case reduced dynamics are rather beneficial than disturbing. Whether an average listener thus perceives a reduced dynamic range as acceptable, or if and when the negative effects of the dynamics reduction outweigh, remains in question.

Nevertheless opinions from audio experts like mastering engineers should be taken seriously because dealing with musical dynamics has been part of their everyday work for decades. And dynamics themselves have been part of music for centuries, but in today's popular music have lost significance. Some listeners (and musicians) might by now have forgotten that music, similar to movies, relies on moods and elements of surprise caused by dynamics.

In this context, yet another phenomenon that temporarily appears in "overcompressed" music becomes important: the so-called "dynamics inversion", which Glenn Meadows describes as follows: "*Spots in the record that should get louder actually get softer because they're hitting the compressor/limiter too hard.*"[48] In this case the "overcompression" leads to a turnaround of the musical intention embodied by the dynamics.

Conclusions

This paper dealt with the so-called "Loudness War", the phenomenon that the loudness of CDs with popular music has increased heavily over the past two decades. In a study with 32 songs and 36 CDs by seven different artists it could be demonstrated that the loudness has been grown nearly uninterrupted since the end of the 1980ies to this day. Thereby, the growth was most intense in the period from 1987-1994. From the mid-

---

[45] Katz (2002): pp. 111, 188; Owsinski (2000), p. 213.
[46] Jenkins (2003), p. 2. Similar: Jackson (2006), p. 2; Fey (2005), p. 31; Owsinski (2000), pp. 10, 215; Katz (2002), pp. 111, 264; Grundman (2002), p. 1.
[47] Jenkins (2003), p. 2. Similar: Owsinski (2000), pp. 212, 230; Katz (2002), p. 128.
[48] Owsinski (2000), p. 11. Similar: Katz (2002), p. 130; Owsinski (2000), p. 246.

1990ies the increase of loudness slowed down but nevertheless the newest CD was in all seven cases the loudest.

Furthermore it could be shown that CDs are made louder especially during the so called mastering and that the "Loudness War" is based on two premises that are linked with each other. First of all with the CD a music storage medium has been invented that is capable of recording music that is as loud as it is nowadays. Secondly music can be made as loud as it is today during the mastering because digital dynamics processors give mastering engineers the chance to do so.

The main reason for the "Loudness War" is the effort of the musicians, A&R Managers and producers to have louder CDs than competing artists. There is a widespread belief in that loud CDs sell better on the market. However not only there is a lack of scientific studies that could affirm this hypothesis but also logic speaks against it. In most cases listeners adjust the loudness of music for themselves. Another reason for the "Loudness War" could lie in the fact the way of listening to music has changed. Music is more and more listened en-route. And one must confess that there are some benefits with dynamics reduced music in those listening situations. A reduced dynamic range (and thus a greater loudness) can help to prevent music that is listened to en-route from vanishing in the background noise. But the dynamic range of the music is reduced way beyond what is necessary to listen to it comfortably en-route.

In the last part two consequences of the "Loudness War" that are frequently mentioned in the literature were presented: the increase of audible distortion and the loss of the dynamics of music. Both are indeed detectable on a physical level. But how they affect the listeners' sensation remains unknown because scientific studies on those topics are missing. Distortion occurs at first because the signal is "clipped" during the mastering in mastering processors like digital limiters to make it louder. Afterwards the distortion is frequently being aggravated for example due to further processing before being broadcasted, while using lossy data compression algorithms or because of overloading electronic devices in listening units like CD players. All that leads to an increase of THD in popular music. However in this context it is important to mention that it seems like the relevance of sound quality for the listeners is declining. So it remains in question if they are bothered by an increasing THD.

Dynamics has been part of music since centuries. The dynamic range of CDs has declined over the past years because increasing the loudness with dynamics processors leads to a decrease of dynamics. How a reduced dynamic range affects the listener's sensation in not known. Some professionals of the audio sector assume that the absence of dynamics makes music lifeless and boring and that such music turns into a stress factor. Further research on this topic and how distortion in music is sensed seems to be necessary.

References

Droney, Maureen: Brian Gardner. *Mix* (March 2002). Available from: http://mixonline.com/recording/interviews/audio_brian_gardner/ (December 2007; cited as: Droney 2002a).

Droney, Maureen: Geoff Emerick. *Mix* (Oktober 2002). Available from: http://mixonline.com/recording/interviews/audio_geoff_emerick/ (December 2007; cited as: Droney 2002b)

EBU Technical Recommendation: The use of high level digital audio material in the production chain. *R117 – 2006.* Genf, Februar 2006 (cited as: EBU 2006).

Fey, Fritz: Leaving New York… Ein Gespräch mit Darcy Proper, Galaxy Mastering. *Studio Magazin* pp. 24-33 (November 2005).

Grundman, Bernie: Mastering the Music: A Dark Art No More. *Mix* (July 2002). Available from: http://mixonline.com/mag/audio_mastering_music_dark/ (December 2007).

Jackson, Blair: Precision Mastering: Two decades in Hollywood. *Mix* (Dezember 1999). Available from: http://mixonline.com/mag/audio_precision_mastering_two/ (December 2007).

Jackson, Blair: Issues in Modern Mastering. *Mix* (Dezember 2006). Available from: http://mixonline.com/recording/mastering/audio_issues_modern_mastering/ (December 2007).

Jenkins, J.J.: Masters on Mastering. *Electronic Musician* (September 2003). Available from: http://emusician.com/tutorials/emusic_masters_mastering/ (December 2007).

Jones, Sarah: The Big Squeeze. *Mix* (December 2005). Available from: http://mixonline.com/mag/audio_big_squeeze/ (December 2007).

Katz, Bob: How to make better recordings in the 21st century - An integrated approach to metering, monitoring, and levelling practices. *Updated from the article published in the September 2000 issue of the AES Journal.* Available from: http://www.digido.com/modules.php?name=News&file=article&sid=9 (December 2007).

Katz, Bob: *Mastering Audio. The art and the science.* Oxford, New York 2002.

Katz, Bob: Compression In Mastering. Available from: http://www.digido.com/modules.php?name=News&file=article&sid=7#part1 (December 2007; cited as: Katz 2004).

Lund, Thomas: Distortion to the people. Oktober 2004. Available from: www.tcelectronic.com/media/lund_2004_distortion_tmt20.pdf (December 2007).

Moore, Brian C.J.: An Introduction to the Psychology of Hearing. 5. Auflage. San Diego, London 2003.

Nielsen, Søren H.; Lund, Thomas: 0 dBFS+ Levels in Digital Mastering. Available from: www.tcelectronic.com/media/nielsen_lund_2000_0dbfs_le.pdf (December 2007; cited as: Nielsen, Lund 2007).

Nielsen, Søren H.; Lund, Thomas: Overload in Signal Conversion. AES 23RD International Conference. Kopenhagen, 23-25 Mai 2003. Available from: www.tcelectronic.com/media/nielsen_lund_2003_overload.pdf (December 2007).

Owsinski, Bobby: *The Mastering Engineer's Handbook.* Vallejo 2000.

von Ruschkowski, Arne: *"Loudness War" – eine psychoakustische Untersuchung von CDs mit populärer Musik –.* Magisterarbeit, Musikwissenschaftliches Institut, Universität Hamburg 2006, unveröffentlicht.

Skovenborg, Esben; Nielsen, Søren H.: Evaluation of Different Loudness Models with Music and Speech Material. *Audio Engineering Society: Convention Paper*, Presented at the 117th Convention, 2004 October 28-31 San Francisco.

Soulodre, Gilbert A.: Evaluation of Objective Loudness Meters. *Audio Engineering Society: Convention Paper*, Presented at the 116th Convention, 2004 May 8-11 Berlin.

Spikofski, Gerhard: Lautstärkemessung im Rundfunk-Stand der internationalen Standardisierung - IRT-Surroundlautstärke-Monitor. *Überarbeitete Fassung des Vortrags zur 23. Tonmeistertagung*, 5.-8.11. 2004 Leipzig.

Stubblebine, Paul: Mastering. As Published by *Mix*. Available from: www.paulstubblebine.com/library/li_ma.php (December 2007; cited as: Stubblebine 2007)

Tischmeyer, Friedemann: *Audio-Mastering mit PC-Workstations*. Bremen 2006.

White, Paul: *Basic Mastering.* London 2000.

Zwicker, Eberhard; Fastl, Hugo: Psychoacoustics. Facts and Models. 3. erweiterte Auflage. Berlin, Heidelberg, New York 2007.

M. Abel

Synchronization of Organ Pipes

Abstract

In this contribution, results on the synchronization of an organ pipe either by a
second pipe or by a loudspeaker are reported, positioned side by side. Classical
theory suggests oscillation death for the synchronization of two organ pipes. The
presented measurements clearly exclude this scenario. Rather, the aeroacoustical
coupling by the oscillating wind sheet at the pipe mouth is identified as the source
of a self-regulation of the phase of the organ relative to the driving source. In
the case of two almost identical coupled organ pipes, the oscillation is antiphase
such that they silence each other, in the case of a loudspeaker driving the organ
pipe, an in-phase movement is observed at the edge of the synchronization region,
which yields a much louder sound of the coupled system at the frequency of the
loudspeaker. This is a way to stabilize an acoustical sound source by a minute
signal - the loudspeaker can be up to 30 dB weaker than the organ pipe, but still
forces the instrument to follow it. To quantify this statement, results on the so-
called "synchronization plateau" are presented for different driving amplitudes of
the loudspeaker.

1   Introduction

Sound production in organ pipes is traditionally described as a generator-resona-
tor coupling. In the last decades, research has been concerned with the complex
aeroacoustic processes which lead to a better understanding of the sound generation in a flue organ pipe. The process of sounding a flue-type organ pipe
employs an airstream directed at an edge, the labium of an organ pipe. An oscillating "air sheet" is used to describe the situation in which the oscillations of
the jet exiting from the flue are responsible for the creation of the pipe sound
[Fabre and Hirschberg, 2000]. Using the "air sheet" terminology, it is pointed out
that the oscillation is controlled not by pressure[Coltman, 1992, Fletcher, 1993],
but by the flow of air [Coltman, 1976, Verge et al., 1997a, Verge et al., 1997b,
Fabre et al., 1996].

When an organ pipe is subject to an external acoustical signal, it can be synchronized to the frequency of the driving sound field. Even more complex, two
organ pipes close to each other sound at the same pitch, if the frequencies are
not too far apart[Rayleigh, 1945, Bouasse, 1929]. The effect can be explained by
nonlinear synchronization theory, a research field that has considerably grown in
recent years. We transfer the results found in so diverse fields as nonlinear oscillator theory, networks of oscillators, coupled map lattices, applications to the life

sciences and chemical systems to nonlinear acoustics. Chaotic synchronization has been investigated [Pikovsky et al., 2001], but synchronization in hydrodynamical turbulent systems has received relatively little attention; this despite early observations in the time of Rayleigh who observed the synchronization of two organ pipes [Rayleigh, 1945]. Because the amplitude of the two coupled pipes decreases considerably to almost silence, the effect was interpreted as oscillation death. This describes the conversion of the whole input power to heat such that a complete silence of both pipes results. We have measured the system similar to the one observed by Rayleigh and could not only confirm his observation but also explain it in the frame of synchronization theory [Abel and Bergweiler, 2007, Abel et al., 2006] Our measurements show that the amplitude decrease is due to a complex coupling of the aerodynamic jet exiting from the pipe mouths which in turn yields an antiphase radiation of the sound; this is then recognized as a decrease in amplitude. In this contribution, precursors of a measurement of the so-called Arnold-Tongue are shown. By an Arnold-Tongue, the size of the synchronization region in dependence on the coupling for an external driving by a loudspeaker is characterized. Here, the synchronization plateau is shown for a series of couplings.

2   Sound generation in organ pipes

Sound generation by organ pipes is a long-standing topic of interest in acoustical research. It is described in [Rayleigh, 1945, Fabre et al., 1996]. Here, the beauty of musical sound generation is paired with complex aerodynamical phenomena, their coupling to the acoustic field has been understood to a reasonable degree in the last years (see the review [Fabre and Hirschberg, 2000]).

In Fig. 1 the tone generation is sketched: The wind supply system drives the system with constant pressure producing a aerodynamical jet exiting from the pipe flue (a and b). The degree of turbulence (or chaos) is characterized by the Reynolds number. Typical Reynolds numbers, corresponding to a free jet are of the order of 10^3, depending on the pressure supplied and the pipe dimensions [Fabre et al., 1996]. The jet exiting from the flue hits the labium of the pipe where a pressure perturbation is generated, travelling inside the pipe resonator (Fig. 1 b) and reflected at the end of the resonator (Fig. 1 c). This pressure wave returns after time T to the labium where it triggers a change of the phase of the jet oscillations (Fig. 1 e). After a few transients, a stable oscillation of an "air sheet" at the pipe mouth is established. This oscillation of the wind field couples to the acoustic modes and a sound wave is emitted (Fig. 1 f).

To model synchronization effects, one can sketch the system in an abstract way: we consider an extended, nonlinear medium. At some region the driving force is applied, point-like as a first approximation, or extended to correspond more reality. At the same region the signal is fed back onto itself. For two organ pipes this sketch is extended accordingly. An acoustical signal hits a pipe at its

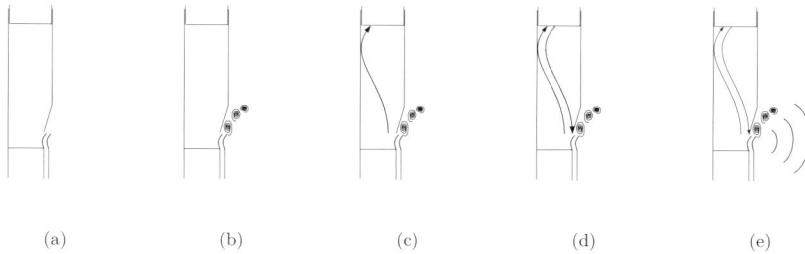

(a)   (b)   (c)   (d)   (e)

Figure 1: Schematic sketch of the interplay between oscillating air sheet and turbulent jet in an organ pipe. The air enters from below, at the top the pipe is closed a) The pipe with -for illustration with the oscillating air sheet, b) a turbulent jet evolves, c) the jet triggers a pressure wave which travels up the resonator, d) the pressure wave travels down and triggers the next detachment of a turbulent eddy, e) sound is radiated from the pipe mouth.

mouth where an air sheet is oscillating. This air sheet is now subject to two forces: the external one and the internal from the oscillations inside the resonator. since the system is highly nonlinear there is the possibility that the frequency adjusts itself to the external one thereby shifting the phase of the air sheet by some fixed amount. When driven with a loudspeaker the sound from the loudspeaker drives the air sheet and couples this way to the pipe.

3 A bit of Synchronization

In his book, Lord Rayleigh states "When two organ pipes of the same pitch stand side by side ... it may still go so far as to cause the pipes to speak in absolute unison in spite of inevitable small differences" [Rayleigh, 1945]. In [Pikovsky et al., 2001] the phenomenon is interpreted as "oscillation death", as explained above. In the following we will rely on synchronization theory to show that *any* pair of self-sustained coupled oscillators generically shows synchronization; later on we will try to give a physical model for the coupling in aero-dynamical terms. Please note that the terms ,,self-sustained" (coming more from Euro-Russian school) and ,,autonomous" (rather used in Anglo-Saxian community) are used as synonyms in the following. Before stepping to the results, we briefly explain the theory of one self-sustained oscillator, driven externally and then step to the synchronization of two coupled self-sustained, nonlinear oscillators.

 Typically, autonomous oscillators exhibit an attracting limit cycle. It appears due to two properties: nonlinearity, and the energy balance between losses and driving. For a linear, damped oscillator a limit cycle solution does not exist, the only possible attractor is the trivial solution. Nonlinearity allows for the dependence of frequency on amplitude which constitutes a mechanism to drive the system towards an amplitude at which the regular oscillations are established. Since the amplitude corresponds directly to the mechanical energy of the system, this is right at the point of equality of losses and supply – the limit cycle.

The dynamics of a self-sustained (frequency ω_0), driven externally by a harmonic signal (frequency $\omega_1 \simeq \omega_0$) is written as

$$\ddot{x} + \omega_0^2 x - \dot{x}\frac{df}{dx} = \omega_1^2 R \cos(\omega_1 t) \ . \tag{1}$$

We have two time scales present in the system: a fast one $t_f = \frac{2\pi}{\omega_1} \simeq \frac{2\pi}{\omega_0}$, and a slow one $t_s = \frac{2\pi}{\omega_1 - \omega_0}$, and $t_s \ll t_f$. We want to investigate now the dependence on the slow time and average over the fast one. With the ansatz $x(t) = A(t) \sin(\omega_1 t + \phi)$, with ϕ the slow phase, one obtains [Pikovsky et al., 2001]

$$\dot{A} = \frac{1}{2}\left(\alpha - \frac{1}{4}\beta A^2\right) A - \frac{\omega_1 R}{2}\cos\phi \ , \tag{2}$$

$$\dot{\phi} = \dot{\Theta}_2 - \dot{\Theta}_1 = \Delta\omega + \epsilon q(\phi) \tag{3}$$

The second equation describes the phase dynamics with the two parameters detuning $\Delta\omega = \frac{1}{2}\frac{\omega_0^2 - \omega_1^2}{\omega_1} \simeq \omega_0 - \omega_1$ and locking term $\epsilon = \frac{\omega_1}{2}\frac{R}{A}$, being proportional to the driving strength. To zero order, one can assume $A \simeq const$ and the phase equation effectively decouples from the amplitude equation. If $q(\phi) = \sin(\phi)$ the paradigmatic Adler equation is found, with two stationary solutions, $\dot{\phi} = 0$, for $|\Delta\omega| \le \epsilon$.

If one wants to investigate the dependence of the synchronization properties, especially the size of the synchronization region, one varies the coupling strength and plots it versus the corresponding synchronization plateau. In this type of plot, the so-called Arnold -Tongue is found, named because the synchronization region becomes smaller with smaller driving amplitude. Here, first results are presented with measurements of a pipe driven by a loudspeaker. The behavior at different sound pressure levels is shown by plotting the respective synchronization plateaus.

Let us turn to two coupled oscillators. Any pair of uncoupled oscillators close to a limit cycle can be written in terms of phase, (Θ_1, Θ_2), and amplitude, (A_1, A_2), in the following form:

$$\dot{\Theta}_i = 2\pi f_i \ , \ \dot{A}_i = -\gamma\left(A_i - A_{i,0}\right) \ , \tag{4}$$

with $i = 1, 2$. For weak coupling, the phase equations are

$$\dot{\Theta}_1 = 2\pi f_1 + \epsilon G_1(\Theta_1, \Theta_2) \ , \ \dot{\Theta}_2 = 2\pi f_2 + \epsilon G_2(\Theta_1, \Theta_2) \ . \tag{5}$$

For $f_1 \simeq f_2$ the phase difference $\phi = \Theta_1 - \Theta_2$ is a slow variable (in comparison with the angle Θ). Averaging yields again the Adler equation

$$\dot{\phi} = 2\pi\Delta f + \epsilon\sin(\phi) \tag{6}$$

where the two parameters are detuning Δf and coupling strength ϵ. This equation has a stationary solution $\dot{\phi} = 0$ if $|2\pi\Delta f| < \epsilon$. This means that $\Theta_1 = \Theta_2$ and the phases are locked. In a typical plot, the frequency difference of the *coupled* oscillators, $\Delta \nu$ is plotted against the frequency difference of the uncoupled ones, $|f_1 - f_2|$. This yields a clearer picture than the use of the absolute frequencies $\dot{\Theta}_1, \dot{\Theta}_2$ because perfect synchronization is observed as $\Delta f = 0$.

Even though it seems appealing to explain the synchronization of organ pipes in such a simple way, it is not completely satisfactory because organ pipes are extended systems and such a simple description does not take into account the aeroacoustics, or the emitted turbulent air jet which is eventually needed for a complete understanding.

4   Results

We present results on the synchronization of an organ pipe with an external loudspeaker signal. For the latter we show synchronization plateaus, which confirm that an extremely weak signal can still yield synchronization in a certain frequency range. To investigate the influences of an external sound source onto the organ-pipe we positioned a loudspeaker directly beside a single, stopped organ-pipe. For the experimental details, please see [Abel et al., 2006]. As a main parameter, the frequency of the pipe was set at 676 Hz, left unchanged during measurement. The frequency of the loudspeaker was increased very slowly, depending on the spectral resolution. This gives the possibility to average the signal four times to suppress noise, an analysis of the noise effects, as imperfect transition etc. is in preparation. The microphone was positioned at the centerline between pipe and loudspeaker at a distance of 15 cm. The experimental setup is shown in Fig. 2

The synchronization can be observed clearly by a plateau in the plot of frequency difference, $\Delta \nu$ against detuning, Δf. As well the predicted square root function is observed at the transition to synchronization. One can see the dependence clearly in each cross-section of Fig. 3 for constant loudspeaker amplitude, more analyses are given in [Abel et al., 2006]. For the amplitude measured at the microphone, we observe a variance from high to low amplitude for since pipe and loudspeaker signals are superposed. This implies the possibility to control the loudness by synchronizing it externally antiphase-wise. The adjustment is system immanent and self-organized. This is fundamentally different to actively controlled systems, because no control unit is necessary. Now, the dependence on the coupling is studied in more detail. In Fig. 3, we show for 11 examples with coupling from 10 dB above to 10 dB below the SPL of the (not driven) pipe. The blue line marks the dependence of the frequency difference on the detuning; the magenta line shows the amplitude measured at the microphone.

In the first place, one notices for 0 difference of pipe and loudspeaker amplitude that the bifurcation type, seen at the edge of the synchronization region is of

Figure 2: The experimental setup. The pipe is located next to the driving source - a loudspeaker.

saddle-node type, recognized by the square-root branching. The amplitudes of speaker and pipe are superposed at the microphone, at the detuning for which a phase difference of π occurs, this superposition results in an anti-phase motion of the pipe and the interference of the signals is destructive - a deep minimum is found. Going to higher SPL of the driving loudspeaker, the bifurcation becomes more and more imperfect, no nice square root is seen any longer. Stepping towards smaller driving, a square root behaviour is found.

The size of the plateaus monotonuously increases with the driving amplitude. With changing amplitude, the position of the minimum changes, this is due to a shift of the relative phase which allows the minimum to be found a bit more to positive detuning. When one leaves the synchronization region the usual beating effect is heard (and measured).

The total measurement time was more than two weeks, it resulted from the high spectral resolution used for small amplitudes - if it is not high enough, the synchronization plateau vanishes inside the frequency resolution. By our precise measurements, we could find an synchronization over a range of 50 dB! at the lower side the loudspeaker was able to force the organ pipe onto its frequency, even though the signal was 500 times weaker than the one of the pipe [Abel et al., 2008].

To measure the mutual synchronization of the two pipes, they were installed on a common bar side by side. One of the pipes was fixed to frequency $170.1 Hz$, the other one was detuned in variable steps. In the following we will use the symbol f for uncoupled frequencies, and ν for measurements of the coupled pipes. As usual for synchronization, we have plotted the frequency difference $\Delta \nu$ versus Δf

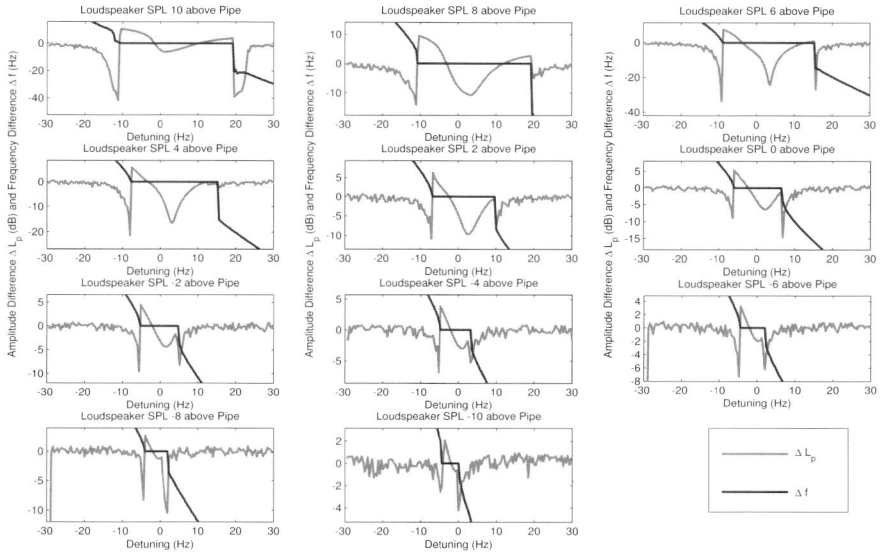

Figure 3: Synchronization plateaus for different coupling, i.e. SPL of the driving loudspeaker.With increasing coupling the synchronization plateau increases, the amplitude shows deeper and deeper minima.

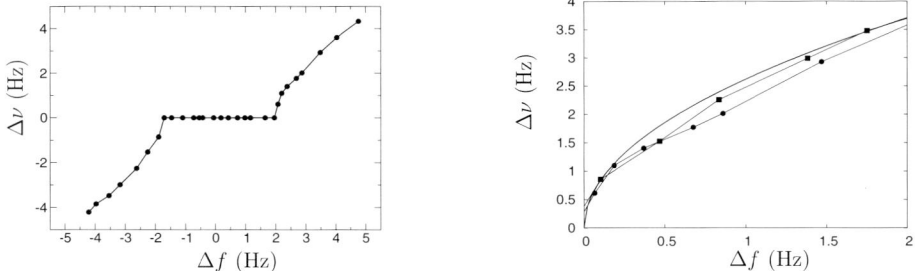

Figure 4: Left: Synchronization of two organ pipes. The plot shows the observed frequency difference $\Delta\nu$ versus the detuning of the uncoupled pipes, Δf. In the synchronization region, a very clean plateau is observed. Right: Transition from the synchronization region. As theory predicts, a saddle-node bifurcation occurs at the edge. The plot shows the mirrored left branch ■ and the left branch • together with a square root fit (straight line).

in Fig. 4. As synchronization theory predicts, the bifurcation close to the ends of the locking region is of saddle node type [Ott et al., 1994], the synchronization plateau is nicely measured.

A detailed investigation of the synchronization of the higher harmonics has been presented in [Abel and Bergweiler, 2007]. In general, the relative phase for the nth harmonic in the synchronization region lies in the interval $(n(\phi_0 - \pi/2), n(\phi_0 + \pi/2))$. This is confirmed by the experiment.

5   Conclusions

Organ pipes are fascinating musical instruments which, when coupled to other sound sources, show highly nonlinear behaviour and influence each other. here, it has been demonstrated that a varying coupling for small driving amplitudes the usual synchronization picture is confirmed. For very high coupling, the synchronization transition changes character. The amplitudes of pipe and loudspeaker interfere at the microphone such that for phase difference of π between pipe and loudspeaker, a deep minimum occurs. The position of this minimum cannot be predicted *a priori*, this depends on the detail of the oscillator equation, which is at the present unknown.

Measurements have been performed on two organ pipes as well. The observed behavior of two pipes, close to each other, is completely consistent with an explanation in the frame of synchronization theory. In a more abstract model, one can describe the system as two driven regions in a wave-guiding nonlinear medium with two different feedbacks applied to these regions. The regions emit chaotic signals which synchronize the two adjacent regions. The synchronization happens by the exchange of information through the medium. Measurements on the influence of the coupling are currently being analyzed, here the coupling is varied by the inter-pipe distance.

From an acoustic point of view, one can address the question of how to position two organ pipes close in frequency. This has been intuitively solved by organ builders by trial and error in the last centuries. Our work might give quantitative hints on how large the inter-pipe distance needs to be to suppress mutual influence, and on details of the coupling mechanism. For example, avoiding an amplitude minimum for the first harmonic is highly desirable.

Current work focuses on the dependence of the synchronization on the distance of two pipes, or oscillators. With increasing distance the chaotic signal emitted from the pipes is less and less synchronizeable. The exact behaviour is, however, not predictable to our knowledge. From our measurements, one can clearly say that the pipes do not show an oscillation death; rather, antiphase sound radiation yields the observed weakening of the amplitude.

Of course, it is very interesting to extend the experimental setup to three, four or even more oscillators in order to see how the self-organization of chaotic oscillators yields the synchronized emission of sound waves for more complex setups.

Acknowledgments

We acknowledge fruitful discussion with M. Rosenblum and A. Pikovsky about synchronization theory. We thank the organ manufacturer Alexander Schuke Potsdam Orgelbau GmBH for providing the organ pipes for our measurements.

References

[Abel et al., 2008] Abel, M., Ahnert, K., and Bergweiler, S. (2008). Synchronized sound. *Nature.* submitted.

[Abel and Bergweiler, 2007] Abel, M. and Bergweiler, S. (2007). Synchronization of higher harmonics in coupled organ pipes. In *Proceedings of the 19th International Congress on Acoustics.* accepted.

[Abel et al., 2006] Abel, M., Bergweiler, S., and Gerhard-Multhaupt, R. (2006). Synchronization of organ pipes by means of air flow coupling: experimental observations and modeling. *J. Acoust. Soc. Am.*, 119(4).

[Bouasse, 1929] Bouasse, H. (1929). *Instruments a vent.* Lib. Delagrave, Paris.

[Coltman, 1976] Coltman, J. W. (1976). Jet drive mechanisms in edge tones and organ pipes. *J. Acoust. Soc. Am.*, 60(3):725–733.

[Coltman, 1992] Coltman, J. W. (1992). Jet behavior in the flute. *J. Acoust. Soc. Am.*, 92(1):74–83.

[Fabre and Hirschberg, 2000] Fabre, B. and Hirschberg, A. (2000). Physical modeling of flue instruments: A review of lumped models. *Acustica - Acta Acustica*, 86:599–610.

[Fabre et al., 1996] Fabre, B., Hirschberg, A., and Wijnands, A. P. J. (1996). Vortex shedding in steady oscillation of a flue organ pipe. *Acustica - Acta Acustica*, 82:863–877.

[Fletcher, 1993] Fletcher, N. H. (1993). Autonomous vibration of simple pressure-controlled valves in gas flows. *J. Acoust. Soc. Am*, 93:2172–2180.

[Ott et al., 1994] Ott, E., Sauer, T., and Yorke, J. (1994). *Coping with Chaos*. Series in Nonlinear Science. Wiley, New York.

[Pikovsky et al., 2001] Pikovsky, A., Rosenblum, M., and Kurths, J. (2001). *Synchronization. A Universal Concept in Nonlinear Sciences*. Cambridge University Press, Cambridge.

[Rayleigh, 1945] Rayleigh, J. W. S. (1945). *The Theory of Sound*, volume 2. Dover Publications.

[Verge et al., 1997a] Verge, M. P., Fabre, B., Hirschberg, A., and Wijnands, A. (1997a). Sound production in recorderlike instruments. i. dimensionless amplitude of the internal acoustic field. *J. Acoust. Soc. Am.*, 101(5):2914–2924.

[Verge et al., 1997b] Verge, M. P., Hirschberg, A., and Causs, R. (1997b). Sound production in recorderlike instruments. i. a simulation model. *J. Acoust. Soc. Am.*, 101(5):2925–2939.

Andreas Beurmann and Albrecht Schneider

Acoustics of the harpsichord: a case study

1. Introduction

With the present study, we want to expand a previous publication (Beurmann & Schneider 2003) in which measurements obtained from several harpsichords, among them an Italian instrument from 1579 (Beurmann 2000, Nr. 4, 24-26), and a two-manual Flemish instrument built by Andreas Ruckers (the Elder) in 1628 (Beurmann 2000, Nr. 24, 86-90) were presented. In this article, the focus will be on a harpsichord by Nicolas Pigalle of Dijon (1709-1786), made in 1771. It is a two-manual French harpsichord (see photo)

which offers the typical design of 8' + 4' (lower manual) and 8' (upper manual). The compass of the instrument is F, ↔ f''' (=F1 ↔ F6) that is, five octaves. The scale length of the strings C, c°, c', c'' in the lower manual and the respective plucking points are given in table 1:

Table 1: Scale and plucking points, harpsichord Nicolas Pigalle, 1771.

Tone	length L (mm)	plucking point l (mm)	ratio L/l
F_1	1837	179	10.262
C	1721	164	10.494
c°	1215	142	8.556
c'	726	115	6.313
c''	374	100	3.74

The diameter and material of the strings is summarized as follows:

F_1	0.52 mm	brass
C	0.42 mm	brass
c°	0.30 mm	iron

If c'' (C5) is taken as a point of reference for the scaling (as is customary, see Henkel 1979, 116), it is obvious that the string length does not double from one octave to the next. The reduction can be expressed thus:

	c''(C5)	c'(C4)	c°(C3)	C(C2)	F,(F1)
Theory	1	2	4	8	12
Measured	1	1.941	3.249	4.602	4.912

At the time of the investigation, the harpsichord was tuned to A_4 (a') = 372 Hz which implies a fundamental frequency for A_2 = 93 Hz, and for A_1 = 46.5 Hz. Consequently, the fundamental frequency for the C_2 (C) is close to 52 Hz. For the measurements, the instrument was tuned in the Valotti and Young temperament.

2. Plucking mechanism, excitation and motion of the string

As is well known, the harpsichord is an instrument whose metal strings are plucked by a plectrum. The material of the plectrum used to be crow quill, and is Delrin (a plastic having similar characteristics) in most modern instruments. The Pigalle at the time of our investigation was equipped with Delrin plectra. As to the plucking mechanism, this process can be divided into five sections: (1) by pressing a key the jack which carries the plectrum is raised so that the plectrum just touches the string; (2) then, the string itself is raised by the plectrum whereby the elongation as well as the tension of the string increases. (3) At a certain point of elongation, the tension of the string causes the plectrum to bend to such an extent that the string begins to slip from the plectrum. (4) At a certain point in this process, the string, apparently rolling to the side from the plectrum is completely free and, due to the restoring force F, is accelerated. The motion, however, is not simply in the equilibrium direction yet is more complex (see below). (5) Finally, the string released from the plectrum performs free vibrations.

It is not necessary here to go into details of the theory of vibrating strings which is one of the fundamental areas of acoustics (see Rayleigh 1894/1896; Kalähne 1913; Wagner 1947, pt III; Morse 1948/1981, ch. 3; Morse & Ingard 1986, ch. 4). Elementary theory of string vibration considers an ideal, that is a homogeneous, very thin string of length L which is treated as if it were a one-dimensional structure. In regard of an ideal string, the boundary conditions could be that the string is free at one or at both ends, simply supported at one or at both ends, clamped at one or at both ends, or any combination of these conditions in regard of the two ends of the string. In the most elementary case relevant for music, the string is considered as a one-dimensional continuum composed of small elements dx along the dimension x ($0 \leq x \leq L$). Since the string has a definite length L, the boundary condition supported-supported (i.e., the string is stretching over two small and sharp-edged bridges) or, alternatively, clamped-clamped should apply.

For the elementary theory of vibration it is assumed that the elongation ζ of the string is very small (or even infinitesimal small) so that it will not cause stretching of the string elements. Further, it is assumed that the elongation is so small that it will not increase the tension of the string while it is plucked.

These assumptions are made to simplify theoretical considerations. However, the situation in a harpsichord string is more complex. First, a real string of course does have a diameter h so that the string elements of finite length dx have a cross section S. Second, the string is composed of a certain material (e.g., iron, brass or similar alloy) so that relevant parameters such as Poisson's ratio and Young's modulus have to be taken into account. Third, because the cross section of the string is not infinitesimal small, and the tension of the string cannot exceed a certain limit before breaking, bending stiffness can occur (depending on the actual size and material parameters). In fact, a real string is composed of a material with mass density ρ and is stretched under a tension, σ.

Given these qualifications, a string plucked at one point $x = l$ is supposed to undergo transversal vibrations since the elongation ζ is orthogonal to the string (for $x = 0$ and $x = L$, $\zeta = 0$). Consequently, transversal motion is normal to the string of dimension x. The transversal motion of the string can be explained in two ways: (1) as a linear superposition of eigenmodes (with their respective eigenfrequencies forming a harmonic series), and (2) as a superposition of two waves of identical speed c which first travel into opposite directions from the point of excitation, and, after reflection at the two ends of the string, combine into a standing wave pattern (see Kalähne 1913, pp. 40, Wagner 1947, Pt III).

In practice, transversal vibration of a string has to be considered as a process that can be nonlinear in regard of the tension and the stretching of a string. If indeed the elongation of the string is large enough to result in stretching of the string elements, an additional tension $\Delta\sigma$ will occur so that the actual tension is $\sigma + \Delta\sigma$. The increase of the restoring force thereby no longer is proportional to the elongation (see Meyer & Guicking 1974, pp. 396). In fact, the eigenfrequencies of the string would raise with increasing elongation. Another factor relevant for nonlinear behaviour of a plucked or struck string is the coupling of transversal and longitudinal modes due to large amplitudes (Morse & Ingard

1986, pp. 856). In this case which is relevant for harpsichords, transversal motion generates longitudinal waves which travel much faster than transversal waves. Nonlinearity of the string is proportional to c[long]^2 - c[trans]^2. Further, one has to take into account that transversal motion of the string is possible in two planes [y, z; figure 1, see below], and that these two transverse modes are coupled as well. Finally, a factor relevant for nonlinear behaviour is bending stiffness which can occur, in particular in relatively short as well as thick strings since the ratio of diameter and length (h/L) no longer satisfies the condition $L \gg h$. Also, bending stiffness increases with low tension of strings. In principle, bending stiffness grows with the thickness of strings (as in wound bass strings of the piano) and gradually turns them into thin bars, to the effect that the equation of motion has to be changed from a 2nd order into a 4th order differential equation. If, in regard of string vibration, an additional tension $\Delta\sigma$ due to large elongation as well as bending stiffness have to be taken into account, proper calculation of the transversal vibration such as found in the steel strings of the piano, leads to a system of two nonlinear differential equations which are coupled (see Lieber 1975). On the other hand, a linear approximation for the plucked (thin) string such as found in a harpsichord is possible if (a) the plucking is treated as a point force, and if (b) geometrical stiffness of the string is very small (Cuesta & Valette 1990).

In an actual harpsichord, however, the string excitation mechanism is quite complex since the plectrum undergoes gradual bending with the raise of the jack while the string remains „glued" to the plectrum due to adhesive frictional forces (see Elfrath 1990). At a certain point which is determined by the friction coefficient, the string begins to slip from the plectrum, in a lateral and sloping direction downwards. This implies that the string is not simply accelerated in a direction perpendicular to the soundboard yet also parallel to the soundboard. Further, due to the slipping from the plectrum bended downwards, the string undergoes some torsional motion. The overall motional pattern of the string in two planes (y, z; see figure 1) hence appears to be elliptic (as in a Lissajou figure resulting from two periodic motions).

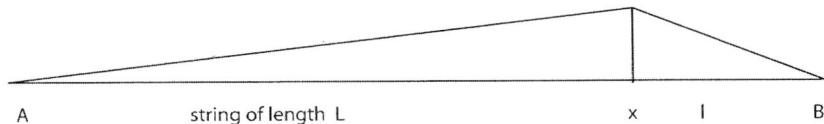

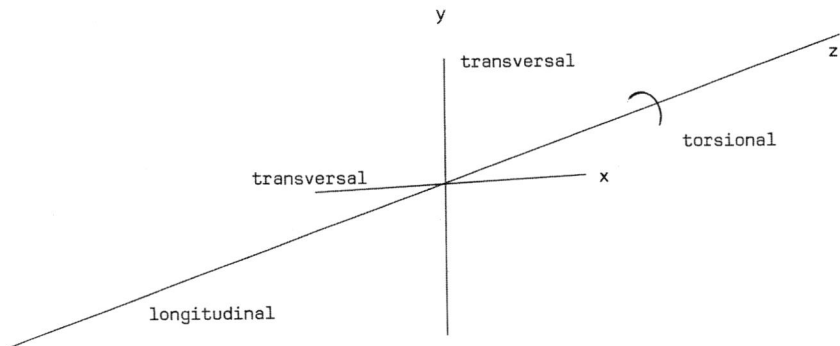

A   string of length L   x | B

y

transversal   z

torsional

transversal

x

longitudinal

figure 1

Though the transversal vibration perpendicular to the plane of the soundboard is most efficient in regard of energy transport into the bridge, and from there on into the soundboard, it is preceded by a longitudinal wave which has been investigated in laboratory experiments employing a mechanical model (Cuesta & Valette 1988, 1989). Longitudinal vibrations have been observed in piano strings where the hammer impulse gives rise to a longitudinal wave which, due to the much higher wave speed of, roughly, $c_l \sim 5000$ m/sec in steel strings, precedes the transversal wave for which the wave speed is given as $c_{tr} \sim 420$ m/sec (Podlesak & Lee 1988, Giordano & Korty 1996). Hence, the ratio of the two wave speeds c[long] and c[trans] for the steel string in question is close to 11:1 or 12:1. The coupling of the 12th partial of the transversal wave to the fundamental of the longitudinal wave has been reported for a harpsichord string (Cuesta & Valette 1989, 114).

The time signal of the note C_2 (C) of the Pigalle 8' recorded with a microphone (Neumann TLM 170, cardioid) close to the vibrating string is shown in figure 2. Before periodicity with a period length of $T \sim 19.1$ ms (corresponding to 52.3 Hz, the fundamental frequency of the C_2 as tuned in this instrument) is established, there is a transient portion of the sound signal lasting for ca 12 ms, and which can be divided into three sections. The very first section which is caused by the plectrum raised against the string, and the lifting of the string by the plectrum, sometimes has been defined as the pretransient (Gäumann 2003), and has been subjected to micro-analysis. With close miking as well as laser trigonometry, a signal can be recorded from the plectrum

245

immediately after the string has slipped. The plectrum itself vibrates (with an amplitude in the range of 1-1.5 mm) at a rather high frequency of ca. 5 kHz.

The spectral content of the transient following the noisy pretransient can be estimated fairly well by means of an autoregressive filter model (Keiler et al. 2003). Since the transient can be expected to contain the longitudinal vibration, this can be measured at the distant end of the string, i.e., at the soundboard bridge. In the case of the note C_2, a small and highly sensitive accelerator was put against the side of the soundboard bridge so as to pick up longitudinal vibration. The time signal (figure 3) is that of a quasi-periodic vibration with a regular decay of the amplitude which lasts for ca. 5.5 ms before the transversal wave sets in. This part of the signal has been subjected to an autocorrelation analysis (figure 4) which yields a period of 44 samples or ca. 0.917 ms. In respect of the sampling frequency of 48 kHz as was applied in the recording, the period T~0.917 ms corresponds to a frequency of ca. 1090.5 Hz. The longitudinal vibration preceding the transversal wave can still be traced on the soundboard (see below).

The velocity of the string resulting from the motion perpendicular to the soundboard was recorded with an inductive measuring device similar to that used by Cuesta & Valette (1989) and Gätjen (1995). Such a device consists of a small yet strong magnet to whose poles metal shoes are attached. The string, moving up and down in the magnetic field between the shoes, induces a current which can be picked up at the two ends of the string. The signal thus obtained is faint and needs amplification which was provided by a measuring amplifier (B & K 2608) before the signal was digitized at 48 kHz/16 bit, and recorded on DAT. The time series of the velocity signal beginning with the onset of the transversal motion is shown in figure 5. The period length of the signal is T = 19.1ms which of course corresponds to the fundamental frequency of the C_2 string. The Fourier transform of the velocity signal (figure 6) yields a fundamental frequency close to 52 Hz. The spectrum shows characteristic minima due to the relation of string length L, and plucking point l. Hence the spectrum is more or less periodic as is the spectrum of the sound of the same note radiated from the instrument (figure 7). Notwithstanding some similarity in regard of the maxima and minima of energy, the two spectra also exhibit some differences due to the resonance mechanism of the instrument (see below).

In regard of the harpsichord, it has been argued that the stiffness of the rather long strings of the harpsichord (as is most obvious in Italian specimen) is slight, and introduces only a small amount of inharmonicity which would result in giving the sound a bit of a bell-like quality (Fletcher 1977). In fact, there is a small amount of inharmonicity inherent in the spectrum even of notes in the low register as the partials raise in frequency above the expected value[1]:

---

[1] Frequencies were measured by analysis of spectral peaks (FFT-length 16384, 32768 and 65536 pts, parabolic interpolation).

Table 2: Frequencies of partials, string/note C_2 (C) and C_3(c°), Pigalle 1771

Partial no.	frequency(Hz)	ratio f_1/fn	frequency(Hz)	ratio f_1/fn
1	51,654	1.0	103,958	1.0
10	517,918	10.0267	1038,837	9.993
20	1039,646	20.1271	2082,212	20.029
30	1569,871	30.392	3135,505	30.161
40	2101,586	40.686	4201,917	40.422
n = 50	2641,831	51.145	5288.284	50.869

The inharmonicity observed can be attributed to the stiffness of the brass strings. However, inharmonicity can also be caused by nonlinear effects of vibration.

In regard of measuring transversal vibrations of the string parallel to the soundboard in addition to perpendicular motion, a specific optical device had been developed by Elfrath (1990, pp. 20) which does not influence the vibrating string.

3. Bridge and soundboard action

Design and construction parameters of historical harpsichords have been the topic of several studies (see Fletcher 1977, Henkel 1979, Kottick 1985, Elfrath 1990, Gätjen 1995). In particular, the geometry of the soundboard, the location of the bridge (or, in case of a 8' + 4' design, the bridges), the variable thickness of the soundboard and the grain structure of the spruce relative to the bridge(s) have been investigated. Also, the input impedance Z at various points along the soundboard bridge has been measured in order to study the energy transfer from the vibrating string into the soundboard.

In regard of the Pigalle of 1771, both the longitudinal and the transversal wave travelling along the string from the plectrum can be easily detected when arriving at the bridge which is glued on the soundboard. With the accelerometer placed on the bridge close to the pin of the string which is played (in this case, C_2), the evolution of the transversal wave as well as its spectral composition can be studied. Figure 8 shows the transversal wave when arriving at the bridge[2]. The transient analysis gives some information as to the spectral composition of the signal which, however, becomes evident with the next frame of the Fourier transform (figure 9). The spectrum thus obtained is more or less periodic with a fundamental frequency close to 52 Hz, and very many partials build thereon. The spectrum contains significant energy up to 15 kHz so that the transversal wave, composed as a broad-band signal, is suited to elicit very many eigenmodes of the soundboard.

The input impedance of the bridge has been studied in great detail by Elfrath (1990) who measured the input impedance along the bridge of four historical harpsichords

---

[2] Of the FFT length of 4096 pts chosen to obtain sufficient frequency resolution (48000/4096 = 11.72 Hz), in this calculation 296 samples (~5.8 ms of sound) are representing the actual onset of the transversal wave to which 3800 samples of zero amplitude have been added. The signal moreover is zero-padded with a factor of 2. For details of signal processing, see Mertins 1996/1999.

which can be regarded as representing different regional traditions[3]. It is interesting to note that the impedance curves for these excellent specimens vary considerably so that it might be difficult to derive a clear pattern from the data which would indicate certain rules. Besides measuring the input impedance for transversal motion perpendicular to the bridge and soundboard, respectively, Elfrath (1990, 108) investigated also input impedances for transversal motion parallel to the bridge and soundboard. As can be expected, for this type of vibration the input impedance of the bridge is considerably higher than for the other transversal mode since parallel vibration does not exert much pressure on the bridge.

For the present study, the input impedance of the bridge of the Pigalle 1771 was estimated rather than measured in a straightforward way. As has been discussed in previous studies (Elfrath 1990, Gätjen 1995), the input impedance Z (kNs/m) which can be regarded as the mechanical resistance of the bridge must be high enough to prevent that the energy contained in the string vibration is absorbed too fast by the bridge as well as by the soundboard. In case of a fast and complete transfer of energy, the sound radiated from the instrument would be very loud yet also very short. With sufficiently high impedance of the bridge and the soundboard, a long decay of the sound radiated from the instrument will occur. The RMS amplitude for the sound of the C_2 string (measured for 300 harmonics by means of a phase vocoder algorithm; Beauchamp 1995) for the attack reaches 80 dB (see figure 10), and then slowly decays. For a decay of 20 dB, it takes about 4 seconds. The slow decay indicates high input impedance of the bridge as well as the soundboard whereas the input impedance of the string is low (as can be inferred from the fact that the mere contact of the string with the small plectrum yields an audible signal).

The soundboard of the harpsichord has been extensively studied by means of modal analysis as well as using drivers to obtain response curves (see Kottick 1985, Elfrath 1990, Savage et al. 1992). The response behaviour of the Pigalle 1771 was studied in several ways: first, we wanted to check whether the longitudinal vibration of the string preceding the transversal wave could be recorded from the soundboard which is 1815 mm long (max. length), and 860 mm wide (max width). To this purpose, an accelerometer was placed on the soundboard between the 4' and the 8' bridge, underneath the strings of either C_2 or C_3 which were set to motion by the normal plucking mechanism. Indeed, the time signal of the longitudinal wave appears undistorted (see figure 11), and the corresponding spectrum of a short-time Fourier transform (zero-padded to allow for a transform length of 1024 pts) contains peaks at about 2012, 3008, and 4012 Hz (figure 12) which can be identified as partials no. 2, 3 and 4 of the longitudinal wave which hence has a fundamental frequency close to 1 kHz (see above). Second, an impulse was applied to the bridge at certain points by means of an impulse hammer, and each impulse response was recorded from the soundboard, again at different places, with an accelerometer (figure 13). The response can be expected to differ in regard of the place of recording since the soundboard is an elastic plate with variable height (with an average of ca. 3 mm) which is divided into smaller

---

[3] A two-manual Flemish harpsichord from Andreas Ruckers (the Elder) 1628, an English two-manual instrument from Jacob and Abraham Kirckman 1783 (Beurmann 2000,Nr. 24 and Nr. 44), an Italian single manual harpsichord (G.B. Giusti 1681) and a German single-manual specimen (Ch. Vater 1738).

panels (by the ribs and the cutoff bar, two bridges, and the 4' hitchpin rail). Moreover, the plate is clamped (for most of its circumference), and is by no means isotropic in its material because of the grain and fibre structure of spruce. In fact, the elactic modulus in the direction of the grain (which, typically, runs parallel to the strings) is about 12 to 16 times that of the respective modulus cross to the grain. Consequently, the velocity of the wave travelling in the direction of the grain is about three to four times that of the velocity of a wave that travels across the grain.

The impulse responses recorded were subjected to an analysis of temporal and spectral features carried out with signal processing tools. In order to secure good resolution in both frequency and time, a combination of the Wigner-Ville and the Fourier transform was applied, and in some cases a LPC algorithm was used to calculate trajectories for spectral components[4]. For example, figure 14 shows a recording from the large panel between the 4' and the 8' bridge where several strong bending modes have been elicited (at about 185, 391 and 470 Hz, respectively), however, with unstable frequencies of vibration. The conventional FFT of the impulse response, on the other hand, calculated for a rather long segment of the time series (16384 samples) yields several strong modes between, roughly 48 and 550 Hz (figure 15). The most salient spectral peaks are found at the following frequencies:

Table 3: Modal frequencies, impulse response of soundboard (Pigalle 1771)

Spectral component No.	Frequency (Hz)	Amplitude(dB)[5]
1	48.06	-61.5
2	69.81	-77.6
3	102.03	-63.4
4	135.2	-65.8
5	152.98	-76.5
6	184.21	-61.8
7	200.29	-63.2
8	220.96	-69.3
9	232.60	-65.5
10	240.14	-64.5
11	277.26	-69.9
12	391.99	-59.2
13	419.44	-68.3
14	442.77	-63.5
15	471.31	-61.2
16	520.39	-67.7
17	535.03	-75.0
18	552.39	-73.1

---

[4] The analysis was done with the SONOGRAM software developed by Hiroshi Momose (1991). The parameter settings are: Wigner+FFT, 2048 pts, Blackman window, dt = 7 pts ~ 0.146 ms hop size.
[5] The dB scale in the software used (Spectro 3.01, Gary Scavone) refers to 0 dBfs as an upper limit. Hence, all amplitudes in an undistorted signal will have a value of $-n$dB (n = real number).

Given the size of the soundboard of the Pigalle (1815 mm max. length, 860 mm max. width; the plane in total is 0.8151 m²), the lowest mode at 48 Hz is not surprising, and is in line with findings obtained in similar measurements (see Elfrath 1990, Savage et al. 1992).

Third, the transversal wave was recorded by an accelerometer placed on the soundboard between the 4' and the 8' bridge. In a long-term average spectrum (LTAS, 131072 samples = 2.73 seconds of sound), very many partials up to 7.5 kHz appear (figure 16). Comparing the pattern of eigenmodes of the soundboard found in the impulse response (Table 3) to the spectrum of the transversal wave as recorded from the soundboard, it is obvious that the signal of the generator (vibrating string) forces the resonator (soundboard) to vibrate in a harmonic manner. The mode frequencies of the transversal string vibration are so many, and are so closely spaced over the spectrum that they will strongly excite resonance frequencies in the soundboard (see Gough 1981, Savage et al. 1992).

4. Air modes

From the construction of a harpsichord which, different from a grand piano, usually does have a massive bottom, one may expect the air enclosed in the cavity made up of soundboard, side walls, and bottom, to work like a Helmholtz resonator. In the Pigalle, the distance between the bottom and the soundboard is ca. 194 mm. Thereby, the cavity formed by the bottom, the soundboard, and the side walls can be estimated to comprise a volume of ca. 0.158m³. However, calculation and measurement of air modes in harpsichords is quite difficult due to the actual geometry and construction (see Savage et al. 1992). Both the rose hole of the soundboard, and the gap found at the bottom close to the lower belly rail are rather atypical structures in regard of a standard Helmholtz box resonator. From previous measurements (Savage et al. 1992) it can be assumed, though, that a coupling of air and structural modes occurs, and that partials of the string will excite soundboard modes as well as air modes of the Helmholtz resonator.

5. Radiation of sound

Finally, in regard of the radiation of sound from the harpsichord, there are two interesting features: first, the large number of partials found in the sounds corresponding to the low notes of the Pigalle as well as other historical harpsichords (see Beurmann & Schneider 2003) provide enough energy to excite many modes of the soundboard which is the most decisive part of the instrument for effective radiation. The lid, however, also is relevant not just in respect of directing the sound radiated from the soundboard yet as a plate that resonates as well. Second, because of the many partials contained in the string vibration, and the many modes excited in the soundboard as well as the air enclosed in the instrument, a very dense sound is generated in which, due to slight inharmonicity, coupling of modes and other factors a small amount of amplitude modulation can be found (see figures 10, 17 and 18). Third, because of the many partials of the transversal wave which set in with a short attack (figure 17: partials no. 1 – 50 of the sound of the note C_2) as well as the transients which can be attributed to longitudinal vibration of the string (plus some noisy, inharmonic components attributable to the ,pretransient'; see Gäumann 2003), the spectral centroid goes up rapidly, and to a rather unusual level. For the note C_2 with a fundamental frequency of ca. 52 Hz, the centroid at the attack reaches 6.3 kHz (figure 18). However, it also falls rapidly when the string vibrates freely, and the sound slowly decays (figure 10). The decay largely is due to the damping out of higher partials whereas the sounds of the low notes can last very long ($t \geq 6$ sec. with a decay of about 10dB). Since the transient section of the sound is very brief, it is just enough to accentuate the attack of each note, on the one hand (the harpsichord supports execution of music in a non-legato or even staccato manner). On the other, the transient indeed is short enough not to hamper building up of periodic vibration as well as a harmonic spectrum rich in partials. Both, of course, are decisive in regard of perception of unambiguous pitches.

6. Conclusion

In the present article, we have summarized data from measurements carried out on a historical harpsichord which was built by Nicolas Pigalle of Dijon, in 1771. Different from some well-known instruments which were investigated previously in regard of acoustics (see Kottick 1985, Elfrath 1990, Gätjen 1995), the harpsichord of Nicolas Pigalle, a fine specimen from the second half of the 18th century, to the best of our knowledge had never been the object of scientific research. We hope that the data and findings reported in this article will add to our understanding of harpsichord acoustics and organology.

References

Beauchamp, James 1995. New methods for computer analysis and synthesis of music sounds. *32nd Czech Conference on acoustics. Speech - music- hearing*. Prague, 7-15.

Beurmann, Andreas 2000. *Historische Tasteninstrumente. Cembali – Spinette – Virginale – Clavichorde*. München, New York: Prestel.

Beurmann, Andreas, Albrecht Schneider 2003. Sonological Analysis of harpsichord sounds. In R. Bresin (ed.). *Proceedings of SMAC 03. Stockholm Music Acoustics Conference 2003*. Stockholm: KTH, Vol. 1, 167-170.

Cuesta, C., C. Valette 1988. Evolution temporelle de la vibration des cordes de clavecin. *Acustica* 66, 37-45,

Cuesta, C., C. Valette 1989. Le transitoire d'attaque des cordes de clavecin. *Acustica* 68, 112-122.

Cuesta, C., C. Valette 1990. Théorie de la corde pincée en approximation linéaire. *Acustica* 71, 28-41.

Elfrath, Thomas 1990. *Physikalische Untersuchungen über die qualitätsbestimmenden Einflußgrößen bei Cembali*. Report No. 6795. Physikalisch-Technische Bundesanstalt Braunschweig.

Fletcher, N.H. 1977. Analysis of the design and performance of harpsichords. *Acustica* 37, 139-147.

Fletcher, N, Th. Rossing 1991. *The Physics of musical instruments*. New York: Springer (2nd ed. 1998).

Gätjen, Bram 1995. *Der Klang des Cembalos. Historische, akustische und instrumentenkundliche Untersuchungen*. Kassel: Bosse.

Gäumann, T. 2003. The pretransient of the harpsichord sound. In R. Bresin (ed.). *Proceedings of SMAC 03. Stockholm Music Acoustics Conference 2003*. Stockholm: KTH, Vol. 1, 163-166

Giordano, N., A.J. Korty 1996. Motion of a piano string: longitudinal vibrations and the role of the bridge. *Journal of the Acoust. Soc. of America* 100, 3899-3908.

Gough, C.E. 1981. The Theory of string resonances on musical instruments. *Acustica* 49, 124-141.

Henkel, Hubert 1979. *Beiträge zum historischen Cembalobau*. Leipzig: VEB Deutscher Verlag für Musik.

Kalähne, Alfred 1913. *Grundzüge der mathematisch-physikalischen Akustik*. Teil II, Leipzig/Berlin: Teubner.

Keiler, F., C. Caradogan, U. Zölzer, A. Schneider 2003. Analysis of transient musical sounds by auto-regressive modeling. *Proc. of the 6th Intern. Conference on Digital Audio Effects (DAFx-03)*, London: St. Mary's, 301-304.

Kottick, Edward 1985. The Acoustics of the harpsichord: response curves and modes of vibration. *Galpin Society Journal* 38, 55-77.

Lieber, E. 1975. Moderne Theorien über die Physik der schwingenden Saite und ihre Bedeutung für die musikalische Akustik. *Acustica* 33, 324-335.

Mertins, Alfred 1996/1999. *Signaltheorie*. Stuttgart: Teubner (engl. translation Signal analysis, Chichester: Wiley 1999).

Meyer, Erwin, Dieter Guicking 1974. *Schwingungslehre*. Braunschweig: Vieweg (2nd ed. 1981).

Momose, Hiroshi 1991. *Sonogram: an acoustic signal analyzer*. Davis: UCD

Morse, Philip 1948/1981. *Vibration and sound*. Reprint of the 2nd ed. 1948. [no place]: Acoustical Soc. of America/American Institute of Physics.

Morse, Philip, K. Uno Ingard 1986. *Theoretical Acoustics*.(Paperback ed.) Princeton: Princeton U.Pr.

Podlesak, Michael, Anthony Lee 1988. Dispersion of waves in piano strings. *Journal of the Acoust. Soc. of America* 83, 305-317.

Lord Rayleigh (W. Strutt), *Theory of sound*. Vol. 1 and 2. 2nd ed. London (Reprint New York: Dover).

Savage, William, Edward Kottick, Thomas Hendrickson, Kenneth Marshall 1992. Air and structural modes of a harpsichord. *Journal of the Acoust. Soc. of America* 91, 2180-2189.

Wagner, Karl W. 1947. *Einführung in die Lehre von den Schwingungen und Wellen*. 2nd ed. Wiesbaden: Dietrich'sche Buchhandlung.

Figures

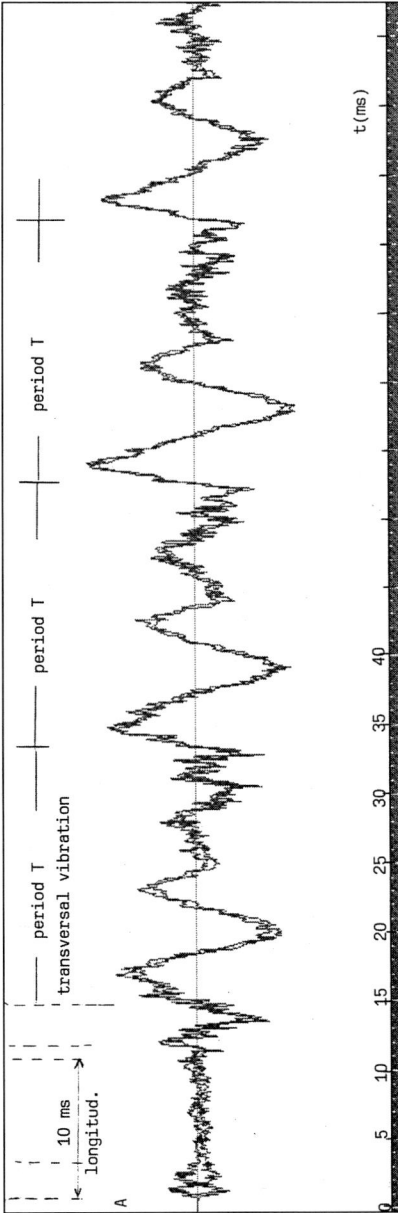

figure 2: Time signal (microphone)

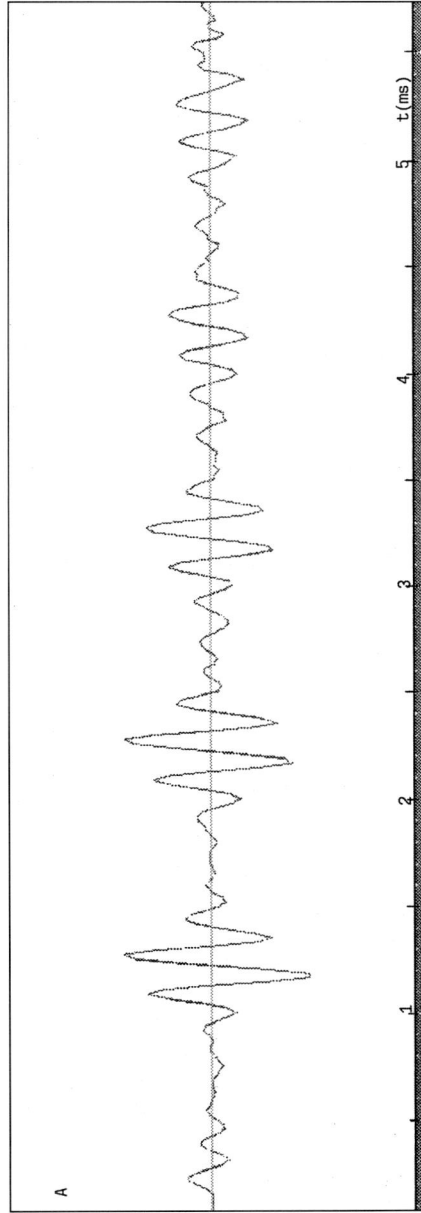

figure 3: Longitudinal wave (string)

253

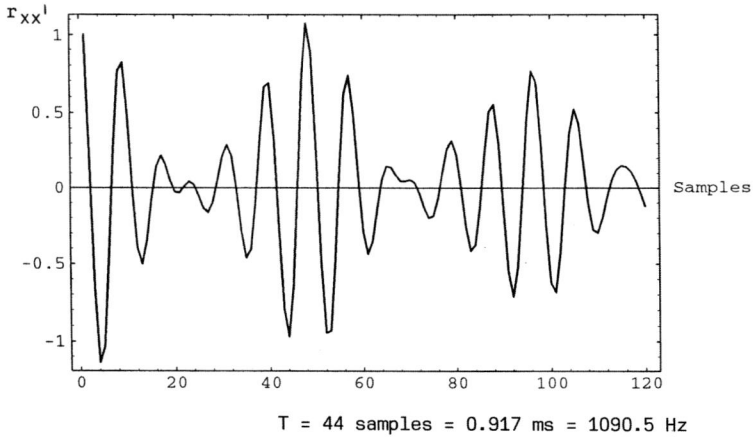

T = 44 samples = 0.917 ms = 1090.5 Hz

figure 4: Autocorrelation of time signal (figure 3)

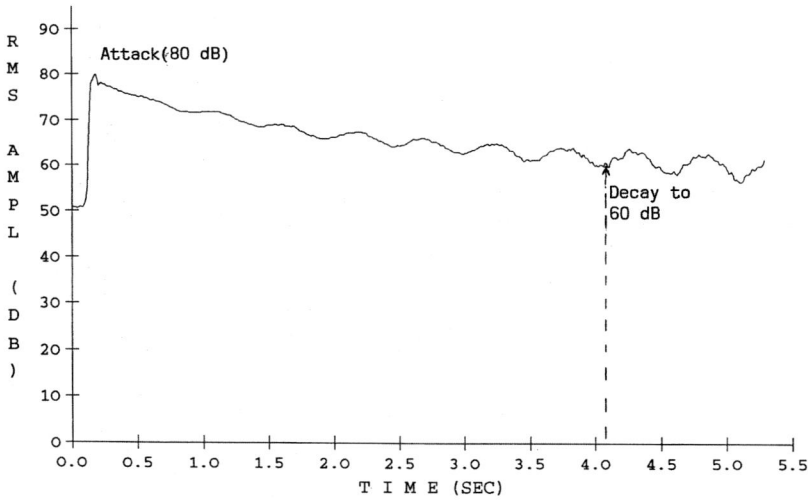

figure 10: Decay of amplitude (RMS), C_2 string

254

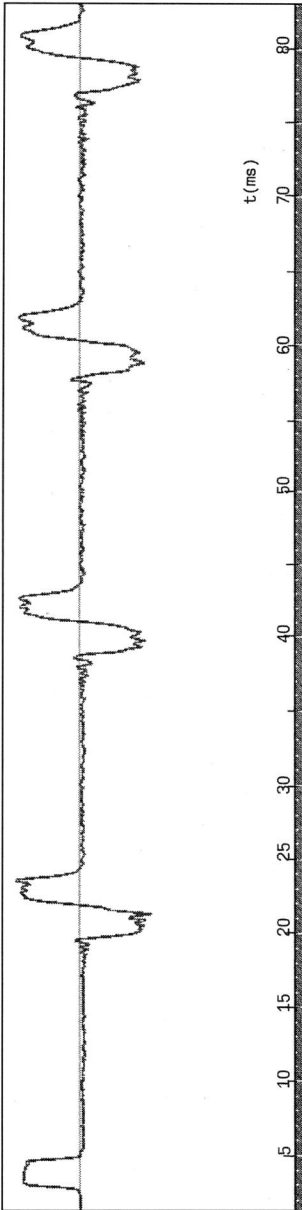

figure 5: String velocity, C_2 string

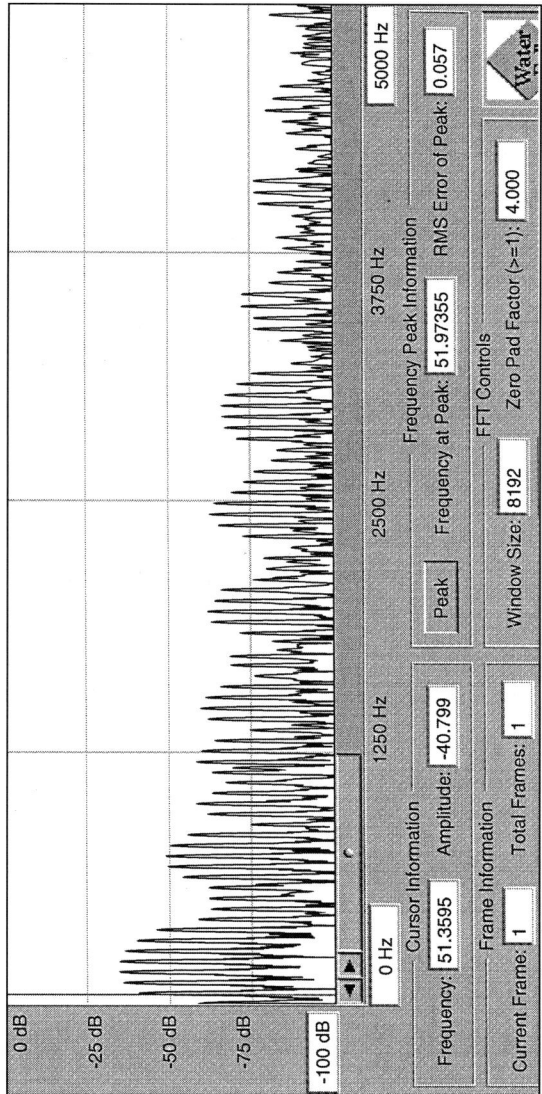

figure 6: Spectrum, string velocity, C_2 string

255

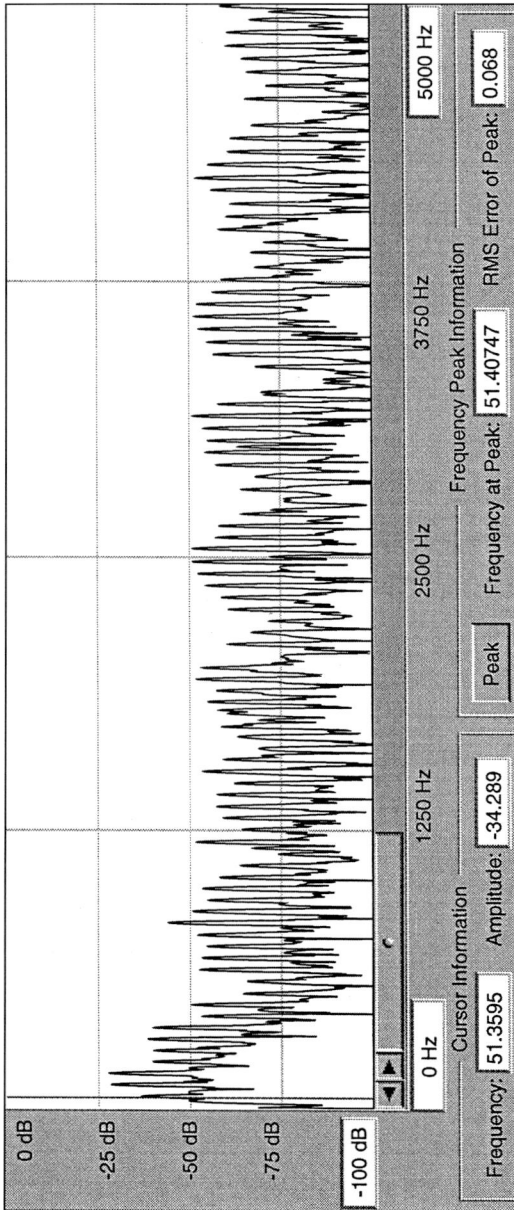

figure 7: Spectrum, microphone signal, C$_2$ string

256

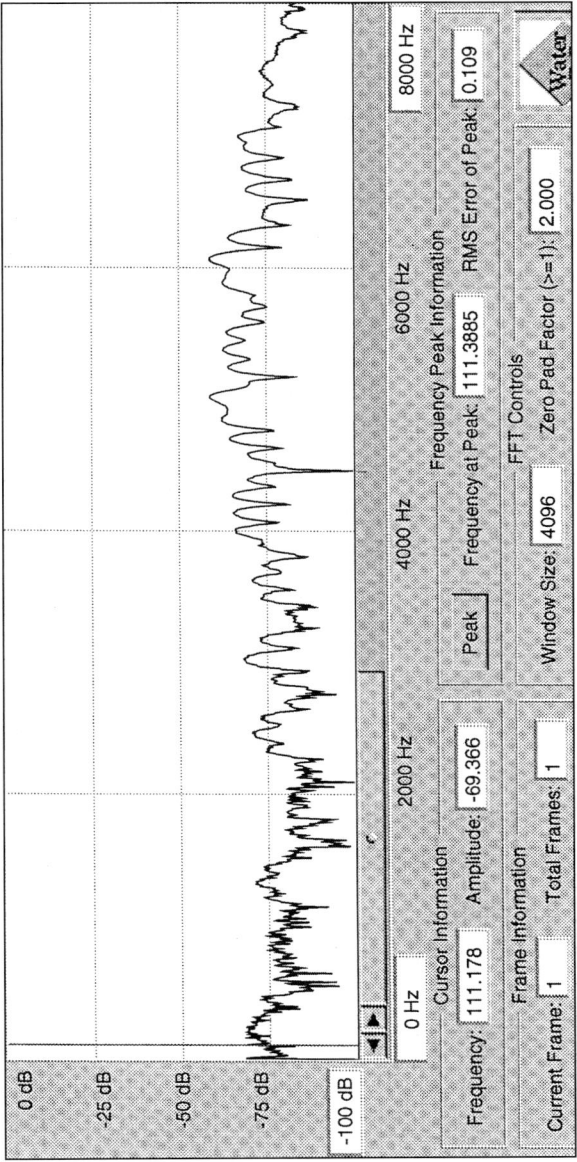

figure 8: Transversal wave arrives at bridge (accelerometer), C_2 string

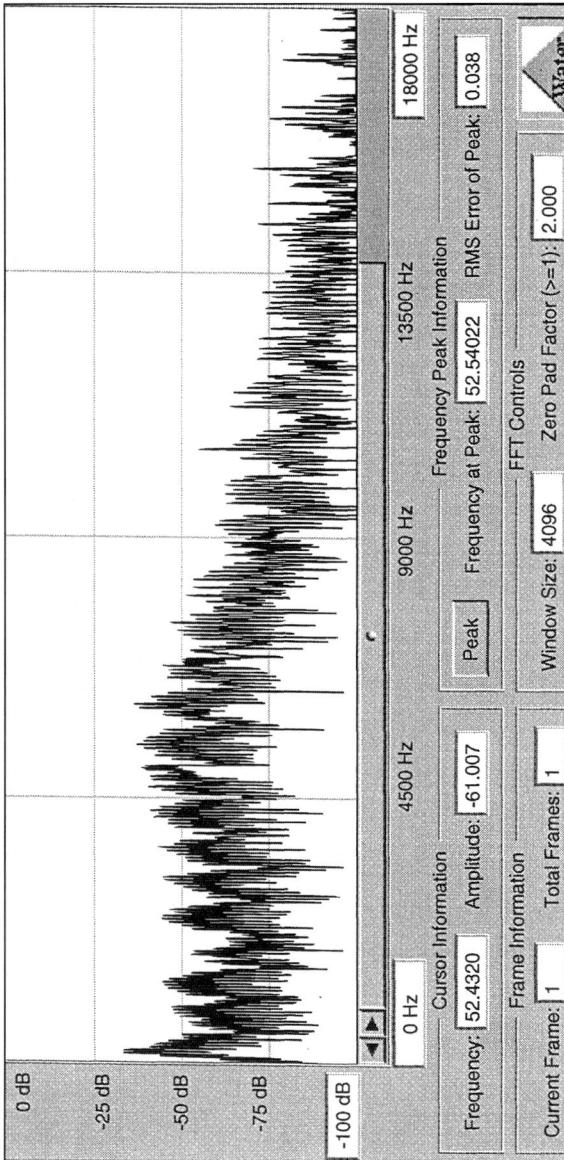

figure 9: Transversal wave recorded at bridge (accelerometer), C_2 string

Pigalle 1771, accelerator on soundboard, longitudinal vibration, note C_2

A

SPECTRUM: /me/Library/SoundWorks/PfgCSwingres.snd

4012.4 Hz

3008.3

2011.8

1367

995

733

0 dB

-25 dB

-50 dB

-75 dB

8 ms

Pigalle 1771, accelerometer on soundboard, longitudinal vibration, note C_2; FFT: 1024 pts, Hann.

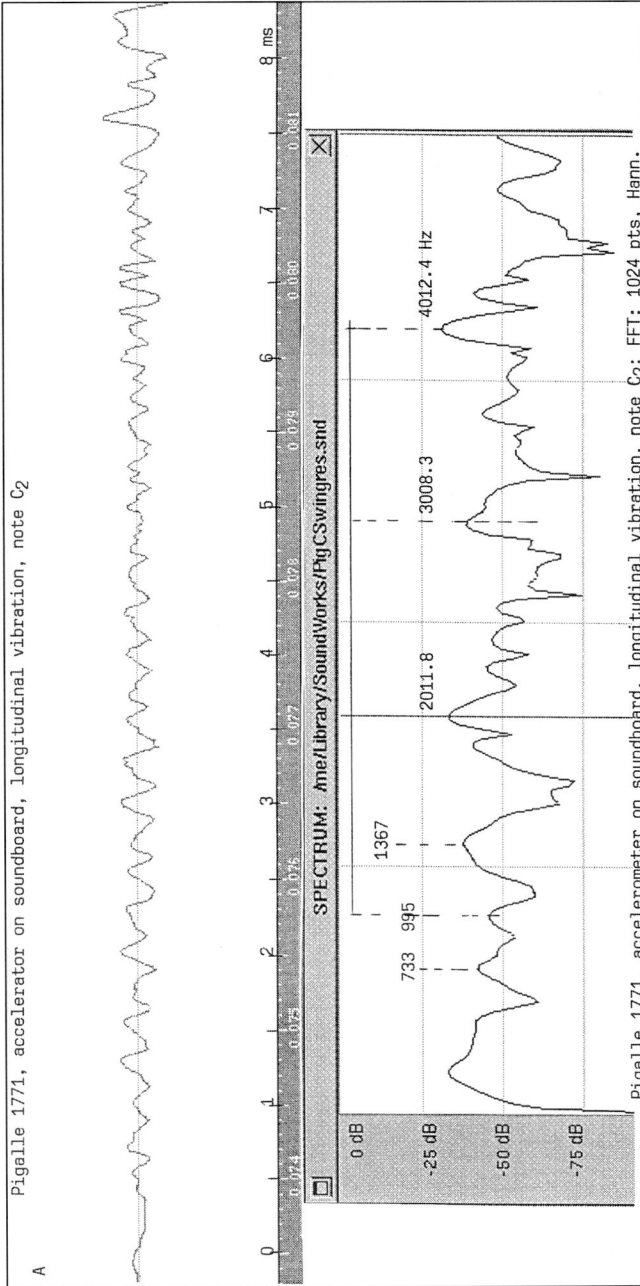

figure 11: Time series   **figure 12:** Spectrum, longitudinal wave on soundboard

259

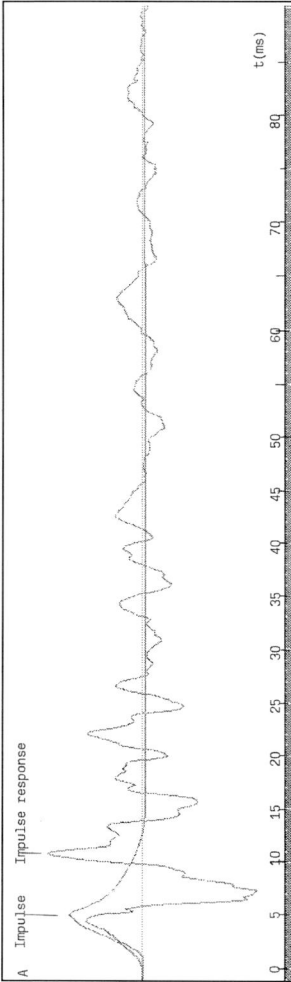

figure 13: Impulse, response

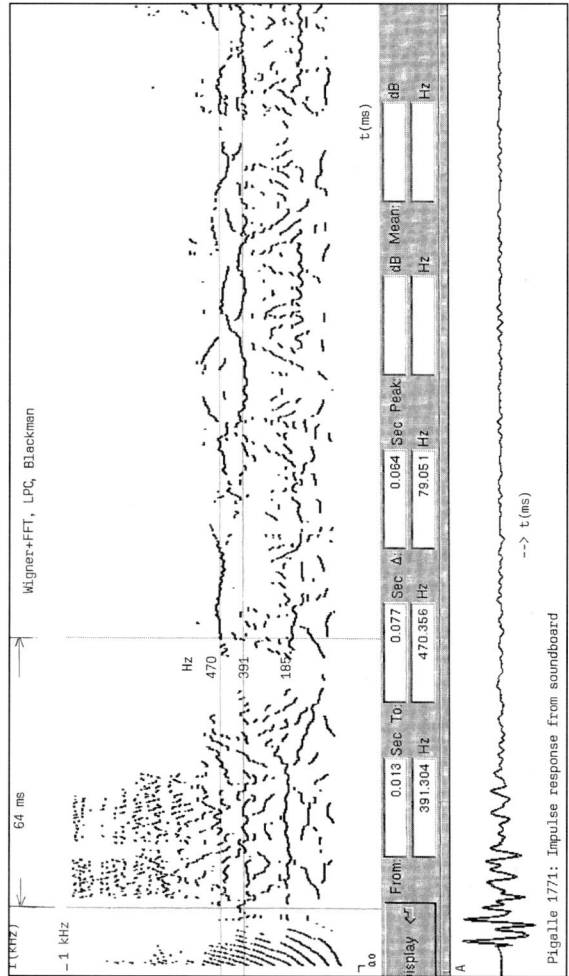

figure 14: Spectrum, impulse response (Wigner/FFT), LPC

260

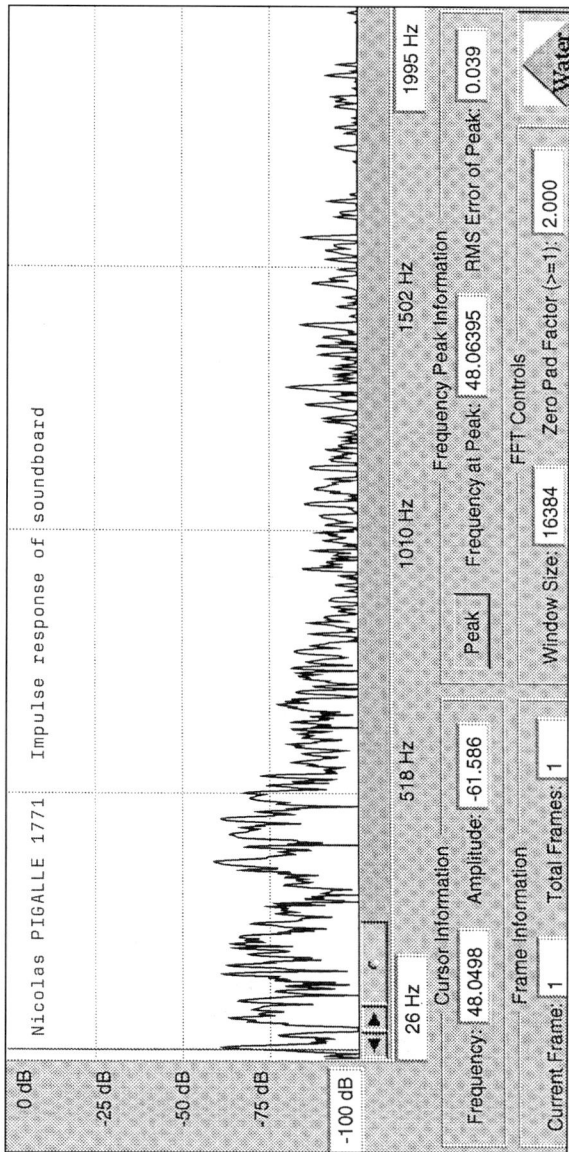

figure 15: Spectrum, bending modes, soundboard

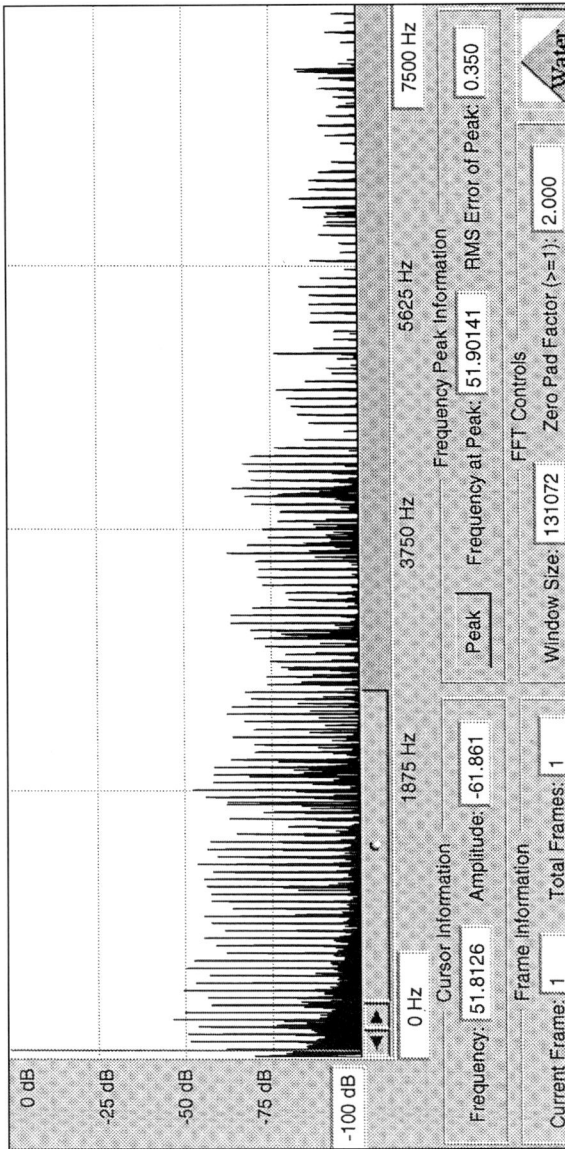

figure 16: Spectrum (LTAS), transversal wave, accelerometer on soundboard

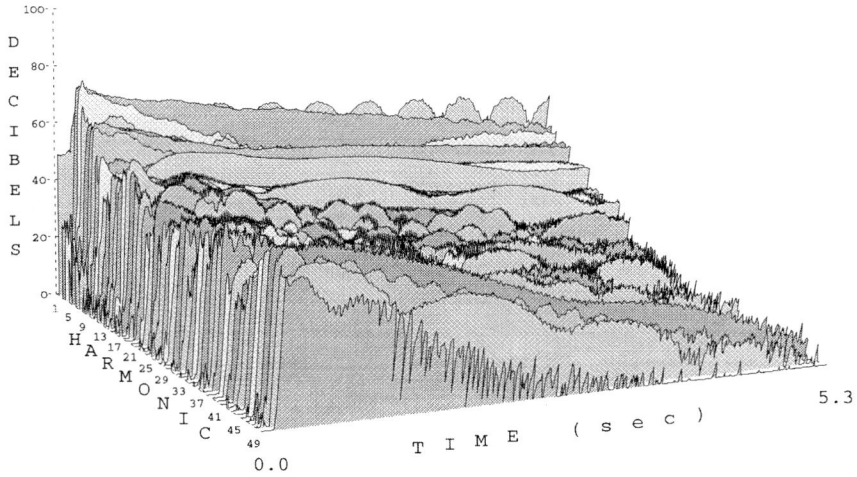

figure 17: 3D-spectrum, radiated sound, C_2 string

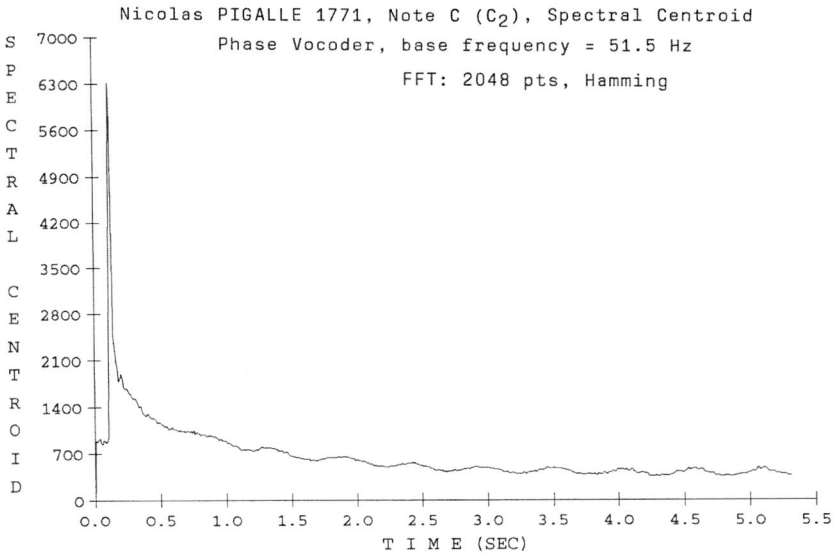

figure 18: Spectral centroid ./. time, radiated sound, C_2 string

263

Kai Stefan Lothwesen

Systematic musicology and Music education.
An empirical investigation into research topics
in German music education.

Abstract

This article looks at the relation between systematic musicology (SM) and music education (ME) in Germany from the perspective of systematic musicology. A starting point
for examining conceptions concerning these disciplines is given by Guido Adler's model
of musicology, where ME is seen as a field of applied musicology under the umbrella of
SM (Adler 1885). It is unclear whether this view is still up to date and what the actual
connections between the two disciplines are. An investigation into research topics
pertaining to German music education can provide more detailed insight; a further study
will elaborate on the results presented here.

The present survey is based on a selection of research papers published in major
German journals about ME which appeared from 1969 to 2007. A total of 1,302 papers
were reviewed using the rules of content analysis and categorised into different fields of
research. In this respect, special reference was made to two main authors (Richter 1997,
Colwell/Richardson 2002). The survey deals with the following questions: How are SM
and ME connected? What topics are examined in ME research? Are such topics in any
way related to SM? Did the main emphasis of research in ME change during the last 40
years? What does this all mean for the relation between ME and SM?

The survey shows how SM and ME are interrelated. Certain topics and fields of research contained in SM are basic requirements for ME. Yet the involvement of SM in
research topics published in ME journals has declined over the last few years. On the
other hand, the connection between SM and ME in fields such as musical development
and reception of music has produced benefits for SM by opening up more research into
practical applications.

Background

Though the history of systematic musicology (SM) and music education (ME) is older
than the names themselves and is rooted in ancient Greek philosophy, an examination of
the relation between SM and ME has to start at the point where they became academic
subjects (see Edler 1987, 9; Oerter/Bruhn 2005, 558). Such an overview with selected
conceptions of musicology prepares the ground for investigating the problems around
this relationship from the perspective of SM.

1. Relation between SM and ME in selected conceptions of musicology

It is appropriate to start with Guido Adler's attempt (1885) at designing a model for all
music-related science, since subsequent conceptions of musicology in general and
especially those of SM throughout the 20th century refer to this model. Adler divided the
field of musicology into two main areas - music history and systematic musicology. The

latter is subdivided into three parts: theory, aesthetics and education (fig. 1). According to Adler, the aim of ME was to systemise the laws of art ("Kunstgesetze") with reference to educational intentions (see Adler 1885, 11). ME was understood as a kind of applied musicology that was supposed to keep musicology in touch with the practice of musical art:

> "Die Aufstellung der höchsten Kunstgesetze und ihre praktische Verwehrtung in der musikalischen Pädagogik zeigt uns die Wissenschaft in unmittelbarer Berührung mit dem actuellen Kunstleben. Die Wissenschaft wird ihre Aufgabe in vollstem Umfange nur dann erreichen, wenn sie im lebendigen Contact mit der Kunst bleibt." (Adler 1885, 15)

Like Guido Adler before him, Hugo Riemann later deemed ME (1914) to be an area for teaching the techniques (greek: tekné) of composition and the basic rules of understanding musical art. Riemann justified the affiliation of ME to musicology by referring to the aims of musicology itself:

> "Aber auch die für die Ausbildung der Tonkünstler im Tonsatz berechnete Theorie der Musik (Kompositionslehre), desgleichen die musikalische Zeichenlehre (Notenschriftkunde) und die Vortragslehre, ja selbst die Gesanglehre und die methodische Unterweisung im Spiel einzelner Instrumente, die Instrumentierungslehre und die Anleitung zum Dirigieren müssen zweifellos der Musikwissenschaft zugerechnet werden, da dieselben fortgesetzt die Verwendung der Mittel des Ausdrucks im Dienste künstlerischer Ideen zum Gegenstande haben." (Riemann 1914, 3)

Although Riemann distinguished a theory of music with a systematic approach from music theory in the sense of propaedeutic instructions, he believed that educational aims were closely connected to the aesthetic terms of music (Riemann 1914, 9). Therefore he recommends the name 'applied aesthetics of music':

> "Die Einführung in die Technik der Komposition, die für den praktischen Unterricht berechnete Musiktheorie ist fortgesetzt gezwungen, mit ästhetischen Begriffen zu operieren, so daß sie als angewandte Musikästhetik definiert werden muß." (Riemann 1914, 9)

This interface between the aesthetics of music and musical teachings as basic tools for musical practice is also found in Albert Wellek's attempt to (re-)establish SM in Germany after 1945 (Wellek 1948). Wellek distinguished between three areas of musicology: music history, systematic musicology and applied musicology, which is "naturally branched off from the systematic attached to it." ("naturgemäß abgezweigt von der Systematischen, bei dieser ansetzend", Wellek 1948, 166).

> "Zur Angewandten Musikwissenschaft gehört im wesentlichen vor allem die Musikpädagogik oder Musikerziehung – ein weites, dabei wissenschaftlich noch sehr wenig geordnetes Feld." (Wellek 1948, 166).

ME is seen as the core of applied musicology, whereas Wellek notes that the field was not yet well-sorted in academic terms (see Wellek 1948, 166). Wellek's description of the competences of ME is akin to those of Adler and Riemann, but goes beyond basic skills and knowledge, since Wellek encouraged the use of psychological findings in ear-training (see ibid.). In Wellek's understanding, ME is divided into music theory and philosophical approaches, which are both based on SM:

> "Als eigentliche Wissenschaft ist alle Angewandte Musikwissenschaft – Musikpädagogik und auch so verstandene 'Musiktheorie' – naturgemäß nur denkbar auf dem Boden einer Systematischen Musikwissenschaft im Vollsinne, insbesondere einer Musikpsychologie. Was die Musikpädagogik anlangt, gibt es aber freilich auch eine philosophische Pädagogik, d.h. eine Theorie und Sinndeutung der Bildungsidee im Rahmen einer 'Philosophischen Anthropologie', eines philosophischen Menschenbildes, und dies allgemein, wie auch im besonderen für die Kunsterziehung. An diesem rein theoretischen Teile also – als philosophische Musikpädagogik – gehört auch diese, die Musikpädagogik, zu den Zweigen der Systematischen, nicht der Angewandten Musikwissenschaft." (Wellek 1948, 166)

As in Wellek's conception of SM (fig. 2), music psychology plays a major role with regard to ME, since it "pervades widely all other disciplines without accounting for them entirely" ("durchdringt weitgehend auch die übrigen Disziplinen, ohne sie allerdings zur Gänze auszumachen", Wellek 1948, 169).

Faced with the given premises and developments, Oskár Elschek stated in 1973 that Adler's conception of SM "did not correspond to today's requirements" ("entspricht nicht den heutigen Anforderungen", Elschek 1973, 422). Elschek suggested a scheme based on an integrative approach to resolve historically grown animosities between SM and music history by deregulating the boundaries of the respective disciplines and converting them into methods and mindsets (see Elschek 1973, 427). The general discrimination of this scheme reveals both theoretical and regional musicology. Theoretical musicology is supposed to solve basic musical problems, which should be examined in three areas with specific responsibilities (scientific, socio-scientific and musical-technical; see Elschek 1973, 429). The structure of the scheme does not necessarily contain a central point, since it aims at an extensive reciprocal exchange:

> "Die einzelnen Disziplinen untersuchen einen kontinuierlichen musikalischen Prozeß, auch wenn sie aus diesem jeweils Teilmomente und spezielle Aspekte herauslösen. Die einzelnen Disziplinen sind deshalb gegeneinander nicht abgeschlossen, sondern dadurch, daß sie verschiedene Formen immer derselben Substanz untersuchen, müssen sie sich auf die Erkenntnisse anderer Disziplinen stützen. Deshalb muß es zu einer breiten Koordination zwischen ihnen kommen, denn Zweck der Musikwissenschaft ist es, ein Gesamtbild von der Musik zu erstellen, Teilresultate in einem Erkenntnissystem zu vereinen." (Elschek 1973, 430)

The various interdisciplinary relationships among the fields of theoretical musicology (No. 1-12) are illustrated with regard to information theory (fig. 3).

The global system of musicology described by Elschek includes ME as a specialised part of theoretical musicology, registered under musical-technical responsibilities. Here ME is related to scopes like "source of information (= the brain)" (I) and "sender of information" (II), which cover topics such as composers, artists, musical instruments, voice, electronic media – basic requirements for the creation of music. But ME is also related to the scope of gnoseological principles of music perception (V). Within this open structure of relation and exchange, ME participates in various academic fields and is defined as an interdisciplinary field of musical science, unspecific in its lack of stricter responsibilities, aims and methods - especially the facets of a propaedeutical musical practice as in previous conceptions.

In 1976 a memorandum considering the situation of German musicology announced that SM included parts of ME "as far as they accrue from applied psychology" ("soweit sie aus angewandter Psychologie erwächst", Dahlhaus et al. 1976, 252; q.v. Karbusicky 1979, 11). The declaration of an interdependent relationship between musicology and ME was used mainly as an argument to strengthen the value of musicology in the education of music teachers (Dahlhaus et al. 1976, 252; see also various publications on this topic, e.g. *Forschung in der Musikerziehung* 1978). The importance of this declaration must be seen with regard to an academic ME evolving since the late 1960s. In the course of the so-called "Curriculumreform", there were changes in the paradigms of educational science which affected affiliated didactics (for historical details see Gruhn 2003, 307 ff.). Contemporary conceptions of ME were linked to scientific principles and an aesthetic adjustment in accordance with the severe criticism already brought forward by Theodor W. Adorno in the late 1950s (Adorno 1956/1991). Though the history of this process is a very interesting topic, it cannot be dealt with here and must be shortened. However, its impact is worthy of note: the "scientification" ("Verwissenschaftlichung") of ME was a controversial issue. As early as 1976, calls for less scientifically orientated music lessons in schools came up (see Gruhn 2003, 355 ff.) and, in retrospect, some authors considered the scientific turnabout and its consequences as a failure caused by misconception (e.g. Reinecke 1970, 148; Kleinen 1985, 336f; Gruhn 1987, 66).

Scientific orientations and approaches in ME can be traced back to the early 19th century. Since then, ME was always associated with psychological and philosophical topics, as was shown by Sigrid Abel-Struths in a detailed overview of the history of ME (Abel-Struth 1985, 583). Many surveys on the development of musical skills during the 1920s dealt with the outer fields of ME, influenced by *Gestaltpsychology* (e.g. Werner 1917, Brehmer 1925, Walker 1927, Briessen 1929, Nestele 1930) – an approach resumed in the late 1950s (see Abel-Struth 1985, 587). Abel-Struth summarises the efforts made in the early 20th century as the basis of systemised fundamental research into ME:

> "Man darf zusammenfassend sagen, daß in den ersten drei Jahrzehnten unseres Jahrhunderts musikpädagogische Grundlagenforschung sich differenziert und zahlreich ausbreitet, erstmals methodologische und systematische Fragen gestellt, erstmals theoretische Ansätze der Musikpädagogik versucht werden. Die Forderung nach musikpädagogischer Forschung und dem wissenschaftlichen Fach Musikpädagogik wird [...] akzeptiert." (Abel-Struth 1985, 587).

In this respect Abel-Struth's distinction of a scientific and a practical ME deserves attention for touching on a basic problem in the relationship between SM and ME (see Abel-Struth 1985, 72f; see also Kleinen/de la Motte-Haber 1982, 309). Whereas scientific ME examines educational acquaintance with music based on the "creative-methodical account of truth and insight" ("der kreativ-methodische Gewinn an Wahrheit und Einsicht", Abel-Struth 1985, 72), practical ME is seen as its realisation in the learning progress measured by the results of educational acquaintance (ibid.). Despite existing problems connected with a proper distinction, as Abel-Struth admits, the basic dualism of theory and practice could only be resolved by abandoning the dogma of instantaneous applicability (see Abel-Struth 1985, 73; see also Bastian 1982, 137; Kleinen 1985, 334). This consistent opening up to other academics presupposes ME to be an interdisciplinary field (see Abel-Struth 1985, 588), and since the main focus of ME is intermediation, music psychology serves here as a pivotal reference: Helga de la Motte-Haber noted that the paradigm shift in educational science had approximated SM and ME, whereas SM acts as a translator for psychological issues (see de la Motte-Haber 1976, 257). Hans Günther Bastian defines music psychology as the controlling authority needed for ME:

> "Musikpsychologie ist also bei allen methodologischen Vorbehalten quasi Kontrollinstanz, die den von Musikpädagogik intendierten Prozeß der Auseinandersetzung auf seine Effizienz hin flankierend untersuchen kann, um Antworten zu finden, welchen Grades der Differenzierung musikalischer Struktur Jugendliche welchen Alters fähig bzw. zu befähigen sind." (Bastian 1982, 126)

Music psychology however bears inherent educational responsibilities. This is pointed out in Vladimir Karbusicky's attempt (1979) to structure SM. Karbusicky extracted four main scopes of SM by systemising courses in musicology with regard to content: a) musical substance, b) music production (historical), c) musical perception (historical and social), d) cultural reference (comparative) (see Karbusicky 1979, 21; see below also Rösing 1986). Karbusicky defined three fields regarding educational matters: a) educational psychology of music, b) ear-training connected with experimental research on perception, and c) music pedagogy. Whereas the third field is localised in the area of musical reception and considered to be part of a theoretical psychology of perception concerning musical listening („Rezeptionstheoretische Psychologie", see Karbusicky 1979, 28), the first and second fields are assigned to the core of music psychology (see Karbusicky 1979, 28). The justification for this systematic approach stems from the philosophical principle of "Ostense", an epistemological basis connected with developmental psychology:

> "Ostense kommt überall zustande, wo etwas 'im Original' gezeigt wird – und das ist in der Musik: Vorführung des Werkes auf einem Konzert, Analyse mit Musikproben, Sendung mit Musikbeispielen, 'Hitparade' usw. = die elementaren Daseinsformen." (Karbusicky 1979, 119)
> "Das Kind verlangt nach Ostense, sie ist der grundlegende Vorgang bei der Festlegung von Bedeutungen der Wortsymbole. Darum ist die Didaktik ohne Ostense unvorstellbar." (Karbusicky 1979, 123)

However, the autonomy of ME as recommended by Abel-Struth remains unaffected by this definition. Regarding SM as a whole, Karbusicky saw ME as an ancillary science for SM concerning theoretical aspects of "Ostense" and creativity:

> "Die Musikpädagogik kommt besonders bei der Theorie der Ostense und den Problemen der Kreativität zu Wort." (Karbusicky 1979, 235)

However, this appreciation of ME as an autonomous academic discipline (the scientific ME according to Abel-Struth) seems slightly diluted in a subsequent article by Vladimir Karbusicky and Albrecht Schneider (1980). The draft of a handbook on systematic and comparative musicology presented here discusses ME on the one hand as part of the applied scopes and disciplines of SM and on the other hand as an equal counterpart (see Karbusicky/Schneider 1980, 100).

2. Expounding the problems from the perspective of SM

A central issue in the relation between SM and ME is the positioning of musicology in general. Wilfried Gruhn (1987) compiled three ways of understanding musicology in the context of ME (Gruhn 1987, 66):

a. Musicology as music history that marks a framework for curricula and legitimation for the selection of musical works
b. Musicology as ancillary science ("Hilfs- oder Zubringerwissenschaft", Gruhn 1987, 66) which ensures the contents of ME via results and facts ("Ergebnisse und Fakten", Gruhn 1987, 66) and operationalises learning targets by fundamental research into music psychology.
c. Musicology as mindset ("Haltung", Gruhn 1987, 66) that regards acquaintance with music as a basically scientific approach.

Whereas the first way clearly aims at historic musicology, the others provide space for SM as well. Hans Peter Reinecke (1970) covered these latter positions in a pointed remark that musicology should not fear being seen as an ancillary science ("Hilfswissenschaft") to reasonable music education ("einer sinnvollen Musikerziehung", Reinecke 1970, 148). For this purpose, Reinecke examined the contemporary circumstances of SM and its relation to ME, which, at the same time, led him to diagnose the inadequacy of Adler's conception.

> "Die Pädagogik [...] ist deutlich mit dem systematischen Aspekt der Musikwissenschaft verknüpft, gewissermaßen als deren pragmatischer Bereich, der sich sinnvoll dem analytischen (musiktheoretischen) und synthetischen (ästhetischen) anschließt. [...] Von diesem Konzept [Adler 1885] ist immerhin der Rahmen – allerdings auch nicht sehr viel mehr – geblieben." (Reinecke 1970, 146)

Reinecke criticised the anachronistic tendencies of musicology in disregarding approaches of SM (Reinecke 1970, 147), an anachronism which becomes a problem for ME – due to the dependance of ME on musicology, it is forced to operate on outdated findings (see Reinecke 1970, 148). Reinecke recommended a consistent updating of musicology by appreciating SM. On the other hand, he stesses that SM should share objectives with ME:

> „Das Wichtigste wird sein, neue Wege der Musikerziehung zu finden, welche den jungen Menschen früh genug ein Fundament allgemeiner Kategorien zu vermitteln imstande sind, die musikalisch-ästhetisches Handeln und Reflektieren, Spiel und Hören ermöglichen – und zwar auch für eine Musik, die wir heute vielleicht noch gar nicht kennen. Dies kann und darf nicht mehr unter alt überkommenen magischen Obligaten, wie etwa dem der 'Reinheit' [pureness of tuning as foundation for music listening and understanding], geschehen, sondern einzig und allein unter dem der wirklich freien Entfaltung der Phantasie, der Ratio wie des Spieltriebs. Diese Aufgaben, die in gleicher Weise an die Erziehung wie an die Forschung gestellt sind und denen sich letztere nicht unter Berufung auf das Postulat der Zweckfreiheit wird entwinden können, sind nur in engem wechselseitigen Kontakt und mit gegenseitiger Hilfe zu lösen." (Reinecke 1970, 150f) [1]

---

[1] This basic recommendation was later elaborated on by Reinecke in collaboration with Hermann Rauhe and Wilfried Ribke and is to be regarded in parts as a practical application of SM (Rauhe/Reinecke/Ribke 1975).

The use of SM in the education of music teachers is obvious: whether SM is defined as a 'translator' or 'controlling authority', it provides an introduction into topics, methods and aims of SM for nascent schoolteachers. Günter Kleinen (1985) detected certain main problems resulting from "insufficient communication between school and science" ("unzureichende Kommunikation zwischen Schule und Wissenschaft", Kleinen 1985, 337):

> "Insgesamt handelt es sich um Probleme eher unzureichender Kommunikation zwischen Schule und Wissenschaft. Zahlreiche Publikationen der Musikpsychologie sind für die Schule absolut uninteressant. Der Forschungsprozeß ist nicht hinreichend auf Erfordernisse des schulischen Alltags abgestimmt; umgekehrt sind die Lehrer oft nicht hinreichend qualifiziert, die Forschungsresultate zu verstehen (Ausbildungsdefizit). Daher sind Mißverständnisse und auch falsche Konsequenzen unumgänglich." (Kleinen 1985, 337)

Kleinen's diagnosis addresses both SM and ME: whereas publications about music psychology are often highly specialised and lack practical relevancy, the teachers often have exaggerated expectations (see Kleinen 1985, 337) – this remains a problem today.

Yet not only was SM regarded as being constricted by mistaken demands of ME, but also by the disregard for historic musicology (see Reinecke 1973; de la Motte-Haber 1976). Helmut Rösing (1986) subsequently localised SM and the attached comparative musicology in a stress field ("Spannungsfeld", Rösing 1986, 98) determinated by ME and historic musicology. By examining the areas of enquiry pertaining to the various academics together with ("Gegenstandsbereiche") their epistemological interests ("Erkenntnisinteresse"), Rösing was able to point out similarities and specific characteristics. The result is shown in a four-dimensional field of diverse points of contact (fig. 4). Relying on this, Rösing certified a general interest of ME in the topics and methods of SM which he regarded as a matter of "existential meaning" for comparative and systematic musicology:

> "Ihre [der MP] prinzipielle Offenheit gegenüber den verschiedensten Inhalten und Methoden des Faches Musikwissenschaft ist aber – zumindest für die Vertreter der Vergleichenden und Systematischen Musikwissenschaft – von existenzieller Bedeutung. Musikpädagogik partizipiert in der Bundesrepublik Deutschland in dem Maße an Aufgabenbereichen der Vergleichenden und Systematischen Musikwissenschaft, wie Historische Musikwissenschaft sich ihnen gegenüber verschließt." (Rösing 1986, 97)

In this way, SM was the kind of ancillary science to ME which Reinecke had already stated. Like Reinecke, Rösing did not assume the need of ME for instantaneous practical application to be a handicap per se (see Rösing 1986, 98). Yet he pointed out the danger that an all-too-close embrace of SM by ME might ulitmately lead to ME absorbing SM:

> "Musikpädagogik als Integrationswissenschaft ist den Fragestellungen, Untersuchungsmethoden und Problemlösungen der Systematischen Musikwissenschaft gegenüber derart offen, daß diese allerdings Gefahr läuft, in der Disziplin Musikpädagogik aufzugehen." (Rösing 1986, 99)

This warning is mainly aimed at the sociopsychological and cultural scopes of SM. Yet the significance of ME is stated vice versa: with reference to overlapping issues, ME is seen as an inspiration for many of the survey topics of SM (see Rösing 1986, 98).

Despite the various theoretical approaches and discussions outlined above, Rolf Oerter and Herbert Bruhn (2005) complained of the insufficient transformation of scientific knowledge into educational practice, a problem especially obvious in the issues relating to the developmental psychology of music (see Oerter/Bruhn 2005, 572). With regard to the discrepancies between music psychology and music didactics, the dualism of theory and practice still appears to be a core problem:

> "Die [musikpsychologische] Grundlagenforschung beschäftigt sich einerseits mit basalen Fragen der musikalischen Wahrnehmung und des Lernens, berücksichtigt aber zu wenig die Komplexität der Lernprozesse beim Singen oder Instrumentalspiel. Die Musikdidaktik ihrerseits hat für die Leistungsentwicklung beim Singen und im Instrumentalspiel eine Fülle von pädagogischen Konzepten und Strategien. Sie sind aus der Unterrichtserfahrung entstanden, fußen jedoch überwiegend auf naiven psychologischen Annahmen (gounded theories) und führen lediglich die subjektiv wahrgenommenen Leistungen einiger weniger Spitzenmusiker als Kriterium oder Beweis für die Effektivität an." (Oerter/Bruhn 2005, 564)

By illustrating such lively scenes, Oerter/Bruhn emphasised contemporary tendencies that would encourage the commitment of SM to issues of ME. Thus the needs of ME and the aims of SM may not be that far apart. Nevertheless, these two issues still have to be weighted.

Synopsis: SM and ME are deeply interlinked as academic areas engaged in various forms of handling music. Remarkably, none of the authors cited connects ME with historic musicology in the same way as they do with SM. Despite having individual conceptions, both academics are designed as interdisciplinary fields. All attempts made here underline the necessity of a closer connection between SM and ME by focussing on different points of view. The main argument is the dualism of theory and practice, the question of instantaneous practical application of scientific knowledge. Even though this question surely cannot be answered in the present study, it should be remembered when discussing the results of the survey.

3. Investigating research topics of German ME in relation to SM

Aims and objectives

This survey picks up the discussions in SM and ME mentioned above and asks about the connections of SM and ME in previous research. The main focus here lies on theory and not on teaching experience, since theoretical conceptions prepare the ground for the practical responsibilities of ME. The fundamental hypothesis of this investigation is the acceptance of two autonomous academics: SM and the scientific part of ME, as pointed out by Abel-Struth. The general aim of this survey is to link the interests and topics of ME to SM.[2] This would provide a basis for more insight into the existing relation between SM and ME.

---

[2] Silvana Klavinius presented a similar attempt in her dissertation (Klavinius 1984). Unlike Klavinius's work the focus here is on research topics in ME and not on theoretical discussions of musicological contents in ME writings. Hermann J. Kaiser's (Kaiser 1989b) approach of exploring the scientific character of ME by examining German ME journals is weighted differently: Kaiser aims at practical issues, not on scientific research, and does not provide a statistical approach, but hermeneutical studies.

The survey was based on the following questions: How are SM and ME connected? What topics are examined in ME research? Are those topics in any way related to SM? Did the main emphasis of research in ME change over time? And what does this mean to the relation between ME and SM?

Method

Publications taken from selected periodicals about German ME were examined using methods of content analysis (see Bortz 1984, 234-237; Mayring 2000; Diekmann 2002, 481-516; Mayring 2003; Früh 2004) to unlock and to systemise the main topics of research in ME. This helped to identify connections with SM and enlighten historical developments. Since it was hardly possible to draw on every single article published in ME, it was decided to work with a sample. This sample covered a time span wide enough to give insight into possible changes in the main emphasis of research in ME. The institutionalisation of ME was defined as an indicator of regular research with scientific approaches.[3] This assumption follows Abel-Struth's differentiation between scientific and practical ME, which sees the former as an independent transmitter of scientific knowledge for the practical application of the latter.

It was decided to select periodicals associated with various institutions, such as research groups and cooperatives attached to university environments via scholars[4] (see fig. 5). For economic reasons, the analysis focussed on the indexes of contents of the periodicals, whereas the titles of the articles were seen as units of analysis. The sample was not analysed automatically but by hand, since the focus was on semantic meaning and not on keywords. In cases of uncertain classification, the abstract of the article or the article as a whole was consulted. Nevertheless, some uncertainties remained. Based on the analysis of the content, basic units were classified and divided into different categories; their interdependence was examined using quantitative methods.

The system of classification was based on theoretical attempts to outline research in ME, as proposed in handbooks and encyclopaedical articles (Helms/Schneider/Weber 1995; Richter 1997; Colwell/Richardson 2002). Following basic principles of content analysis, this system was revised in the process of classifying. The system presented here is a combination of theoretical and empirical approaches (see Früh 2004, 144f.).

A combination of two categorisational approaches was used to enable further comparison of research topics in German and international ME: Christoph Richter (1997) suggests a free and partially unspecific categorisation for explicit German research. An international perspective was taken from *New handbook of research on music teaching and learning* edited by Richard Colwell and Carol Richardson (2002). Though both attempts coincide in their basic scope, the specific outline sometimes differs strongly. The benefit of the scheme presented here lies in its openness and flexibility to assimilate new perspectives and facets and provide insights into the specific characteristics of research in German ME without neglecting international attempts. By combining the

---

[3] For an overview concerning various aspects of ME institutionalisation see Kaiser 1989a, and, in particular, Antholz 1989.
[4] Though investigations of the institutions' histories and the impact of scholars are certainly a main basis for understanding the history of German ME and SM as well, they are omitted here to allow more space for focussing SM perspective on the relation of the two academics. A comparison with research on ME topics in SM and music psychology is scheduled in a following study.

273

attempts of Richter and Colwell/Richardson, it allows a basic comparison of both German and international research in ME. Since the system of classification constructed in this way is empirically founded, it is the first of various results given here.

Results

The categorisations of Richter (1997) and Colwell/Richardson (2002) feature different approaches: whereas Richter offers a specific German perspective, Colwell/Richardson offer an attempt dominated by the perspective of Anglo-American research besides a few contributions by German scholars. So a combination of these two has to be used to form a consistent model. Yet both attempts lack certain aspects which should be mentioned before presenting the results of the analyses.

Neither Richter nor Colwell/Richardson provide a consistent systematic order of categories. Especially the model proposed by Richter cannot be accepted as a taxonomical system, because it does not offer selective categories and lacks fundamental conditions.[5] Yet the categories offer insights that can be regarded as hypotheses in the context of this survey. A profound revision of these categories and their criteria is a necessary precondition before referring to Richter's categories in examining research in ME. This revision was made possible in an empirically orientated analysis.[6] The categories extracted from the outline of the handbook by Colwell/Richardson had to be treated the same way.

In combining the two attempts, the categories of Colwell/Richardson (2002) were defined as superordinate classes, since they cover more open and unspecific topics, while the categories of Richter (1997) were defined as subordinate classes that were revised closely during the analysis. A brief exemplification will illustrate this: Richter added special weight to "historical research" which Colwell/Richardson simply lacked; yet no autonomous category entitled "outcomes in general education", as proposed in Colwell/Richardson, could be provided following Richter, since this is covered in his category classroom research ("Unterrichtsforschung") and the subordinate "educational approaches" (see Richter 1997, Sp. 1455). Whereas Richter presented "comparative music education" as an autonomous field of research, Colwell/Richardson do not cover this. However, neither attempt discerns the field of popular music studies. So it seemed appropriate to add the latter categories as superior classes to the model presented here. To retain their autonomous and interdisciplinary approaches, they cannot to be filed under any of the other classes. Concerning genuine musicological issues (composers, works, music history, gender issues, musical ability and giftedness, etc.) the classification distinguished between scientific and didactic perspectives provided by the articles. Thus

---

[5] In just listing themes and topics of research, the categories do not distinguish scientific from educational approaches. A clear division of these approaches should provide insight into the weighting and grounding of such topics. Yet it could also obliterate the boundaries of SM and ME, so that Rösing's (1986) warning of a vanishing SM has to be remembered.

[6] There are certain difficulties in building a consistent system of categories for the purpose displayed here. The necessities of a profound theoretical background and the need for discussing constraints and developments of the academics' histories and epistemological interests are beyond question, yet this had to be shortened here. These issues will be dealt with in a following study. The attempt presented here is to be regarded as a work in progress; nevertheless, it reveals noteworthy tendencies for further discussion.

individual topics may appear in an educational context and from a scientific perspective (this is noted in fig. 6).

Christoph Richter offered a structured overview on research topics of German ME (Richter 1997, Sp. 1454ff) without any commentary going deeper than listing various topics. Richter differentiated:

1. Topics in music psychology ("musikpsychologische Themen"): Basic topics founded in sociopsychological approaches and developmental psychology.
2. Listening to music ("Hören von Musik"): A basic topic following discussion of ME since Adorno's harsh notes on ME, attached to sociopsychological approaches. This topic is covered by the field of music psychology research on music perception in a broader sense. The categories and articles were classified according to Richter's principles. Thus the topic was dispensed with.
3. Classroom and teaching research ("Unterrichtsforschung"): A major field of ME, since it contains a connection between scientific knowledge and practical application, e.g. via evaluating teaching methods. Richter distinguished between curricular and educational approaches with subordinate classes.
4. Historical research ("historische Forschung"): With a focus on biographical issues and conceptions, on the history of ME, on the educational profession, ("Berufsstand") and on ME in the 19th and early 20th century and during the "Nazizeit".
5. Acquaintance with music ("Umgang mit Musik"): This comprises musical analysis, music theory, music history and music-making in an educational context.
6. Anthropological substantiation ("anthropologische Begründung"): Anthropological approaches examining foundations of music and music-making.
7. Understanding music ("Verstehen von Musik"): Richter distinguished between philosophical-hermeneutical approaches and psychological-neuroscientific approaches.

The outline of the handbook edited by Richard Colwell and Carol Richardson (2002) presents the following categories that are commentated with regard to Richter's scheme:

1. Policy and philosophy – a topic neglected by Richter.
2. Educational context and the curriculum – affiliated in Richter "Unterrichtsforschung" and its subordinates.
3. Musical development and learning.
4. Musical cognition and development – part of Richter's music psychology topics.
5. Social and cultural contexts – combined scope of music sociology and music psychology, not explicitly covered by Richter's categories.
6. Music teacher education – though not explicitly mentioned by Richter, this is a topic widely discussed in German ME.
7. Music education – topics like music and the arts are not explicitly covered by Richter's categories.
8. Neuroscience, medicine, and music – Richter addressed these approaches under the methodological perspective of understanding music and not as autonomous fields of research.

9. Outcomes in general education – not clearly presented in Colwell/Richardson; in Richter's scheme, these aspects are touched on with respect to research on teaching methods and educational conceptions. Thus this category was dispensed with.

10. Research design, criticism, and assessment in ME – a topic not mentioned as an autonomous field by Richter in 1997.

The model presented here is commented on with reference to the statistical distribution of the codings of the selected publications. A total of 1,578 units were coded, which are distributed as follows: the greatest number were extracted from *AMPF* (588 codings = 37%) and *DiskMP* (487 = 31%), followed by *ForumMP* (237 = 15%) and *FidME* (221 = 14%); the smallest number were taken from *ZfkMP* (46 = 3%). The distribution of codings clarifies the main points of research in ME (fig. 6).

According to the coded articles, the main emphasis is on educational matters ("Educational context and the curriculum" with 475 codings altogether, which equals 30.08% of the total number of codings). This category is made up of research on the conditions of teaching ("Unterrichtsforschung") and topics to be taught ("educational acquaintance with music"). Another broad field of interest comprises "Social and cultural contexts" (293 = 18.56%), followed by articles dealing with political issues and basic constraints of science defining the scientific branch of ME ("Policy and philosophy", 264 = 16.72%). Fundamental issues dealing with the education of music teachers ("Music teacher education", 142 = 8.99%) are followed by aspects of musical development ("Musical development and learning", 125 = 7.92%; "Musical cognition and development", 66 = 4.18%).

According to Colwell/Richardson's outline, the shares of SM are divided into several categories to get a more clearly defined insight into the scope of ME. In summing up these shares, it becomes apparent that SM has 35.53% of the total number of articles coded. Therefore the following categories were merged: "Musical development and learning", "Musical cognition and development", "Social and cultural contexts", "Neuroscience, medicine, and music" (8 = 0.51%), the subordinate class "Research methods" (34 = 2.15%) and the field of studies on "Popular music" (32 = 2.03%) which is dominated by sociological and sociopsychological perspectives. This shows that SM has shares in 6 of 12 categories of research in ME (disregarding the category of unclear classifications).

Comparing the adjustments of the periodicals on research topics reveals several similarities (fig. 7a). The periodicals *Musikpädagogische Forschung* (*AMPF*) and *Diskussion Musikpädagogik* (*DiskMP*) share certain main points ("Educational context and the curriculum": *DiskMP* 32.65% / *AMPF* 29.79%, "Social and cultural contexts": 20.94% / 23.81%, and "Policy and philosophy": 16.84% / 15.99%). Yet, when accessing the relevant categories as named above, it becomes obvious that *Musikpädagogische Forschung* (*AMPF*) is more closely related to topics of SM than *Diskussion Musikpädagogik* (*DiskMP*) (fig. 7b).

Regarding the development of these categories over the time span covered by the publications in the sample, it is obvious that the number of SM-related topics steadily declines after reaching a maximum of 74 codings in 1990 (fig. 8a). This has to be put into perspective by regarding the total number of units coded in the analysis (fig. 8b). It becomes clear that the number of SM in the ME-related research publications is relatively stable, yet with a wide range (AM: 11.44, SD: 7.96; that equals a mean of 33.22 % with a range of 19.98 %) – except for a minimum in the year 1972: here only 6 articles were counted in total, and none of them touched on a topic related to SM. The decline of SM topics is measurable, although the focus on these topics varies across the time span examined. Whereas aspects of musical development and sociological and sociopsychological aspects are clearly predominant most of the time, other topics vary in their occurrence and quantity (fig. 9). Research methods have been treated irregularly since the early 1970s, but with a peak in the late 1980s and early 1990s; also aspects of neuroscientific research appear very rarely; popular music is treated more or less regularly since 1983.

One can ask if the categories subsuming SM-related topics are in any way linked to one another or if they must be regarded as independent categories. Using SPSS, correlations were calculated to examine possible relations (fig. 10). The result shows that only a few categories correlate more or less on a medium level. The categories "Musical cognition and development" (code K_04_cogn) and "Social and cultural context" (code K_Soci) appear to be of interest, since they each correlate with two other categories. Whereas the correlation of the former with the category "Musical development and learning" (code K_03_deve, $r = .473$) could have been expected with regard to content, it seems astonishing that the correlation with research methods (code K_10_Rese) is even higher ($r = .517$). The correlation of socio-cultural issues is equally surprising: The respective category correlates with research methods ($r = .385$) and with neuroscientific aspects (code K_08_Neur; $r = .319$) – one possible explanation for the surprising result can be seen in the almost uninterrupted occurrence of this category throughout the time span (see fig. 9): in that case, this relation would have to be regarded as a statistical artefact. The same could be said about articles on popular music, yet the effect does not seem to be so great: studies on popular music (code K_12_Popu) appear to be largely autonomous, since they only correlate slightly (with research methods, K_10_Rese: $r = .030$ and musical cognition, K_04_cogn: $r = .096$) or even in the opposite direction (as with issues of musical development, K_03_deve: $r = -.064$ and topics of neuroscience, K_08_Neur: $r = -.161$).[7]

In accordance with the correlations discussed above, a multivariate data analysis was used to find out whether there is a relation between the distribution of the categories (as dependent variables) and the distribution of publications (with the total number of articles as an independent variable) over the time span (fig. 11). The result points to significant discrimination in the sample ($p = .003$). Regarding the effects of the particular dependent variables, it becomes obvious that the significance is predominantly caused by the category K_12_Popu ("Popular music").

Discussion and outlook

The total of 35.53% concerning topics related to SM or even genuine topics of SM in the sample clearly indicate a strong integration of SM in ME research. Furthermore, the

---

[7] Regarding content, the interdisciplinary field of studies on popular music shows a lot of reference to sociology and cultural studies. These results should be seen as hypotheses serving as guiding questions for deeper examination that could also draw on hermeneutical methods. Such options will be discussed in a following study.

correlations of SM-related topics discussed above reveal certain inherent connections. Thus it seems appropriate to define the field of studies on popular music as being largely autonomous except for sociological aspects. The distinct need of ME in handling youth cultures and their music is reflected by the extension of this topic since the 1980s. Regarding the distribution of categories by various publications, it could be assumed that the number of articles on popular music is related to content of the particular publication – yet this point cannot be dealt with in the present study.

Concerning the institutionalisation of ME and SM in the late 1960s and early 1970s, it becomes obvious that a connection of both academics was mainly influenced by the curricular reform brought about by the demand for a scientific basis in music lessons at school. So musicology and SM in particular were integrated into the education of music teachers. Thus the profiles of many musicological departments in Germany were founded.[8] Apart from inherent problems and particular developments over the years, a more intense kind of relationship has strengthened the involvement of SM in ME research topics, as Oerter/Bruhn (2005) stated:

> "Die wachsende Sensibilität gegenüber pädagogischen Problemen und die Forderung danach, psychologisches Wissen nutzbar zu machen, hat die Zeit reif werden lassen für intensivere psychologische Forschung auf dem Gebiet der Musikpädagogik." (Oerter/Bruhn 2005, 610)

An extension of this survey could provide more insight into the history of research in German ME, and even a comparison with international research. For this purpose, it would be necessary to draw on hermeneutical approaches besides the statistical analyses proposed here. Concerning the involvement of scholars and institutions, details on the history, needs, and topics of ME and relevant research into SM would become clearer. This, in turn, could provide deeper insight into the institutionalsiation of both SM and ME.

Theoretical discussions would also help to redefine the relation of the two academic fields. As shown in the introductory overview, this relation has to be defined in a contemporary context. According to approaches like those of Karbusicky (1979) and Rösing (1986), an examination of topics and contents as well as of epistemological pretensions could be helpful in rethinking the relations under the prevailing circumstances in music and musical culture. Though SM is not to be regarded as a simple ancillary science, it shares certain fields with ME, e.g. music learning, musical practice and musical development. Following musicological conceptions as introduced above and accepting ME as an autonomous science (as the scientific part of ME), the aims of SM can be seen as answering the needs of ME by providing relevant scientific knowledge, accompanying and reflecting educational practice empirically as well as theoretically, and endowing impulses for both scientific and practical ME. In respecting the practical needs of ME, SM could offer support in transferring its results and knowledge in order to minimise the risk of an inevitable didactical reduction (see Kleinen 1985, 335f). The decline of SM commitment in examining topics of ME interest should be seen as a challenge for future research: SM has to remember its inherent educational issues and should take part in the process of reflecting on the relation between these two academic fields.

---

[8] Despite this, the idea of a connection between SM and ME is not that far away, since even undergraduates appreciate pedagogics related to SM (see Schneider 1993, 165).

References

Abel-Struth (1985). *Grundriß der Musikpädagogik*, Darmstadt: Wissenschaftliche Buchgesellschaft / Mainz: Schott.

Adorno, Theodor W. (1956/1991). *Dissonanzen. Musik in der verwalteten Welt*, therein: Kritik des Musikanten; Zur Musikpädagogik, Göttingen: Vandenhoeck/Ruprecht (7th ed.).

Adler, Guido (1885). Umfang, Methode und Ziel der Musikwissenschaft, in: *Vierteljahrsschrift für Musikwissenschaft*, ed. by Friedrich Chrysander, Philipp Spitta, Guido Adler, vol. 1, 1885, 1. Heft, Leipzig: Breitkopf & Härtel, 5-20.

Antholz, Heinz (1989). Musikpädagogik – institutionelle Aspekte einer wissenschaftlichen Hochschuldisziplin, in: *Musikpädagogik. Institutionelle Aspekte einer wissenschaftlichen Disziplin*, ed. by Hermann J. Kaiser, Mainz: Schott, 8-27.

Bastian, Hans Günther (1982). Musikpsychologie und Musikpädagogik. Zur Systematik und Relevanz einer musikwissenschaftlichen Teildisziplin, in: *Musikpädagogik. Historische, systematische und didaktische Perspektiven. Heinz Antholz zum 65. Geburtstag*, ed. by Hans Günther Bastian und Dieter Klöckner, Düsseldorf: Schwann, 119-140.

Bortz, Jürgen (1984). *Lehrbuch der empirischen Forschung für Sozialwissenschaftler*, Berlin et al.: Springer.

Brehmer, Fritz (1925). *Melodieauffassung und melodische Begabung des Kindes*, Leipzig: Barth.

Briessen, Maria van (1929). *Die Entwicklung der Musikalität in den Reifejahren*, Langensalza: Hermann Beyer & Söhne.

Colwell, Richard / Richardson, Carol (ed.)(2002). *The new handbook of research on music teaching and learning*, Oxford University Press.

Dahlhaus, Claus et al. (1976). Memorandum zur Lage der Musikwissenschaft, in: *Die Musikforschung*, vol. 29, 1976, 249-256.

Diekmann, Andreas (2002): *Empirische Sozialforschung. Grundlagen, Methoden, Anwendungen*, Reinbek bei Hamburg: Rowohlt (8th ed.).

Früh, Werner (2004): *Inhaltsanalyse. Theorie und Praxis*, Konstanz: UVK Verlagsgesellschaft.

Edler, Arnfried (1987). Zum Verhältnis Musikpädagogik – Musikwissenschaft aus Sicht der Musikwissenschaft, in: *Musikpädagogik und Musikwissenschaft*, ed. by Arnfried Edler, Siegmund Helms, Helmuth Hopf, Wilhemshaven: Noetzel, 9-39.

Elschek, Oskár (1973). Entwurf einer neuen musikwissenschaftlichen Systematik, in: *Die Musikforschung*, vol. 26, 1973, 421-434.

Gruhn, Wilfried (1987). Musikwissenschaft in den vorliegenden Curricula. Eine kritische Bestandsaufnahme, in: *Musikpädagogik und Musikwissenschaft*, ed. by Arnfried Edler, Siegmund Helms, Helmuth Hopf, Wilhemshaven: Noetzel, 61-81.

Gruhn, Wilfried (2003). *Geschichte der Musikerziehung. Eine Kultur- und Sozialgeschichte vom Gesangunterricht der Aufklärungspädagogik zu ästhetisch-kultureller Bildung*, Hofheim: Wolke (3rd ed.).

Helms, Siegmund / Schneider, Reinhard / Weber, Rudolf (1995). *Kompendium der Musikpädagogik*, Kassel: Bosse.

Kaiser, Hermann J. (ed.)(1989a). *Musikpädagogik. Institutionelle Aspekte einer wissenschaftlichen Disziplin*, Mainz: Schott.

Kaiser, Hermann J. (1989b). Der Wissenschaftscharakter der Musikpädagogik im Spiegel musikpädagogischer Zeitschriften, in: *Musikpädagogik. Institutionelle Aspekte einer wissenschaftlichen Disziplin*, ed. by Hermann J. Kaiser, Mainz: Schott, 83-95.

Karbusicky, Vladimir (1979). *Systematische Musikwissenschaft. Eine Einführung in Grundbegriffe, Methoden und Arbeitstechnik*, München: Fink.

Karbusicky, Vladimir / Schneider, Albrecht (1980). Zur Grundlegung der Systematischen Musikwissenschaft, in: *Acta Musicologica*, vol. 52, 1980, 87-101.

Klavinius, Silvana (1984). *Musikwissenschaft und Musikvermittlung Eine Inhaltsanalyse des musikdidaktischen Schrifttums*, Frankfurt am Main u.a.: Lang.

Kleinen, Günter / Motte-Haber, Helga de la (1982). Wissenschaft und Praxis, in: *Systematische Musikwissenschaft* (= Neues Handbuch der Musikwissenschaft, Bd. 10), ed. by Carl Dahlhaus and Helga de la Motte-Haber, Laaber: Laaber, 309-344.

Kleinen, Günter (1985). Musik als Mittel der Erziehung, in: *Musikpsychologie. Ein Handbuch in Schlüsselbegriffen*, ed. by Herbert Bruhn, Rolf Oerter, Helmut Rösing, München: Urban & Schwarzenberg, 331-338.

Mayring, Philipp (2000): Qualitative Inhaltsanalyse, in: *Qualitative Forschung. Ein Handbuch*, ed. by Uwe Flick, Ernst von Kardorff, Ines Steinke, Reinbek bei Hamburg: Rowohlt, 468-475.

Mayring, Philipp (2003): *Qualitative Inhaltsanalyse. Grundlagen und Techniken*, Weinheim und Basel: Beltz (8th ed.).

Motte-Haber, Helga de la (1976). Systematische Musikwissenschaft in der Lehrerausbildung, in: *Forschung in der Musikerziehung 1976* (= Musikpädagogik in der Studienreform), Mainz: Schott, 252-262.

Nestele, Albert (1930). *Die musikalische Produktion im Kindesalter. Eine experimentalpsychologische Untersuchung der kindlichen Melodik*, Leipzig: Barth.

Oerter, Rolf / Bruhn, Herbert (2005). Musikpsychologie in Erziehung und Unterricht, in: *Spezielle Musikpsychologie* (= Enzyklopädie der Psychologie, Serie VII, Themenbereich D, Musikpsychologie Bd. 2), ed. by Rolf Oerter and Thomas Stoffer, Göttingen et al.: Hogrefe, 555-624.

Richter, Christoph (1997). Art. Musikpädagogik, A. Versuch einer Systematik der Musikpädagogik, in: *Die Musik in Geschichte und Gegenwart*, second edition, ed. by. Ludwig Finscher, Kassel et al.: Bärenreiter, Sp.1439-1473.

Riemann, Hugo (1914). *Grundriß der Musikwissenschaft*, Leipzig: Hesse (2nd ed.).

Reinecke, Hans-Peter (1970). Musikwissenschaft und Musikerziehung, in: *Jahrbuch des Staatlichen Instituts für Musikforschung Preußischer Kulturbesitz*, Kassel: Merseburger/Berlin: de Gruyter, 1970, 14-151.

Rauhe, Hermann / Reinecke, Hans-Peter / Ribke, Wilfried (1975). *Hören und Verstehen. Theorie und Praxis handlungsorientierten Musikunterrichts*, München: Kösel.

Rösing, Helmut (1986). Systematische Musikwissenschaft im Spannungsfeld von Historischer Musikwissenschaft und Musikpädagogik, in: *Musicologica Austriaca*, vol. 6, 1986, 89-105.

Schneider, Albrecht (1993). Systematische Musikwissenschaft. Traditionen, Ansätze, Aufgaben, in: *Systematische Musikwissenschaft* (= Theoretische und methodische Aspekte. Stand der Forschung), vol. 1/2, 1993, Bratislava: ASCO, 145-180.

Themenkatalog für Forschungsaufgaben in der Musikerziehung, in: *Forschung in der Musikerziehung*, vol. 1 (I), 1969, Mainz: Schott, 34-35.

Walker, Erwin (1927). *Das musikalische Erlebnis und seine Entwicklung* (= Vergleichende Untersuchungen zur Psychologie, Typologie und Pädagogik des ästhetischen Erlebens, 4. Heft, ed. by. Oswald Kroh), Göttingen: Vandenhoeck & Ruprecht.

Wellek, Albert (1948). Begriff, Aufbau und Bedeutung einer Systematischen Musikwissenschaft, in: *Die Musikforschung*, vol. 1, 1948, 157-171.

Werner, Heinz (1917). Die melodische Erfindung im frühen Kindesalter. Eine entwicklungspsychologische Untersuchung, in: *43. Mitteilungen der Phonogramm-Archivs-Kommission* (= Kaiserliche Akademie der Wissenschaften in Wien, Philosophisch-historische Klasse, Sitzungsberichte, 182. Band, 4. Abhandlung, vorgelegt in der Sitzung am 10. Mai 1916), Wien: Alfred Hölder.

Figures

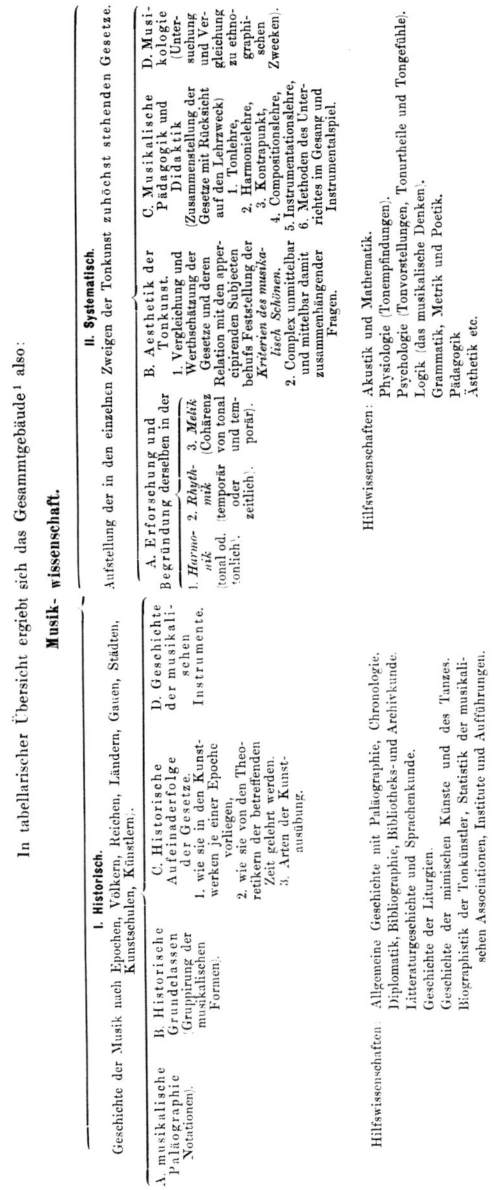

In tabellarischer Übersicht ergiebt sich das Gesammtgebäude[1] also:

Musik- wissenschaft.

I. Historisch.

Geschichte der Musik nach Epochen, Völkern, Reichen, Ländern, Gauen, Städten, Kunstschulen, Künstlern.

A. musikalische Paläographie (Notationen).

B. Historische Grundclassen (Gruppirung der musikalischen Formen).

C. Historische Aufeinanderfolge der Gesetze.
1. wie sie in den Kunstwerken je einer Epoche vorliegen,
2. wie sie von den Theoretikern der betreffenden Zeit gelehrt werden.
3. Arten der Kunstausübung.

D. Geschichte der musikalischen Instrumente.

Hilfswissenschaften: Allgemeine Geschichte mit Paläographie, Chronologie, Diplomatik, Bibliographie, Bibliotheks- und Archivkunde.
Litteraturgeschichte und Sprachenkunde.
Geschichte der Liturgien.
Geschichte der mimischen Künste und des Tanzes.
Biographistik der Tonkünstler, Statistik der musikalischen Associationen, Institute und Aufführungen.

II. Systematisch.

Aufstellung der in den einzelnen Zweigen der Tonkunst zuhöchst stehenden Gesetze.

A. Erforschung und Begründung derselben in der
1. *Harmonik* (tonal od. tonlich).
2. *Rhythmik* (temporär oder zeitlich).
3. *Metrik* (Cohärenz von tonal und temporär).

B. Aesthetik der Tonkunst.
1. Vergleichung und Werthschätzung der Gesetze und deren Relation mit den appercipirenden Subjecten behufs Festellung der *Kriterien des musikalisch Schönen*.
2. Complex unmittelbar und mittelbar damit zusammenhängender Fragen.

C. Musikalische Pädagogik und Didaktik (Zusammenstellung der Gesetze mit Rücksicht auf den Lehrzweck).
1. Tonlehre,
2. Harmonielehre,
3. Kontrapunkt,
4. Compositionslehre,
5. Instrumentationslehre,
6. Methoden des Unterrichtes im Gesang und Instrumentalspiel.

D. Musikologie (Untersuchung und Vergleichung zu ethnographischen Zwecken).

Hilfswissenschaften: Akustik und Mathematik.
Physiologie (Tonempfindungen).
Psychologie (Tonvorstellungen, Tonurtheile und Tongefühle).
Logik (das musikalische Denken).
Grammatik, Metrik und Poetik.
Pädagogik
Ästhetik etc.

fig. 1: Adler 1885: Scheme of music related sciences (Adler 1885, 16-17).

Zusammenfassend kann gesagt werden, daß sich die Systematische Musikwissenschaft aus folgenden Teilfächern aufbaut:

1. als naturwissenschaftlicher Hilfs- und Voraussetzungswissenschaft:

   A k u s t i k a) physikalische

   　　　　　　b) physiologische (H ö r - und Stimmp h y s i o l o g i e);

2. G e h ö r - (Ton-) p s y c h o l o g i e

   (psychologische Akustik);

3. M u s i k p s y c h o l o g i e;

4. M u s i k ä s t h e t i k (Musikphilosophie);

   sodann a n e i n e m T e i l e :

5. M u s i k s o z i o l o g i e (soweit nicht historisch)

6. M u s i k p ä d a g o g i k (soweit nicht angewandt).

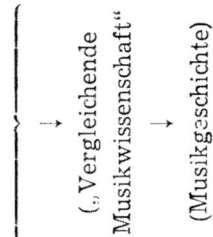

} → („Vergleichende Musikwissenschaft" → (Musikgeschichte)

fig. 2: Wellek 1948: Scheme of SM (Wellek 1948, 169).

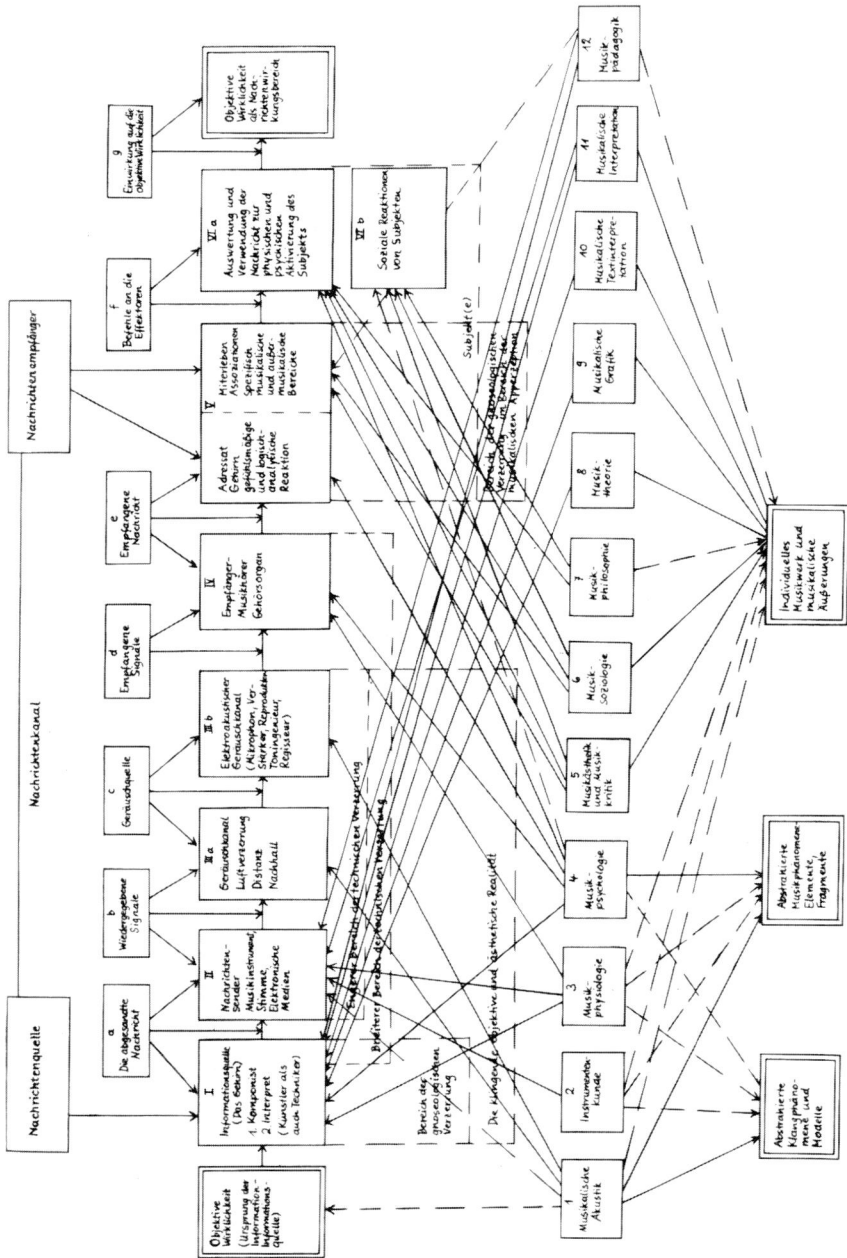

fig. 3: Elschek 1973: Scheme of interdisciplinary relations between the fields of theoretical musicology (Elschek 1973, 431).

284

Gegenstandsbereich
Musik und Geschichte
(Schwerpunkt: Noten)
Historische Musikwiss.
Musiktheorie, -ästhetik
Musikethnologie/Popularmusik

Gegenstandsbereich
Gesellschaft und Musik
(Schwerpunkt: Klang)

Musiksoziologie
Musikethnologie
Popularmusik

Gegenstandsbereich
Person und Musik
(Schwerpunkt: Akustische
Struktur/Klang)
Musikalische Akustik
Hörphysiologie
Musikpsychologie

Gegenstandsbereich
Vermittlung / praktische
Anwendung musikbezogener
Sachverhalte
Musikpädagogik
Angewandte Musik-
psychologie/Musiktherapie

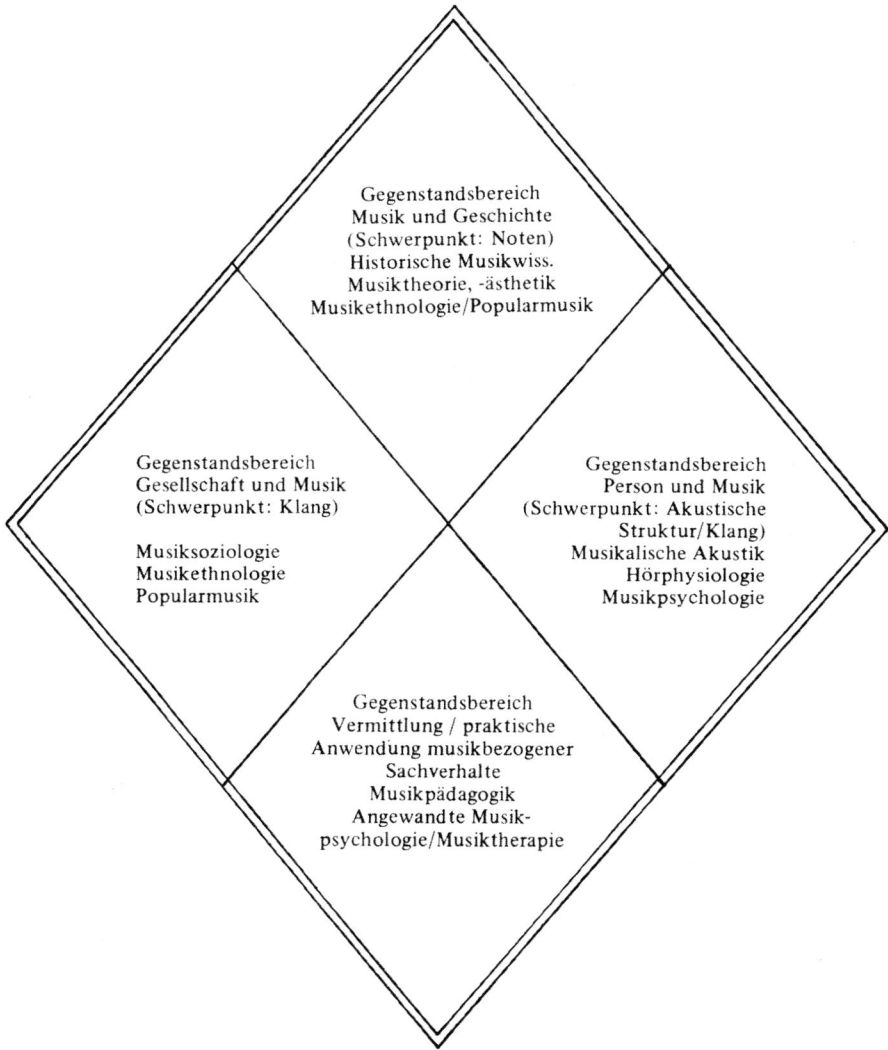

fig. 4: Rösing 1986: Scheme of positioning SM vs HM, ME and Ethnomusicology (Rösing 1986, 101).

285

selected periodicals	code	issues	frequency	amount of contributions
Forschung in der Musikerziehung	FidME	vol. 1974-1981	anually	180
Musikpädagogische Forschung (= proceedings of the Arbeitskreis Musikpädagogische Forschung, AMPF)	AMPF	vol. 1980-2006	anually	465
Musikpädagogische Forschungsberichte (from the periodical: Forum Musikpädagogik, ed. by Rudolf-Dieter Kraemer)	ForumMP	vol. 1/1992, vol. 2/1993, vol. 3/1994, vol. 4/1995, vol. 5/1996, vol. 6/1997, vol. 7/1998, vol. 8/2001, vol. 9/2004	continously (unregularly since vol.7)	207
Diskussion Musikpädagogik	DiskMP	vol. 1999-2007	quarterly	406
Zeitschrift für Kritische Musikpädagogik (= online paper)	ZfKM	vol. 2002-2007	continously	44

fig. 5a: List of selected periodicals.

year	DiskMP	AMPF	FidME	ForumMP	ZfkMP	total
1969	0	0	14	0	0	14
1970	0	0	21	0	0	21
1971	0	0	7	0	0	7
1972	0	0	6	0	0	6
1973	0	0	7	0	0	7
1974	0	0	8	0	0	8
1975	0	0	5	0	0	5
1976	0	0	32	0	0	32
1977	0	0	8	0	0	8
1978	0	0	22	0	0	22
1979	0	0	10	0	0	10
1980	0	16	21	0	0	37
1981	0	14	19	0	0	33
1982	0	14	0	0	0	14
1983	0	14	0	0	0	14
1984	0	22	0	0	0	22
1985	0	19	0	0	0	19
1986	0	17	0	0	0	17
1987	0	17	0	0	0	17
1988	0	18	0	0	0	18
1989	0	0	0	0	0	0
1990	0	74	0	0	0	74
1991	0	21	0	0	0	21
1992	0	22	0	14	0	36
1993	0	15	0	26	0	41
1994	0	10	0	24	0	34
1995	0	12	0	56	0	68
1996	0	13	0	0	0	13
1997	0	20	0	32	0	52
1998	0	13	0	20	0	33
1999	44	8	0	0	0	52
2000	46	12	0	0	0	58
2001	48	17	0	19	0	84
2002	51	13	0	0	16	80
2003	43	21	0	0	9	73
2004	52	11	0	16	6	85
2005	43	13	0	0	5	61
2006	53	19	0	0	5	77
2007	26	0	0	0	3	29
total	406	465	180	207	44	1302

fig. 5b: Distribution of codings by periodicals from 1969-2007.

	FidME	AMPF	ForumMP	DiskMP	ZfkMP	total
01_Policy and Philosophy	26	94	40	82	22	264
01_a_epistomological remarks	3	3	0	1	3	10
01_b_institutions	14	16	3	36	0	69
01_c_policy of education	1	1	0	7	0	9
01_d_ME as academic	3	16	1	2	4	26
01_e_anthropological substantiaton	1	8	0	1	0	10
01_f_historic research	1	1	0	0	1	3
01_f.1_biographical issues	0	13	12	14	11	50
01_f.2_conceptions	0	9	8	14	3	34
01_f.3_history of ME	0	9	3	4	0	16
01_f.4_educational profession	2	2	0	2	0	6
01_f.5_19ᵗʰ and early 20ᵗʰ century. Nazi-era	1	16	13	1	0	31
02_Educational Context and the Curriculum	58	175	72	159	11	475
02_a_"Unterrichtsforschung"	0	0	0	0	0	0
02_a.1_teachers, teaching methods, curriculum	0	0	0	0	0	0
02_a.1.1_music teachers: role, attitude, typology	3	17	2	6	1	29
02_a.1.2_analysis of schoolbooks	0	4	1	5	0	10
02_a.1.3_vocal and instrumental lessons	2	15	3	4	0	24
02_a.2_educational and pedagogical aspects	1	2	0	3	1	7
02_a.2.1_curriculum	3	4	0	13	2	22
02_a.2.2_aims of music lessons	3	6	0	25	1	35
02_a.2.3_music teaching and learning	6	14	8	12	1	41
02_a.2.4_methods of instruction	1	3	6	4	0	14
02_a.2.5_disign and analysis of instruction	0	0	0	0	0	0
02_a.2.5.1_practical sketches for instruction	1	5	0	4	0	10
02_a.2.5.2_empirical analysis of instruction	2	19	1	3	1	26
02_a.3_young people's interests regarding music lessons	2	3	1	0	0	6
02_a.4_extracurricular impartation of music	0	7	2	12	0	21
02_b_educational aquaintance with music	0	1	2	2	0	5
02_b.1_music listening	5	4	1	2	0	12
02_b.1.1_music and movies, scores	0	8	6	2	0	16
02_b.2_music history (educational)	3	3	4	9	1	20
02_b.3_musical practice: music making, singing	4	17	4	7	1	33
02_b.3.1_songs and singing	2	1	16	0	0	19
02_b.4_music theory and analysis (educational)	4	4	0	10	0	18
02_b.5_sociology of music (educational)	0	0	0	0	0	0
02_b.5.1_youth and music (educational)	0	2	2	3	1	8
02_b.5.2_sociology of music and music lessons	3	0	1	0	0	4
02_b.5.3_musical socialisation (educational)	1	3	0	1	0	5
02_b.6_media	1	19	9	13	0	42
02_b.7_ethnomusicology (educational)	5	1	1	3	0	10
02_b.8_music psychology (educational)	2	0	1	1	0	4
02_b.9_aesthetics of music (educational)	1	3	1	4	1	10
02_b.10_music therapy (socio-educational)	0	1	0	1	0	2
02_b.11_popular music and music lessons	1	3	0	2	0	6
02_c_theory of music (musicological)	2	6	0	8	0	16
03_Musical Development and Learning	18	42	44	20	1	125
03_a_musical ability and aptitudes	10	16	18	4	1	49
03_b_music learning (psychological)	0	6	5	14	0	25
03_c_practice	0	4	13	0	0	17
03_d_motivation and emotion	7	14	7	1	0	29
03_e_music therapy (psychological)	1	2	1	1	0	5
04_Musical Cognition and Development	13	29	18	5	1	66
04_a_perception of music	6	13	4	0	0	23
04_b_musical performance	6	14	12	1	0	33
04_c_understanding music	0	0	0	0	0	0
04_c.1_philosophical-hermeneutical	0	1	2	4	1	8
04_c.2_psychological-neuroscientifical	1	1	0	0	0	2
05_Social and Cultural Contexts	23	140	27	102	1	293
05_a_musical preferences and reception of music	11	24	7	5	0	47
05_b_sociology and social history of music	6	13	2	5	0	26
05_b.1_youth and music	1	15	2	7	0	25
05_b.2_musical socialisation	0	27	4	7	0	38
05_b.3_gender issues	0	9	3	0	1	13
05_c_ethnomusicology	2	7	0	2	0	11
05_d_media and music technology	1	14	4	4	0	23
05_e_music history (in general)	1	12	4	9	0	26
05_e.1_composers, works, musicians	0	7	1	41	0	49
05_e.2_aesthetics of music (historical)	1	3	0	22	0	26
05_e.2.1_musc and visual arts	0	9	0	0	0	9
06_Music Teacher Education	64	10	6	56	6	142
06_a_music teachers' education, activities, self-concepts	5	3	3	12	0	23
06_b_program of studies (educational, academical)	52	7	3	18	1	81
06_c_on educational reforms	7	0	0	26	5	38
07_Music Education Connections	3	12	3	9	0	27
07_a_sports	0	1	0	0	0	1
07_b_religion	0	0	2	0	0	2
07_c_arts and education, arts and science	3	4	1	6	0	14
07_d_music and visual arts	0	7	0	3	0	10
08_Neuroscience, Medicine, and Music	0	1	3	3	1	8
09_Outcomes in General Education	0	0	0	0	0	0
10_Research Design, Criticism, and Assessment in ME	10	56	15	14	3	98
10_a_objects and state of research	0	11	1	0	0	12
10_b_theory and methods of classroom research	7	19	9	14	3	52
10_c_research methods	3	26	5	0	0	34
11_Comparative ME	5	13	6	15	0	39
12_Popular Music	1	13	2	16	0	32
classification unclear	0	3	1	6	0	10

fig. 6: Distribution of codings.

	FidME		AMPF		ForumMP		DiskMP		ZfkMP		total	
	f(x)	%	f(x)	%	f(x)	%	f(x)	%	f(x)	%	f(x)	%
Policy and Philosophy	26	11,77	94	15,99	40	16,88	82	16,84	22	47,83	264	16,72
Educational Context and the Curriculum	58	26,24	175	29,76	72	30,38	159	32,65	11	23,91	475	30,08
Musical Development and Learning	18	8,14	42	7,14	44	18,57	20	4,11	1	2,17	125	7,92
Musical Cognition and Development	13	5,88	29	4,93	18	7,59	5	1,03	1	2,17	66	4,18
Social and Cultural Contexts	23	10,41	140	23,81	27	11,39	102	20,94	1	2,17	293	18,56
Music Teacher Education	64	28,96	10	1,7	6	2,53	56	11,51	6	13,04	142	8,99
Music Education Connections	3	1,36	12	2,04	3	1,27	9	1,85	0	0	27	1,71
Neuroscience, Medicine, and Music	0	0	1	0,17	3	1,27	3	0,62	1	2,17	8	0,51
Outcomes in General Education	0	0	0	0	0	0	0	0	0	0	0	0
Research Design, Criticism, and Assessment in Music	10	4,52	56	9,52	15	6,33	14	2,87	3	6,52	98	6,21
Comparative Music Education	5	2,26	13	2,21	6	2,53	15	3,08	0	0	39	2,47
Popular Music	1	0,45	13	2,21	2	0,84	16	3,29	0	0	32	2,03
classification unclear	0	0	3	0,51	1	0,42	6	1,23	0	0	10	0,63
frequencies in total	221	99,99	588	99,99	237	100	487	100	46	99,98		
total amount in percentages	14		37,24		15,01		30,84		2,91			

fig. 7a: Periodicals' adjustment by content.

	FidME	AMPF	ForumMP	DiskMP	ZfkMP	total	
	%	%	%	%	%	f(x)	%
Policy and Philosophy	9,85	35,61	15,15	31,06	8,33	264	100
Educational Context and the Curriculum	12,21	36,84	15,15	33,47	2,32	475	99,99
Musical Development and Learning	14,4	33,6	35,2	16	0,8	125	100
Musical Cognition and Development	19,67	43,94	27,27	7,58	1,52	66	99,98
Social and Cultural Contexts	7,85	47,78	9,22	34,81	0,34	293	100
Music Teacher Education	45,07	7,04	4,23	39,44	4,23	142	100,01
Music Education Connections	11,11	44,44	11,11	33,33	0	27	99,99
Neuroscience, Medicine, and Music	0	12,5	37,5	37,5	12,5	8	100
Outcomes in General Education	0	0	0	0	0	0	0
Research Design, Criticism, and Assessment in Music	10,2	57,14	15,31	14,29	3,06	98	100
Comparative Music Education	12,82	33,33	15,38	38,46	0	39	99,99
Popular Music	3,13	40,63	6,25	50	0	32	100,01
classification unclear	0	30	10	60	0	10	100

fig. 7b: Periodicals' adjustment toward categories of research.

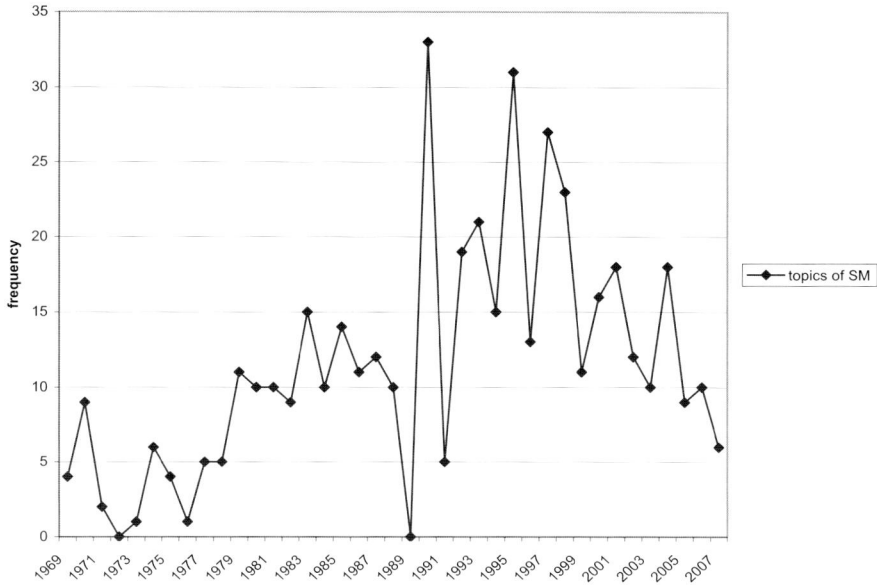

fig. 8a: Developing of the amount of SM related topics.

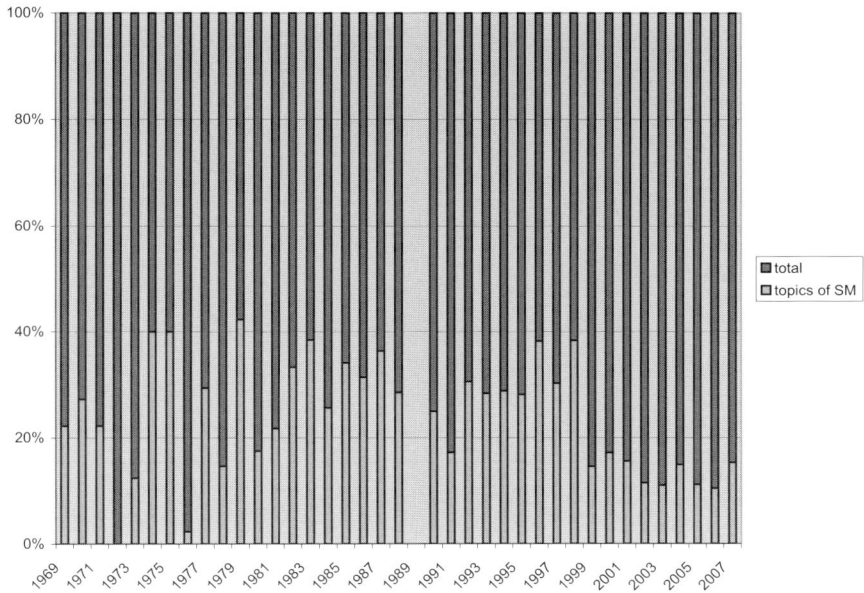

fig. 8b: Developing of the amount of SM related topics related to the whole.

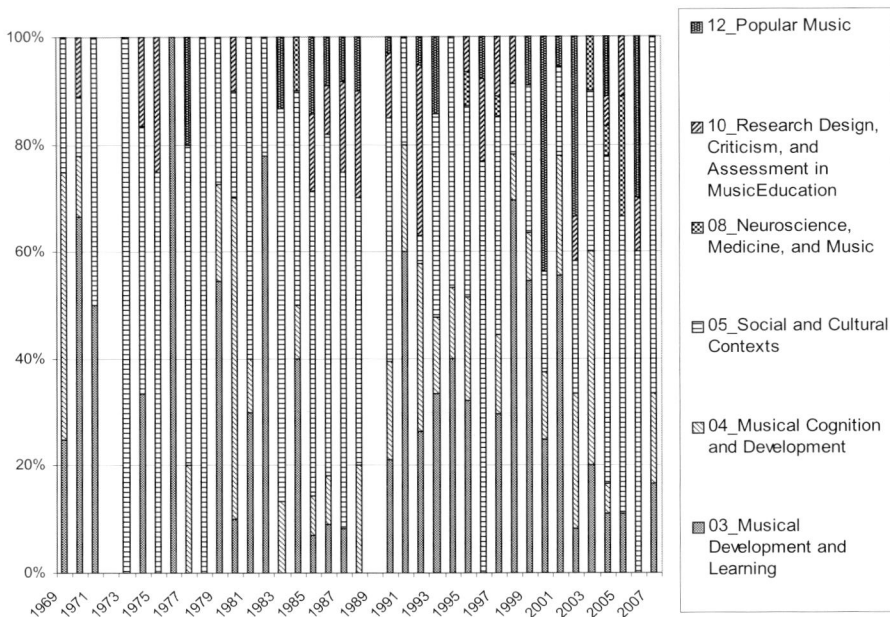

fig. 9: Developing of distribution of SM related topics by content.

Legend:
- 12_Popular Music
- 10_Research Design, Criticism, and Assessment in MusicEducation
- 08_Neuroscience, Medicine, and Music
- 05_Social and Cultural Contexts
- 04_Musical Cognition and Development
- 03_Musical Development and Learning

Korrelationen

		K_03_deve	K_04_cogn	K_05_Soci	K_08_Neur	K_10_Rese	K_12_Popu
K_03_deve	Korrelation nach Pearson	1	,473**	,159	,172	,241	-,064
	Signifikanz (2-seitig)		,002	,333	,294	,139	,700
	N	39	39	39	39	39	39
K_04_cogn	Korrelation nach Pearson	,473**	1	,301	,225	,517**	,096
	Signifikanz (2-seitig)	,002		,063	,168	,001	,562
	N	39	39	39	39	39	39
K_05_Soci	Korrelation nach Pearson	,159	,301	1	,319*	,385*	,200
	Signifikanz (2-seitig)	,333	,063		,048	,015	,223
	N	39	39	39	39	39	39
K_08_Neur	Korrelation nach Pearson	,172	,225	,319*	1	,117	-,161
	Signifikanz (2-seitig)	,294	,168	,048		,477	,328
	N	39	39	39	39	39	39
K_10_Rese	Korrelation nach Pearson	,241	,517**	,385*	,117	1	,030
	Signifikanz (2-seitig)	,139	,001	,015	,477		,857
	N	39	39	39	39	39	39
K_12_Popu	Korrelation nach Pearson	-,064	,096	,200	-,161	,030	1
	Signifikanz (2-seitig)	,700	,562	,223	,328	,857	
	N	39	39	39	39	39	39

**. Die Korrelation ist auf dem Niveau von 0,01 (2-seitig) signifikant.
*. Die Korrelation ist auf dem Niveau von 0,05 (2-seitig) signifikant.

fig. 10: Correlations of categories concerning SM related topics.

Multivariate Tests[c]

Effekt		Wert	F	Hypothese df	Fehler df	Signifikanz	Partielles Eta-Quadrat
Konstanter Term	Pillai-Spur	,968	20,069[a]	6,000	4,000	,006	,968
	Wilks-Lambda	,032	20,069[a]	6,000	4,000	,006	,968
	Hotelling-Spur	30,103	20,069[a]	6,000	4,000	,006	,968
	Größte charakteristische Wurzel nach Roy	30,103	20,069[a]	6,000	4,000	,006	,968
total	Pillai-Spur	5,160	1,905	174,000	54,000	,003	,860
	Wilks-Lambda	,000	2,619	174,000	31,840	,001	,931
	Hotelling-Spur	193,516	2,595	174,000	14,000	,022	,970
	Größte charakteristische Wurzel nach Roy	129,941	40,327[b]	29,000	9,000	,000	,992

a. Exakte Statistik

b. Die Statistik ist eine Obergrenze auf F, die eine Untergrenze auf dem Signifikanzniveau ergibt.

c. Design: Intercept+total

fig. 11: MANOVA: total amount of coded articles and categories concerning SM related topics.

293

Bruno Nettl

COMPARATIVE STUDY AND COMPARATIVE MUSICOLOGY: COMMENTS ON DISCIPLINARY HISTORY

This is a meditation about the concept of comparison in ethnomusicology and its history. I wish to contemplate some of the central literature defining comparative study, sketch briefly the history of some of the major landmarks of this endeavor, and also – since some conclusions come from observation of oral rhetoric and discourse – bring in a personal perspective. In the last two years, some important surveys of this history have been published, particularly by Albrecht Schneider (2006), Mervyn McLean (2006), and Victor Grauer (2006), and a bit earlier, by Martin Clayton (2003). My comments cover much the same ground, though with a slightly different perspective due to my research experience as an ethnomusicologist and anthropologist (see Nettl 2000, 2006). I will try to contribute to the dialogue about essential aspects of the history and future of ethnomusicology (including comparative approaches) that has in effect been addressed in a number of recent publications (among them being those mentioned above).

Let me begin with three observations, upon which I then take the liberty of expanding.

1. The term "comparative musicology" and its non-English equivalents, principally "vergleichende Musikwissenschaft" and "musicologie comparée," existed without much controversy for about half a century. Then, after 1950, they were abandoned rather suddenly and rapidly, replaced by "ethnomusicology," "ethnographie musicale," and "Musikethnologie" (along with some synonyms), terms which have actually never been defined unanimously or with precision.

2. In music research, the concept of comparison has, over the last fifty years, come to have a questionable and even unsavory reputation; nevertheless, a large proportion of the most significant research depends on comparison of one sort or another for its identity and effectiveness. Some of the concepts of greatest currency in recent scholarship – e.g., "world music," universals, evolution of music, diasporas – require, for their development, some kind of comparative approach

3. Comparative studies in music are subject to difficulties and problems that require fine-tuning of method and careful insight into the relationship of cultures, cultural domains, and musical elements. Despite these difficulties, there are important aspects of music that lend themselves particularly and perhaps uniquely well to inter- and intra-cultural comparison.

While Schneider's view, and to a degree those of McLean and Grauer as well, place comparative study in the center of early research on non-Western and folk music, seeing it as a methodology that generally declined over the course of the twentieth century, but it is now encouraged by a kind of revival, my interpretation differs slightly. I am inclined to accord comparative study itself a position of modest prominence throughout this history but suggest that its prestige, and the perception of its position at the center (or the outskirts) of the discipline, have had a more oscillating history.

From Adler's "Musikologie"

In my days as a student, ca. 1950, my principal teacher, George Herzog, who was considered by many the leading scholar of non-Western music in North America and the vicar, if you will, of Hornbostel in the New World, talked unabashedly about "comparative musicology." In 1950, and again in 1955, Jaap Kunst (Kunst 1950, 1959) was still using the term, though with caveats. As late as 1957, Marius Schneider (1957:1-2) headed the first section of his survey of "primitive music" (1957:) "Comparative Musicology." But of course the term goes back to the beginning of the late 19th century. If eventually the term was used to refer to syntheses or compendia of non-Western music, it is interesting to see that the first lengthy survey, in the first volume of August Wilhelm Ambros's monumental music history (1862), which is full of comparative statements, does not use the term "comparative musicology." Jonathan Stock (2007), indeed, makes a good case for designating Alexander John Ellis (1885) as the first comparative musicologist, although to my knowledge he did not use the term.

I am unable. In fact, to ascertain when the term was first used, but it does appear in the same year as Ellis's publication in Guido Adler's 1985 article in which he famously laid out the field of musicology, with its two main branches – historical and systematic – and mentions as part of the latter something he calls "Musikologie". In the tabular outline (1885:17), it is defined thus: "Musikologie (Untersuchung und Vergleichung zu ethnographischen Zwecken)," which brings up several questions. "Untersuchung," best glossed as "investigation," is general enough, but what is to be investigated? "Vergleichung," comparison, is again vague, as its basis might be the world's cultures, one culture, one composer's oeuvre, etc., but the purpose, "zu ethnographischen Zwecken", is acknowledgment of the presence of a variety of cultures in the world, and hints also at an interest in some kind of relationship of music to other domains of culture. The concept of "ethnographie," in that period ordinarily defined as the description of culture without the theoretical underpinnings that might have required use of the term "ethnologische Zwecke," is also significant.

In his text commenting on the outline, Adler goes further: Although the outline puts "Musikologie" into the systematic branch, the text (p. 14) gives it a status of a complementary subject ("Nebengebiet dieses systematischen Teils"), foreshadowing the tripartite scheme of musicology now widely used. Also in the text (p. 14), there now appears, as a synonym for "Musikologie," the term "vergleichende Musikwissenschaft," whose task it is, says Adler, to compare the world's musics and to classify them. Why the word "Musikologie" is used at all is not clear, but my impression is that this formulation –i.e., use of the suffix "logie" – may have given the concept a bit of a scientific aura, an attitude on later finds in Robert Lach's contemplation of the field (Lach 1924, 1925). In any event, possibly Adler, whose interest in Western art musics was significantly aesthetic, saw the world's other musics as of interest mainly to science-like contemplation. At least for the time being.

It seems unlikely to me that Adler believed that classifying was all that the musicological profession should do with non-Western music. Rather, I suspect that he saw this as a first step. Confronted with a vast body of hitherto unknown, material, the first thing one might do (or maybe the first thing a proper Germanic scholar might do) was to impose some kind of order; to classify and group. Adler says: "vergleichen und nach der Verschiedenheit ihrer Beschaffenheit zu gruppiren." (1885:14). The fact that he described "vergleichende Musikwissenschaft" as a new and "dankenswert" ("rewarding" may be the closest gloss) field, a field with lots of potential, suggests that he expected much more to be done than simple comparison and classification. And the repeated use of the term "ethnographische Zwecke" suggests that he saw the results of this field to have an important role in ethnography, ethnology, anthropology.

It's important to remember two other aspects of the context of this article. First, this was a brave statement by a young scholar, a man who wanted to push ahead and probably saw this outline as the first of various future attempts. Born in 1855, Adler was only 28 and 29 years old when he wrote this article (to be sure, although he continued working as a scholar for another 55 years, he never revised it). And his forward-looking conception of "vergleichende Musikwissenschaft" had to be based on a tiny body of research and literature

The term "vergleichende Musikwissenschaft" evidently then sneaked unheralded into the terminology of the newly established discipline of musicology in 1885. It took twenty years for it to experience a kind of formal introduction. It occurs, interestingly, in an anthropological journal where the technical advance of sound recording is set forth (Abraham and Hornbostel 1904), but its first significant appearance in a musicological context occurred in 1904-5 when Hornbostel, in an article originally delivered as a lecture for the Vienna chapter of the International Music Society, began by saying, "Einem jungen Spezialgebiet einer Wissenschaft fällt die Aufgabe zu, seine Daseinsberechtigung zu erweisen." Hornbostel then turns to a defense of comparison, pointing out, in light of its significance in epistemology, the need to start by comparing the new with the known, and from this, thorough analysis of the individual manifestation may follow. Extolling the successes of comparative linguistics and comparative anatomy, he proceeds to suggest that the reasons for the relatively slow entry of musicology into the comparative realm was lack of technology for acquiring reliable data, a situation which, however, was in the process of being mitigated by the recent development of the phonograph, which would now become an indispensable tool. The article goes on to discuss in detail aspects of transcription, interval measurement, and analysis, but in the end it does not go into the matter of comparison very much.

Conceptually, the field then remained on a kind of plateau, a period of about fifty years during which the term "comparative musicology" was widely used but not widely examined. An occasional series, *Sammelbände für vergleichende Musikwissenschaft*, appeared in the 1920s, and the journal, *Zeitschrift für vergleichende Musikwissenschaft*, was published from 1933 to 1935. An important contrary example is the mentioned monograph by Robert Lach (1924), which introduces the field to an academic public but emphasizes the potential of comparative musicology for an understanding of the evolution of music, in a manner related to the methodology of parallel disciplines such as comparative linguistics and comparative anatomy, and, more emphatically a year later (Lach 1925), to art history. In important ways, Lach re-establishes the cooperative relationship of comparative musicology and historical musicology, rather in contrast to the attitude of other scholars, for whom the two musical discipline represent opposite poles of a continuum. Lach's work, and a more clearly introductory book by Curt Sachs (1930) also had the function of encouraging wider acceptance of the term.

But while some clearly comparative work was carried out under its rubric, the term "vergleichende Musikwissenschaft" denoted, it seems to me, two additional things – first, obviously, the study of non-Western music, and of Western music outside the scope of Western art music, and second, an attitude to the effect that somehow, one could discuss all of the world's music under a single umbrella. In most respects, comparison was an informal discourse resulting from a desire to give broad characterization for surveying the world's musics, and to falsify widely held generalizations about human music. Responding, for example, to beliefs that pentatonicism characterizes only certain cultures, comparativists might have been inclined to reply, "no, pentatonic scales of various kinds are found in all corners of the world," or, in reply to assertions that all cultures have musical instruments, "no, the people of xxx seem not to have any." But the literature on non-Western and folk music from 1900 to 1950 does not include much in the way of comparative statements. The "comparative musicologists" didn't do all that much outright comparing. They did, I think, believe that insights could be gained from comparison, and that the term "comparative" suggested that one could look at all of the world's musics from the perspective of one lens; and that comparison could lead to a new understanding of history.

Comparative Musicology and Comparative Method

In some of the literature (e.g. Lach 1924, see discussion in McLean 2006:310-17, Schneider 2006), there is the implication that "comparative musicology' requires a rather rigorous "comparative method," somewhat like that of "comparative linguistics" (see Antilla 1972) or perhaps the (otherwise named) "historical-geographic method" of folklore (see Nettl 2005:323-24), or in a more general way, of comparative literature. Each of these fields developed a method of intercultural or interlingual comparison leading to a class of conclusions. Comparative study, as the terminology usually suggests, was thought to be the centerpiece of these disciplines. But in comparative musicology, no single comparative method was developed. While the concept of comparison may have been, perforce, at the bottom of a contemplation of the world's musics, the great majority of published research studies before 1950 did not actually engage in comparison.

Nevertheless, a proper interpretation of disciplinary history leads us to several bodies of work – projects, they might be named as a group – in which a technique of comparison is fundamental. Among them, let me mention these as examples:

1. *Find a way of describing musical style that facilitates the comparison of styles.* Many of the studies of individual repertories by Stumpf (1886, 1911), Hornbostel (e.g. 1906), and the collaboration of Abraham and Hornbostel (e.g.1906) appear to try to establish a method of stylistic description that would make comparison possible and convenient. Thus, what has sometimes been called the "Hornbostel paradigm" – focusing on scalar structures and pitch relations, and giving attention to singing style and tone color – seems to have been developed in part for establishing an approach to description of music that might facilitate a comparative method. The purpose of enabling comparison was actually not

emphasized (however, see Lach 1924 as a contrastive example), but perhaps these early scholars simply took it for granted that a single, broadly applicable approach would be essential at least for the early development of this discipline. Hornbostel's approach was taught, though only occasionally followed, by George Herzog, and it is in a sense the basis for schemes of comparative description that were developed, after 1950, by Kolinski (see bibliography), and of the cantometrics projects of Alan Lomax of the 1960s and 1970s (see bibliography). There were other attempts to provide templates; I mention only a statistical approach promulgated by Merriam (Freeman and Merriam 1956) and a broadly applicable approach to analysis suggested by Herndon (1974). A natural accompaniment to these schemes for comparing musical styles is the considerable number of schemes for describing and comparing instruments, the best-known of which is that of Hornbostel and Sachs (1914). Some classification schemes for instruments found in a variety of cultures are themselves subjected to comparative study by Kartomi (1990).

2. *Find a way of reconstructing history through the geographic distributions of style traits and instruments.* The study of geographic distribution of music, important in music studies from ca. 1900 into the 1970s, has naturally always required comparison. Much of this research makes use of comparison as an informal way of imparting information, but more specifically, several approaches were used for a wide body of data, or in contrastive world areas or musical domains, justifying the term "comparative method." Most prominent of these in the first half of the 20th century were the so-called "Kulturkreis" approach, whose results were analyzed in detail by Albrecht Schneider (1978), and were shown to have had far-reaching scholarly consequences. Among the influential studies following this approach let me just mention Curt Sachs's study of instrument distributions and the resulting chronology (1929); Marius Schneider's summary world history of polyphonic styles (1934), based substantially on geographic distributions; and the relationship of pentatonicism and matriarchal/matrilineal social structures in the work of Werner Danckert (see Schneider 1978; Danckert 1939). Although hardly as rigorous as the methodology of comparative linguistics, the attempts to present relationship clusters as historical strata can be considered "a" comparative method, though one whose general usefulness has not been established.

The approach of the musical studies that borrow concept and approach from the development of the "culture area" concept were more informally conceived and had limited ambition (see Nettl 1954 and 1965; Merriam 1964:295-96, McLean 1979; also Collaer 1958, 1960), placing more emphasis on taxonomy and less on historical reconstruction. Classifying the typical musical styles of Native American tribes or nations and grouping them requires, of course, comparisons of style traits – scales, rhythmic types, forms, sound ideals – and determining the degree of homogeneity and diversity within a repertory all require some kind of systematic comparison (see also Lomax 1968). Musical style has turned out to lend itself to comparison of this sort better than many other domains of culture. Music as an aspect of culture – what Merriam called "behavior" and "concept," are less easily quantified and have lent themselves less well to a comparative grid. The notion of musical areas belongs mainly to the period between 1935 and 1960.

Although the assumption, in the construction of culture areas (by scholars such as Kroeber 1947, Wissler 1917, and Driver 1961) was that they would have relevance to the reconstruction of history, using among guiding tools such rather vague concepts as "culture climax" – intensity of concentration of a cluster of characteristics – musical areas have not been widely used for speculating about history.

3. *Find a way of reconstructing history through the geographic distributions – in contrast to considerations of style – of units of musical content.* By "content" I mean identifiable works – usually compositions, but conceivably other units such as themes or subdivisions such as lines – that can be identified even when some of their style traits change. This may refer for example to pieces that retain their identity through change of scale or mode in folk song variants (for theoretical discussion, see, e.g., Bayard 1950, Salmen 1954, Jardanyi 1962), transformation of themes, arrangements, re-orchestrations, and even divergent interpretations in performance. The concept of "musical content" in ethnomusicology has largely been used in comparison of folk song variants. Indeed, the concept of variants and versions, of tune families and tune types, have depended on the comparative study of units of musical content that are – or might be – arguably in some sense related. The distinction between stylistic similarity and genetic relationship has played a major role here.

In the study of "content" distribution, one of whose earliest examples is Wilhelm Tappert's (1890) suggestion that European tunes wander through the international art and folk music repertories, is one of the major genres of research in European and Euro-American folk music into the middle of the 20th century. A very large number of scholars has participated in this genre of study; besides those listed above, Bela Bartok (1931), Walter Wiora (1953), and Bertrand H. Bronson (1959) should be mentioned. Each of these scholars was involved in distinctive national approaches to the issue. Fundamental to the study of tune relationships is the development of classification systems, which began with the need to classify melodies in the burgeoning collecting movements that began before 1900, and whose formal beginning goes back to an exchange between Oswald Koller (1902-3) and Ilmari Krohn (1902-3). Classification of folk tunes declined in interest after ca. 1960 although it continued to have a presence especially in Eastern Europe (see Stockmann and Steszewski 1973), but it also influenced the establishment of tune classification in other domains of music such as hymn tunes (Temperley 1998). Reconstructing the history of melodies by comparing presumed variants continued, though with diminished interest, into the late 20th century (e.g. Cowdery 1990, Hungarian Academy of Sciences 1992).

While our interest here is largely in the pursuit of intercultural comparative study, it is important to point out that comparative work of many sorts within a musical culture or repertory has never been abandoned, but in some respects, it too, like its intercultural analogue, has encountered conceptual as well as political difficulties. Some of the methodological problems – measuring degrees of difference and similarity, for example – are faced at all levels. Lists of studies making large-scale comparisons would occupy pages, and they include work as contrastive as comparisons of classification systems in Indian music (as an example, see Powers 1970), comprehensive map-making such as the musical atlas of western Rajasthan (e. g., Neuman et al 2006), and comparisons of performances in one mode by one musician (Nettl and Riddle 1974).

Arguments about Terminology

The bodies of literature just mentioned make significant use of comparison in various ways. The degree to which they are explicitly "comparative" might be questioned, but they do not, on the whole, go into the question of comparison, provide no rigorous comparative method, and in the end probably do not constitute a very large proportion of the studies on non-Western and folk music. Looking, for example, at the large body of literature on Native American music from before 1950, only a few publications (importantly including Roberts 1936) engage specifically in intercultural comparisons; and only one (Herzog 1936) presents itself as having a principally comparative purpose, with its title, "A Comparison of Pueblo and Pima Musical Styles." Jaap Kunst was surely correct in pointing out (1955:9) that "comparative musicology" does not engage directly in comparison any more than other fields.

Kunst is said to have introduced the term "ethno-musicology" in 1950, but it is possible (this information comes from my memory of conversations) that some American scholars (Melville Herskovits, Richard Waterman, Alan Merriam), using as models words such as "ethno-linguistics," "ethnohistory," and "ethnobotany," also developed the term independently and were already using it informally at the same time. For Kunst, it was the subject content – all music outside the scope of Western art and popular music – that was diagnostic for defining it; for the Americans, it was the association of music with the other domains of culture. It is striking, however, that the term "comparative musicology," and its German and French equivalents, enjoying a relatively calm existence for a half century, was – as I suggested above – rather suddenly abandoned and replaced. Very soon after 1950, one saw the old term only occasionally, and "ethnomusicology," sometimes rendered as "Musikethnologie" or "musikalische Völkerkunde"(see Bose 1953, Reinhard 1968, Olsen 1974) took over and appears frequently throughout the literature. There seemed at the time to be little in the way of resistance, and the change is sometimes mentioned with little explanation. When the Society for Ethnomusicology was founded, in the early 1950s, no one questioned the term (though the hyphen was briefly an issue of debate). Indeed, the notion of comparative study, growing in a number of social disciplines (see Sarana 1975; Warwick and Osherson 1973) played a decreasing role in statements about the principal questions of ethnomusicology (see e.g. Rice 1987). Like Rice, Egger (1984), in an analysis of ethnomusicology (defined as the study of non-Western and of European folk music) in its relationship to other disciplines and fields, devotes only a brief page (1984:59) to discussion of comparison, treating it almost as a minor area of activity.

Actually, a very conscious shifting of gears becomes evident soon after 1950. Thus, Curt Sachs, in the 1959 revised edition of his 1930 survey, *Vergleichende Musikwissenschaft: Musik der Fremdkulturen*, points out the shift: "[Ihr] alter Name [dieser Wissenschaft] „Vergleichende Musikwissenschaft" führt irre und ist allgemein aufgegeben worden...sie ist Musikgeschichte geworden...In den Ländern englischer Sprache ist der offizielle Name Ethnomusicology und in Frankreich, Ethnomusicologie oder ethnographie musicale." (1959:5). In his last book, *The Wellsprings of Music*,

Sachs also introduced the new term, though with some trepidation. He admits that "comparative" is misleading, but "with or without hyphen, the word [ethnomusicology] is somewhat unwieldy and its meaning obscure to people who have not even a clear idea of musicology without a prefix. The "musikalische Völkerkunde" of the Germans and the ethnographie musicale of the French seems to put an exaggerated stress on the ethnological part of the aggregate" (Sachs 1962:15).

Interestingly, this issue of terminology and the ambivalence regarding terms appears already in the previously mentioned first book devoted principally to theory and methodology of our field, by Robert Lach (1924). He asks why the term "vergleichende Musikwissenschaft" should be used for a study of the world's traditional musics, when this field does not engage in comparative work more than other humanistic fields. Contemplating Adler's "Musikologie" he finds it etymologically indefensible. "Musikalische Folklore" is too explicitly devoted to European folk music, and "musikalische Ethnographie" is unsatisfactory because it implies study of one individual culture at a time. Thus, he defends "vergleichende Musikwissenschaft," which suggests to him, given certain caveats, the concept of all traditions from the perspective of a world of music (distinct musics?), a definition congruent with some – or at least parts of – modern definitions of ethnomusicology.

For Lach, the relationship of comparative musicology to natural sciences is primary; rather than considering the individual phenomena of music simply in their historical and cultural setting, comparative musicology contemplates them in the much broader framework of events that are scientifically observable, as part of a structure of a natural process of evolution (Lach 1924:8, 12).

In any event, the arguments about the validity of the term "comparative musicology" and the role of a comparative approach to the world of music, seen as a recent phenomenon by some, has actually been around for a long time. So, while the "comparative musicologists," even including Lach, seemed to have a wide area of agreement on what they were about, the scholars who called themselves ethnomusicologists have had difficulty agreeing on definitions of their field (see Merriam 1977).

Objections to Comparison: Responding to McLean

One would think that this change of terminology, from comparative musicology to ethnomusicology, would accompany a significant change in scholarly activity. It is possible to make a case for this shift, and indeed, Mervyn McLean (2006:314-16), in providing a synthesis of the history of the field, sees a general avoidance of comparative study as characteristic of the second half of the twentieth century. He thinks that the change in terms may actually have stimulated a kind of flight from comparative study, but suggests several more seriously conceived reasons for what he considers an unjustified abandonment. He cites Mantle Hood, who in several publication and many lectures inveighed against intercultural comparison because he felt that it was being done before the cultures, musics, works, systems, etc. that were to be compared had become thoroughly understood. Other reasons given by McLean include the association of the concept of comparison with early, and eventually abandoned, conclusions of comparative study, particularly the Kulturkreis school; the complexity of music, which has both structure and meaning each of which may be interpreted differently by cultural insiders and outsiders; and simply the difficulty of comparative study.

One of the issues that has confronted comparative studies is the difficulty of measuring degrees of similarity and difference in music itself, and even more, in musical behavior and conceptualization. Musics that sound similar to some may appear thoroughly different to others, and although both Hornbostel's analytical paradigm and Lomax's Cantometrics method try to overcome the problems, lots of questionable conclusions have been drawn (see for example Barbeau 1934, 1962).

I find myself in substantial agreement with McLean, but yet it seems to me that the criticisms of comparison cited by McLean could easily be swept away. It makes sense to say that, faced with an apple and an orange, one should not compare them before having examined each, though one could learn something important just from noting differences in color and acidity and thickness of skin, and perhaps geographic provenance, and from similarities in shape and size – without insisting on the most thoroughgoing possible chemical and biological examination. We can learn something significant, for example, from the recognition that typical structures of geographically distant Native American musics such as the standard public ceremonial songs of Blackfoot of the Northern Plains, the Peyote songs of the Oklahoma Kiowa, and the Californian majority of songs of the Yahi (i.e., the songs of Ishi) share an important feature – they are binary but use asymmetrical (sometimes called "incomplete") repetition – and this is significant even absent an accounting for other aspects of style, and laying aside (for the time being) the interpretation that singers in any of these cultures might attach to the mentioned form types. Thus (*pace* Hood 1963:233 and Blacking 1971:108), it's not required that one must know "everything" about a music before making comparisons, and one doesn't constantly have to invoke the difference between structure and meaning. McLean's last reason, difficulty of comparative study, appears to suggest the importance of sloth in determining research design. Surely each ethnomusicologist has moments of laziness, some more than others, but on the other hand, most research thrives on the difficulty of the task, so here I am not convinced.

McLean suggested, also, that comparative study was abandoned because its early manifestations – the work of the Kulturkreis school (he mentions Marius Schneider and Curt Sachs) in particular – came to be discredited, producing "an irrational distaste for the whole idea of comparison" (McLean 2006:315). Fundamentally in agreement with this interpretation of McLean's, I wish to offer some additional comments. After World War II, three questions seem to me to have been important in the general discourse of ethnomusicology in the English-speaking world: 1) Is comparative study valid? 2) Does it have political ramifications? 3) Should it be the centerpiece of this discipline? These questions lead to further considerations.

On the third question: If we undertake to engage in comparative studies, does this necessarily mean that they should be the identifying marker of the discipline? Some non-Western musicians – from Japanese to Indian to African to Native American – have over the years quizzed me along several tracks relevant to this question. Did the term "comparative musicology" suggest that we – Europeans and North Americans – studied their music only in order to compare it to ours, or non-Western musics to each other? What could possibly be the purpose of such comparison, if not to prove which music is "better," to glorify one at the expense of others, or to determine what stage a music

303

occupies in a world history of music? Such questions clearly hit their mark: As late as 1957, Marius Schneider, in a sub-chapter titled "Comparative Musicology," maintains that although the available materials on tribal music is "of recent origin," he wishes to "bring into historical order the medley of primitive, transitional, and advanced cultures which still exist side by side..." (1957:1-2). According to him, comparative musicology – the discipline – had as its primary aim "the comparative study of all the characteristics, normal and otherwise, of non-European art." (1957:1).

But I also remember, drawing on personal memories, frequently hearing the question, just what it was that was so interesting about the music of the Arapaho, or the Basongye, that a person should devote years to their study. Often my answer and that of my colleagues at the time, unable to be convincing about the intrinsic complexity of even numerically limited musical systems, took recourse to the reconstruction of history, or the functionality of the music, or the understanding of the musical world and its universals, all of them dependent on large-scale intercultural comparison.

National and Disciplinary Politics

Expanding further upon McLean's thoughts: It seems to me that while comparative study with historical agenda occupied scholars before 1950 only to a limited extent, it began nevertheless to be seen by some as the central marker and activity. After World War II, when scholars from English-speaking nations (plus some Dutch and Scandinavians) began to play a major role in the study of non-Western and folk music, the centrality of comparative study came to be disreputable for several reasons which are not directly connected with the concept of comparison. Broadly speaking, all have political foundations involving oppositions and developments that followed and to some degree resulted – often quite indirectly – from World War II, the defeat of the governments of the main German-speaking nations; the pressure to decolonize much of Asia, Africa, Oceania, and in some respects, parts of the Americas; the dominance of American- and British-derived styles of anthropological thought; and the growth of American music education.

The concept of "comparative musicology" with its interest in Kulturkreis theory, folk music classification, and the Hornbostel paradigm were seen in the militarily and also academically victorious nations as essentially German or Germanophone, and thus associated – unjustly in most cases – with the racist theories of the Nazi movement, never mind that a number of the scholars associated with these positions were themselves victims of Nazi ideology. To many younger American and British scholars of the 1950s, it was important to get away from the old, the "German," the speculative, and certainly from anything that had racist implications. Thus, while the founder of the Society for Ethnomusicology expressed respect for Hornbostel and Stumpf, for folk songs scholars such as Bartók, and even sometimes for the stands of the Kulturkreis school (see Merriam 1964:289), they and their colleagues wished to move in other directions, placing distance between themselves and the Germans and Austrians. The notion that musical style elements might be genetically (i.e., racially) determined, promulgated by some ethnomusicologists (e.g. Bose 1952) were abandoned for half a century for ideological as well as scientific reasons (see Födermayr 1971).

This attitude went hand-in-hand with newly conceived ideas about the relationship between scholars (from Western, "developed" nations) and the people whose music they studied. (for an early statement of the position, see Gourlay 1978.) This is an area deserving lengthy historical treatment, but let me just say that with the early manifestations of globalization in communication, musicians and scholars coming from, say, India, Japan, or Africa saw no reason for having their music associated with what was merely a subfield of the "real" musicology, and that their music was worth noting only in the context of intercultural comparison. The same kind of problem soon arose with the development of the term and concept of "ethnomusicology," and the occasional use of the term "ethnomusic" to denote the non-Western and Western "other."

One of the most important innovations in post-1950 ethnomusicology was the creation of training systems that included the study of performance. A development most associated with Mantle Hood (1960, 1971:230-45) and his successes at UCLA, and secondarily with David McAllester and Robert E. Brown at Wesleyan University, it was substantially aided by certain other conditions of its time. The interest of Western composers – but especially of Americans such as Colin McPhee, Lou Harrison, Henry Cowell, Roy Harris – in Asian music, and of such devices as the Orff-gamelan, led to an increased academic interest in non-Western music in American and other Western music education systems. The centrality, in American universities, of hands-on approaches to music teaching, and the increased interest of American music educators in giving students first-hand performing experience, moved towards the privileging of Asian art music systems – particularly the Gamelan traditions – and on concentration on the uniqueness of these systems. Quite appropriately, as funds for extended fieldwork by ethnomusicologists and their graduate students became more widely available, scholars began to specialize more. Recognizing the complexity of even small musical cultures, and devoting themselves to individual societies and repertories, they put comparison on the back burner.

The comparative study of folk music, although often totally devoid of national issues, seems to me to have suffered also for political reasons, being seen by some as an expression of no longer valid nationalism and even irredentism, and by others as an expression of radical political causes (Bohlman 1996, 2002). Nevertheless, the concepts initiated by folk music researchers – tune types and families, for examples – continued into the later twentieth century (e.g. List 1979; Hungarian Academy of Sciences 1992).

Finally, there is a somewhat ambiguous role of anthropology. The decrease of interest in comparative study in the dominant schools of thought in anthropology – the disciples of Franz Boas, A. H. Radcliffe-Brown, B. Malinowski, and Claude Levy-Strauss – significantly influenced musical studies. For comparative study, this was importantly true for Melville J. Herskovits (1945), who tried to measure similarities and differences in various cultural domains in a study of several African-derived New World cultures. It is of course true that many anthropologists engaged in comparative study (see Lewis 1956), but these researches decreased in significance as anthropology increased its emphasis from quantitative to qualitative methods, and with the increased emphasis on reflexivity and interpretive discourse. To be sure, the occasional forays into comparative methodology in ethnomusicology – e.g. those of Kolinski and Lomax – were, I believe, received with more interest by anthropologists than by music-oriented scholars. And also, to be sure, the central figure in anthropology-oriented ethnomusicology after 1950, Alan Merriam, encouraged comparison (McLean 2006:315) and once admitted to me, in the context of criticizing "comparative musicology" as interested only in history, that in fact we in ethnomusicology (meaning even himself) seem to spend most of our time making comparisons.

The most vocal opponent of comparative study, as pointed out above and by McLean (2006:315), was Mantle Hood, who considered it a major obstacle to progress, criticizing such faults as "a premature concern with the comparison of different musics [which] has resulted in an accumulation of broad generalities and oversimplifications" (1963:233) on various occasions (see also Hood 1971:343). Nevertheless, Hood too acknowledged the usefulness of comparative study – once the cultures being compared are sufficiently well understood – for solving certain problems and answer particular questions (1971:342-44). Merriam, usually presented as intellectually opposed to Hood's approaches, does not look at comparison all that differently, having proposed, in the 1960s, a different method and purpose of comparison from the pre-1950 period, and insisting "that the approach must be cautious, that like things must be compared, and that the comparison must have bearing upon a particular problem and be an integrated part of the research design" (1964:53). During the period in which comparison (as a concept) seemed to be particularly unpopular, Merriam (1982) – in what was probably his last work, published posthumously – wrote a lengthy article defending it against arguments proposed by Hood and Blacking.

But if the term "vergleichende Musikwissenschaft" seems to have been used most in connection with so-called tribal societies, its most prominent use in French appeared in the title of a work by Alain Danielou as late as 1959. His Traité de musicologie comparée, which was published in a series devoted to science and engineering, is actually a comparison of the tone systems of Chinese, Indian, ancient Greek, and European scales and theoretical systems, following a discussion of music universals which serves as a jumping-off point. Interestingly, Danielou on various occasions objected to the term "ethnomusicology" as degrading to complex art musics such as Indian (Danielou 1973:34-46). Quite likely, the title of his comparative study is intended as specific to his project, and not as a designation of the discipline in which he was working.

Opposition or Synthesis? The Y2K Era

For reasons suggested above, it has been widely believed that ethnomusicology started out "comparative" and after 1950 abandoned this approach; and that various schools of American ethnomusicology claimed superiority over others by avoiding comparative study. In fact, however, I would maintain that the studies of non-Western and folk music before 1950 were not, as Kunst also pointed out, "especially" comparative, and that after 1950, comparative study continued to play a major role. The change in terminology, away from "vergleichende," was the result of changes in political relationships among nations and parts of the world, and of changes in the nationality of the principal population of the field.

It's also widely believed that there developed an opposition in ethnomusicology between the anthropologists, who consider comparative study essential though sometimes dangerous, and the musicians, who consider musical systems unique and comparison dangerous and in the end impossible. Another strand of conventional wisdom has been to present the history of ethnomusicology as moving away from comparison. I suggest, however, that while this conventional reading of history reflects the dominant rhetoric, in actual practice the attitudes toward comparison have been fairly consistent, and comparative study has played a significant though not dominant role throughout the century.

It is interesting to see the continued appearance, and 1965, of publications that support and encourage comparative study. The term "comparative musicology" is of course gone, but there is plenty of comparative method. An important survey of what had been done appeared among the many works of Walter Wiora (1975) who, interestingly, distinguishes between "vergleichende Musikforschung," by which he suggests individual research projects in which comparison plays a role, and "vergleichende Musikwissenschaft," which he takes to be the (unsatisfactory and obsolete) designation of a discipline. Wiora (1975:7) criticizes the substitution of "Musikethnologie" for "vergleichende Musikwissenschaft" (i. e., ethnomusicology for comparative musicology), but does not propose a better terminology. He then proceeds to survey several dozen studies, largely from post-1950 and many from the years just before his publication, which are in fact comparative. The developments in the world of music in the era of globalization have also given rise to comparative studies, such as Slobin's identification of "micromusics" (Slobin 1992). Clearly, comparative study has not been abandoned; it has only ceased to be the diagnostic feature of ethnomusicology, and in some respects its existence has been "under the radar."

If comparative study has ceased to be regarded as the centerpiece of the discipline by most, that was not true of Alan Lomax. The best-known interculturally oriented comparative project after ca. 1960 has been Lomax's cantometrics project, and there is no doubt (though perhaps he did not say so in print) that he considered this work central to our field. Though seemingly abandoned for a time, it has recently – since Lomax's death – been revived, though also revised, by Victor Grauer. In a lengthy essay, Grauer (2006) argues that a more sophisticated approach to cantometrics – both the analytical method and the assessment of the relationship of music and culture – can provide answers to the most fundamental questions about music: its origins, its worldwide history, its role in society. Grauer seemed to be proposing, in 2006, a paradigm-shift to a return to comparative study as central to ethnomusicology.

Grauer's approach connects not only to cantometrics, with its interest in large musical areas of varying degrees of homogeneity, but also to the interest in universals that produced a number of publications in the 1970s (e.g. Blacking 1977, Harrison 1977, Wachsmann 1977; see Nettl 2005:42-49). In the pre-1950 period in ethnomusicology, comparative study emphasized the diversity of the world's musics and the dominant discourse included a desire to deny that all of the world's musics had anything in common. It was the continuing interest in comparative study after 1950 that moved the search for universals to a position of greater prominence, to the extent that many scholars felt motivated to weigh in on the issue from one perspective or another.

This thread continued into the early 21st century, together with an increased interest, particularly in the English-speaking world, in systematic musicology including cognitive studies, psychology and biology of music, and what has come to be known as "evolutionary musicology." (see e.g. Wallin at al 2000). Here a renewed interest in the origins of music has stimulated a relationship of ethnomusicologists to scientists reminiscent of the association of Hornbostel and Stumpf with the methods of psychologists and physicists, and of Lach's interest in evolution. Comparative study has come to be broadened, seeking, for example, universals in human music to provide a base for comparison with forms of animal communication.

The need for a return to comparative study, but with a higher degree of sophistication, has been emphasized in an essay by Martin Clayton (2003), which suggests that comparison of one parameter of musical sound or structure (or of musical culture) must be made against a moving and varied template, a kind of moving target. For example, presentation of a comparison of melodic structure of two cultures must be made with attention to the differences between the ways in which they conceive of music – their theories of music. Clayton proposes to "address the relationship among sound, as an integral aspect of human interaction; the experience of producing, perceiving, and responding to that sound; and the processes by which people imagine that sound to possess structure or to convey meaning" (2003:66).

This is surely what many of Clayton's predecessors had in mind. The difficulty they have had, illustrated constantly in Lomax's work, is the (relative) ease of dividing musical sound into elements that appear to be easily quantified or characterized (e.g. the number of pitches in a scale, or the number of phrases in a stanza) or classified (iterative, progressive, and reverting forms) as compared with the difficulty of drawing such lines among societies in the way they conceive of music. Thus, dividing the world into pentatonic and heptatonic cultures would appear to be easier than separating cultures on the basis of their conception of the creation of songs. Easier, to be sure, but perhaps also misleading, and possibly not capable of leading to worthwhile conclusions. A problem with comparative study has been our inability to find satisfactory ways of comparing, with equal degrees of confidence, all aspects of musical culture and sound. Albrecht Schneider (2006) therefore proposes a renewed association of ethnomusicology and systematic musicology, with scientifically-based comparative studies of musical structure (see also Schneider 2001).

How then to outline the history of comparative study in music research? Historians of Western art music have "always" engaged in a lot of comparison, but it has of course involved limited fields – a variety of versions of one work, the wandering of a motif through the works of one composer, the relationship of a composer's folk-derived style to the rural folk repertory he had heard, the similarities and differences between schools of opera as developed in different Italian cities, the question of periodization. Only in a few specialized studies (e.g. Becking 1928, whose classification of composers by rhythmic character into groupings headed by Mozart and Beethoven foreshadows cantometrics) did music historians attempt the kinds of things typical of ethnomusicological comparisons. Intercultural comparison (e.g. "central" and "peripheral" styles in the Renaissance) has, to be sure, been carried out for generalized orientation.

But the discourse in the world of Western art music – the response of audiences and the relationships among musics – is unremittingly comparative. Discussion of composers, works, performances almost always takes place within a context that invites comparison (other Baroque composers, other concertos by Mozart, other interpretations of the Waldstein I've heard, other recordings of "Death and the Maiden," and "when I last heard her play this..."). Comparison in terms of quality, and merciless ranking. Small wonder, perhaps, that Indian and Chinese and Native American musicians who are acquainted with Western conversational habits think that "comparing" means deciding which is better.

In ethnomusicology, responsible comparative study has never been judgmental, and one wonders why this issue should have become such a bone of contention. That comparative study may be difficult and requires careful methodology, that one must avoid drawing unwarranted conclusions, that one must be aware of the contexts in which the elements selected for comparison exist, these things one readily stipulates. Beyond this, the reason for the controversy surrounding the value of comparison has been largely an issue of terminology.

To summarize: The history of comparative study has been two-pronged. As a practice, it has always been with us, subject in its individual projects to sometimes justified, sometimes unreasonable criticism. We have not been able to get on without it. In a kind of parallel history, the term "comparative" and the concept have had their ups and downs. Before 1950, the term was used, often with insufficient justification, as comparison (we were reminded of this by Kunst, Sachs, Merriam, and others) did not play a special role. After about 1950, the term "comparative" began, sometimes justly and often not, to be associated with various undesirable qualities – racism and "culturism," prematurity, superficiality, neglect of contexts, the understanding that in comparative study, some data will have to come from sources other than the investigator's own fieldwork, unwillingness to recognize that each culture was worthy of study on its own. Even those studies that were clearly inter- or intra-culturally comparative – to say nothing of the field as a whole – withdrew from the comparative terminology. More recently, and particularly in the 21st century, we may again be ready to admit that much of what we have always done has had a basis in comparison. Comparative study is again becoming respectable among a variety of recognized methodologies of the ethnomusicological arsenal.

Publications Cited

Abraham, Otto and Erich M. Von Hornbostel. 1906. "Phonographierte Indianermelodien aus Britisch-Columbia. In *Anthropological Papers Written in Honor of Franz Boas*. New York: Stechert, pp. 447-74.

Adler, Guido. 1885. "Umfang, Methode und Ziel der Musikwissenschaft." *Vierteljahrschrift für Musikwissenschaft* 1 :5-20.

Ambros, August Wilhelm. 1862. *Geschichte der Musik*. Breslau: F. E. C. Leuckart.

Anttila, Raimo. 1972. *An Introduction to Historical and Comparative Linguistics*. London: Macmillan.

Barbeau, Marius. 1934. "Asiatic Survivals in Indian Songs." *Musical Quarterly* 20:107-16.

----- 1962. "Buddhist Dirges of the North Pacific Coast." *Journal of the International Folk Music Council* 14:16-21.

Bartók, Béla. 1931. *Hungarian Folk Music*. London: Oxford University Press.

Bayard, Samuel P. 1950. "Prolegomena to a Study of the Principal Melodic Families of British-American Folk Song." *Journal of American Folklore* 63:1-44.

Becking, Gustav. 1928. *Der musikalische Rhythmus als Erkenntnisquelle*. Augsburg: B. Filser.

309

Blacking, John. 1972. "Deep and Surface Structures in Venda Music" *Yearbook of the International Folk Music Council* 91-108.

---- 1973. *How Musical Is Man?* Seattle: University of Washington Press.

----- 1977. "Can Musical Universals Be Heard?" *World of Music* 19/1-2:14-22.

Bohlman, Philip V. 1996 "Pilgrimage, Politics, and the Musical Remapping of the New Europe." *EM* 40:375-412.

----- 2002 *World Music: A Very Short Introduction*. Oxford: Oxford University Press.

Bose, Fritz. 1952. "Messbare Rassenunterschiede in der Musik." *Homo* 2/4: 1-5.

----- 1953. *Musikalische Völkerkunde*. Zürich: Atlantis.

Bronson, Bertrand H. 1959. "Toward the Comparative Analysis of British-American Folk Tunes." *Journal of American Folklore* 72:165-91.

Clayton, Martin. 2003. "Comparing Music, Comparing Musicology. In Martin Clayton, Trevor Herbert, and Richard Middleton, ed. *The Cultural Study of Music*. New York: Routledge.

Collaer, Paul. 1958. "Cartography and Ethnomusicology." *EM* 2:66-68.

----- 1960 *Atlas historique de la musique*. Paris: Elsevier.

Cowdery, James R. 1990. *The Melodic Tradition of Ireland*. Kent, OH: Kent State University Press.

Danckert, Werner. 1939. *Das europäische Volkslied*. Berlin: J. Bard.

Danielou, Alain. 1959. *Traité de musicologie compareé*. Paris: Hermann.

----- 1973 *Die Musik Asiens zwischen Missachtung und Wertschätzung*. Wilhelmshaven: Heinrichshofen. (Originally published in French, 1971)

Driver, Harold E. 1961. *Indians of North America*. Chicago: University of Chicago Press.

Egger, Kurt. 1984. *Ethnomusikologie und Wissenschaftsklassifikation*. Wien: Böhlau.

Ellis, Alexander J. 1885. "On the Musical Scales of Various Nations." *Journal of the Royal Society of Arts* 33:485-527.

Elschek, Oskar, and Doris Stockmann, ed. 1969. *Methoden der Klassifikation von Volksliedweisen*. Bratislava: Verlag der slowakischen Akademie der Wissenschaften.

Elschekova, Alica. 1966. "Methods of Classifying Folk Tunes." *Journal of the International Folk Music Council* 18:56-76.

Erickson, Edwin Erich. 1969. "*The Song Trace: Song Styles and the Ethnohistory of Aboriginal America*." Dissertation, Columbia University.

Födermayr, Franz. 1971. *Zur gesanglichen Stimmgebung in der aussereuropäischen Musik*. Vienna: Stiglmayr.

Freeman, Linton C., and Alan P. Merriam. 1956. "Statistical Classification in Anthropology: An Application to Ethnomusicology." *AA* 58:464-72.

Gourlay, K. A. 1978. "Towards a Reassessment of the Ethnomusicologist's Role." *EM* 22:1-36.

Grauer, Victor. 2006. "Echoes of Our Forgotten Ancestors.' *World of Music* 48(2):5-59. With responses by Bruno Nettl, Jonathan Stock, and Peter Cook.

310

Harrison, Frank Ll. 1977. "Universals in Music: Towards a Methodology of Comparative Research." *World of Music* 19/1-2:30-36.

Harrison, Frank, Mantle Hood, and Claude Palisca. 1963. *Musicology*. Englewood Cliffs, N.J.: Prentice-Hall.

Herndon, Marcia. 1974. "Analysis: The Herding of Sacred Cows?" *EM* 18:219-62.

Herskovits, Melville J. 1945. "Problem, Method, and Theory in Afroamerican Studies." *Afroamerica* 1:5-24.

Herzog, George. 1930. "Musical Styles in North America." *Proceedings of the 23rd International Congress of Americanists* (New York), pp. 455-58.

----- 1936. "A Comparison of Pueblo and Pima Musical Styles." *Journal of American Folklore* 49:283-417.

Hood, Mantle. 1960. "The Challenge of Bi-Musicality." *EM* 4:55-59.

----- 1963. *"Music, the Unknown."* In Harrison, Hood, and Palisca (1963).

----- 1971. *The Ethnomusicologist*. New York: McGraw-Hill.

Hornbostel, Erich M. von. 1905. "Die Probleme der vergleichenden Musikwissenschaft." *Zeitschrift der internationalen Musikgesellschaft* 7:85-97.

----- 1906. "Phonographierte tunesishe Melodien," *Sammelbände der internationalen Musikgesellschaft* 8:1-43.

----- 1911. "Über ein akustisches Kriterium für Kulturzusammenhange." *Zeitschrift für Ethnologie* 3:601-15.

Hornbostel, Erich M. von, and Otto Abraham. 1904. "Über die Bedeutung des Phonographen für die vergleichende Musikwissenschaft, *Zeitschrift für Ethnologie* 36:222-233.

Hornbostel, Erich M. von, and Curt Sachs. 1914. "Systematik der Musikinstrumente." *Zeitschrift für Ethnologie* 46:553-90. English translation by Anthony Baines and K. P. Wachsmann, "Classification of Musical Instruments," G*alpin Society Journal* 14:3-29, 1961.

Hungarian Academy of Sciences, Institute for Musicology. 1992. *Catalogue of Hungarian Folk Song Types Arranged According to Styles*. Vol. I. [by László Dobszay and Janka Szendrei]. Budapest.

Jardanyi, Pal. 1962. "Die Ordnung der ungarischen Volkslieder." *Studia Musicologica* 2:3-32.

Kartomi, Margaret. 1990. *On Concept and Classifications of Musical Instruments*. Chicago: University of Chicago Press.

Kolinski, Mieczyslaw. 1956. "The Structure of Melodic Movement, a New Method of Analysis." In *Miscelanea de Estudios Dedicados al Dr. Fernando Ortiz*. Havana: Sociedad Economica de Amigos del Pais), 2:879-918.

----- 1959. "The Evaluation of Tempo." *EM* 3:45-57.

----- 1961. "Classification of Tonal Structures." *Studies in Ethnomusicology* (New York) 1:38-76.

----- 1962. "Consonance and Dissonance." *EM* 6:66-74.

----- 1965a. "The General Direction of Melodic Movement." *EM* 9:240-64.

311

----- 1965b. "The Structure of Melodic Movement – A New Method of Analysis." *Studies in Ethnomusicology* (New York) 2:95-120.

----- 1973. "A Cross-Cultural Approach to Metro-Rhythmic Patterns." *EM* 17:494-506.

----- 1978. "The Structure of Music: Diversification versus Constraint." *EM* 22:229-44.

Koller, Oswald. 1902-3. "Die beste Methode, volks- und volksmässige Lieder nach ihrer melodischen Beschaffenheit lexikalisch zu ordnen." *Sammelbände der internationalen Musikgesellschaft* 4: 1-15.

Kroeber, Alfred Louis. 1947. *Cultural and Natural Areas of Native North America*. Berkeley: University of California Press.

Krohn, Ilmari. 1902-3. "Welche ist die beste Methode, um volks- und volksmässige Lieder nach ihrer melodischen (nicht textlichen) Beschaffenheit lexikalisch zu ordnen?" *Sammelbände der internationalen Musikgesellschaft* 4:643-60.

Kunst, Jaap. 1950. *Musicologica*. Amsterdam: Royal Tropical Institute.

----- 1959. *Ethnomusicology*. 3d ed. The Hague: M. Nijhoff.

Lach, Robert. 1924. *Die vergleichende Musikwissenschaft, ihre Methoden und Probleme*. Vienna: Akademie der Wissenschaften.

----- 1925. *Vergleichende Kunst- und Musikwissenschaft* . Vienna: Oesterreichische Akademie der Wissenschaften.

Lewis, Oscar. 1956. "Comparison in Cultural Anthropology." In W. L. Thomas, ed., *Current Anthropology, a Supplement to Anthropology Today*. Chicago: University of Chicago Press, pp. 259- 92.

List, George. 1979. "The Distribution of a Melodic Formula: Diffusion or Polygenesis?" *Yearbook of the International Folk Music Council* 10:33-52.

Lomax, Alan. 1959. "Folksong Style." *AA* 61:927-54.

----- 1962. "Song Structure and Social Structure." *Ethnology* 1 :425-51.

----- 1968. *Folk Song Style and Culture*. Washington: American Association for the Advancement of Science.

----- 1976. *Cantometrics*. Berkeley: University of California.

McLean, Mervyn. 1979. "*Towards the Differentiation of Music Areas in Oceania*." Anthropos 74:717-36.

----- 2006. *Pioneers of Ethnomusicology*. Coral springs, FL: Llumina Press.

Merriam, Alan P. 1964. *The Anthropology of Music*. Evanston, Ill.: Northwestern University Press.

----- 1977a "Definitions of 'Comparative Musicology' and 'Ethnomusicology': An Historical-Theoretical Perspective." *EM* 21:189-204.

----- 1982. "On Objections to Comparison in Ethnomusicology." In Robert Falck and Timothy Rice, ed., *Cross-Cultural Perspectives on Music* (Toronto: University of Toronto Press), pp.174-89.

Nettl, Bruno. 1954 *North American Indian Musical Styles*. Philadelphia: American Folklore Society.

----- 1964. *Theory and Method in Ethnomusicology*. New York: Free Press.

----- 1969. "Musical Areas Reconsidered." In *Essays in Musicology in Honor of Dragan Plamenac*. Pittsburgh: University of Pittsburgh Press, pp. 181-90.

----- 1974. "Thoughts on Improvisation, a Comparative Approach." *Musical Quarterly* 60:1-19.

Nettl, Bruno and Philip V. Bohlman, eds. 1991. *Comparative Musicology and Anthropology of Music*. Chicago: University of Chicago Press.

Nettl, Bruno, and Ronald Riddle. 1974. "Taqsim Nahawand, a Study of Sixteen Performances by Jihad Racy." *Yearbook of the International Folk Music Council* 5:11-50.

Neuman, Daniel, Shubha Chaudhuri, and Komal Kothari. 2006. *Bards, Ballads ad Boundaries: An Ethnographic Atlas of Music's Traditions in Western Rajasthan*. Oxford: Seagull Books.

Olsen, Poul Rovsing. 1974. *Musikethnologie*. Copenhagen: Berlingske Forlag.

Powers, Harold S. 1970. "An Historical and Comparative Approach to the Classification of Ragas." *UCLA Selected Reports of the Institute of Ethnomusicology* 1/3:1-78.

Reinhard, Kurt. 1968. *Einführung in die Musikethnologie*. Wolfenbüttel: Mosiler.

Rice, Timothy. 1987. "Toward the Remodeling of Ethnomusicology." *Ethnomusicology* 31:473, 1987.

Roberts, Helen H. 1936. *Musical Areas in Aboriginal North America*. New Haven, Conn.: Yale University Publications in Anthropology, No. 12.

Sachs, Curt. 1929. *Geist und Werden der Musikinstrumente*. Berlin: J. Bard.

------ 1930. (1959). *Vergleichende Musikwissenschaft -- Musik der Fremdkulturen*. Heidelberg: Quelle und Meyer.

----- 1937. *World History of the Dance*. New York: Norton.

----- 1943. *The Rise of Music in the Ancient World, East and West*. New York: Norton.

----- 1962. *The Wellsprings of Music*. The Hague: M. Nijhoff.

Salmen, Walter. 1954. "Towards the Exploration of National Idiosyncracies in Wandering Song-tunes." *Journal of the International Folk Music Council* 6:52-56.

Sarana, Gopala. 1975. *The Methodology of Anthropological Comparisons: An Analysis of Comparative Methods in Social and Cultural Anthropology*. Tucson: University of Arizona Press (Viking Fund Publications in Anthropology, no. 53).

Schmidt, Wilhelm. 1939. *The Culture Historical Method of Ethnology*. New York: Fortuny's.

Schneider, Albrecht. 1976. *Musikwissenschaft und Kulturkreislehre*. Bonn: Verlag für systematische Musikwissenschaft.

----- 1979 "Vergleichende Musikwissenschaft als Morphologie und Stilkritik: Werner Danckerts Stellung. ..." *Jahrbuch für Volksliedforschung* 24: 11-27.

----- 2001. "Sound, Pitch, and Scale: From Tone Measurements to Sonological Analysis in Ethnomusicology." *Ethnomusicology* 45:498-515.

----- 2006. "Comparative and Systematic Musicology in Relation to Ethnomusicology: A Historical and Methodological Survey." *Ethnomusicology* 50:236-58.

Schneider, Marius. 1934. *Geschichte der Mehrstimmigkeit*. Vol. 1. Berlin: J. Bard.

----- 1957. "Primitive Music." In Egon Wellesz, ed., *Ancient and Oriental Music*. London: Oxford University Press, pp. 1-82.

Slobin, Mark 1992. "Micromusics of the West: a Comparative Approach," *Ethnomusicology* 36:1-87.

Stock, Jonathan. 2007. "Alexander J. Ellis and His Place in the History of Ethnomusicology." *Ethnomusicology* 51:306-25.

Stockmann, Doris, and Jan Steszewski 1973 Eds., *Analyse und Klassifikation von Volksmelodien*. Krakow: Polskie wydawnictwo muzyczne.

Stumpf, Carl. 1886. "Lieder der Bellakula-Indianer." *Vierteljahrschrift für Musikwissenschaft* 2:405-26.

----- 1911. *Die Anfänge der Musik*. Leipzig: J. A. Barth.

Tappert, Wilhelm. 1890. *Wandernde Melodien*. 2. vermehrte und verbesserte Ausgabe. Leipzig: List & Francke.

Temperley, Nicholas. 1998. *Hymn Tune Index: A Census of English-Language Hymn Tunes*. Oxford: Oxford University Press.

Wachsmann, Klaus. 1971. "Universal Perspectives in Music." *Ethnomusicology* 15:381-84.

Wallaschek, Richard. 1893. *Primitive Music*. London: Longmans, Green. German ed. 1903, with title Anfänge der Tonkunst.

Wallin, Nils and others, ed. 2000. *The Origins of Music*. Cambridge: M.I.T. Press.

Warwick, Donald P., and Samuel Osherson 1973 Eds., Comparative Research Methods. Englewood Cliffs, N.J.: Prentice-Hall.

Wiora, Walter. 1953. *Europäischer Volksgesang. (Das Musikwerk, no. 4.)* Cologne: Arno Volk. English trans. ca. 1966, by Robert Kolben, *European Folk Song: Common Forms in Characteristic Modification*. New York: Leeds.

----- 1975. *Ergebnisse und Aufgaben vergleichender Musikforschung*. Darmstadt: Wissenschaftliche Buchgesellschaft.

Wissler, Clark. 1917. *The American Indian*. New York: McMurtrie.

Tiago de Oliveira Pinto

Music and the Tropics:
On Goals and Achievements of Ethnomusicology in Brazil

Introduction

In 2005 the Society for Ethnomusicology (SEM) celebrated its fiftieth anniversary.[1] On the occasion of this special anniversary, the society gave opportunity to the representatives from different countries to inform the assembly about their contribution to the discipline. The same year can also be considered the centenary of ethnomusicology as a whole (Oliveira Pinto, 2005). Considering that in 1908 the first field sound recordings for research purposes were made in Amazonia by German ethnologist Wilhelm Kissenberth in 1908, Ethnomusicology can celebrate its jubilee in Brazil in 2008. Since jubilees are always a welcome opportunity to reflect about what is being celebrated, the following statements aim to reveal some remarks about ethnomusicology outside of North America and Europe, that are rarely made in recent history of this academic field.

Paraphrasing Michael Weber (1990), who referred to ethnomusicology as "the other musicology", the present paper will reveal some ethnomusicological landmarks in Brazil, which, on behalf of the "another ethnomusicology", will present some examples extracted from the history of the discipline in Latin America in general.[2]

The history of an academic field of study, or discipline, within the humanities, is always related to the sum of several regional histories and developments, as there are little areas of scientific research that can belong exclusively to one country or region without relations to others. At the same time, history and reality of the discipline in Latin America reveal certain specificities, some of are addressed in this essay.

I.

The early stage of ethnomusicology in Brazil coincides with the beginnings of the discipline as a "neues Spezialgebiet der Wissenschaft" (specific field of musicological study), to quote Hornbostel, 1905. There are two strong connections that bind Brazilian ethnomusicology to the first phase of the discipline, known as comparative musicology:

1. Music anthropological research in Brazil has played an important role for the development of the beginning of the discipline, almost a century ago. The so-called "Berlin School of Comparative Musicology" under Erich M. von Hornbostel, benefited from the fieldwork and the first major sound recordings realized in Brazil by German ethnographers. Musical materials gathered in the Amazon (Brazil) were used as primary tools for building the universal theories of music as a cultural expression of mankind, defined among diffusionist ethnologists of that time (Schneider, 1976).

2. Shortly after, research and documentation of traditional and popular musics took place in Brazil, revealing new approaches that brought into mind of intellectuals,

folklorists, music teachers and composers, the importance of the fieldwork in the country. It is pertinent to note, that the essence of what anthropology and comparative musicology in Europe and North America were focusing on within the first half of the 20th century – the quest for the "authentic" musical forms – , were not necessarily always at the centre of attention of Brazilian music research.

Hearing was the last of the European inhabitant's five senses to gain experience from distant sensorial universes. When they returned to their countries of origin, those who traveled to the tropics brought back curious objects, images and sketches (later photography), from far-off regions. They also brought reports of fascinating destinations, smells, tastes and even material that offered new tactile experiences, but never included the respective sounds. For this to take place, a technological invention was needed to preserve elements from an "ex-acoustic" universe (since "exotic" stems from *ex-optic*, "from a point of view"). Although the Edison phonograph was invented in 1877, it started to be used in field research only in 1890.

The preservation of sounds (the possibility of transporting them and making them reecho outside their original contexts) afforded the Europeans the opportunity to substantially renew their knowledge of the "other" and also of themselves through the sense of hearing. Recorded sounds from the tropics were essential in this process of the acoustic recognition of human manifestations. Without a doubt, the longest of the processes of sensorial assimilation of the world, often painful and giving rise to countless controversies and debates ranging from the conceptual and the aesthetic to the prejudiced and the racial.

As a discipline ethnomusicology started to exist at the same time that Europeans became aware of different sound concepts from different parts of the world. To my knowledge, no other discipline from the humanities came into existence in the same period that its main subject was experienced. This experience being the result of the discipline's first attempt to define its goals and aspirations. And Brazilian sounds were among the first to arrive in the centre of the beginning of the ethnomusicological thought, analysis and theory in Berlin. They contributed enormously, for instance, to Erich M. von Hornbostel's "Blown Quint Circle Theory" in the 1920's (Hornbostel…).

The first collection of Brazilian music recorded in the field was made between 1908 and 1913, by anthropologists Wilhelm Kissenberth (1878–1944) and Theodor Koch-Grünberg (1872–1924). They conducted research and collected samples of indigenous culture for the Berlin Museum of Ethnology, then called the Königliches Völkerkundemuseum zu Berlin (The Royal Ethnological Museum of Berlin). In addition to the realized recordings of music among the Kayapó and Karajá and the gathering of valuable collection of dance masks, Kissenberth's collection of wax phonograph cylinders remained practically unnoticed in the storage of the museum until very recently (cf. CD, 2006). For his part, Theodor Koch-Grünberg visited Brazil in 1899 but conducted research from 1903 to 1905, from 1911 to 1913, and in 1924. Unlike his colleague Kissenberth, Koch-Grünberg published the results of his research, maintained contact with other researchers, and strove to make the largest possible number of phonographic recordings, especially after having been prepared for the second trip by comparative musicologist Erich M. Von Hornbostel.

Question can be raised here: was the research object – indigenous music – as attractive to the Latin-American scholars as it was to the Europeans? The Brazilian physician and ethnologist Edgar Roquette Pinto recorded indigenous music during his field research in Mato Grosso in 1912. During his visit to the Pareci and Nambikwara Indians, Roquette Pinto recorded the first field sound document by a Brazilian (Roquette Pinto, 1917). The Edison cylinders of this research trip are stored in the ethnological sector of the National Museum in Rio de Janeiro. Although other sound documents have been collected in this institution since, indigenous music did not receive the minimum attention from Brazilian anthropologists until the 1950s. This becomes also evident with the first recordings by Roquette Pinto, as music was rather an offshoot activity conducted between his data collection; a completely different situation when compared with those of Kissenberth or Koch-Grünberg, who gave music a constitutive space in their research and documentation goals.

In the 1920s, the Brazilian poet, cultural activist, ethnographer and musicologist Mário de Andrade became aware of the important work of Koch-Grünberg and requested copies of the recordings made in the Amazon from the Berlin collection. In addition to the recordings and their musical analyses, the ethnography published by Koch-Grünberg (1923) made another great contribution to the Brazilian culture with the myths that the anthropologist had registered. This was the Makuxi myth about the hero Maku-Naima, who in 1928 became the protagonist of Mário de Andrade's great modernist novel, *Macunaíma*.

After obtaining copies of the Koch-Grünberg recordings, Mário de Andrade also asked the Berlin museum for a phonographic field-recording device. The equipment arrived in Brazil in 1938 and was placed into the hands of the singer and guitar player Olga Praguer Coelho, who recorded religious Afro-Brazilian Candomblé songs in Bahia. As far as is known, these are the first sound recordings ever made of this repertoire.

To record Afro-Brazilian music instead of indigenous repertory led to what I am calling the "authenticity dispute" between Mário de Andrade and Marius Schneider, who succeeded Erich M. von Hornbostel in the position of head of the Berlin *Phonogrammarchiv* in 1934. In a short exchange of letters in 1938 between Andrade and Schneider evinced different arguments about the nature of the authenticity in traditional music. These points of view stood for two basic ideological principles of comparative and of folklore music research of the period. While Schneider was interested only in the "veritable musique indienne et non pas du folklore brasilien" (True Indian music and not Brazilian folklore). In his reply to the Schneider's (May 6, 1938) letter, Andrade showed little sensibility for this exclusive need of comparative musicology:

> Je regrette, cher Monsieur, de ne pas pouvoir vous donner que ces quelques indications fort incomplète sur la bibliographie musicale des indigènes du Brésil. Mon domaine est tout autre; je suis restreint au folklore, et j'ose même vous envoyer ci-joint une monographie où j'ai essayé de présenter l'apport de négre d'Afrique, dans le Samba afrobrésilien (Mário de Andrade, São Paulo, June 23, 1938).

It is pertinent to note, that until 1938, the *Phonogrammarchiv* in Berlin did not have a single sample of Afro-American music from South-America. This situation was strange enough to the many sound-collections from this subcontinent that had already reached the institution (cf. Ziegler, 2006). This was probably due to the idea of "authenticity". For the comparative musicology, Afro-American was neither African nor native of America. Therefore he was not really authentic. The *candomblé*-recordings made by Andrade were probably the first of this kind to enter the Berlin archives. This was significantly due to the effort of a Latin American, and not of a European scholar.

Among the early Brazilian intellectuals and artists, the quest for sounds meant challenge of discovering the cultural resources of the country. Driven by the hope of the existence of a musical *eldorado*, deep in its essence and unheard in other parts of the world, these scholars believed that manifestations of the descendants of African slaves or those of the different kind of *mestizo* population could also be included in this musical treasure. Brazilian scholars contemporary of Andrade were not primarily interested in the purity and the authenticity of possible origins of culture. Therefore, Mário de Andrade could not understand why the German musicologist had their eyes and ears for something he considered as pure and unpolluted. Few years prior to Andrade's complaint about a German traveller he met in his trip to the Northeast, who said that "*indio é mais brasileiro que mestiço* [Indian is more a Brazilian than the *mestizo*] (Andrade, 1937). Compared to this European imperative on authenticity, Andrade's study "Samba Rural Paulista" (Andrade, 1934) is more advanced in its anthropological approach than those of most of his contemporary European or North-American musicologists; since he had abandoned completely the idea of purity in favour of the focus on the musical performance as a phenomenon elevated by social meanings.

Whereas authenticity for the foreign researcher meant purity from an ethnic point of view, authenticity for Mário de Andrade represented genuineness of expression, i.e., music performance as practiced in a live and original contextual setting. The fact, that the <u>expression</u> itself may have had different origins, was not a problem as such, as long as the overall <u>impression</u> of the performance and its vivid interchange with the community were in the spotlight.

The "authenticity dispute" discussed above proves once again the basic difference of expectation between the research conducted in Europe with the vision to the world, and the research realized at home, with a self observation focus. Each one of these positions would necessarily influenced any methodological *mise au point* to cultural research. Since the groundbreaking *oeuvre* of traveller and natural scientist Alexander von Humboldt in the first half of the 19th century, "Measuring of the World" ("Die Vermessung der Welt") is a *topos* for almost any natural and geographical study in Europe. Exemplified by Humdoldt's travels through South America, "measuring" by Europeans conflicted with the "discovering of the self" in the folklore research in Latin America from the turn to the 20th century on until its 2nd half.

If "measuring of the world" was a fundamental motivation to natural and cultural sciences that became also important to comparative musicology of the beginning 20th century, Brazilian's efforts during the same period were less engaged in the <u>measuring,</u> but more so in the <u>discovering</u> of the self in order to contribute to a higher ideal – the construction of a nation in terms of its (new) identity. Such a question was certainly not central to the foreign research. Instead, the over posed goal in comparative musicology had less local or national, and much larger universal ambitions:

> (…) Unsere Wünsche fliegen noch höher: wir möchten die fernste, dunkelste Vergangenheit entschleiern und möchten aus der Fülle des Gegenwärtigen das Zeitlose, Allgemeine herausschälen; mit anderen Worten: wir wollen die entwicklungsgeschichtlichen und die allgemein-ästhetischen Grundlagen der Tonkunst kennen lernen (Hornbostel, 1905).

It is quite understandable therefore that Brazil did not have a Hornbostel, but instead a Mário de Andrade; Brazil never measured intervals, but attempted to listen carefully to them in their proper context. Brazil accomplished this in order, to discover itself for having remained unknown to its own population and to the rest of the world until the Word War II, and to contribute to the scientific methodology of a world discipline.

How did Andrade proceed to discover his country through cultural research at in the beginning of the 20th century? He travelled in the search of specificities and originalities, without separating categories such as the genuine and the "less unique" in advance. He was open to find anything, regardless of its supposed origin. In its utmost final consequences, discovering native culture expressions would lead to a higher ideal, to the invention of a nation. This was Andrade's and his contemporary modernist thinkers' goal.

The rise of a broad-based ethnomusicological research in Brazil came out of this general quest for the discovery and for the building of a nation by itself. At the same time there was the need to face a dilemma caused by modernity through the ongoing urbanization of the country. While the concern of Horbostel, first pronounced in 1905, regarded the danger of irrecoverable loss of musical manifestations around the world as a result of the contact with Western influences (Hornbostel, 1905), Andrade and his collaborators faced a more ambiguous situation: there was the need of documenting endangered manifestations of the country, although the final goal was not primarily to preserve them, but mainly to lay upon them in order to formulate cultural references of a new nation.

The 1930s and 1940s experienced the most impressive, multidisciplinary grounded research missions to the different corners of the country. Mario de Andrade himself, holding the position of the head of the Cultural Department of the municipality of São Paulo, organized a team under the designation of "Missão de Pesquisas Folclóricas" that travelled through different states of the Northeast Brazil filming, sound recording, photographs and protocols the main popular and traditional musical manifestations of the region. Although he did not participate himself in this mission, Andrade had previously carried out research in the Northeast of the country (Andrade, 1927). He was able to advise the team members in detail about their itineraries (CD SESC, cf. bibliography).

In technological terms, this mission inaugurated the era of magnetic field recordings in South America, by using the most advanced devices available at that time. From the musicological realm, the conceptual framework of the research was strongly centred on Constatin Brailoiu's *Esquisse d'un méthode de folklore musical* from 1930. An aesthetical input to the research motivation came from Andrade himself, who in 1928, had published his *Ensaio sobre a música brasileira*, a literary account to Brazil's musical traditions, and a manual not only for those who were interested to undertake musical research, but also to young composers as an aid to their search for a national art music.

In the United States, the term "musicology" was widely discussed first in 1915 (Reese, 1972). Likewise, in Latin America, up until the 1930s, "musicologia" was the subject that included *estudos musicais*, *historia da musica* or *estudos de folk-lore musical*. Even though, musicology and especially ethnomusicological research, existed before the terms "musicologia" and "etnomusicologia" were introduced. The same happens to the term "música tradicional" which also did not appear until the 1940s. "Estudos de Folk-lore" was the main research task of the team from São Paulo, as commented in 1938 chronicles.

In this same year, an important institutional foundation for musicology in Latin America was created by Francisco Curt Lange of the "Istituto Inter-Americano de Musicologia" in Montevideo. Francisco Curt Lange, born 1903 in Eilenburg, near Leipzig, in Germany, adopted the Uruguayan citizenship, while he lived and worked in different Latin American countries since 1927 (Uruguay, Argentina, Brazil, Venezuela). He was the only active musicologist on the subcontinent, who could be named among several prominent teachers as Erich Moritz von Hornbostel and Curt Sachs (Bispo, 1984). Curt Lange did research in historical musicology. He is responsible for a monumental work that, for the first time, shed light on a vivid and highly expressive and original musical life in colonial Latin America, almost in straight connection to clerical traditions between the 17th and the 19th centuries. In spite of this accomplishment, Lange expressed his interest in the ethnomusicological research. As editor of several periodicals and collective editions, he encouraged and published numerous ethnomusicological texts by his colleagues, among them Mário de Andrade's essay on the *Calunga* puppet in *Maracatu* music performance from Recife (Andrade, 1935). Lange was certainly one of the most prominent representatives of the 20th century musicological thinking in Latin America. In 1934, he gave lectures in São Paulo speaking with enthusiasm about his idea concerning an "Americanismo Musical", a joint musicological initiative for the whole of Latin America,[3] which he realized outside of the "Instituto Inter-Americano de Musicologia". Throughout his life Lange carried out restless and incomparable fruitful research activities that resulted in plenty of spectacular musicological discoveries.

Different premises for research in Latin America have to do with those who do ethnomusicology, but those who do ethnomusicology are not always ethnomusicologists in an official definition. The term arises only rather hesitantly in the 1970s.

Musicians, especially composers where among the first to document and analyse orally transmitted music in Latin America. It becomes evident, that composition and ethnomusicology always related one to another in different countries and diverse stylistic phases of music history in 20th century Latin America. Ana M. Ochoa refers to a large group of "sonic transculturators" in Latin America, among them musicians, folklorists and composers (Ochoa, 2005). Composers like Heitor Villa-Lobos or Mozart Camargo Guarnieri devoted themselves at least as students to the search of traditional sounds, both to study unknown materials as well as to get inspiration for own creative work; but also scholars that later became rather prominent in ethnomusicology often started as composers, like Argentinian born Isabel Aretz (…) or her Venezuelan husband Luis Felipe Ramón y Rivera (…).

In the decades between the 1930s and the 1960s, ethnomusicological research was mainly carried out within the framework of folklore studies, and the upcoming studies in popular music remained in the domain of historians, musical journalists, and even historical musicologists. Within this panorama, one name among Brazilian scholars must be mentioned. Luiz Heitor Correa de Azevedo (1905-1992) was this man gave the main impetus to the study of regional musical manifestations. As the head of the Unesco music department in Paris, he oversaw the music related matter in the entire Latin America. The Rio de Janeiro born Azevedo studied music in his hometown. As a young man, he wrote music reviews for the local newspapers. His interest also included the analysis of ethnographic documents from the National Museum; writing of an academic thesis on the scale of indigenous music (based on the 1937 field recordings of previously mentioned by Roquette Pinto. His discussion of the interchange nature of the Brazilian Indians culture and musical traditions, points to a conceptual dilemma that some decades later, would become again a concern in Lévi-Strauss "Le cru et le cuit" (1963). In 1941 Azevedo spent a sojourn in the US, where he met Alan Lomax. In 1943 Azevedo founded the "Centro de Pesquisas Folclóricas" at the Music School of the Federal University of Rio de Janeiro. In the same year he conducted a documentation field research trip intending to continue the efforts initiated by the "Missão de Pesquisas Folclóricas" before. Field recordings where made between 1942 and 1943 (CD Library of Congress, cf. bibliography).

Mário de Andrade and Luiz Heitor Correa de Azevedo are the most important scholars of early phase of ethnomusicology in Brazil. Whereas Mario de Andrade, the elder of the two, was an accomplished poet and cultural activist who never really invested in an academic carrier, was not a musicologist or ethnomusicologist, but the position of lecturer in music history at the "Conservatório Dramático e Musical de São Paulo". Luiz Heitor Corea de Azevedo, on the other hand, was more than a scholar devoted to the academy. His main interests were in the academically based musical science. He conducted musical analysis, based on field research methods, later named ethnomusicology.

	Mário de Andrade	Luiz Heitor Correa de Azevedo
Activities	Poet, music critic, cultural coordinator, music history etc.	Musicologist, music historian, researcher and field worker
Research	Essayist and coordinator of field documentation and data collection	Field worker and musicologist with analytical approach in one
Praxis	Little own recordings. Many own published transcriptions	Own field recordings, transcriptions and analysis
Intention	The search for National questions that go beyond music itself	Music research (pure) within academic concepts of a specific discipline (musical folklore and musicology).
Nacional institutions	Cultural Documentation, cultural politics and mediation with governmental support, without binding at an university	Academic oriented "Centro de Pesquisas Folclóricas" of the School of Music, Federal University of Rio de Janeiro
Internacional institutions	Contact by correspondence and exchange of materials with international institutions	Researcher and teacher of musicology and Brazilian music. Guest at North American institutions and universities, director of an Unesco affiliated Council and regular courses at French universities
Continuity	Discoteca Municipal, Oneyda Alvarenga	EM da UFRJ, *Dulce Martins Lamas*. IMC, IFMC
Dissertation or thesis	No academic thesis	Academic thesis with ethnomusicological focus on "Escala, melodia e ritmo da música indígena no Brasil" (1937)
Students and followers	Oneyda Alvarenga at the Discoteca Publica (Public Library) and Rossini Tavares de Lima (Museu do Folclore, SP)	Henriqueta Braga, Dulce Martins Lamas at the "Centro de Pesquisas Folclóricas"

Fig. 1: Mário de Andrade & Luiz Heitor Correa de Azevedo.

II .

In this section I will comment some approaches and orientations in Brazilian and Latin American ethnomusicology after the Andrade era, which is from 1945 on. The following brief remarks, which could easily be expanded to several more, will be limited to the following ten issues:

Music education
Musical anthropology
Afro-Brazilian specificities
Debate on ethnicity
Local hearing
Tropical sounds
World music
Cognitive questions
Applied ethnomusicology
Academic presence of ethnomusicology

Research orientation and goals addressed below can be distinct, behave antagonised, or combine in several ways. A number of the *modi operandi* and approaches discussed occur at the same time in different works or places, or get even together in the work and brain of a single researcher. Certain approaches can be abandoned, or be overtaken again somewhere else. Similar to the early phase of ethnomusicology in Brazil, also New Brazilian ethnomusicology – from the end of the 1970s on – is not characterized by unified methods or objects of study, not even represented only by ethnomusicologists in a narrow sense. Brazilian and also other music researcher in Latin American in general, belong to different and diverse fields of knowledge and have their own multiple backgrounds.

The educational concern - The worry with educational matters is as old as is musicology as academic discipline. In the first academic proposals on the goals of musicology by Guido Adler, musical education is also included (Adler, 1884). Besides the search for music as national expression, composers too dealt with music education. The composer Heitor Villa-Lobos was one of the main music educators in Latin America, responsible for large efforts in the formalization and the music education practice maintained by the State. With the support of the nationalist government of Getúlio Vargas, Villa-Lobos built up a national program for children education based on collective chant, which probably has no other parallel in the Americas (Lange, 1935). The composer was convinced that similar to the acquisition of language, children can only learn music in a lively way. They should sing and listen to music, before learning to read musical scores and music theory. Villa-Lobos was persuaded that musical education of Brazilian children would succeed best with musical folklore, their creative conscience to be trained musically with this traditional repertoire. Such a requirement would necessarily encourage research in traditional music from all over the country. In fact, music teacher in schools were among those who helped in collecting folklore for educational purposes. Villa-Lobos' enthusiasm for his program filled up soccer stadiums with up to thirty thousand school children, who sang in honour of the President or to commemorate the independence day (Oliveira Pinto, 1987). Despite its enormous repercussion, Villa-Lobos' "canto orfeônico" soon lost importance after his dead in 1959.

While Villa-Lobos' music education is originally found on the collection of orally transmitted music, arranged by the composer for children's choir, a completely differently organized program has become visibility in Rio de Janeiro in recent years through applied ethnomusicological research, where the goal of specific communities is to learn more about culture and society through research measures in with the own community (Araújo, 2006).

The importance of ethnomusicology in connection to music education in Brazil has more and more become evident at the annual meetings of the music educators association (ABEM) but also at the meetings of the national association for post-graduate studies in music (ANPPOM), where a significant portion of the presented papers from the 1990s on dealt with ethnomusicological matters. The very first concrete effort of creating a Brazilian Society for Ethnomusicology was articulated in such a meeting of music educators by the end of the 1990s and could finally come to concretion at the 38th World Conference of the International Council for Traditional Music (ICTM) in Rio de Janeiro, July, 2001.

The anthropological challenge – While musical folklore studies en vogue until the 1970s focussed the local view, different from the musicological approach that could get beyond the country, envisaging also a larger historical contexts – like for instance Curt Lange's research in an "Inter-American" comprehended music history – anthropology soon managed to cover both, the global and the local. This might be one of anthropology's main strategically contributions to ethnomusicology, which adopting its methods also became able to face local manifestations and to simultaneously set them in a broader context, at the same time that it contributed to the understanding of the transformations caused by global processes (see Erlman's [(1999] discussion about "global imagination", and for Latin America cf. Ochoa [2003]).

Social Anthropology in Brazil has a remarkable trajectory. The first department for anthropology was established in 1935 at the University of São Paulo and its curriculum was advised by Claude Lévi-Strauss, one of the first scholars to teach the subject in Brazil (Lévi-Strauss, 1953). Together with the institute for anthropology at the National Museum in Rio de Janeiro, anthropology from São Paulo has been responsible for the high quality training on post-graduate level of at least 75% of Brazilian social anthropologists. The field of Brazilian anthropologists is mainly inside the country. Anthropologists play an important advisory role in the government, orienting questions regarding Indian land and minority matters; but also in the countries actual socio-cultural debate, anthropology has a strong voice.

It is significant, that the first three monographs with a new ethnomusicological approach on Brazilian music appeared in the biennium 1978/79, having anthropologists as authors. The first is Rafael José de Menezes Bastos' *A Musicologica Kamayurá* (Bastos, 1978), an absolutely original account on the musical thinking of an Amazonian people. The second "breathtaking" study in this end of the 70s is Gerhard Kubik's *Angolan Traits in Black Music, Games and Dances of Brazil* (Kubik, 1979). Both studies, although different in approach and focus one from the other, entered the scene with completely new insights, and remained this past three decades far from loosing their importance and actuality. African elements in the musical interaction across the Southern Atlantic is also the subject of Kazadi wa Mukuna's *Contribuição Bantu na Música Popular Brasileira* (Kazadi, 1979). Different from the two previous, here aspects of popular music productions are also in the core of the authors' interest. Whereas books by Bastos and Kazadi are based on their theses in Social Anthropology, Kubik's book, published in Portugal, represents the first account of the author regarding his field research in Brazil in 1974, done under the perspective of his almost fifteen years of research experience in Africa.

The term ethnomusicology is not mentioned in these oeuvres. Bastos book has the subtitle: "A contribution to the anthropology of communication" (and not "ethnomusicology"!). Kubik always maintained a certain distance to the term, on the other side, to speak publicly of ethnomusicology was rare and would evoke question marks in Brazil of those days. In one of the initial chapters Bastos discusses ethnomusicology, defining it as an item belonging to anthropology, arguing this field should more precisely be understood as a musical anthropology (Bastos, 1978). Soon after the three mentioned books, another anthropologist who was teaching at the Museu Nacional in Rio, Anthony Seeger, published his first book *Os Indios e Nós* (The Indians and Us) in 1980. In the only chapter on music no reference is made to ethnomusicological methods or to the field as such (Seeger, 1980).

It is truly hard to find a book publication in Brazil discussing term and signification of ethnomusicology in the period until the end of the 1970s. One of it is João Baptista Siqueira's *Os Cariris do Nordeste* (Siqueira, 1978), a research on local culture of the Northeastern *cariri* people, with some incursions into music. For Siqueira, ethnomusicology is clearly the term for studies in primitive music (Siqueira, 1978). As we can see, the terminus was gaining space rather cautiously. Another two interesting articles on the tonal system of Xavante Indian traditional music by the anthropologist Desidério Aytai where published making explicit emphasis on ethnomusicological transcription and analysis. Aytai's research presents some influence from North American ethnomusicology of the 1960s and 1970s (Aytai, 1976, 1979).

The main innovation in methodological approach in the three mentioned music centred anthropological studies is the dissociation from merely sound descriptions as such, to the search for broader structural connections and to the cognitive level of musical manifestations. The surface level of tone production was abandoned in favour of the deepness of native musical theories and of intra and intercultural musical thinking, exemplarily demonstrated in Kubik's African pattern discussion as appearing in a new – the Brazilian– environment, or Bastos' discernment of a native sound concept that goes far beyond physical sound itself, when analysed within its different semantics and in connection to its social embeddings. The knowledge of linguistics and the conviction that language is the bearer of theory is common to the three of the above mentioned works. This might be responsible for the large step ethnomusicology did in Brazil in this phase, conveying really new insight to the plan and into discussion. This large stride forward was an important way for ethnomusicology in Brazil to start getting more visibility among the other human sciences.

The transatlantic connection – Under new perspectives the mentioned books of Kubik and Kazadi deal with the transatlantic connection between Brazil and Bantu-speaking Africa, but they were not the first to address this issue. After the pioneer studies on Afro-Brazilian religions by Nina Rodrigues (1910) and Arthur Ramos (1934) –with a few remarks on music and musical instruments– studies of the transatlantic connection where introduced by Herskovits in Surinam (1936) and later in Brazil (1941) and by Fernando Ortiz in the Caribbean, especially in Cuba (1950).

Among Brazilian folklorists Luiz da Camara Cascudo and Renato Almeida where the first to address questions and to formulate proposals for the interpretation of the presence of African music and dance elements in Brazil. Both scholars have also been to Africa, a fact that granted them distinction among other folklorists of their time (Cascudo, 1961; Almeida, 1962).

While social sciences have long remained flanked by the antagonist concepts of cultural contribution on one side and cultural resistance on the other to characterize the presence of African cultural heritage, or "roots", on Brazilian ground, Kubik proposes an entirely innovative argumentation, suggesting with reference to his in dept knowledge of African music, especially from Angola, that the presence of Africa in Brazil could rather be imagined as cultural "extensions":

> In my own approach I am unable to perceive African music merely as the "roots" of something else. I consider African music/dance forms as the products of people living in various African cultures which have changed continuously in history, absorbing and processing elements from inside and outside the continent, creating new styles and fashions all the time. Afro-American music then appears as a consequent and creative *extension overseas* of African musical cultures that have existed in the period between the 16th and 20th centuries.
>
> From this perspective Afro-American music cannot be described adequately in terms of "retentions" and "survivals", as if African cultures in the Americas were doomed from the outset and perhaps only by some act of mercy to "retain" certain elements (Kubik, 1979:8).

Gerhard Kubik is the first scholar to present solid examples from selected music genres, dance performances and organology, where African cultural "extensions" can be perceived in Brazil. His time-line-pattern concept for Brazilian *samba* opens the opportunity on behalf of an entirely reinterpreted view on the subject, since nothing comparable had been done in Brazil by folklorists or music historians regarding common pattern perceptions, music processes and common instrumental skills between Africa and Brazil. Kubik's main contribution was to demonstrate, that African cultural traits regarded as stable in their original settings, have been maintained in Brazil in their structural composition, but where reinterpreted according to the new environment in the New World (Kubik 1979, 1986, 1991). An example for this can be observed in the use of different African time-line-pattern in Brazil (cf. Oliveira Pinto, 1999).

Comprehended in this way, studies on *samba* and Afro-Brazilian performance would clearly deal with Brazilian expression, even if a number of components recall African structures, concepts, and instrumental proficiency, as they have been incorporated and re-signified. Going further, we can comprehend a coca-cola tin filled with rice as a "genuine" Afro-Brazilian musical instrument, from the moment on that it is used with the respective mental musical conception and struck according to specific performance patterns, a mental process that can occur in similar ways also in Africa (Oliveira Pinto,

1991). Research under this heading has been continued and substantially enlarged in the 1980s and 1990s (Kazadi & Oliveira Pinto, 1994; Oliveira Pinto, 1999; Kazadi, 1999).

The ethnicity / identity debate – The old debate on ethnicity and, related to it, on identity have experienced a phase of relative importance in Latin America, in different ways and forms. It is sufficient to note, that music, musical performance and its related genres have frequently been used to explain ethnic origins or ethnic identities. As a composer, devoted to the search for specificities in Brazilian musical forms from all social groups or from the most diverse parts of the country, Villa-Lobos is the one who tried to systematize ethnic affiliations in Brazil, in order to gain a better image of the whole of the nation's cultural identity. This experience, of course, didn't prospect, but it reflected a real concern from the 1930s to the 1950s. With his diagram on the different ethnic influences, Villa-Lobos aimed to stress "universal" roots of the music in Brazil (Villa-Lobos, 1939).

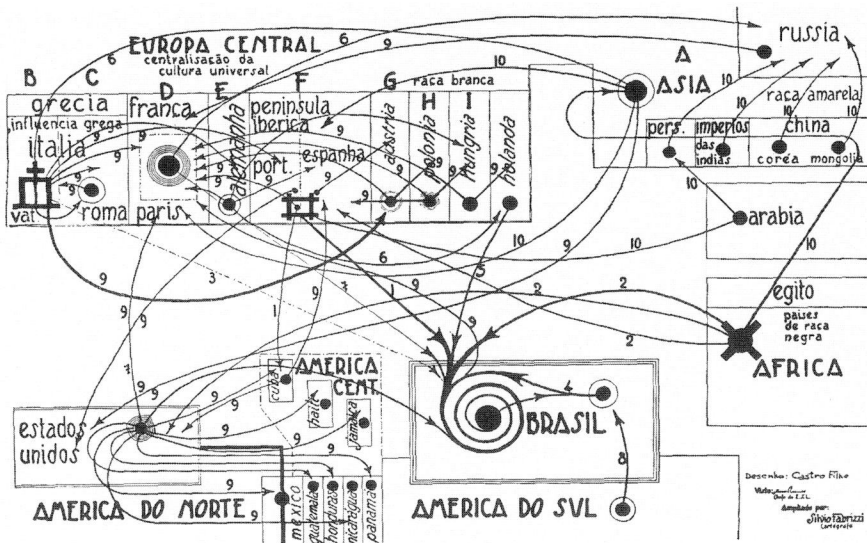

Fig. 2: Scheme of Villa Lobos: "Legenda do gráfico planisférico etnológico da origem da música no Brasil".

Today ethnicity as terminus is less in use than a few decades ago. It became complicated to detect ethnic filiations, even in connection to expressive culture. In Brazil anthropology moved towards to accept ethnic identities on the ground of the auto-identification of a group, and of the identification through the wider social context of this very group (Carneiro da Cunha, 1986). This has become particularly important for the recognition of land to indigenous groups, or to *quilombos* – the villages of descendents of escaped African slaves in the 18th and 19th centuries – and to any other auto-defined ethnic minorities. These processes always require the expertise of national anthropologists. The efforts of a determined social group, applying for a proper ethnic identity, are often enough emphasized by musical practices (cf. CD Encontro dos Tambores). While in these cases credit is given to difference, the lack of precisely defined so called ethnic boundaries induces concepts regarding miscegenation or evokes hypotheses on cultural hybridism, Africanisms, etc. Fact is, although, that the music in the Brazilian and other Latin American tropics most seldom evince a total blending of its different cultural elements. Vestiges of its origins remain intact as in few other domains of culture; no amount of mixing is able to completely dilute the marks and structures of the origin of the styles. Thanks to its own methodological approach, ethnomusicology is able to demonstrate to cultural studies in Latin America that music manages to be a manifestation of the present while continuing to simultaneously evince its past.

The Anthropology of Hearing – Hearing is allotted cultural importance in determined societies more than in others. The auditory perception that the indigenous people of the lowlands of South America have developed in relation to their natural and supernatural worlds is certainly very keen and highly refined. Based on his experience with the Marubo people from Rondonia, Guilherme Werlang stated that:

> … for certain indigenous peoples of Amazonia, music has a higher epistemological density than that of a structural-linguistic sign, i.e. the arbitrary designation of something that is beyond itself. The Amazonian Marubo, with whom I worked, designate their "music" as *saiti,* referring specifically to a festival where they perform myths in a specific musical form: their *saiti* "mythchants", the form that establishes the ontological origins of these peoples and those of the world where they live (Werlang, 2001).

Also among the Kamayurá from Upper Xingu, whose musical culture has been studied by Rafael José de Menezes Bastos since 1968, the notion of *ihu* is a general category that means "all the sounds," among which are found all the possible forms of perceiving and producing the universe by means of sound, from the breaking of a branch in the forest to the voices of rattles (*maraka*). These sounds occupy a predominant position in the sensorial culture of this Amazonian people.

Bastos shows in his work that the Kamayurá people from the Xingu river in Amazonia perceive sound as a category which is sofisticately differentiated in various levels. While *ihu* means the totally flow of sounds, this overal sound is the sum of many diverse sound and noise categories, where to be find also music by singing or by instrumental practice (Fig. 3). The author's main interest is to understand the "musico-logic" of this people.

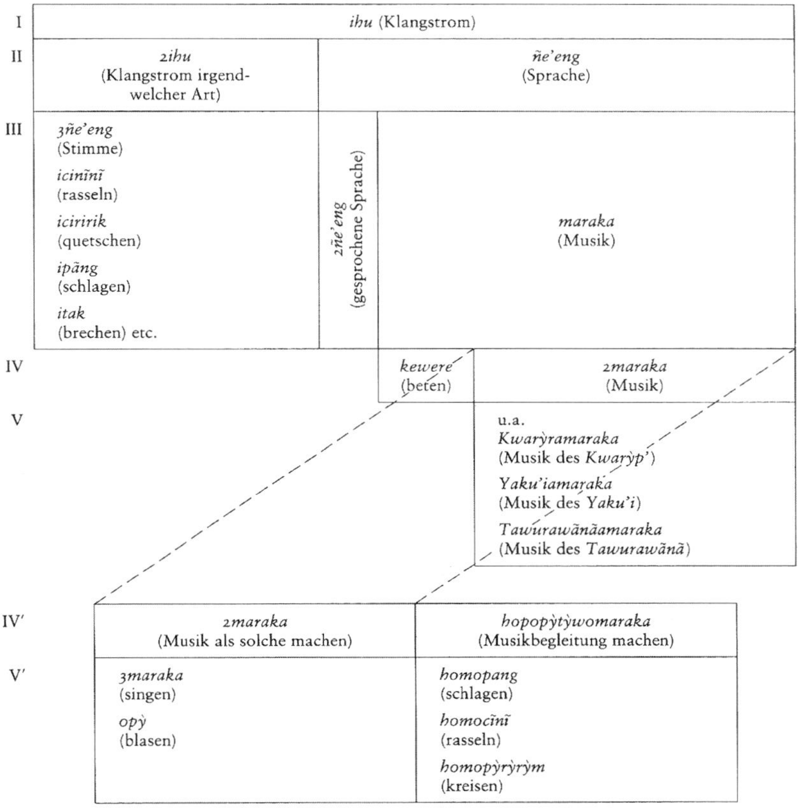

I	ihu (Klangstrom)		
II	2ihu (Klangstrom irgend- welcher Art)	ñe'eng (Sprache)	
III	3ñe'eng (Stimme) icinīnī (rasseln) iciririk (quetschen) ipāng (schlagen) itak (brechen) etc.	2ñe'eng (gesprochene Sprache)	maraka (Musik)
IV		kewere (beten)	2maraka (Musik)
V			u.a. Kwarỳramaraka (Musik des Kwarỳp') Yaku'iamaraka (Musik des Yaku'i) Tawurawānāamaraka (Musik des Tawurawānā)

IV'	2maraka (Musik als solche machen)	hopopỳtỳwomaraka (Musikbegleitung machen)
V'	3maraka (singen) opỳ (blasen)	homopang (schlagen) homocīnī (rasseln) homopỳrỳrỳm (kreisen)

Fig. 3: Native classification of Kamayura musical instruments (R. Menezes Bastos, 1978).

Inhabitants of the tropical forests really seem to hear in a different manner from the urban man. Raoni, a Kaiapó leader whom I accompanied traveling by boat down the Xingu River in the 1970s, could hear from far away when a capybara plunged from the riverbank into the water. The sound of the splash told him that it was this species, and not another kind of animal.

Distinguishing sounds that convey something within an auditory spectrum seems indeed to be a special skill of the indigenous cultures of Amazonia. I could experience this from 1996 to 1998 while engaged with a cultural reconstruction project among the Apalai from northern state of Para (Oliveira Pinto, 1996). When a group of young people from Apalai Village, of the Upper Parú gathered around a small transistor radio, all I could hear was a static noise, as though it were tuned to some station less point on the dial. However, the concentration of these Apalai youths piqued my interest, and I finally noted that there was a weak, almost unrecognizable signal, from a distant radio broadcaster. When asked what they were listening to, the Apalai youths explained, "it's Roberto Carlos". Untouched by the bad and almost unrecognizable noise from the little

329

radio, the young man had recognized the voice of this old and popular Brazilian singer. I myself would not have been able to do the same.

Tropical sounds and the World Music wave – After centuries of European projection concerning the tropics in Asia, Africa and Latin America, of expectations couched in the imaginary of what the exotic was or could be, there is a perceptible return to the auditory diversity committed with the sounds of nature, of the forest, the coastline, the mangroves, the strange timbres and the microtonalities, added to the fragments of speech, the noise of machines, of cities and airplanes. Many composers and intellectuals like Villa Lobos have already expressed the close relationship of their ouvre to the tropical nature. The sociologist from Recife, Gilberto Freyre, initiated an academic curriculum he called "tropicologia", believing that the Luso-African encounter in the Brazilian tropical environment had produced a specific, entirely new society (Freyre, 1936). In fact, the strongest impact of a Brazilian cultural movement around tropics was a musical one: "Tropicália" in 1968. Here the tropic makes itself heard through electric guitars, keyboards, loudspeakers, colors, rhythms and silence. These are sound and ideas, that arose metaphorically from the clichés of the past, irreverently assuming that everything within modernity's wide auditory spectrum, coupled with the sounds of the tropics, would be used for a musical response to the world. This movement characterized by manifestoes and appropriations of sounds has become one of the most innovating cultural and artistic movements not only in Brazil, but in all the tropics, for being founded in the idea of tropicality as a wide-ranging aesthetic expression. Reverting the worldwide tendency for the standardization of the sound of pop music, while significantly widening the diversity of sound, structure, style and timbre, has been Tropicália's great contribution. More than this, the free incorporation of elements alien to the pop repertoire, from vanguard, traditional, African and Oriental music anticipated World Music, which was to arise officially in Europe fifteen years later. With the great advantage of incorporating the timbres of other cultures, World Music follows the process laid out by Tropicália – from the tropics to the world – but in the opposite direction.

Although the listening to Brazilian musics, as done from abroad, was not always in tune with that of the few specialists in the country – remember the dispute between Mário de Andrade in Brazil and Marius Schneider in Europe– the believe in the pure and "natural" power of Brazilian sounds remained all over the 20th century. After being explored by comparative musicology in order to sustain universal scientific questions – questions never rose in Brazil – several musical styles of the country were expected as ideal natural resources to be used (and misused) for World Music purposes in the last decades of this very same century. This is why another form of "interest" in the music of Brazil has appeared at least since the end of the 2nd World War. Obviously, the fact that there is a place where musical "natural resources" are so varied and abundant as in Brazil, makes the country an interesting one for the music industry and for international artists as well. In exactly this sense Paul Simons "Rhythm of the Saints" is based on *bloco-afro* rhythms that the artist himself recorded in a live performance in the streets of Salvador. Another popular music star, Sting, has appeared in the early 90s in the Amazon rain forest, side by side with Kaiapó-Indians (amongst them also with my friend and former travel companion Raoni). Or remember the images of one of the latest video-clips of Michael Jackson captured in Rocinha, the biggest favela slum of Rio de Janeiro. They all benefited of this "natural music resources" Brazil has to offer.

Initially imprisoned in the wax cylinders of Edison's phonograph and in magnetic tapes, to be confined to collections, the sounds of Brazil and other tropical countries gained more and more space with the advance of the 20th century, finally abandoning the collections and hallowed halls of study to inhabit vinyl records, audio CDs and – marking the turn of the new millennium – MP3 players or down load files. Twentieth-century worldwide pop music would be unthinkable without the African offbeat, introduced to the globe through North American jazz and Latin American popular music.

Since sound is the main feature that determines world music (as a music industry category alone), this new development around world music is finally being detected and accompanied by an ethnomusicology in Brazil, through its own methods of listening and research.

The electronic era and the power of loudness – More than any other region, the tropics are characterized by discriminatory uses of the musical sounds. This is another challenge to local ethnomusicology. The difference for the 21st century is that globalization and the democratization of access to the means of mass communication has brought those who were once dominated, into positions of dominance, where they incorporate the ethnocentric prejudices of the former dominators; they impose tempered scales, harmonies of the most tonic-dominant elementary functionality through the oppressive acoustic resource of loudness, thanks to electronic technology, a strong ally of this process of domination.

The tape recorder, and later the radio and other equipment made sound more mobile, bringing it at close range; even when it originated in faraway places, the mobility of the sounds and noises became local. The "ghetto blaster" – the mobile sound equipment of the young people of the slums – brought the rap or funk music of one house, corner or block to another; mobile sound trucks blast advertisements for political candidates along the streets, and even private automobiles with their doors swung open, parked in the public squares of small towns and cities of the interior, with their volume turned up to the max, prove that in the tropics whoever has the loudest sound wields the power. This becomes especially evident through political propaganda short before elections, whereas sound is much more effective than other sensitive means (Fig. 4: photo of a "sound-car").

Fig. 4: Photo of a "sound-car".

Suggesting an "ethnomusicology of loudness", I have argued elsewhere, that one of the main differences between the regions of tropics and of the poles don't rest alone in the temperatures but also in the opposite noise propagation:

> There are elements such as the relation between sound and silence, which can also be essentially different from one region of the globe to another. Thus, the auditory continuum of the regions near the poles is precisely the opposite of that of the tropics: while here the silence breaks the nearly constant noisy flow, there it is the noise – of an avalanche of snow, for example – which interrupts the silence (Oliveira Pinto, 2008).

The cognitive question – Despite its insistent and noisy propagation, through the mentioned domination of loudness, the tonal system of the Old World is resisted in the Southern American tropics, for instance in the Brazilian Northeast or in Colombia. Several examples of this resistance to the diatonic scales include the interval of the neutral third used in northeast Brazil (located between the minor and major third), an "irrational" interval played by fife-and-drum bands, the so-called *bandas de pífanos*, and also in the sung cattle-herding calls of the cowboys in the hinterlands of Pernambuco. This principle has persisted despite modernization, and, oddly enough, it is not isolated – it lives together with a tonal repertoire as when, for example, a fife is accompanied by an accordion, or when in a local radio studio a fife band plays together with an electronic keyboard. One of the many questions which are being studied in recent years in regard

332

to this phenomena, points out that not "bi-musicality", in the sense given to the term by Mantle Hood (1971), is in the focus of investigation, but rather the phenomenon of "by-musicality", or "co-musicality" (Eira, 2006).

Applied ethnomusicology and research – Ethnomusicologists are often confronted with situations in which their social responsibility is requested. In this cases research means to help solving existing problems, extending as such the usual academic paradigms, by acting both inside and ahead of usual institutional frameworks.

Ethnomusicological knowledge can be used to influence social interaction. Practical results of the research and documentation work is based on the common efforts by the academic researcher and members of the community whose music is being documented. Not only a final result, but also the focus of the research, a proper development and involvement by people outside the academia is intended. The goals of the project are formulated together and in close agreement by all parts involved. At a more advanced stage of the research project the ethnomusicologist can even become dispensable, since the community might overtake the research by its own.

Community based ethnomusicological projects are coming more and more into evidence in Brazil in this new century. In Bahia, Francisca Marques (2005) is already carrying out documentation together with local community members from Cachoeira since 2001, who jointly built up a studio to mix and to make editions of sounds and programs for educational purposes and for the local radio broadcast. Theses efforts have gained recognition by UNESCO's educational program.

Another important endeavour in the sense to support citizenship to youths in peripheral communities in Rio de Janeiro with a high percentage mainly of drugs criminality has proved to be enormously efficient by encouraging self reflection and practical research (Araujo, 2006). These are only two of many examples, where ethnomusicology gives back at least some of its knowledge production to the interested communities.

The rise of national ethnomusicology and its academic presence – In quantitative matters the most important development of the past two decades undoubtedly refer to programs devoted to ethnomusicology at different universities in the country, what also fosters a stronger presence of ethnomusicology within the humanities and in the media. Also in qualitative matters we are much further. Without the increase of serious programs of ethnomusicology one would not explain the presentation of approximately 200 papers delivered at the 3rd Conference of the "Brazilian Ethnomusicological Association" (ABET) in São Paulo, in November 2006. At least 90% of the presented topics dealt with music in Brazil, delivered by scholars and students living, studying and researching in the country.[4]

But not only universities contribute to 21st ethnomusicology in Brazil. Other institutions like NGO'S and private archives, studios, broadcasting stations, dance houses, *sedes de agremiações*, or even Lan houses are occupying the "ethnomusiological space". Even indigenous villages in Amazonia or local festivals such as in *quilombos*, can nowadays quite obviously be transformed in ethnomusicological settings. The new information I got, is that the Xavante Indians from Pimentel Barbosa, Mato Grosso, opened their village for cultural tourism. In this very special case, musical performances will certainly play an important role, but under entirely redefined settings.

Many other approaches could have been listed and discussed, as, for instance, the linguistic contributions, the historiography of music, or the popular music studies, with a long tradition and a huge output in Latin America. Far from having come to a final conclusion, or to have numbered all important aspects in the history and in the present state of ethnomusicology in Latin America – especially stressed in this essay ethnomusicology in Brazil – I will end this section by summing up some relevant features that have become of prominent importance to ethnomusicological research in the Subcontinent:

1. First of all, not "what is music" is an important question, but what it is made for, what is the purpose behind its performance.
2. Instead of the objective analytical deconstruction of expression, the overall impression of the same comes mainly into the focus. Therefore, specific contexts evince that it makes more sense to get an impression of the broad meaning of the manifestation, than to stress the exclusive look to single elements it expresses.
3. Of interest is rather the authenticity of occasions than the singularity of the musical form per se. Questions deal first with the mix, caring less with the authenticity of single elements of this mix.
4. Instead of leaving behind the structures to look after their meanings, like in recent ethnomusicology abroad, the equal look on both aspects becomes important in Latin American ethnomusicology.
5. Folklore studies and, simultaneously, popular music interpretations are on the plan from the very beginnings of music research in Latin America.
6. Research: From the discovery of the own, to the contribution to the global.
7. Practitioners (composers, musicians etc): the appropriation of the global to the improvement of the own.
8. Recent ethnomusicological work brings the social dimension into a closer plan; therefore the research on communal musics is replaced by community based projects where, instead of scholarly rhetoric's, communal speeches gain new significance.
9. The practical use of documentation build up privately, or by different kinds of institutions, is as important as growing archives which stay mainly devoted to scholars and to academic research.

Outlook

One final aspect that can be mentioned, differentiating Brazil from many other countries, resides in the relation of its people to music. In a recent inquiry campaign published by the magazin *Isto É* we learn, that 66% of Brazilians are of the opinion that their music is the main subject to be proud of fascia the international community (*Isto É*, September, 2005). This percentage is even higher than the overall opinion about Brazilian soccer as a national argument for pride. But the most important fact about the inquiry on music is that it expresses an absolutely democratic view, since it reflects a consensus in all social classes, regions and among all age groups and genders. Here we certainly can recognize the most recent demand Brazilian ethnomusicologists face in their country, despite all the difficulties[5] that have overcome in the past one hundred years: because of the national esteem of music, our activities are becoming more and more acknowledged by a broader community of non-specialists, suggesting that we are far away from doing an exotic job, like, for instance, our colleagues in European countries, whose field of study is sometimes regarded to belong to the so-called "Orchideenfächer".

On the occasion of different jubilees – the 100 years of ethnomusicology in 2005, the 50th anniversary meeting of SEM on local developments of ethnomusicology, also in 2005, or the beginning of ethnomusicological fieldwork in Brazil one century ago in 1908 – my final statement is that work and thinking which differ from those from Anglo-American or European branches, must get more visibility in the scope of present day ethnomusicology, both from the content of a rich variety of expressions, as well as from the adopted approaches and gained insights of local, national, and even sub-continental "other ethnomusicologies".

The richness of our discipline is also the richness of different approaches, realized projects of documentation, goals and academic output. This is to say, that the history of ethnomusicology can not be less than the sum of many histories, one of them definitely to be found in South America. After having listened for almost a century to exotic – or "ex-acoustic" – sounds, it certainly remains one of the "world ethnomusicology's" main tasks in this dawn of the 21st century, to listen with a better care also to echoes which resound also from the sayings of those who live in midst and think about the soundscapes from afar.

Notes

[1] In 2005 we were confronted with several jubilees. Bruno Nettl reminded in the SEM Newsletter from May that year, that besides the 50 years of SEM, we have to commemorate 120 years since the break-through article of John Alexander Ellis "On the musical scales..." as a pioneer study for ethno-musicological thought. Timothy Rice, president of SEM in 2005, considered the issues that were important 25 years before for his society and how research improved from that time on. In my opinion, we have also to consider that our field of research, ethnomusicology, as a discipline, has completed 100 years of existence this year. I show the arguments and suggest this completely neglected anniversary in an article I wrote recently for the Brazilian Ethnomusicological Association (ABET).

[2] To give just an example: not even under the sub-title "other ethnomusicologies" in the entry ethnomusicology (Pegg et al., 2001) of Grove Dictionary of Musics and Musicians (Sadie, 2001) a single mention regarding Latin American ethnomusicology is made. Different from Africa and Asia as regions within this paragraph on "other ethnomusicologies", Brazilian or Latin American scholars simply are "not on the map" (Nettl, 2005) of an officially understood ethnomusicology.

[3] In a report in the Diário de São Paulo from November, 1934, Mário de Andrade informs about a lecture given by Curt Lange in the Conservatory. For him the 30 years old speaker belonged at that time already to "the most interesting figures of the American musicology" (Andrade, 1993:262).

[4] As a comparison, at the SEM 45th meeting in Toronto in 2000, approximately 200 papers were delivered.

[5] Speaking for Brazil, we have to consider some important aspects which brought difficulty to the ethnomusicological labour: twice a totalitarian regime in the 20th century, the language barrier (not only for us, but for the international scholarly community who had no access to our writings), different mentality and diversity of acting fields; last but not least also the lack of possibilities for earning a living through "pure" ethnomusicology.

Acknowledgements

The author expresses his gratitude to Kazadi wa Mukuna, who kindly read a previous version of this paper, making valuable comments. Thanks are also due to Samuel Araújo and Flavia Camargo Toni, who shared the session on Brazilian ethnomusicology at the 50th Conference of the Society for Ethnomusicology in Atlanta, November 2005.

References

Adler, Guido (1884) "Umfang, Methode und Ziel der Musikwissenschaft", *Vierteljahrschrift für Musikwissenschaft*, vol. 1: 5-20

Almeida, Renato (1962) "Caracterização do fato folclórico. A posição dos folcloristas brasileiros" *Jornal de Letras*, 14 (155)

Andrade, Mário de (1927) *O turista aprendiz*. São Paulo

Andrade, Mário de (1935) "A calunga dos maracatus", *Congresso afro-brasileiro 1*, Recife

Andrade, Mário de (1937) "O samba rural paulista", *Revista do Arquivo Municipal*, 4 (41), São Paulo

Andrade, Mário de (1993) "Prof. Curt Lange", *Música e Jornalismo: Diário de São Paulo*, São Paulo: Edusp, 262

Araújo, Samuel et al. (2006): "Conflict and Violence as Theoretical Tools in Present-Day Ethnomusicology: Notes on a Dialogic Ethnography of Sound Practices in Rio de Janeiro". *Ethnomusicology*, vol. 50, no. 2, 287-313

Aytai, Desidério (1976) "O sistema tonal do canto xavante" *Revista do Museu Paulista*, nova série, vol. XXIII, São Paulo: USP

Aytai, Desidério (1979) "O sistema tonal da música karajá" *Revista do Museu Paulista*, nova série, vol. XXV, São Paulo: USP

Bispo, Antonio A. (1984) "Francisco Curt Lange: 80 anos", *Boletim da Sociedade Brasileira de Musicologia*, no. 2, São Paulo

Cascudo, Luiz da Câmara (1961) *Made in Africa*. Rio de Janeiro

Carneiro da Cunha, Manuela (1986) *Antropologia do Brasil. Mito, história, etnicidade*. São Paulo: Edusp

Eira, Cristina (2006) *Historicidade e aculturação nas bandas-de-pífanos do Brasil*. MA project, São Paulo: USP

Erlmann, Veit (1999) *Music, Modernity and the Global Imagination: South Africa and the West.* New York and Oxford: Oxford University Press

Freyre, Gilberto (1936) *Casa Grande e Senzala*. Rio de Janeiro

Herskovits, Melville J. (1936) *Suriname Folk-Lore*. New York: Columbia University Press

Herskovits, Melville J. (1941) *The Myth of the Negro Past*. New York: Harper

Hornbostel, Erich M. von (1905) "Die Probleme der vergleichenden Musikwissenschaft", *Zeitschrift der internationalen Musikgesellschaft*, vol. 7 / 3: 85-97

Hornbostel, Erich M. von (1928) „Die Maßnorm als kulturgeschichtliches Forschungsmittel", W. Koppers (ed.) *Festschrift P. W. Schmidt*. Vienna

Kazadi wa Mukuna (1979) *Contribuição Bantu na Música Popular Brasileira*. São Paulo: Global (3rd ed. 2007)

Kazadi wa Mukuna (1999) "Ethnomusicology and the Study of Africanisms in the Music of Latin America". J. Codgell DjeDje (ed.) *Turn up the Volume. A Celebration of African Music*, Los Angeles: UCLA

Kazadi wa Mukuna & Oliveira Pinto, Tiago de (1990) "The Study of African Musical Contribution to Latin-America and the Caribbean: A Methodological Guideline", *Bulletin of the International Committee on Urgent Anthropological Research*. Vienna

Koch-Grünberg, Theodor (1923) *Vom Roraima zum Orinoco*. Stuttgart:

Kubik, Gerhard (1979): *Angolan Traits in Black Music, Games and dances of Brazil. A study of African cultural extensions overseas*. Lisboa: Junta de Investigações Científicas do Ultramar

Kubik, Gerhard (1986),"Afrikanische Musikkulturen in Brasilien", T. de Oliveira Pinto (ed.): *Brasilien. Einführung in Musiktraditionen Brasiliens*, Mainz etc: Schott

Kubik, Gerhard (1991) *Extensionen afrikanischer Kulturen in Brasilien*. Aachen: Alano

Lange, Francisco C. (1935) "Villa-Lobos, un Pedagogo-Creador", *Boletin Latinoamericano de Musica*, vol. 1, Montevideo

Lévi-Strauss, Claude (1953) *Tristes Tropiques*. Paris: Gallimard

Marques, Francisca (2004): "O samba de roda na Festa da Boa Morte: Entre o ritual e o divertimento das mulheres negras baianas". *Sinais Diacríticos* no. 2, São Paulo: SOMA - USP

Menezes Bastos, Rafael J. (1978) *A Musicológica Kamayurá. Para uma antropoloia da comunicação no Alto-Xingu*. Brasília: Funai

Menezes Bastos, Rafael J. (1986), "Die Musik der Kamayura", T. de Oliveira Pinto (ed.): *Brasilien. Einführung in Musiktraditionen Brasiliens*, Mainz etc: Schott

Nettl, Bruno (2005) "A Year of Anniversaries", *SEM Newsletter*, 39 / 3: 5

Nina Rodrigues, Raimundo da (1903) "O problema da raça negra na América Portuguesa", *Jornal do Comércio*. Rio de Janeiro

Ochoa, Ana Maria (2003), *Musicas locales en tiempos de globalización*. Bogotá: Editorial Norma

Ochoa, Ana Maria (2006), "Purification and the Aural Public Sphere in Latin America", *Social Identities*, Vol. 12, Issue 6, p. 803 - 825

Oliveira Pinto, Tiago de (1986): *Brasilien. Einführung in Musiktraditionen Brasiliens*, Mainz etc: Schott

Oliveira Pinto, Tiago de (1987) " 'Art is Universal' - On Nationalism and Universality in the Music of Villa-Lobos", *The World of Music*, vol. 24 (2), Wilhelmshaven, 104-116

Oliveira Pinto, Tiago de (1991): *Capoeira, Samba, Candomblé. Afro-Brasilianische Musik im Recôncavo, Bahia*. Berlin: Reimer.

Oliveira Pinto, Tiago de (1994) "Local Thoughts on Global Music", Womex '94, Berlin

Oliveira Pinto, Tiago de (1996) "The Discourse about Other's Music: Reflecting on African-Brazilian Concepts", in *African Music. Journal of the International Library of African Music*, vol. 7, no. 3, Grahamstown

Oliveira Pinto, Tiago de (1999): As cores do Som. Estruturas sonoras e concepção estética na música afro-brasileira. In: *Revista África* (22 / 23): 87-110.

Oliveira Pinto, Tiago de (2005) "Cem anos de Etnomusicologia e a 'era fonográfica' da disciplina no Brasil", A. Lühning (ed.) *Etnomusicologia: lugares e caminhos, fronteiras e diálogos. II Encontro Nacional da ABET.* Salvador: UFBA

Oliveira Pinto, Tiago de (2006): "The Invention of Brazil: The Ethnography, Folklore and Musicology of Mário de Andrade". T. de Oliveira Pinto & M.Izabel Ribeiro (ed.) *The Idea of Brazilian Modernismo.* Berlin, New York, London: LIT, 128-151

Oliveira Pinto, Tiago de (2008) "'Crossed Rhythms': African structures, Brazilian practices, and Afro-Brazilian meanings", I. P. Rheinberger & T. de Oliveira Pinto (eds.): *AfricAmerica. Itineraries, Dialogues, and Soundscapes.* Madrid, Frankfurt: Vervuert

Ortiz, Fernando (1950) *La africania de la música folklórica de Cuba.* Habana

Ramos, Artur (1934) *As culturas negras no Novo Mundo.* São Paulo: Ed. Nacional

Reese, Gustav (1972) "Perspectives and Lacunae in Musicological Research: Inaugural Lecture", B. S. Brook (ed. et al.) *Perspectives in Musicology.* New York: Norton

Roquette Pinto, Edgard (1917) *Rondônia.* Rio de Janeiro

Sandroni, Carlos (2001*): Feitiço decente. Transformações do samba no Rio de Janeiro (1917-1933).* Rio de Janeiro: Zahar

Schneider, Albrecht (1976) *Musikwissenschaft und Kulturkreislehre.* Bonn: Orpheus-Verlag

Seeger, Anthony (1980) *Os índios e nós.* Rio de Janeiro

SESC (2006) *Responde a roda outra vez. Música tradicional de Pernambuco e da Paraíba no trajeto da Missão de 1938.* São Paulo (CD and booklet)

Siqueira, João Baptista (1978) *Origem do Termo Samba.* Rio de Janeiro: MEC

Villa-Lobos, Heitor (1939) "A música: fator de comunhão entre os povos", *Anuário Brasileiro,* no. 3

Weber, Michael (1990) *Eine andere Musikwissenschaft.* Frankfurt/Main: Peter Lang

Werlang, Guilherme (2001), *Emerging Peoples: Marubo Myth-Chants.* Phil.Diss. University of St. Andrews

Wolff, Marcus (2007) "Entrevista com Samuel Araújo*", Etnomusicologia Online,* no.2, Salvador: UFBA

Ziegler, Susanne (2006) *Die Wachszylinder des Berliner Phonogrammarchivs.* Berlin: Ethnologisches Museum

Jukka Louhivuori

Lutheran Hymn Singing in African context
Lobe den Herren, den mächtigen König der Ehren vs. Reta Morena wa matla!

Background

Change in music was one of the major topics at the beginning of last century among folk music researchers and later music anthropologists and ethnomusicologists (Koller 1902, Krohn 1902-1903, Roberts 1925, Densmore 1930, Poladian 1942, Dincsér 1947, Elscheková 1975, Freeman 1956). The reason for interest in this topic was connected to the findings of researchers who had collected huge amount of folk songs. Many of the melodies were found in different shapes (variants, tune families etc.), and it was not at all clear which melodies should be described as being the "same" or variants or which belong to the same tune family. Another question was about the origin of melodies and how melodies change in time. Hundreds of articles have been published about these topics, but still today the questions of change and similarity in music is relevant. Especially the rapid development in music information retrieval has kept researchers active in these topics (Typke 2007, Deliege 2007).

Although the questions of change in music and similarity of melodies are still relevant, the focus of researchers has changed from the description of melodic changes towards attempts to understand the phenomena from the point of view of cognitive processes. Instead of trying to answer questions like: "which parameters in music are sensitive to change, and what remains untouched?", researchers are more interested for example in how musical change and perception of similarity can be understood from the cognitive point of view: how the functions of human mind could explain musical change and perception of similarity (Selfriedge-Field 2004, Eerola et al. 2001.)

Another approach, more oriented towards ethnomusicology, looks at musical change from cultural point of view: what is the role of culture in musical change, what happens when a musical piece, for example a tune, is transferred from one culture to another. Is there any regularity in how cultural similarities or differences are reflected in a transformation process? (Merriam, 1955 and 1964.)

In this article, one European hymn melody "Lobe den Herren, den mächtigen König der Ehren" has been taken as a "test tune". The aim is to analyse what has happened to this well-known European hymn when adapted by South African singers (hymn "Reta Morena wa Matla!"), and to look at how South African traditional music, and music culture in general may have influenced the shape of it. In addition to musical parameters also interpretation praxis will be compared.

Change in music – early studies

Although it became very soon clear that almost every parameter in music is open to change, such as rhythm, melody, scales, intonation, structure, timbre, etc. (Wiora 1941, 193, 195), differences between musical parameters about their sensitivity to change were reported: musical deep structures (scales, intonation, melodic contour, meter) did not change as much and quickly as surface structures (melody, ornamentation, rhythm). For example, Densmore found out at the beginning of the last century that most differences between variants were found in structurally unimportant notes (Densmore 1918, 51). Suppan mentioned that the ends of phrases and structurally strong notes were stable (Suppan 1964, 20). This was also the main finding of Krohn, who based his classification system of melodies on structurally strong notes inside phrases and on phrase endings (cadences) (Krohn 1899). Inspired by the Gestalt psychology some researchers analysed melodic contours and found out that melodic contours did not change a lot, although single pitches can be unstable. Ling and Jersild applied statistical methods, and they found out that the relative frequency of occurrence of certain pitches remain stable (Ling and Jersild 1965, 104).

Although some disagreement existed between the findings of researchers, some agreement could be found: musical parameters are not equally related to their sensitivity to change; basically every parameter can change, but deep structures are more stable than surface structures.

The opinion of some authors was that actually more interesting than change in music is what is not changed (Blacking 1977, 6). Other researchers pointed out that also musical genres differ in their sensitivity to change. Ritual and spiritual music was believed to be more stable than secular and especially popular music. The argument was that the more music is related to the basic values of the society, the more music stays untouched (Blacking 1977, 5). Changes in religious music may reflect significance changes in theological thinking and values of the society. This argument is of special interest from the point of view of the present article, because the topic is about religious tunes (Lutheran hymns).

Nettl discussed how cultural identity might be connected with musical change. He argued that special characteristics of music could be important for the identity of people. These special characteristics in music might be glued so deep into the minds of people that they stay untouched although other aspects in music would be changed. (Nettl 1964, 234.)

Nettl was interested also in the direction of change. He argued that music changes towards increasing specialization. The problem of the direction of change becomes more relevant when we think about how cultures influence each other. According to Nettl, cultures that are close to each other become more similar through assimilation. (Nettl 1964, 234-235.) In addition to assimilation, acculturation is one of the key concepts related to change in music. What happens when two cultures are in touch with each other? What are the preconditions without which acculturation won't happen? Cultures take features from each other the easier the more they have similarities (Nettl 1964, 172).

It is not clear if minor groups might have a strong influence on the culture of major groups. John Blacking argues that the key point is not if cultures have contacts with each other or not. The question is more about individuals, key persons, who make decisions about what aspects they accept and assimilate into their musical style (Blacking 1977, 12). If this is the case, major cultures may take some special aspects of minor groups because of certain key individuals in the society who make decisions about acceptances or rejections. Even single persons can have a crucial role in accepting or rejecting unfamiliar influences from other cultures, and thus are influencing cultural change.

Research design

Lutheran hymns and religious music in general give an especially interesting possibility to study change in music. One reason for the benefits of hymns as test material is the fact that their history is often well documented. In most cases we know the composer and even have an access to the original handwriting.

From social and cultural point of view hymns are worth of studying, because societies give often special attention to hymns: they are related to religious rituals and other cultural habits that are important expressions of the values in society. Thus, it is not unimportant for people how hymns are sung and in what shape they appear. Many examples could be given how sensitive people are in this respect. In Finland, discussion continues about the changes of hymn melodies that were made more than twenty years ago, in 1986: people are still arguing about the melodic and textual changes made to the hymns that were close to them, especially Christmas carols.

An interesting and useful fact for researchers is that missionaries have carried out hymns to many cultures around the world. This gives a very special opportunity to make cross-cultural comparisons, and to see for example what is the influence of culture into changes of melodies.

In this article a well-known hymn "Lobe den Herren, den mächtigen König der Ehren" by Joachim Neander (1650-1680) is chosen as a test hymn. The aim is to compare the shape of the hymn and hymn singing style in South African and European context.

The hymn was videotaped from seven singers in Limpopo province, Sekhukhune area. In addition to the analyzed hymn they sang five other hymns from the local hymnbook (Difela tsa kereke, 2005) (Appendix 1).

The abovementioned hymn was chosen to be analyzed more carefully because it contains from analytical point of view several useful features: The hymn has both upwards and downwards stepwise melodic movements, which gives a good opportunity to measure intonation practices. Both European and South African singers know this hymn well and it represent a hymn that belongs to the basic repertoire of the singers.

Although solo singing is not the most natural singing context for hymns, it gives an ideal condition for measuring intonation. Because of the "unnatural" context of solo singing the hymn was recorded as a group singing act as well. In addition to group singing I have had an opportunity to record the hymn during Sunday service in its natural singing context in Pretoria (St Paul's Lutheran Church, Mamelodi).

Edward Lebaka videotaped the hymns in the Catholic Centre located in Schoonoord (Limpopo, Sekhukhune, see the map in Appendix 5) in March 2002. None of the singers are professional musicians, but two of them are music teachers, and one acts as a church elder.[1]

Lutheran hymns in South African context

Historical and cultural background

The first group of missionaries of the Berlin Missionary Society arrived to South Africa in 1834 (Boshoff 2004, 447). This article deals with hymn singing in Limpopo province (see map in Appendix 5), that is north from the area where the first Berlin missionaries

---

[1] Sound exerpts of the analyzed singing acts can be heard in the www-site: http://www.jyu.fi/~louhivuo/RetaMorena

341

started their missionary work. In addition to Limpopo area, I have recorded hymn singing in other areas as well, mainly in Pretoria. In Limpopo province, the most influential group of missionaries have been Germans belonging to a group called Berlin Missionary Society. This group was, from a dogmatic point of view, strict; for example, the use of drums in service was not allowed. Only in recent times the use of drums has become more acceptable. First mentions of the Berlin mission's influence in Limpopo are from the late 19th century. In addition to Lutheran missionaries also Catholic, Anglican and other Christian movements and sects have influenced the lives of people in Limpopo province.

Most of the people living in the area where the recordings have been made (Sekhukhune) belong to Pedi people. The Pedi are people living in the Limpopo province, in an area bordered by the Limpopo Vaal and Komati Rivers. They have their own language, Pedi, also known as Northern *Sotho* (*sepedi*). The music of the Pedi people consists of call and response singing and drumming, including polyrhythms that arise both in the accompaniment and in its relation to the singing (Kaemmer 1998). The national dance of the Pedi is the *Dinaka* (Pedi reed pipes), which involves the rhythmic movement of the legs and drumming to the music of end-blown pipes with different pitches (pentatonic or heptatonic scale) played in *hocket* –i.e., with the individual tones of a melody alternating between different players in close succession (Kaemmer 1998). Sometimes the spectators support the performers by hand clapping. The musical scale used appears to be basically pentatonic (Barz 2003) although Blacking (1970) has characterized the music of the neighbouring *Venda* people as strongly diatonic. However, this may be a result of Christian missions, which have had a strong influence on African music in general (Kaemmer 1998, 718): the missionaries brought with them Christian hymns and military music, and they often translated the hymns into African languages while disparaging the use of African music (Kaemmer 1998, 716).

The influence of the Christian missionaries has been quite complex. The elements they brought blended with indigenous southern African music and formed the *makwaya*, meaning choral singing that uses formalized western four-part harmonization and tempered intervals (Coplan 1998 and 2003).

Hymn books and singing practice

In South Africa several different hymnbooks are in use. Because of the twelve official languages, the hymnbooks must contain hymns translated at least for the most commonly used languages. It is a common practice, that people from different cultural and linguistic background are present in the same service. Because of this fact, the cantor tells before the singing act the number of the hymn in different languages. Hymns are often sung simultaneously in many languages. It was interesting to observe that sometimes the priest may give his sermon in many languages by continuously changing the language in every few minutes. People are able to follow the content of the talk although the language changes, because short periods of foreign languages are not too long for preventing people to follow the main idea of the sermon.

Hymnbooks contain four part harmonisations of the hymns in tonic sol-fa (Appendix 2). Sometimes people sing the hymns using tonic sol-fa syllables instead of the original lyrics of the song. The explanation I was given was that this helps some people to sight read hymns that are not familiar for them.

Traditional beliefs and Christianity

Although Christianity has had a strong influence on Pedi culture, traditional beliefs still have an important role in people's lives. Edward Lebaka mentioned during our discussion, that "Pedi people are Christians during the daytime and during the nights they walk to sanatoriums and practice traditional beliefs".

The role of traditional healers in the society is still strong and healing methods are practiced weekly in Sekhukhune area. According to Lebaka, "This form of communication is still dominating. It appears that the Pedi, in addition to linear historical time with its commencement and termination, are aware of a Great Eternal Time. From this Great Eternal Time all life originates and to this Great Eternal Time it returns. This concept of time, as perceived by the Pedi, is related to their ancestor-worship. Man stands between the Great Eternal Time and linear time." "It would perhaps be better to say that there are many aspects of Pedi religion. This includes for example the belief in a creator God through ancestors. There is also the belief in the ancestors and ritual action (e.g. making offerings to the ancestors)". (Lebaka 2001).

The aim of this article is not to argue that Pedi traditional beliefs would have a direct influence on hymn singing. Instead of looking at the influence of doctrines the main aim of this article is to see how for example typical scales, rhythmic patterns and melodic structures of Pedi traditional music may influence the shapes and singing style of Lutheran hymns.

Changes in musical parameters

In this chapter comparisons will be made between the European version of the hymn "Lobe den Herren, den mächtigen König der Ehren" by Joachim Neander (1650-1680) and variants found in South Africa. Comparisons are made about melody, scale, intonation, meter, rhythm, harmony, vibrato, body movements, usage of instruments, and interpretation practice.

Melody. The melody of the hymn "Lobe den Herren, den mächtigen König der Ehren" is only slightly changed by one singer in solo singing situation. The difference can be found in bars 4 and 12. The melodic movement is the same in both bars: ascending movement from the sixth degree towards the first degree (tonic). In variants a and b the leading note is replaced with the first degree (tonic; see figure 1, bars 4 and 12). In group singing the leading note in the bar 15 is replaced in the same way (variant a).

Fig. 1. European version from Finland ("Kiitos nyt Herran") of the hymn "Lobe den Herren, den mächtigen König der Ehren", and two variants with minor melodic changes.[2]

It is noteworthy that in group singing the singers used a different variant compared with solo singing version. In group singing, only that variant was used in which the leading note is replaced by repeating the tonic. In solo singing, only one of the singers used this variant. In group singing just a few of the singers sang the hymn melody, because in this situation some of the singers improvised new melodic lines for harmonizing purposes. In solo singing the singers were not consistent: sometimes they used the leading note, and sometimes they didn't.

---

[2] The European version is from the Finnish hymn book from 1986, no. 329 ("Kiitos nyt Herran!"; compare the German version of the hymn in Appendix 4).

Reta Morena wa Matla!

Group singing act in Sekhukhune, Schoonoord 2002

Fig. 2. Harmonized version of the first cadenza in group singing situation.

The use of the variant in group singing may be seen as an example of how traditional way of harmonizing hymns "forces" the singers to make changes in the melody, although the singers know the "correct" version of the hymn melody. Because of the harmonizing practice in group singing situation the singers change the melody to make it fit better with the underlying harmony.[3]

   It is also noteworthy that in the descending melodic movement the leading note appears just as in the original version of the hymn (bar 3). Thus, the leading note is missing only in the ascending melodic line. The same phenomenon can be heard in the group singing.

   The question of harmonization hymn melodies in South Africa is a separate research topic, and should be more carefully studied.

Scale and intonation. The question of the missing leading note can be studied from another point of view as well, by looking for typical Pedi scales. As mentioned above, a typical scale in Pedi culture is pentatonic, but because of the influence of Venda people

---

[3] The harmonies used in the hymnbook are written in tonic solfa (Appendix 2). Tonic solfa notation is transcribed into staff notation in Appendix 3.

also the heptatonic scale is known. In both scales, the leading note is missing. In figure 3, intonations used by a few African tribes in heptatonic, hexatonic and pentatonic scales are described (Tracey 1958, 19).

TYPICAL AFRICAN SCALES

HEPTATONIC SCALES				HEXATONIC SCALES				PENTATONIC SCALES			
1. *Chopi.* (43-125) Moçambique		2. *Bemba.* (L2W-9) N. Rhodesia		3. *Ndau.* (CMR-46) S. Rhodesia		4. *Kanyoka.* (L3D-1) S. Congo		5. *Soga.* (F3P-6) Uganda		6. *Yogo.* (F4H-15) N. Congo	
Vs.	Cents.	Vs.	Cents.	Vs.	Cents.	Vs.	Cents.	Vs.	Cents.	Vs.	Cents.
504	1200	280	1200								
	173		182	736	1200	392	1200			448	1200
456	1027	252	1018		285		309	520	1200		267
	193		143	624	915	328	891		197	384	933
408	834	232	875		115		201	464	1003		190
	179		173	584	800	292	690		257	344	743
368	655	210	702		175		201	400	746		237
	157		173	528	625	260	489		221	300	506
336	498	190	529		136		139	352	525		248
	173		192	488	489	240	350		254	260	258
304	325	170	337		243		119	304	271		258
	168		172	424	246	224	231		271	224	0
276	157	154	165		246		231	260	0		
	157		165	368	0	196	0				
252	0	140	0								

Fig. 3. Typical African scales and intonations measured by Hugh Tracey (1958, 19).

As can be seen from the figure 3 the second degree in pentatonic scale is much higher compared with the height of the second degree in tempered scale. The use of the high second degree by the singers in Sekhukhune may thus be a reflection of the pentatonic scale commonly used in Pedi traditional music.

In addition to the high second degree some of the singers use a very low third degree. In some cases (singers B and F) the intonation is almost exactly between a major and a minor third (that is, yielding a neutral third). Other singers also use intonation which results in a pitch between major and minor third (see table 1). The use of a neutral third may be a reflection of traditional intonation practices of Pedi people, but this argument needs to be more carefully studied.

In table 1 different ways of the seven singers to intonate descending melodic movement from the fifth to the third degree (minor third) and from the second to the first degree (major second) are described. In figure 4, the places (notes, intervals) of intonation measurements are indicated.

Reta Morena wa Matla!

Original hymn

Neutral third (ca 350 c)   Missing leading note   High second (ca 250 c)

Variant

O H

Missing leading note   Missing leading note   High second (ca 250 c)

V

Fig. 4. Intonation measurements have been made of the interval between the third and fourth note (minor third; c – a), of the leading note in ascending melodic line (bar 4, second note; bar 12, third note), and of the second degree in the cadence of the first and last phrases (major second; g – f). Equal-tempered intonation of the major third would be 400 cents, minor third 300 cents, major second 200 cents, and minor second 100 cents.

Singer	Cents (c-a)	Cents (g-f)
A	378	252
B	350	252
C	360	217
D	341	221
E	341	270
F	357	274
G	315	260

Table 1. Different ways of the singers to intonate the descending minor third from the fifth to the third degree of the scale (F-major: c-a), and the second degree (F-major: g-f) in cadence melodic movements (at the end of the first phrase f-g-f; at the end of the last phrase a-g-f).

As can bee seen in table 1, intonation varies a lot: the difference between largest and smallest third is 63 cents. Most of the singers use a very large descending minor third (c-a), which is in most cases between major and minor third (neutral third, ~350 cents). Closest to the equal-tempered intonation is the singer G, who uses a minor third of 315 cents.[4]

Intonation of the second degree of the scale is often very high, only the singers C and D are quite close to the equal-tempered intonation (C: 217 cents, D: 221 cents). Other singers use a much too wide second which is between minor third (300 cents) and major second (200 cents). Difference between the largest (widest) and smallest (narrowest) major second is 57 cents.

---

[4] The intonation practices of the singers were analyzed with Praat (version 5.0). An interval of 315 Cents corresponds to a just minor third (frequency ratio 6/5, 316 Cents).

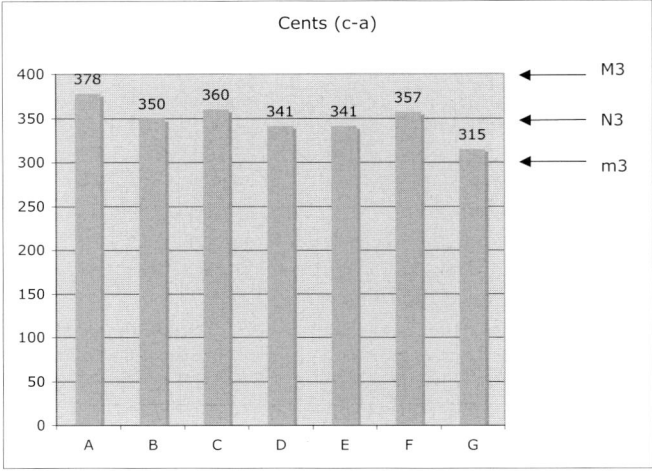

Fig. 5. Intonations of the descending minor thirds compared with equal-tempered values. M3 = Equal-tempered Major third, 400 cents; N3 = Equal-tempered neutral third, 350 cents; m3 = Equal-tempered minor third, 300 cents.

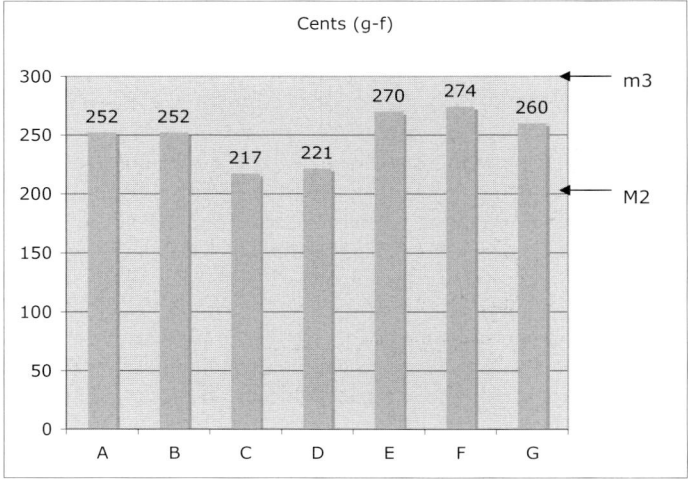

Fig. 6. Intonations of the major second compared with equal tempered intonations. M2 = Equal tempered Major second, 200 cents; m3 = Equal-tempered minor third, 300 cents.

From the figures 5 and 6, it can be seen how close the intonation practice of the singers is to the pentatonic scale measurements in table 1. The missing leading note may be explained by the influence of the pentatonic scale commonly used in Pedi culture. Why the leading note is missing only in ascending melodic movements can't be explained as easily. The relationship between the direction of the melody and intonation or scale systems in general should be studied more carefully.

Meter and rhythm. Meter is not changed very much, and also rhythm remains almost untouched. The only difference noticed was the style in group singing to stress almost every single note. This is more about interpretation practice, but can be interpreted as a reflection of a different way of understanding meter in South African context. Instead of a smooth and fluctuating way of singing, the hymns are thought to be sung in a steady meter. This argument is supported by the fact that the way of singing is changed when the singers start singing Lutheran hymns instead of traditional hymns (*makwaya*). In Lobethal, the church elder who was leading hymn singing during the service, started to conduct and to count loudly measure numbers when the congregation started to sing Lutheran hymns. Instead of a floating way of singing a more strict and stiff way of singing is thought to be the right way to sing; counting loudly helps to sing in steady meter.

Vibrato. A clear difference between European and South African ways of using vibrato can be heard in the Sekhukhune area. Differences in vibrato can be compared with the different styles of making vibrato in violin playing: Sekhukhune vibrato is close to so-called bow vibrato, which is made by regularly changing the bow pressure instead of moving (swinging) the finger smoothly up and down on the finger board. The effect of this kind of vibrato is very different from the vibrato used by European hymn singers, but actually not so far for example from jazz musicians' way to produce it.

In the vibrato of the singers F and G the difference can be seen clearly. In most cases they use typical European vibrato, but on some occasions they change into a vibrato style which is closer to diaphragmatic vibrato. In figures 7 and 8, respectively, two different kind of vibratos can be compared. In figure 7, the start of the vibrato goes in asynchrony with the frequency. In figure 8, the vibrato is very wide: actually between a fourth and a fifth (550 c). Vibrato used by Pedi people in Sekhukhune is close to dia-phragmatic vibrato, in which the diaphragm pulsates during a sustained tone (Seashore 1932, Sundberg 1987). In figure 9 another example is given for typical Pedi vibrato, which is fast, narrow in frequency modulation, and in which amplitude and frequency are in asynchrony.

349

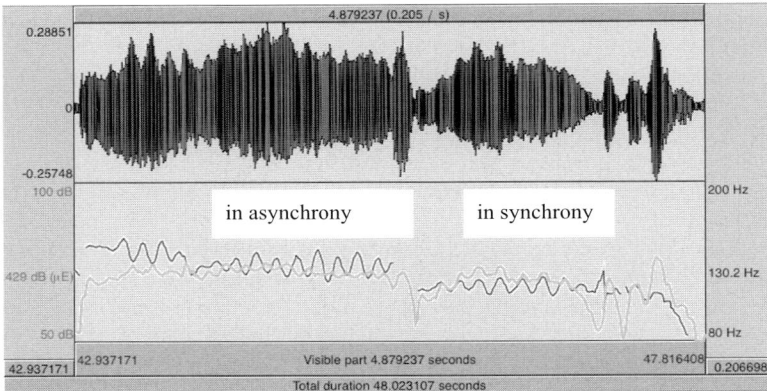

Fig. 7. At the beginning of the vibrato of the singer G the frequency and amplitude are in asynchrony, which gives a special effect for the sound.

The characteristics of the vibrato style in Sekhukhune area is a topic that should be studied more carefully. How widely this type of vibrato is used in South Africa, and how it is produced from a physiological point of view are topics of special interest.

In some cases vibrato can be very wide, as can be seen in the figure 8. Wide vibrato makes the voice to be separated from other voices easier.

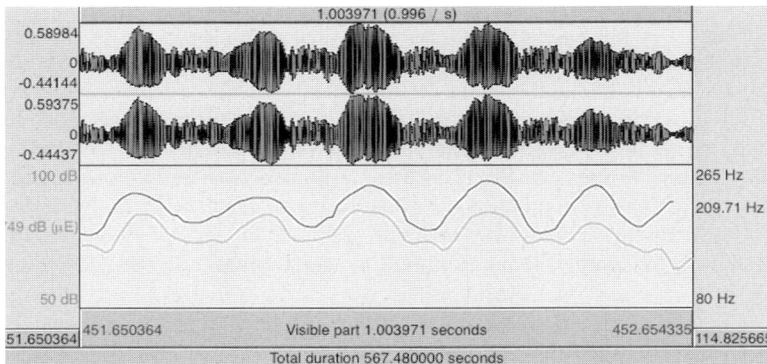

Fig. 8. In this example the singer F uses very wide vibrato. The amplitude of vibrato can sometimes be almost a fifth (245,42 Hz – 178,7 Hz = 550 cents). Also in the vibrato of the singer F amplitude and frequency are sometimes in asynchrony.

For comparison purposes, an example has been given in figure 9 from a Sunday service in Sekhukhune (Lobethal Lutheran Centre).[5] The leading voice (soprano) used a typical

---

[5] The recording was made by the author of this paper in Sekhukhune, Lobethal Lutheran service in December 2000.

fast and narrow type of vibrato. Also in this example the asynchrony of amplitude and frequency can be clearly seen.

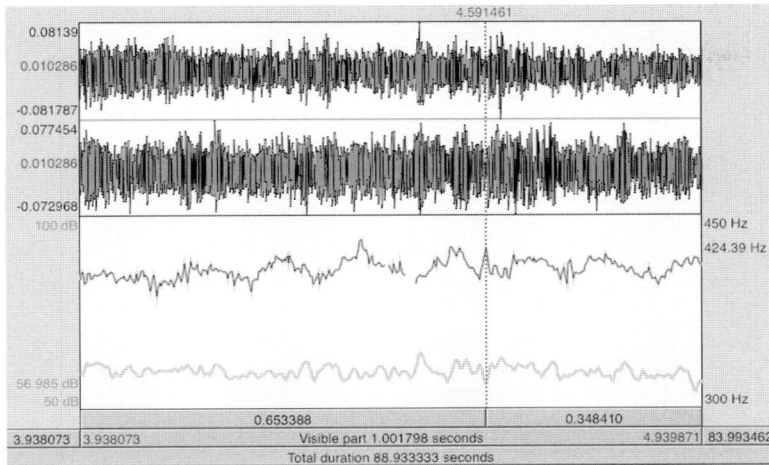

Fig. 9. Typical vibrato style from Sekhukhune area in which the amplitude and frequency are in asynchrony. Another characteristic feature is the fast speed and narrow frequency modulation of the vibrato. The narrowness of the vibrato is an example of the other extreme compared to the very wide vibrato in figure 8.

Body movements. Body movements that are typical in South African choir singing are not used in Lutheran hymn singing. People sit still just like during European hymn singing acts. Immediately when the first notes of traditional hymns (*makwaya*) are heard people stand up and start dancing, clapping hands and using hymn books as drums. Thus South Africans in Sekhukhune have adapted the European tradition of singing hymns without dancing or using other strong body movements.

Instruments. In the case an organ or piano exists in the church building, it can be used as an accompanying instrument, but otherwise instruments are not widely used. Drums are not accepted by Lutherans especially in the Limpopo province, but the congregation use hymn books in making rhythmic accompaniment during singing traditional hymns (*makwaya*). In the Pretoria area and south from Pretoria where the influence of Hermann Missionary has not been as strong as in northern parts of South Africa, drums and other rhythm instruments are more frequently in use.

Conclusions

The basic shape of the hymn "Lobe den Herren, den mächtigen König der Ehren" sung by the informants in Sekhukhune area is melodically very close to the European version. Only a few melodic changes were found in versions of some of the singers who didn't use the leading note in the ascending stepwise melodic movement. The main differences were found in intonation practice: most of the singers used a very low third degree, and

351

some of the singers used a very high second degree compared to equal temperament. It is argued in this article that the intonation practice is influenced by the pentatonic scale and traditional intonation practice, which has been widely used in Sekhukhune area. The fact that a lot of differences in intonation practice were found between individual singers tells that the intonation practice at the moment is in an unstable state. Some of the singers are more influenced by the Western type of intonation than others.

The other differences between European and South African versions of the hymn concerned the way to produce vibrato, harmonizing practice in group singing, and the special way to stress single notes in hymn singing compared with the fluctuating way of singing traditional South African hymns (*makwaya*). During a group singing situation all the singers used, as far it was possible to hear from the recordings, neutral thirds and a variant in which the leading note was absent in ascending stepwise melodic movements. In solo singing all but one of the singers used the leading note version. This interesting difference between solo and group singing may be related to the traditional way of harmonizing melodies in the Sekhukhune area.

In general the findings give an impression that the hymn is in an unstable position. Differences exist between singers about how much they are influenced by the traditional intonation system of Pedi people. Influences of traditional music can be heard in the use of neutral thirds, high second degree and in the unstable use of the leading note.

The vibrato used by some of the singers was different compared to the vibrato normally used by European singers. Perhaps singing practices that are more physiological (vibrato) than cognitive (melody) in nature are more stable and resistant to change.

The hymn singing in South Africa is in a rapid process of change. In addition to Lutheran hymns new types of mixtures of traditional songs and hymns are sung in churches (*makwaya*). These songs are more close to the traditional African singing style, but many of those have roots in Lutheran hymn melodies. These religious hymns resemble spiritual folk hymns known from many European countries, in which traditional folk song style and Lutheran hymn melodies are mixed with each other (Louhivuori 2006). Traditional hymns in *makwaya* style should be studied more carefully, because in those hymns features of traditional South African music can be heard stronger than in hymns that are closer to their European origins.

References

Barz, G. F. (2003). Sotho/Tswana music. In L. Macy (Ed.), *The new Grove Dictionary of music online*. Retrieved from http://www.grovemusic.com

Blacking, J. (1970). Tonal organization in the music of two Venda initiation schools. *Ethnomusicology, 14*, 1–56.

Blacking, J. (1977): Some problems of theory and method in the study of musical change. *Yerbook of the International Folk Music Council 9*, 1-26.

Coplan, D. (2003). Popular styles and cultural fusion. In L. Macy (Ed.), *The new Grove Dictionary of music online*. Retrieved from http://www.grovemusic.com

Deliege, I. (2007). Similarity relations in listening to music: How do they come into play? *Musicae Scientiae, 9-37.*

Densmore, F. (1918) *Teton Sioux Music*. Washington: US Goverment Printing Office.

Densmore, F. (1930): Peculiarities in the singing of the American Indians. *American Anthropologist 32, 651-660.*

Difela tsa kereke. Tse di nago le. Dinota tsa tonic sol-fa (1960). E.L.C.T. book depot. First edition 1960. Revised edition 2005. Morija Pringing Works. Pietersburg.

Dincsér, O. (1947*). Die Probleme der Varianten in der Musikforschung.* Geneve.

Eerola, T., Järvinen, T. Louhivuori, J. Toiviainen, P. (2001): Statistical Features and Perceived Similarity of Folk Melodies. *Music Perception Mar 2001, Vol. 18, No. 3: 275–296.*

Elscheková, A. (1975). Systematizierung, Klassifikation und Katalogisierung von Volskliedweisen. *Handbuch des Volksliedes*, Band II. München.

Freeman, L. C. (1956). The changing functions of a folksong. *Journal of American Folklore 70, 215-220.*

Kaemmer, J. E. (1998). Southern Africa: An introduction. R. M. Stone (Ed.), *The Garland Encyclopaedia of World Music. Volume 1: Africa* (pp. 700-721). New York: Garland Publishing.

Koller O. (1902). Die bäste Methode, Volks-, und volksmässige Lieder nach ihrer melodischen Beschaffenheit lexikalisch zu ordnen? *Sammelbände der International Musikgesellschaft IV, 1-15.* Leipzig.

Krohn, I. (1899). *Über die Art und Entstehung der geistlichen Volksmelodien in Finnland.* Helsinki.

Krohn, I. (1902-1903). Welche is die beste Methode, um Volks-, und volksmässige Lieder nach ihrer melodischen (nicht textlichen) Beschaffenheit lexikalisch zu ordnen? *Sammelbände der International Musikgesellschaft IV, 1.* Leipzig.

Lebaka, M. E. K. (2001). *The ritual use of music in indigenous African religion: a Pedi perspective.* Unpublished master's thesis, University of Pretoria, Pretoria, South Africa.

Ling, J. & Jersild, M. (1965). A Method of Cataloguing Vocal Folk Music. A Description of the System Used at the Svenskt Visarkiv. *Svenskt Visarkiv 21, 103-114.*

Louhivuori, J. (2006). Spiritual Folk Hymn Singing in Finland – Beseecherism. *Spiritual Folk Singing. Nordic and Baltic Protestant Traditions.* 85-96.

Merriam, A. P. (1955). The use of music in the study of a problem of acculturation. *American Anthropologist 57, 28-34.*

Merriam, A. P. (1964). *The Anthropology of Music.* Northwestern University Press. USA.

Nettl, B. (1964). *Theory and Method in Ethnomusicology.* New York: Free Press of Glencoe.

Poladian, S. (1942). The problem of melodic variation in folk song. *Journal of American Folklore 55, 204-211.*

Roberts, H. (1925). A Study of Folk Song Variants based on Field Work in Jamaica. *Journal of American Folklore 38, 149-216.*

Sass Bak, K. and Nielsen, S. (Eds.) (2006*). Spiritual Folk Singing. Nordic and Baltic Protestant Traditions.* Aka-Pring A/S.

Seashore, C. E. (1932). *The Vibrato.* Iowa City, Iowa : University of Iowa.

Selfriedge-Field, E. (2004). Towards a measure of cognitive distance in melodic similarity. *Computing in musicology, 13, 93-112.*

Suomen evankelis-luterilaisen kirkon virsikirja (2005). Kirjapaino Raamattutalo. Pieksämäki.

Sundberg, J. (1987). *The Science of the Singing Voice.* Illinois: Northern Illinois University Press.

Suppan, W. (1964). Die Beachtung von "Original" und "Singmanier" im deutschsprachigen Volkslied. *Jahrbuch für Volksliedforschung 9, 12-30.*

Tracey, H. (1958). Towards an assesment of African scales. *African music. 2 (1) , 15-20.*

Typke, R. (2007*). Music retrieval based on melodic similarity.* Dissertation. Universiteit Utrecht.

Wiora, W. (1941). Systematik der musikalischen Erscheinungen des Umsingens. *Jahrbuch für Volksliedforschung 7, 128-195.*

Appendix 1. The hymns sang by the informants are from the hymn book "Difela tsa kereke" (1960).

Hymn no 12: "A nke re ye le Badisa" -
Hymn no 35: "Tlang, tlang badumedi"
Hymn no 218: "Ke ratile Jesu fela"
Hymn no 245: "Retamo Rena wa matla!"
Hymn no 252: "Yomokgethwakgethwa"
Hymn no 271: "Jesu swika le mehleng"

Appendix 2. Reta Morena in Tonic Solfa (Difela tsa kereke, 1960).

245.   Reta Morena wa matla!

```
KEY G
{|d   :d   :s  |m  :—.r :d  |t₁  :l₁  :s₁ |l₁  :t₁  :d  |r   :—   :—
 |s₁  :s₁  :s₁ |s₁ :—.s₁:l₁ |s₁  :f₁  :m₁ |f₁  :f₁  :m₁ |s₁  :—   :—
 |Re - ta  Mo-|re  -  na wa|ma- tla! Ke |Mong wa kgo-|di-
{|Pe - lo, tha -|be -  la wa|le - go - di -|mong ka kga-|hli-
 |Re - nda Mu-|re   -  na Ra-|maa-nda, mu-|la - ya  ma-|ho-
 |Mbi-lu  ta -|ka  -  la, mu|lo - she, u |kho- de  vhu-|ho-
 |m   :m   :r |d  :—.r :m  |m   :d   :d  |d   :r   :d  |d   :t₁.l₁:t₁
 |d   :d   :t₁|d  :—.t₁:l₁ |m₁  :f₁  :d₁ |f₁  :r₁  :l₁ |s₁  :—   :—

        D.C.
{|d   :—   : |s  :s  :s |l  :—  :— |m  :f  :s |s  :—.f :m
 |s₁  :—   : |d  :s₁ :d |d  :—  :— |d  :d  :t₁|d  :—.t₁:d
 |šo.
{|šo.        |Kgo-bo - ka|nang,     |ba - hla- be -|le -  di tso -
 |si.        |Vu -wa - ni -|ha      |vha - i - mbi|vha  dzi-ngo-
 |si.
 |d   :—   : |m  :r  :m |f  :—  :— |s  :d  :r |m  :—.f :m
 |d₁  :—   : |d  :t₁ :d |f₁ :—  :— |d  :l₁ :s₁|d₁ :—.r₁:m₁

{|r   :—   :— |s₁ :l₁ :t₁ |d  :r  :m |r  :—   :— |d  :—  :—
 |t₁  :—   :— |s₁ :fe₁:s₁ |s₁ :t₁ :d |d  :t₁.l₁:t₁|d  :—  :—
 |gang!       |A  nke le  |kwa-tše tu -|mi -     |šo.
{|sha,        |kha ri mu  |re - nde nga|mbi-     |lu.
 |s   :—   :— |t₁ :d  :r  |m  :f  :s |s  :—   :— |m  :—  :—
 |s₁  :—   :— |m₁ :l₁ :s₁ |m₁ :r₁ :d₁|s₁ :—   :— |d₁ :—  :—
```

2. Reta Morena e a lokišang tše go fela,
E a go sokolotšeng mo o beng o timela.
Mo tshepelong o go išitše khutšong
Mo o kgahlwang ke go phela.

3. Reta Morena, gobane ke mmopi wa gago,
E a go thabišitšeng, e a beng a na nago;
Gomme mehleng yohle a go ntšha bobeng.
A bo bušetša morago.

4. Reta Morena e a go fileng hlogonolo,
A go tšhetšeng ka lerato la gagwe gagolo.
Bea pelong tše di tšwileng Modimong,
Kgoši modiramehlolo.

5. Reta Morena, le nna a nke ke mo kgahliše;
Batho ka moka ba fase le ba mo tumiše.
Se lebaleng e a re bonegetšeng.
Amen! A re mo godiše.

Appendix 3. Four part harmonization of the Reta Morena wa Matla! in staff notation (transcription by Jukka Louhivuori).

Reta Morena wa matla!
From the Hymn book "Difela Tsa Kereke" Pietersburg, South Africa in 1960

Appendix 4. Lobe den Herren, den mächtigen König der Ehren (Katholische Rezeption im 20. Jahrhundert) (http://www.liederlexikon.de/lieder/lobe_den_herren_den_maechtigen_koenig/editiond)

Text und Melodie: nach Joachim Neander

1. Lo - be den Her - ren, den mäch - ti - gen Kö - nig der Eh - ren;
lob ihn, o See - le, ver - eint mit den himm - li - schen Chö - ren.

Kommet zu - hauf, Psal - ter und Har - fe, wacht auf, las - set den Lob - ge - sang hö - ren.

Gotteslob. Katholisches Gebet- und Gesangbuch. Ausgabe für das Erzbistum Freiburg. Hrsg. von den Bischöfen Deutschlands und Österreichs. Freiburg 1975, S. 317f. (Nr. 258).
DVA: V 2/1027

Dort folgende Herkunftsangabe: "T: Joachim Neander 1680, M: Stralsund 1665 / Halle 1741".

357

Appendix 5. Sekhukhune area locates in Limpopo Province. The recordings way made in Catholic Centre in Limpopo Province, Sekhukhune area, Schoonoord.[6]

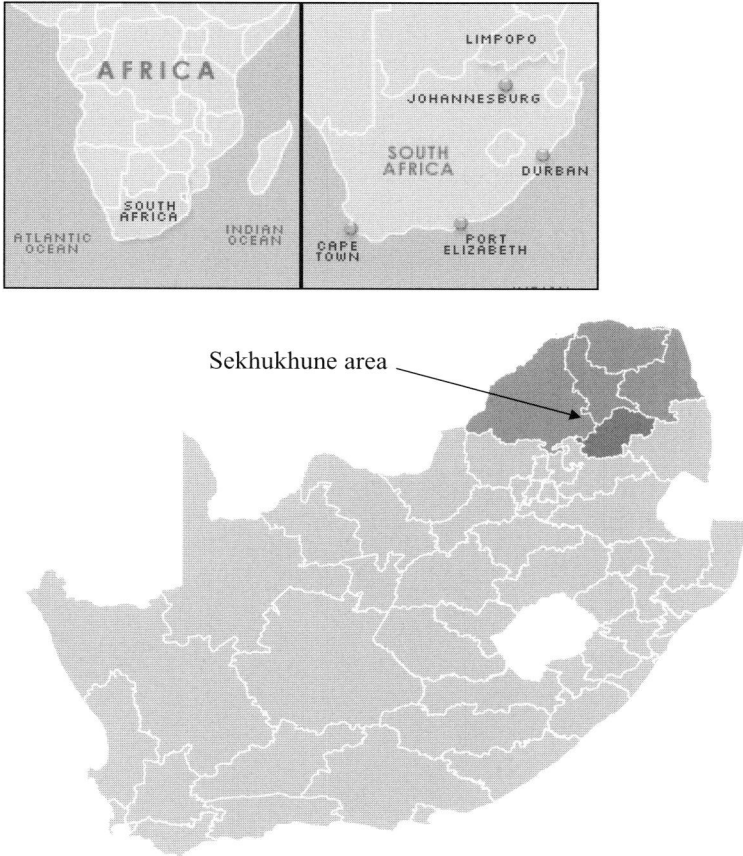

Sekhukhune area

Acknowledgements. I wish to thank Edward Lebaka for his great help in finding the informants and videotaping the hymns. Edward Lebaka, MA, has been an educator, a school director, an account executive at Buyers Network Unlimited (BNU) in Pretoria, South Africa, Regional Co-ordinator (Arts and Culture) in Limpopo, and Research Assistant at the University of Pretoria. Without Edward Lebaka's cultural knowledge and networks in Sekhukhune Area, this study could not been done.

Sanna Salminen and Aino Peltomaa have transcribed the four-part harmonization of the group singing version (figure 2).

---

[6] Limpopo map source:
http://www.safarinow.com/destinations/limpopo-province/map.aspx
Sekhukhune map source:
http://en.wikipedia.org/wiki/Image:South_Africa_Districts_showing_Sekhukhune.png

Gerhard Kubik

Zur Mathematik und Geschichte der afrikanischen time-line-Formeln

Einleitung

Wahrscheinlich schon vor zwei bis dreitausend Jahren oder mehr haben Vorfahren der heutigen Sprecher von Kwa -(I.A.4)- Sprachen an der Guinea-Küste und Benue-Cong - (I.A.5)- Sprachen im Raum Ostnigeria/Westkamerun entdeckt, wie man eine ungerade Anzahl von Schlägen auf Stein oder Holz, etwa 5, 7 oder 9, über den Zyklus einer geraden Anzahl von Elementarpuls-Einheiten optimal verteilt. Der Auslöser weiterer Entwicklungen und Diffusionen war dann das Aufkommen einer westafrikanischen Metallurgie, als man Eisenglocken zu schmieden begann.

Eine brauchbare Definition der afrikanischen time-line-Formeln ist vielleicht jene, die ich für den Artikel "Africa" im <u>Grove</u> 2000 erarbeitete. Dieser Text – dort mit einigen editorialen Veränderungen abgedruckt – sei hier in der Originalfassung, etwas gekürzt, wiedergegeben:

> "Time-line patterns are mostly single-pitch, occasionally double-pitch rhythm patterns that are struck on objects of penetrating timbre, such as a bell, the body of a drum, concussion sticks, etc. These patterns are characterized by an irregular, asymmetric structure within a regular cycle, and they range from ubiquitous eight-pulse cycles, 3 + 3 + 2, common in musical traditions of the Maghrib, to the most complex asymmetries filled into a 24-pulse package, such as the 24-pulse pattern struck on a percussion beam in the *moyaya* dance of the Bangombe pygmies, Central African Republic. A time-line pattern often represents the structural core of a musical piece, something like a condensed and extremely concentrated representation of the rhythmic-motional possibilities open to the participants (musicians and dancers)."

So weit uns bekannt ist, findet sich nichts Vergleichbares in anderen Musikkulturen der Welt. Rhythmen auf dem Balkan und in der Türkei sind mit den west- und zentralafrikanischen time-line-Formeln nicht vergleichbar und von anderer Genese. In den Kunstmusik Bereichen Europas ist jedoch das Verteilungsprinzip nicht unbekannt, manifestiert sich dort aber visuell und nicht auditiv. Auf der Tastatur eines Pianos (Cembalos etc.) entspricht die Verteilung der weißen Tasten optisch einer 7-Schlag 12-Pulsformel; die Verteilung der schwarzen Tasten ihrem Komplementärbild: der 5-Schlag-Version (cf. Kubik 1992:367-8). (Abb.1)

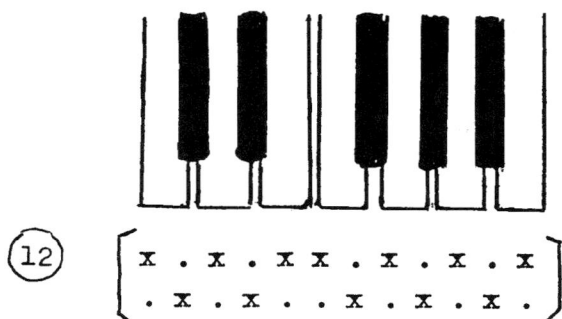

⑫ $\begin{bmatrix} \text{x . x . x x . x . x . x} \\ \text{. x . x . . x . x . x .} \end{bmatrix}$

Abb. 1

Die Asymmetrie 7 gegen 5 innerhalb der Zahl 12 (Tasten) ergibt sich hier strukturell aus dem temperierten Tonsystem, das ja letztendlich aus der im Mittelmeerraum in der Antike verbreiteten Heptatonik hervorgegangen ist.

Die Struktur der asymmetrischen time-line-Formeln Afrikas, ihr Verhältnis zueinander wie zu den Zyklen ist mathematischen Gesetzen unterworfen. Die im sub-saharanischen Afrika generell verwendeten Zyklen, definiert durch die Anzahl der Elementarpuls-Einheiten, die sie umfassen (cf. Kubik 1961:198 - 9) sind 8, 12, 16, 24, 32, 36, 48 und ihr Vielfaches; weniger häufig, aber doch nicht unbedeutend, sind in manchen Kulturen die Zykluszahlen 9 und 18. Referentielle Elementarpulsation ist eine der Grundlagen afrikanischer Musikpraxis. Wir verstehen darunter ein subjektiv wahrgenommenes Maß, einen inneren, sehr engen Zeitraster, der allen Gestaltungen zugrunde liegt.

Die wichtigsten time-line-Formeln in der afrikanischen Musik lassen sich demnach wie folgt beschreiben:

(1) über einen Zyklus von 8, 12, 16 oder 24 Elementarpulswerten wird eine ungerade Schlaganzahl, durch die der Zyklus nicht teilbar ist, möglichst ebenmäßig verteilt; (2) Man kann die zu jedem Zyklus gehörenden Schlaganzahl-Werte k_1 und k_2 errechnen, indem man die Zykluszahl halbiert und 1 dazuzählt beziehungsweise abzieht. Bei höheren Zyklen (ab 16) erhält man zusätzliche Werte und damit weitere Formeln, indem man den Zyklus viertelt, 1 dazuzählt bzw. abzieht, oder aber halbiert und eine andere Zahl, z.B. 3 addiert bzw. subtrahiert.

n   sei die Zykluszahl (in der älteren Literatur zur afrikanischen Musik auch Formzahl genannt, (cf. Kubik 1961:199), ausgedrückt in der Anzahl der Elementarpulswerte, die der Zyklus zusammenfasst

k   sei die Anzahl der Schlagimpulse (Perkussion auf Trommel, Glocke etc.), die über den Zyklus verteilt werden.

Die Schlaganzahl der wichtigsten afrikanischen time-line-Formeln ergibt sich demnach mathematisch wie folgt:

$$k_1 = \frac{n}{2} + 1 \qquad\qquad k_2 = \frac{n}{2} - 1$$

Die beiden k-Werte, die man auf diese Weise erhält, geben die Schlaganzahl zweier sich jeweils komplementär ergänzender time-line-Formeln an. Beispiel: Der Zyklus (n) sei 12. Daraus errechnet sich die Schlaganzahl der beiden zugehörigen time-line-Formeln wie folgt:

$$k_1 = \frac{n}{2} + 1 = \frac{12}{2} + 1 = 7$$
$$k_2 = \frac{n}{2} - 1 = \frac{12}{2} - 1 = 5$$

Es gibt also eine 5-schlägige und komplementär dazu eine 7-schlägige, asymmetrisch strukturierte 12-Puls-timeline-Formel. Beide ergänzen sich zur Summe der Elementarpulswerte, denn:

$$n = k_1 + k_2 = \left(\frac{n}{2} + 1 \right) + \left(\frac{n}{2} - 1 \right)$$

Komplementärbilder

Schon vor einiger Zeit wurden wir auf diese komplementäre Fächerung der asymmetrischen time-line-Formeln in den afrikanischen Kulturregionen aufmerksam. In einer älteren Schrift (cf. Kubik 1972:172) nannte ich die Komplementärbilder "patrix" und "matrix". Bei der asymmetrischen 12-Puls-Formel beispielsweise ist die Relation wie folgt (Abb. 2, vgl. auch Abb.1):

$$\text{⑫} \begin{bmatrix} x \cdot x \cdot x\,x \cdot x \cdot x \cdot x \\ \cdot\ x \cdot x \cdot\cdot\ x \cdot x \cdot x \cdot \end{bmatrix} \qquad \begin{array}{l} \text{7-Schlag-Version} \\ \text{5-Schlag-Version} \end{array}$$

Abb. 2: "Patrix" und "Matrix" der asymmetrischen 12-Puls-Formel.

Die Integration der beiden Komplementärbilder – ganz gleich, ob sie tatsächlich geschlagen oder nur gedacht werden – ergibt immer die Elementarpulsation.

Wir konnten ferner feststellen, daß in Afrika meist eine Komplementärform regional dominiert, zum Beispiel die 7-Schlag-Version der 12-Puls-Formel oder ihr 5-Schlag-Gegenbild. Bei den Mpyεm im Südwesten der Zentralafrikanischen Republik war zur Zeit unserer Feldforschungen 1964 und 1966 nur die 5-Schlag-Version gebräuchlich und sie wurde in einem sehr langsamen Tempo geschlagen, in der Regel auf einer Glasflasche, um *kembe-* (Lamellophon-)Musik zu begleiten, aber auch andere Genres. Dagegen stand bei den Yoruba 1960 und den Fò 1970 zur Zeit meiner Feldforschungen in Nigeria und Togo die 7-Schlag-Version im Vordergrund; die andere war eher latent, wenn auch nicht völlig abwesend. Der "Gegenrhythmus" kann jeweils mit einem Finger mitvollzogen werden, wie ich dies bei dem wandernden Spielmann Sosu Njak in Togo beobachten konnte (cf. Kubik 1972:171-2). Das Tippen des Fingers war unhörbar.

Schließlich gibt es Kulturen, in denen eine time-line-Formel gemeinsam mit ihrem Komplementärbild angeschlagen wird, wie etwa bei den -Luvale in Nordost-Angola, wo man beim *kachacha* genannten Tanz-Genre die asymmetrische 16-er Formel mit zwei Stäbchen auf das Korpus einer Trommel schlägt, die 9-Schlag-Version mit dem rechten, die dazwischen fallende 7-Schlag-Version mit dem linken Stäbchen.

Der Kegelstumpf

Bald wurde auch klar, daß man die Ordnung der afrikanischen time-line-Formeln als Periodizität wie ein gleichschenkeliges Trapez darstellen kann (cf. Kubik in Simon ed., 1983: 336). Daraus ließen sich charakteristische Strukturbeziehungen erkennen (Abb. 3):

Formzahl	Struktur der Formel	Notation (Einsatzpunkte in verschiedenen Kulturen variabel)
8	3 + 5	[x x . ǀ x . x x .]
12	5 + 7	[x . x x . ǀ x . x . x x .]
16	7 + 9	[x . x . x x . ǀ x . x . x . x x .]
20	(9 + 11)	[x . x . x . x x . ǀ x . x . x . x . x x .]
24	11 + 13	[x . x . x . x . x x . ǀ x . x . x . x . x . x x .]

Abb. 3: Beziehung der time-line-Formeln zueinander (Abbildung reproduziert aus Kubik in Simon 1983:336).

Man kann diese Darstellung auch räumlich auffassen, als Kegelstumpf, denn die time-line-Formeln sind doch zirkulär wiederkehrend; ihr Ablauf ist wie ein Ring, der den Grundriß des Objekts bildet.

In meiner Darstellung oben (Abb. 3) ist eine Zykluszahl 20 aufgenommen, obwohl wir bislang in keiner afrikanischen Musikform eine asymmetrische Formel mit dieser Zykluszahl nachweisen konnten. Sie ist wie ein "missing link". Ich will damit nicht ausschließen, daß es irgendwann, irgendwo eine solche gegeben hat – man darf nicht vergessen, wie sehr auch der afrikanische Kontinent einem "worldwide greyout of culture" (cf. Lomax 1973:475) unterworfen ist, einem Nivellierungsprozeß mit scharfer Reduktion der Formenvielfalt – aber wahrscheinlich handelt es sich um ein übersprungenes Glied. Wegen der afrikanischen Präferenz für Zykluszahlen, die durch 2, 3, 4, 6 und 8 teilbar sind, dürfte es nicht zur Bildung einer time-line-Formel mit Zykluszahl 20 gekommen sein. 20 wäre durch 5 in vier Abschnitte zu teilen.

Strukturell ist diese nicht-operationelle Formel dennoch von Bedeutung, denn nur so stellt sich heraus, daß die Zykluszahlen aller asymmetrischen Formeln in unserem Kegelstumpf eine arithmetische Folge bilden. Ihr Bildungsgesetz lautet:

$$a_{n+1} = a_n + 4 \; ; \; a_1 = 4 \; ; \; n = \langle 1,2,3,4,5,6 \rangle$$

$$
\begin{aligned}
\text{Daher:} \quad a_2 &= a_1 + 4 &= 8 \\
a_3 &= a_2 + 4 &= 12 \\
a_4 &= a_3 + 4 &= 16 \\
a_5 &= a_4 + 4 &= 20 \\
a_6 &= a_5 + 4 &= 24
\end{aligned}
$$

Die ersten drei Zyklen, 8, 12, 16, sind für die Bildung des Systems die wichtigsten. Die 24-er time-line-Formel, die Djenda und ich 1966 bei den Pygmäen des oberen Sangha-Flusses, Zentralafrikanische Republik, fanden, war ein außergewöhnlicher Fund, der zu vielerlei Spekulationen Anlaß gegeben hat.

Zyklus 24 und darüber hinaus

Es gibt in verschiedensten Gebieten Afrikas Musikformen, vor allem auch älterer Entstehung, die auf anderen Zykluszahlen beruhen. Auch die regulären Zyklen 8, 12, 16 und 24 bringen eine Vielzahl rhythmischer Gestaltungen hervor, die nicht notwendigerweise asymmetrisch sind. Das prominenteste Kulturgebiet für unge-wöhnliche Zykluszahlen – ohne Gebrauch von time-line Formeln – umfaßt die alte Hofmusik von Buganda, von der ich in den 1960er Jahren immerhin 102 Kompositionen in ihren Xylophon-Versionen aufzeichnen konnte. Die meisten sind inzwischen vergessen, unter heutigen Musikern längst nicht mehr bekannt. Studenten lernen sie von meinen Transkriptionen. Die häufigsten Zykluszahlen in der Kiganda-Xylophonmusik waren die Kombinationen $2 \cdot 12$, $2 \cdot 18$ und $2 \cdot 24$, daneben gab es aber auch Kompositionen mit Formzahl 50 ($2 \cdot 25$) und 54 ($2 \cdot 27$), und ein Stück hatte $2 \cdot 35$ Elementarpulswerte als Zyklus. Auffallend ist die Abwesenheit von 16-er und 32-er Zyklen. Dies mag damit zusammenhängen, daß die präferentielle Tanz-Beat-Formierung in der Kiganda-Musik sich auf $2 \cdot 3 = 6$ Elementarpulswerte stützt; auch $2 \cdot 27$ ist ja durch 6 teilbar. Bei den seltenen Zyklen, die auf der Zahl 25 oder 35 beruhen, muß der Beat in 5-er-Pulseinheiten zusammengefaßt worden sein, wenn man nicht so wie Joseph Kyagambiddwa in seiner Transkription (1955:231-2) ständigen Taktwechsel hineinhören will.

In der Kiganda-Hofmusik ist es zur Bildung von vielerlei irregulär bis asymmetrisch strukturierten Zwei-Ton-Phrasen gekommen, die auf den beiden obersten Platten eines *amadinda*-Xylophons geschlagen werden. Sie ergeben sich als inhärente Gestalten aus dem Gesamtbild der zwei ineinandergreifend kombinierten Basis-Parts. Es handelt sich bei diesen *okukoonera*-Gestalten jedoch nicht um Formeln wie in der Musik an der Guinea-Küste oder in West-Zentralafrika, die das Ensemble leiten sollen, sondern um einen Aufputz oft recht langer Schlagfolgen. In der Kiganda-Hofmusik beruhen schon die kürzesten Kompositionen auf der Zykluszahl 24. Hier kann es gelegentlich auch zu formelbildenden Erscheinungen kommen, ja sogar zu asymmetrischen Strukturen, wie etwa in dem Stück "Basubira malayika" für *akadinda*, aufgenommen 1950 von Hugh Tracey am Hof des Kabaka in Kampala (Cf. AMA Records TR 137, 1950, Analyse in Kubik 1994:80). Dort ergibt sich faktisch eine melodisch ausgelegte 5-Schlag l2-Puls time-line-Formel als inhärentes Pattern!

Ansonsten kann man aber inhärente Patterns – ein audiopsychologisches Phänomen (cf. Kubik 2004) – nicht grundsätzlich mit time-line-Formeln wie in West- und Zentralafrika vergleichen. Sie dienen auch nicht als Orientierungslinie für die Musiker, sondern sind das Ergebnis einer Umgruppierung in der menschlichen auditiven Wahrnehmung, bei der Tiefenstrukturen an die Oberfläche kommen. Eine Art Formel ist vielleicht der *okukoonera*-Part von "Ennyana ekutudde":

$$\text{㉔} / \; 1.22.11.2...1.21.11.2.../$$

Er beruht rhythmisch auf dieser Gestalt:

$$\text{⑫} / \text{x.xx.xx.x...} /,$$

die aber nicht asymmetrisch ist. Formelhaftigkeit ist keine generelle Eigenschaft der *amadinda*-Musik. Am ehesten entsteht sie bei kurzen Zyklen.

Rekonstruktionsversuch einer Erfindungsgeschichte

Eine wahrscheinliche Erfindungsgeschichte der asymmetrischen time-line-Formeln läßt sich aus ihrer gegenwärtigen Verbreitung und der Liaison dieser mit linguistischen und kulturgeographischen Daten gewinnen. Vor der rezenten Verwischung der Konturen ihrer alten Verbreitungsgebiete durch pan-afrikanisierte Popmusik waren die time-line-Formeln auf ganz bestimmte Zonen konzentriert. Sie waren überwiegend in der Musik der Guinea-Küste, dem Raum der I.A.4 (Kwa)-Sprachen zu finden, sowie im westlichen Zentralafrika, in den beiden Kongos, Angola und angrenzenden Gebieten, im südlichen Katanga bis hinein nach Zambia; und dann gab es einen Ausläufer ins Zambezi-Tal und in den Raum des Nyasa.

Korreliert mit den Sprach-Superfamilien Afrikas, läßt sich postulieren, daß die time-line-Formeln eindeutig eine Erscheinung sind, die mit Sprechern von Niger-Kongo-Sprachen einhergeht, aber auch hier nur mit bestimmten Gruppen, vor allem den Sprechern der I.A.4-Sprachfamilie (von der Côte d'Ivoire über Ghana, Togo, das südliche Nigeria bis nach Ostnigeria), und des "Western Stream" der Benue-Congo-Sprachen, sowie den bereits erwähnten Ausläufern ins Untere Zambezi-Tal und zum Nyasa, wo die fünfschlägige 12-Puls-Formel etwa bei den -Yao, aber auch bei den -Lomwe vorkommt.

Sprecher afro-asiatischer Sprachen, nilo-saharanischer Sprachen und Khoisan-Sprachen fallen größtenteils außerhalb der Verbreitungszonen der 12-er und 16-er asymmetrischen time-line-Formeln. Die Idee einer time-line als ständig wiederholte Schlagfolge zur rhythmischen Orientierung spielt nur in Randgebieten zu den Niger-Congo-Sprachen noch eine Rolle, etwa bei den Alur im West Nile District, Uganda, die auf dem *olodhuru*-Schlagbalken zur Begleitung einer Harfe (*adungu*) komplexe time-line-Formeln ausführten, als ich bei ihnen im Jahr 1960 Aufnahmen machte (cf. no. B 5010 - 5022 im Phonogrammarchiv Wien). Möglicherweise kam die Inspiration dazu in der fernen Vergangenheit, auf dem Umweg über die Logo (II.E.2-Sprecher) im Kongo, von Adamawa-Ost (I.A.6)-Sprechern wie den Azande, die komplexe vielfach asymmetrisch organisierte rhythmisch-melodische 24-er Zyklen, etwa in der Harfenmusik, verwenden (cf. Stücke wie "Wen' ade gbua" und "Ngbadule o", cf. Kubik 1994:150 - 153). Die 16-er time-line-Struktur in der *kponingbo*-Xylophonmusik (cf. Kubik 1994:106), melodisch ausgelegt, ist dagegen selbst ein Import aus südlicheren Teilen des Kongo.

In Ost- und auch in Südafrika waren bis zur Mitte des 20. Jahrhunderts die bekannten asymmetrischen time-line-Formeln (außer der ubiquitären 8-er oder Rumba-Formel) gleichfalls unbekannt. Ihre Geschichte ist also eindeutig innerhalb einer relativ kleinen Zone von Sprechern von Niger-Kongo-Sprachen zu entschlüsseln und muss vor der Bantu-Ausbreitung ab 1000 - 200 v .u.Z. begonnen haben, als Niger-Kongo-Sprecher nur in Westafrika zu finden waren. Und innerhalb dieser Sprach-Superfamilie ist es wahrscheinlich, daß die Erfindung der komplexen time-line-Formeln in jenem Gebiet entlang der westafrikanischen Küste erfolgte, wo sie bis heute prominent sind, also zwischen dem heutigen Siedlungsraum der Baule im Westen und der Igbo im Osten.

Ein besonderer Fall ist die 24-Puls-Formel, die Maurice Djenda und ich im *moyaya*-Tanz der Bangombe-Pygmäen, als einer auf dem Schlagbalken geschlagenen Formel in Linjombo, oberes Sangha -Flußgebiet, Zentralafrikanische Republik, dokumentierten. Für Forscher, die von der Hyphothese einer unilinearen Entwicklungsgeschichte der Kulturen der Menschheit ausgehen – nach dem Schema "vom Einfachen zum Komplexen" – müsste dies überraschend sein, weil dann eine der aus dieser Sicht "primitivsten" Gruppen Zentralafrikas die längste und am meisten komplexe time-line-Formel verwendete! Unser Fund 1966 war auch für uns eine Überraschung, nicht weil wir solche Ansichten vielleicht teilten , sondern weil offenbar keiner der Nachbarn der Bangombe-Pygmäen, weder die Mpyɛm, noch die Pomo und andere, diese lange Formel verwendeten. Dies ist ein Gebiet, das auch auf der Congo-Seite der Grenze intensiv durchforscht wurde, zuerst 1946 in der berühmten Mission Ogooué von André Didier und Gilbert Rouget, Musée de l'Homme, Paris (cf. Rouget 1948, 2004). Auf beiden Seiten der Grenze war die 5-Schlag 12-Puls-Formel präsent. Bei den Mpyɛmo in der R.C.A wurde sie zur Zeit unserer Feldforschungen 1966 mit dem Terminus ma umschrieben, inzwischen ein unbekanntes Wort bei den jüngeren Leuten.

Die Überraschung für uns war also nicht, daß die Bangombe-Pygmäen die längste time-line-Formel in unserer Kegelstumpf-Darstellung benutzten, sondern daß sie in dieser Kenntnis offenbar allein dastanden. Bei den benachbarten Ethnien fanden wir diese Formel nicht, obwohl sie so manches von der Pygmäen-Musik, vor allem ihre Polyphonie und die Jodel-Technik der Frauen entlehnt hatten. Es gibt verschiedene Möglichkeiten der Erklärung, drei seien hier erwähnt: (a) entweder wurde diese 24-Puls-

Formel von den entfernten Vorfahren dieser Pygmäen erfunden, vielleicht schon vor mehreren tausend Jahren und so wie andere charakteristische Pygmäenmusik-Merkmale und -techniken bis heute tradiert. Daß wir bei den wesentlichen Stilmerkmalen der Pygmäen-Musik mit sehr alten Überlieferungen rechnen können, diesen Standpunkt hat jüngst auch Victor A. Grauer (2007), ein bedeutender Mitarbeiter an Alan Lomax` Cantometrics Project (1968), vertreten; (b) oder es war so, daß andere Erfinder im Benue-Congo-Sprachraum die Formel entwickelten und in diese Waldregion brachten, worauf die Sangha-Pygmäen sie übernahmen, während sie in den Gebieten ihrer Erfinder inzwischen in Vergessenheit geraten ist. Das wäre ein Fall, wie er aus der Migrationsgeschichte von Musikinstrumenten und anderen Kulturgütern in vielen Teilen der Welt nicht unbekannt ist; (c) es könnte auch sein, daß diese Pygmäen irgendwann in der fernen Vergangenheit, als sie mit Musikformen Bantu-sprachiger Einwanderer in Kontakt kamen, aus einem 12-er Modell bei den letzteren ihre Formel entwickelten. Kofi Agawu in einem Fachgespräch an der Princeton University, wohin er mich zum International Symposium on the Music of Africa, October 10-11, 2003 eingeladen hatte, meinte, als ich ihm die Pygmäenformel vorklopfte, daß sie wohl zusammengesetzt sei. Ich war etwas überrascht, verstand aber, daß er die Formel zweiteilig auffaßte, jeden Teil über 12 Pulseinheiten. Demnach unterteilten sechs Schläge den ersten Abschnitt von 12 Pulseinheiten regelmäßig und sieben Schläge dann den zweiten Abschnitt in Verschiebung. Zwei rhythmische Überlagerungen eines Dreier-Beat wären aneinandergekoppelt. Allerdings macht in diesem Fall der zweite Teil, isoliert gesehen, keinen Sinn. Würde man ihn als solchen wiederholen, dann erfolgten drei Schläge in der Elementarpulsation aufeinander. Das wäre keine asymmetrische Formel. Kofi Agawu`s Auffassung erscheint mir daher unwahrscheinlich. Aber sogar wenn dies die Erfindungs-geschichte der 24-Plus-Formel der Sangha-Pygmäen sein sollte, müsste man sie als Zeugnis eines gewaltigen Innovations-Sprunges in der fernen Vergangenheit ansehen, denn aus Zweier-Überlagerungen eines Dreier-Beat, in Grundform und dann verscho-ben, ergibt sich nicht notwendigerweise eine asymmetrische Formel, die so genau in unser Kegelstumpf-Schema passt. Dazu ist die Aktivierung eines weiteren mentalen Komputations-Prozesses nötig; ob bewußt oder unbewusst, wäre hier nicht von Belang.

Ich kann mich jetzt für keine der drei Möglichkeiten unseres Rekonstruktionsversuchs entscheiden. Jede hat ihre Relevanz. Sehr komplexe Untersuchungen – auch allgemein über den Rahmen kognitiver und rechnerischer Fähigkeiten des Menschen, plus kulturgeographischer Umstände – sind nötig. Da es sich um Ereignisse der fernsten Vergangenheit handelt, ist dies besonders schwierig.

Ansonsten können wir aber schon einiges zur wahrscheinlichen Erfindungsgeschichte der afrikanischen time-line-Formeln aussagen. Aus dem Verbreitungsbild (cf. KARTE) um die Mitte des 20. Jahrhunderts – noch vor dem exzessiven Impakt der Musik der Massenmedien – sowie linguistischer wie auch kulturgeographischer Überlegungen lässt sich vermuten, daß die asymmetrischen 12-er und 16-er time-line-Formeln in West-afrika, dem Raum zwischen Ghana und Ostnigeria von Vorfahren der heutigen I.A.4-(Kwa-) Sprechern und I.A.5 (Benue-Congo) Proto-Bantu-Sprechern erfunden wurden. Eine Liaison mit den Anfängen des Eisenzeitalters in Westafrika, besonders einer bestimmten Eisentechnologie, die zur Entwicklung von Einfach- und Doppelglocken führte (auf denen time-line Formeln vielfach geschlagen werden), ist wahrscheinlich, ebenso zu einer Reihe anderer Kulturgüter wie Geheimbünden, Maskenwesen etc. Ich versuchte diese Zusammenhänge in einer Karte in der Garland Encyclopedia of World Music darzustellen (Kubik 1998:308). (Abb.4)

FIGURE 6   The approximate African distribution of masked dancing, timelines, and iron bells, ca. 1965; compiled from the evidence of sound and cinematographic recordings, using major European collections and private sources.

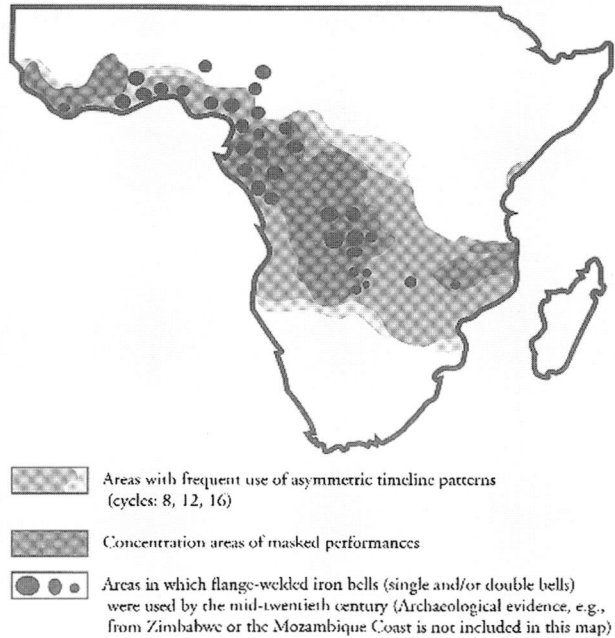

Areas with frequent use of asymmetric timeline patterns (cycles: 8, 12, 16)

Concentration areas of masked performances

Areas in which flange-welded iron bells (single and/or double bells) were used by the mid-twentieth century (Archaeological evidence, e.g., from Zimbabwe or the Mozambique Coast is not included in this map)

Abb. 4: Verbreitungs-Karte: Time-line-Formeln, Maskentänze und Eisenglocken.

Mit dem Sprachbild korreliert und den wahrscheinlichen Migrations-Routen – ihre Chronologie aus archäologischen Daten rekonstruierend (cf. Phillipson 1977 und andere) – scheint die Erfindungsgeschichte ganz besonders in Richtung I.A.4 Sprachfamilie zu weisen, weitaus mehr als I.A.5, denn die erste langsame Ausbreitung früher Bantu-Sprecher aus dem sogenannten Bantu-Nukleus (Zentral-Kamerun/Cross-River-Gebiet Ostnigerias) zwischen ca. 1000 und 400 v.u.Z. entlang der Nordgrenze des äquatorialen Waldlandes zu den großen ostafrikanischen Seen brachte eine solche Kenntnis offenbar nicht nach Ostafrika. Aus dem Gegenwartsbefund wissen wir, daß mit Ausnahme von Enklaven an der Kenya/Tanzania-Küste, die auf maritime Kontakte mit anderen Teilen Afrikas zurückgehen, die bekannten time-line-Formeln bis ins 20. Jahrhundert in Ostafrika unbekannt waren. Die zweite Welle Bantu-sprachiger und des Eisens kundiger Auswanderer aus dem Raum Ostnigeria/Westkamerun dürfte dann diese Kenntnis ab ca. 200 v. u. Z. in das Congo-Waldland gebracht haben. Nach dem Durchstoßen der von Pygmäen bevölkerten Waldlandzone, möglicherweise entlang des von Norden nach Süden fließenden Sangha-Flusses, wie auch durch Gabon, dürften sich diese Kenntnisse in den Südwesten und Süden der heutigen Demokratischen Republik

Congo und bis nach Angola verbreitet haben, wobei die bedeutendste weitere Ausbreitung, nämlich von Katanga über ganz Ostangola wohl erst im 17. Jahrhundert erfolgte, nach dem Zusammenbruch des Lunda-Reiches und der damit ausgelösten Auswanderungen. Schließlich gelangte die Kenntnis von time-line-Formeln aus Angola ins untere Zambezi-Gebiet und zum Nyasa vielleicht überhaupt erst mit den Reisen der pombeiros und anderer Handelskarawanen mit ihrem vielköpfigen Begleitpersonal von Luanda über Lunda-Kazembe zu den Stationen am Zambezi, vor allem Tete, gegründet 1532.

Ich will mit diesen spekulativen Äußerungen nicht den Eindruck erwecken, das letzte Wort zu dieser Thematik gesagt zu haben. Ich schätze mich schon glücklich, wenn sie nur in groben Zügen stimmt; Details in jeder Menge können nach dem Stande unseres sich entwickelnden Wissens dann eingefügt werden.

Intrakulturelle Vorstellungen und externe Analyse

Die meisten Musiker in den fraglichen Gebieten in Afrika erklären oder geben sonst irgendwie zu verstehen, daß sie sich eine time-line-Formel als Ganzes, als pattern vorstellen. Dies entwertet nicht analytische Auffassungen, wie sie einst A.M. Jones vertreten hatte (Jones 1954, 1959), der die 12-er Formeln additiv als 5 + 7 bzw. 2 + 3 + 2 + 3 + 2 darstellte.

Da die verschiedenen Referenzebenen beim Spiel weitgehend unbewußt wirksam werden, d.h. das tatsächliche rhythmische Verhalten kommt durch konditionierte Reflexe zustande, ist es unrealistisch, von den Ausführenden auch noch analytische, wissenschaftliche Reflexion zu erwarten. Indirekt verrät sich ihre Konzeption der Formeln trotzdem, wenn man etwa beobachtet, wie sie Kindern oder Lernenden gezeigt werden, oder wie die Tänzer mit ihren Schritten auf die Formeln reagieren, etc. Ein Kapitel in Volume 2 meines Buches *Theory of African Music* (cf. Kubik, in press) enthält vielerlei Feldbeobachtungen zu diesem Fragenkomplex.

Kommunikations-Schwierigkeiten zwischen Forschern und lokalen Musikern haben auch abstruse Theorien über die intrakulturelle Konzeptualisierung der time-line-Formeln hervorgebracht; u.a. daß sie nie gegen einen regelmäßigen Beat gedacht würden oder daß man sie nur auf den "fastest pulse", d.i. die Elementarpulsation bezieht. Das letztere ist grundsätzlich nicht möglich, weil die Elementarpulsation an sich keinen Anfang und kein Ende hat, also an jedem ihrer Punkte anfangen und enden kann. Der Musiker muß aber einen zyklischen Anfangspunkt konzeptualisieren, auch wenn er von der Elementarpulsation und nicht vom Beat ausgeht, eine 1, wenn man will. Wo die Eins steckt, ist dann eine weitere Frage (cf. Schneider 1994). Die time-line-Formeln sind einem bestimmten Musikstück immer eindeutig zugeordnet. Das Verständnis für die richtige Zuordnung kann auch transkulturell wirksam sein, wie eine unserer jüngsten Erfahrungen nahe legt. Für ein Konzert vor Studenten am 16. November 2007 im Institut für Musikwissenschaft der Universität Wien reaktivierte ich meine *likembe*, ein Lamellophon, das ich in Angola 1965 spielen gelernt hatte. Ich holte das alte Instrument heraus. Aber mir fehlte die Begleitung. Glücklicherweise waren die beiden Musiker-Komponisten Sinosi Mlendo und Christopher Gerald aus Malawi gerade bei uns in Europa, denn wir waren auf Tournee in Italien gewesen. Ich bat Christopher, mich auf der Rassel zu begleiten, sagte ihm aber nur, er könne spielen, was er für richtig halte.

Darauf intonierte ich ein Stück (Zyklus 24, hexatonische Stimmung, asymmetrischer Aufbau), das er noch nie gehört hatte. Prompt spielte er auf der Rassel die 7-Schlag 12-Puls-Formel! Er hing sie am einzigen Angelpunkt an das Stück, der uns allen möglich schien, nachdem er sekundenlang beim ersten Anlauf daneben gegangen war und von Sinosi korrigiert wurde. Sehr aufmerksam hörte er auf die Elementarpulsation in meinem Spiel <u>und</u> auf ein <u>inhärentes pattern</u> in der tiefen Klangregion. Als ich einmal einen Fehler machte, hielt er kurz an und setzte neuerlich ein, sobald meine Gestalt retabliert war. Christopher war noch nie in Angola gewesen.

"Panafrikanisches Musikverständnis" sollte man da nicht postulieren; auch "cultural memory" ist kein Erklärungsmodell. Christopher kennt die Formel und ordnete sie sinngemäß zu. Aus praktischem Nachvollzug wissen wir, daß es dabei mehrere Bezugsebenen gibt (Elementarpulsation, Beat, Zyklus, aber auch <u>inhärente Strukturen</u>), die alle gleichzeitig wirksam werden. Das geschieht in einem raschen Erkennungsprozeß. Dieser lässt sich erlernen, aber nicht mit jedermann diskutieren. Die Wiedergabe einer Rhythmusformel aktiviert mentale Prozesse, die verschieden sind von denen einer theorie-orientierten Strukturanalyse. Die letztere ist für das praktische Spiel ebenso irrelevant wie die Bewußtmachung grammatikalischer Regeln beim Gebrauch einer Sprache (außer man will Sprachunterricht geben).

Musiker mögen daher strukturelle Analysen unverständlich und manchmal als überflüssig empfinden. Das soll uns nicht hindern, Zahlenbeziehungen hinter den time-line-Formeln aufzuspüren (mit den Methoden empirischer Forschung und begrifflicher Überlegungen), so wie sich ein Nuklear-Physiker nicht daran hindern läßt, Unterscheidungen zu treffen, an denen sich das bloße Auge nicht orientieren kann. In der praktischen Musikübung analysiert man nicht gleichzeitig, weil das zu Spielende psychisch funktioniert und diese Funktion zum praktischen Gebrauch hinreicht.

Bei Analysen muß man aber zweierlei auseinanderhalten, <u>Strukturen</u> (die unveränderlich sind) und <u>Zuordnungen solcher Strukturen</u> zu anderen Maßeinheiten. In ihrer Struktur sind die asymmetrischen time-line-Formeln mathematisch definiert und nicht veränderbar. Wie wir schon früh erkennen konnten, geben sie uns daher auch ein Mittel in die Hand, um historische Kulturzusammenhänge zu rekonstruieren, etwa zwischen regionalen Kulturen Afrikas und afro-amerikanischen Kulturen. Sie dienen uns als "diagnostic marker" (cf. Kubik 1979). Ihre Absenz aus einer afro-amerikanischen Kulturzone ist dabei ebenso signifikant historisch wie ihre Präsenz (cf. Kubik 1999). Bei Transplantation in andere Kulturen können sie ihre Spielgeschwindigkeit, ihre Akzentuierungen, die Instrumente, auf denen man sie schlägt, aber auch ihren Beat-Bezug verändern. Auf das letztere hat wiederholt Tiago de Oliveira Pinto mit Bezug auf die angolanische 16-Puls *kachacha*-Formel hingewiesen.

Im brasilianischen Samba wird sie auf den Tanz-Beat meist anders bezogen als in Ostangola (Pinto 1999). Unter welchen Einflüssen und konzeptuellen Veränderungen eine time-line-Formel ihren Beat-Bezug verändert, also "umgekippt" wird, ist selbst eine hoch interessante Frage, die uns zur Untersuchung kognitiver Vorgänge bei Kulturkontakt führt. Auch innerhalb Afrikas gibt es kulturell bedingte Unterschiede. So etwa wird die 7-Schlag 12-Pulsformel bei den Yoruba Nigerias anders auf den Tanz-Beat bezogen als bei den -Luvale, -Lucazi und verwandten Populationen in Angola und Nordwest-Zambia.

Mathematische Empirik

Mathematische Entdeckungen in einer Kultur müssen nicht immer durch Theoreme verbalisiert werden. Man kann sie auch durch praktisches Verhalten implicite weitergeben. Das alte Afrika war prall von Mathematik (cf. Ascher 1991). Ich selbst und meine Forschungs-Teams konnten hierzu die dichtesten Erfahrungen machen. Die nonverbal transmittierte Mathematik äußert sich u.a.

a. im visuellen Bereich, z.B. in den *tusona*-Ideogrammen Angolas, die ja charakteristischerweise im Sande auch völlig wortlos, stumm, gezeichnet werden (siehe die ausführliche Darstellung in meinem Buch, Kubik 2006). Die verbale Erklärung erfolgt nachher, was die Trennung dieser Vorgänge unterstreicht.

b. im visuell-motionalen Bereich. Viele arithmetische Rätsel werden in Afrika im Sinne darstellender Kunst gelöst, d.h. man verschiebt Objekte etc. (cf. unseren Film no. 16/187, Zambia, "*Kafuta* – Luchazi arithmetical puzzle", archiviert im Ethnologischen Museum, Berlin). Auch bei Brettspielen (*bao*) ist das Bewegungs-element im Handlungsablauf wichtig. In diesen Bereich gehört auch Körper-dekoration, die choreographisch eingesetzt wird.

c. im auditiven bzw. auditiv-motionalen Bereich, so in der Struktur spezifischer Rhythmus-Formeln, Melodieformen, Formrelationen etc. wie den Verzahnungs-techniken in den meisten Holmxylophon-Stilen Ostafrikas.

Wir beschäftigen uns in diesem Aufsatz vor allem mit Punkt c, im besonderen mit den Rhythmus-Formeln. Gestützt auf die Erkenntnis, daß die Ebenen der Orientierung in den meisten afrikanischen Musikkulturen (a) der subjektive Raster der Elementarpulsation, (b) die Zyklen aus spezifischen Zahlensummen und (c) strukturelle Zahlenbeziehungen untereinander sind, hat Alfons M. Dauer in einer 1966 veröffentlichten Schrift von "unbenannten Zahlenerlebnissen" gesprochen (reprint in A. Simon 1983:41). Damit war mit anderen Worten das ausgesprochen, was Neurowissenschaftler wie Roger Gelman, UCLA und Stanislaus Dehaene, Institute de la Santé et de la Recherche Médicale, Paris, inzwischen experimentell bestätigt haben, daß in unserem Gehirn Zahlenoperationen unabhängig von Sprache und den Sprachzentren erfolgen. Aus ihren Forschungen ergab sich, daß die menschlichen Fähigkeiten des Zählens, Rechnens und des Auswendig-lernens (etwa von Multiplikationstafeln) von verschiedenen Netzwerken in unserem Gehirn, einige in der rechten, einige in der linken Hemisphäre, bewerkstelligt werden.

Es ist heute keine Frage mehr, daß es non-verbale Prozesse mathematischer Einsicht gibt, unabhängig von sprachlichen Prozessen der Konzeptualisierung. Solche Einsichten können sich z.B. (a) geometrisch, oder (b) in der Kreation musikalischer Strukturen äußern, was erst seit den 1990er Jahren, vor allem im Zusammenhang mit der Erforschung der afrikanischen Musik, die Aufmerksamkeit einiger Forscher auf sich gezogen hat (cf. Chemillier 2004 und andere). Die Ergebnisse passen recht gut in

Michael Gazzaniga's (1998) Modultheorie der Organisation neuronaler Abläufe im Gehirn.

In vielen Kulturen wurden mathematisch fundierte Gebilde hervorgebracht, in visuellen Darstellungen, in der Musik, ohne daß die Träger solcher Traditionen diese Gebilde in den Konventionen mathematischer Theorie – wie in der europäischen Wissenschaft – diskutierten. Das zeigt nicht etwa mangelndes Abstraktionsvermögen, sondern einfach, dass diese Mathematik von Netzwerken in unserem Gehirn gesteuert wird, die unabhängig von verbaler Konzeptualisierung arbeiten.

Tusona-Ideogramme, wie sie in Angola von Experten in den Sand gezeichnet werden, haben eine komplexe Struktur, deren Beschreibung und Erfassung mittels europäischer mathematischer Konzepte gar nicht so einfach ist. Hier kam Wolfgang Jaritz in einer wenig bekannten Studie der Lösung mancher meiner Fragen nahe (Jaritz 1983; Kubik 2006). Aber Ideogramme wie *tusona* sind eine komplexe Tradition; sie sind nicht auf nur eine mathematische Einsicht festgenagelt. Es war in der fernen Vergangenheit ein ständiges Experimentieren dieser Zeichner in meditativer Stimmung, die sie zu ihren Entdeckungen von Zusammenhängen einer eigenartigen Geometrie aus Punkten und aus Linien führte, die diese Punkte umfahren und nach langer Strecke unweigerlich in sich selbst zurückkehren.

Permutationen

In einem 1988 erschienenen Aufsatz befaßte sich Alfons M. Dauer mit unilinearen, d.h. auf einen Ton beschränkten "Rhythmen", und zwar in einem Versuch, alle rhythmischen Möglichkeiten zu erfassen, die sich ergeben, wenn man eine bestimmte Anzahl von Impulsen (Schlägen) über einen bestimmten Zahlen-Raster verteilen will.

In der europäischen Mathematik beschäftigt sich die Kombinatorik mit solchen Problemen. Dauer ging von meiner Darstellung der Zyklen aus, die in fast der gesamten afrikanischen Musik als Konstruktionsbasis verwendet werden und dabei immer eine bestimmte Anzahl von Kleinstwerten, den Elementarpuls-Werten, zusammenfassen. Eine Anzahl von Schlägen kann in vielfacher Weise über einen solchen Rahmen verteilt werden. Es gibt eine berechenbare Anzahl von Permutationen. Jede Permutation wird in irgendeinem Musikstück irgendwann ausgenützt, und sei es nur in einer Variation.

Dauers Projekt war wie die Bestandsaufnahme eines multiplen Universums. Aber einige besonders auffällige und wichtige Permutationen sind eben in West- und Zentralafrika zu Standard-Formeln, time-line patterns, geworden. Angeregt durch Rhythmus-Studien eines Angehörigen der damaligen Hochschule für Musik und Darstellende Kunst in Graz, Rudolf Derler, unternahm Dauer den Versuch, mittels der Kombinatorik alle Möglichkeiten der Verteilung einer gegebenen Schlaganzahl auf eine gegebene Anzahl von Elementarpuls-Werten in einem Computer-Programm durchzuexerzieren. Der Computer spielte dies durch, indem er systematisch immer einen Impuls unter den zunächst in die linke Ecke gedrängten Impulsen nach rechts verschob, bis alle Permutationen durchgeführt waren. Dies gab uns auch einen interessanten Einblick in die Systematik einer solchen Verschiebungstechnik. In seinem Programm hatte Dauer dem Computer folgende Aufgaben gestellt: Alle Möglichkeiten durchzuspielen und visuell darzustellen, die es gibt, um eine gegebene Anzahl von Impulsen, zum Beispiel 7, über das Schema eines Zyklus von zum Beispiel 12 Elementarpuls-Werten zu verteilen. Implicite war damit auch die Frage gestellt, wann, das heißt bei welchem Glied innerhalb der Kette von Permutationen, der Computer die afrikanische Standard-12er time-line-Formel ausspuckt. Es stellte sich heraus, dass es immer die letzte Permutation in der Reihe ist (Dauer 1988:130-131).

Man kann beide Fragen auch als mathematische Aufgabe ohne Computer lösen. Darüber hinaus kann man eine solche Aufgabe analog zu dem, was in vielen Kulturen geschieht, wenn Kindern oder Jugendlichen solche Aufgaben gestellt werden, auch mit Inhalten ausstatten, die ein konkretes Problem darstellen, das abstrakt zu lösen ist. Wir wollen dies an einem Beispiel vorzeigen. Die nun folgende Aufgabe wurde erstmalig im Text unseres Theaterstückes "Return to the Planet of People" (uraufgeführt in der Minoritenkirche, Krems a.d. Donau, am 14. Oktober 2006), konzipiert gemeinsam mit Sinosi Mlendo und Christopher Gerald (beide aus unserer Jazzgruppe in Malawi), mit den Schauspielern dort durchgespielt.

Fünf Delegierte sollen sich an einen runden Tisch setzen, um den man zwölf Stühle rund herum in gleichen Abständen angeordnet hat. Frage 1: Wie viele Möglichkeiten gibt es für die Delegierten, sich zu setzen? Dabei ist zu beachten, daß sie alle "clones" sind und daher untereinander austauschbar. Sie haben keine Namen, keine Individualität. Aber sie können einander nicht leiden. Daraus ergibt sich Frage 2: Wie sollen sie sich optimal verteilt setzen, so daß sie, wie Arthur Schopenhauers Stachelschweine in einem seiner Aphorismen, stets die größtmögliche Distanz zueinander halten, ohne die nachbarliche Körperwärme völlig entbehren zu müssen?

Die erste Frage können wir mittels der Kombinatorik lösen. Man kann die Aufgabe als "ungeordnete Stichprobe ohne Wiederholung" ansehen. Die Anzahl der Permutationen errechnet man dann – so scheint es – mit einer Formel, die aus Lehrbüchern höherer Schulen bekannt ist. n sei die Anzahl der Elementarpuls-Einheiten, k die Anzahl der Schläge (Impulse), die über den Zyklus verteilt werden sollen.

$$C_n^k \ = \ \frac{n!}{(n-k)! \cdot k!}$$

Doch Vorsicht! Leider führt sie zu einem falschen Ergebnis! Der Tisch ist ja rund! Eine geometrische Darstellung dieser Aufgabe würde uns daran erinnern, dass wir vor einer zirkulären Struktur stehen; die zwölf Stühle sind wie die Stunden-Markierungen einer Uhr. Wenn wir beginnen, ein Element (einen der Delegierten) solange zu verschieben, bis alle Möglichkeiten durchspielt sind, entsteht das Problem, daß die Ausgangsposition – alle Delegierten sitzen zuerst nebeneinander, also

⑫ [xxxxx......]

372

sich in dem Augenblick wiederholt, in dem ein Delegierter ans Ende der Sitzreihe geschoben wird.

Die oben zitierte Anordnung ist also identisch mit der folgenden:

$$\textcircled{12} \, [\mathtt{xxxx} \ldots \ldots \mathtt{x}]$$

Verschiebe ich die Person auf Platz 12, dann konstituiert sich wieder die Grundfigur von fünf nebeneinander sitzenden Personen. Ich muß also im Zähler von n (= Gesamtzahl der Stühle) einen Stuhl abziehen. Veränderungen im Nenner bewirkt dies nicht.

Die Standardformel für die Beantwortung unserer Frage 1 nach der Anzahl möglicher Permutationen lautet daher:

$$c_n^k \; = \; \frac{(n-1)!}{(n-k)! \; \cdot \; k!}$$

In den Zähler muß man n minus 1 faktoriell setzen, denn der letzte Elementarpulswert in dem Kreis des Tisches ist auch die Schwelle zur Wiederholung des Zyklus.

Die Rechnung lautet dann:

$$c_{12}^5 \; = \; \frac{(12-1)!}{(12-5)! \; \cdot \; 5!} \; = \; \frac{11 \cdot \cancel{10} \cdot \cancel{9} \cdot \cancel{8} \cdot \cancel{7} \cdot \cancel{6} \cdot \cancel{5} \cdot \cancel{4} \cdot \overset{3}{\cancel{3}} \cdot \overset{2}{\cancel{2}}}{\cancel{7} \cdot \cancel{6} \cdot \cancel{5} \cdot \cancel{4} \cdot \cancel{3} \cdot \cancel{2} \cdot \cancel{5} \cdot \cancel{4} \cdot \cancel{3} \cdot \cancel{2}} \; = \; 66$$

Westafrikaner, scheint es, haben die Lösung schon vor sehr langer Zeit auditiv und motional gefunden; durch Perkussions-Erfahrungen. Sie fanden nicht nur alle rhythmischen Verteilungen, die sich ergeben – insgesamt sind es 66 Permutationen – sondern auch die optimale Verteilung der Impulse. Und dies ist die 5-Schlag 12-Puls time-line-Formel. Analog dazu gibt es bei der Kombination $C\,\frac{7}{12}$ – also dem Komplementärbild – auch 66 Möglichkeiten.

Visuell läßt sich die optimale Verteilung eindrucksvoll darstellen. Alle Delegierten (sprich: Schläge in der Rhythmusformel) halten zueinander größtmöglichen Abstand. Die Sitzplätze konstituieren sich aus 2 + 2 + 3 + 2 + 3 Distanzen. Optisch hat jeder Teilnehmer, würde er einen roten Punkt ihm gegenüber fixieren, einen weiteren Teilnehmer im linken und einen im rechten Gesichtsfeld (Abb. 5).

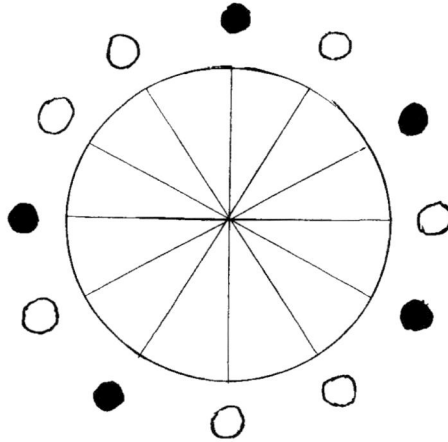

Abb. 5: Struktur der 5-Schlag 12-Puls time-line-Formel: Optimale Verteilung von fünf Personen auf 12 Stühle um einen runden Konferenztisch.

Da solche Permutationen in der Musik sich zyklisch manifestieren, sind sie visuell auch immer kreisförmig darzustellen. Eine lineare Darstellung in Musiknotationen jeder Art verschleiert diese Tatsache. So hat man bei den sieben möglichen Permutationen einer anderen Formel, n = 8 / k = 3, wenn man auch ihre acht möglichen Startpunkte einbezieht, scheinbar 56 (7·8) mögliche "Rhythmen": aber der Startpunkt einer Formel als Variable hat bei zirkulären (unendlich ablaufenden) Wiederholungen auf die Struktur der Formel keinen Einfluß. Daher ist strukturell

$$\text{⑧} \begin{bmatrix} x & . & . & x & . & . & x & . \end{bmatrix}$$

identisch mit

$$\text{⑧} \begin{bmatrix} x & . & x & . & . & x & . & . \end{bmatrix}$$

Abb. 6

und die zwei folgenden Darstellungen der 12-er Standard-Formel Westafrikas sind ebenso identische Strukturen:

$$\text{⑫} \begin{bmatrix} x & . & x & . & x & x & . & x & . & x & . & x \end{bmatrix} \quad \text{und} \quad \begin{bmatrix} x & . & x & . & x & . & x & x & . & x & . & x \end{bmatrix}$$
$$ 1 2 3 4 1 2 3 4$$

Abb. 7

In der linken Umdrehung oben haben wir die Yoruba/Fõ–Version mit ihrem Beat-Bezug vor uns, in der rechten die ostangolanische. Das muß man wissen, um der in der

Literatur nicht selten zu findenden Konfusion zwischen der Struktur einer time-line-Formel und ihrer Drehung in Bezug auf den Beat zu entgehen.

Die tiefere Beziehung zwischen den Komplementärbildern einer time-line-Formel zeigt sich gleichfalls mathematisch und visuell; mathematisch indem die Anzahl der Permutationen über n = 12 sowohl bei $k_1 = 7$ wie bei $k_2 = 5$ immer 66 ist. Visuell zeigt sich diese Relation in unserer Abbildung 5, in der die weißen Ringe – also die unbesetzten Stühle – uns die Verteilung der Impulse bei der 7-Schlag 12-Puls time-line Formel zeigen. Die 66. Permutation ist die am meisten ebenmäßige Verteilung der 7 oder 5 Schläge innerhalb des Rahmens von 12 Elementarpuls-Einheiten. n = 12 / k = 7 und n = 12 / k = 5 ergibt dieselbe Anzahl möglicher Permutationen. Alfons M. Dauer (1988:130-131) hatte ermittelt, daß in allen Fällen die afrikanische time-line-Formel immer als "letzter Rhythmus", also als die letzte Permutation erscheint, die der Computer konstruiert, hier als die 66te. Als zufällig kann man das nicht hinnehmen.

Wir können unsere Untersuchung nun weiterführen, indem wir errechnen, was bei den anderen Kombinationen n = 8 / k = 3 oder 5 und n = 16 / k = 7 oder 9 herauskommt.

Es zeigt sich dann:

Bei n = 8, k = 3 oder 5, gibt es 7 Möglichkeiten der Verteilung.
Bei n = 12, k = 5 oder 7, gibt es 66 Möglichkeiten der Verteilung.
Bei n = 16, k = 7 oder 9, gibt es 715 Möglichkeiten der Verteilung.

Damit sind die wichtigsten asymmetrischen time-line-Formeln in der afrikanischen Musik und ihr Permutations-Hintergrund mathematisch erfaßt.

Aber hinter diesen Zahlen verbirgt sich noch etwas: auch jene Werte, die die Anzahl der Permutationen angeben, stehen in einer Beziehung zueinander. Es handelt sich um die Folge:

$$\langle 7 \quad 66 \quad 715 \rangle$$

Das Bildungsgesetz dieser Folge läßt sich ermitteln und in einer Rekursionsformel darstellen:

$$a_{n+1} = (a_n - 1) \cdot 11 \quad ; \quad a_1 = 7 \quad ; \quad n = \langle 1,2,3 \rangle$$

Hier zeigt sich neuerlich, dass die west/zentralafrikanischen time-line-Formeln Teil eines Systems sind. Bei den nächsten Stufen in unserem Kegelstumpf ergeben sich allerdings divergierende Resultate, wenn man etwa die time-line- Formeln n = 24 / k 1 = 11; k 2 = 13 nach C_n^k für Permutationen durchrechnet und mit dem vergleicht, was bei einer Weiterführung der Rekursionsformel herauskäme.

Auch eine Einschränkung anderer Art unserer C $\frac{k}{n}$-Standardformel ist zu beachten. Die Anzahl der Permutationen bei k Schlägen innerhalb einer Zykluszahl n kann mit ihr nicht in allen Fällen ermittelt werden. Ist n durch k teilbar, würde die Berechnung mit dieser Formel einen Dezimalwert ergeben.

Bei n = 12 / k = 3 kann man zum Beispiel die drei Schläge asymmetrisch wie folgt verteilen: 5 + (5 - 1) + (5 - 2) = 5 + 4 + 3 = 12 (Abb. 8). Das macht musikalisch Sinn.

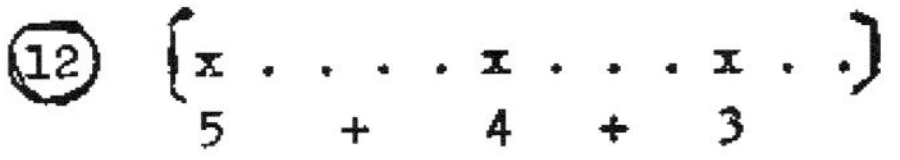

Abb. 8: Asymmetrische Verteilung von drei Schlägen über 12 Pulse

Die optimale Verteilung ist aber in diesem Falle die symmetrische. Die Gesamtheit der Permutationen ist 19 und man kann sie in vier Blöcken darstellen, die sich jeweils um die Anzahl 3 diminuieren:

1 + 1 + 10	2 + 8 + 2	3 + 6 + 3	4 + 4 + 4
1 + 2 + 9	2 + 7 + 3	3 + 5 + 4	
1 + 3 + 8	2 + 6 + 4	3 + 4 + 5	(optimale Verteilung)
1 + 4 + 7	2 + 5 + 5		
1 + 5 + 6	2 + 4 + 6		
1 + 6 + 5	2 + 3 + 7		
1 + 7 + 4			
1 + 8 + 3			
1 + 9 + 2			

$$9 \quad + \quad 6 \quad + \quad 3 \quad + \quad 1 \quad = \quad 19$$

Die Formel, mit der man die richtige Anzahl der Permutationen bei n = 12 / k = 3 ermittelt, lautet:

$$C_n^k = \frac{n \cdot (n - 2)!}{(n - k)! \cdot k!} - 1$$

Sie weicht im Zähler von der C $\frac{k}{n}$-Standardformel erheblich ab. Das -2 dient dazu, das zweite Glied in n! (eine Primzahl) auszuschalten. Dadurch wird der Zähler durch den Nenner teilbar. Und aus Gründen der Redundanz muß noch 1 abgezogen werden.

Generell läßt sich sagen, daß unsere C $\frac{k}{n}$-Standardformel nur dann gilt, wenn k eine Zahl ist, die n nicht teilen kann, zum Beispiel n = 12 / k = 5, oder n = 9 / k = 4 etc. (Fall I). Das Ergebnis ist immer eine Zahl, die sich aus höheren Primfaktoren zusammensetzt; so etwa lösen sich die 715 Möglichkeiten der Verteilung bei n = 16 / k = 9 in die Faktoren 5 · 11 · 13 auf.

376

Wenn dagegen k eine Zahl ist, die n teilt, zum Beispiel n = 8 / k = 4 oder n = 6 / k = 3, dann gilt die folgende Formel zur Berechnung der Permutationen:

$$c_n^k = \frac{n \cdot (n-2)!}{(n-k)! \cdot k!} \qquad (\mathrm{F\ a\ l\ l\quad II})$$

In einigen Fällen allerdings, wie weiter oben gezeigt, muß man von dieser Formel noch einen Wert, und zwar l, manchmal auch nur 1/2 abziehen, um die richtige Anzahl der Permutationen zu ermitteln.

Ich kann hier nicht im Detail ausbreiten, wie ich auf diese Varianten – nach einigen Missgeschicken – gekommen bin, noch warum dies so ist, denn es würde uns von unserem Thema der time-line-Formeln allzu weit in rein mathematische Probleme führen. Der Leser kann selbst experimentieren. Wichtig ist, daß sich mit den für Fall I und Fall II eruierten Kombinatorik-Formeln die Anzahl aller "Rhythmen" bei den untersuchten Zyklen bestimmen lässt.

Alfons M. Dauer hat auf eine weitere, sehr interessante Zahlenbeziehung hingewiesen, die erkennbar wird, wenn man beispielsweise die Anzahl der Permutationen einer Zykluszahl 8 mit Schlaganzahl k = 2 oder 3, 4, 5 oder 6 als Folge darstellt. Es bildet sich eine Kette, die aus spiegelverkehrten Hälften besteht. Das Prinzip der Komplementarität stellt sich auf diese Weise mathematisch dar.

Bei Zykluszahl 8 führte er diese Folge als 4 - 7 - 8 - 7 - 4 an, denn bei n = 8 / k = 2 ergaben sich vier Permutationen, bei k = 3 dann sieben usw. Leider ist ihm bei k = 4 aber ein Fehler passiert. Meine rechnerische Ermittlung ergibt zehn Permutationen und nicht nur acht. Es sind die folgenden (Abb. 9):

n = 8	x x x	1 + 1 + 1 + 5
k = 4	x x x . x . . .	1 + 1 + 2 + 4
	x x x . . x . .	1 + 1 + 3 + 3
	x x x . . . x .	1 + 1 + 4 + 2
	x x . x . . x .	1 + 2 + 3 + 2
	x x . . x . x .	1 + 3 + 2 + 2 *
	x x . . . x x .	1 + 4 + 1 + 2
	x . x . . x x .	2 + 3 + 1 + 2
	x x . . x x . .	1 + 3 + 1 + 3 *
	x . x . x . x .	2 + 2 + 2 + 2

Abb. 9: * Die Rhythmen Zeile 6 und 9 fehlen in Dauers Tabelle (1988: 128).

Dem Autor sei damit kein Vorwurf gemacht. Es entwertet auch nicht seine Entdeckung der spiegelverkehrten Hälften, aber die richtige Folge lautet eben 4 - 7 - 10 - 7 - 4. Das ist wichtig, weil seltsame Zahlenrelationen auch zu höheren Zyklen bestehen. Diese Folge definiert sich als $a_{n+1} = a_n + 3$; $a_1 = 4$; $n = \langle 1, 2, 3 \rangle$ bei $n = \langle 4, 5 \rangle$ dann - 3.

Wenn wir alle Permutationen für n = 12 mit den k-Werten 2 oder 3, 4, 6, 8, 9 und 10 ermitteln, kommt ebenso eine Folge zustande:

$$\langle 6, 19, 45, 84, 45, 19, 6 \rangle;$$

auch bei ihr wird Dauers Fund der Spiegelverkehrtheit in der diminuierenden Phase, d.i. nach dem Kulminationspunkt 84, bestätigt. Die Folge selbst konstituiert sich nach einem Bildungsgesetz, das sich wie folgt manifestiert:

6 - - - - - - - - 19 - - - - - - - - - 45 - - - - - - - - - 84

6 + 13   19 + 2 · 13   45 + 3 ·13

Das Bildungsgesetz der Folge lautet: $a_{n+1} = a_n + 13n$; $a_1 = 6$;

$n = \langle 1, 2, 3, 4 \rangle$

Daher:

$a_2 = 6 + 13 \cdot 1 = 19$
$a_3 = 19 + 13 \cdot 2 = 45$
$a_4 = 45 + 13 \cdot 3 = 84$

Man kann das Spiel mit n = 16 / k = 2 oder 4 oder 8 etc. fortsetzen. Wie Dauer richtig erkannt hat (1988:129), sind die spiegelverkehrten Teile auch ein Ausdruck "der Komplementarität aller Letzten Rhythmen", womit er die in den Computer-Tabellen in der letzten Zeile herauskommenden Permutationen meinte.

Es sei hier auch daran erinnert, daß unsere x und . (Punkte) ein binäres Notationssystem darstellen, wie die 0 und 1 im Computer. Es gibt nur zwei Aktionen in der mathematischen Struktur der time-line-Formeln: Schlag (x) und Nicht-Schlag (.), ganz analog zu "switch on" (1) und "switch off" (0) von elektrischen Impulsen. Die nicht mathematisch bestimmten Aspekte im Spiel von time-line-Formeln wie Spielgeschwindigkeit, Beat-Bezug, Akzente, Wahl der Musikinstrumente, Timbre-Folgen etc. sind nicht Gegenstand der hier vorliegenden Untersuchung.

Optimale Verteilung

Es war kein Zufall, daß bei der dem Computer gestellten Aufgabe, 5 oder 7 Impulse (Schläge) über einen Zyklus von 12 Elementarpulswerten zu verteilen, immer am Ende der Tabellen eine prominente afrikanische time-line-Formel herauskam. Dasselbe trifft auch auf die anderen Permutationen einer ungeraden Schlaganzahl über einem geraden Zyklus zu, etwa 3 oder 5 Schläge über 8 Elementarpulswerten verteilt, wenngleich die

Anzahl der Möglichkeiten in diesem Fall schon bei 7 erschöpft ist. Prompt ist aber der 7. "Rhythmus" die bekannte "Rumba"-Formel.

Der Computer arbeitet die Möglichkeiten so durch, wie es Dauer (1988) gezeigt hat: immer wird ein Element aus dem Cluster – den in einer Ecke zusammengedrängten x, bei Dauer sind es I – losgerissen und verschoben. In der letzten Zeile, der letzten Verschiebung ist dann das weiteste Spacing erreicht (Abb. 10).

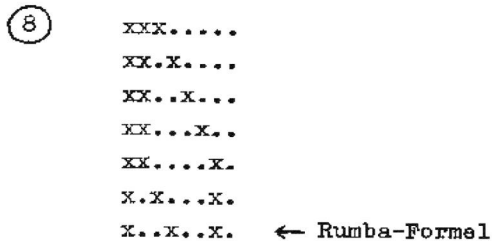

① (8)

```
xxx.....
xx.x....
xx..x...
xx...x..
xx....x.
x.x...x.
x..x..x.    ← Rumba-Formel
```

Abb. 10: Permutationen von n = 8 / k = 3 in systematischer Darstellung.

Abbildung 10 macht auch nochmals deutlich, daß man ein x nur bis zum vorletzten Elementarpulswert des Zyklus schieben darf (siehe Zeilen 5 bis 7 der Abbildung), weil dies eine lineare Darstellung ist. Würde man das x weiter an den Rand, auf den letzten Elementarpulswert drängen, wäre wieder die Anfangsgestalt, so wie in Zeile 1 mit den drei aufeinanderfolgenden x erreicht. Bei den 8-er Zyklen mit Schlaganzahl 3 oder 5 gibt es nur 7 Permutationen, wobei die letzte in der Reihe die optimale ist, nämlich die bekannte Rumba-Formelstruktur 3 + 3 + 2 , die man natürlich auch beliebig umdrehen kann, ohne daß sich ihre Struktur verändern würde.

Was heißt nun aber optimal?

Als optimal bezeichnen wir die am meisten gleichmäßige Verteilung einer ungeraden Anzahl von Impulsen also 3, 5, 7, 9 etc., über eine gerade Anzahl von Elementarpuls-Werten, 8, 12, 16 etc. die durch die jeweils gewählte Zahl der Impulse nicht teilbar ist. Dies führt ja zu der für die afrikanischen time-line-Formeln charakteristischen Asymmetrie. Optimal heißt, daß die Impulse – weil keine Teilung des Zyklusses möglich ist – so gleichmäßig wie möglich, so äquidistant wie möglich gesetzt werden. Und damit ist mathematisch auch ein Charakteristikum dieser time-line-Formeln ausgesprochen: die annährende Äquidistanz ("pen-equidistance" mit einem Begriff von Klaus Wachsmann, 1967, wenn es um Tonsysteme geht).

Die am meisten gleichmäßige Verteilung ist somit jene, bei der die Impaktpunkte alle zueinander den im Rahmen eines spezifischen Zyklus' größtmöglichen Abstand haben; und wenn sie besonders zahlreich sind und ihre Verteilung daher besonders dicht, dann soll es so selten wie möglich vorkommen, daß zwei Impulse unmittelbar aufeinander folgen. Optimale Verteilung heißt demnach, daß die Schläge (Impulse) in der Zeit bei

379

größtmöglichem Abstand voneinander in größtmöglicher Ebenmäßigkeit verteilt werden.

Äquidistanz ist ein Organisationsprinzip, das in vielen afrikanischen Kulturen, im visuellen wie im auditiven Bereich, eine große Rolle spielt. Sie ergibt sich aus der Übertragung einer gewählten Spanne über eine Ebene, oder durch einen Raum, oder in der Dimension der Zeit. Dieses Ordnungsprinzip manifestiert sich unter anderem in folgenden Bereichen:

a. in bestimmten Formen graphischer Darstellung, zum Beispiel in der Konstruktion vieler der schon erwähnten *tusona*-Ideogramme im Ostangola-Kulturraum. Hier wird die Spanne zwischen Zeige- und Ringfinger der rechten Hand strikte eingehalten, um Punktreihen in den Sand zu drücken, gleichmäßig in verschiedenen Richtungen auf der Sandfläche zu übertragen, sodaß bald ein Netzwerk von Punkten gleicher Distanz entsteht. (Cf. unseren Film no. 75 *Tusona*, Zambia, Sept.- Okt. 1987; archiviert im Ethnologischen Museum Berlin)

b. in bestimmten afrikanischen Tonsystemen, die wir äquipentatonisch bzw. äquiheptatonisch nennen. Hier ist es ein Intervall zwischen zwei Tönen, das als Spanne konzeptualisiert und dann systematisch transponiert wird, so daß am Ende eine größere Spanne, nämlich eine Oktave mit fünf oder sieben Tönen in ungefähr gleichem Intervallabstand ausgefüllt wird (Cf. Kubik 2004).

c. im Konzept einer annährend äquidistanten Verteilung von Impulsen ungerader Anzahl über einen geradzahligen Raster. In der Musik Afrikas ist dieses Prinzip vor allem bei den sogenannten time-line-Formeln verwirklicht, bei denen eine regelmäßig teilbare Zahl von Elementarpuls-Werten, zum Beispiel 8, 12 oder 16 durch eine Folge von Schlägen ausgefüllt wird, die eine Primzahl bilden, also 3, 5, 7 etc. Die Verteilung findet nun so statt, daß der Zyklus der Elementarpulsation trotzdem möglichst ebenmäßig (d.h. möglichst einer Äquidistanz nahekommend) unterteilt wird. Eine solche Verteilung nennen wir dann optimal.

In den Fällen *b* und *c* wird die annähernde Äquidistanz eigentlich erzwungen. Bei *b* ist eine genaue Äquidistanz der Tonimpulse innerhalb einer Oktave, also 240 Cents im äquipentatonischen bzw. 171.4 Cents im äquiheptatonischen System, gehörsmäßig nicht erreichbar. Die Schwankungen (Abweichungen) vom äquidistanten Mittel sind erheblich und haben viele Forscher verwirrt. Manche haben ihnen eine Bedeutung beigemessen, die sie nicht besitzen; bei näherer Untersuchung kann man jedoch eine Konzeptualisierung von mehreren unterschiedlichen. Intervalltypen -- etwa enge (ca. 220 Cents), im Gegensatz zu mittleren (ca. 240 Cents) und größeren (ca. 270 Cents) in den Vorstellungen der Musiker vor Ort nicht nachweisen. Andere Forscher haben gemeint, daß das menschliche Ohr gar nicht in der Lage sei, Äquidistanz zum sensorischen Ausgangspunkt des Abstimm-Verhaltens zu machen. Es würden sich immer "reine" Quarten und Quinten aufdrängen, wie sie in der natürlichen Partialtonreihe vorkommen. Diese Autoren räumen allerdings die Möglichkeit der Existenz einer Temperierung ein, im Sinne eines Sekundärvorganges, daß man also auf dem Umweg über die

Wahrnehmung "reiner" Intervalle, in denen man auch singt, bei Instrumenten wie Xylophonen, Lamellophonen etc. aus bestimmten Gründen zu einer äquidistanten Temperierung übergegangen sei.

Was die afrikanischen asymmetrischen time-line-Formeln betrifft, ist die Tendenz zu einer möglichst äquidistanten Verteilung innerhalb eines Zyklus unverkennbar. Eine solche wird angestrebt, obwohl der Zyklus durch die Anzahl der Schläge nicht teilbar ist, wie bei 12:7 oder 16:9. Jene Verteilung wird gewählt, bei der alle Schläge in größtmöglichem Abstand zueinander stehen sollen. Wenn es nicht möglich ist, die Aufeinanderfolge zweier Schläge zu vermeiden, wie eben bei 12:7 oder 16:9, dann soll dies so wenig wie möglich vorkommen. Bei der 9-schlägigen *kachacha*-Formel aus Ostangola, über Zyklus 16, lässt sich dies zweimal nicht vermeiden: (Abb. 11)

(16) [x . x . x . x x . x . x . x x .]

Abb. 11

Jedoch ist auch optimal, daß die beiden Doppelschläge <u>zueinander</u> den größten Abstand haben, genau 5 Elementarpuls-Werte in der einen und 7 in der anderen Richtung. Dies kommt einer Äquidistanz oder balancierten Verteilung der Impulse über den ganzen Zyklus am nächsten. Jede andere Verteilung würde die Doppelschläge näher aneinanderrücken, zum Beispiel in dieser Form (Abb. 12)

(16) [x . x . x . x . | x x . x . x x .]

Abb. 12

Das ist dann nicht mehr <u>eine</u> zusammenhängende asymmetrische Formel, sondern es sind zwei aneinandergekoppelte Gestalten, was ich in Abb. 12, oben, durch den Trennungsstrich veranschaulicht habe. Der erste Teil ist divisiv gegliedert, 8:4, der zweite Teil ist eine Rumba-Formel. Eine solche zweiteilige Form gibt es in der afrikanischen Musik zwar auch, das ist aber Rumba, nicht *kachacha*; als Ganzes ist sie nicht mehr asymmetrisch, und die Impulse sind auch nicht mehr annährend äquidistant verteilt.

Die Struktur der *kachacha*-Formel wird genauso wie bei den anderen asymmetrischen time-line-Formeln so am besten sichtbar, wenn man sie kreisförmig darstellt. Man stelle sich vor, daß 16 Stühle um einen runden Konferenztisch angeordnet sind und wir 9 Delegierte optimal verteilt setzen wollen. (Abb. 13)

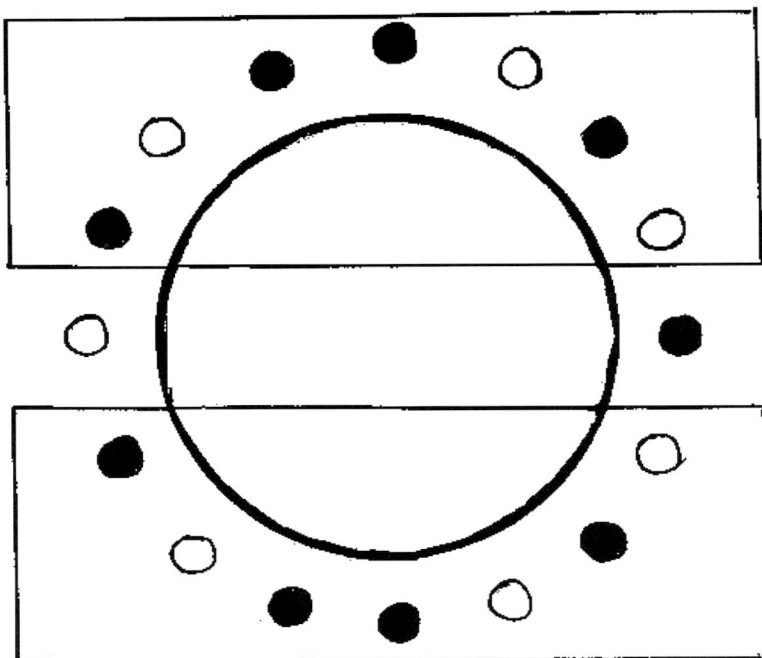

Abb. 13: Struktur der *kachacha*-Formel (Angola), in Brasilien *samba.*

Aus Abbildung 13 läßt sich erkennen, daß nicht nur die 9 Personen (schwarzen Punkte) optimal verteilt sind, das heißt den weitest-möglichen Abstand zueinander haben, auch die leeren Stühle, also das Komplementärbild n = 16 / k = 7, zeigt entsprechend optimale Verteilung. Und die zwei Schlagelemente, die aneinander gerückt sind, haben immerhin zu einer Seite hin jeweils einen leeren Stuhl. Aus der visuellen Darstellung kann man noch eine weitere Entdeckung machen; wir haben sie durch Einzeichnung zweier rechteckiger Rahmen hervorgehoben: Die Formel hat zwei spiegelverkehrte Teile. Der Inhalt des oberen Rechtecks aus vier besetzten und drei leeren Stühlen stellt sich im unteren Rechteck spiegelverkehrt dar. Und in der Mitte entsteht eine horizontale Achse, in der ein besetzter Stuhl einem unbesetzten gegenüber direkt zugeordnet ist. Die ganze Figur hat rhythmisch eine unerhörte Balance; brasilianische Musiker würden hier von balanço reden. Sollte Brasilien seine Nationalflagge ändern wollen, wäre dies, mit den symbolischen Farben Brasiliens versehen, das kulturell richtige Muster für die neue Fahne!

Berechnung der optimalen Verteilung

"Optimale Verteilung", "annähernde Äquidistanz" bleiben trotzdem zunächst Begriffe vagen Inhalts und als solche von noch zu erweisendem wissenschaftlichen Wert. Kann man eindeutig feststellen, berechnen, was eine optimale Verteilung von Impulsen innerhalb einer Asymmetrie der besprochenen Art sein soll?

Wir wollen es versuchen, denn nur so läßt sich auch die genaue Platzierung der Impulse innerhalb eines gegebenen Zyklus unentrinnbar ermitteln. Längst haben wir ja gelernt, daß es nur eine Möglichkeit, eine Permutation ist, die wir optimal nennen können, die der Computer als "Letzten Rhythmus" in Dauer's Programm ausgespuckt hat. Wenn man die genaue Verteilung der Impulse eines solchen "Letzten Rhythmus" im Sinne einer annähernden Äquidistanz rechnerisch ermitteln will (ohne Computer), geht man schrittweise vor. Zuerst muß man bei allen Formeln, die sich aus k = n/2 ± 1 konstituieren, ermitteln, wie oft ein größtmöglicher Abstand zwischen den Impulsen überhaupt zu realisieren ist. n sei 12, k sei 5, und wir wollen die 5 Schläge möglichst gleichmäßig über die 12 Pulse verteilen, ohne daß wir die Pulse selbst unterteilen könnten. Wir ermitteln zunächst den Durchschnittsabstand, der beträgt 12 : 5 = 2 .4 Pulse. Da dies immer ein Dezimalwert ist, kann sich die Verteilung nur aus den nächst höheren und nächst kleineren ganzen Zahlen konstituieren. Das wären also in diesem Fall die Zahlen 2 und 3.

Das bedeutet also, die fünf Schläge müssen über die 12 Elementarpulse so verteilt werden, daß ihre Abstände manchmal 3 und manchmal 2 Elementarpulse umfassen. Aber wieviele 3er und wieviele 2er Werte brauchen wir, damit sich dies ausgeht, und – was schwieriger ist – in welcher Reihenfolge müssen wir sie anordnen?

Die erste Frage kann man durch eine einfache Gleichung mit zwei Unbekannten lösen. x sei die Anzahl der benötigten 3er und y die der benötigten 2er Werte. Ihre Summe muß 12 betragen. (siehe Gleichung I). Aber noch eine zweite Bedingung muß erfüllt werden. Die Summe der Anzahl aller benötigten 3er und 2er Werte muß in unserem Beispiel 5 sein (= 5 Schläge). (Gleichung II).

Die Rechnung lautet daher:

$$
\begin{array}{llll}
\text{I} & 3x + 2y & = & 12 \\
\text{II} & x + y & = & 5
\end{array}
$$

$$
\text{(II)} \quad x = 5 - y \quad \text{in Gleichung I einsetzen:}
$$

$$
3(5 - y) + 2y = 12
$$
$$
15 - 3y + 2y = 12
$$
$$
-y = -3
$$
$$
y = 3
$$

Jetzt y = 3 in Gleichung II einsetzen:

$$
\text{II} \quad x + 3 = 5 \quad \longrightarrow \quad x = 2
$$

Wir brauchen also dreimal 2er Werte und zweimal 3er Werte: (Abb. 14)

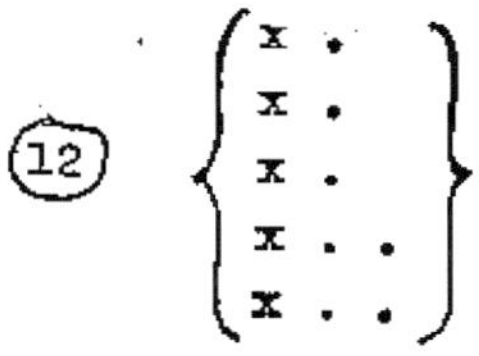

$$\text{(12)} \quad \left\{ \begin{array}{l} \mathbf{x} \ . \ . \\ \mathbf{x} \ . \ . \\ \mathbf{x} \ . \ . \\ \mathbf{x} \ . \ . \ . \\ \mathbf{x} \ . \ . \end{array} \right\}$$

Abb. 14

Was uns die Lösung der Gleichung zunächst nicht mitteilt, ist in welcher Reihenfolge wir nun die 2er und 3er Werte anordnen sollen, damit sich die Formel nach dem Prinzip optimaler Verteilung über 12 Elementarpulse konstituiert. Die einfachste (nicht-rechnerische) Methode, um das zu lösen, ist, die beiden Werte abwechselnd aneinander zu reihen und die Lücke mit dem übrig gebliebenen Wert auszufüllen:

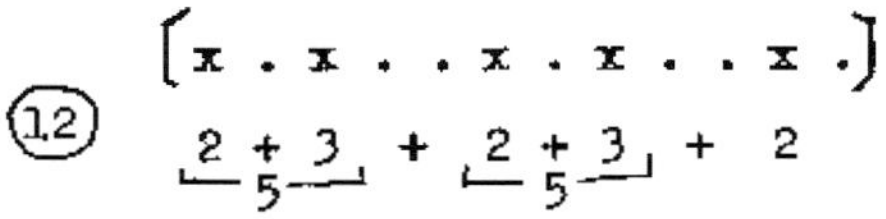

$$\text{(12)} \quad \left[\mathbf{x} \ . \ \mathbf{x} \ . \ . \ \mathbf{x} \ . \ \mathbf{x} \ . \ . \ \mathbf{x} \ . \right]$$
$$\underbrace{2 + 3}_{5} + \underbrace{2 + 3}_{5} + 2$$

Abb. 15

Die Reihenfolge ist ganz egal; auch umgekehrt führt es zum selben Ergebnis:

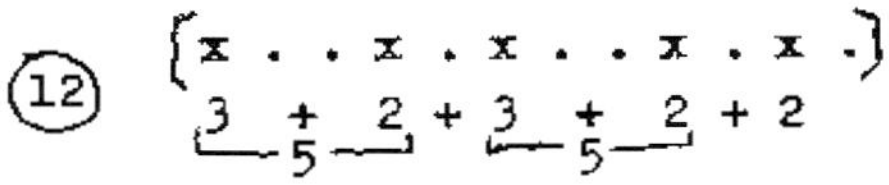

$$\text{(12)} \quad \left\{ \mathbf{x} \ . \ . \ \mathbf{x} \ . \ \mathbf{x} \ . \ . \ \mathbf{x} \ . \ \mathbf{x} \ . \right\}$$
$$\underbrace{3 + 2}_{5} + \underbrace{3 + 2}_{5} + 2$$

Abb. 16

Leider geht dies so intuitiv nicht bei allen Formeln; schon beim Komplementärbild der obigen Formel n = 12 / k = 7 muss man einen anderen Weg beschreiten. Hier ergeben die Gleichungen mit zwei Unbekannten nämlich fünf 2er Werte (x = 5) und zwei 1er Werte (y = 2), die optimal aneinander gereiht werden sollen.

Was macht man da? Da jede Formel aus zwei (asymmetrischen) Teilen bestehen soll, teilt man die zunächst höhere Anzahl in die Hälfte; hier also 5 : 2 = 2.5 Immer kommt ein Dezimalwert heraus, wir ignorieren ihn aber und runden ab, nicht auf. Daher: 2. Dasselbe tun wir mit dem y-Wert. 2 : 2 = 1, also einmal. Nun reihen wir zweimal den 2-er Wert aneinander, gefolgt von einmal dem 1er Wert. Dies wiederholen wir solange, bis der Rahmen (Zyklus) fast ausgefüllt ist und schließen den übriggebliebenen Wert einfach an; also:

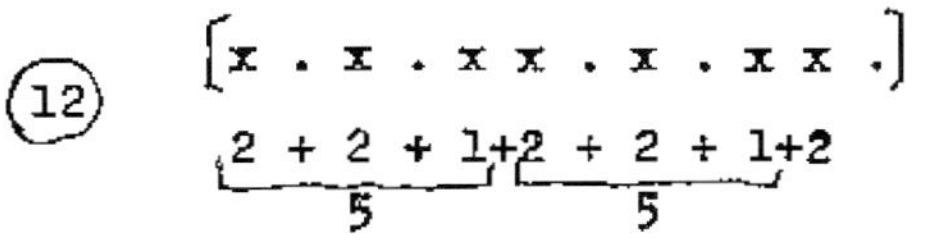

$$\text{(12)} \quad \left[x \cdot x \cdot x\,x \cdot x \cdot x\,x \cdot \right]$$
$$\underbrace{2 + 2 + 1{+}2}_{5} \; \underbrace{+ 2 + 1{+}2}_{5}$$

Abb. 17

Mit dieser Methode haben wir eine eindeutige, optimal strukturierte Verteilung der Werte durchgesetzt und damit den Formelaufbau rechnerisch konstituiert. Intuitiv kann man natürlich zum gleichen Ergebnis auch auf visueller Basis, mit dem runden Tisch und den Stühlen, kommen.

Die optimale Verteilung läßt sich also tatsächlich rechnerisch ermitteln. Um dies völlig klarzustellen, wollen wir die Methode noch an den längeren Formeln durchexerzieren. Wir berechnen jetzt die optimale Verteilung der Schläge an den Formeln $n = 16 / k_1 = 7$, $k_2 = 9$.

Berechnung $n = 16 / k = 7$: Daher $16 : 7 = 2.28$, die Abstände zwischen den Schlagimpulsen der Formel sind daher manchmal 2 und manchmal 3.

$$
\begin{array}{ll}
\text{I} & 3x + 2y = 16 \\
\text{II} & \underline{x + y = 7} \\[4pt]
\text{II} & x = 7 - y \\[4pt]
\text{I} & 3(7 - y) + 2y = 16 \\
 & 21 - 3y + 2y = 16 \\
 & -y = -5 \\
 & + \quad + \\
 & y = 5 \\[6pt]
\text{II} & x + 5 = 7 \\
 & x = 2
\end{array}
$$

Wir brauchen also zwei 3er Werte und fünf 2er Werte zur Konstituierung dieser time-line- Formel. Die Hälfte von 5 ist 2.5, abgerundet: 2, und die von 2 ist 1. Wir reihen also zwei 2-er Werte aneinander, gefolgt von einmal einem 3-er Wert.

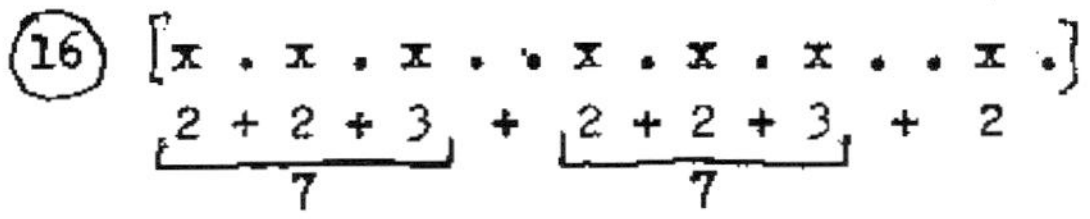

$$\text{(16)} \quad \left[x \cdot x \cdot x \cdot \cdot x \cdot x \cdot x \cdot \cdot x \cdot \right]$$
$$\underbrace{2 + 2 + 3}_{7} + \underbrace{2 + 2 + 3}_{7} + 2$$

Abb. 18

Wie geht es bei der Komplementärformel n = 16 / k = 9? 16 : 9 = 1.7, die Abstandsgrößen sind daher 2 und 1.

$$
\begin{array}{llll}
\text{I} & 2x + y & = & 16 \\
\text{II} & x + y & = & 9 \quad / \ - \\
\hline
\text{I} - \text{II} & x & = & 7 \\
\text{II} & 7 + y & = & 9 \quad =====\!\!\!\Rightarrow \quad y = 2
\end{array}
$$

7 : 2 = 3.5, wir runden ab auf 3; 2 : 2 = 1. Bei der Konstituierung dieser Formel müssen also jeweils drei 2er Werte aufeinanderfolgen und dann ein 1er Wert, daher:

$$
\text{(16)} \quad \left[\begin{array}{c} x \ . \ x \ . \ x \ . \ x \ x \ . \ x \ . \ x \ . \ x \ x \ . \end{array} \right]
$$

$$
\underbrace{2 + 2 + 2 + 1}_{7} + \underbrace{2 + 2 + 2 + 1}_{7} + 2
$$

Abb. 19

Berechnung n = 24 / k = 13

Die längste uns bekannte asymmetrische time-line-Formel in der afrikanischen Musik ist jene der Bangombe-Pygmäen am oberen Sangha-Fluß in ihrem mit Schlagbalken und Trommeln begleiteten *moyaya*-Tanz. Auch sie können wir nach demselben Verfahren mathematisch wiedererschaffen. 24 : 13 = 1.8 Die Formel konstituiert sich daher aus 2er und 1er Werten. Wieviele sind nötig?

$$
\begin{array}{llll}
\text{I} & 2x + y & = & 24 \\
\text{II} & x + y & = & 13 \quad / \ - \\
\hline
\text{I-II} & x & = & 11 \\
\text{II} & 11 + y & = & 13 \\
& y & = & 2
\end{array}
$$

11 : 2 = 5.5 Wir runden ab auf 5. Und 2 : 2 = 1 . Wir müssen also jeweils fünf 2er Werte gefolgt von einem 1er Wert aneinanderreihen.

$$
\text{(24)} \quad \left[\begin{array}{c} x \ . \ x \ . \ x \ . \ x \ . \ x \ . \ x \ x \ . \ x \ . \ x \ . \ x \ . \ x \ . \ x \ x \ . \end{array} \right]
$$

$$
\underbrace{2 + 2 + 2 + 2 + 2 + 1}_{11} \, \underbrace{2 + 2 + 2 + 2 + 2 + 1}_{11} \, 2 +
$$

Abb. 20

Es sei hier auch darauf hingewiesen, daß es bei n = 24 / k = 13 und entsprechend beim Komplementär bild n = 24 / k = 11 nicht weniger als 104006 Permutationen gibt, wie die Berechnung mit der entsprechenden Permutationsformel zeigt. Die Pygmäen-Formel ist die optimale Verteilung der Impulse unter den 104006 Möglichkeiten.

$$C_{24}^{13} = \frac{(n-1)!}{(n-k)! \cdot k!} = \frac{23 \cdot 22 \cdot 21 \cdot 20 \cdot 19 \cdot 18 \cdot 17 \cdot 16 \cdot 15 \cdot 14}{21 \cdot 10 \cdot 9 \cdot 8 \cdot 7 \cdot 6 \cdot 5 \cdot 4 \cdot 3 \cdot 2}$$

$$= 23 \cdot 7 \cdot 19 \cdot 17 \cdot 2 \quad = \quad 104006$$

Non-Standard Formeln

Neben den Standard time-line-Formeln, die wir oben behandelt haben, gibt es noch eine weitere Gruppe, die etwas aus dem Rahmen fällt, entweder weil n eine der seltenen Zykluszahlen darstellt, oder aber weil k einen anderen, noch nicht behandelten Wert hat.

Zu n = 9 / k_1 ,= 4 / k_2 = 5 ergeben sich nach unserer Berechnung 14 Möglichkeiten der Verteilung:

$$C_9^5 = \frac{8!}{4! \cdot 5!} = \frac{8 \cdot 7 \cdot 6 \cdot 5 \cdot 4 \cdot 3 \cdot 2}{4 \cdot 3 \cdot 2 \cdot 5 \cdot 4 \cdot 3 \cdot 2} = 14$$

Die systematische Verteilung sieht wie folgt aus:

387

⑨

```
XXXXX....
XXXX.X...
XXXX..X..
XXXX...X.
XXX.X..X.
XXX..X.X.
XX.X.X.X.
XX.X..XX.
XX..XX.X.
XX..X.XX.
XX...XXX.
.XX..XX.
..XX.XXX.
```

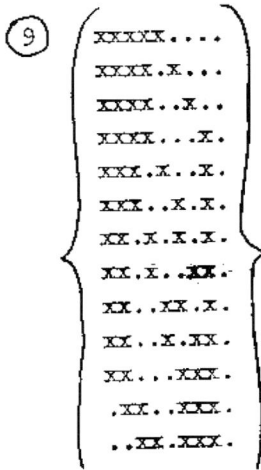

Abb. 21: N.B. Permutationen, in denen nicht mehr als zwei Schläge unmittelbar aufeinanderfolgen, sind als time-line verwendbar.

Das zweite Beispiel, das wir bringen wollen, betrifft Zyklus n = 16, den man auch noch durch eine weitere Schlagzahl asymmetrisch teilen kann, neben 9 und 7, nämlich durch 5. Hier ist die Beziehung zwischen den zwei Komplementärbildern wie folgt:

$$k_1 = \frac{16}{2} - 3 \quad \text{ist komplementär zu} \quad k_2 = \frac{16}{2} + 3$$

Eine Formel mit der Schlaganzahl 5 (k_1) ist also komplementär zu einer mit Schlaganzahl 11 (k_2) im Zyklus n = 16. Wieviele Möglichkeiten der Verteilung aber gibt es insgesamt? Dies erfahren wir mittels unserer bekannten Formel:

$$C_{16}^5 = \frac{(16-1)!}{(16-5)! \cdot 5!} = \frac{15 \cdot \overset{7}{14} \cdot 13 \cdot \overset{3}{12} \cdot 11 \cdot 10 \cdot 9 \cdot 8 \cdot 7 \cdot 6 \cdot 5 \cdot 4 \cdot 3 \cdot 2}{11 \cdot 10 \cdot 9 \cdot 8 \cdot 7 \cdot 6 \cdot 5 \cdot 4 \cdot 3 \cdot 2 \cdot 5 \cdot 4 \cdot 3 \cdot 2} = 21 \cdot 13$$

Es gibt also 273 Permutationen (Möglichkeiten der Verteilung). Die optimale Verteilung kann man visuell oder rechnerisch ermitteln; rechnerisch indem wir n durch k teilen, also 16 : 5 = 3.2 Die benötigten Randwerte konstituieren sich also aus 3er und 4er Einheiten; wieviele das sein müssen, ergibt sich aus dem uns inzwischen bekannten Berechnungs-Schema:

$$\begin{aligned}
\text{I} \quad & 4x + 3y = 16 \\
\text{II} \quad & x + y = 5
\end{aligned}$$

$$\text{II} \qquad x = 5 - y \quad \text{(in I einsetzen)}$$

$$\begin{aligned}
\text{I} \quad 4(5 - y) + 3y &= 16 \\
20 - 4y + 3y &= 16 \\
-y &= -4 \\
y &= 4
\end{aligned}$$

$$\text{II} \quad x + 4 = 5 \quad \Longrightarrow \quad x = 1$$

Wir brauchen also zum Aufbau der optimalen Verteilung vier 3er und einen 4er Wert. Das ist sehr einfach, da in diesem Fall eine einmalige Aneinanderreihung den Zyklus umspannt:

$$(16) \quad \left[x \ . \ . \ x \ . \ . \ x \ . \ . \ x \ . \ . \ x \ . \ . \ . \right]$$
$$ \quad \ \ 3 \ + \ 3 \ + \ 3 \ + \ 3 \ + \ 4$$

Abb. 22

Eine solche Gestalt gibt es in der afrikanischen Musik; nicht notwendigerweise als Formel, sondern als Struktur einer temporären Dreier-Überlagerung eines Beat aus vier Elementarpulswerten. Alfons M. Dauer hatte bereits darauf hingewiesen, daß diese Struktur auch in der Bossa Nova (Brasilien) vorkommt (Dauer1988:139) und daß dies der "Letzte Rhythmus" unter 273 Rhythmen sei. Die Struktur findet sich auch vielfach in Jazz-Improvisationen, und formalisiert (beinahe formelhaft, wenn auch nicht durchlaufend) zum Beispiel im rhythmischen Aufbau des mit Saxophonsatz gespielten Themas von Glenn Miller`s "A String of Pearls" (CD Glenn Miller, American Patrol FABCD 186 Acrobat).

Die kubanische Clave-Formel

Wir wissen, daß es noch eine weitere, sehr populäre Formel gibt, bei der fünf Schläge über 16 Pulse verteilt werden: die kubanische Clave-Formel. Eine Aufsehen erregende Studie erschien 1986 in Form des Buches von Rolando Antonio Pérez Fernández über die "binarización" ursprünglich ternärer afrikanischer Rhythmen in Lateinamerika. Die Grundthese von Fernandez ist, daß eine Reihe ursprünglich als "Dreier-Rhythmen" gedachter Bewegungsformen in den afrikanischen Musikkulturen nach ihrer Transplantation in die Neue Welt, insbesondere nach Lateinamerika, dort in "Zweier-Rhythmen" umgedeutet wurden. Allerdings geht der Autor von einer Prämisse aus, die eine Verallgemeinerung enthält, nämlich einer angeblich absoluten Vorherrschaft (predominio absoluto) binärer Taktteilungen in lateinamerikanischer Musik afrikanischen Ursprungs, und andererseits ternärer Teilungen in afroamerikanischen Kulten wie in der afrikanischen Musik. (Fernández 1986). Fernández' Feststellung richtet sich gegen die ältere spanisch-sprachige Literatur, in der binäre Rhythmen in Lateinamerika vielfach mit Afrika und ternäre mit Spanien in Verbindung gebracht werden. Überall geht man hier auch von den (europäischen) <u>Takt</u>-Vorstellungen aus, die entweder "binär" oder "ternär" untergeteilt seien.

Das Buch bekam verdienterweise den Premio de Musicologia, weil es doch eigentlich kognitionspsychologisch versucht, an ein kulturgeschichtlich relevantes Thema und menschliches Verhalten bei Kulturkontakt heranzugehen. Vieles von dem konstatierten Problem ist jedoch phantomhaft und wirkt zurechtgebogen, verallgemeinernd. Die Datenbasis, besonders aus Afrika, ist schwach. Andererseits ist der Grundgedanke oder zumindest die Grundbeobachtung, nämlich daß in der Neuen Welt gelegentlich afrikanische rhythmische Patterns binarisiert wurden, auch psychologisch einleuchtend. Dies betrifft nicht so sehr eine plötzlich Verhaltensänderung von Afro-Lateinamerikanern gegenüber ihren überlieferten afrikanischen Traditionen, sondern es trifft vor allem auf jene Kontaktsituationen zu, in denen Hispano-Amerikaner diese Traditionen zu übernehmen begannen. Hier trat der von Melville J. Herskovits theoretisch formulierte Prozeß der Reininterpretation massiv ein. Ähnliches ist auch in den U.S.A. im Laufe der Jazz- und Blues-Geschichte zu beobachten. Viele im Süden der U.S.A. von Afro-Amerikanern entwickelte Bluesformen haben eine ternäre Innenstruktur, daß heißt, es sind eigentlich (im afrikanischen Sinne) 12-Puls-Formen; der Vierer-Beat wird bei jedem Schlag dreigeteilt und zwar ganz ebenmäßig im Sinne der referentiellen Elementarpulsation (ohne Präakzentuierung). Von anderen Traditionen herkommende Gitarristen scheinen damit oft Schwierigkeiten zu haben. Sie präakzentuieren manchmal die "Triolen", und in ihrem Repertoire findet sich oft eine Tendenz zu überwiegend binären Formen; die ternären Formen werden entweder gemieden oder in binäre Formen umgedeutet; aus [♩ ♪] wird [♩ ♪].
In Kuba ist in diesem Zusammenhang die entfernte Geschichte der berühmten Clave-Formel interessant, die sich über 16 Elementarpuls-Werte erstreckt. Abgesehen von den jüngeren Einflüssen kubanischer Son-Musik (Rumba) in Zentralafrika, scheint diese Formel in den alten Kulturen Zentralafrikas in dieser Form nicht auffindbar, dort gibt es eine Formel mit derselben Anzahl von Schlägen, nämlich fünf, aber diese sind über 12 Elementarpuls-Werte verteilt (wie wir bereits dargestellt haben). Ist die kubanische Clave-Formel somit eine hispano-kubanische Reinterpretion der 5-Schlag/12-Puls Formel Afrikas? Fernández hat hier ein interessantes Thema zur Diskussion geführt.

Seine Ansicht, daß die Clave-Formel ihre spezifische Schlag-Verteilung einem Prozess der Binarisation verdankt, der in Kuba schon bei den ersten Begegnungen spanischer Deszendenten mit der afrikanischen asymmetrischen Formelwelt stattfand, ist im Prinzip nicht abwegig. Reinterpretation dieser Art findet bei jedem Kulturkontakt statt. In Brasilien wurde die ostangolanische *kachacha*-Formel, also n = 16 / k = 7 oder 9, zur Grundlage vieler Formen des Samba. Meist ist sie in ihrem Tanzbeat-Bezug reinterpretiert (cf. Pinto 1991), aber auch der angolanische Beat-Bezug überlebt gelegentlich, wie eine Aufnahme, die wir 1975 in einem Vorort von Salvador/Bahia am Strand von einer lokalen Samba-Gruppe machten, belegt (cf. Tonaufnahme G. Kubik/Dieter Föhr, 12. Oktober 1975 aus Itapoa, Gesang, Trommeln und "cuica"-Reibetrommel, auf der die

Formel gespielt wurde). Aus der Struktur des Gesanges der Leute ergibt sich eindeutig der Beat-Bezug .

Daß sich eine Schlagfolge auch in ihrem internen "Spacing" in der auditiven Wahrnehmung von Leuten anderen kulturellen Hintergrunds verändern kann, ist uns gleichfalls aus vielen Kontaktsituationen bekannt. Die west- und zentralafrikanischen time-line-Formeln, besonders jene über 12 Elementarpulseinheiten, werden regelmäßig von Angehörigen anderer Kulturen perzeptorisch umgebogen. Darüber hat bereits A.M. Jones (1959: 223) uns einiges mitgeteilt und in graphischer Darstellung gezeigt, weshalb diese Fehlwahrnehmung so leicht zustandekommt . Nach unseren heutigen Forschungs-Erfahrungen geschieht sie immer dann, wenn der Rezipient (Zuhörer etc.) nicht imstande ist, gehörsmäßig den intrakulturell richtigen Bezug der time-line-Formel zur Elementarpulsation herzustellen. Daß dies nicht nur Leuten mit überwiegend europäisch-klassischer Musikausbildung passiert, sondern auch Personen aus afrikanischen Kulturen ohne time-line-Formeln, darauf stieß ich in Uganda bereits in den 1960er Jahren. Einmal, bei einem Vortrag vor Baganda-Studenten der Musik in Kampala, spielte ich die 5-Schlag/12-Puls-Formel Zentralafrikas vor und forderte die Studenten dann auf, sie zu notieren. Einer hatte den Mut dazu; er notierte sie, ohne bei den anderen deshalb Widerspruch zu erregen, im 7/4-Takt, und zwar so:

Abb. 23

Wenn man also, mit der 5-Schlag/12-Puls-Formel konfrontiert, nicht imstande ist, sie auf die darunter liegende unhörbare Elementarpulsation zu beziehen, sondern sie auf internalisierte Metren bezieht, dann kommt es zu vorhersagbaren Reaktionen. Es kann sein, daß die Formel auf ein ungerades Metrum bezogen wird, oder es wird Taktwechsel hineingedacht, wie es vielen Musikwissenschaftler bei ihren Notationen afrikanischer Musik von Schallaufzeichnungen anfangs des 20. Jahrhunderts ergangen ist. Oder aber es findet eine minimale Umdeutung anderer Art statt, besonders wenn es sich um sensible Musiker handelt.

Wenn Fernández' These von der Binarisation stimmt, wäre ein solcher Fall in Kuba zustandegekommen. Der Unterschied zwischen dem Spacing der Schläge in der afrikanischen 5 Schlag/12-Puls-Formel und der kubanischen Clave-Formel ist relativ gering und – was hier besonders wichtig erscheint – man kann beiden Formeln den gleichen ground beat unterlegen, ohne sie zu zerstören. Auf dem ersten und dem vierten Grundschlag stimmen beide überein (Abb. 24)

391

Clave-Formel Kubas im Vergleich

(a) Kubanische Clave-Formel:

$$\boxed{16} \quad \left[\; x \;\cdot\; \cdot\; x \;\cdot\; \cdot\; x \;\cdot\; \big|\; \cdot\; \cdot\; x \;\cdot\; x \;\cdot\; \cdot\; \cdot\; \right]$$

(b) 5-Schlag/12-Puls-Formel
    Zentralafrikas:

$$\boxed{12} \quad \left[\; x \;\cdot\; x \;\cdot\; x \;\cdot\; \big|\; \cdot\; x \;\cdot\; x \;\cdot\; \right]$$

Grundschlag: (Tanz-Beat)

$$\boxed{12} \quad \left[\begin{array}{c} x \\ 1 \end{array} \qquad \begin{array}{c} x \\ 2 \end{array} \quad \big| \begin{array}{c} x \\ 3 \end{array} \qquad \begin{array}{c} x \\ 4 \end{array} \right]$$

Abb. 24

Wer nur vom Grundschlag ausgeht und nicht von den <u>zwei verschiedenen Elementarpulsebenen</u> dieser Formeln, für den stellen sich die Diskrepanzen als "mikrorhythmisch" dar. Es ist denkbar, daß kubanische Audienzen in einer frühen Kontaktphase mit afrikanischen Sklaven aus dem Bantu-Sprachraum deren Formel in diesem Sinne umdeuteten.

Obwohl die Abweichungen der Formeln voneinander aus Kleinstwerten bestehen, können sie gerade deshalb wahrnehmungspsychologisch so leicht an eine andere innere Vorstellung regelmäßiger Pulsketten geankert werden. Dieser Effekt der Regularisierung ist uns allen von Reisen im Schlafwagen alter Züge bekannt, bei denen man das Holpern der Räder über die Schienenlücken rhythmisch umdeutet. Mit anderen Worten: jemand, dem die 5-Schlag 12-Pulsformel fremd ist, weil er oder sie "metrisch" denkt und den Bezug zur Elementarpulsation nicht herstellen kann, wird bei der Umdeutung von den ersten und letzten on-beat Schlägen als Bezugspunkte ausgehen. Er/sie wird diese Stellen metrisch als Taktteil 1 und 4 reinterpretieren und den Rest der Formel wahrnehmungsmäßig so zurechtbiegen, wie die Räder-Rhythmen auf alten Eisenbahnen.

Allerdings wäre auch eine andere Rhythmusformel als Hintergrund für die Entstehungsgeschichte der Clave-Formel denkbar. Wenn man die asymmetrische $n = 16$ / $k = 5$-Formel zum Vergleich heranzieht, zeigt sich, daß der Unterschied zwischen dieser und der kubanischen Clave-Formel in <u>nur einem einzigen Schlag</u> besteht (Abb. 25):

Clave-Formel
16

$$\left[\; x \;\cdot\; \cdot\; x \;\cdot\; \cdot\; x \;\cdot\; \cdot\; \cdot\; x \;\cdot\; x \;\cdot\; \cdot\; \cdot\; \right]$$

Formel
$n = 16$ / $k = 5$

$$\left[\; x \;\cdot\; \cdot\; x \;\cdot\; \cdot\; x \;\cdot\; \cdot\; x \;\cdot\; \cdot\; x \;\cdot\; \cdot\; \cdot\; \right]$$

Abb. 25

Wie Alfons M. Dauer in seinem Artikel (1988) gezeigt hat, sind beide Formeln Permutationen von C_{16}^5. Die Clave-Formel erscheint allerdings in der Computer-Tabelle nicht als "Letzter Rhythmus". So gäbe es vielleicht auch ein strukturelles Argument zugunsten von Fernández' These: Alle asymmetrischen afrikanischen time-line-Formeln sind in Dauer`s Computer-Tabellen "Letzte Rhythmen", repräsentieren also optimale Verteilungen der Impulse; die Clave-Formel ist es dagegen nicht. Sie könnte also dem System der afrikanischen time-line-Formeln nicht direkt zugeordnet werden, was ihre Entwicklung außerhalb des Kontextes einer afrikanischen Musikkultur (also etwa in Kuba) in den Bereich des Möglichen rückt.

Auch der historische Befund könnte Fernández' These, daß die Formel in Kuba entwickelt wurde, stützen. In Westafrika erscheint sie im gesamten Sample unserer Aufnahmen seit 1960 immer mit Musikimporten aus der Karibik assoziiert, also mit neueren Formen afrikanischer Populärmusik in der ersten und zweiten Hälfte des 20. Jahrhunderts. Daß sie in der neueren Kongo-Musik vorkommt, ist bekannt. Dort geht ihre Verwendung in "moderner" gitarren-basierter Musik ab den 1950er Jahren eindeutig auf den Import kubanischer Schallplatten zurück und auf die Inspiration, die sie lokal in den urbanen Zentren Kinshasa, Brazzaville etc. auslösten.

Mindestens seit den 1930er Jahren ist ein heftiger Import populärer Musikformen aus der Karibik, Calypso, Rumba etc. an der westafrikanischen Küste zu spüren, mit Sicherheit nachweisbar in manchen Formen der Yoruba-Musik, wobei ja die Geschichte des Rückflusses afro-karibischer und afro-brasilianischer Kulturelemente in vielen Bereichen des Lebens spürbar ist und in Lagos auf Rücksiedlungen von Afro-Brasilianern nach der Abolition 1888 zurückgeht. 1960, als ich meine Dokumentation von Yoruba-Musik in dem Städtchen Oshogbo und anderswo in West-Nigeria begann, war die Clave-Formel längst etabliert, und nicht nur in der *juju*-Musik prominent, sondern sie war von dorther sogar in ein Märchenlied "Adu aja mio" (cf. Kubik 1989: 175) vorgedrungen. Sie wurde zwar nicht direkt beim Gesang als Begleitung geschlagen, war aber strukturell in dem Lied impliziert. Auch der Playright Duro Ladipọ benützte die Formel in seinen Musikdramen, ganz explizit.

Das Problem hier ist dennoch kaum zu lösen; denn wenn immer die Clave-Formel in Afrika auftaucht, ergibt sich berechtigterweise der Verdacht, daß rezenter, transatlantischer Rückfluss vorliege. Ihre Abwesenheit in Musik-Genres älterer Prägung im heutigen West- und Zentralafrika scheint dies zu unterstützen, ist aber auch anders erklärbar. Es könnte sein, daß die Clave-Formel im 16., 17. oder 18. Jahrhundert sehr wohl in West- oder Zentralafrika etabliert war, aber – wie vieles in afrikanischen Kulturen – inzwischen verloren gegangen ist, nachdem sie vorher noch in die Neue Welt exportiert wurde. Kulturgeschichtlich wäre dies ja kein einzigartiger Fall. Sie hätte demnach abseits ihres ursprünglichen Verbreitungsgebietes an der "Peripherie" überlebt, dort eine bleibende Nische gefunden, wie so manches andere in Diaspora-Kulturen, das in den Heimatkulturen längst verloren gegangen ist.

Im Candomblé Brasiliens beispielsweise überleben Formeln, die in den Yoruba-Kulten Nigerias längst nicht mehr benützt werden. Und eine ist genau die Clave-Formel. Wie

Tiago de Oliveira Pinto im Recôncavo, Bahia, dokumentierte, erscheint sie dort in einem *toque* genannt *ramunha* oder *avamunha* und wird auf der Einfachglocke *gã* geschlagen. (Abb. 26)

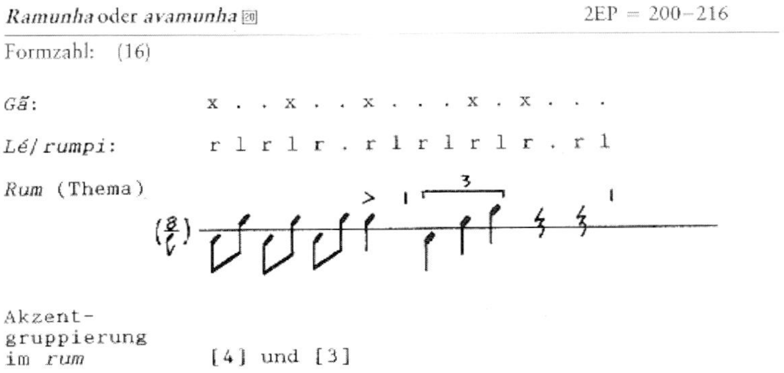

Ramunha oder avamunha 📞   2EP = 200–216

Formzahl: (16)

Gã: x . . x . . x . . . x . x . . .

Lé / rumpi: r l r l r . r l r l r l r . r l

Rum (Thema)

Akzent-
gruppierung
im *rum*   [4] und [3]

Abb. 26: *Gã*–Formel im Candomblé, Recôncavo, Bahia (reproduziert aus Pinto 1991:187).

Es ist wohl nicht anzunehmen, daß diese Formel aus der populären Musik Kubas übernommen wurde, sondern sie wird direkt mit der Orixa-Religion aus Westafrika nach Bahia gekommen sein.

Man kann auch Fernández' These in ihrer Formulierung modifizieren und annehmen, daß die kubanische Clave-Formel strukturell mit der 5-Schlag/12-Pulsformel in Afrika gar nichts zu tun hat, sondern viel mehr von der ubiquitären 3 + 3 + 2 -Formel abgeleitet ist, die auch in der fernsten uns bekannten Geschichte längst nicht nur im sub-saharanischen Afrika, sondern im Maghreb und – mit der maurischen Präsenz – in Spanien, sowie durch weiteren Kulturkontakt in anderen Mittelmeerländern bekannt war. Man kann die kubanische Clave-Formel als aus zwei Hälften bestehend auffassen, die erste Hälfte mit der Struktur 3 + 3 + 2, die zweite in divisiver Teilung des darunter liegenden 4/4-Metrums. Die Verbindungen mit dem sub-saharanischen Afrika bestünden dann vor allem in diesen Merkmalen: (1) der Übernahme der west/zentralafrikanischen Grundidee einer time-line –Formel; daß diese Version eben als time-line funktioniert; (2) daß sie auf Gegenschlag-Stäbchen ausgeführt wird; (3) daß sie Teil einer Perkussionsgruppe ist, deren Organisation breiten afrikanischen Überlieferungen folgt. In diesem Sinne wäre auch ein konzeptuelles Überblenden der Erfahrung anderer afrikanischer time-line-Formeln wie sie von Yoruba, Ewe und Kongolesen nach Kuba gebracht wurden, in die Entstehungsgeschichte der Clave-Formel denkbar.

Der Mangel an Quellenmaterial aus früheren Jahrhunderten zu diesen Fragen beeinträchtigt unsere Forschung. Andererseits kann uns manchmal auch eine vorsichtige Anwendung von ein wenig Psychologie bei der Einschätzung universellen menschlichen Verhaltens um einen kleinen Schritt weiterhelfen. Die Psychologie des Menschen ist doch letzthin eine Konstante, wenn sie auch immer mit verschiedensten Inhalten der "Kultur" und der persönlichen Lebenserfahrung aufgefüllt wird. Wir haben gelernt, daß im Zuge der Reinterpretation einer time-line-Formel bei Kulturkontakt nicht nur der Beat-Bezug der Formel verändert werden kann, sondern es kann auch eine

Elementarpulsebene gegen eine andere ausgetauscht werden. In diesem Sinne sind die 5-Schlag/12-Pulsformel Zentral- und Südostafrikas und die 16-Puls Clave-Formel Kubas gegenseitige Annäherungen. Die Ähnlichkeit der Verteilung der Schlagimpulse bei beiden Formeln ist zwar frappant, wird aber vom jeweils unterliegenden Elementarpuls-Schema relativiert.

Dabei haben wir des öfteren eine Beobachtung gemacht, die wichtig scheint: Personen, die in ihrem Leben zuerst die Clave-Formel aus Kuba gelernt haben und gut beherrschen, haben regelmäßig Schwierigkeiten, die zentralafrikanische 5-Schlag/12-Pulsformel in den genauen Abständen zu treffen, sollten sie in die Lage kommen, an einer solchen Musik teilzunehmen. Entsprechende Experimente habe ich gemeinsam mit Maurice Djenda in den 1960er Jahren auf unseren Forschungsreisen mit verschiedenen Leuten in der Zentralafrikanischen Republik und anderen Staaten gemacht, aber auch an uns selbst durchgeführt (siehe meinen Bericht in *Theory of African Music*, Vol. 2). Die 5-Schlag/12-Plus-Formel ist die dominierende time-line in Djenda's ethnischer Gruppe im Südwesten der R.C.A.: den Mpyɛm. Djenda hatte sie als Kind zuerst (also als "erste Sprache") erlernt, und später mit seinem Interesse an Kongo-Populärmusik auch die Clave-Formel. Er beherrschte somit beide "Sprachen". Wer aber von der kubanischen Clave-Formel als "erster Sprache" herkommt, sie also zuerst gelernt hat, wie es auch bei mir in meiner eigenen Geschichte der Fall war, tendiert nun dazu, bei Begegnung mit der anderen Formel den vierten Schlag verzögert zu spielen, weil er/sie eben doch unwillkürlich immer noch von einer 16-er Elementarpulsation oder gar von einem 4/4-Metrum ausgeht. Es braucht einige Zeit, bis man umgelernt hat. Es gibt aber auch Personen, für die beide Formeln "Fremdsprache" bleiben; diese neigen dann nicht selten dazu, sie "additiv" aufzufassen.

Die ersten drei Schläge werden von manchen Personen dann eher als eine Dreier-Überlagerung eines 4/4-Taktes verstanden (siehe das Notationsbeispiel in Jones 1959: 223). Aber den nächsten Schlag an der richtigen Stelle zu artikulieren, gelingt dann nicht mehr, denn es setzt voraus, daß man von der richtigen 12-er Elementarpulsation ausgeht, da sie (und nur sie) den internen, fast unbewußten Raster von relevanten Bezugspunkten repräsentiert. Auch das ist natürlich erlernbar.

Ich gewann den Eindruck (und stütze mich dabei auf Beobachtungen bei Donald J. Kachamba auf unseren vielen Tourneen, als er mich mit der 5-Schlag 12-Pulsformel bei meinem *likembe*-Spiel begleitete), daß das Umsteigen von der 5-Schlag 12-Puls-Formel auf die kubanische Clave-Formel bei Personen, die in der ersteren Tradition aufgewachsen sind, müheloser gelingt, als umgekehrt.

Danksagung

Die Forschungen, die zu dieser Untersuchung über die afrikanischen time-line-Formeln geführt haben, wurden im Rahmen unseres vom Wissenschaftsfonds Wien finanzierten Dreijahres- Projekts P 17751 G06 (15. März 2005 -15.März 2008) durchgeführt. Ohne die neuerlichen gemeinsamen Feldforschungen mit Dr. Moya A. Malamusi in Moçambique, Malawi, Tanzania und Uganda und die praktische Zusammenarbeit mit den Musiker-Komponisten Sinosi Mlendo und Christopher Gerald wäre diese Arbeit noch lange nicht fertiggestellt worden. Für die Einladung an das Institut für Musikwissenschaft der Universität Hamburg im Mai 2007, wo ich etwas von unseren jüngsten Forschungen in Uganda vermitteln konnte, danke ich Prof. Dr. Albrecht

Schneider, der mit mir viele dieser Interessen teilt. Dies gilt in gleicher Weise auch für meinen "Zwillingsbruder", Prof. Dr. Tiago de Oliveira Pinto – wir sind am gleichen Tag, aber nicht im selben Jahr geboren – der mit mir seit vielen Jahren das Interesse an den time-line-Formeln in Afrika wie in Brasilien gemeinsam hat. Schließlich danke ich unserem Projekt-Mitarbeiter Yohana Malamusi, der den Computer-Satz dieses Artikels, ausgehend von meinem Maschine-getippten Originalmanuskript, hergestellt hat.

Literaturhinweise

Ascher, Marcia

    1991   *Ethnomathematics. A Multicultural View of Mathematical Ideas*. Belmont: Wadsworth, Inc.

Chemillier, Marc
    2004   Représentations musicales et représentations mathématiques", *L'Homme. Revue Française d'Anthropologie*. Musique et Anthrolopologie. No. 171 – 172, juillet/décembre, pp. 267 – 283

Dauer, Alfons M.
    1966   „Musik-Landschaften in Afrika", *Afrika Heute*, Sonderbeilage 23. – Nachdruck in Artur Simon, ed., *Musik in Afrika*, 1983:41 – 48

    1988   „Derler 1: Ein System zur Klassifikation von Rhythmen. Musktheoretische und musikhistorische Aspekte", *Jazzforschung – Jazz Research* 20: 117 – 154

Dehaene, Stanislaus
    1997   *The Number Sense*. New York: Oxford University Press

Dehaene, Stanislaus and Cohen L.
    1997   „Cerebral pathways for calculation: Double dissociations between Gerstmann's acalculia and subcortical acalculia", *Cortex* 33: 219 – 250.

Fernandez, Rolando A. Pérez
    1986   *La Binarizacion de los Ritmos Ternarios Africanos en America Latina.* La Habana :

Gazzaniga, Michael A.
    1998   *The Mind's Past*. Berkeley: University of California Press

Grauer, Victor A.
    2007   „New perspectives on the Karahari debate: a tale of two ‚genomes'", *Before Farming*, no. 2, article 4 http://music000001.blogspot.com

Greenberg, Joseph H.
    1966   *The Languages of Africa*. Research Center for the Language Sciences, Indiana University, Bloomington: Indiana University Press

Guthrie, Malcolm
    1948   *The Classification of the Bantu Languages*. London: Oxford University Press

Herskovits, Melville J.
    1941   *The Myth of the Negro Past*. New York: Harper & Brothers

Jaritz, Wolfgang
    1983   "Über Bahnen auf Billardtischen oder: Eine mathematische
               Untersuchung von Ideogrammen angolanischer Herkunft" Bericht
               Nr. 207 *Mathematisch-Statistische Sektion*, Forschungszentrum Graz.

Jones A. M:
    1934   „African drumming. A study in the combination of rhythm in African
               music", *Bantu Studies*, 8 (1) : 1 - 16

    1954   "African rhythm" , *Africa*, 2 (1) : 26 – 47

    1959   *Studies in African Music*, Vol. 1 and 2. London: Oxford University Press.

Kubik, Gerhard
    1961   "Musikgestaltung in Afrika" *Neues Afrika* 3 (5): 195-200; Nachdruck mit
               Ergänzungen in Artur Simon: *Musik in Afrika*, 1983: 27 – 40

    1972   „Oral notation of some West and Central African time-line patterns",
               Review of Ethnology, 2 (22): 169 – 176

    1979   *Angolan Traits in Black Music, Games and Dances of Brazil. A Study of
               African Cultural Extensions Overseas.* Estudos de Antropologia Cultural 10.
               Lisabon: Junta de Inestigações do Ultramar.

    1989   "Àló – Yoruba chantefables : An Integrated Approach Towards West African
               Music and Oral Literature", in: Jacqueline Cogdell DjeDje and William
               G. Carter, eds.: *African Musicology: Current Trends*. Volume 1.
               A Festschrift presented to J.H. Kwabena Nketia. Los Angeles: African
               Studies Center & African Arts Magazine, University of California,
               pp. 129 – 182

    1992   „Analoge Strukturen im auditiven und visuellen Bereich afrikanischer
               künstlerischer Gestaltung" , *Jahrbuch Bayerische Akademie der Schönen
               Künste* 6. München: Oreos Verlag, pp. 326 – 368

    1993   *Theory of African Music*. Volume 1. Wilhelmshaven: Noetzel

    1998   "Intra-African streams of influence", in: *The Garland Encyclopedia of World
               Music*. Volume 1: *Africa*. Ruth M. Stone, ed., New York and London:
               Garland Publishing Inc., pp. 293-326.

    1999   *Africa and the Blues*. Jackson: The University Press of Mississippi. – Italian
               Translation by Fabio Polese: *L'Africa et il Blues*. A cura di Giorgio Adamo.
               Subiaco: Fogli Volanti Edizioni, 2007 (with accompanying CD)

    2004   "Inherent patterns – Musiques de l'ancien royaume Buganda: étude de
               psychologie cognitive", *L'Homme – Revue Française d'Anthropologie*,
               no.171 – 172, Juillet/décembre, pp. 249 – 266, plus CD.

    2005   *Tusona – Luchazi Ideographs. A Graphic Tradition of West –Central Africa*.
               Second enlarged edition. Münster: LIT Verlag

  In press *Theory of African Music*. Volume 2. Chicago: University of Chicago Press

Kyagambiddwa, Joseph
  1955   *African Music from the Source of the Nile.* New York: Praeger

Lomax, Alan
  1968   *Folk Song Style and Culture.* American Association for the Advancement of
          Science, Publication 88. Washington: American Association for the
          Advancement of Science.

  1973   "Cinema, Science and Culture Renewal", *Current Anthropology* 14 (4),
          October, pp. 474 – 480

Phillipson, David W.
  1977   *The Later Prehistory of Eastern and Southern Africa.* London: Heinemann

Pinto, Tiago de Oliveira
  1991   *Capoeira, Samba, Candomblé. Afrikanische Musik im Recôncavo Bahia.*
          Veröffentlichungen des Museum für Völkerkunde Berlin. Neue Folge 52,
          Abteilung Musikethnologie VII. Berlin: Staatliche Museen Preußischer
          Kulturbesitz.

  1999   As cores do Som. Estruturas sonoras e concepção estética na música afro-brasileira. In:
          Revista África (22 / 23): 87-110.

Rouget, Gilbert
  1948   Musiques pygmées et nègres d'Afrique Equatoriale Française. 3 disques 30
          cm/78tm BAM 108-109-110 Mission Ogooué-Congo 1946. Réédition LP 1957

  2004   „L'efficacité musicale: musiquer pour survivre. Le cas des Pygmées",
          L'Homme – Revue Française d'Anthropologie no. 171 – 172, juillet/décembre,
          pp. 27 – 52 (avec CD)

Schneider, Albrecht et al
  1994   „Wo ist die 'Eins' ? Zur Wahrnehmung und Apperzeption (afro-)rhythmischer
          Gebilde", in: *For Gerhard Kubik. Festschrift ...* August Schmidhofer und
          Dietrich Schüller eds. With a foreword by David Rycroft. Frankfurt a. Main:
          Peter Lang, pp. 479 - 501

Simon, Artur, Hg.
  1983   *Musik in Afrika. 20 Beiträge zur Kenntnis traditioneller afrikanischer
          Musikkulturen.* Veröffentlichungen des Museum für Völkerkunde Berlin.
          Neue Folge 40, Abteilung Musikethnologie VII. Berlin: Staatliche Museen
          Preußischer Kulturbesitz.

Tracey, Hugh
  1973   *Catalogue of the Sound of Africa Recordings.* 210 Long Playing Records on
          music and songs from Central, Eastern and Southern Africa by Hugh Tracey,
          Vol. I and II. Roodeport (South Africa): The International Library of African
          Music.

Wachsmann, Klaus Peter
  1967   "Pen-Equidistance and Accurate Pitch: A Problem from the Source of the Nile",
          in: *Festschrift für Walter Wiora zum 30. December 1966.* L. Finscher & C.-H.
          Mahling, eds. Kassel: Bärenreiter, pp. 583-592

Ulrich Morgenstern

Der *Skobarja* von Velikie Luki und angrenzende instrumental-vokale Formen im Gebiet Tver' (Ethnische und ethnomusikalische Identität)[1]

Vorbemerkungen

Fragen von Ethnizität und ethnischer Identität stehen seit Jahrzehnten im Zentrum des ethnologischen Interesses. In der Volkskunde / Europäischen Ethnologie wie auch vielfach in der europäischen Ethnomusikologie haben diese Leitbegriffe den des „Volkes" seit geraumer Zeit abgelöst. Als wissenschaftliches Konzept erscheint dieser axiologisch konnotiere Basisbegriff der traditionellen Folkloristik zumindest wegen seiner Doppeldeutigkeit im Kontext sowohl ethnischer („das russische Volk", „das deutsche Volk") wie auch sozialer Distinktion („das Volk und die Partei") als problematisch. Dies bedeutet im übrigen keineswegs, daß man den Entlarvungsgestus und die fortdauernde Gehässigkeit teilen muß, mit der in den Kulturwissenschaften vielfach vermeintliche oder tatsächliche Nachwirkungen der romantischer Ästhetik „ideologiekritisch" vorgeführt werden.

Betrachtet man den gesellschaftlichen und politischen Diskurs der letzten Jahrzehnte in den europäischen Ländern, so ist unschwer festzustellen, daß „Volk" als Leitbegriff nur sehr selten anklingt. Sein früheres Pathos wird vor allem in ritualisierten Situationen aktuell, wenn an die gesellschaftliche Solidarität und Loyalität appelliert wird. In der Bundesrepublik Deutschland werden Gerichtsurteile „im Namen des Volkes" ausgesprochen, bei ihrer Vereidigung berufen sich die höchsten Amtsträger im Staat ebenfalls auf das Volk. Mithin wurde der Volksbegriff auch im Zusammenhang mit gesellschaftlichen Konflikten eingesetzt – seien es real existierende („Wir sind das Volk!" als Parole gegen das kommunistische Regime Ostdeutschlands) oder eingebildete („Power to the people!" als sozialromantischer Slogan der akademischen Jugend in der westlichen Welt, dessen Vertonung 1971 nach Lohn Lennons Eingeständnis gleichwohl zehn Jahre zu spät kam).

Wurzelnd in der vorindustriellen Ständegesellschaft wird der Volksbegriff (ganz überwiegend in Zusammensetzungen) heute zudem im Kontext kultureller Phänomene gebraucht, die historisch mit einem Milieu verbunden sind, das den sozialen oder wissenschaftlichen Eliten gegenübergestellt wurde. Wir sprechen von „Volksetymologien", „Volksmedizin" usf. – und auch der Begriff der *Volksmusik* erscheint durchaus nicht obsolet, wenn wir es etwa mit der musikalischen Praxis in bäuerlich geprägten Gemeinschaften zu tun haben, die vormals von Adel, Kaufleuten oder Klerus geschieden waren. Dessen ungeachtet ist auch in historisch-rekonstruktiv orientierten ethnomusikologischen Studien der Terminus *Volksmusik* weitgehend durch den auf außereuropäische

---

[1] Der vorliegende Beitrag ist eine leicht veränderte Fassung meines Aufsatzes „«Velikolukskij Skobar'» i ego vostočnye sosedi. Ètničeskaja i ètnomuzykal'naja identičnost'", der für den zehnten Band der von Aleksandr Sergeevič Gerd herausgegebenen Reihe *Severnorusskije govory* (Philologische Fakultät der Universität St. Petersburg 2008) vorgesehen ist. Ich danke dem Herausgeber für die freundliche Genehmigung zur Veröffentlichung der deutschen Version.

Verhältnisse besser anwendbaren Begriff der *traditionellen Musik* ersetzt worden, der gleichwohl eher als Notbehelf gelten muß (Elschek 1991). Besonders in der US-amerikanischen Forschung spricht man neuerdings weniger von traditionellen, sondern von *lokalen* Musikstilen, Musikern, Musik-Konzepten usf. Dieser Begriffswandel beansprucht eine geringere kategoriale Reichweite, wie sie der Begriff der *Volksmusik* und auch der *traditionellen Musik* impliziert, der von sozial und stilmäßig mehr oder weniger abgrenzbaren Musikkulturen ausgeht. Mit solchen hat es ethnomusikologische Forschung auch in Zeiten der Globalisierung vielfach immer noch zu tun (Brandl 2003) – ungeachtet aller lustvollen Überbetonung der Transformation und des Hybridhaften (Greve 2002).

Der der Ethnologie entstammende Begriff der *ethnischen Gruppe* ist – bei aller neuerdings geäußerten Skepsis – auch in der Ethnomusikologie zum Basiskonzept geworden (nicht jedoch der Terminus *ethnische Musik*, der vor allem auf dem Tonträgermarkt gebräuchlich ist). Nach Bettina Beer kann die «ethnische Gruppe» oder die «Ethnie» als „eine überwiegend endogame familienübergreifende Gemeinschaft definiert werden, deren Mitglieder in der Abgrenzung von anderen Menschen ein «Wir-Gefühl» entwickelt haben, eine gemeinsame, sie von anderen unterscheidende (angenommene) Abstammung, gemeinsame Geschichte und meist einen gemeinsamen Kanon an Werten und Normen teilen" (Beer 2006: 54). Ein so verstandenes Konzept der ethnischen Gruppe verzichtet auf eindeutige Zuschreibungen von Ethnizität als gleichsam zwingend notwendiger Eigenschaft jedes Individuums sowie auf eine hierarchische Taxonomie von Ethnien.

Der Vorteil der modernen ethnologischen Konzepte kann in der Abkehr von der ausschließlichen Fixierung auf die vielfach nur konstruierte historische Kontinuität gesehen werden und von den axiologischen Implikationen, die den Konzepten von *Volk* und *Stamm* häufig zugrunde liegen[2]. In der russischen Ethnologie hat ein solcher Ansatz, der Ethnizität nicht als etwas Naturgegebenes ansieht, sondern auf das Selbstbewußtsein der jeweiligen Gruppe abhebt, eine lange Geschichte. Schon 1947 hielt P.I. Kušner einen Vortrag mit dem Titel „Das nationale Selbstbewußtsein als ethnischer Indikator"(Grigor'eva/Martynova, Hg., 2005: 29). Auch wenn die Suche nach solchen „Indikatoren" uns heute reichlich essentialistisch erscheinen mag, so zeigt doch die Hervorhebung des kollektiven Bewußtseins als einer grundlegenden Voraussetzung von Ethnizität vor 60 Jahren, daß der Gedanke von ihrer „sozialen Konstruiertheit" (Tiškov 2003: 120-124) weit mehr ist als eine modische Phrase im Geiste der Postmoderne.[3] Wenngleich

---

[2] Gerade das in der traditionellen europäischen Folkloristik häufig spürbare Bestreben, den untersuchten Kulturgütern und kollektiven Verhaltensmustern möglichst viele archaische, volkstümliche und ethnische oder nationale Eigenschaften zuzuschreiben, hat vielfach, besonders in totalitären Systemen, eine seriöse Prüfung solcher Vermutungen behindert. Als unrühmliches Beispiel für kann das Schicksal von Vladimir Karbusickys Studie zu den tschechischen Epen gelten (Karbusicky 1980). Als sich abzeichnete, daß diese Epen weder als national, noch als volkstümlich noch als Relikt archaischer Zeit gelten können, mußte der Gelehrte seine Forschungen im Geheimen weiterführen. Nicht weniger verhängnisvoll erweisen sich solche ideologischen Verengung aber auch dadurch, daß sie vielfach zum – mithin durchaus willkommenen – Anlaß genommen werden, jedes Interesse an historischer Forschung in den Kulturwissenschaften zu diskreditieren, das sich nicht auf die so beliebte „Dekonstruktion" von *invented traditions* beschränkt.

[3] Gleichwohl mag der Ethnomusikologe nicht ohne weiteres der Position Tiškovs zustimmen, nach der „die Kultur selbst schweigsam" sei. (2003: 116).

der Konstruktivismus nicht als ein auf alle Lebensbereiche anwendbares Erklärungsmodell gelten kann, so scheint er doch für die Klärung ethnischer Prozesse in der modernen Welt wie in der historischen Perspektive vielfach hilfreich.

Der prozessuale Charakter der Ethnizität, ihre Fähigkeit, sich mit biographischen oder politischen Rahmenbedingungen zu transformieren, betrifft durchaus nicht nur die Wandlungsprozesse in einer globalisierten Welt, etwa die vielfältigen Migrationsströme. Er kann auch Aktualität erlangen, wenn wir es mit relativ isolierten bäuerlich geprägten Gemeinschaften im ostslawischen Raum zu tun haben. Und in solchen Transformationsprozessen können *ethnic markers* wie Musik und Tanz eine wichtige Rolle spielen.

Der *Skobarja* von Velikie Luki und sein Verbreitungsgebiet

Lokale Musikkulturen bilden ihre Identität in erster Linie durch Abgrenzung von anderen Kulturen oder ethnischen Gruppen (Barth 1969). In dieser Hinsicht teilen traditionelle Musiker den vergleichenden Ansatz mit den Ethnomusikologen[4]. Ein besonders geeignetes Material ist das weithin vernachlässigte Feld der traditionellen russischen Instrumentalkultur mit ihrer klaren regionalen und lokalen Differenzierung der Gattung *pod pesni*, also nichttänzerische instrumental-vokale[5] Formen, die Festtagsumzüge der Dorfjugend begleiteten[6]. Der in diesem Zusammenhang häufig verwendete, jedoch ethnomusikologisch wenig ausgearbeitete Begriff der *častuška* (oder des *častuška*-Stücks) weicht stark von der traditionellen Terminologie ab und erscheint aufgrund struktureller und funktionaler Befunde für dieses Repertoire als ungeeignet. Dies gilt freilich nicht für Untersuchungen der monostrophischen Liedtexte der Gattung *pod pesni*, die dem Versmaß der *častuška* (Vierzeiliger, vierfüßiger Trochäus) entsprechen und vielfach zwischen beiden musikalischen Gattungen austauschbar sind.[7]

Die vorliegende Arbeit ist dem südöstlichen Typ der Instrumentalform *Skobarja* aus dem Gebiet Pskov (*Pskovskaja oblast'*) gewidmet, seinem Verbreitungsgebiet, seiner musikalischen Spezifik und seinem ethnokulturellen Kontext. In Anlehnung an volksterminologische Befunde und im Hinblick auf das Zentrum seines Verbreitungsgebiets Velikie Luki, im Süden der *Pskovščina*, ist *Velikolukskij skobar'* (resp. die in den meisten Publikationen bevorzugte akkusativische Form *Skobarja*) als typologische Bezeichnung geeignet. In seinen traditionellen Bezeichnungen überwiegt die funktionale Terminologie: *Pod pesni*[8] (Liedbegleitung), als funktionale Varianten: *K devkam* („Zu den Mädels", also zum Tanzabend), *Ot devok* („Von den Mädels"). *Pod draku* („Zur Prüge-

---

[4] Karbusicky spricht von der „psychischen Notwendigkeit des ständigen Vergleichs" als einer „anthropologischen Qualität" (1979: 213). In der sowjetischen/russischen Folkloristik und Ethnomusikologie wurde die bereits von Pëtr Bogatyrëv, Vladimir Propp und anderen Vertretern des Strukturalismus ausgearbeitete vergleichende Methode erfolgreich für historische Untersuchungen verwendet (Zemcovskij 1975, für die Ethnoorganologie: Tynurist 1975).

[5] Dieser Terminus von Jurij Bojko verweist auf den dominierenden Instrumentalpart.

[6] Zur Struktur des Instrumentalrepertoires s. Morgenstern 2003, 2007.

[7] Ausführlicher s. meinen Beitrag „Častuška kak ètnomuzykovedčeskaja problema" (Die *častuška* als ethnomusikologisches Problem) in der Festschrift zum 70. Geburtstag von Izalij Zemcovskij *Fol'klor i my: tradicionnaja kul'tura v zerkale ee vosprijatij* (Die Folklore und wir: Traditionelle Kultur im Spiegel ihrer Wahrnehmungen), Sankt-Peterburg, in Vorbereitung.

[8] Die Gattungsbezeichnung tritt hier als Titelbezeichnung auf und wird daher groß geschrieben.

lei"), *Po derevne* („Durch das Dorf"). Ethnonymische (*Skobarja*) und toponymische[9] (*Velikolukskaja*) Terminologie, mithin hilfreich für eine typologische Nomenklatur, haben in der Tradition selbst keine tiefen Wurzeln (Morgenštern 2005).

Typologische Bezeichnung[10]	Traditionelle Bezeichnungen	Verbreitungsareal	Harmonisches Schema[11]
Porchovskaja (nach der Stadt Porchov)	*Skobarja*, *Milaška*, *Pod pesni*, *Pod draku*, *Dlinnaja* („Das lange Stück") *Sobakovskaja*	Südlicher Kreis (*rajon*) Porchov, östlicher Kreis Dedoviči	2/4 |CG|CG|Ga|GG|
Novorževskaja (nach der Stadt Novoržev)	*Skobarja*, *Popolam* („Zweigeteilt"), *Pod pesni*, *Pod draku*, *Dlinnaja*,	Kreis Novoržev, Norden und Südosten des Kreises Bežanicy, nach indirekten Quellen auch Kreis Puškinskie Gory	2/4 |FC|GC|FC|GC| |Ga|GC|Ga|GC|
Sumeckaja (nach dem ehem. Bezirk *Sumeckij*)	*Skobarja*, *Sirotinka* („Das Waisenkind"), *Pod pesni*, *Pod draku*, *Nemoevskaja* (toponymisch)	Ungefähr in einem Areal mit den Eckpunkten Pskov, Čichačëvo, Vybor, Ostrov	2/4 |aG|Cd|CG|aa|

Die Bezeichnung *Skobarja* ist identisch mit der Selbstbezeichnung der Bewohner des ehemaligen Gouvernements von Pskov. Nach veröffentlichten und Felddaten aus dem

---

[9] Im Grenzgebiet von Pskov und Tver' wurde die seltene Bezeichnung *Velikolukskaja* (erg.: *igra*, also: „Das Instrumentalstück von Velikie Luki") von A.V. Poljakova nachgewiesen, vgl. den Aufsatz *Gudošnaja tradicija* („Die Tradition des Gudok"): http://www.ru.narod.ru/sta/gudok-2.htm.

[10] Die typologischen Bezeichnungen entstammen meiner Arbeit „Die Musik der Skobari" (Morgenstern 2007). Eine knappe typologische Nomenklatur wurde auch von den Autoren der umfangreichen Publikation „Traditionelle Volkskultur des Gebiets Pskov" (hg. von Anatolij Mechnecov 2002, Bd. 1, 639) vorgelegt. Diese Publikation erhöht wesentlich den dokumentarischen Wert der seinerzeit von Mechnecov (1987) veröffentlichten Schallplatten zur traditionellen Instrumentalmusik von Pskov, bei denen weitere Ortsangaben fehlen. In der genannten Dokumentation unterscheiden die Autoren folgende Typen der Gruppe *pod pesni*: 1) *Milaška*, 2) *Pskovskaja pod pesni*, 3) *Skobarja*, 4) *Sumeckaja*, 5) *Novorževskaja*. Die Gegenüberstellung dieser Nomenklatur mit der hier verwendeten wird dadurch erschwert, daß in der Arbeit lediglich Bezeichnungen der Instrumentalformen aufgelistet werden, die auf keinerlei Weise mit einer typologischen Charakterisierung, oder wenigstens mit den in dem Werk aufgeführten Transkriptionen oder den anderweitig veröffentlichten Tonaufzeichnungen in Beziehung gesetzt werden. Die erste Instrumentalform entspricht höchstwahrscheinlich unserer *Porchovskaja*, die dritte dem Velikolukischen Typ des *Skobar'*. *Sumeckaja* und *Novorževskaja* sind durch die relativ einheitliche Volksterminologie unschwer zuzuordnen. Von einer „flächendeckenden" Verbreitung der letztgenannten Instrumentalform im Kreis Porchov kann gleichwohl allenfalls dann gesprochen werden, wenn wir die zufällige Auswahl durch einen Musiker bei der Gestaltung seines individuellen Repertoires (verbunden zumeist mit einer eher schematischen Darbietung) nicht von einer festen Verwurzelung und funktionalen Bindung an ein lokales Repertoire unterscheiden, was in der Regel mit einem vollwertigen, virtuosen Spiel einhergeht.

[11] Die harmonischen Stufen können variieren. Rhythmische Abweichungen und Vorhalte, auch von systematischem Charakter, bleiben hier unberücksichtigt.

Gebiet Pskov tragen den Namen *Skobarja* außer dem Velikolukischen mindestens drei weitere Instrumentalformen, die in der Tabelle aufgeführt sind. In ihr sind nur solche Zeugnisse berücksichtigt, die auf die feste Verankerung einer Instrumentalform im lokalen Repertoire schließen lassen.

In einigen Dörfern des Kreises Toropec im Gebiet Tver' wird als *Skobarja* auch eine vereinfachte Variante des Velikolukischen bezeichnet, die sich an das gesamtrussische *častuška*-Schema anlehnt, also: 2/4 |CC|GG|DD|GG|. Der Velikolukische selbst trägt dort die ältere Formbezeichnung *Pod pesni*.

Nach den zugänglichen Quellen ist der *Velikolukskij skobarja* hauptsächlich in den zentralen und südlichen Teilen des ehemaligen Gebiets Velikie Luki bekannt. Die erste veröffentlichte Aufzeichnung – wenn man die entfernt ähnliche *Bologovka* bei Kotikova (1961: 68) außer acht läßt – stammt aus der Toropecker Sammlung von Izalij Zemcovskij (1967: № 110a-b). Auf der von Mechnecov (1987: № 12) herausgegebenen Schallplatte ist eine Harmonika-Balalaika-Version des *Skobarja* mit Gesang aus dem Dorf Lešno im Kreis Pustoška vertreten, eine Balalaikaversion hat Ol'ga Veličkina in Aksent'evo, Kreis Zapadnaja Dvina (Düna), Gebiet Tver', aufgezeichnet (Košelev 1990: № 16.). Teilweise entspricht diesem Typen des *Skobarja* das Geigenstück von Vasilij Muravickij (1923–1993) aus Kamenistik, Kreis Velikie Luki (Mechnecov/Lobkova 1989: № 8). In der Sammlung Razumovskajas (1998: № 166–68) sind drei Varianten des Velikolukischen dokumentiert, die von dem Harmonikaspieler Dmitrij Podstežonok (1937–2005) aus Andronovo, Kreis Kun'ja, stammen. Nicht weniger virtuos spielte den *Skobarja* der aus der Umgebung von Puchnovo stammende Harmonikaspieler Vladimir Jakovlev (1937-2007), der seinerzeit mehrfach das Petersburger Publikum begeisterte und auch in dem Film „Abschied von Mechowoje" von Jochen Kraußer (Ursendung 1998, Arte) mitwirkte. Weiter südlich, in dem an Weißrußland angrenzenden Kreis Usvjaty, hat Jurij Bojko (2002: Beispiel 3) einen *Skobarja* des Velikolukischen Typs aufgezeichnet, der als harmonisches Schema dargestellt ist.

Im Jahr 2005 konnte ich gemeinsam mit Aleksandr Romodin und Igor' Stesev im Süden des Landkreises Bežanicy mehrfach den *Velikolukischen Skobarja* mit der lokalen Bezeichnung *Bologovka* (*Bologoločka*, *Galagoločka*) aufzeichnen und im Kreis Loknja mit der Bezeichnung *Pod pesni* oder *Skobarja*. Der Formtyp findet sich häufig, in leicht vereinfachter Form, unter der Bezeichnung *Po derevne* („Durch das Dorf"), seltener *Kalinka* (möglicherweise toponymisch nach Kalinin/Tver') in den Kreisen Zapadnaja Dvina und Žarkovskij des Gebiets Tver'. Die nordöstlichste Ausdehnung des *Velikolukischen Skobarja* ist der Norden des Kreises Andreapol' (s. u.). Insgesamt jedoch unterscheiden sich die skobarischen Stücke im Kreis Andreapol' im Instrumentalpart etwas von dem Velikolukischen Typ. Östlich der Stadt Peno, hinter den Seen Veslug und Peno beginnt, nach orientierenden Befragungen, bereits ein anderes Areal der instrumentalen Melogeographie, das in Richtung Seližarovo und Ostaškov weist. Weder die Bezeichnung *Skobarja* noch das für die Instrumentalformen von Velikie Luki und Andreapol' charakteristische asynchrone Verhältnis von Instrumental- und Vokalpart konnten hier dokumentiert werden.

Im Nordwesten grenzt das Verbreitungsareal des *Velikolukischen Skobarja* an das der *Novorževskaja*. Im Westen (offenbar im den Kreisen Pustoška oder Opočka) verläuft die Grenze zu dem Verbreitungsgebiet des *Gorbatogo* (der ein wenig der *Porchovskaja* ähnelt). Irgendwo im Kreis Usvjaty, nahe der heutigen weißrussischen Grenze, verliert sich der S*kobarja*, während im angrenzenden Kreis Haradok (Gorodok) des weißrussischen Gebiets von Vicebsk (Vitebsk) zweiteilige Instrumentalformen der Gattung *pod pesni*, die harmonisch der *Novorževskaja* ähneln, recht ausgeprägt sind.[12] Die Bezeichnung *Raschožaja* (weißruss: *Raschadnaja*) verweist hier auf eine der Funktionen der nichttänzerischen Instrumentalformen *pod pesni*. Mit ihnen kündigte der Musiker das Ende einer Tanzunterhaltung an. Ähnliche Formtypen mit der gleichen Bezeichnung finden sich auch in dem an Rußland angrenzenden Kreis Rossony. In den südlicher und westlicher gelegenen Landkreisen Verchnedvinsk, Polack (Polock) und Hlubokoe (Glubokoe) sind sie dagegen unbekannt.[13]

Die ethnische Situation des Areals – Skobari und Poljakí

Bevor wir uns dem *Velikolukischen Skobarja* als musikalischer Form zuwenden, zunächst einige Worte über sein ethnokulturelles und ethnomusikalisches Areal. Die südöstliche Grenze der skobarischen Instrumentalformen entspricht ungefähr der Südostgrenze des ehemaligen Gouvernements von Pskov. Der *Skobarja* findet sich auch etwas südlicher dieser Grenze, etwa im Süden des Kreises Zapadnaja Dvina, jedoch weist hier einiges auf sein späteres Auftauchen in der lokalen Instrumentalpraxis hin. „Die *Skobari* haben es uns gelehrt", erklärte der aus dem Dorf Počinok gebürtige Nikolaj Rjabikov (*1931) unter Verweis auf Musiker aus dem am Westufer der Düna gelegenen Chlebanicha (Kreis Kun'ja). 1938 zeichnete Fedosij Rubcov in Il'ino, unweit der Heimat unseres Gewährsmannes, neben anderen Instrumentalmelodien zwei Geigenstücke mit der Bezeichnung *Pripevki* und ihre vokalen Versionen auf, die keinerlei Ähnlichkeit mit dem *Skobarja* aufweisen. Als weitere *častuška*-Form ist die *Čyganočka* vertreten[14]. Offensichtlich war der *Skobarja* den lokalen Musikern zu jener Zeit noch nicht bekannt, andernfalls hätte der Forscher kaum die Möglichkeit versäumt, ihn zu dokumentieren. Bezeichnend ist auch die Bemerkung einer älteren Gewährsfrau des Bezirks (*volost'*) Baranovo (Landkreis Kun'ja), dessen Bewohner sich traditionell nicht als Skobari ansehen. Als ihr Nachbar ein etwas ruppiges Lied zum *Skobarja* anstimmte, bemerkte sie: „Das sind skobarische Lieder."

Hinsichtlich der ethnischen Grenzen des untersuchten Areals bemerkt der Petersburger Ethnolinguist Aleksandr Gerd, daß die Selbstbezeichnung Skobari „nicht über die Grenzen des Pskover Kerngebiets hinausgeht. Die Bewohner südlicher von Opočka–Velikie Luki nennen sich nicht Skobari, sondern Poljakí" (Gerd 1995: 49).[15] Die historisch-

---

[12] Tonaufnahmen bei Romodin/Romodina (1989: *Dva ritual'nykh naigryšej pod draku*), Transkription bei Nazina (1989: № 148).

[13] Nach Feldforschungen von Aleksandr Romodin (Rußländisches Institut für die Geschichte der Künste) und dem von ihm geleiteten Ensemble „Studio St. Petersburg" im Gebiet Vicebsk 1989 unter Beteiligung des Verfassers. Es sei bemerkt, daß zahlreiche hier behandelte Fragen und Ideen bereits zu jener Zeit in ständigen Gesprächen gegenwärtig waren und in vielerlei Hinsicht den laufenden Forschungen die Richtung wiesen.

[14] Die Aufzeichnungen befinden sich im Phonogrammarchiv des Instituts für russische Literatur der Rußländischen Akademie der Wissenschaften (Puškin-Haus) unter den Signaturen VF ВФ 4532 (№°3-5) und VF 5195 (№°3). Ich bedanke mich freundlichst bei den Mitarbeitern des Phonogrammarchivs Aleksandr Kastrov und Vladimir Šiff für die Bereitstellung von Kopien dieser wertvollen Materialien.

[15] Die Selbstbezeichnung der südlichen Nachbarn der Skobari wird im Gegensatz zu der russischen Bezeichnung für die *Polen* meistens endbetont und als eigenes Lexem wahrgenommen. Als Adjektiv wird hier die Form *poljakisch* verwendet.

kulturelle Zone des Pskover Kerngebiets (*pskovskoe jadro*) wurde nach archäologischen, historischen und linguistischen Befunden herausgearbeitet (Gerd/Lebedev 1991). Nach unseren vorläufigen Daten verläuft die Südgrenze des Ethnonyms *skobari* in den Landkreisen Velikie Luki etwas weiter südlich, nämlich über die Punkte Mart'janovo (nördlich von Poreč'e) – Sapronovo – Turnoe (am See Ordosno) – Lipicy (vgl. Karte 4). Die Grenze deckt sich also recht genau mit der alten Grenze der Gouvernements Pskov und Vicebsk. Etwas weiter südlich verlief die Grenze Rußlands mit Polen bis zur Ersten polnischen Teilung 1772. Die Bewohner zu beiden Seiten der Grenze zwischen Skobari und Poljakí nennen als markantestes Unterscheidungsmerkmal das frikative /g/ der Poljakí und das velare der Skobari.

Der Geograph Andrej Manakov, der die aktuelle ethnische Situation im Gebiet Pskov untersucht hat, weist darauf hin, daß „bis heute das Andenken an das Gebiet [*oblast'*] Velikie Luki lebendig ist, das ungeachtet dessen kurzen Bestehens (13 Jahre) die Grundlage für die Formierung der subregionalen Identität sowohl im Gebieten Pskov als auch in dem von Tver' wurde" (Manakov o. J.: 5). Im Lichte der historischen und ethnolinguistischen Untersuchungen erscheint die von Manakov bemerkte territoriale Identität durchaus nicht so zeitgenössisch. Gerd unterstreicht die „tiefe historische Motiviertheit der alten Südgrenze des Gebiets Pskov mit dem Gebiet Velikie Luki" (1988: 82.).

Obgleich die Dorfbewohner, in der Regel, keine gesteigerte Aufmerksamkeit auf die ethnische Zugehörigkeit dessen richten, mit dem sie in Kontakt treten – man erinnert sich häufig an freundschaftliche Beziehungen zu von fern zugezogenen Arbeitskollegen –, so hatte doch die territorial-ethnische Grenze zwischen Skobari und Poljakí (wie auch zwischen anderen lokalen ethnischen Gruppen) noch vor wenigen Jahrzehnten eine enorme Bedeutung. Sie war spürbar in den Vorstellungen von Differenzen in Sprache, Mentalität und sogar in physisch-anthropologischen Merkmalen. Hiervon zeugt eine Vielzahl von Redensarten, Spottversen und individuellen Bemerkungen – zu beiden Seiten der skobarisch-poljakischen Grenze. Verständlicherweise erfuhren die Bedeutung dieser Grenze vor allem Migranten, wie die aus Kupuj, Kreis Velikie Luki, stammende Tamara Kozlova (*1949), die seit ihrer Heirat in Žigari, südlich von Poreč'e, lebt: „Als ich hierher zog, hieß es von allen Seiten: Skobar'ka! Und ich zurück: Poljakí!" Der Geograph und Heimatforscher Vjačeslav Grinëv aus Kun'ja (*1959 in Kožino) schilderte in einem Gespräch folgendermaßen die Situation an der Grenze:

> Unsere nannten sie Waldmenschen (*lesuny*) und Poljakí. Sie ärgerten uns: „Moskali, Skobari!" Die Jungs ärgerten uns über den Fluß [*Rulinskaja* oder *Puchnovskaja*] hinweg. Dann wurden wir in einem Landkreis vereinigt. [. . .] Wenn Jungs von Usmyn' zu einem Wettbewerb kamen, zum [Sportwettkampf] GTO [. . .], ärgerte und hänselte man sie bei uns. Also, weil sie so hochgewachsen und schlank waren. Sie waren schlanker, höher als wir. Und das Gesicht schlanker. Sie haben eine andere Anthropologie. Mehr so leicht verlangsamt sind sie – aber von aufmerksamer Ernsthaftigkeit [*vdumčivye*]. Wenn er sich einer Sache annimmt, dann macht er es wirklich [. . .]. Deswegen kamen viele in leitenden Funktionen in der Kreisverwaltung aus Usmyn'. [. . .]
>
> Alles in allem, sie lebten in ihrer Welt, und sie wollten nicht viel mit uns zu tun haben. Und wir wollten es nicht, selbst in den Siebzigerjahren. Diese Besonderheit hat sich sehr stark gehalten. Wir verstanden, daß man sie nicht umdrehen kann, sie hatten nicht vor, sich zu ändern. Sie hatten ihre Art zu leben, ihre Denkweise. Das konnte man merken.

Weniger greifbar ist die Ostgrenze des skobarischen Territoriums. Hierzu Manakov: „an der östlichen und besonders der südöstlichen Grenze des Gouvernements [Pskov] ist die

Verwendung der regionalen Bezeichnung [*skobari*] merklich geringer" (Manakov o. J.: 21). Aleksandr Gerd nannte als Ostgrenze die Bahnstation Ochvat zwischen Andreapol' und Peno im Gebiet Tver'[16]. Seine Einschätzung deckt sich somit annähernd mit der Meinung des Direktors des Heimatkundlichen Museums von Andreapol', Valerij Linkevič, der in einem persönlichen Gespräch als Grenze die Düna nannte. Die Bewohner des Kreises Andreapol' kennen für die östlichen Nachbarn im Kreis Peno den nicht sehr freundlichen Spitznamen *kozly* (Ziegenböcke), der im Gegensatz zu *poljakí* als Selbstbezeichnung freilich ausfällt.

Zahlreiche, mithin kontrovers diskutierte Fragen stellen sich im Zusammenhang mit der sprachlichen und ethnischen Charakterisierung der Poljakí. Auf der „Dialektologischen Karte der russischen Sprache in Europa von 1914" (Zacharova/Orlova [2]2004: Anhang) ist das Territorium der Poljakí den weißrussischen Mundarten zugeteilt. Fedosij Rubcov versah die erwähnten Tonaufnahmen aus dem Dorf Il'ino (heute Kreis Zapadnaja Dvina, Gebiet Tver') in der Rubrik „Volk" mit dem Vermerk „Weißrussen". Die „Dialektologische Karte der russischen Sprache von 1964" (Zacharova/Orlova: ebd.) ordnet die gleichen Mundarten dagegen der „westlichen Gruppe" des Südrussischen zu. Die Koautoren der auf aktuellen empirischen Untersuchungen beruhenden ethnologischen Monographie „Das weißrussisch-russische Grenzgebiet" sprechen hinsichtlich der Bewohner der ehemals weißrussischen Gebiete von „Übergangsmundarten" (*perechodnye govory*) und einer *„Mischsprache" (smešannyj jazyk*, s. Grigor'eva/Kasperovič 2005b: 103-105). Aleksandr Romodin indessen, der seit Jahrzehnten die ethnomusikalische Kultur zu beiden Seiten der heutigen Staatsgrenze untersucht, spricht sich (auch unter Verweis auf ältere dialektologische Befunde) entschieden für die „Einheitlichkeit der nordweißrussischen musikalisch-ethnographischen Tradition" aus (Romodin 1996). Von scharfer Kritik nicht verschont blieb auch die Sprachpolitik der Sowjetzeit, „die einen nicht wiedergutzumachenden Schaden dem lebendigen Volksdialekt zufügte" (Romodin/Romodina 1990a: 205).

Die Veränderung der politischen Grenzen in den 1920er Jahren hatte nachhaltige Konsequenzen für das ethnische Selbstbewußtsein. Überzeugende Belege für „eine sehr leicht transformierbare ethnische Identität" haben Grigor'eva und Kasperovič (2005a: 63) angeführt. So verringerte sich die Zahl der Weißrussen in den Landkreisen Veliž, Nevel' und Sebež, die 1924 in das Gebiet Pskov eingegliedert wurden, nach der Volkszählung von 1926 „im Vergleich zum Jahr 1897 [. . .] um das Siebenfache" (ebd.). In derselben Untersuchung (103-105) sind ausführliche Zeugnisse dargelegt, die ein starkes Bewußtsein von der sprachlichen Einheit zu beiden Seiten der heutigen weißrussisch-russischen Grenze deutlich werden lassen – was im Hinblick auf die gänzlich anders verlaufenden dialektalen Grenzen auch nicht sonderlich verwundern kann. Demgegenüber ist in der an den Staatsgrenzen orientierten Untersuchung die für die Bewohner des südlichen Gebiets von Pskov so bedeutsame Opposition Skobari – Poljakí nicht berücksichtigt.

Nach einigen Befunden wird die verstärkte russische Identität unter den Trägern der weißrussischen Mundarten (Poljakí) in deren Bewußtsein der der nördlichen Nachbarn, der Skobari, gegenübergestellt. Bezeichnend ist hier eine im Kreis Sebež aufgezeichnete Replik: „Wir sind Russen. Und dort ist Pskov. Das ist schon die *Skabščina*" (Mechnecov 2002, Bd. 2, 604). Eine ähnliche Opposition Russen – Skobari betonten auch Gewährs-

---

[16] Persönliche Auskunft von Prof. Dr. Aleksandr Gerd im Sommer 2006.

leute aus dem Kreis Usvjaty. Die heutige ethnische Situation im Südwesten des Gebiets Pskov ist in vielem dadurch bestimmt, daß in der Perestroika- und Postperestroikazeit, mit ihrem verstärkten Interesse für die „kleinen Heimat"[17], die Selbstbezeichnung Skobari ein höheres Prestige gewann. Das Ethnonym, das lange Zeit (besonders in St. Petersburg) pejorativ konnotiert (und kaum druckfähig) war, diente in den 90er Jahren zunächst als Bezeichnung einer ethnographischen Fernsehsendung, später als Titel einer Stadtillustrierten, eines Almanachs der Pskover Schriftsteller und einer Reihe von weiteren Unternehmen und allerlei Warenprodukten. Die offenkundige Anziehungskraft des Wortes *Skobar'* begünstigte auch die Ausdehnung des als skobarisch wahrgenommenen Territoriums. Nach Manakovs Ansicht „begann sich erst gegen Ende des 20. Jahrhunderts, als das Wort *Skobar'* unter der örtlichen Bevölkerung seine negative Schattierung wegen des Weggangs der Generationen, der realen Träger des Spitznamens verlor, das Wort allmählich über das ganze Gebiet [*oblast'*] als regionale Selbstbezeichnung zu verbreiten. Hierbei machte sich deutlich eine positive Schattierung in der Verwendung der Selbstbezeichnung fest: Sie wurde zum eigentümlichen Symbol des Patriotismus im Gebiet Pskov" (Manakov o. J.: 22f.).

Diese Beobachtung ist äußerst wichtig für das Verständnis der aktuellen ethnokulturellen Prozesse, gleichwohl ist zweifelhaft, ob für die örtliche Bevölkerung das Ethnonym *Skobar'* jemals mit einer negativen Schattierung verbunden war. Von seiner positiven Wahrnehmung zeugt die unerschütterliche Volksetymologie, nach der die Skobari kräftige und geschickte Handwerker waren, die zum Erstaunen Peters des Großen Stahlklammern (*skoby*) mit bloßen Händen zu biegen in der Lage waren. Im Bewußtsein der Bauern in der mittleren *Pskovščina* ist ein Skobar' ein verläßlicher, kräftig zupackender Mann – mit dem man allerdings keinen Streit anfangen sollte. Wenn das Ethnonym *Skobar'* in der ersten Hälfte des 20. Jahrhundert im mittleren Gebiet von Pskov eine negative Schattierung getragen hätte, hätte es zu dieser Zeit niemals den Status der Bezeichnung von lokalen Instrumentalformen erlangt. Dies zeigt einmal mehr, wie das ethnomusikalische Bewußtsein als deutliches Zeugnis ethnischer Identität hervortreten kann.

Heute zählen sich die Nachfahren der Poljakí im Gebiet Pskov nicht selten zu den Skobari – wenngleich hauptsächlich dann, wenn der auswärtige Feldforscher diese Frage aufwirft. Gleichzeitig ist in der Verwendung der Selbstbezeichnung *Skobar'*, wenn sie durch den Wohnort innerhalb der heutigen Gebietsgrenzen motiviert ist, eine gewisse Unschlüssigkeit zu spüren. „Gebiet Pskov – also Skobar' und fertig!" sagte ein aus dem Dorf Cholm (Kreis Kun'ja, zeitweise Gebiet Smolensk) stammender älterer Gewährsmann. Es ist unschwer zu erkennen, daß das Selbstgefühl als Skobar' hier schwach entwickelt ist. Die stolze Erklärung „Ich bin ein reinblütiger Skobar'" ist von den Bewohnern der vormals zum Gouvernement Vicebsk gehörenden Teile des Pskover Gebiets kaum zu hören. Überaus aufschlußreich ist hier ein Gespräch mit einem älteren Ehepaar des Velikolukischen Dorfes Sapronovo, das mehrfach in dem nördlich gelegenen Bezirk Kupuj als erste Siedlung der Poljakí genannt wurde. Die Frau bemerkte auf Nachfrage etwas gleichgültig: „Wir sind Skobari. Pskov – also Skobari." Unvermittelt rief ihr Ehe-

---

[17] Den Begriff gebraucht der 1960 in Ivano-Frankivsk (Stanislau) geborene ukrainische Schriftsteller Jurij Andruchowytsch. Die Hinwendung zu lokalen Kulturtraditionen, die gleichsam weniger durch den Identifikationsbedarf des Großmachtchauvinismus korrumpiert sind, ist typisch auch für die politischen Jugendbewegungen im Westen in den 70er und 80er Jahren des 20. Jahrhunderts, besonders für die Ökologiebewegung.

mann, der dem Gespräch zunächst schweigend gefolgt war, mit Feuer in den Augen aus: „Wir sind aber Poljaki!" Seine Frau fühlte eine gewisse Verlegenheit und antwortete, nicht ohne leichte Ironie: „Jetzt sind alle Skobari." Wir sehen also, daß die politischen Grenzen die ethnischen Prozesse nicht nur auf der Ebene der Selbstbestimmung der Volkszugehörigkeit beeinflussen (die sog. *nacional'nost'* war nach russischem Melderecht noch bis vor kurzem eine neben der Staatsangehörigkeit amtlich erfaßte Kategorie). Die Grenzen können auch das Zugehörigkeitsgefühl zu einer *lokalen* Gruppe formieren, wobei das Prestige dieser Gruppe eine wesentliche Rolle spielt. Und dieses Zugehörigkeitsgefühl kann sich wiederum im ethnomusikalischen Bewußtsein niederschlagen. So charakterisiert der Leiter des Kulturhauses von Urickoe im südlichen Gebiet Velikie Luki, der Harmonikaspieler Viktor Burov (*1962), die Identifikationskraft des *Skobarja* folgendermaßen: „Die Hymne Rußlands ist eine Sache – das aber ist die Hymne der Gegend."

Ungeachtet der „Skobarisierung" des Südrandes des Gebiets von Pskov sind sich die Bewohner ihrer dialektmäßigen Verbindung zu den Bewohnern des heutigen Weißrußlands vielfach bewußt. Besonders betrifft dies die Vertreter der dörflichen Intelligenz, obgleich sie diese Vorstellung nicht als Selbstverständlichkeit ansehen. Der ehemalige Lehrer Pëtr Pašetko (*1939) aus dem Dorf Smol'ki im Kreis Kun'ja erinnert sich: „Ich schrieb sogar so eine Arbeit [. . .] Dialektwörter für das Institut [. . .] einige tausend Wörter. Und als ich diese Wörter sammelte, überzeugte ich mich davon, daß die Bevölkerung bei uns mehrheitlich gerade weißrussisch sprach." Michail Begunov (*1961) aus dem Nachbardorf Bulavkino wurde die dialektale Zugehörigkeit seiner Heimat auf andere Weise bewußt: „Als ich bei der Armee diente, nannten mich alle *bul'baš* [ironische Fremdbezeichnung für die Weißrussen]. Die weißrussische Identität ist im Süden der *Pskovščina* auch deshalb nicht besonders ausgeprägt, da das Ethnonym *belarus* bis zum Ende des 19. Jahrhunderts generell wenig gebräuchlich war.

Ethnomusikalische Grenzen

Die Dorfmusiker zeigen generell ein großes Interesse an Repertoire- und Stilgrenzen, wobei sie in der Regel anderen Lokaltraditionen überaus wohlwollend gegenüberstehen. Gleichzeitig kann zwischen den einzelnen Musikern (vor allem wenn es sich um Berufsmusiker handelt) das Verhältnis „durch scharfe Berufskonkurrenz bestimmt" sein (Romodin/Romodina 1989). Nach Beobachtungen von Aleksandr Romodin im Dorf Kresty, im äußersten Süden des Kreises Kun'ja, bewerten selbst Verwandte und Nachbarn der örtlichen Harmonikaspieler deren Niveau einigermaßen zurückhaltend und favorisieren neidlos die weiter nördlich ansässigen Musiker (Romodin 1999: 8). Der velikolukische Harmonikaspieler Nikolaj Panov (*1948) aus dem Bezirkszentrum Čerpessa gibt der *Maripčelskaja* (Notenbeispiel 1) den Vorzug gegenüber der vom Vater übernommenen lokalen Variante des *Skobarja* (Notenbeispiel 2), die nach melischer Entwicklung und spieltechnischem Raffinement klar hinter der erstgenannten zurückbleibt. Für diesen Musiker erwiesen sich ästhetische Kriterien bei der Auswahl für das eigene Repertoire als wichtiger als die Treue zu den Traditionen des Heimatdorfes. Stilistische Grenzen zwischen großräumigeren Repertoire-Arealen werden bisweilen mit leichter Ironie bedacht. Der Harmonikaspieler Vasilij Lavrenov (*1932) aus dem Kreis Belyj, Gebiet Tver', (wo man zur *Zalivočka* Vierzeiler im Achtelrhythmus singt) charakterisierte folgendermaßen die für ihn ungewohnten skobarischen Exklamationen zwischen den Liedzeilen: „Dort [in Andreapol'] sind Skobari. Dort singt man anders. Man sagt zwei Worte – und dann: aaah! [belustigt]. Ich kann gar nicht singen auf deren Art."

In der uns interessierenden Region verlaufen mehrere Grenzen zwischen ethnomusikalischen Arealen, die durch unterschiedliche gattungs- und stilmäßige Merkmale gekennzeichnet und in unterschiedlichen geschichtlichen Phasen entstanden sind. In erster Linie sind hier die vor allem auf dem Territorium der Poljakí angesiedelten Lieder des Jahresbrauchtums zu nennen, nach Romodin und Romodina (1998: 323) „für den poozer'e [Nordweißrussische Seenplatte] die gattungs- und wesensmäßige Dominante". Die Autoren stellen Lieder des Dorfes Ragozy (Kreis Usvjaty) vor und verweisen auf Parallelen sowohl im Kreis Haradok des Gebiets von Vicebsk wie auch in den Kreisen Nevel' und Velikie Luki des Gebiets Pskov. Eigens wird diese Frage in einem umfangreichen Beitrag der Petersburger Ethnomusikologin Ajšat Gadžieva (2001) behandelt, der nach den Worten der Herausgeber A.S. Gerd und G.S. Lebedev „deutlich die historische Geschlossenheit der historisch-kulturellen Zone von Dnepr und Düna zeigt"[18].

Eine weitere Grenze markiert der nordöstliche Ausläufer des Verbreitungsareals der instrumentalen Hochzeitsmelodien. Die Petersburger Forscherin Elena Razumovskaja (1996: 9f.) sieht die Düna als Ostgrenze der Hochzeitsmärsche an, die mit den Bewegungen der Hochzeitsteilnehmer zwischen den vorgesehenen Stationen verbunden sind – und die, wie die Autorin bemerkt, tatsächlich oft wenig mit Marschmusik gemein haben. Auf der dieser Arbeit beigefügten Karte reicht das Areal der Märsche im Nordosten bis nach Kun'ja, obgleich alle von Razumovskaja angeführten Quellen – wie auch die Feldforschungsmaterialien Mechnecovs (Hg. 2002) – einem Areal entstammen, dessen Nordostgrenze mit der des ehemaligen Gouvernement Vicebsk zusammenfällt. Dies stützt Razumovskajas Vermutung von einer polnisch-weißrussischen Herkunft dieser Gattung – wobei eine vergleichende Untersuchung mit den Hochzeitsmärschen in Schweden, Österreich, der Schweiz, in Frankreich und anderen europäischen Ländern wünschenswert wäre. Wie die Märsche so sind auch die anderen Hochzeitsmelodien (etwa die *Nadeljannaja* bei der rituellen Beschenkung der Braut), die vor allem Romodin in zahlreichen Veröffentlichungen behandelt, in den traditionell skobarischen Nordteilen der Gebiete Velikie Luki[19] und Kun'ja – und um so mehr in der mittleren *Pskovščina* unbekannt. Das gleiche gilt für den „Professionalismus [Hervorhebung nicht im Original] der nordweißrussischen Instrumentalisten" (Romodin 1999: 10), dessen hauptsächliche Sphäre „die rituelle Hochzeitspraxis ist" (ebd.). Als entscheidendes Kennzeichen der nordweißrussischen Instrumentaltradition nennt Romodin (2006: 9) ebenso den Ensembletyp, bestehend aus Violine, Hackbrett und einigen anderen Instrumenten. (Gleichzeitig verweist er auf eine weite Verbreitung ähnlicher Ensembles in Süd- und Osteuropa.) Dieser Ensemblestil, für den die solistische Violine vor dem Hintergrund einer harmonischen und/oder einer Baßbegleitung, eventuell unter Verwendung des Tamburins, kennzeichnend ist, "can be said to mirror a seventeenth and eighteenth century development in the music of social elite in Central Europe"[20]. Andererseits bevor-

---

[18] Vgl. S. 6, Anm. 1 im Vorwort. Der Titel des Beitrags wurde mißverständlich vertauscht. Das Zitat der Herausgeber kann sich jedoch inhaltlich nur auf den Beitrag von Ajšat Gadžieva beziehen.

[19] Eigene Feldforschungen im Sommer 2006.

[20] William Henry Noll: *Peasant Music Ensembles in Poland. A Cultural History.* University of Washington Ph.D., University Microfilms International 300 N. Zeeb Road, Ann Arbor, Mi 48106, USA,

zugen, nach der Sammlung Nazina (1989) zu urteilen, gerade die Instrumentalensembles im Gebiet von Vicebsk eine heterophone Faktur, die möglicherweise mit der lokalen Vokalpraxis zusammenhängt (Romodin 1997).

Zur Frage nach dem Vordringen der westeuropäischen Instrumente Violine und Hackbrett in die weißrussischen Dörfer ist die schon von Vladimir Gippius bemerkte Nähe der weißrussischen zur jüdischen Instrumentaltradition von einiger Bedeutung. Der Forscher verweist auf „rein instrumentale Tanzlieder[21], deren Repertoire (und teilweise auch deren Vortragsstil) sich berührt mit der instrumentalen Volksmusik der jüdischen Geiger. In der weißrussischen und der jüdischen instrumentalen Volksmusik brechen sich auf vielfältige Weise Melodiegestalten [*intonacii*] und Rhythmen der europäischen und der russischen städtischen Tanzmusik" (Gippius 1941: 121). Igor' Macievskij unterstreicht „die Einwirkung der zigeunerischen und jüdischen Tanzmusikkapellen" auf den Ensemblestil der *troista muzyka* in der Ukraine (Macievskij (1985: 101). Schon 1888 führte der Organologe Michail Petuchov einige „liegende Harfen" auf, die sich „bei einigen unserer Fremdstämmigen finden" und nicht die Bezeichnung *gusli* tragen: „das finnische *kantele*, das mit diesem identische lettische *kukles* und litauische *kankles* und das jüdische Hackbrett" (Petuchov 1888: 826). Offensichtlich wurde im Rußland des späten 19. Jahrhunderts das Hackbrett eben als jüdisches Musikinstrument wahrgenommen. Es sei hier auch an das Bild des jüdischen Hackbrettspielers Jankel aus Adam Mickiewiczs Versepos „Pan Tadeusz" erinnert, dessen Handlung im heutigen Weißrußland spielt. Über die jüdischen Hackbrettspieler im Kreis Lepel (Gebiet Vicebsk) schrieb Nikolaj Findejzen (1926). Allgemein bekannt ist die „klassische" Klezmerbesetzung Geige – Hackbrett – Tamburin. Überaus aufschlußreich ist in diesem Zusammenhang, daß das Hackbrett, nach den erwähnten Arbeiten von Romodin und Mechnecov und ebenso nach der Kartei des Pskover Gebietswörterbuchs[22] zu urteilen, in der Umgebung der früheren jüdischen Zentren Sebež, Nevel' und Veliž sehr stark vertreten ist, jedoch nördlich der im Zarenreich festgeschriebenen jüdischen Besiedlungsgrenze schlagartig verschwindet. Zweifellos geht also die weißrussische instrumentale Ensemblekultur in bedeutendem Maße auf die jüdischen Berufsmusiker, die Klezmorim, zurück.

Oben wurden bereits die Instrumentalformen *pod pesni* aus dem Kreis Haradok erwähnt. Offensichtlich endet hier, im Nordosten Weißrußlands, die gesamtrussische Tradition dieser nichttänzerischen und funktional wie lokal äußerst differenzierten Instrumentalformen. Sie treten in Weißrußland zurück hinter die Kultur der Polka, einer der führenden Instrumentalgattungen der polnisch-weißrussischen Tradition mit zahllosen strukturellen und funktionalen Varianten. Zur gesamtrussischen Instrumentalkultur gehört auch die berühmte *pljaska*-Melodie *Kamarinskaja*, die nach Beobachtung von Inna Nazina gerade in den an Rußland angrenzenden Gebieten Vicebsk und Mahyljaŭ (Mogilëv) als *Ljavonicha* bekannt ist.

1986: 250. Zit. nach Bielawski 1992: 54. Zu diesem Ensemblestil im Hinblick auf die nordweißrussische Tradition s. auch Morgenstern (2006: 156f.).

[21] Wörtl.: *pljasovye pesni* – obgleich wohl eher das gesamteuropäisch beeinflußte Repertoire (*tanec*) und weniger das slawische (*pljaska*) gemeint ist.

[22] Das von der Philologischen Fakultät der Universität St. Petersburg herausgegebene „Pskovskij oblastnoj slovar'" (seit 1967) gehört zu den genauesten und umfangreichsten dialektologischen Quellensammlungen in Rußland.

Wenn die Instrumentalmusik *pod draku* noch den Nordosten des Gebiets Vicebsk erfaßt (Romodin/Romodina 1989), so findet sich der Kampftanz *lomanie* im Gebiet Pskov ausschließlich auf dem Territorium der Skobari.[23] Die Poljakí mochten sich von der Harmonika zur Prügelei anstacheln lassen, vor dem Kampf tanzte man jedoch nicht. Das Areal dieses (leider völlig unerforschten) Tanzes steht den unter gewissen Liebhabern des russischen Faustkampfes[24] populären Vorstellungen über seine Verbindung zu dem baltisch-ostslawischen Stamm der Kriwitschen (*kriviči*)[25] entgegen. Auf den nachweislich den Kriwitschen zuzurechnenden Territorien (Smolensk, Polack) ist nichts bekannt, was auch nur entfernt an das *lomanie* der Skobari erinnern könnte. Auf die Herkunft und das hohe Alter dieses Tanzes können seine zoomorphen „offensichtlich bärenartigen Züge" hindeuten, die der Spezialist für Spielkultur Igor' Morozov (1995: 54) beobachtet hat, und ebenso der Umstand, daß der Tanz ausschließlich auf dem Gebiet der finnougrischen Hydronymie nachweisbar ist. Auf die Nähe der skobarischen Tänze zu den finnougrischen wies mich persönlich auch Igor' Macievskij nach einem Auftritt des Ensembles von Andrej Gruntovskij im Institut der Geschichte der Künste hin.

In der mittleren und jüngeren Generation der Skobari ist ein deutliches Interesse an den Kampftänzen und den Instrumentalstücken *pod draku* zu verzeichnen wie zu dem gesamten Komplex der ritualisierten Schlägereien, die gewöhnlich nur aus den Erzählungen der Älteren bekannt sind. Bezeichnend sind hier die lebhaften Schilderungen eines ungefähr 55 Jahre alten Bewohners des Dorfes Ozerec im Kreis Toropec, Gebiet Tver'. Der Gewährsmann, der sich unter leichter Alkoholeinwirkung befand, berührte nicht ohne Stolz das Thema des Kampfes – sowohl im Hinblick auf die kriegerischen Geschichte seiner Heimat wie auch (eher harmlos) auf die eigene Biographie: „Wir haben immer mit irgendwem Krieg geführt, aber da [zeigt nach Osten in Richtung Toropec] hat keiner gekämpft." „Wenn ich mich nicht schlage [als Grundschüler mit den Schülern aus den Nachbarsdörfern], dann ist der Tag umsonst gewesen. [. . .] Sogar die Mädchen haben uns Steine gebracht [. . .]. Und ich bin ein Bursche aus Ozerec, ich muß die anderen besiegen." Äußerungen im Stil von „Ich bin ein reinblütiger Skobar'" unterstrich der Gesprächspartner durch angedeutete Bewegungen des Kampftanzes: hervorgehobene Brust, die Fäuste in Achselhöhe gegen die Seiten gestemmt, scharfe Bewegungen der Schultern und Ellenbogen. Offensichtlich hat das *lomanie* und sein situativer Kontext bewußt oder unbewußt auch in unserer Zeit einige Bedeutung für das Selbstgefühl der Skobari.

Musikalische Besonderheiten des *Velikolukischen Skobarja*

Nach seiner emotionalen Verfaßtheit und seiner psychischen Wirkung auf der Hörer unterscheiden sich alle in der *Pskovščina* beheimateten Formen des *Skobarja* in Abhängigkeit von dem außermusikalischen Kontext und der entsprechenden Artikulationsart. Sehr häufig wird dem *Skobarja* ein suggestiver, fast aggressiver Gestus zugeschrieben. „*Zadi-*

---

[23] Nach Volksterminologie, Ästhetik und Stil ist dieser Tanz von der russischen *pljaska* stark unterschieden. Deswegen kann er, wenngleich er „zur Prügelei" gespielt wurde, zu den nichttänzerischen Gattungen (im Sinne von *pljaska* und *tanec*) gerechnet werden. Zur wahrscheinlichen Herkunft des *lomanie* s. ausführlicher: Morgenstern 2007 (Bd. 1, 357ff.).

[24] Zu Faustkampf und Faustkampf-Revival s. die eingehende Untersuchung von Wolfdietrich Junghanns (2003).

[25] S. etwa die Internetseite www.buza.ru.

ristaja igra" (eine anstachelnde Musik) ist eine sehr häufige Charakterisierung, die direkt auf eine seiner Hauptfunktionen verweist: das Instrumentalspiel *pod draku* – zur Prügelei, also ein musikalisches Mittel zur Entfachung von rituell vorbereiteten, durchaus harten Auseinandersetzungen zu den Patronatsfesten, an denen in ihrer territorialen Zugehörigkeit unterschiedliche Gruppen der männlichen Jugend, mithin aber auch Erwachsene teilnahmen. „Durch den *Skobarja* wurde der Charakter erzogen, der Mut", wie es der Harmonikaspieler Anatolij Grinёv (*1939) aus Kožino im Kreis Kun'ja ausdrückte. Gleichzeitig ist dem *Skobarja* aber auch ein Element tiefster Schwermut eigen. Aleksandr Romodin führt eine Erinnerung an den berühmten Ivan Kondrusev an: „Pul'ka [wörtl.: „die Kugel", Spitzname des Harmonikaspielers] spielte den *Skobarja* so, daß man weinen konnte" (Romodin 1999: 10). Entsprechende Bemerkungen von Dorfnachbarn über besonders herausragende Musiker sind sehr häufig. Ivan Plesnjakov (*1939) aus Troica, Kreis Velikie Luki, drückte halb im Scherz auf folgende Weise die Doppelgesichtigkeit des *Skobarja* aus: „Wer ihn gut spielt, der kann dich zu Tränen rühren – oder auch zu Heldentaten anspornen."

Die unterschiedlichen emotionalen Schattierungen und strukturell-artikulatorischen Charakteristika des *Velikolukischen Skobarja* sind in der Volksterminologie klar reflektiert. Strukturell unterscheiden zahlreiche Musiker den *Kurzen* (*Korotkij*) und den *Langen Skobarja* (*Dlinnyj/Dolgij skobar'*, vgl. etwa Razumovskaja 1998: № 166-167). Der Erste ist gekennzeichnet durch die Kürze der Form, durch schroffe, abgerissene Tongebung und, auf der Baßseite der Harmonika, gewöhnlich durch eine Folge von Baß und Akkord im Achtelrhythmus. Gerade der *Kurze Skobarja* wird charakterisiert als „anstachelnd" (*zadiristyj*), „scharf" (*rezkij*), lustiger (*po-veselee*). Dem *Langen Skobarja* ist mehr ein zurückhaltenderes Tempo eigen, mithin eine elaboriertere Formgestaltung, vor allem aber eine breitere, getragene Artikulation im Instrumentalspiel wie im Gesang. Auf der Baßseite der Harmonika überwiegt eine einstimmige Faktur (ohne Akkordtasten), eine häufige Verwendung von Vierteln und häufiges Legato.

Den *Kurzen Skobarja* unterscheiden einige Musiker nicht von dem *Skobarja pod draku*, der, natürlich, in erster Linie mit dem männlichen Repertoire verbunden ist. Der *Lange Skobarja* mit seinem eher lyrischen Gestus, entspricht mehr dem weiblichen Repertoire. Aber auch innerhalb des Männerrepertoires existiert eine Differenzierung zwischen einem „lustigeren" (*po-veselee*) Spiel (neben dem *Skobarja pod draku*) und einem schwermütigen (*skučnoj*) Gestus. Situativ ist diese atmosphärisch-artikulatorische Opposition verbunden mit dem Weg zum Tanzabend in gehobener Stimmung einerseits und andererseits der Rückkehr nach Hause – nach dem schweren Abschied von der weiblichen Gesellschaft. Entsprechend sind *K devkam* („Zu den Mädels") und *Ot devok* („Von den Mädels") selbständige und vollgültige Titelbezeichnungen, analog dem *Kurzen* bzw. dem *Langen Skobarja*.

Den *Skobarja* nennt Romodin zu Recht „Gegenstand des besonderen Stolzes" für die besten lokalen Harmonikaspieler" (1999: 11). Gerade in ihm (wie auch in anderen lokalen Varietäten des Repertoires *pod pesni*) äußern sich melischer Einfallsreichtum des Musikers, virtuoseste Spieltechnik, mithin die Fähigkeit zu komplizierter polyphoner Faktur – im instrumentalen Solospiel wie im Zusammenwirken mit einem Sänger. Dem *Skobarja* ist in heutigen Zeit bei weitem nicht jeder Harmonikaspieler gewachsen. Ältere Musiker bemerken häufig, daß das Erlernen jüngeren Musiker erhebliche Schwierigkeiten bereitet, die auch Musikern aus traditionsorientierten Revival-Ensembles wohlbekannt sind.

Diese Schwierigkeiten entstehen auf zwei Ebenen – der der Wahrnehmung und der Fähigkeit, eine Melodie vor dem inneren Ohr wiederzugeben, und auf der Ebene der eigentlichen Spieltechnik. Einmal mehr sei daran erinnert, wie selbst ein Boris Asaf'ev sich mit der prinzipiellen Unfaßbarkeit des traditionellen instrumentalen Melos konfrontiert sah. Im Hinblick auf die nordrussische Harmonikamusik bemerkte der Gelehrte:

> Ich habe einmal versucht, das, was ich aus Beobachtungen auf diesem Gebiet des volkstümlichen Scherzo gewonnen habe, für mich zusammenfassend aufzuzeichnen. Ich mußte mir eingestehen, wie begrenzt der Horizont meines Gehörs ist. Vergleichsweise leicht fällt dagegen die Klärung auf dem Gebiet des volkstümlichen gedehnten Liedes [*protjažnaja pesnja*]. Das Gebiet des Scherzo (das spannungsreichste, lebendigste und beweglichste) ist der Beschreibung durch Worte unzugänglich (ich meine dies im Hinblick auf das gestalthaft-strukturierende Verfahren [*intonacionno-konstruktivnaja technika*]). (Asaf'ev 1947[26], zit. nach: Zemcovskij Hg. 1987)

Dieses gestalthaft-strukturierende Verfahren ist in erster Linie auf die Überwindung jedweden Schematismus gerichtet. Man kann von der Virtuosität und Beweglichkeit nicht nur der Spielfinger, sondern des musikalischen Bewußtseins, also von *mentaler Virtuosität* sprechen. Besonders den älteren und versiertesten Harmonikaspielern ist die bei konzertanten Bajanspielern so beliebte Sequenztechnik und vielfach auch die prägnante Hervorhebung der Form und ihrer Teile zutiefst fremd. Gleichzeitig ist im Instrumentalspiel der traditionellen Musiker das Prinzip der Motivwiederholung relativ weit verbreitet, das die Wahrnehmung der Form erschwert, welche eher durch die melodische Initiative[27] des Baßparts der Harmonika bestimmt ist. (Beispiel 5, 11, 15). Wahrscheinlich hatte diese ästhetisch ungemein produktiven Schwierigkeiten ein aus der Umgebung von Kartašovo im Kreis Toropec stammender Gewährsmann (*1938) im Sinne, als er auf die Frage nach der wichtigsten lokalen Instrumentalform zunächst nicht deren Bezeichnung (*Pod draku*) angab, sondern nach einer gewichtigen Pause langsam das eine Wort *chitraja* („ein trickreiches") aussprach.

Freilich ist auch die Virtuosität der Spielfinger von enormer Bedeutung. Ein wesentlicher Teil des Repertoires auf der gleichtönigen Harmonika (*chromka*) läßt sich mit drei Fingern der rechten und zwei der linken Hand spielen; irgendwie bekommt man auf diese Art auch einen *Skobarja* hin. Anspruchsvolle Musiker werden sich damit jedoch niemals zufriedengeben. Die rechte Hand muß nach Ansicht des bekannten Virtuosen Ivan Ivlev (1931-2007) aus dem Kreis Haradok das motorisch weit schwierigere Spiel mit vier Fingern beherrschen (der Daumen fällt als Greiffinger aus): „Wenn du die Hand so zurichtest, dann kannst du gut spielen" (Romodin/Romodina 1990b). Auch Vladimir Jakovlev sagte von sich mit berechtigtem Stolz: „Ich bin notenloser Profimusiker. Profi und Autodidakt! Deswegen spiele ich mit allen vier Fingern." Die „zugerichtete Hand" erweitert entscheidend den melischen Horizont des Musikers, seine *künstlerische Suche* (Romodin 2005: 115) – die rechte Hand ist für die Beweglichkeit der Hauptmelodie verantwortlich, die linke für die Ausweitung des melisch-linearen Elements und für eine verstärkte Beweglichkeit von Timbre- und Registerwahl (Grundbaß und/oder Akkord).

---

[26] Erstveröffentlichung in tschechischer Sprache: *Tempo*, R. XIX, Praha 1947: S. 2f., russische Version: *Sovetskaja muzyka*, Heft 2, 1949: S. 62-65.

[27] Formulierung von Jurij Bojko.

Eins wie das andere ist von prinzipieller Bedeutung für die musikalische Ästhetik der Skobari.

In Abhängigkeit von der künstlerischen Konzeption des Musikers kann der *Skobarja* als bis in die feinsten melischen Bewegungen elaborierte, stabile Komposition erscheinen – oder als beständige Improvisation bis hin zur Brechung der Periodizität der Form. Als Beispiele können die *Pskovskaja pod pesni* von Vasilij Muravickij (Mechnecov/Lobkova 1989) einerseits, der *Skobarja* von Dmitrij Podstežonok (Razumovskaja 1998: № 166-68) andererseits gelten.

Die am weitesten verbreitete Form des *Velikolukischen Skobarja* besteht aus vier Zweivierteltakten. In manchen Fällen legt die metrorhythmische Artikulation der achtschlägigen Periode eher eine auftaktige Lösung mit gemischtem Metrum nahe (Beispiel 2). Auf die erste Zählzeit fällt gewöhnlich eine Bewegung vom tonalen Zentrum (standardisiert: g^1), seltener von der Oberquinte oder -oktave zu dem Achtelschritt c^2 – h^1 (mit Umspielung des zweiten Tons) auf der zweiten Zählzeit. Dieser Schritt wird im Baßpart der Harmonika gewöhnlich durch den Schritt S – T unterstützt. Besonders deutlich tritt das Initialmotiv in den Beispielen 1, 5 und 8 hervor. Der auf dieses Motiv folgende zweite Takt wird in der Regel durch zwei Spielfiguren zu vier Sechzehnteln ausgefüllt, die mehr oder minder der Viertelbewegung (variabler) Nebenakkord – Hauptakkord (T) entsprechen. In der zweiten Hälfte der Grundform entfaltet sich meist eine rhythmisch bewegliche Melodie, die auf einer Kadenz im vierten Takt endet, obgleich besonders versierte Musiker häufig bestrebt sind, die Formkonturen durch melische Übergänge gleichsam zu verwischen. Diese erste Variante des *Velikolukischen Skobarja* ist durch die Beispiele 1–4 vertreten. In der zweiten Variante kann das Motiv des zweiten Taktes wiederholt werden, um im vierten Takt zur Kadenz überzuleiten (Beispiel 11a). Gleichwohl kann dieses Hauptmotiv mithin auch öfter wiederholt werden (Beispiel 5, 6a), wodurch sich die viertaktige Form erweitert. Diese zweite, motivwiederholende Variante des Velikolukischen kommt in der *Pskovščina* südlich der Städte Kun'ja und Velikie Luki vor. Eine dritte Variante ist im Nordosten des Kreises Žarkovskij im Gebiet Tver' beheimatet (am Unterlauf der Velesa, einem linken Düna-Zufluß). Sie ist durch eine Periodizität niedrigeren Niveaus gekennzeichnet – beide Hälften der achtschlägigen Form sind fast gleich gestaltet (Beispiel 7). Nur selten schaffen die lokalen Harmonikaspieler eine entwickeltere Komposition auf Grundlage der sehr einfachen Formel. Beispiel 8 zeigt eine (mit einigen Variationen im Baßpart) sich beständig wiederholende Form in der Ausführung von Michail Lebedev (*1937).

Die harmonische Bewegung der ersten Variante des *Velikolukischen Skobarja* läßt sich nicht immer auf eine stabile Formel reduzieren, häufig jedoch findet man eine Abfolge wie in Schema 1:

Schema 1

♩ ♪♪	♩	♩	♩	♩
G C G	a	G	D	G D G

Für den *Velikolukischen Skobarja*, wie allgemein für die vokal-instrumentalen Formen der *Pskovščina*, ist ein solistischer Vortrag des Vokalparts charakteristisch. Wenn meh-

414

rere Singende beteiligt sind, werden die monostrophischen Vierzeiler im *častuška*-Versmaß reihum gesungen. (Hierin besteht ein Unterschied zu den Formen *pod pesni* in anderen nordwest- und in nordrussischen Regionaltraditionen.) Die rhythmische Bewegung der Vokalstrophe verläuft in Achteln mit den beiden ersten Silben als Auftakt, ähnlich dem bekannten Tanzlied *Ach vy seni, moi seni*. Die letzten zwei Silben der ungeraden Zeilen können zu Vierteln verlängert werden (Beispiel 4). Die niemals direkt hintereinander gesungenen Zeilen werden entweder durch Wortwiederholungen vor den geraden Zeilen verlängert – wie in der *Spasovskaja* zwischen Volchov und Sjas (Bojko 1985, 1993) – oder auch durch Pausen oder durch charakteristische Exklamationen, die mal Drohgebärde sind (in den Männerliedern zur Prügelei), mal aber auch zarte seelische Empfindungen (nicht nur in Frauenliedern) ausdrücken. Die rhythmische Organisation ist gewöhnlich die folgende: Der Abstand vom ersten Akzent der ungeraden Zeile (Verssilbe 3) bis zum Finalis beträgt (letzteren nicht gerechnet) 10 Zählzeiten.

Wie *Porchovskaja* und *Spasovskaja* so ist auch der *Velikolukische Skobarja* durch ein asynchrones Verhältnis von Vokal- und Instrumentalpart gekennzeichnet. Hierbei sind nicht nur die Kadenzen, sondern auch das Metrum der Parts gegeneinander versetzt. Leider wird dieses wichtige Prinzip in den vorhandenen Transkriptionen häufig nicht berücksichtigt, so daß die Taktstriche der Parts zusammenfallen. Der Instrumentalpart wird zumeist gewaltsam an das Metrum des Vokalparts angepaßt. Hierdurch wir die reale Heterometrie verschleiert und die Wahrnehmung der Instrumentalform erschwert.

Im *Velikolukischen Skobarja* fällt recht häufig die erste Verssilbe (ohne Berücksichtigung von Exklamationen) auf das siebte Viertel der Instrumentalperiode. Entsprechend fällt der Finalis der Vokalstrophe (gewöhnlich das tonale Zentrum, aber auch die kleine Unterterz) auf das zweite Viertel des Instrumentalparts[28]. Das hieraus resultierende Zusammenfallen von Finalis in vokaler Strophe und Halbstrophe mit der Subdominante im Instrumentalpart (häufig auch in der *Porchovskaja*) verleiht dem instrumental-vokalen Ensemble eine unnachahmliche Dynamik. In Beispiel 4 fällt Verssilbe 1 mit dem fünften Viertel der Instrumentalperiode zusammen, obgleich die Sängerin wie auch der Musiker den Gesang auch zwei Takte früher beginnen kann. Die Empfindung von Asynchronizität verdankt sich dann dem Nichtzusammenfallen von starken und schwachen Zählzeiten (Auftakt im Vokalpart – Volltakt im Instrumentalpart). Das gleiche heterometrische Prinzip finden wir in Beispiel 6b, wo, durch den improvisatorischen Charakter des Stücks kaum zu erkennen ist, ob der Vokalpart irgendeiner stabilen Instrumentalform entspricht.

Die östlichen Nachbarn des *Velikolukischen Skobarja*

Anhand der wenigen zur Verfügung stehenden Publikationen ist nicht feststellbar, wo die Ostgrenze des *Velikolukischen Skobarja* verläuft und wie das Instrumentalrepertoire jenseits dieser Grenze strukturiert ist. Daher war die Klärung der instrumentalen Melogeographie im Westen des Gebiets von Tver' eine der Hauptaufgaben der Feldforschungen 2005 und 2006. Wie sich herausstellte, verläuft zwischen dem Areal der nach den Aufzeichnungen von Sergej Starostin aus den Landkreisen Olenino (Košelev 1990: № 10.) und Nelidovo (Krasnopevceva/Veličkina 1990) bekannten *Zavidovskaja* (*Zavido-čka*) und dem Areal des Velikolukischen eine deutliche Grenze in den undurchdringli-

---

[28] Beispiele bei: Zemcovskij (1967: № 110b), Mechnecov (1987: № 12), Bojko (2002: № 3).

chen Sümpfen südwestlich der Stadt Nelidovo – obgleich in der Zeit nach dem Zweiten Weltkrieg die *Zavidovskaja* auch westlich dieser Grenze, etwa im Kreis Žarkovskij, in Gebrauch kam. Im Kreis Belyj wird der Formtyp auch *Zalivočka* genannt, im Hauptverbreitungsgebiet überwiegen jedoch wie gewohnt funktionale Bezeichnungen: *Po derevne* („Durch das Dorf") oder *Pod pesni.*

Schema 2 zeigt die metrisch-rhythmische Struktur des Instrumentalparts der *Zavidovskaja* und die Baßlinie auf der Harmonika, wobei die Buchstaben sowohl Einzelbässe wie auch Akkorde bezeichnen können. Die Rhythmusformel des Liedes *Ach vy, seni*, die wir aus dem Vokalpart unterschiedlicher vokaler Vertreter des *Skobarja* kennen, bildet hier die Grundlage der Instrumentalperiode. Ein Kennzeichen der *Zavidovskaja* ist ihr bitonaler Charakter. Auf den starken Zählzeiten kämpfen a-Moll und G-Dur gleichsam um das stärkere Gewicht im Bewußtsein des Hörers. Einer Wahrnehmung als Dur-Tonalität kommt in gewissem Grade die Kadenzwendung der Melodie auf dem letzten Viertel entgegen (Beispiel 10). In Richtung Moll tendiert häufig der Finalis der Vokalstrophe.

Schema 2

♪ ♪	♪ ♪	♪ ♪	♪ ♪	
C G	a a	C a	G G	Nikolaj Kožanov (Beispiel 9)
C G	a a	a a	G G	Vasilij Lavrenov (Beispiel 10)
C G	a a	e F	G G	Vitalij Korguzov (Molodoj Tud, Kreis Olenino)
C G	a a	e a	G G	Konstantin Basov (Nikitino, Kreis Olenino)

Der Vokalpart deckt sich in seiner metrisch-rhythmischen Grundlage mit dem Instrumentalpart. Der *častuška*-Vers (8+7, 8+7) wird hier in Achteln gesungen. Asynchronizität ist gleichwohl auch hier im Spiel – in dem Sinne, daß die erste Silbe der Liedform auf das fünfte Achtel der Instrumentalperiode fällt.

Interregionale Parallelen zur *Zavidovskaja* lassen sich finden, wenn man ein höheres Abstraktionsniveau als das des harmonischen Schemas wählt. Wenn in Instrumentalformen die harmonischen Stufen stark variieren, ist es mitunter hilfreich die realen Funktionen auf zwei Kategorien zu reduzieren: Hauptakkord (0) und Nebenakkorde (1), was den Begriffen *ustoj* und *neustoj* aus der russischen Harmonielehre entspricht. Ein solcher Ansatz ist auch perspektivenreich für die Analyse des Repertoires der mittleren und südwestlichen *Pskovščina*, wo – besonders in den Guslistücken – stabil nicht die harmonische Formel, sondern lediglich die Verteilung von Haupt- und Nebenakkorden ist. Man kann von einer *binären Funktionsharmonik* sprechen, die auf der Spannung zwischen zwei Zentren beruht – im Unterschied zur westeuropäischen dreistufigen Harmonik.[29] Im Falle der *Zavidovskaja* ist allerdings ein hierarchisches Verhältnis von Haupt- und Nebenakkord nicht zweifelsfrei auszumachen. In Schema 3 wird das Dur-Zentrum mit 1, das Moll-Zentrum mit 0 bezeichnet. Die letzten beiden Harmoniefolgen aus

---

[29] Vgl.: Morgenstern (2007: 326-330). Ein Ähnliches Reduktionsverfahren verwendet auch Veličkina (1993) bei der Analyse der südrussischen Panflötenmusik.

Schema 2 weisen in dem abstrakteren Schema 3 eine komplementäre Verteilung der harmonischen Funktionen in den beiden rhythmischen Vier-Achtel-Sequenzen.

Schema 3

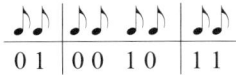

01 | 00 10 | 11

Ein ähnliches Grundmuster finden wir häufig in den Gusli- und Balalaikastücken (*Pod pesni*) im Nordosten des Gebiets von Novgorod (Morgenstern [Morgenštern] 1998a, 1998b).[30], wo die harmonischen Funktionen mithin ausschließlich durch den Dur- und den sekundverwandten Molldreiklang repräsentiert sind. Weiter ist dieses Grundmuster in ähnlicher Form auch im Kreis Ust'ja im Gebiet von Archangel'sk vertreten[31].

Nach den derzeit verfügbaren Feldforschungsdaten verläuft die Grenze des *Velikoluki-schen Skobarja* nördlich des Areals der *Zavidovskaja* weniger klar. Im Kreis Toropec ist der Velikolukische recht häufig vertreten. Im Kreis Andreapol' spielte ihn lediglich ein Musiker aus Solovenec am Nordrand des Landkreises, an der Grenze der Gebiete Tver' und Novgorod, der Harmonikaspieler Vasilij Šaljapin (*1930). In der Heimat dieses herausragenden Musikers verläuft somit die Nordostgrenze des Verbreitungsgebiets des *Velikolukischen Skobarja*. Das von Šaljapin gespielte Stück beginnt mit dem charakteristischen Initialmotiv im ersten Takt und einer darauffolgenden melisch aktiven Phrase mit Motivwiederholung. Die Baßlinie wird variiert und hält nicht immer die für diesen Formtyp charakteristischen regelmäßigen Wechsel von Haupt- und Nebenakkord ein (Beispiel 11a, b).

Andere Musiker aus dem Kreis Andreapol' verwenden im *Skobarja* das Initialmotiv des Velikolukischen, auf das ein melisch relativ beweglicher Takt folgt. Der dritte Takt eröffnet nun eine melisch und harmonisch einigermaßen unbewegliche Phrase (Beispiele 13, 14), was allen anderen lokalen Formen des *Skobarja* entgegensteht, für die im allgemeinen Sechzehntelbewegungen (teils mit Achteln durchsetzt), jedoch sehr selten Viertel oder längere Werte charakteristisch sind. Das Verhältnis von Instrumental- und Vokalpart entspricht dem oben beschriebenen Prinzip des Velikolukischen: Die erste Verssilbe fällt auf das siebte Viertel der Instrumentalperiode, der Finalis auf deren zweites Viertel. So singt den *Skobarja* Aleksej Vladimirov (*1930) aus dem ehemaligen Bezirk Žukovskij (Beispiel 13 zeigt die Instrumentalversion). Aleksandr Semënov (*1930) dagegen, der aus dem selben Bezirk stammt, beginnt die Instrumentalperiode mit dem hier auftaktig verwendeten siebten Viertel des Grundmusters (Beispiel 14). Auf diese Weise verliert sich der für den *Velikolukischen Skobarja* so charakteristische Eindruck der Asynchronizität. Eine elaboriertere Form bevorzugt Nikolaj Škadov (*1927) aus Fomino, südlich von Andreapol' (Beispiel 15). Hier fehlt das Initialmotiv des Velikolukischen. Eine bewegliche melische Figur wird leicht variiert, worauf wiederum eine melisch und harmonisch wenig bewegliche Phrase folgt, die zur Schlußwendung überleitet.

---

[30] Vgl. Morgenštern (1998a № 7), teilweise auch Morgenstern (1998b: № 1).

[31] Vgl. die am Musikwissenschaftlichen Institut der Universität Hamburg in Vorbereitung befindliche Videodokumentation *Russian Traditional Instrumental Music*. In dieser sind auch zahlreiche der hier transkribierten Feldaufzeichnungen vertreten.

Der Musiker kombiniert nicht nur gerade und ungerade Takte, in der Schlußwendung wird auch die regelmäßige metrische Pulsation durchbrochen.

Im Bezirk Žukopa, am Ostrand des Kreises Andreapol', wo Beispiel 12 aufgezeichnet wurde, stellen die Musiker dem lokalen *Skobarja* den in den Vierzigerjahren übernommenen Formtyp *Zalesica* gegenüber, was auf sein Herkunftsgebiet „hinter den Wäldern" hindeutet. Er erweist sich als identisch mit der *Zavidovskaja*, die uns aus dem südlich gelegenen Landkreis Nelidovo bekannt ist. Die ursprünglichen Verbreitungsareale der beiden Formtypen sind durch das unbewohnte Sumpf- und Waldgebiet an der Grenze der Landkreise Andreapol' und Nelidovo getrennt, das heute das berühmte Biosphärenreservat „Central'nyj lesnoj zapovednik" bildet.

Auch im Landkreis Peno konnte in Vorošilovo, westlich des zur oberen Wolga gehörenden Peno-Sees, bei einem Kurzbesuch ein *Skobarja* von Anatolij Gusarov (*1957) aufgezeichnet werden. Im allgemeinen ähnelt das Stück den lokalen Instrumentalformen von Andreapol' (Initialmotiv + melische Wendung zum unteren Grundton + melisch relativ unbewegliche Phrase, s. Beispiel 16). Ungewöhnlich ist die starke Variierung rhythmischer Kombinationen im letzten Takt. Die Transkription zeigt (unberücksichtigt des Auftaktes) den Finalakkord aus zwei Vierteln und ebenso aus einer Viertel und einer Halben. In anderen Instrumentalperioden verwendete der Musiker auch eine Kombination eines punktierten mit einem einfachen Viertelwert des Schlußakkordes. Diese ungewöhnlich freie Rhythmik überwindet die sonst für vergleichbare russische Instrumentalformen so charakteristische gleichmäßige metrische Pulsierung. Die Konzentration des Musikers und seine bewußte Akzentgebung schließen eine fehlerhafte Ausführung als Grund für die freirhythmischen Kombinationen aus. Die Sängerinnen aus Vorošilovo, wie auch Gusarov selbst, sangen zu seiner Harmonika die typisch skobarischen Kurzlieder – mit markanten Exklamationen am Zeilenanfang und schroff akzentuierten Endungen. Eben so singt zur Balalaika der Vater des Harmonikaspielers, Nikolaj Gusarov (*1932, Beispiel 17). Aus der Transkription geht nicht zweifelsfrei hervor, ob die aperiodische Gestalt des Instrumentalparts der künstlerischen Konzeption des Musikers entspringt oder ob sie einer gewissen Unsicherheit des Musikers geschuldet ist, der immerhin die selbständige Singstimme mit seinem Spiel zu koordinieren hat. Das Beispiel sei hier vor allem als eindrucksvolles Zeugnis skobarischen Gesangs an der Ostgrenze des ehemaligen Gouvernements von Pskov angeführt. Leider waren die Feldforschungen im Kreis Peno zeitlich begrenzt. Seine völlig unerforschte, jedoch zweifellos ausgesprochen reiche Instrumentaltradition verdient eine besonders hohe Aufmerksamkeit von seiten der Ethnoorganologie.

Schluß

Abschließend läßt sich sagen, daß für die Bewohner des untersuchten Territoriums – besonders in den Grenzen des ehemaligen Gouvernements von Pskov die lokale ethnische Identität einen hohen Stellenwert einnimmt. Ihr Zusammengehörigkeitsgefühl als Skobari ist untrennbar mit dem ethnomusikalischen Bewußtsein verbunden. Sowohl die ethnische wie auch die musikalische Seite des Begriffs „Skobar'" können eine große Anziehungskraft auf die südlichen Nachbarn des skobarischen Territoriums ausüben. Die Träger der nordweißrussischen Dialekte, die Poljakí, übernahmen mit der Zeit nicht nur die russische, sondern auch die skobarische Identität. Die instrumental-vokale Form *Skobarja*, deren südöstlicher Typ hier vorgestellt wurde, ist nicht nur der Stolz jedes traditionellen Musikers im ehemaligen Gouvernement Pskov und darüber hinaus, sondern auch der Stolz der traditionellen Musikkultur des Pskover Landes.

Anmerkungen zu den Notenbeispielen

Außer dem Balalaikastück (№ 17) wurden alle transkribierten Stücke auf der gleichtönigen Harmonika (*chromka*) gespielt. In diesen bezeichnet eine doppelte Ligatur einen verwischten Übergang zwischen zwei Tönen mit minimaler Überschneidung. Ein Pfeil über einer Note im Vokalpart verweist auf eine Alteration um ungefähr einen Viertelton, eine geringere Alteration wird durch einen seitlich abgeschnittenen Pfeil gekennzeichnet. Ein Kreuz als Notenkopf bezeichnet eine eher rezitativische Artikulation, ein eckiger Notenkopf einen ausgesungenen, jedoch „heiseren" Ton mit hohem Geräuschanteil, wie er im skobarischen Gesang ausgesprochen häufig ist.

Außer dem Verfasser waren an den Aufzeichnungen die folgenden Personen beteiligt: Elizaveta Borodulina, (4, 10), Vladimir Jaryš (8, 11, 16, 17), Rostislav Košelev (10), Dr. Aleksandr Romodin (4, 10), Igor' Stesev (1–3, 5, 6, 12–15) und Valentin Vinogradov (7, 9).

Gebiet Pskov

1. *Skobarja (Maripčelskaja)*. Aufgezeichnet am 9. Sept. 2006 in Čerpessa, Kreis Velikie Luki, von Nikolaj Ivanovič Panov (*1948 in Gajdukovo[32]).

2. *Skobarja (Čerpesskaja)*. S. № 1.

3. *Skobarja*. Aufgezeichnet am 20. Sept. 2006 in Tronino, Kreis Velikie Luki, von Vasilij Andreevič Ul'janov (*1931 in Temrevo).

4. *Skobarja dlinnogo, razlivnogo* (der lange, verfließende *Skobarja*). Aufgezeichnet am 2. Aug. 2006 im Kreiszentrum Kun'ja von Anatolij Arsent'evič Grinëv (*1936 in Kožino) und Tat'jana Fëdorovna Grinëva (*1935 in Kožino).

5. *Skobarja*. Aufgezeichnet am 14. Sept. 2006 in Belavino, Kreis Kun'ja, von Andrej Filippovič Danilov (*1930).

6a-b. *Pod draku* („Zur Prügelei"). Aufgezeichnet am 17. Sept. 2006 in Uspenskoe, Kreis Velikie Luki, von Nikolaj Borisovič Kušakov (*1952 in Kamen'ka).

Gebiet Tver'

7. *Po derevne* („Durch das Dorf"). Aufgezeichnet am 21. Okt. 2005 in Kaščёnki, Kreis Žarkovskij, von Ivan Vasil'evič Miščenkov (*1952 in Zaluž'e).

8. *Po derevne*. Aufgezeichnet am 24. Aug. 2006 im Kreiszentrum Andreapol' von Michail Ivanovič Lebedev (*1937 in Zabor'e, Kreis Žarkovskij).

9. *Po derevne* oder *Zalivočka*. Aufgezeichnet am 12. Okt. 2005 in Lipovka, Kreis Olenino, von Nikolaj Ivanovič Kožanov (*1932 in Karskoe, Kreis Belyj).

10. *Zalivočka*. Aufgezeichnet am 16. Juli 2003 in Verchov'e von Vasilij Micheevič Lavrenov (*1932 in Dunaevo).

---

[32] Angaben zum Geburtsort werden nur dann gemacht, wenn sie vom Ort der Aufzeichnung abweichen.

11a-b. *Skobarja.* Aufgezeichnet am 25. Aug. 2006 in Andreapol' von Vasilij Ivanovič Šaljapin (*1930 in Solovenec).

12. *Skobarja.* Aufgezeichnet am 26. Aug. 2006 in Žukopa von Ivan Stepanovič Koptilin (*1928 in Šelegovka, Kreis Peno).

13. *Skobarja (Pod pesni).* Aufgezeichnet am 25. Sept. 2006 in Andreapol' von Aleksej Vladimirovič Vladimirov (*1930 in Zachod, Bezirk Žukovskij).

14. *Skobarja (Pod pesni).* Aufgezeichnet am 25. Sept. 2006 in Andreapol' von Aleksandr Michailovič Semënov (*1930 in Pokrovskaja, Bezirk Žukovskij) und Aleksej Vladimirov (s. № 13).

15. *Pod draku* („Zur Prügelei"). Aufgezeichnet am 26. Sept. 2006 in Andreapol' von Nikolaj Kuz'mič Škadov (*1927 in Fomino, heute Bezirk Kozlovskoe).

16. *Skobarja.* Aufgezeichnet am 26. Aug. 2006 in Vorošilovo, Kreis Peno, von Anatolij Nikolaevič Gusarov (*1957 г. in Gora).

17. *Novgorodskaja.* Aufgezeichnet am 26. Aug. 2006 in Vorošilovo, Kreis Peno, von Nikolaj Fëdorovič Gusarov (*1932 in Gora).

Literatur

Barth, Frederik

1969 (Hg.)   *Ethnic Groups and Boundaries. The Social Organization of Cultural Differences.* Bergen; London 1969.

Beer, Bettina

2006   „Ethnos, Ethnie, Kultur", in: *Ethnologie: Einführung und Überblick*, hg. von Bettina Beer und Hans Fischer. Berlin: Reimer ⁶2006.

Bojko, Jurij Evgenievič

1985   „Sovremennye formy bytovanija Spasovskoj častuški bassejna Volchova i Sjasi i perspektivy ich razvitija" (Zeitgenössische Existenzformen der *častuška Spasovskaja* im Becken von Volchov und Sjas' und die Perspektiven ihrer Entwicklung), in: *Artes Populares. A Folklore Tanszék Eevkönyve. Yearbook of the Dpt. of Folklore.* Budapest 1985, S. 78-94.

1993   „Intonacionnye elementy Spasovskoj častuški" (Gestaltelemente der častuška Spasovskaja), in: *Aktual'nye teoretičeskie problemy ėtnomuzykoznanija. Gippiusovskie čtenija V, 7-9 dekabrja 1993, materialy konferencii.* Sankt-Peterburg: Rossijskij institut istorii iskusstv 1993, S. 30-34.

2002   Sootnošenie teksta i napeva v russkoj častuške (Verhältnis von Text und Weise in der russischen *častuška*), in: Iskusstvo ustnoj tradicii. Istoričeskaja morfologija. Sbornik statej posv. 60-letiju I.I. Zemcovskogo, hg. Von Nailja Junisovna Al'meeva. Sankt-Peterburg: Rossijskij institut istorii iskusstv 2002, S. 216-225.

Brandl, Rudolf M.

2003   „Si tacuisses Greve – der notwendige Erhalt der Musikethnologie", in: *Die Musikforschung*, 56. Jg., 2002, S. 166-389.

Elschek, Oskár

1991 „Traditional Music and Cultural Politics", in: *Music in the Dialogue of Cultures: Traditional Music and Cultural Policy* (Intercultural Music Studies, vol. 2), hg. von Max Peter Baumann. Wilhelmshaven: Florian Noetzel 1991, S. 32-55

Findejzen, Nikolaj Fëdorovic

1926 „Evrejskie cimbaly i cimbalisty Lepjanskie" (Jüdische Hackbretter und Hackbrettspieler von Lepel), in: *Muzykal'naja ètnografija*, hg. von N.F. Findejzen, Leningrad 1926, S. 38-43.

Gadžieva, Ajšet [richtig: Ajšat] Achmedovna

2001 „Kalendarnye napevy Verchnego Podneprov'ja i Podvin'ja" (Die Kalendermelodien des oberen Dnepr- und des Dünagebiets), in: *Očerki istoričeskoj geografii. Severo-Zapad Rossii: Slavjane i finny.* Sankt-Peterburg: Izdatel'stvo Sankt-Peterburgskogo universiteta 2001, S. 139-187.

Gerd, Aleksandr Sergeevič

1988 „Istorija formirovanija dialektnych granic vokrug Pskova" (Die Geschichte der Herausbildung der Dialektgrenzen um Pskov), in: *Srednerusskie govory: sovremennoe sostojanie i istorija.* Kalinin: Kalininskij gosudarstvennyj universitet 1988, S. 77-87.

1995 Vvedenie v ètnolingvistiku (Einführung in die Ethnolinguistik). Sankt-Peterburg: Izdatel'stvo Sankt-Peterburgskogo universiteta 1995.

Gerd, Aleksandr Sergeevič / Lebedev, G. S.

1991 „Èksplikacija istoriko-kul'turnych zon in ètničeskaja istorija Verchnej Rusi (Explikation der historisch-kulturellen Zonen und die ethnische Geschichte der Oberen Rus'), in: *Sovetskaja ètnografija*, H. 1, 1991, S. 73-85.

Gippius, Evgenij Vladimirovič

1941 „Zamečanija o belorusskoj narodnoj pesne" (Anmerkungen über das weißrussische Volkslied), in: *Belorusskie narodnye pesni*, hg. von Zinaida Èval'd. Moskva, Leningrad 1941, S. 121-123

Greve, Martin

2002 „Writing against Europe. Vom notwendigen Verschwinden der ‚Musikethnologie'", in: *Die Musikforschung*, 55. Jg., 2002, S. 239-251.

Grigor'eva R.A.; Kasperovič, G.I.

2005a „Identičnost' i demografičeskaja charakteristika naselenija" (Identität und demographische Charakteristik der Bevölkerung), Kapitel 1 aus Grigor'eva/Martynova (Hg) 2005, S. 37-84.

2005b „Russkij i belorusskij jazyki: status i arealy rasprostranenija" (Russische und weißrussische Sprache: Status und Verbreitungsareal), Kapitel 2 aus Grigor'eva/Martynova (Hg) 2005, S. 87-107.

Grigor'eva, M.A. / Martynova, M.Ju. (Hg.)

2005 *Belorussko-russkoe pograničʹe. Ètnologičeskoe issledovanie* (Das Weißrussisch-russische Grenzgebiet. Eine ethnologische Studie). Moskva: Izd. Rosijskogo universiteta družby narodov 2005.

Junghanns, Wolf-Dietrich

2003 „Daj boju – Drauf und dran! Traditioneller ostslawischer Faustkampf und heutige Popularisierungen eines „russischen Stils", in: *Berliner Debatte Initial*, Jg. 14 (2003), H. 4/5, S. 63-113.

421

Karbusicky, Vladimir

1979 *Systematische Musikwissenschaft: Eine Einführung in Grundbegriffe, Methoden und Arbeitstechniken.* München: Wilhelm Fink 1979.

1980 *Anfänge der historischen Überlieferung in Böhmen. Ein Beitrag zum vergleichenden Studium der mittelalterlichen Sängerepen.* Köln: Böhlau 1980.

Košelev, Aleksandr Sergeevič

1990 *Russkie narodnye balalaečnye naigryši* (Russische volkstümliche Balalaikastücke). Moskva: Sovetskaja Rossija 1990.

Kotikova, Natalija L'vovna

1961 *Russkie častuški, stradanija, pripevki* (Russische *častuški, stradanija, pripevki*). Leningrad: Goz. muz. izd. 1961.

Krasnopevceva, E.A. / Veličkina, Ol'ga V.

1990 „Proekt detskoj školy narodnogo tvorčestva" (Das Projekt der Kinderschule für Volkskultur), in: *Sochranenie i vozroždenie fol'klornych tradicij*, vyp. 1, S. 177-195

Macievskij Igor' Vladimirovič

1985 „Troista muzyka. K voprosu o tradicionnych instrumental'nych ansambljach" (*Troista muzyka*), in: *Artes Populares. A Folklore Tanszék Évkönyve. Yearbook of the Department of Folklore.* Budapest 1985, S. 95-119.

Manakov, Andrej Genad'evič

ohne Jahr[33] „Kul'turnye granicy i identičnost' (na primere severo-zapada Evropejskoj Rossii)" (Kulturelle Grenzen und Identität. Am Beispiel des Nordwestens des europäischen Rußland) www.dartmouth.edu/~crn/groups/geographies_group_papers/ Finalpapers/ Manakov02.pdf.).

Mechnecov, Anatolij Michajlovič

1987 *Jarmaročnaja igra* (Jahrmarktsmusik), Schallplattenserie: *Gudi gorazdo. Narodnye muzykal'nye instrumenty Pskovskoj oblasti* (Dröhne laut. Volksmusikinstrumente des Gebiets von Pskov), Folge 1. Leningrad: Melodija 1987, S20 26011 002.

Mechnecov, Anatolij Michajlovič (Hg.)

2002 *Narodnaja tradicionnaja kul'tura Pskovskoj oblasti* (Traditionelle Volkskultur des Gebiets Pskov), Bd. 1, Pskov 2002.

Mechnecov, Anatolij Michajlovič / Lobkova, Galina Vladimirovna

1989 *Napevy rodiny Musorgskogo* (Weisen der Heimat Musorgskijs), Schallplatte. Leningrad: Melodija 1989, S20 28761 001.

Morgenstern, Ulrich

1998a [Morgenštern, Ul'rich] „K voprosu o kornjach sovremennoj tradicii igry na balalajke i na gar-monike v Rossii" (Zur Frage nach den Wurzeln der heutigen Tradition des Balalaika- und des

---

[33] Der Beitrag ist möglicherweise identisch mit dem gleichnamigen Aufsatz des Verfassers in dem Sammelband *Identičnost'i geografija v postsovetskoj Rossii* (Sankt-Peterburg 2003, 114-139), der in Deutschland leider nicht zugänglich ist.

Harmonikaspiels in Rußland), in: *Sud'by tradicionnoj kultury. Sbornik statej i materialov pamjati Larisy Ivlevoj*. Sankt-Peterburg: Dmitrij Bulanin 1998, S. 164-186

1998b „Zur Tradition der Flügelzither Gusli im Gebiet Novgorod", in: *Berichte aus dem ICTM-Nationalkomitee Deutschland, VI/VII. Musik und Symbol – Musik und Region – Freie Berichte*, hg. von Marianne Bröcker. Bamberg: Universitätsbibliothek Bamberg 1998, S. 183-196

2005 [Ul'rich Morgenštern] „My daže ne znali, čto éto «Skobar'»" (Wir wußten nicht einmal, daß das der *Skobar'* ist), in: *Problemy instrumentovedčeskoj terminologii*, hg. von D.A. Abdu'nasyrova und Ju.E. Bojko. Sankt-Peterburg: Rossijskij institut istorii iskusstv, S. 9-10.

2006 „Concepts of the National in Russian Ethnoorganology" in: *Tautosakos darbai XXXII 2006 (Studia instrumentorum musicae popularis XVI)*, Vilnius, S. 148-160.

2007 *Die Musik der Skobari. Studien zu lokalen Traditionen instrumentaler Volksmusik im Gebiet Pskov (Nordwestrußland)*. Göttingen: Cuvillier 2007.

Morozov, Igor' Alekseevič

1995 „Ékspedicija v Vaškinskij rajon Vologodskoj oblasti" (Feldforschung im Kreis Vaškinskij, Gebiet Vologda), in: *Živaja Starina* (1995), H. 2 (6), S. 54.

Petuchov, Michail O.

1888 „Gusli" Niva (1988) , № 33. S. 826.

Razumovskaja, Elena Nikolaevna

1996 „*Plač pod jazyk* i *pod ikan'e* – osobye vokal'no-ansamblevye formy pričetnoj tradicii" (Die Klage „pod jazyk" und „pod ikan'e" [unterschiedliche Typen der Vokalimitation] – besondere Vokalformen im Ensemble), in: *Ékspedicionnye otkrytija poslednych let. Narodnaja muzyka, slovesnost', obrjady v zapisjach 1970–1900-ch godov. Stat'i i materialy (Serija „Fol'klor i fol'kloristika)"*, hg. von Michail Aleksandrovič Lobanov. Sankt-Peterburg: Dmitrij Bulanin, S. 9-60.

1998 *Tradicionnaja muzyka russkogo poozer'ja (po materialam ékspedicij 1971-1992)* (Traditionelle Musik des Poozer'e. Nach Materialien aus Feldforschungen der Jahre 1971 bis 1992 [mit 3 Musikkassetten]). Sankt-Peterburg: Kompozitor 1998.

Romodin, Aleksandr Vadimovič

1996 „O edinstve severobelorusskoj muzykal'no-étnografičeskoj tradicii" (Über die Einheit der nordweißrussischen musikalisch-ethnographischen Tradition), in: *„Pašlju seru zjazulj'ku na padzinušku". Sbornik statej i referatov Nevel'skoj meždunarodnoj gumanitarnoj konferencii*. Sankt-Peterburg, Nevel' 1996, S. 43-45.

1997 „Rol' tembra v stanovlenii severobelorusskoj narodnoj instrumental'noj muzyki. Poozer'e – pograničʼe Pskovskoj, Smolenskoj i Vitebskoj oblastej" (Die Rolle der Klangfarbe in der Herausbildung der nordweißrussischen instrumentalen Volksmusik. *Pooser'e* – Grenzregion der Gebiete Pskov, Smolensk und Vicebsk), in: *Tradicionnoe iskusstvo i čelovek: Tezisy dokl.XIX naučnoj konferencii molodych fol'kloristov pamjati A.A: Gorkovenko 15-17* aprelja 1997, hg. von Marija I. Roditeleva. Sankt-Peterburg: Rossijskij institut istorii iskusstv 1997, S. 54-58.

1999 „Narodnye muzykanty juga Pskovščiny" (Volksmusiker der südlichen Pskovščina), in: *Živaja starina*. 1999. № 4(24).

2005   Tradicionnye rasskazy o severobelorusskich muzykantach-instrumentalistach (Traditionelle Erzählungen über nordweißrussische Volksmusiker), in: Muzykant v kul'ture: koncepcija i dejatel'nost', hg. von Alisa A. Timošenko. Sankt-Peterburg: Rossijskij institut istorii iskusstv 2005, S. 102-120.

2006   in: *Tradicionnaja kul'tura. Poiski. Interpretacii. Materialy: Sbornik statej po materialam konferencii pamjati L.M. Ivlevoj*, hg von Anna Fëdorovna Nekrylova. Sankt-Peterburg: Federat. Agenstvo po kul'ture I kinematografii, Rossijskij institut istorii iskusstv 2006, S. 9-18.

Romodin, Aleksandr Vadimovič / Romodina, Irina Aleksandrovna

1989   *Obrjadovaja muzyka* (Brauchtumsmusik), Schallplattenserie: *Tradicionnoe iskusstvo poozer'ja* (Traditionelle Kunst des Poozer'e), Folge 1. Leningrad: Melodija 1989, S20 29387 000.

1990a   „Rasskazy o posidelkach. Publikacija ėkspedicionnych materialov" (Erzählungen über die Spinnstuben. Dokumentation von Feldforschungsmaterialien), in: *Zreliščno-igrovye formy narodnoj kul'tury*, hg. von Larisa Michajlovna Ivleva. Leningrad: Leningradskij gosudarstvennyj institut teatra muzyki i kinematografii 1990, S. 204-213.

1990b   *Večerinočnaja Muzyka* (Musik der Tanzabende), *Tradicionnoe iskusstvo poozer'ja* (Traditionelle Kunst des Poozer'e), Folge 2. Leningrad: Melodija 1990, S20 30043 002.

1998   „Pesni derevni Ragozy. Publikacija ėkspedicionnych materialov" (Lieder des Dorfes Ragozy. Dokumentation von Feldforschungsmaterialien), in: *Sud'by tradicionnoj kultury. Sbornik statej i materialov pamjati Larisy Ivlevoj*. Sankt-Peterburg: Dmitrij Bulanin 1998, S. 322-359.

Tiškov, Valerij Aleksandrovič

2003   *Rekviem po ėtnosu. Issledovanija po socialno-kul'turnoj antropologii* (Requiem auf das Ethnos. Untersuchungen zur Sozialen und Kulturanthropologie). Moskva: Nauka 2003.

Tynurist [Tõnurist], Igor'

1977   „Gde vo gusli zvonili? Opyt kartografirovanija narodnych muzykal'nych instrumentov" (Wo wurden die Gusli geläutet? Versuch einer Kartierung von Volksmusikinstrumenten), in: *Ėtnografičeskie issledovanja Severo-Zapada SSSR*. Leningrad: Nauka 1977, S. 16-29.

Veličkina, Ol'ga V.

1993   „Sochranenie kurskoj tradicii mnogostvol'noj flejty" (Die Erhaltung der Tradition der Mehrfachflöte des Gebiets von Kursk), in: *Sochranenie i vozroždenie fol'klornych tradicij*, vyp. 2, čast' I. Moskva, S. 77-100.

Zacharova, K.F. / Orlova, V.G

2004   Dialektnoe členenie russkogo jazyka. Moskva: Ėditorial URSS ²2004 [¹1970].

Zemcovskij, Izalij Iosifovič

1967 (Hg.)   *Toropeckie pesni. Pesni podiny M. Musorgskogo* (Toropecker Lieder. Lieder der Heimat M. Musorgskijs). Leningrad: Muzyka 1967.

1975   *Melodika kalendarnych pesen* (Die Melodik der Kalenderlieder). Leningrad: Muzyka 1975.

1987 (Hg.)   *B. Asaf'ev. O narodnoj muzyke* (B. Asaf'ev. Über Volksmusik). Leningrad: Muzyka 1987.

Notenbeispiele

1. Skobarja (Maripčelskaja)

N. I. Panov: Harmonika Chromka

2. Skobarja (Čerpesskaja)

N. I. Panov: Harmonika Chromka

3. Skobarja

V. A. Ul'janov: Harmonika Chromka (Kirillovskaja)

4. Skobarja dlinnogo, razlivnogo

A. A. Grinёv: Harmonika Chromka
T. F. Grinёva: Gesang

1. Го - во - рят, кар - то - шку съе - ли,

ой ко - ло - рад - ски - е жу - ки.

А не ну - жно нам кар - тош - ки,

а лишь бы бы - ли му - жи - ки.

5. Skobarja

A. F. Danilov: Harmonika Chromka

6a. Pod draku

N. B. Kušakov: Harmonika Chromka

6b. Pod draku

N.B. Kušakov: Harmonika Chromka, Gesang

7. Po derevne

I. V. Miščenkov: Harmonika Chromka

8. Po derevne

M. I. Lebedev: Harmonika Chromka

9. Po derevne (Zalivočka)

N. I. Kožanov: Harmonika Chromka

10. Zalivočka

V. M. Lavrenov: Harmonika Chromka

1.Как по э - той, по де - ре - вень - ке хо - жу семь-над - цать раз. [Не - у -] же - ли мо - я ми - ла - я на пить - ся не по - дасть?

11a. Skobarja

V. I. Šaljapin: Harmonika Chromka

11b Skobarja

V. I. Šaljapin: Harmonika Chromka

12. Skobarja

I. S. Koptilin: Harmonika Chromka

13. Skobarja

A. V. Vladimirov: Harmonika Chromka

434

14. Skobarja

A. M. Semёnov: Harmonika Chromka, Gesang
A. V. Vladimirov: Gesang

15. Skobarja

N. K. Škadov: Harmonika Chromka

16. Skobarja

A. N. Gusarov: Harmonika Chromka

17. Novgorodskaja

N. F. Gusarov: Balalaika, Gesang

1. Эх, как нов-го-род-ска-я скоп-ска-я, о-

ох, как зем-ля-ни-чень-ка мо-я. Ох,

как са-ма сто-ишь три ко-пей [ки]. О-

ох, как су-шишь маль-чи-ка ме-ня.

Karten

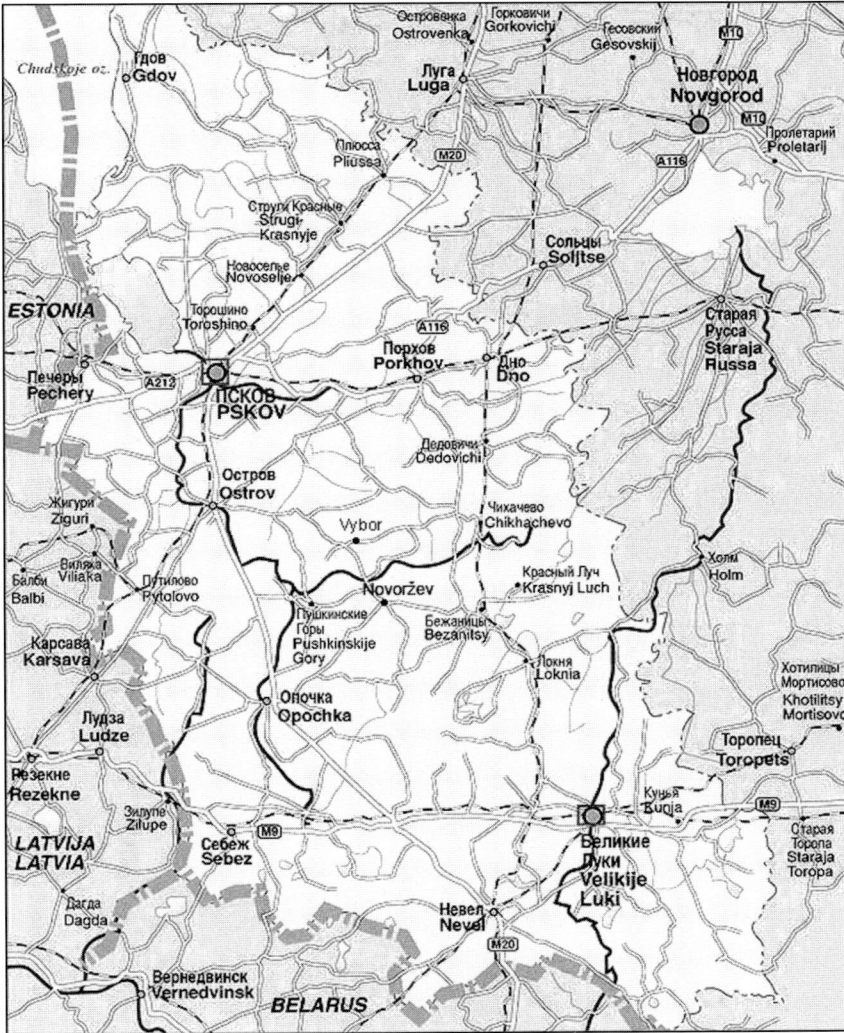

Karte 1 Das heutige Gebiet Pskov (*Pskovskaja oblast'*)

Karte 2 Das Forschungsgebiet

Karte 3 Die Südostgrenze des Gouvernement Pskov (*Pskovskaja Gubernija*)
Ènciklopedičeskij slovar' (hg. von I. E. Andreevskij), Bd. 49, Leipzig: Brockhaus, Sankt-Peterburg: Èfron 1898, Stichwort: „Pskovskaja Gubernija". Unter Verwendung der Internetquelle: http://gatchina3000.ru/brockhaus-and-efron-encyclopedic-dictionary/084/84087.htm

440

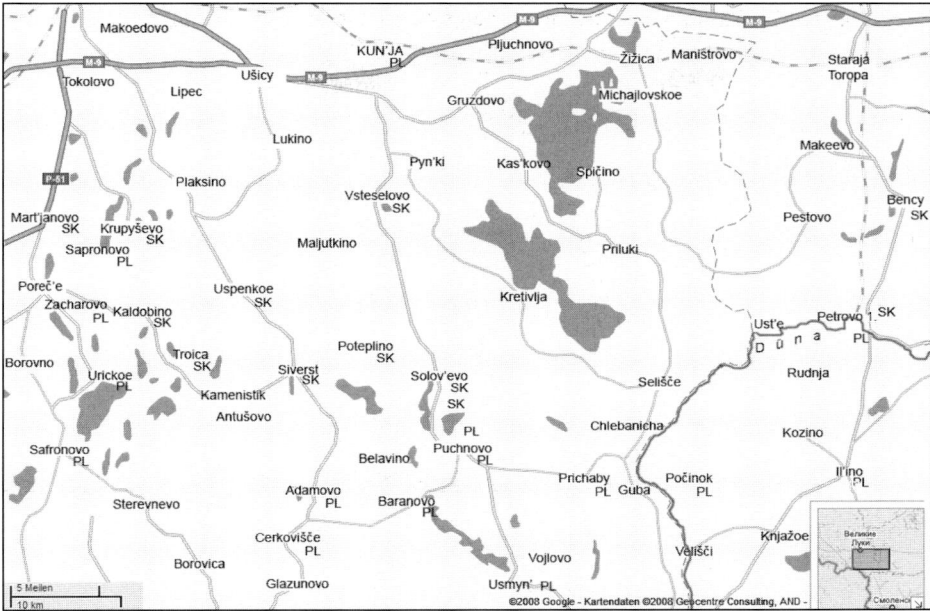

Karte 4 Siedlungen von Skobari (SK) und Poljaki (PL)

Danksagung

Die in der vorliegenden Arbeit verwendeten Feldforschungsdaten wurden im Südosten des Gebiets von Pskov und im Westen des Gebiets von Tver' in den Jahren 2005 und 2006 gesammelt. Die Feldforschungen wurden im Rahmen des von der Deutschen Forschungsgemeinschaft geförderten und am Musikwissenschaftlichen Institut der Universität Hamburg angesiedelten Projekts „ ‚Ich spiele nicht auf eure Art.' Stil und Repertoire der traditionellen russischen Instrumentalmusik im Grenzgebiet zu Weißrußland als Faktor für die Bildung von ethnischer und Generationenidentität" durchgeführt. An den Teams von jeweils zwei bis vier Teilnehmern waren meine Kollegen vom Rußländischen Institut für die Geschichte der Künste (St. Petersburg) Dr. Aleksandr Romodin und Valentin Vinogradov beteiligt sowie der Journalist Igor' Stesev, die Musiklehrerin Elizaveta Borodulina und der Student des Konservatoriums und Fotograf Rostislav Košelev. Die Arbeiten im August 2006 in den Landkreisen Andreapol' und Peno des Gebiets von Tver' wurden gemeinsam mit Vladimir Jaryš (Velikij Novgorod) begonnen und im September desselben Jahres mit Igor' Stesev und zeitweise mit Aleksandr Romodin fortgeführt. Für besonders tatkräftige Unterstützung der Forschungsarbeiten habe ich dem Leiter des Kreiskulturamtes Andreapol', Herrn Anatolij Ivanov, zu danken, für äußerst wertvolle Hinweise und Empfehlungen dem Leiter der Abteilung für künstlerische Kultur der Gebietskulturbehörde Velikie Luki, Herrn Viktor Pašin. Wesentliche Unterstützung erhielten wir ebenso von der Leiterin des Kreiskulturamtes Olenino (Ge-

441

biet Tver'), Frau Nina Ivanova. Ebenso standen uns zahlreiche weitere Mitarbeiterinnen und Mitarbeiter der kulturellen Einrichtungen vor Ort mit kundigen Ratschlägen, vielfachem Beistand bei mithin auftretenden organisatorischen Problemen zur Seite.

Notes on the authors of this volume

Markus Abel (Dr. rer. nat. habil.) is a physicist affiliated with the University of Potsdam and the Institute of Musicology, University of Hamburg.

Rolf Bader (Dr. phil. habil.) works as a professor of Systematic Musicology in the Institute of Musicology, University of Hamburg.

Andreas Beurmann (Dr. phil.) studied musicology and physics at Göttingen. He did teach in Systematic Musicology at the University of Hamburg as a Honorary professor.

Oskár Elschek (Dr. phil. habil.) is professor emeritus of musicology, Comenius University Bratislava, Slovakia. He was also Head of the Dept. of Musicology of the Slovac Academy of Sciences. He still teaches musicology in the University of Vienna, Austria.

Klaus Frieler (Dipl.-Phys.) is a physicist and musicologist affiliated with the Institute of Musicology, University of Hamburg where he teaches in Systematic Musicology.

Rolf Inge Godøy (Dr. phil.) is a professor of musicology teaching and doing research in the Institute of Musicology, University of Oslo, Norway.

Gerhard Kubik (Dr. phil. habil.) is an africanist and ethnologist who did teach as a professor at various academic institutions, among them the Universities of Vienna, Austria, and Mainz, Germany.

Marc Leman (Dr. phil.) is professor of Systematic Musicology in the Institute of Musicology and Head of the Institute of Psychoacoustics and Electronic Music (IPEM) of the University of Ghent, Belgium.

David Lewis (PhD.) is a Research Fellow in the Department of Computing, Goldsmiths College, University of London, United Kingdom.

Kai Lothwesen (Dr. phil.) works in music education and is affiliated with the Institute of Musicology, University of Frankfurt/Main, Germany.

Jukka Louhivuori (Dr. phil.) is a professor of musicology with a specialization in cross-cultural music cognition at the University of Jyväskylä, Finland.

Ulrich Morgenstern (Dr. phil.) is an ethnomusicologist working in a research project on Russian folk music funded by the DFG. He is affiliated with the Institute of Musicology, University of Hamburg.

Daniel Müllensiefen (Dr. phil.) is a Research Fellow in the Department of Computing, Goldsmiths College, University of London, United Kingdom.

Bruno Nettl (PhD., Dr. h.c.) is professor emeritus of ethnomusicology and anthropology, Dept. of Music, University of Illinois at Urbana-Champaign, USA.

Christiane Neuhaus (Dr. phil.) is a postdoc research associate in the Max Planck-Institute for Human Cognitive and Brain Sciences, Leipzig, Germany.

Tiago de Oliveira Pinto (Dr. phil.) is an ethnomusicologist teaching in the Departamento de Antropologia, Universidade de São Paulo, Brazil, and as visiting professor in the Institute of Musicology at Hamburg.

Arne von Ruschkowski (M.A.) is a scientific co-worker in the Institute of Musicology, University of Hamburg, currently preparing his PhD-dissertation.

Albrecht Schneider (Dr. phil. [habil., Comenius University Bratislava]) is a professor of Systematic Musicology in the Institute of Musicology, University of Hamburg.

Geraint Wiggins (PhD., PhD.) is professor of Computational Creativity in the Department of Computing, Goldsmiths, University of London, United Kingdom.

HAMBURGER JAHRBUCH FÜR MUSIKWISSENSCHAFT

Herausgegeben vom Musikwissenschaftlichen Institut
der Universität Hamburg

Das *Hamburger Jahrbuch für Musikwissenschaft* besteht seit 1974. Jeder Band ist thematisch gebunden, wobei wechselweise musikalische Gattungen, Epochen der europäischen Musikgeschichte, bedeutende Komponistenpersönlichkeiten oder fachsystematische Grundsatzfragen ins Zentrum treten.

Die Bände 1-13 sind im Laaber-Verlag, 93164 Laaber, erschienen.

Ab Band 14 erscheint diese Reihe im Verlag Peter Lang, Europäischer Verlag der Wissenschaften, Frankfurt am Main.

Band 14 Peter Petersen/Hans-Gerd Winter (Hrsg.): Büchner-Opern. Georg Büchner in der Musik des 20. Jahrhunderts. 1996.

Band 15 Annette Kreutziger-Herr (Hrsg.): Das Andere. Eine Spurensuche in der Musikgeschichte des 19. und 20. Jahrhunderts. 1998.

Band 16 Peter Petersen/Helmut Rösing (Hrsg.): 50 Jahre Musikwissenschaftliches Institut in Hamburg. Bestandsaufnahme – aktuelle Forschung – Ausblick. 1999.

Band 17 Constantin Floros/Friedrich Geiger/Thomas Schäfer (Hrsg.): Komposition als Kommunikation. Zur Musik des 20. Jahrhunderts. 2000.

Band 18 Hans Joachim Marx (Hrsg.): Beiträge zur Musikgeschichte Hamburgs vom Mittelalter bis in die Neuzeit. 2001.

Band 19 Helmut Rösing / Albrecht Schneider / Martin Pfleiderer (Hrsg.): Musikwissenschaft und populäre Musik. Versuch einer Bestandsaufnahme. 2002.

Band 20 Peter Petersen (Hrsg.): Hans Werner Henze. Die Vorträge des internationalen Henze-Symposions am Musikwissenschaftlichen Institut der Universität Hamburg. 28. bis 30. Juni 2001. 2003.

Band 21 Claudia Maurer Zenck (Hrsg.): Der Orpheus-Mythos von der Antike bis zur Gegenwart. Die Vorträge der interdisziplinären Ringvorlesung an der Universität Hamburg, Sommersemester 2003. 2004.

Band 22 Claudia Maurer Zenck (Hrsg.): Musiktheater in Hamburg um 1800. 2005.

Band 23 Beatrix Borchard / Claudia Maurer Zenck (Hrsg.): Alkestis: Opfertod und Wiederkehr. Interpretationen. 2007.

Band 24 Albrecht Schneider (ed.): Systematic and Comparative Musicology: Concepts, Methods, Findings. 2008.

www.peterlang.de